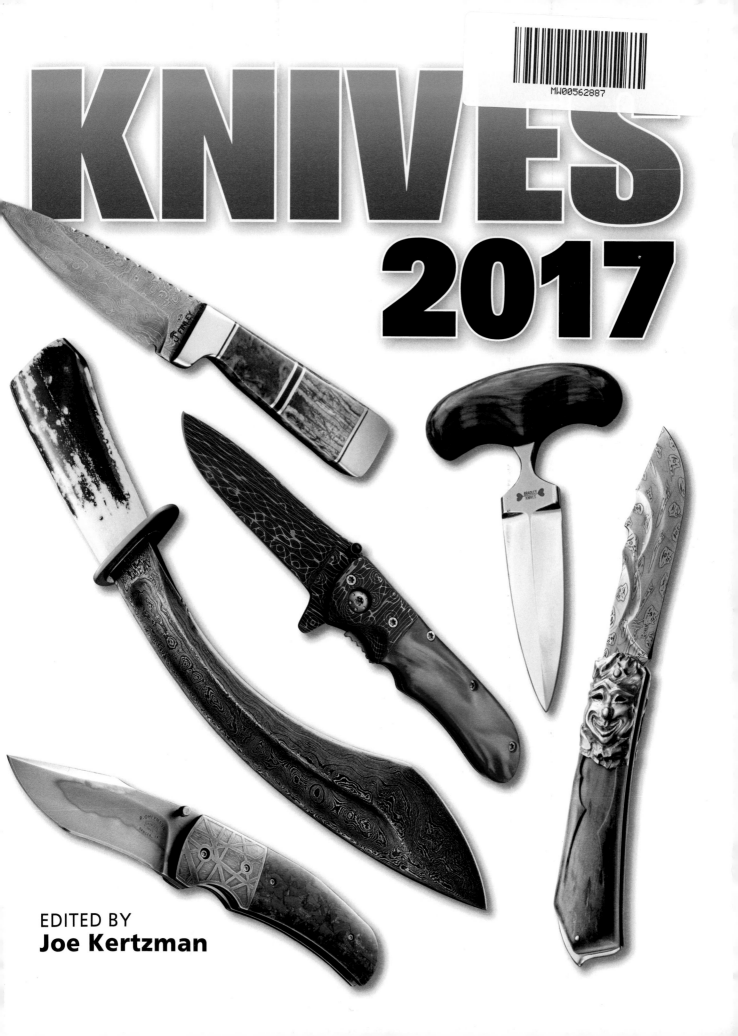

KNIVES
2017

EDITED BY
Joe Kertzman

Published by

Krause Publications a division of F+W Media, Inc.
700 East State Street • Iola, WI 54990-0001
715-445-2214 • 888-457-2873
www.krausebooks.com

To order books or other products call toll-free 1-800-258-0929
or visit us online at www.shopblade.com

Cover photography by Kris Kandler

ISSN: 0277-0725
ISBN-13: 978-1-4402-4678-4
ISBN-10: 1-4402-4678-5

Cover Design by Sharon Bartsch
Designed by Dane Royer
Edited by Corrina Peterson

Printed in the United States of America

10 9 8 7 6 5 4 3 2 1

Dedication and Acknowledgments

BLADE Magazine Cutlery Hall Of Famer® Ken Onion is a co-founding member of Alaska's Healing Hearts, a national foundation "Serving the Battle Wounded and Battle Weary." The organization offers year-round outdoor recreational opportunities for America's brave, wounded soldiers and their families, including rehabilitation activities like fishing, hunting, skiing, rodeo, dog sledding tours and various other outdoor pursuits. Jim Zumbo, a prominent firearms and hunting commentator and writer, the host of Jim Zumbo Outdoors on The Outdoor Channel and a former hunting editor for Outdoor Life magazine, is the president of Alaska's Healing Hearts. For his part, Onion has dropped everything many times to assist in projects for wounded veterans.

A story titled "Knives For Charity" on blademag. com (http://www.blademag.com/blog/knives-charity) starts, "There's never been a shortage of charitable acts within the knife industry. For as long as there have been knifemakers, there have been knives given to those in need, particularly soldiers, farmhands, friends and neighbors, or blades donated for auction to raise money for good causes." The story goes on to explain that the American Knife & Tool Institute (AKTI) announced in 2015 that it planned to hold a "1st Annual Giving Back Event" featuring knives donated by Ron Lake, D'Alton Holder and others at the 2016 BLADE Show. It took place Friday, June 3rd, 2016, from 6-9 p.m. at the Renaissance Waverly Hotel, where knives from some of the world's finest custom knifemakers were contributed for auction to "give back" and help the knife community and its favorite charities. Fifty percent of the proceeds went directly to charities, and 50 percent went to AKTI's many efforts to "keep knives in our lives."

A Google search for "knives for charity" turns up too many knifemakers, manufacturers and knife sales to mention all, but some of the results include: Weige Knives, a small business that has donated knives to raise money for many causes and charities, including the Leukemia and Lymphoma Society of Dallas and the Junior League of Austin; KnifeCen-ter.com, which supports Habitat For Humanity and Us Too Prostate Cancer Education & Support, among many others; Emerson Knives, which has put up several knives for auction, including its new Sheepdog knife and a CQC-7 carried during the raid on Osama bin Laden's compound in Pakistan, to raise money for St. Jude and charities benefiting Special Operations Forces, among others; Cutco Corp. and KA-BAR Knives, Inc., two brands under the same corporate umbrella that give back to charities with a focus on health, education and communities; knifemaker Calvin Robinson, who has fashioned numerous knives to raffle off and raise money for the Marine Memorial Tower in Pensacola, Florida, the American Cancer Society and others; Ramos Knives, which has auctioned knives to raise money for the New Mexico Christian Children's Home and for a mission trip to Ecuador; and Victorinox Knives, maker of the Swiss Army Knife that invited 2016 SHOT Show attendees to build their own Wounded Warrior Project knives at the company's booth to raise money for wounded warriors (incidentally, many knifemakers have sold knives to raise money for the Wounded Warrior Project, a favorite charity among makers).

Shortly after the attack on the World Trade Center, September 11th, 2001, authorized officials gave select knifemakers pieces of the tangled steel girders to forge blades from and donate the proceeds from the sales of the knives to charity. (See page 7 herein for an update). And every time a knifemaker becomes seriously ill, a knife shop burns down or a maker falls on hard times, his or her fellow makers tend to gather in droves, build knives, sell them and donate money to help their colleagues in need.

To all the knifemakers and companies, and I realize I have missed many and apologize now, who have donated money from the sales of knives to charities, worthy causes, fellow makers and more, I acknowledge your compassion and dedicate the *KNIVES 2017* book to you. □

Joe Kertzman

Contents

Introduction 6
2017 Wooden Sword Award 7

Features

Blade Wizardry in Burgundy 8
Desert Ironwood Is One Hot Burl 15
Visceral Allure of the Bowie 20
How Real Smiths Smelt Steel 26
Fine Tuning Folders 32
Kantou: Appreciation of Japanese Swords 36
Survival of the Bush-Craftiest 42
Taking Knife Passion to the Next Level 46
The Magical Swords of Norse Lore 52

Trends Section 57

Chef's Specials 58
Flipper Folder Flair 60
Ti-Dyed Timascus 65
Tacti-Turns 66
BFF's—Bowie/Fighters Forever 68
Guarded Swords & Daggers 75
Folder Fancy 78
Crosscut Mammoth & Some Molars 86
A Synthetic Aesthetic 88
Steel-Tipped Boots 95
Nation Builders 96
Throwback Bowies 99
Palpable Pulps 102
Straight-Up Daggers 110
Pocket Wares 114
Forward Tanto Thrust 117
"Game On!" Blades 118
More Love for Loveless 126
Keen Campers 128

State of the Art Section 130

Complete Knife/Sheath Packages 131
A Sculpture Park 136
An Engraving Conversation 138
Carvings Come to Knife 146
Jigged, Filigreed, Stippled, Textured & Chased 148
The Draw of Scrimshaw 150
Touches of Turquoise 153
Uncommon Play in Handle Inlay 154

Steel-ustrators 156
Singular San Mai Steel 160
Gold Veins 162
Powerful Pattern Welds 164

Factory Trends Section **173**
Black Beauty, Not Just Another Horse Story 174
Hawks 'n Hatchets 178
Refined Folders 179
Military Units 180

Directory **201**
Custom Knifemakers 202
Knifemakers State-by-State 291
Knifemakers Membership Lists 300
Knife Photo Index 303
Sporting Cutlers 305
Importers 308
Knifemaking Supplies 310
Mail Order Sales 312
Knife Services 314
Organizations 318
Publications 319

On The Cover

It's never dull in the land of *KNIVES* book covers, and the blades featured front and center on *KNIVES 2017* do not disappoint! Tucked in and partially folded at upper left is a Shane Sibert "Metronaught" model sporting a 2.75-inch Chad Nichols "wave pool"-damascus blade with a signature Sibert blade fuller. It includes an exclusive "Randomania"-pattern G-10 handle, a matching, accented G-10 thumb disk, accented barrel back spacers, titanium pivot head screws and a sculpted titanium pocket clip. Engraved by Antonio Montejano and parading 22-carat-gold foil inlay, the fully integral Riccardo Mainolfi fixed blade at bottom left is based off a Bob Loveless Hideout and is one piece of mirror-polished RWL-34 steel engraved with Medusa on one side of the handle and Perseus of Cellini (shown)—a bronze sculpture by Benvenuto Cellini—on the other. At bottom-center lies a Herman J. Schneider double-hollow-ground 440C dagger showcasing a fluted fossil walrus ivory handle, and a sculpted and carved 416 stainless steel guard and pommel. It stretches 11.5 inches overall. To its right, and the largest of the cover knives, is a Steven Ramos "Cygnus" model showing off an 8-inch, fileworked CPM 154 blade with integral, pointed guard, a 304 stainless steel bolster and pommel, and a relatively rare (only found in Africa) green Verdite stone handle. It comes with a leather sheath boasting six cane toad skin inlays. Not disappointing is becoming a habit of *KNIVES* book covers. (cover photo by Kris Kandler) □

Introduction

Unpretentious, without airs, modest or perhaps just living closer to the earth, regardless, it's always dangerous to label an entire segment of the population. You can't paint people with a broad stroke. There should be no preconceived notions, stereotypes or generalizations. One can only attempt to describe a population of people, such as handmade knifemakers, from his or her own field of experience. And that's where the lack of pretension comes in. The makers this *KNIVES 2017* book editor has met, shaken hands with, chatted up—laughing, talking and sharing ideas—have been regular folk, nonjudgmental, honest and sincere. They put on their pants just like you or me.

I picture their homes as lived in and comfortable, not pristine and intimidating, yet there's a danger there. Everyone is different, even in the knife community. People who make tools by hand, though, do tend to have an appreciation for the simple things in life, the necessities. Take food, shelter and clothing for example. One might surmise that if someone is pounding out a knife blade from a billet of steel, or forging blades in charcoal furnaces, they might just have a fruit tree or two in the yard, maybe even a garden, a garden shed, barn or workshop. There could be a sewing machine or ironing board in one of the rooms of the house. If a knifemaker fixes his or her tools by hand, fashions their own knife parts, screws and springs, do you think they might sew a tear in a shirt seam? Or maybe patch cracks in walls and give them a fresh coat of paint? Could such people can their own vegetables, shoot deer in season or pick an apple from a tree? A person can't make assumptions about such things.

Not all knifemakers build utilitarian knives, hunters, old-time pocketknives, combat knives or household cutlery. Many fashion art knives, highly engraved, scrimshawed, sculpted and jewel-inlaid pieces. Maybe the makers of high-end knives are the sophisticates of the blade builders, attending operas, dining in fine restaurants and reading classic novels. That could be. Therein is the catch. You cannot assume. What you can do is state the facts, and the fact is the knife industry is not only a great place to work and visit, but it is a healthy, expanding, vibrant and exciting market. The variety of knives is downright astounding. It can unequivocally be stated that many knifemakers are self-sufficient, industrious, innovative, creative and skilled craftsmen and women, artists and artisans, technologically advanced and mechanically inclined. More than a select few have perfected the marrying of utility with aesthetics, a feat that has not gone unnoticed by enthusiasts and collectors.

Trends within the *KNIVES 2017* book include "Flipper Folder Flair," "Nation Builders," "Steel-Tip Boots," "Keen Campers," "Palpable Pulps," "Chef's Specials," "Pocket Wares," "Folder Fancy," "Throwback Bowies," "Tacti-Turns," "Game-On Blades" and "Straight-Up Daggers."

Of course there are those aforementioned and presumed sophisticates, the artistically inclined creating State Of The Art pieces that fall into such categories as "Powerful Pattern Welds," "Touches of Turquoise," "The Draw of Scrimshaw," "An Engraving Conversation," "A Sculpture Park," "Complete Knife/Sheath Packages," "Uncommon Play In Handle Inlay," "Singular San Mai Steel," "Steel-ustrators," "Gold Veins" and "Carvings Come to Knife."

Some informative articles seemed in line, and the front of the book is filled with them—features covering everything from ironwood to Japanese swords, and from pursuing one's true knife passion to fine tuning folders. Smelting steel is covered, as are bushcraft knives, a French husband-and-wife knifemaking team and swords of Norse mythology.

Make no mistake—the 37th Edition of the *KNIVES* annual book is an unpretentious affair. It welcomes you into its fold and asks you to stay awhile, soaking up its surroundings, features and focus, the knives within its realm, the handmade pieces and works of art, utilitarian tools and sharp objects of beauty. Everyone is welcome. There are no exclusions. It's a place for enthusiasts to congregate and enjoy. □

Joe Kertzman

2017 WOODEN SWORD AWARD

Shortly after the attack on the World Trade Center, September 11th, 2001, authorized officials gave a couple select knifemakers pieces of the tangled steel girders to forge blades from and donate the proceeds from the sales of the knives to charity. The knifemakers raised funds for families of victims, including the loved ones of police officers and firemen and women who lost their lives responding to the scene. Knifemaker John Young is written into a new chapter of the sad saga, having fashioned a bronze letter opener from pieces of The Sphere that once stood in the middle of Austin J. Tobin Plaza—the World Trade Center plaza. After the attack on 9/11, the heavily damaged sphere, a sculpture by German artist Fritz Koenig, was saved and moved to Battery Park to show the ability of New Yorkers and Americans to withstand the attack and return strong and resolved. The sphere had to be restored and abated to remove asbestos that was disturbed from the collapse of the Twin Towers. The New York and New Jersey Port Authority chose Lou De Santo and his men to do the job, and since they completed the work ahead of schedule and under budget, Lou was rewarded with pieces of the sphere that the falling girders had punched out. On one side of the bronze letter opener handle is "WTC" for World Trade Center, and on the other "9-11-01." For his role in preserving part of the sphere for generations to come, and in such a beautiful way with the incredibly clean letter opener, it is a pleasure to award knifemaker John Young with the 2017 Wooden Sword Award. □

Joe Kertzman

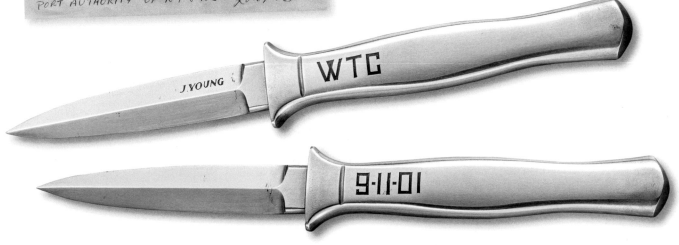

CERTIFICATE OF AUTHENTICITY

THE BRONZE (LETTER OPENER) THAT YOU HAVE RECEIVED WAS CRAFTED FROM PIECES OF THE SPHERE THAT STOOD AT WORLD TRADE CENTER PLAZA. AFTER THE ATTACK ON 9/11, THE SPHERE WAS CHOSEN TO SHOW OUR ABILITY TO WITHSTAND AN ATTACK AND RETURN STRONG AND RESOLVED.

THE SPHERE HAD TO BE RESTORED AND ABATED TO REMOVE ASBESTOS THAT WAS DISTURBED FROM THE COLLAPSE OF THE TOWERS. I AND MY MEN WERE CHOSEN BY THE PORT AUTHORITY TO DO THE JOB. WE COMPLETED THE WORK AHEAD OF SCHEDULE AND UNDER BUDGET, SO I WAS REWARDED WITH PIECES OF THE SPHERE THAT THE FALLING GIRDERS HAD PUNCHED OUT. I RECEIVED THESE PIECES FROM THE PORT AUTHORITY OF NY & NJ   Lou De Santo

Blade Wizardry in Burgundy

Husband and wife, warriors and knifemakers, a French duo works up wizardly blades

By James Morgan Ayres

©MLAyres images except where otherwise noted

Deep in the heart of France's Burgundy wine country region is a delightful house, a house that radiates a little magic. Surrounded by forest on three sides, and with a vineyard of wine grapes on the other side, the house sits next to a long footpath that was once a railroad track. Previously a *gare*—a railway station—now, after much work in the conversion, it looks like a wizard's home, with many levels, hidden rooms and secret nooks. There are books on arcane subjects stacked everywhere, odd medieval-looking tools used as paperweights, and an eclectic selection of antique wood cabinets, chairs and tables sharing space with hand-thrown pottery cups and bowls, and with knives … many knives.

The first thing I noticed when we were ushered into this wizard's lair were the knives—blades on the shelf of a coat rack in the entryway, knives on the kitchen worktable, on racks lining the kitchen walls, more on the dining table and sideboard, and blades on the coffee table next to a low-slung leather couch in the sunlit salon. There were old knives, new knives, ordinary kitchen knives and antique fixed blades with stag handles like Daniel Boone carried.

There were Opinels and Douk Douks, Spanish horn-handled folders with blades like willow leaves, tiny hideout blades, hand-filling

bowies, sleeve daggers, push daggers, curved claw blades and bejeweled knives that could only belong to a warrior princess from another world. No doubt there were knives hidden away and ready for instant use. Nestled here in lush forest, far from city streets and the strife and cares of the outside world, this is the home, workshop and sanctuary of Fred Perrin and Elsa Fantino, knifemakers extraordinaire, wizards of the blade, warriors.

While spending a few months in France, my wife and companion of a hundred adventures, Mary Lou

At home deep in the heart of France's Burgundy wine country, Elsa Fantino and Fred Perrin forge, grind, polish and craft a wide variety of blades. *(Elsa Fantino and ©MLAyres images)*

(ML), and I had the opportunity to visit Fred and Elsa. After we endured a long day's travel from a village near the Spanish border, Fred met us at the train station in a nearby town. Perrin stands well over 6 feet, with broad shoulders, lean muscles and the long arms and legs of a natural swordsman. He moves with the grace and economy of a trained martial artist, and has the situational awareness of a combat veteran. Greeting us with a friendly smile, Fred escorted us to his truck. After leaving town, we drove for miles through twilight-lit forest, deer fleeting at the edges of our headlights, and finally arrived at his hideaway.

Elsa greeted us at her door and immediately put us at ease with her charming smile and colloquial English. When speaking English, she has no trace of a French accent and sounds like a California girl. ML asked her, "Are you sure you're French?" Turns out Elsa spent many years in America as a working professional artist in her chosen medium: iron. In addition to knives, Elsa forges decorative ironwork, gates, tables, dragons, jewelry and, well, anything in iron.

Fantino is a strikingly beautiful woman, with strong features, ink-black hair and clear green eyes. Compact and athletic, she moves with the deliberation of the highly trained martial artist that she is. There is, however, no hint in appearance of her past as a champion kickboxer. No broken nose, no cauliflower ears or scarred eyebrows. From the lack of visible scars I figured that, like a knife fighter with no scars, she must have been a very good kick boxer. Hollywood has featured many actresses as warrior princesses, but neither the directors nor actresses ever got it right. Elsa is a warrior princess. She's also a very nice lady.

Over dinner and a bottle of the local white Burgundy wine, Fred and Elsa made us welcome in their home. We told stories, shared backgrounds, stayed up late and got to know one another. The next morning Elsa showed us around the grounds of their place. In back there is a large green lawn, two cabins and a vegetable garden from which she gathered greens for our lunchtime salad.

A Fred Perrin Neck Bowie (left) and Ken Onion-designed CRKT Eros II are ready for lunch duty.

Elsa Fantino's fantasy-inspired but practical knives include, from right, the Avatar Claw, a bejeweled dagger and two tiny hideout blades.

A COAL-FIRED FORGE

Close behind the house is the workshop they share, with a thousand ancient-looking hand tools, anvils and hammers, grinding wheels and files, and a coal-fired forge. We watched for hours as they forged, hammered, polished and crafted a wide variety of blades.

Elsa's stunning blades create their own aesthetic, a unique fusion of feminine art, power and purpose. Medieval, otherworldly or from a dream world, I've never before seen their like. If your imagination is captured by Elsa's work, as was mine, be assured that these brilliantly designed and crafted blades are functional tools and weapons, not only creative craft.

During cutting tests in the shop and in the nearby forest where we cut saplings for primitive shelters and weapons, Elsa's blades performed as a bladesmith's blades should perform; they cut well and efficiently, and held their edges. In the shop, they cut rope, thickly rolled fabric and heavy cardboard

with ease. She used her "Avatar"—a knife inspired by the film of the same name and that has a blade like a giant raptor's claw, including a bejeweled hilt that characterizes most of her work—to bring down saplings. Elsa's work is new to most Americans, but it won't be for long. She is a rising star.

Perrin is a former French Army Commando, a national tae kwon do champion, an all-Europe full-contact stick fighting champion, and a master of *savate*—hard core, full contact French kickboxing. Fred has considerable real world combat experience, and teaches CQB (Close Quarter Combat), which includes blade work, unarmed combat, and the combat use of handguns and shoulder weapons, to military, covert units and selected students in many European countries. He also teaches edged weapons defense to various police units. This background and experience is reflected in his knives.

He is well known in the United States for his production and semi-production knives, such as the

A knife enthusiast or hard-core user could do far worse than this collection of Neck Bowies by Fred Perrin.

Elsa Fantino forged and crafted the tiny but piercingly pointed poniards.

After cutting many feet of nylon webbing and polypropylene rope, Fantino's little jewel of a blade was still razor sharp. Meanwhile, Perrin's Shark cut hanging polypropylene rope with ease.

Street Beat, Street Bowie and PPT folder, made by Spyderco, and others from his own production. Such would include the La Griffe, the Shark and the Neck Bowie. Designed as weapons suited for the modern world, these knives are also graceful and elegant, well made and tough. In addition to their self-defense function, they work well as all-around utility knives.

During our stay, we used many of Fred's designs to cut hanging rope, polypropylene and hemp, as well as 6-inch-thick rolls of denim and other fabrics, heavy cardboard, tissue-thin paper and oak saplings. All fell to Fred's blades.

With a short cutting edge and a finger hole to provide a secure grip, the La Griffe was a revolutionary concept in self-defense blades when Fred first introduced it some years ago. The knife has been copied many times, but none of the copies have the quality and integrity of the original. When used as designed, it is an excellent defensive knife and has stood the test of time. Many covert operators use the compact and effective La Griffe as a backup blade, and it is, as the saying goes, unseen it all the best places.

SMALL EFFECTIVE BLADE

Similar to the La Griffe in concept, the Shark is what Fred describes as "the smallest effective blade I could design." The slim sliver of steel fits in my wallet or on a key ring. Worn slung from a dog tag chain around the neck, the Shark is almost as light as dog tags and barely noticeable. The large finger ring, handle and lanyard make for a comfortable and effective grip.

I've used the tiny Shark in cutting competitions, and it has outperformed many larger blades. The Shark cuts hanging rope, slashes through water-filled plastic bottles and press-cuts through 22 layers of tightly rolled denim. It's also a handy tool to open envelopes and boxes, and cut rubber hose. I've used the Shark in the kitchen and found that it will slice a flank steak into strips for barbecue just as well as any of my kitchen knives.

ML has used her Street Beat to prepare vegetables, meat and fish to make delicious meals in kitchens and around campfires in 20 countries, and to make kindling for those campfires. She has also employed the knife to assist me in making survival shelters for classes we teach. It is one of her two favorite knives, and rarely am I allowed to use it.

Once, when locked out of a chateau in which we were staying in France, she let me use her Street Beat to jimmy open the 3-inch-thick, solid oak, ironbound doors with no damage to the little blade. Small, handy and non-threatening in appearance, the Street Beat is balanced and secure in hand, has a cutout for an index finger and functions as an everyday carry survival knife.

A couple of years ago, while wandering along the Turkish coast just across from the Greek Islands, I used a Perrin Neck Bowie to make a fish trap from a discarded plastic water bottle. By cutting off the tapered top of the plastic bottle and slicing off the lid, I inverted the resulting cone inside the bottle and used tuna scraps as bait. I used rocks to wedge the trap in place underwater with the opening of the bottle facing the outgoing tide. While waiting for

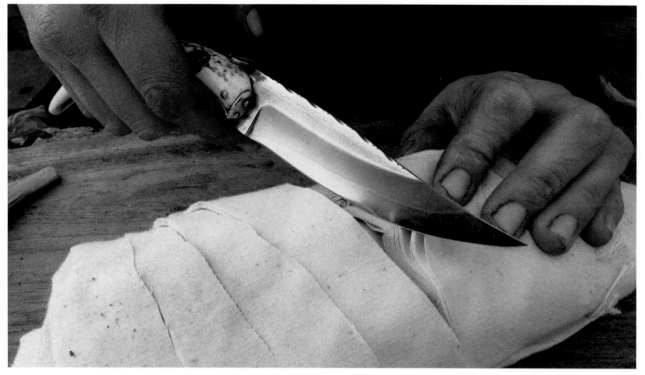

Fantino's friction folder sliced cleanly through 26 layers of tightly rolled fabric.

our fish trap to produce, we went foraging. The hills above the Mediterranean are covered with edible plants, and some require local knowledge to identify; others include familiar dandelion greens, rose hips, wild peppers and prickly pear cactus. Prickly pear pads can be eaten raw in a salad, grilled or cooked with tomatoes to make a delicious Mexican dish.

While foraging, I used the Neck Bowie to cut shelter poles to make a tripod, secured a "space blanket" as a covering, then cut tall grass to cover the ground under our shelter. When we returned to the water, we found two small fish in our trap. While anticipating the tasty dinner to come, we set up the results of our foraging for photos. However, as we fiddled with cameras a feral cat crept up, snatched one of the fish and made off with it.

Deprived of our fish dinner, we fell back on emergency rations—a block of goat cheese and a bottle of white wine, which we had with the wild green salad at our little shelter while watching the sun sink into the sea.

PUNCHED INTO AN OAK TREE

I continued to use the little Neck Bowie in the kitchen for a few weeks. Then, wondering just how strong this little knife really was, I gave into temptation and punched it into an oak tree, hard. The blade

penetrated well and with no damage. The butt of the Neck Bowie's handle is nicely curved and fits comfortably into the base of my palm. It is so well formed that there was no discomfort on impact.

The Street Bowie, with its 5-inch blade, is big brother to the Street Beat, and will do anything the Street Beat will do with more blade length. It is an

Perrin sharpens a spear point using one of his re-forged custom blades.

Perrin takes down a sapling with two strokes of his 7-inch bowie.

Nothing but the hand-filling Fantino Avatar Claw, named after the movie, would do for fashioning a spear point.

incredibly versatile knife that is ideal for utilitarian and personal-defense applications. A small fixed blade, it transitions well from urban to wilderness conditions.

Perrin makes a wide range of custom knives, some variations on the styles for which he is known, and others being unique, forged, high-carbon-steel blades with stag and wood handles. Often re-forged from old carbon steel that he finds in French flea markets, many of them have a rustic look reminiscent of American frontier knives. They perform as well as Fred's modern designs, and with their thin, uncompromising blades, cut like the winter wind in Siberia.

I've used two of Fred's small, rustic custom knives at a cabin in the foothills of Bulgaria's Stara Planina Mountains for outdoors and kitchen work. Either could be used to peel an apple or a pear in one thin spiral, and sliced meat as well as any sushi knife. The larger one, which has a 4-inch blade, splits kindling and shaves wood curls for nightly fires with ease. When I first received these knives they were scary sharp, and a month later they still were.

Perrin also makes a series of carbon fiber blades. The non-metallic blades weigh next to nothing and cut reasonably well, albeit not as well as steel blades. The carbon fiber blades do not hold their edges cutting wood or other hard material, but do well enough on meat and soft cutting media. They are easy to sharpen on just about any sharpener or on emery cloth.

Having been trained in various martial arts, including blade arts, which I've practiced for 50 years, and having been obliged to protect my life with a

blade during overseas service, I know a little about these topics. Fred knows a lot. He is a specialist and taught me a few things. During our brief visit, I learned certain things, important things, by watching Fred and by closely examining the knives he has designed. Tools teach their own lessons. If you are interested in these topics, get a Perrin knife and pay close attention to it. You might learn some things.

The morning of our departure came too soon. I was not ready to leave, but obligations required it. I took a last look around the workshop and around the comfortable and slightly magical redoubt that together Fred and Elsa have created, hidden deep in the French countryside, home to wizards and warriors. Then we headed down the road, memories firmly held. ☐

Desert Ironwood Is One Hot Burl

A hard, colorful, highly figured handle material, ironwood is a knifemaker's dream

By Mike Haskew

Michael Tyre's Dog Bone Dagger showcases an exhibition-grade desert ironwood handle to complement the 340-layer, ladder-pattern damascus blade.

(PointSeven Studios image)

To quote the Kris Kristofferson song, *Pilgrim*, it's "a walkin' contradiction, partly truth, partly fiction." Even the name ironwood is a bit of a mixed metaphor, and depending on whom you talk to, it is known as desert ironwood, Arizona ironwood or simply ironwood. In Mexico, it goes by the moniker palo fierro. Scientists like to use the term Olneya tesota. In any iteration or language, it remains one of the best known but least understood of natural knife handle materials.

From the world's great custom knifemakers to those who are just establishing themselves, ironwood is a traditional choice for fine knife patterns. Its color ranges from dark, robust brown to shimmering gold and sometimes seems to mimic the rays of the sun. With a specific gravity of 1.2, it is among the densest of woods, making it both easy and challenging to work.

"Arizona ironwood is extremely dense, and only a few other species in the world have a density in this range," explained Rob Bradley, president of Arizona Ironwood, LLC. "It is so dense it will sink in water and so hard it was used as wheel bearings before steel bearings were invented. Customers often tell us that Arizona ironwood is their preferred handle material. We often hear that it is easier to work with than other types of wood because it is forgiving and can be finished right along with the blade."

Renowned custom knifemaker Jerry Fisk began earning a living at the forge in 1987. His proficiency with ironwood is a hallmark of his long career, and while there is an art to working with the material, he acknowledges the benefits too. "On one hand it is hard to work

Wayne Whittaker's folder sports an ironwood handle, nickel silver bolsters engraved by Bert Edmonston and a Mike Norris "crazy lace"-pattern damascus blade. *(PointSeven Studios image)*

Courtesy of Arizona Ironwood, LLC, the blocks of desert ironwood reveal the intricate and varied patterns that the material embodies, making it ideal for knife handles.

with, but it has advantages as well," he reasoned. "It is both a hard wood and an oil-based wood. That means it will gum up your sanding belts. Forget about it if you use a dull belt. The best thing for knifemakers is that you do not have to seal the wood since it is oil based. Just sand and polish it."

Allen Surls is a relative newcomer to custom knives, but he has latched onto ironwood and pursued it with gusto. Its beauty pulls him toward its possibilities like a magnet. "Ironwood has deep, rich colors," he commented. "Depending on the piece, there is a gold sheen that can jump out at you and that is unsurpassed as far as I am concerned. The natural properties of the wood allow it to be considered very stable with less chance of warping, cracking and checking."

"The natural oils make it so stable that conventional stabilizers will not work," Surls continued. "Even if the stabilization process is done correctly, under vacuum and pressure, the ironwood will not take the resins. Another very nice feature of it is its toughness

and resistance to dents and such from use."

Fisk is also a collector. While ironwood may be resistant to dents, when Jerry looks at the material from an investment perspective he has a different take. "As a collector, I do not buy knives with desert ironwood," he admitted. "The grain darkens over time, and the wood has a tendency to 'check,' with miniature cracks, most often shallow but they are there. As a collector, when I buy a wood handled knife, my first choice is a gunstock wood."

In contrast, Wayne Whittaker, a maker of straight knives beginning in 1970, and who branched into folders nearly 30 years later, has experienced virtually no issues with ironwood checking or shrinking. His biggest headache is in the sanding process. "If you use sharp belts, it is easy to work with," he said, "but the end grain will burn easily. So you have to be careful there. I finish it with 2,000-grit paper and a good coat of wax."

A POWERFUL STENCH

Some say that ironwood gives off a powerful stench during sanding, something similar to that of dirty socks. To minimize the unpleasantness and collect the fine dust that is a byproduct of the sanding process, good ventilation and vacuum systems are a must. One other concern may arise with the oil or resin in the wood. Contact with the skin can cause an irritation for those prone to allergies, although such reports are rare.

A veteran of three tours in Vietnam with the

⌃ Allen Surls chose the ironwood burl handle scales well for his version of a Bob Loveless Wilderness pattern, also featuring black G10 liners and a hollow-ground A2 tool steel blade.

⌄ Two Chris Brookshire knives sport desert ironwood handles, the 52100 blade at left heat-colored a plumb brown, and the knife at right featuring an Alabama Damascus blade. *(PointSeven image)*

101st Airborne Division, Michael Tyre has been a custom knifemaker for 16 years, and he has been an ironwood devotee the entire time. "I have never had a problem with ironwood shrinking or swelling," he asserted. "It drills well and shapes easily. It helps to use a small amount of oil when you are sanding."

Shanna Kemp of Jantz Supply calls ironwood a personal favorite. "Desert ironwood is, in my opinion, one of the most eye catching woods available," she commented. "The color ranges from yellow and auburn to a darker reddish-brown with black streaks. Some pieces can be almost entirely black with light tones that seem to shimmer or even glow. The overall effect is a rich mixture of colors."

An investment of time and effort will yield spectacular results for the custom knifemaker who is willing to learn the art of working with ironwood. "It will achieve a lustrous polish with patient sanding, using fine grade sandpaper or micron polishing paper, once the final shape of the knife handle is achieved," Kemp advised. "Some knifemakers like to

also use pink, scratch-resistant polishing compound on a sewn muslin wheel as a final finish, and then coat the wood with Renaissance Wax to offer extra protection and resistance to darkening. Though darkening happens naturally with age, since desert ironwood is already old by the time it comes to market, customers can expect little color change for some time."

When asked if ironwood is really as hard as its name and reputation suggest, Fisk responds with an emphatic, "Yes! One of North America's main candidates for the crown of hardest wood species is desert ironwood. It is that hard."

Although its appeal is broad among the knifemaking and buying public, the flowering desert ironwood tree grows only in a localized area of the Sonoran Desert in the American Southwest and northern Mexico. It is a member of the Fabaceae family and a distant relative of pea and bean plants. It is considered a keystone species, a nurse plant and a habitat modifier. Therefore, it has been a protected species

This stylish cross-section of desert ironwood demonstrates the variety of colors and intricate patterns found in the material. *(Myles Gilmer, Gilmer Wood Company image)*

A group shot of Chris Brookshear's work in desert ironwood exemplifies the many looks, both bold and subtle, that may be achieved with the handle material. *(PointSeven Studios image)*

since the 1970s in the state of Arizona and since 1993 in Mexico.

"Years ago, you could harvest a fallen ironwood tree but not cut one down," noted Fisk. "Now they do not want you to harvest a fallen tree as I understand it."

Kemp added, "Desert ironwood is becoming more difficult to source. Since it is highly sought after by woodcrafters, furniture makers and artisans, the supply has become more limited. For this reason, harvesting has been restricted to protect the ecology and sustainability of desert ironwood."

JUST ASK THE SERI

"Historically, the Seri Indians used desert ironwood for tool handles," she continued, "and today members of the tribe produce highly prized art carvings with the wood using hand tools. It is a dream for the woodcarver and sculptor, making it perfect for the knifemaker looking to take their handles to the next level artistically. Knifemakers love desert ironwood for its stability and beauty. Its popularity is increasing, and we see a surge in people using it in knifemaking. A few years ago we featured desert ironwood on the cover of our catalog, which allowed knifemakers to really see the beauty of the wood when sanded and finished."

Despite restrictions on harvesting and distribution, ironwood remains in good supply for knifemakers, and it is affordable. As the quality or grade of a particular ironwood slab or set of handle scales in-

creases, the price goes up accordingly. "Finer grades of desert ironwood can be quite expensive, but I feel it is worth it because it belongs on quality knives that are built to last for generations," Tyre said.

"We grade desert ironwood on two bases," related Bradley. "These are clarity of wood and figure quality. Premium quality is defect free, as in our 'standard' and 'figured' stock-size blanks. Colors range from chocolate to a light gold. Standard quality includes mostly solid colors with little figure, while figure quality includes mixed colors such as black straight growth lines over gold. The higher figure grade is found in ironwood burl, and burl is graded on the tightness of grain and color configuration."

Arizona Ironwood, LLC works with customers to provide specific sizes and colors whenever necessary. "It is our specialty," Bradley confirmed, "so around our shop it is the most popular wood type we sell, and it seems to grow in demand with the growing industry. Many of our customers ask for our ironwood by name, as well as the figure quality and the specific size they need. If we don't have it in stock, we can usually custom mill the size in the figure quality they want."

"Desert Ironwood can be all over the board in figure and color," he laughed, "from flat black to bright yellow with black lines. Figure can be straight with contrasting lines, while burl can be wildly swirled, bizarrely patterned, revealing faces and shapes limited only by the imagination. We responded to customer requests by creating a website where photos and a list of about 1,500 individual wood blanks can be found at any given time. Customers can now browse through our website pages, select the exact piece of wood they like and buy it on the spot."

At Jantz Supply, a tiered grading system indicates to prospective customers the relative characteristics of a given ironwood sample. "Grading is the process of categorizing the wood based on color, contrast and burl," commented Kemp. "The more contrast, color and burl, the rarer and therefore more expensive the wood.

"High contrast is characterized by a bright color contrast with darker lines, which produces a luminosity effect when polished," said Shanna. "Exhibition contains burl and rich patterning, which is the result of the tree growing in a deformed manner and creating growth that changes the typical grain patterns. Burl often appears as swirls of light and dark patterning across the wood. Presentation grade is the most rare and has extreme contrast and figure throughout the wood."

IRONCLAD INVESTMENT

For quality and value, Kemp recommends desert ironwood as a solid, economical choice to add to the aesthetics and durability of a personal knife or a custom knife for resale.

"Since we cater to knifemakers, our desert ironwood is sold in precut scales and priced according to size and grade," she added. For example, High Contrast Ironwood scales measuring .25 inches by 1.25 inches by 4 inches sell for $14.95, while the same size in Exhibition Burl costs $27.95, and Presentation Burl runs $36.95.

Over the years, Fisk has consistently used two familiar ironwood patterns. "I have bought two basic colors," he said, "brown/black and the one that is brown/black with a bit of gold/yellow color. I prefer the one with the bit of gold/yellow color in it. The wood can be classed as grades A, B, C and D also, with grade D being straight grain and no movement in the grain structure. The A grade can look very stunning with all the twists and turns of the burl

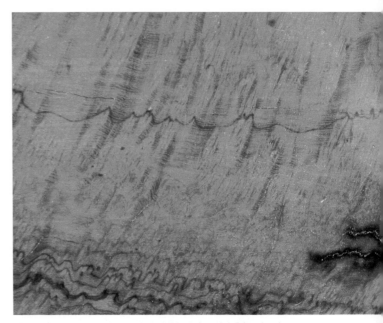

The desert ironwood sample exhibits a burnished red color, adding subtle beauty and highlights to any knife. *(Myles Gilmer, Gilmer Wood Company image)*

lines. Ironwood will last on a knife handle for years, and since it is an oil-based wood it will have less shrinkage," he concluded.

Custom knifemaker Chris Brookshear uses ironwood on about a third of his work and finds it particularly well suited as a complement to his damascus blades. He purchases most of his ironwood inventory at the BLADE Show. Its popularity and the reasonable price for mid-range pieces help drive his handle choices. Then, of course, there is the kaleidoscope of color.

"Every piece is different with unlimited grain variations," Chris noted. "I see the demand as surging, and the difference in the grain patterns is a big reason for that."

Echoing that sentiment, Whittaker remarked, "Most people like wood, but ironwood is the favorite. I always have a couple of desert ironwood knives on my table at shows. The interest in ironwood has been about the same year after year. There have always been some people that only like wood handles, and most of them prefer desert ironwood."

Surls says ironwood is a "classic that can't be beat!"

For custom knifemakers, suppliers and those who treasure their collections, knives with ironwood handles attract attention, set apart by the hardwood's timeless beauty, romantic aura and historic elegance. □

Visceral Allure of the Bowie

The author and thousands of people like him have been deeply affected by the bowie knife

By Les Robertson

A knife collector, custom knife entrepreneur/dealer/ purveyor and expert, Robertson owns Robertson's Custom Cutlery, robertsoncustomcutlery.com

September 19, 1827, on a sandbar between Louisiana and Mississippi, there was first a duel and then a fight. The fight between Col. Robert Crain and Jim Bowie purported to last only 90 seconds, and those 90 seconds have been discussed and reviewed since that day. While the sandbar fight started the Bowie legend, man and knife, it was probably an 1831 incident in Texas that solidified the legend. Three armed men, hired to kill him, attacked Bowie. The story goes that even though the attackers were armed with rifles, Bowie was the only man to walk away.

Bowie dispatched all three attackers using his knife. If interested in an in-depth look at the start of the Bowie legend, I highly recommend Dr. James Batson's book titled *James Bowie and the Sandbar Fight: Birth of the James Bowie Legend and Bowie Knife*. Batson is not only an excellent researcher and writer, but also an American Bladesmith Society (ABS) master smith. His firsthand knowledge of crafting bowie knives gives him a special insight into the creation of Jim Bowie's original knife.

Of all the great knifemakers and designers in the world, none of them have an entire category of knives named after them like Bowie does. The style of knife used by Bowie—now known simply as a bowie or bowie knife—saw some changes after the confrontation at the

Well balanced and exceptionally quick in the hand, ABS journeyman smith Steve Randall's bowie boasts an 8.5-inch san mai steel blade, a Sambar stag handle, and a blued high-carbon-steel guard, ferrule and pommel, the latter filed to match the grooves of the stag. *(PointSeven image)*

sandbar. Most notable were the addition of double guards to most bowies, and sharpened clip points with the appearance of the forward third of the blade spines being clipped off.

The knives bearing Bowie's name gained such a reputation and following that they began to be mass-produced in Sheffield, England. Renowned makers such as Joseph Rodgers and George Wostenholm started making bowie knives. Estimates are that upwards of 70 percent of the bowies that went West with the first wave of pioneers came out of Sheffield.

The bowie knife enjoyed "must have" status for many soldiers on both sides of the Civil War. The bowie's diversity was summed up by a historian of the time who described the knife style as, " … long enough to use as a sword, sharp enough to use as a razor, wide enough to use as a paddle, and heavy enough to use as a hatchet."

What is and what is not a bowie is the subject of numerous debates. Rezin Bowie, Jim's brother who had the first knife made for his sibling, indicated the historic knife had a 9 ¼-inch blade. Given that there

Lightweight and with great balance, Cladio and Ariel Sobral's stag-handle bowie dons a 10-inch, satin-finished san mai steel blade, stainless steel fittings and a Marcelo Sobral custom leather sheath. *(Ward image)*

is no photo of the knife, we can only go by information historians have gathered. My take on the blade length of the first bowie is that it was between 9 and 11 inches.

I'd like to say I based this on Rezin's comments but that is not the case. Certain blade lengths favor particular tasks. Bird-and-trout blades are usually between 2 and 4 inches. Hunters and skinners generally have blades in the 3- to 5-inch range. Camp knives often feature blades stretching from 5-7 inches, and fighters commonly sport blades in the 6-8-inch range.

Based on Rezin's comment that the blade made for his brother was 9 ¼ inches, combined with the variety of chores that could be done with the bowie, the 9-11-inch range is where I place the bowie's blade. All of the blade lengths mentioned are generalizations. Blade lengths are subjective, and different categories will often feature shorter or longer blades. I have seen gent's or a gambler's bowies with 4-inch blades and hunting knives parading 10-inch blades. When I

see knives sporting blades that defy the conventional lengths of their category, I am reminded of my 7th-grade shop teacher who always reminded us to use the "right tool for the job."

BOWIE LEGEND LIVES, NOT FADING AWAY

Many objects of legend and lore fade after 189 years, but not the bowie knife. Thanks in no small part to the ABS and the men and women of this organization, the forged blade has been kept alive around the world. Bill Moran, the patriarch of the ABS, is credited with reintroducing modern knife enthusiasts to the art of forged damascus blade steel.

Another of the founders of the ABS who does not receive enough credit is B.R. Hughes. Hughes was there at the beginning, in 1976, along with Bill Moran, Don Hastings and Bill Bagwell when the ABS was formed. Hughes' 40-plus years of writing about the forged blade has done much to educate and inform makers and collectors, leaving no doubt that

Of frame-handle construction with a mosaic-damascus guard and ferrules, a fileworked bronze spacer and liners and domed handle pins, Terry Vandeventer's mosaic-damascus swayback bowie also showcases a mammoth ivory handle and custom leather sheath. *(Ward image)*

he is the finest knife writer in the business.

In 1988, at a small knife show in Lexington, Kentucky, I saw my first damascus bowie. Master smith Keith Kilby had made the knife, and though damascus blades had been available for several years, it was my first encounter with pattern-welded steel. Despite the damascus being in a basic random pattern, I became intrigued with not only the look, but also the forging process. This was before the Bill Moran School of Bladesmithing opened, there were no hammer-ins, and the Internet didn't exist, so information was on the scarce side. At the time, the knife was out of my price range, but Kilby informed me that a similar knife in a plain, high-carbon-steel blade would be less money.

It was at the 1989 BLADE Show that I got to see another incredible bowie, this one with a 10-inch, high-carbon-steel blade, rope filework on the guard, a stag handle and a shooting star logo. Picking up the bowie for a closer look, I was amazed at how light and balanced the large knife was. The hook was set. That purchase from master smith Jim Crowell set me on the path to purchasing several thousand forged blades.

The visual and visceral allure of the bowie knife

is undeniable. Without exception, every year over the last 25 years that I've paid for a table at the BLADE Show as a custom knife entrepreneur and dealer/purveyor, the "fight" has broken out. Several times each show, someone would pick up a bowie off of my table and start moving it as if having an imaginary fight. Once the "fight" was complete, they'd look at me with a sly grin. I would always inquire, "Did you win?" That question never failed to turn the sly grin into a smile.

Defining bowies often involves their handles, forged steel blades and overall material makeup. I often equate steel to baked goods. You have the category of cakes or pies. What determines the type and consistency of a cake or pie are the ingredients and often the baker. The same is true for steel. All steel contains carbon, however after that the recipe can branch out in hundreds of directions.

While stainless steel has been forged, the primary type of alloy used on forged bowie knives is high-carbon steel. It is wise to consider the pros and cons of a steel alloy, particularly for the job the blade is intended to perform, if and when purchasing or perhaps making a forged blade. At most knife shows are forged blades made from old saw blades, railroad spikes, truck leaf springs and even files. If it is carbon steel, it can be forged. That is not to say it will cut better or worse than manufactured steel. With manufactured steel, you generally know what you are getting with regards to the composition of the steel and how best to work it.

Below are popular steels that are and have been used to forge blades. However it is not, nor is it intended to be, a complete list. The comments are intended to inform about the steel and not a maker's ability to get more out of it than what is intended. It is more of a starting point for a conversation.

With the 10 series of steel, which would be 1095, 1084, 1070, 1060 and 1050 alloys, the higher the number the better the edge holding and the lower the number the tougher the steel. 1095 and 1084 are most often used for forged blades.

- O1: This steel has a reputation for being forgiving while being worked. It takes a very good edge, is tough but will rust easily.
- W2: It holds an edge well, is tough, and by a skilled bladesmith can show an excellent

A Tad Lynch sub-hilt bowie parades an 11.5-inch W2 blade with distinct *hamon* (temper line), a stainless steel guard and sub-hilt, and a stabilized Turkish walnut handle. *(Ward image)*

hamon, or temper line.

- 5160: This steel features good edge holding and is extremely tough.
- 52100 ball bearing steel: It is similar to 5160 with better edge holding ability, yet is not as tough as 5160.

Most forged blades are flat ground, or have flat-ground edges. Simply put, this means the blade thicknesses taper all the way from the spines to the edges, and on both sides of the blades. A flat grind is difficult to achieve, as the maker has to remove a lot of metal. The advantage gained is a lighter blade that maintains its integrity. Another technique utilized with forged blades is differential heat-treating the blades, creating hard edges and soft spines. After differential heat-treating and finishing/polishing a blade, a temper line generally forms, revealing the intersection of the hard and soft parts of the blade.

While other alloys can and do produce a temper line, over the last five years W2 steel has become a favorite of collectors, as exquisite temper lines can be achieved in differentially heat-treating the steel. It is the use of a clay coating on the blade, and then heating and tempering, that have found favor with both makers and collectors. Through this technique, the uncoated portion of the blade heats to a higher temperature than the clay-coated part, and a temper line forms. W2 might be a favorite blade steel right now, but temper lines can be achieved using the 10 series of blade steels as well.

There are three basic types of handles. A hidden-tang handle is one in which a hole is drilled and shaped lengthwise through the center of a handle to make room for the blade tang. Epoxy is often used as an adhesive to hold the steel tang and handle material together. Depending on the material and maker, the handle may or may not have a pin through the

Exhibiting a beautiful feather-pattern damascus blade and exceptional handle ergonomics, Michael Deibert's take on a bowie/fighter also includes a blued high-carbon-steel guard and ferrule, a bronze spacer and a desert ironwood grip. *(SharpByCoop image)*

handle material and into the tang to further secure it.

A hidden-tang handle also lends itself to a takedown style of knife. A takedown handle is built in a similar fashion to a standard hidden-tang grip, but with no glue used to secure the tang and handle material. Instead, the handle is held together with a nut or finial that screws onto the end of the tang, providing the necessary pressure to keep the handle secured between the nut and guard, bolster or blade. Generally a tool is provided to remove the pommel nut or finial.

A mortise-tang handle is one with a shorter tang, and handle material that is split lengthwise. The inside of each handle half has a slot cut evenly, lengthwise, allowing the tang to be sandwiched in between both pieces of handle material. This technique almost always requires a combination of epoxy and some type of pin through the handle. Two

advantages to this type of handle are the reduction of weight, which can really help on a hunter/skinner that is carried in the field, and overall better balance of the knife.

Lastly is a frame-handle knife. For a frame handle, the blade tang is slotted into the frame of a knife, and handle material is added to each side. When completed, it gives the illusion that the knife has a full tang. Generally constructed with both hidden pins and those that show, this is the most complex method of knife handle making. Expect to pay more for this type of grip.

FIRST STOP FOR BOWIE FANS

A first stop for any bowie knife fan or enthusiast of the forged blade should be online at www.americanbladesmith.com. Here a myriad of information awaits you about what it takes to achieve different

The W2 blade of Will Morrison's bowie/fighter is etched and polished to show a hamon, and accompanied by an ironwood handle, a stainless steel guard, and black G-10 and bronze spacers. *(Ward image)*

bladesmith certifications (stamps), about the location, dates and times of hammer-ins, the backgrounds of makers and other useful information. If you've only had a chance to see forged blades in a magazine or online, attend a show and handle the knives. The two-dimensional photography belies the subtleties in the different steels and construction techniques.

Currently the three best shows to see bowies and other forged blades are: The Art of Steel Show held in Little Rock, Arkansas, in February; the BLADE Show in Atlanta each June; and the International Custom Cutlery Exposition (ICCE) taking place in Kansas City, Missouri, in September.

The exchange of information that is available on forging knives has opened the door to hundreds if not thousands of new makers worldwide. The information provided here merely scratches the surface of what a knife enthusiast should know to get the best

bowie for the money.

For a collector or potential owner of bowies and/or forged blades, the information is out there. Use it. Learn as much as you can about construction techniques and methods. Understand what is and what is not acceptable of the different levels of knifemakers. Do you know the difference between a $700 and a $1,000 bowie? If not, find out *before* you buy a bowie, not *after*.

If you are a knife user, learn about blade and edge geometry to help get the most out of a blade. Make sure you know what your knife can and can't do. The steel type, type of guard and even sheath will have a bearing on how your knife performs and carries. Remember the advice of my 7th-grade shop teacher— use the right tool for the job—and take heed. □

How Real Smiths Smelt Steel

The magic is in the smelting when turning raw iron ore into a bar of steel for a knife blade

By Tim Zowada

Making iron and steel using the bloomery smelting process is both expensive and labor intensive. A *bloomery* is a type of furnace used for smelting iron from its oxides. Making steel in this way is so inefficient, the bloomery method was rendered obsolete well over 150 years ago by the Bessemer process and other steelmaking methods. Yet, over the last decade, the production of iron and steel by bloomery smelting has increased dramatically. There is something magical about taking raw iron ore and converting it into a bar of iron, or steel, at home.

The resurgence of smelting in the United States has been mostly due to the efforts of craftsmen. Lee Sauder, Darrell Markewitz, Michael McCarthy, Ric Furrer and several others, including myself, have spent a great deal of time, money and effort to bring the bloomery smelting process back from the pages of history. As with most things, "We stand on the shoulders of giants." Those who've been able to get involved in smelting relatively quickly owe a lot to the efforts of others before them.

In 2006, I had the privilege of watching a smelting demonstration by Michael McCarthy. It was fascinating, and Michael pulled a huge iron bloom from his smelter. While I enjoyed learning about the process, I must admit I wasn't very interested

in trying it on my own. The biggest reason was the effort involved in collecting, cooking and crushing the ore. I suppose I may just be lazy at heart, but all that work with rocks wasn't very appealing.

Everything changed after talking to knifemaker and American Bladesmith Society master smith Kevin Cashen. He explained that, in Michigan, we have an iron ore source that is nearly ready for the smelter—the black sands of Lake Superior. I attended a smelt at Kevin's house where the sand was used. Kevin made a beautiful, high-carbon bloom. He even gave me half of it. After making a knife and razor from Kevin's bloom, I was hooked.

That trip to Kevin's led me to formulate some very specific goals for my smelting. First, I wanted to produce high-carbon blooms. A lot of smelting is

The chimney of the smelter is a simple construction of a flue, ceramic wool and sheet metal.

⩘ The flue is wrapped with one layer of ceramic wool, which is wired in place.

⩘ The chimney assembly is wrapped with sheet metal and secured with hose clamps.

aimed at producing low-carbon iron. That's fine for the blacksmiths, but I need steel for making knives and razors. Many smelting processes yield a bloom that has greatly varying carbon content throughout. These blooms are usually forged flat, cut into smaller pieces, and then sorted by carbon content. My hope was to produce a bloom that, when forged and folded onto and over itself, would result in a bar of steel averaging .85-to-1 percent carbon.

My second goal was to keep the smelt, and bloom size, manageable for just one person. Most of the smelting done these days produces wonderfully large blooms. Two or more workers are required to keep things efficient. Where I live, help is hard to find. Keeping the smelter and bloom size down means I can be much more flexible in planning and working the process.

MODULAR SMELTER DESIGN

The above goals led to a modular smelter design. It is fast and easy to build. All the materials are available locally. Most importantly, after the smelt is finished, the furnace may be disassembled one piece at a time to investigate bloom formation and placement. This has been a huge help in learning how to

make a bloom with the properties I desire.

The smelting furnace is basically a vertical cylinder, or rectangle, open on the top. The bottom section houses the area for the combustion air to enter, and the bloom to form. Charcoal and iron ore are fed in the top. When the process is completed, the bloom is removed from the bottom area of the furnace.

The heart of the modular smelter is an 8 ½-inch-square chimney flue. This provides the stack into which the charcoal and iron ore are added. Such flues are available at most brick or construction supply houses. The flue is wrapped with a 1-inch layer of ceramic wool insulation. On the outer surface, a piece of sheet metal is secured with hose clamps to hold everything together.

The base of the smelter is constructed from ordinary cement blocks and firebricks. First, a base layer of cement blocks is laid and leveled. Eight blocks are laid in a square shape to support the main part of the smelter. Two additional blocks are placed off the left side to serve as a base for the *tuyere* (a pipe

A cement block base is leveled and filled with sand.

The first layer of blocks is filled with sand for stability.

The firebrick layer is where the bloom will form.

through which air is blown into a furnace) assembly. This base should be as level and smooth as possible. The areas between the blocks are then filled in with dry dirt or sand to hold everything in place. Someday I will stop procrastinating and pour a cement base to replace my layer of blocks.

The next level is also made from cement blocks. Four blocks make up the bottom level of the smelter chimney. I normally use two full-size blocks and two half blocks, but four full-size blocks certainly suffice. I make sure they fit tightly together and are level. The spaces are also filled in with dry sand or dirt. During the smelting process, the bottom of the bloom will form close to the top of this block layer.

The next stage involves standard firebricks. The corresponding photos in the story show the proper placement. This firebrick layer is where the bloom forms. It is important to have all the blocks fit tightly together because the smelter will work much better if there are no gaps or leaks. In fact, it is a good idea to seal all the vertical seams with ordinary furnace cement.

The firebrick layer is also where the air tuyere enters the smelter. The tuyere for this smelter is fashioned from pipe fittings. A water-cooled tip allows for placement experimentation without worry-

ing about the tip melting. The inner section is simply ¾-inch pipe, while the outer casing is 1 ½-inch pipe. It is very important that the water-cooled tip does not leak! Adding water to a 2,800-degree Fahrenheit smelter would be a very bad thing! For safety's sake, most accomplished smelters prefer a heavy copper tuyere. For more information on smelter construction and tuyeres, visit www.leesauder.com/smelting_research.php.

OUTFITTED WITH A PEEPHOLE

Another interesting feature of a typical, modern tuyere is the peephole on the end. The end opposite the furnace is made from a few PVC fittings, and the

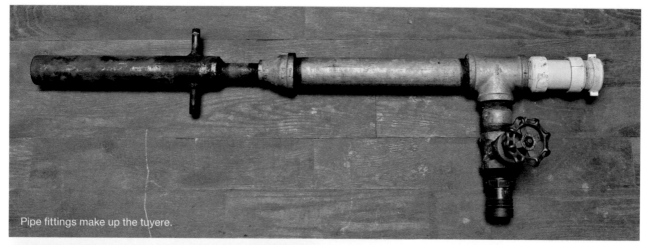

Pipe fittings make up the tuyere.

⌃ A viewing port or "peephole" is made from a #3 welding lens and PVC pipe fittings.

⌄ The tuyere angle and insertion depth are set while building the firebrick layer.

end cap is a #3 welding lens, allowing the steelmaker to see what is going on in the smelter from the end of the tuyere. The cap is also easily removable for clearing the business end of the tuyere when required.

The tuyere angle influences the shape and carbon content of the bloom. In general, lower angles produce low-carbon blooms and higher angles create high-carbon blooms. A range of 15 to 30 degrees is common. For high-carbon blooms, 25 to 30 degrees has been ideal.

The chimney flue assembly is set on top of the brick base, and any minor gaps around the tureye are plugged with ceramic wool and a little furnace cement. The air supply for the smelter is nothing

more than a cheap "bouncy house/moon bounce/ inflatable castle" blower, several of which have been and usually are listed on eBay.

While the more ambitious iron and steel makers also make their own charcoal, the store-bought variety works fine. With the increasing popularity of hardwood charcoal grilling, most of the big box stores now carry hardwood charcoal in 20-pound bags. Real hardwood charcoal, not briquettes, works well. The only problem with the commercial charcoal is that it is usually rather large, and must be crushed or cut to size. I shoot for about 3 1/2-inch pieces, without a lot of dust from crushing the charcoal, and find that I need between 80 and 100 pounds of charcoal per run of the smelter.

The ore used for this smelt is black sand from the southern shore of Lake Superior. It is a mixture of magnetite and hematite, and has a fair amount of silica sand mixed in as well. The Internet is an excellent source for finding iron ore in any location.

Start by filling the base section with finely crushed charcoal. This charcoal base helps determine where the bottom of the bloom will form. A few inches below the tuyere is about right. It is easiest to do this before putting the chimney flue on the top of the smelter.

A small fire is then started in the smelter at the tuyere level. The air is started, and the fire is allowed to grow slowly. As the fire grows, more charcoal is added from the top of the chimney flue. Slowly, the air blasts from the tuyere, and the amount of charcoal is increased. Eventually, the charcoal is to the top of the chimney flue, and a healthy flame is coming from the top of the smelter. Once the smelter is burning at the desired rate, alternating charges of charcoal and iron are added.

The feed rate of charcoal and the ratio of charcoal to iron ore are extremely important. Sauder has found a charcoal feed rate formula of .3 to .4 grams of fuel/minute/cm2 of furnace area works consistently well. For this furnace, that works out to the equivalent of a #10 tin can of charcoal every 6 ½ to 7 minutes. Fussy smelters will weigh every charcoal charge.

The ratio of ore to charcoal is usually done by weight. Those smelting to produce low-carbon blooms usually use a ratio of one part charcoal to one part ore. Smiths seeking a higher carbon product often decrease the ratio to as low as one part iron to two parts charcoal, by weight.

SLAG FORMATION

The adding of charcoal and iron ore continues for several hours. After an hour or two, slag will begin forming at the end of the tuyere. It is easily seen when looking down the peephole on the end of the tuyere. Left alone, this slag will eventually clog the

Running the smelter is a constant process of feeding iron ore and charcoal.

tuyere and end the smelt.

There are two ways to clear the slag. The first is to remove the peephole assembly and run a steel rod down the tuyere, clearing the slag buildup. The second is to pre-form a "slag tap" from a small steel bar. To tap the slag, the front, center firebrick is removed. The slag tap is used to probe at about the top level of the cinder block. If done correctly, a molten stream of liquid slag flows from the furnace. These methods help clear the tuyere and allow the bloom formation to continue.

A time will come where, no matter how often

A modular smelter design allows for the investigation of bloom formation and easy bloom removal.

the tuyere is cleared, or the slag is tapped, the furnace just slows down. The charcoal burn rate will decrease dramatically, even though nothing has been done to change the amount of air entering the furnace. The feeding of the smelter is at an end.

The air is kept running and the charcoal level allowed to burn down. When the chimney flue is about a third full, the flue can be removed and placed to the side … carefully. At this point, all parts are extremely hot! The firebricks are removed to reveal the bloom, which may be slightly stuck to some of the bricks, though careful plying and a little hammering should free it.

This is the best point and time to begin forging the bloom. It is as hot and as thoroughly heated as it will ever be. This is also the best time to cut the bloom into smaller pieces for easier handling later.

Yield rates vary depending on the ore used and details of the smelting process. Low-carbon blooms often yield a bloom as heavy as 35 percent of the weight of ore used, and high-carbon blooms 20 percent of the ore weight

Before the bloom is forged to the final shape, high-carbon blooms are usually folded and welded several times, helping work out impurities and homogenize the carbon content throughout the bar of steel. Typically, a bloom is folded and welded anywhere from five to 15 times.

Something to remember: smelting is very dangerous! It is advisable to wear protective equipment at all times. All in all, smelting is a wonderful way to produce iron or steel at home. Although the process is not very efficient, the work involved in smelting steel is ultimately gratifying. The best way to describe waiting for the smelter to burn down so it can be opened, revealing the bloom, is comparing it to the anticipation a child feels on Christmas morning, waiting to open presents—truly wonderful! □

Fine Tuning Folders

Improved and evolved LinerLock and flipper folders can be tuned, tweaked and tightened

By Wally Hayes, ABS master smith

After starting to write this article on fine-tuning or tuning up folding knives, I realized it was just as important to look at the evolution of folders over the years. As folders evolved and improved with each new invention, they began to work smoother and faster while also becoming safer.

I remember around the time I started to make knives that my first LinerLock® folder was a wedding gift from my wife. It was a beautiful damascus and pearl locking-liner folder. The liners were stainless steel and there was no detent ball bearing in the locking tab. Years later, I met Michael Walker, who invented, popularized and patented the modern LinerLock, at the New York Custom Knife Show. Michael was the first maker to use a ball bearing as a detent in the lock. This holds the folder closed. Michael was also the first person to use a hardened stop pin.

In no particular order, following is information about each individual part of LinerLock and flipper folders and how they have changed over time.

Pivot screws have certainly evolved through the years. My first folder from knifemaker Mick Langley was pinned together and soldered, and the pivot pin was peened on each side of the bolster. The knifemaker had one chance to get it right. If he peened the pivot pin too tightly, it would seize the blade to where it could not be opened or closed.

Next, I saw folders with bronze bushings to help make the folding action smoother. Some makers started creating their own pivot pins and screws. Later, I witnessed makers fashioning really fine screws, with 80 threads per inch, thus making it possible to control how tight or loose the blades of folders were when opening or closing them.

Now, custom CNC-machined (Computer Numerically Controlled) screw heads are popular and even being made out of titanium. Michael Sheffield at Sheffield Knifemakers Supply has been producing some killer parts. He has the largest assortment of pivot screws I have ever seen.

Washers have evolved over the years as well. When Langley started making knives, he also cut out his own washers from .010-to-.015-inch-thick bronze sheet stock. Later, makers started producing their own washers from sheets of Nylatron, and then came ready-made washers of all thicknesses, available from suppliers and such online sites as KnifeKits.com. I think the big breakthrough in washers was the development of the Ikoma Korth Bearing System (IKBS) by knifemakers Flavio Ikoma and Rick Lala.

For their IKBS system, the makers drill out a "step" in the liners of a folder and make a washer that integrates ball bearings. The ball bearings incorporated into the washer ride around the pivot pin. A lot of top makers have used this system for years, and still do. Then someone figured out how to press ball bearings into stainless steel washers. Others pressed ball bearings into plastic and other fibrous materials. I found the washers that were made to fit loosely worked best (thanks to knifemaker Michael Burch's advice at last year's BLADE Show).

WASHERS, LINERS & BLADES

Employing ball bearing washers, a knifemaker decides how deeply to set them into the liners, with the washers sticking up at whatever height he or she prefers. This, in turn, gives the maker more versatility in blade thickness without having to surface grind each blade to a standard washer or bearing thickness.

It also makes it easier to match up standoffs or back spacers to blade thickness. Speaking of standoffs, they've also changed over time. When LinerLock folders became popular, most knifemakers put a stainless steel or damascus spacer between the two liners, giving the blade room to rotate open and closed freely between handle liners. Then someone

Illustrated in the image is the development over time, from left to right, of washers and pivot screws that are used in folding knives.

Knifemaker Michael Burch carburizes the end of titanium lock for a folder. *(Michael Burch image)*

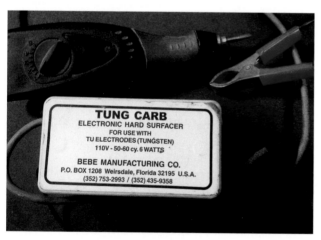

This is a typical carbide-coating machine used to carburize the end of a folding-knife lock. *(Wally Hayes image)*

came up with thick washers or standoffs, eliminating the necessity of spacers, though many knifemakers still use spacers. Afterwards came standoffs with shoulders to make folders more stable and solid.

Now with CNC machinery, Michael from Sheffield Knifemakers Supply and others are creating custom standoffs. I think it is so cool to use titanium ones. Alpha Knife Supply has started to offer #2-56 screws in titanium, making it possible to put a folder together with all titanium parts—minus the pivot pin. It enables a knifemaker to anodize the titanium parts so they're either in the same, complementary or matching colors.

At the last BLADE Show in Atlanta, I was told some makers are using ceramic ball bearings. The jury is still out as to the benefits of ceramic over stainless ball bearings. Some guys are saying ceramic bearings are faster, and others not.

Washer thickness has also changed over time. When Langley started making knives in the 1970s, I think washers were about .010-inch thick. When I started years later, washers were .015- or .020-inch thick. Now some makers use .040-inch-thick washers. Why? With thicker washers, there is more clearance between the frame or liners and the blade. You don't have to worry about the lock pushing the blade over to one side and scratching it. It also gives more clearance for cleaning tactical folders.

At the BLADE Show, I found a knife parts supplier who offered hardened washers for the ball bearing washers to ride on. This prevents any gouging of the blade.

Tuning a folder includes oiling or greasing the ball bearings and pivot pins. I prefer to use HI-SLIP grease by Sentry Solutions, but WD-30 mixed with STP also works well, and there are many options for grease.

REFINED TUNING

I spent the last 10 years refining the art of tuning folders, with part of that time spent talking to most of the top makers, only to discover that we all build and tune folders differently. Each maker grinds and fits up the locks differently. I think tangs of folders were first ground to a flat 5-degree angle for the lock to rest against. Some makers later started scooping out, or concaving, the tang by grinding it to a 5-7-degree angle using an 8-inch contact wheel. It was no longer flat.

I grind the tang of my blade with a 7-degree block on a disc grinder. This works great. Then I knock off the corner of the tang of the folder blade using a Scotch-Brite wheel so the lock transitions on and off the tang smoothly.

The liner material makers use has also progressed over the years, from stainless steel to titanium with a carbide coating. Carbide coating is applied by a little handheld machine that welds

Michael Walker invented and patented the LinerLock® folder. Note at bottom right how the lock of his stunning folder fully engages the tang of the damascus blade. *(SharpByCoop image)*

carbide onto the locking liner, creating a very hard surface. This prevents the titanium lock from sticking to the tang of the folder. Some people like to flame-harden the end of the lock, but I think most knifemakers have been carburizing the lock end.

Detent balls have played a major role in tuning folders. Most knifemakers set a 1/16-inch stainless steel ball bearing into the lock with a modified punch. Others start to set the ball, but without fully setting it, turn the liner over onto a steel plate, and with a steel washer of the thickness they want exposed, they hit the liner with a hammer. If done right, it leaves the height of the ball bearing sticking out of the liner the same thickness as that of the washer being used. If the washer is .020-inch thick, then .020-inch of ball bearing protrudes above the liner. This knifemaking practice has remained fairly standard over the years, but what has changed is the hole in the blade that the detent ball falls into.

The norm for years was to use a No. 56 drill bit that made a .046-inch hole in the blade where the ball bearing would rest. Later, some knifemakers rounded the corners of the hole for a smoother action. Following that, designers moved the hole .010-inch further away from where the ball travels. This makes the ball want to fall still further into the hole when closed. Progressing with new ideas, some makers opened up the hole on the far side only. This lets the ball pull the blade in more, creating a snug closing.

I think the big breakthrough for tuning flipper folders was making the hole in the blade bigger. This makes the blade build up more energy before the ball bearing is released out of the hole, and thus propelling the blade open quicker when the flipper mechanism is flipped. A lot of the first flippers didn't pop open very well.

I thought the blade size and weight made a difference in how fast a flipper folder could be opened, only to find out later this was not the case. The bigger hole made the difference for the blade to snap

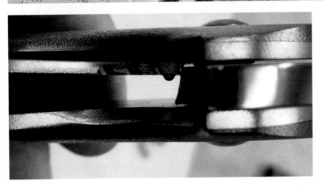

The blade tang of Burch's locking-liner folder is scooped out/concaved, and the tang engages roughly three-quarters of the thickness of the locking liner. *(Michael Burch image)*

A relatively new innovation is the ball bearing washer, illustrated here on a Wally Hayes flipper folder. *(Wally Hayes image)*

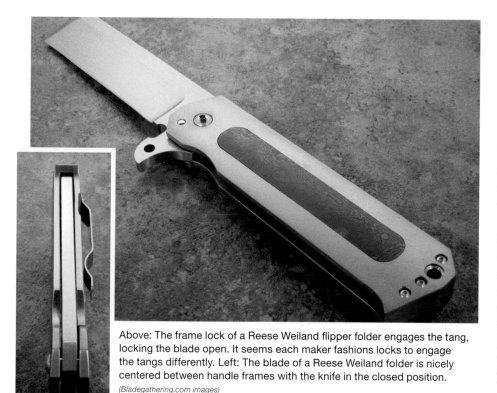

Above: The frame lock of a Reese Weiland flipper folder engages the tang, locking the blade open. It seems each maker fashions locks to engage the tangs differently. Left: The blade of a Reese Weiland folder is nicely centered between handle frames with the knife in the closed position.
(Bladegathering.com images)

open in a flipper. I use a No. 54 drill bit that makes a .055-inch hole in the blade. These days some makers are using .056- or .057-inch holes for even more resistance.

RAMPING THE EDGE

A new idea incorporated into fine-tuning folders is to ramp the edge of the tang so the ball bearing moves smoothly onto the tang of the blade. This helps a lot. It is also important to polish the inside of the pivot hole in the blade after heat-treating the steel. I also polish the pivot pin on my buffer.

Another variable that affects the working of a folder is the amount of contact between the lock and the tang of the blade. Too much contact makes the folder difficult to unlock. Not enough contact, and the lock can slide off the tang and result in the blade closing on your fingers! I grind the tang of the blade so it engages the bottom 1/8-inch of the lock.

Knifemaker Reese Weiland says he likes the entire face of the lock to match up with the blade, and another maker I know likes to grind a 2-degree angle away from the bottom of the lock. Along with how much of the face is in contact with the lock, how far the lock travels across the blade tang is also important. I prefer .030- to .040-inch of travel. I have seen other folders work perfectly with more or less

travel. With a blade fully open and the lock engaged, I test each of my folders by gently tapping the back, or spine, of the open blade against my workbench to ensure it won't override the lock and close. I also make sure my fingers are not in the way of the blade edge in case the lock fails!

Adjusting a flipper or LinerLock folder is a lot of fun once you become comfortable with all of the variables. Looking at a folder in the closed positon, it's imporant that the point of the blade is centered between the handle frame halves or liners. When I put a folder together, the bottom pivot screw is tightened right up. This is the side the lock is on. The top screw is tightened until the point of the blade moves into the center of the handle. This is pretty cool.

If the blade is too hard to move once I get the blade tip in the center, there is other troubleshooting to do. First I take the folder apart and make sure the liners are straight. I rest a liner on a precision parallel bar and hold it up to a light source to see if there are any bends in the liner itself. It does not take much bend in the liner to throw the point of a blade off center.

I also check the bend of the lock. I prefer it to bend a little less than three-quarters of the way over toward the liner on the opposite handle when there is no blade in the folder. I usually have to take out a little bit of the bend. Too much bend pushes the blade over and off center. I also check that the ball bearing is not protruding up higher than the face of the washer. I use digital calipers for this.

Once comfortable with all the different scenarios, troubleshooting turns into a game and an investigation. Sometimes a folder will go together and work perfectly the first time. Other times, it is necessary to test all the different variables. I hope this sheds some light on tuning folders and the evolution in materials, parts and techniques that has taken place over the years. □

Kantou: Appreciation of Japanese Swords

Carefully examining sword blades can reveal clues as to when, where and how they were forged

By Leon Kapp

Japanese swords have been made and appreciated in Japan for almost 1,600 years, and there is a systematic protocol to use in looking at and evaluating traditional Japanese swords. The first step in the study of a sword is to remove it from its mounting or *koshirae* and to study the bare blade alone. Any impressions from the accompanying mounting or fittings are completely ignored. The koshirae is studied and evaluated independently of the blade.

Kantou means appreciation of the sword. This type of study is not influenced by value or accompanying fittings, but focuses strictly on the blade itself. Another oft-used term, *kantei*, means an appraisal that can include value, provenance, acknowledgment of an accompanying mounting and other factors.

There are several elements or features of the sword that must be examined, and because the sword is made of steel, the condition of the steel or its polish is very important. A polish should be in good condition so the details in the steel can be observed, but the different parts of the sword normally have slightly different finishes. If a sword is in good condition and has a good polish, all parts of the blade can be easily examined.

For the *ji*, or body of the sword, the individually forged steel exhibits a distinctive color or texture, as well as a visible surface pattern created from folding the steel over

A 1243 A.D. painting depicts a prince carefully handling and examining a sword, suggesting that the polishing process was already sophisticated.
(photo from the Kitano Tenmangu Shrine)

⌃ To examine the shape of a Japanese sword, it is held upright at arm's length. *(Aram Compeau photo)*

⌄ The sword is aimed at a point below a light source, and the *hamon*, or temper line, details should be very clear around the reflection of the light on the blade. *(Compeau photo)*

In examining the *jihada*, or surface and surface pattern, the blade is held low and parallel to the ground. The light source should be above and in front of the viewer's head. *(Compeau photo)*

onto itself, usually an average of 12 times during the forging process. Traditional Japanese craftsmen are extremely strict, meticulous and methodical, and in the past, each group (or school) of swordsmiths had a characteristic protocol to follow in making their steel from *tamahagane* (quality Japanese steel smelted from iron-rich sand). They forged and folded the steel, forging the blade to shape using specific temperatures and other methods, and differentially heat-treated the blade to achieve a *hamon* (temper line) and a hardened, martensitic edge.

This means that, with study, most well made swords not only have recognizable colored and textured steel surfaces and surface patterns (*jihada*), but also characteristic shapes and hamons. The forging process is when the characteristic details are formed. The swordsmith literally forges the characteristics into the steel when he folds and forges the tamahagane.

The polishing process is conducted using extremely fine, abrasive, natural limestone, and no chemicals or etching agents. The visible lines that make up the jihada are generally formed by the presence of oxides between the steel layers. In some cases these lines are coarse and prominent, and on other swords, they're tight, fine and barely visible. The

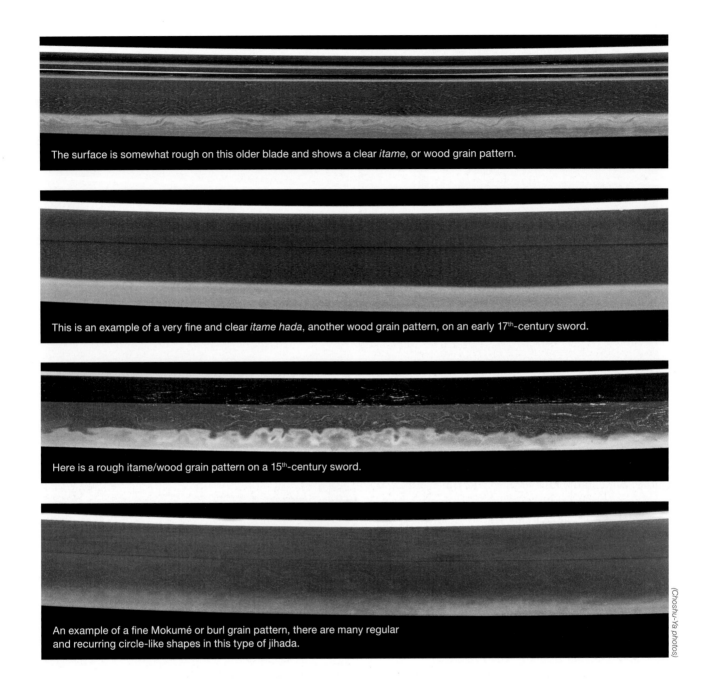

The surface is somewhat rough on this older blade and shows a clear *itame*, or wood grain pattern.

This is an example of a very fine and clear *itame hada*, another wood grain pattern, on an early 17th-century sword.

Here is a rough itame/wood grain pattern on a 15th-century sword.

An example of a fine Mokumé or burl grain pattern, there are many regular and recurring circle-like shapes in this type of jihada.

(Choshu-Ya photos)

exact appearance depends on forging techniques and temperatures used, and on the makeup and origin of the tamahagane steel.

In general, forging at higher temperatures produces fine jihada lines or patterns, while using lower quality tamahagane steel and forging at lower temperatures leaves more oxides in the steel and produces coarser appearing patterns.

DEFINING TEMPER LINE

The differentially heat-treated blade and resulting temper line, or hamon, is the most recognizable feature of a Japanese sword. This is also a characteristic feature in the work of specific schools and groups of smiths. The appearance of the hamon and its details depends on how the steel was forged, the quality of the steel, and how it was heated and quenched.

A good, quality polish allows many fine details within the hamon to become visible. Usually the hamon area is polished to make it lighter and to contrast with the body, or ji, of the sword. However, if the hamon is over-polished, or polished until it is extremely bright or white, the details inside of the hamon can be obscured or rendered invisible. An excessively whitened hamon area can also make it difficult to examine the adjacent ji and jihada.

The shape, or *sugata*, of a Japanese sword is formed by forging and then filing, and is then refined

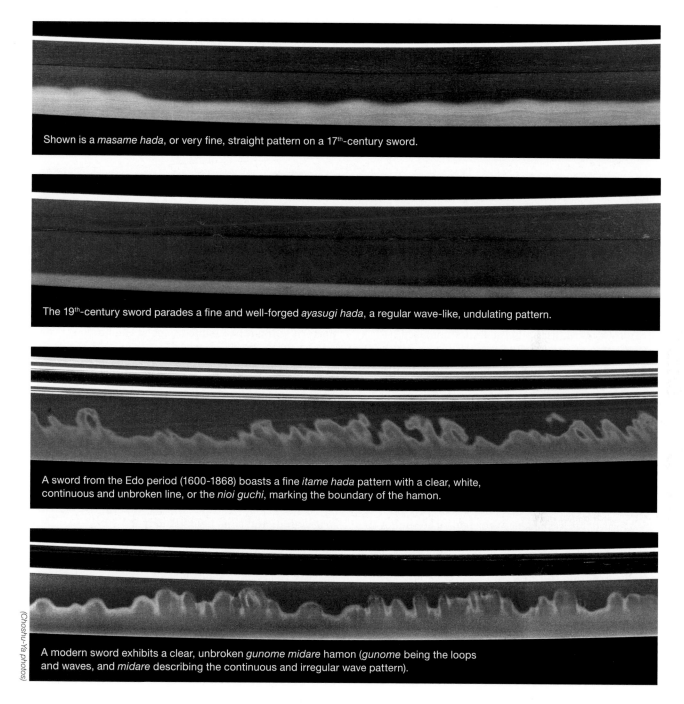

Shown is a *masame hada*, or very fine, straight pattern on a 17th-century sword.

The 19th-century sword parades a fine and well-forged *ayasugi hada*, a regular wave-like, undulating pattern.

A sword from the Edo period (1600-1868) boasts a fine *itame hada* pattern with a clear, white, continuous and unbroken line, or the *nioi guchi*, marking the boundary of the hamon.

A modern sword exhibits a clear, unbroken *gunome midare* hamon (*gunome* being the loops and waves, and *midare* describing the continuous and irregular wave pattern).

(Choshu-Ya photos)

by polishing after the smith finishes his work. The lines should be clear and sharp, the longitudinal ridge line—*shinogi*—should be crisp, the point well defined, and the upper surface—*shinogi ji*— above the longitudinal ridge line should be flat, with the back, unsharpened surface—*mune*—also defined by flat surfaces.

The shinogi ji and mune are burnished to produce a clear, reflective surface. However, the burnished surface is polished so it appears dark, reflective and translucent. A highly reflective burnished surface is often bright enough to obscure or dull the important

details in the ji just below the shinogi.

A well-polished Japanese sword also has a balanced polish. The ji has a visible color and pattern or jihada. The hamon is well defined by using the traditional polishing process, but the finish on the hamon permits a clear examination of the details, or *hataraki*, inside of the hamon.

These details mean that a properly polished Japanese sword must be finished in a way that balances the final appearance or polish on all of the three primary surfaces (the ji, the hamon, and the shinogi ji) so that details on all of the surfaces are visible and

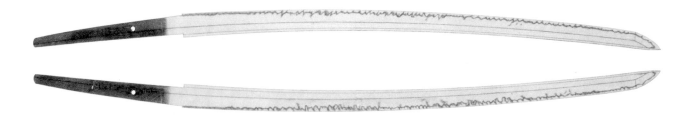

This type of *oshigata* image—a tracing of a 19th-century Naotane sword with the hamon drawn in by hand—is the traditional way to show hamon detail. *(Tanobe Michihiro tracing)*

clear. Since the sword is made out of steel, there is a narrow range of optimal finishes that make it easy to simultaneously view all parts of the sword.

Traditional polishing materials are a series of water-lubricated stones, starting with rough stones (granite was traditionally the first stone used) to very fine limestone for the final steps. Burnishing the shinogi ji and mune surfaces is done with specially shaped and sized steel burnishing needles. Some modern synthetic stones are occasionally used in the very first stages of the polishing process when shaping the sword, but otherwise, no modern abrasive materials or chemicals are used to obtain a fully traditional polish.

SOUL OF THE SWORD

A swordsmith considers the steel—the soul of the sword—the most important part of the sword, and all of the other properties of the sword depend on and are derived from the steel and its properties. The tamahagane is smelted in a charcoal-fired furnace, just as in the past, resulting in the steel used to forge the sword. Each sword is individually made, so there can be a lot of variation between individual swords and schools of sword making.

Optimally the steel is heated to a very high temperature just short of melting before being drawn out and folded. If the steel is overheated or partially melted during this folding process, there will either be no or very little visible jihada or other fine details in the body of the sword. A high forging temperature is more important than the number of times the steel is folded.

Once the sword is forged to shape, two types of clay are used to form the hamon: one type coats the area to be the hamon and another type covers the rest of the sword. The sword is then heated to the critical temperature, where magnetic activity is lost, or above, and quenched in room-temperature water. If this process is done correctly, the hardened edge region will

be clearly defined and there will be a visible, continuous boundary (a *nioi-guchi*) separating the hardened edge from the softer body of the sword blade.

In general, a hamon should have a clear, continuous, unbroken border to define it, and the jihada pattern will not be visible inside of the hamon. Frequently, the outline of the hamon or its overall shape is described by terms such as *suguha* (straight), *gunome* (regular loops), *midare* (wave-like), *choji* (loops shaped like the outline of a clove bud) and many others. *Hataraki* are additional details, shapes or lines visible inside of the hamon area and serve to break up the otherwise uniformly hard martensitic edge, making it less brittle and less likely to develop large chips or cracks from use. Hataraki also can be characteristic of the area and period where the sword originated, and thus help identify it.

The features visible in the ji indicate that the sword was forged and heat-treated in a way intended to leave the steel inhomogeneous—not a completely uniform, martensitic region, but one with areas of variable hardness. It is striking that all of the most famous swords from the past, including national treasures and important cultural properties, have an abundance of such features in the body or ji and in the hamon, indicating that these visible details were a very important indication of the quality of the sword.

The shape or sugata of Japanese swords can also help identify the time and place a sword was made. The most common shape for a long sword or katana has a single, hardened edge, some curvature, some tapering (i.e. *fumbari*) from the base to the point, and also a tapered thickness from the base of the blade to the point. A standard degree of tapering from the base to the point is about 20 to 30 percent, and the thickness tapers the same amount as the blade itself.

A well-made blade appears graceful, is comfortable and easy to hold and move, and usually has a regular uniform curvature (*sori*) so it can be placed

Top: A photo shows the shape, color and the straight (*suguha*) hamon of a modern Shoji Yoshihara sword, but no details of the steel surface (*jigane*) or surface pattern (*jihada*). Bottom: This image shows the shape of a polished Yoshindo Yoshihara sword blade and the outline of the hamon, but no fine details in the steel surface or inside of the hamon. *(Compeau photos)*

into and removed easily from a scabbard. The degree of curvature can vary from almost straight to very strongly curved. The type or style of curvature varied with the time and place where the sword was made. The shape can be wide, narrow, show large or small degrees of tapering, and the length of the blade can vary over a large range. Technically, a katana or long sword is defined as having a length of 24 inches or more, and some older 14th-century examples are 36-48 inches long.

SHINE A LIGHT ON THAT BLADE!

There is a narrow range of lighting that allows someone to examine a Japanese sword carefully and see all of the important details, and there is a standard or customary set of conditions and lighting to use. First, the sword is removed from its scabbard, and dusted with a fine powder called *uchiko*. The uchiko is wiped off, and this process should remove all oil, dirt or dust from the sword blade. For a good view of the sword's details, the brightness or level of light in a room should be low, or even dim.

To examine the hamon, the sword is aimed below a source of light such as a bare light bulb. The details of the hamon can be easily examined by looking just below or above the reflection from the light on the blade. As the reflection of the light source is moved along the blade, it is possible to examine the entire hamon. Under these conditions, all of the details of the hamon and hataraki in the hamon should be visible.

To carefully examine the ji of the sword, the blade is held flat and the body of the blade is nearly parallel to the ground. Under these conditions, the light source should be above or slightly in front of the observer's head, and details on the ji should be visible around the reflection of the light source on the blade. To examine the shape of the sword, it is held upright by the tang.

From these traditional considerations, what should

one expect to see in a good sword? One would not expect to see a featureless and bright steel surface in a traditional Japanese sword. The shape should be clean and graceful, and have traditional and expected details present such as a clear hamon and some curvature, and be formed in such a way that it is comfortable and balanced when holding or moving it. It should be in good condition and not "tired" or excessively polished to the extent that the shape is altered or noticeably worn from its original condition.

There should graceful and appropriate proportions between the length, width, thickness, curvature and point. The steel should be non-reflective, somewhat dark, and have a clear texture or pattern visible on it. There should be a pattern (the jihada) present from folding and forging the steel, although the pattern could be strong and clear, or subtle and difficult to see.

The hamon should be clearly visible against the body of the sword and have an unbroken boundary separating it from the body or ji of the sword. In general, the hamon boundary is not a simple thread-like line, but can have a complex structure with loops, waves, projections and a wide or complex boundary or nioi-guchi. The origin of the complex hamon with hataraki was originally meant to tie the martensitic hamon into the softer body or ji of the sword, in a manner akin to forming a zipper between the ji and hamon, the two steel parts of the sword. Consequently, an interesting and functional hamon often has a continuous, complex and interesting structure.

All of these structural details produce interesting and beautiful (although functional) details that make each well-forged and well-made Japanese sword distinctive and unique. Under these conditions, with some experience, it should be possible to observe, appreciate and evaluate all of the fine details of the shape, hamon and surface or ji in a traditional Japanese sword. □

Survival of the Bush-Craftiest

A preeminent manufacturer of no-nonsense survival knives hones its bushcraft blade skills

By Pat Covert

ESEE Knives has always been known for making no-nonsense survival knives. It is in the company's DNA and burned into the minds of a cult-like following who often find enough in the ESEE line that they need no other knives. In a great sense, they're right. From the small Candiru drop-point, integral fixed blades to the Junglas machete/choppers designed for the Latin American jungle, there are plenty of offerings to slake any knife user's cravings, including six other standard models in the line. And that's not counting the new Camp-Lore series of bushcraft knives.

All of ESEE's knives are made in the U.S.A., which no doubt appeals to many of their loyal flock. If a machete is desired, the company offers one manufactured in South America, complete with a Micarta® handle for a firm, durable grip. Plus there are a couple of ESEE branded folders produced offshore.

Jeff Randall is the president and co-founder of TransEquatorial Solutions, Inc., the parent company to ESEE Knives and Randall's Adventure & Training. Randall's Adventure & Training (acronym R.A.T.) offers a host of task specific survival programs to individuals, corporations and government entities around the world. R.A.T. was formed in 1997 as a jungle survival school for individuals, pilots and military personnel seeking terrain and environment training. Shortly thereafter the company signed a contract with the Peruvian military to run students through a Special Operations jungle survival course.

ESEE Knives was formed as an offshoot of R.A.T., and the ESEE acronym stands for Escuela de Supervivencia (survival school), with the E's representing Escape and Evasion. Using the vast knowledge gained from jungle survival experience, Randall, along with co-founder and business partner Mike Perrin, saw a need for a line of rugged, no-frills survival knives and set out to accomplish that goal. If anything they far exceeded it. ESEE knives are used in harsh environments worldwide.

With its 4.1-inch cutting edge and handle designed for extended periods of use, the ESEE-4 fits the generic parameters of a bushcraft knife nicely. *(Pat Covert image)*

THE ESEE-4 FACTOR

Ironically, and unbeknownst to Randall and Perrin when introducing one particular knife model to customers, ESEE released a perfectly sound bushcraft knife—the ESEE-4 model—around the same time the bushcraft movement started taking root here on American shores. The ESEE-4, debuted in 2007, sports a 4.5-inch 1095 high-carbon-steel blade, an alloy overwhelmingly preferred by bushcrafters for its ease of sharpening in the wild. And while the early enthusiasts of the genre preferred a Scandinavian, or zero-bevel, blade grind, commonly referred to simply as a "Scandi grind," the full, flat V-ground blade of the ESEE-4 has since found wide acceptance alongside convex and saber grinds.

The bushcraft knife, dating back to the early written works of Horace Kephart in the 1890s, the writings and broadcasts of Les Hiddins of Australia and Mors Kochanski of Canada in the 1980s, and more recently Ray Mears of England, is primarily a wood crafting knife. A medium-to-light-duty knife, a typical bushcraft blade is geared toward such tasks as shaving bark off tree branches, sharpening tent pegs and carving notches for traps and such. It is not a chopper per se, but can be used for preparing a meal, dressing game and light shelter building. The ESEE-4 performs all these functions in easy fashion, hence its wide acceptance by bushcrafters.

"It is probably the best all-around camp/bush knife we sell right now," Perrin states.

And it would also be a part of the impetus for bushcraft knives to come for the ESEE brand. "The ESEE-4, being a favorite among bushcrafters, naturally led us into knives that were more directly associated with the finer techniques of the craft," Randall informs.

CAMP-LORE IS BORN

While Randall and Perrin are not bushcraft aficionados, several of their instructors at R.A.T. are extremely well versed in the practice, and the company owners turned to them for design expertise. "The guys we collaborated with on designs for the Camp-Lore series worked closely with us for quite a while, and we have a lot of respect for them," Perrin notes. "They develop their designs the same way Jeff and I do—through hard use, trial and error."

"Reuben Bolieu, designer of the Camp-Lore RB3, is a highly experienced woodsman and world traveler," says Randall, "and suggested we use the name based on an old book named *Camp-Lore and Woodcraft* by author Daniel C. Beard. We liked the idea and it stuck. As far as Reuben goes, he's a great instructor and extremely knowledgeable when it comes to woods skills. He's one of our assistant instructors in our jungle survival class in South America and also helps us teach some of our domestic classes."

The Camp-Lore RB3 hearkens back to the beginnings of the modern bushcraft movement, including a 3.5-inch, drop-point 1095 high-carbon-steel blade with a Scandi grind and a stonewashed finish. At 8.2 inches overall, it boasts palpable green canvas Micarta handle scales. Each of the Camp-Lore knives includes a natural cowhide sheath with belt loop.

"James Gibson was simply born in the wrong century," Perrin states in describing the designer of the Camp-Lore JG3 model. "He would have been hanging around with the likes of [Daniel] Boone and [Davy] Crockett, and flint knapping points with Tecumseh."

"One of the nicest, most honest guys I have met in this whole industry," Randall adds, "James Gibson

Randall's Adventure & Training (R.A.T.) lead instructor Patrick Rollins demonstrates the wood splitting technique of "batoning."
(Randall Adventure Training image)

The ESEE Camp-Lore knives (the RB3 shown at left and JG3 on right) went through rigorous testing before they were released to the knife buying public. *(Reuben Bolieu image)*

is probably the most skilled man I have ever met when it comes to being in the woods with a knife. He instructs a few of our classes and brought one of his new designs to a class a couple of years ago. When I saw it, I immediately snapped a picture and sent it to my partner, Mike Perrin, and our manufacturer, Shon Rowen, along with a simple statement: 'We have to make this knife!' Gibson agreed and the rest is history. Of everything ESEE makes, the JG3 is my favorite backpacking fixed blade. It just works and fits like it's suppose to."

FITS LIKE A GLOVE

The Gibson-designed Camp-Lore JG3 is a departure from mainstream bushcraft Zeitgeist. At 7.625 inches in overall length, the knife is more compact than its RB3 sibling. It also differs from all other ESEE knives in that it has more curves than the brand's typical fare. The handle, topped with sculpted green Micarta handle scales, is curvaceous and fits the palm like a glove. The flat-ground blade is a 3.5-inch drop point, canted slightly downward in similar fashion to the ESEE Izula II.

While certainly able to perform wood crafting chores, the JG3 is also ideally suited for hunters. The drop point blade is the most ideal style for skinning game, efficiently riding under the surface of flesh

without snagging viscera and puncturing organs. Like the RB3, it comes with a stonewashed blade and a leather belt-loop sheath.

Randall's Adventure & Training is located in Gallant, Alabama, a semi-mountainous region with plenty of flat terrain and downright steep limestone cliffs to train in. Lead instructor Patrick Rollins describes the facility: "We have approximately 180 acres, a classroom, rappel tower, firing range and plenty of woods. We offer classes in survival, navigation, single rope techniques, rope rescue, firearms, human tracking, search and rescue, bushcraft and wilderness medicine."

"We also still teach Jungle Survival in the Peruvian Amazon," Rollins adds. "Students range from military and law enforcement personnel to attorneys, I.T. [information technology] folks, factory workers and everyone in between. We take the training very seriously and strive to provide the best instruction for the students."

Knives play a key role in all of R.A.T.'s classes, performing a myriad of functions ranging from general camp use to wilderness medicine applications. In his various duties, Rollins teaches a veritable gamut of cutting chores. "I teach knife safety and skills in any class where the students will be using them," he says. "We discuss sheathing a knife when it's not in use, being aware of your follow-through [with the blade tip and sharp edge], keeping others out of your 'blood circle' [360 degrees around anywhere your knife could reach] and so on."

"I teach snap-cutting—bending the sapling or branch until the fibers are stressed, then cutting through them—and V-notching—using a baton with the knife to take down larger saplings," Rollins expounds. "We also teach all the basic notches used for traps and shelter construction. Batoning is taught for processing standing deadwood for fire making. I know some folks are against batoning, or striking the spine of a blade with a baton to force the edge through wood, but without an axe it is the best way to get to the drier inside of the wood, a must for fire making in wet environments. I also teach students how to make feather sticks and shavings in order to light wood using a Ferrocerium rod. The classes where we use knives most are the field survival and bushcraft seminars."

THE TRAIL AHEAD

Having successfully launched the Camp-Lore line, Randall and Perrin see expansion in the future. "Oh, we have a lot of designs lying around on paper napkins," Randall remarks. "Most of this series will see growth from the direction of collaborations, more so than ESEE's ideas. We tend to grow our company carefully and slowly instead of just throwing out an idea every few months to try to gain more sales. That way, whatever we put out is in the production system without too many hiccups. With that said, we have a smaller Camp-Lore knife coming out in 2016 and our lead survival instructor, Patrick, has been working on a Kephart design that we'll be producing."

"Bushcrafters have both general needs and some very specific needs, just like most knife communities," Perrin adds. "Revisiting some inherently traditional designs might be a direction, since bushcraft is heavily dependent on tradition. There are also some cool, smart people thinking outside of the box, and who are decidedly non-traditional, so we look to those folks and see what they have to offer. But ideas in knife design are a 'one works and nine don't' deal. Just putting out a bunch of different designs doesn't work."

Designed by knifemaker and bushcraft/survival instructor James Gibson, the curved handle and arched profile of the Camp-Lore JG3 distinguish if from other ESEE knives. *(Pat Covert image)*

ESEE designs don't come fast and furious. Rather, a lot of thought, planning and testing go into an ESEE before it ever sees the factory. Jeff notes, "We always build several handmade prototypes and put them out to designers and experienced woodsmen for 'beta testing.' Once we are all satisfied and have the design tweaked to work for its intent, as well as for a manufacturing setup, the final production process starts."

"Most of the time, you will see our designs and ideas years before they come to fruition at the factory—it's just our process and we refuse to build something based on anyone's timeline except our own," Jeff concludes.

In other words, don't look for ESEE to pop out new models like Krispy Kreme donuts. That's never been the company's *modus operandi* and never will be, but their position in the bushcraft community is now well established and ESEE fans can look forward to enticing new additions in the future! □

ESEE Knives are sold through dealers. For a dealer near you, call 256-613-0372, or visit eseeknives. com. For general inquiries for ESEE Knives and Randall's Adventure & Training, contact the company at P.O. Box 99, Gallant, AL 35972 256-613-0372, info@eseeknives.com.

Taking Knife Passion to the Next Level

For some knife enthusiasts, collecting and using knives just isn't enough. So what then?

Words & Images by David W. Jung

There's a defining moment in the lives of many knife enthusiasts—a time when they choose whether or not to take their interest in knives to another level. Fortunately, we can look at the paths others have taken, and as it turns out, there are paths aplenty.

The first step is education. Better yet, let's call it discovery. It's best to learn the history of knives, from early stone tools to their high-tech descendants. Knives were mankind's earliest tools, and were as indispensable in early days as their modern counterparts are today.

Visiting history museums online or in person to see early examples of stone tools is a good idea, as is learning how to flint knap knives like early man. Most college archeology departments have practitioners of this primitive technology, along with local flint-knapping groups that are happy to share the ancient skill. This easy-to-learn facet of knifemaking provides an understanding of how knives work, and costs almost nothing.

Exploring the metal age of knives opens up even more opportunities. Knife collecting is a great place to start. Knife collectors usually begin collecting *everything*, though they can specialize and build a collection based on defined interests. Others are so prolific that they become dealers out of financial necessity.

If you want to play in the high-dollar knife market, it is crucial to understand market pricing. Knife collections can include $1 knives or $10,000 knives. Deciding a budget and trying to stick with it is prudent. Some of the most knowledgeable knife experts started as highly motivated collectors.

Tony Berg of Tacoma, Wash., is an antique dealer who specializes in high-end vintage knives. He became interested in collecting knives at the age of 10, and later, when he was working as a prep cook next door to a knife show, he ventured in and traded his interests in cooking for knife collecting and selling. He states, "Antique dealing pays the bills, but knives are my happy place." His tips are, "Research before you buy, and buy the best you can afford." The knives in his personal collection have meaning to him, with

Washington knifemaker Matt Caldwell shows off some of his Bob Loveless-inspired mid-tech (semi-production) knives that boast N690 blades and Kydex® sheaths.

Knifemaker Peter Carey designed the Spyderco Firefly, featuring a 2.74-inch VG-10 stainless steel blade, carbon fiber front bolsters and polished, orange G-10 handle scales.

the most significant, notably, tattooed on his arm.

Becoming a new knife dealer is easy to do, but can also get a person in financial trouble. The reality is that we live in an online world, and we also compete for customers in that same world. While most retailers prefer a brick and mortar store, they need to be realistic about the new norm of shopping. Great frustration exists for the proprietor each time a knife customer enters the store, examines a product, and then buys the knife online for a few dollars less.

Knife dealers compete with the lowest price Internet sites that don't have to spend time physically showing the knife. To compete, many storefronts now also have e-commerce websites. Learning the business as an employee, either behind the counter or behind the scenes is also advisable. By learning the ropes from others, a new knife dealer can avoid pitfalls and improve his or her chances for success. Fine knives sell themselves, and learning about quality helps everyone.

MAKING MODIFICATIONS

Most knife collectors at some point decide to modify their knives. This can be as simple as replac-ing the handle scales on a well-worn hunting knife, or even embellishing a brand-new knife. Embellishing handles with engraving or scrimshaw can be a fulfilling endeavor and increase the value of the knives significantly. Other modifications include changing the finish on a knife, or even modifying the blade shape. Mechanisms of knives can be disassembled for study, or even modified, though any warranty will probably be void after modifications.

The late Phil Boguszewski began his knifemaking career by disassembling Case brand knives to learn the fit and finish. By learning how to replicate known designs, he went on to fashion incredibly precise folders known for their smooth actions and impeccable workmanship.

Starting with a hot fire, anvil, hammer and an old file, one can begin to forge knives. There are many in the knifemaking community who feel that forging is the best approach to becoming a true knifemaker. The stock-removal process, taking a bar or billet of steel and grinding away "what isn't a knife," has resulted in countless great knives as well.

Knifemaking is best learned from others. Luckily, knifemakers are some of the nicest and most gener-

Gary Martindale, who names Todd Begg and Thad Buchanan as mentors, made the leather sheath that goes with his Bob Loveless-inspired boot knife in a stag handle and CPM 154 blade.

One of the best aspects of going to knife shows like the BLADE Show in Atlanta are the live demonstrations. Here John Conway demonstrates blade forging using his portable forge.

ous people in the world. Sharing knowledge is crucial, and joining a knife club or bladesmithing group can be a great start. There are also numerous books and magazines written by knife experts that can put a burgeoning knifemaker down the right path.

Jeremy Spake began his knifemaking journey with the purchase of a custom knife while bicycling through France. Using that knife daily changed his perspective on blades. His education in metalsmithing and jewelry making has led him to a career in film animation, making the metal armatures for stop-motion movies like *Coraline*, *ParaNorman* and *The Boxtrolls*. A positive reaction to his first knife led him to create more knives, specializing in kitchen knives and Scandinavian designs. At this point he considers it a hobby. He says, "It doesn't pay for itself yet, but I enjoy doing it, and would like it to pay at some point."

Matthew Caldwell began selling knives at a young age. He says that, "I was too young to be a gun dealer, and I always liked knives since I was a kid." Selling Chris Reeve production knives, as well as handmade pieces, he states that, "Competition made being a dealer difficult, and making knives would give more control."

Starting in 2006 he began making mid-tech (semi-production) knives based on proven Bob Loveless designs with high-end steel, like CPM 154, and Micarta® handle scales. He now uses N690 steel. Mid-tech knives open new opportunities for knifemakers. It allows successful custom makers to sell versions of their handmade knives at a lower cost. Other knifemakers like Caldwell go straight to the mid-tech sales model after prototyping and testing.

Jeremy Spake studied metalsmithing and jewelry making, which led to a job making the internal metal armatures of stop-motion figures used in motion pictures, and eventually into knifemaking.

A former Air Force F-111 pilot, Tom Sterling engraved the flat stainless steel handle frame of a Spyderco Cricket. He began making Japanese netsuke figurines and transitioned into art knives.

Doing limited product runs allows for good quality control with small out-of-pocket expenses.

DESIGNING THE DREAM KNIFE

Designing your own dream knife for production can be rewarding, but can also be frustrating. Knife enthusiasts often approach company executives with designs on paper ready for their big break. It is a hard lesson when they learn that a knife design on paper is like an airplane design on paper. It might look good, but that doesn't mean it will fly. The obstacles in the way of the knife designer are numerous.

That is why many knife companies choose to collaborate with established custom knifemakers, a concept introduced by Sal Glesser of Spyderco when he partnered with Bob Terzuola to produce the Spyderco Terzuola folding knife in 1990. Many knife companies offer custom collaborations, allowing executives to judge the potential success of a knife based on the popularity of the custom version. The side benefit for the customer is that they get to purchase a knife with custom-made attributes at a greatly reduced price.

If a new knifemaker has a unique design, it is worth making a prototype or having one made. Most knife prototypes go through a number of stages, including cardboard, Plexiglas™ or even wood. Ergonomics and basic function can then be tested and improved. The best way to explore this is to attend a major knife show such as the BLADE Show in Atlanta, where numerous knifemakers, vendors, major knife companies and collectors gather together. Knife people are very approachable and happy to help.

Peter Carey, a knifemaker building stunning pieces that can fetch thousands of dollars each, landed two custom collaborations with Spyderco. As a child he owned and used knives, even taking them to school. After metal and wood shop classes, he became a welder. He remembers, "I always wanted to try my hand at making a knife, so one day when my welding job got rained out, I made a fixed blade and was hooked. Then, when I got burned out on welding, we sold everything and moved to Texas. I told my wife I wanted to try going full time as a knifemaker and she gave me two years to be successful."

Along the way he picked up Bob Terzuola's book *The Tactical Folding Knife*. He says, "That book had all the answers to get started!" He also gained knifemaking knowledge from the "Steel Dust Junkies" forum group on the Usual Suspect Network—usualsuspect.net. His final word of advice, "Get some steel and practice grinding; you can get all the guidance in the world, but you don't really learn until you put the steel to the wheel!"

Yet another approach to knife design is to use software programs. Since most knife companies live in a CAD/CAM world of machine milling, having a 3D-engineered knife design is like a prototype

One of many knife enthusiasts who choose to focus their efforts on sharpening blades, Dennis Morgan can put up to a 6,000-grit, mirror-polished edge on a blade using an Edge Pro Sharpener.

Tony Berg traded a cook's knife for a bunch of knives as an antique dealer who now specializes in vintage blades. Here he shows the knives that are significant enough for him to "wear them."

model onscreen. While many designers produce 3D models without an engineering background, the right engineering education can allow the designer the ability to understand the materials, stresses that will be applied to those materials through knife use and needed tolerances that might otherwise take many hours of trial and error.

Glenn Klecker is an engineer who depends on 3D computer programs. Growing up in Michigan, he joined the Marines after high school and then used the military scholarship program to get an engineering degree. His experience in the Marines led him to a job in the automotive industry. He states, "It wasn't until later at Ford that I discovered I had a knack for making things better and less expensive." This led to a design job at Leatherman Tools and later as a knife designer with his unique Klecker knife lock and KLAX ax design.

Working in a knife factory can also be a great way to learn about knives. Many knifemakers got their start working for a company prior to striking out on their own. Willingness to work hard, even at entry-level positions, can lead to big things.

TAKING THE PLUNGE

Taking the plunge into knife manufacturing is a little bit like deciding to race boats, cars or horses. You can start with a large amount of money and end up with a little. Legacy knife companies like Buck, Ontario and Case have a long history of knife manufacture in the United States. Knife manufacturing is tough, and those behind the companies have made numerous sacrifices in order to pursue their dreams. Considering a business plan carefully and talking to those who have succeeded, and those that have not, is essential to success.

One area often overlooked is knife sharpening. While every knife enthusiast should learn how to sharpen knives, for those lacking patience, there are people who specialize in honing blades. While it is tough to make a living sharpening knives, those who become masters easily stay busy. Knowledge leads to success, and practice (or seeking advice of those in the field) makes perfect.

Dennis Morgan of The Grateful Edge in Scappoose, Oregon, worked in a meat packing plant where a sharp knife was necessary. After being introduced to personnel from Timberline Knives and taking a knifemaking course from Wayne Goddard, he decided on something different.

Morgan says, "It felt like there was a big crowd of knifemakers in the 1990's, and I don't like crowds." After reading an article on Edge Pro Sharpeners in Hood River, Oregon, he spent time with the owner and walked out with a machine. Starting with farmer's markets, then gun shows and finally knife shows, he is not quite a full-time knife sharpener, but almost. He states that, "We get to know the knife from the heel to the tip, plus the knife crowd is therapeutic."

Almost every fixed blade needs a sheath. While many custom knifemakers make their own sheaths, others farm out the practice. Quality leather sheath making is an art that can rival the beauty of the knife itself. More contemporary synthetic sheaths, such as Kydex®, are easier to make, especially for the tactical market, but still take some level of skill. Materials are inexpensive and easy to find, and once again, learning from others in the field proves invaluable.

While there are other avenues worth considering, such as knife writer/blogger/photographer, martial arts knife expert, BladeSports competitor and more, there is one more area deserving of a knife enthusiast's passion. It is protecting the right to own, carry and use knives. Doug Ritter formed the Knife Rights organization after reading an anti-knife-slanted article in the July 25th, 2006 edition of the *Wall Street Journal*. With no previous experience in the

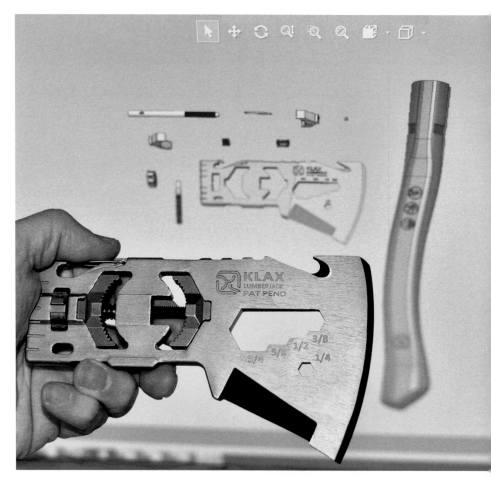

Glenn Klecker worked on parts of the Klecker KLAX Lumberjack, awarded "Most Innovative Design" at the 2014 BLADE Show, and assembled them digitally using a 3D modeling program.

legislative or legal field, he formed Knife Rights to protect knife owners and, more importantly, to work aggressively helping knife owners living where their right to own or carry knives is restricted.

When asked about how people can get involved, he replied, "Visit kniferights.org and send money, or if a knifemaker, donate a knife to the Ultimate Steel™ fundraiser!" In addition, he says, "One of the most important actions is to make calls and send emails to congressmen, senators and legislators when a knife rights bill is up for a vote. Calls and emails make an impact, they cost nothing but a few minutes and they are a huge help. Spread the word about Knife Rights. The more folks know about us, the more support we gain, and the more effective we become."

There are numerous ways to expand your interest in knives, not limited to those mentioned above. Luckily for us, the knife community is composed of great people anxious to share their knowledge and enthusiasm for the benefit of all. Enjoy your adventure. □

The Magical Swords of Norse Lore

Some amazing blades play significant roles in the tales of Norse gods and warriors

By Leslie Jordan Clary

Swords and Vikings just seem to go together like herrings and sour cream. A sword was likely the most valuable possession a Norse warrior might have, and it was generally passed down as an heirloom from generation to generation. Its value was determined not only by its craftsmanship, but by how many battles it had fought in. Double-edged, with each side equally sharp, these blades were wielded single-handed while the other hand clutched the shield.

If you're traveling to Norway and are interested in Viking culture, the Lofotr Viking Museum in Norway offers a rich, interactive recreation of this ancient society. As well as seeing the world's largest longhouse, visitors can take part in a Viking feast, try a hand at archery and ax throwing or listen to a traditional storyteller re-imagine the past.

Many Norse legends have their roots in fact, but over time the Viking story has grown to include a rich cast ruled over by gods and goddesses. In addition to warriors and shield maidens, you're likely to hear about berserkers, who were known for their frenzy in battle, and Valkyries, handmaidens of Odin whose main role was to conduct fallen warriors to Valhalla.

Norse myths have established a place in popular culture as well. The popular HBO series *Game of Thrones*, books by J.R.R. Tolkien such as *The Hobbit* and *The Lord Of The Rings*, as well as many role-playing games like "Dungeons and Dragons" all have echoes of the ancient Vikings in them. In many

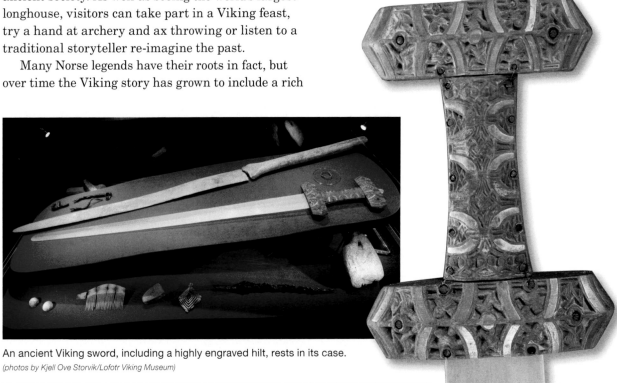

An ancient Viking sword, including a highly engraved hilt, rests in its case.
(photos by Kjell Ove Storvik/Lofotr Viking Museum)

Modern day berserkers recreate a Viking battle scene. *(photo courtesy of Kampshow Lofotr Vikingfestival Museum Nord)*

of these stories, the sword plays a central role. It usually has a name, magical powers and sometimes a curse. Here are three stories from Norse legends with a magical sword (or two) at their core.

HERVOR THE SHIELD MAIDEN

Hervor's father was a Viking warrior, Angantyr, who died in battle before she was born. Much to the dismay of the village women, Hervor grew up reckless and unruly. She shunned typical girl's chores like sewing and cooking. Instead she learned to shoot a bow, wield a sword and fight with the boys, who more often than not fled home in tears to their mothers by the time Hervor was finished with them.

If you're a *Lord Of The Rings* fan, you might recognize traces of Hervor in Eowyn, who was described as a shield maiden of Rohan, the warrior who brought down the King of the Nazgul in the final battle.

As Hervor grew into a young woman, she became even wilder. With flaming red hair and a charismatic personality, Hervor was soon leading raiding parties along the shorelines to rape, pillage and plunder the villages (I'm using rape here in the ancient meaning—to take what doesn't belong to you; however, with Hervor, you never know).

Raiding villages might have been enough for a typical Viking, but Hervor was anything but usual. She had hubris in excess. Somewhere along her travels she learned that her father, Angantyr, had been buried with a magical sword called Tyrfing.

Hervor became obsessed.

Long ago, an evil king had kidnapped two dwarves and forced them to forge a blade with a golden hilt and that could cut through stone as easily as if it were cloth. As anyone who has even slightly tested the waters of fantasy knows, dwarves make the best blades. However, dwarves also hate to be forced to do anything, so although they made

A painting by Peter Nicolai Arbo depicts Hervor, daughter of Heidrek, taking her last gasps.

the blade, they put a curse on it as well. Each time it was drawn, it would kill someone. And it would ultimately lead to the downfall of whoever wielded it.

None of this deterred Hervor. With her fleet of ships and her crew of Vikings, she sailed off for her father's grave on the island Munarvagr. As they drew near, flames shot up from the murky shores of the island and a host of ghosts flew across the water shrieking at them. The crew was terrified. Hervor gave them a tongue-lashing for being such a sorry lot of spineless Vikings, and set off alone to confront her father's ghost.

Ax-bearing demons and fire-breathing spirits threw just about every roadblock imaginable in her way, but Hervor never flinched. Eventually, she managed to summon her father forth from his grave. It wasn't exactly a warm reunion. Angantyr warned her to leave Tyrfing where it belonged: with him in the grave. He told her it was no good. He admonished her that it was cursed and would only bring her unhappiness.

Hervor retorted that her father was dead and what did a dead man need with a magical sword? It was her rightful inheritance and she wasn't going to leave the island without it. Hervor's uncles, the ghosts of her father's 11 berserker brothers, stormed out of their graves and gave the same warning. Leave the island, they told her. Forget the sword and leave it alone. She ignored them as well, and eventually managed to secure the sword from her father's dead grip.

When she returned to her shoreline, she was in for another surprise. Her crew had fled in terror, leaving her alone and stranded on the haunted island. Somehow Hervor found her way home where she continued her career of fighting and pillaging. With Tyrfing in hand, she became an even more ferocious opponent.

Eventually, however, she got tired of the warrior's life, married, settled down and had some kids. She may have died comfortably as an old woman, or according to some versions of the story, she felt the lure of battle and headed back out to the battlefield where she was killed.

But a magical sword has to fulfill its destiny.

Hervor's son Heidrik inherited Tyrfing. He used the sword to kill both his brother and foster son. Later Heidrik died in battle, ending Hervor's bloodline, and Tyrfing vanished from legend.

Above: The dwarf, Mime, tries to re-forge the sword, Nothung, into one piece. Right: Valkyries storm down from the sky with their swords drawn. *(illustrations by Arthur Rackham/ photos by Leslie Clary)*

SIGURD THE DRAGON SLAYER

Magical swords and golden rings in deep subterranean caverns have inspired mythmakers from the beginning of time, and the Norse were no exception. The story of Sigurd the Dragon Slayer is an ancient Norse myth, but perhaps no one has immortalized the story as richly as Wilhelm Richard Wagner in the opera *The Ring of the Nibelung*, where Sigurd is resurrected as Siegfried, and the sword, Gram, is known as Nothung.

The story of Sigurd is a convoluted one with curious plot twists and characters that reappear under different names. Several swords show up in this story, but the main one is usually called Gram, which Odin himself thrust into a tree. Although many tried, no one was able to remove it until a warrior named Sigmund stepped up to the trunk and easily pulled it out.

Unfortunately, Sigmund was killed in battle, but not before passing on the fragments of the broken sword to his pregnant wife, Hjördís. He told Hjördís that someday their son would re-forge the magical blade into a great weapon and become a great warrior.

Hjördís gave birth to a son, Sigurd, remarried another man, and her second husband sent Sigurd to be fostered by the dwarf, Regin (known as Mime in Wagner's opera). It wasn't the best foster arrangement, and Regin's main interest in the boy was that he would fulfill his destiny to slay the dragon, Fafnir, and regain for him the gold in the dragon's lair.

When Sigurd was grown, he gave Regin the sword, Gram, and he forged it into a powerful weapon. Sigurd headed off to the mountain to kill the dragon. Along the way, he met Odin in disguise, who passed along some words of wisdom. After slaying the dragon, he was to bathe in its blood, which would make him invulnerable, and to drink some as well, which would give him the gift of understanding birds and wild animals.

Sigurd did as he was instructed and was told by the birds that Regin planned to kill him when he returned. When he learned of his foster father's deceit, he returned home and killed Regin instead, leaving Sigurd free to head off for more adventures and to add many more episodes and plot twists to the story line.

BEOWULF, THE GEATISH WARRIOR

Beowulf wouldn't exist without the presence of two powerful and magical swords: Hrunting and a very special giant's sword. For those of you who

In an illustration by Johannes Gehrts, Freyr holds his magical sword.

The recreation depicts a Viking ship on the North Sea.
(courtesy of Per Christian van Borssum Waalloes, ©Ruben Schipper Fotografie VOF)

slept through high school English class, Beowulf was a Geatish warrior who sailed to Denmark to assist King Hrothgar in ridding the kingdom of the monster, Grendel, who had been terrorizing the place for years. Night after night, Grendel would creep into the mead hall where he decapitated warriors and made off with their bodies.

Once Beowulf arrived at the kingdom, he didn't waste any time getting down to business. The very night he arrived, he retired to the mead hall and pretended to sleep. When Grendel skulked in for his grisly deeds, Beowulf fought the demon single-handed, finally defeating him by tearing off Grendel's arm, which he later hung in the hall as a trophy.

The mortally wounded Grendel made off for his lair to die. That might have been the end of it except none of them had reckoned on dealing with an even worse monster: Grendel's mother. His mother was a swamp hag and offspring of Cain himself. Fearless, ruthless and tough as nails, she made her son seem about as threatening as the Pillsbury Doughboy.

After Grendel died in her arms, she went on a veritable frenzy of murderous rage. Instead of decapitating just one warrior at time, Grendel's mother was soon slaying in the double digits. In the process she killed Aeschere, one of the king's most beloved advisors.

Beowulf had his work cut out for him. As he and his men prepared to battle the swamp hag, King Hrothgar, overcome with grief over the death of Aeschere, presented Beowulf with "a rare and ancient sword named Hrunting." As legend has it, "The iron blade with its ill-boding patterns had been tempered in blood. It had never failed the hand of anyone who hefted it in battle."

Beowulf gratefully accepted the weapon and praised the sword's craftsmanship. Then he headed off for the swamp. When he arrived, the warrior fearlessly jumped into the dark waters. He sank, battling off a host of demons before finally arriving at the bottom where an epic fight took place. Beowulf swung Hrunting with all his might time and again, but magnificent as the sword was, it was powerless against the supernatural Grendel's mother.

Then, he spied in the corner just what he needed, a giant's sword, "an ideal weapon, one that any warrior would envy." Beowulf hefted the sword and in one swoop brought down Grendel's mother. He replaced the giant's sword to its corner, picked up Hrunting and made his way to the surface. He returned Hrunting to Hrothgar, but not without giving it proper praise and assuring Hrothgar that only a supernatural sword could have done the deed. With the monsters slain, his quest was over and he sailed back home with his crew.

SWORDS OF THE GODS

It probably goes without saying that any sword owned by a god is going to do some awesome thing. Some amazing blades have small but significant parts in the tales of Norse gods. The sword Hofund

The world's largest Viking longhouse can be seen at Lofotr Viking Museum in Norway. *(photo by Kjell Ove Storvik/Lofotr Viking Museum)*

was a dwarvish blade owned by the god Heimdall. Odin cast an enchantment on Hofund, and Heimdall was able to use the sword to command cosmic forces and wield blue flames that came straight from the stars. The sword also gave him the ability to pass himself off as a mortal man.

The Norse fertility goddess, Freya, is often depicted with a helmet and sword. As one of the Vanir, a group of gods who represent nature, love and magic, Freya was also leader of the Valkyries. She created the Northern Lights riding through the night sky with her sword and chariot.

Freya's twin brother, Frey, was chief of the Vanir, but the power of love led to his downfall and the loss of his magic sword that was able to fight on its own if the person who wielded it also had wisdom. One day as Frey was looking out over the world he spied the giantess, Gerda, and fell head over heels in love. Gerda married him, and for a while, it seemed like things might work out. Frey had to fight the giant, Beli and defeated him by stabbing him with an antler. Later, though, a fire giant defeated him during the great battle, Ragnarok, in which a number of major gods are also destroyed.

In Norse mythology the sword archetype is particularly mysterious. Its very origins are cloaked in secrecy. From the fires of the forge, swordsmiths made the magical transformation of ore to iron. It's not surprising these amazing creations found their way into stories where they could breathe fire, cast spells and bestow immortality on the warriors that wielded them. □

TRENDS

Talk about two completely different knife patterns—chef's knives and flipper folders—yet each has reached the pinnacle of popularity. Chef's knives gained steam during the Great Recession of the 1990s when people tended to entertain in their houses as opposed to dining out, and many gathered in their kitchens. At the same time, a movement toward organic and self-sufficient farming—growing and cooking one's own food—made chef's knives a staple. People began remodeling the centers of their households, making modern kitchens a mainstay. It was also a time when the Food Network and just about every other TV enterprise added at least one cooking show to their programming. Chef's knives exploded!

And then there are flipper folders, the latest entry into the tactical folder fray. The little extension of the blade tang that extends through the handle halves when a folder is closed is sure fun to flick with the forefinger. And upon flicking it, the blade rotates out at a speed fast enough to "click" into place when it hits the stop pin in the fully open position. Those ceramic ball bearings, bronze bushings and pivot rings sure help, practically making for friction-free blade opening.

Nothing is new under the sun, but innovative knifemakers ensure there will always be Trends in knives, with this year's slate including "Ti-Dyed Timascus," "Tacti-Turns," "BFF's—Bowie/Fighters Forever," "Steel-Tipped Boots" and some "Forward Tanto Thrust." They're all completely different knife patterns, yet as popular as Jennifer Lawrence at an Oscars party, and yes, that's probably a trend. □

Chef's Specials	58	Nation Builders	96
Flipper Folder Flair	60	Throwback Bowies	99
Ti-Dyed Timascus	65	Palpable Pulps	102
Tacti-Turns	66	Straight-Up Daggers	110
BFF's—Bowie/Fighters Forever	68	Pocket Wares	114
Guarded Swords & Daggers	75	Forward Tanto Thrust	117
Folder Fancy	78	"Game On!" Blades	118
Crosscut Mammoth & Some Molars	86	More Love For Loveless	126
A Synthetic Aesthetic	88	Keen Campers	128
Steel-Tipped Boots	95		

Chef's Specials

« JEREMY SPAKE

Having smelted his own crucible steel blade, the maker added a stabilized maidou burl and redwood lace grip for an overall comely composition, or tasty dish.

« BILL BURKE

Dizzy up the damascus, dice the tomatoes and dish up the dessert.

(PointSeven image)

« TIM TABOR

The damascus blade of the maple-burl-handle chef's knife has more layers—448 to be exact—than a royal wedding cake.

(PointSeven image)

⌃ MICHAEL McCLURE

Which one is spicier—the damascus blade or stabilized California buckeye burl handle?

(Patrick Cashmore image)

⌃ THOMAS HASLINGER

The "New Generation Chef" dons an 8-inch CPM S35VN stainless steel blade, distal tapered for balance and excellent edge geometry, and a stabilized curly koa handle.

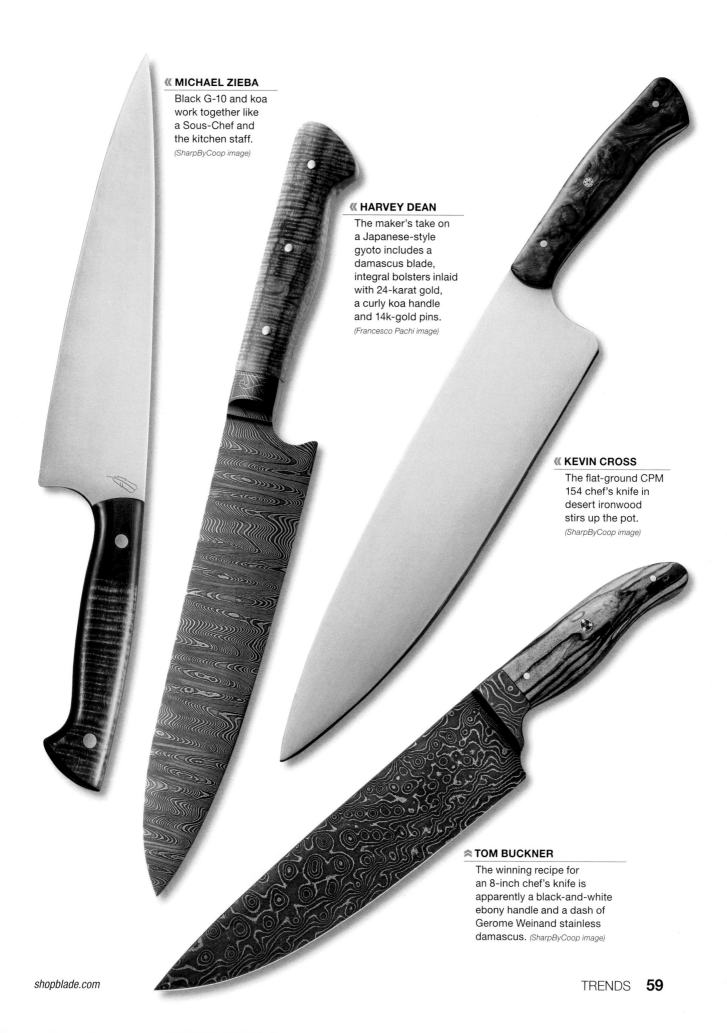

« MICHAEL ZIEBA
Black G-10 and koa
work together like
a Sous-Chef and
the kitchen staff.
(SharpByCoop image)

« HARVEY DEAN
The maker's take on
a Japanese-style
gyoto includes a
damascus blade,
integral bolsters inlaid
with 24-karat gold,
a curly koa handle
and 14k-gold pins.
(Francesco Pachi image)

« KEVIN CROSS
The flat-ground CPM
154 chef's knife in
desert ironwood
stirs up the pot.
(SharpByCoop image)

⌃ TOM BUCKNER
The winning recipe for
an 8-inch chef's knife is
apparently a black-and-white
ebony handle and a dash of
Gerome Weinand stainless
damascus. *(SharpByCoop image)*

Flipper Folder Flair

Not since the LinerLock® or frame-lock folder, the pocket clip or the thumb stud has a folding knife innovation revolutionized the industry as much as the flipper folder, named such because it flips open with the flick of a forefinger. An extension off the base, or tang, of the blade protrudes through and rises above the handle when the folder is in the closed position. By flicking it with the forefinger while holding the handle, the blade flies open faster than a novelty shop near a cruise ship landing.

Bronze bushings, pivot rings and ceramic ball bearings aid in smooth, nearly friction-free blade opening. Flipper folders are fun to flick and as quiet as a librarian, until that telltale, audible "click" sounds when the blade hits the stop pin in the fully open position, ready for use or to hold upright toward the light and admire.

It's amazing how far the folding knife has come in such a short period of time. Early tactical folders look more like boxy, awkward affairs compared to today's lightweight, sleek, ergonomic, stylish and curvaceous examples. With anodized titanium frames and bolsters, damascus blades, engraving, gold inlays and exotic materials, the folders have become art forms, though tactically handy and utilitarian cutting tools. They are tough, reliable workhorses, and with some flipper folder flair to spare. □

« RON BEST
The dress flipper folder is curved, contoured, anodized and delivered, in a re-curved damascus blade, no less, and an unobtrusive carbon fiber pocket clip. *(SharpByCoop image)*

⌃ SCOT MATSUOKA
Wood of the padauk variety was a fine choice for a CPM 154 flipper folder in zirconium bolsters.
(PointSeven image)

⌄ BRIAN TIGHE
The anodized titanium handle of the Damasteel flipper folder is striking in more ways than one.
(Cory Martin Imaging)

» JONATHAN MCNEES

Meet the "Bonedaddy" dress tactical folder fashioned from a 5.5-inch W2 blade with wavy temper line, and a Mokuti handle and pivot collars. Glow features in the back spacer and under the handle scales can be viewed through the holes in the grip. *(SharpByCoop image)*

⌄ JASON CLARK

Who knew ivory Micarta, Mokuti and damascus would combine for such an attractive ensemble, utilitarian in design and aesthetic in execution? *(SharpByCoop image)*

⌄ WES CRAWFORD

Built like a "Tank," and named such, the titanium-frame flipper folder features a CPM S30V blade and a black-and-green G-10 handle. *(SharpByCoop image)*

⌄ BRIAN NADEAU

The maker offers the 6AL-4V-titanium frame of his "Typhoon" flipper folder in a variety of colors and patterns. The 4-inch blade rides on a stainless ball bearing thrust washer. *(SharpByCoop image)*

» JERRY MOEN

The "Blue Max" flipper folder relies on a multi-ground PSF-27 steel blade and contoured carbon fiber handle scales.

(Steve Woods image)

⌄ DAVID SHARP

Blending tradition and innovation, the "Frame Horn" folder enlists a CPM 154 blade, titanium frame and bolsters, integral back spacer and clip, and stag handle scales.

(SharpByCoop image)

« BILL COYE

The textured titanium frame and CPM 154 blade of frame-lock folder are treated to a stonewashed finish.

(PointSeven image)

» SEAN FLORIAN

Titanium with dual-color anodizing makes for a lasting impression on a pair of 154CM flipper folders. *(PointSeven image)*

« RICHARD ROGERS

The "Axiom" flipper blends Chad Nichols "tuxedo"-pattern damascus with bronze bolsters and standoffs, bronze-lightning-strike carbon fiber handle scales, and a titanium frame, pivot, screws and liners. *(SharpByCoop image)*

« RICK BARRETT

Just in case there's any fallout, the "Fallout" flipper folder might come in handy, including a san mai damascus blade with an Elmax core, a titanium frame and Timascus overlays. *(Cory Martin Imaging)*

« MICHAEL ZIEBA

It's the copper and black nickel finish of the titanium frame-lock flipper folder that elevates it to new heights. *(SharpByCoop image)*

⯈ BUTCH BALL

As smooth as it looks, the Damasteel and pearl "Skorpion XL" opens when asked. *(PointSeven image)*

⯈ TODD BEGG

Almost entirely blacked out, the "Bodega" flipper folder showcases a Cerakote-covered blade, carbon fiber handle scales and then a gold-anodized lock bar and pocket clip. *(Cory Martin Imaging)*

» ERIC OCHS

A harpoon-shaped CPM 154 blade defines the Tatsu tanto flipper folder in a hand-rubbed satin finish, Timascus handle and chipped-zirconium pocket clip, back spacer and Rick Hinderer LBS lock stabilizer.

⌃ LEE WILLIAMS

A thin copper spacer separates the meteorite bolsters from the green Micarta handle scales of the flipper folder, which also sports a copper back spacer and liners. *(PointSeven image)*

⌃ DAVID S. KULIS

Carbon fiber and Timascus team up for the handle of a claw-shaped, hollow-ground CPM S30V flipper folder.

(SharpByCoop image)

» KIRBY LAMBERT

"Augustus" comes in a marbled carbon fiber handle, a Zircuti front bolster and a Chad Nichols "blackout" damascus blade and integral flipper.

(SharpByCoop image)

Ti-Dyed Timascus

⌄ MIKE ZSCHERNY

Timascus doesn't get any more colorful than the handle of the folding tanto featuring a Chad Nichols damascus blade. The pocket clip parades more Timascus.
(SharpByCoop image)

⌄ STAN WILSON

Timascus highlights the highly fit and finished folder with tightly patterned damascus blade.
(PointSeven image)

≫ LEE WILLIAMS

Timascus drips down over the mother-of-pearl handle of the "Iceman" folder like the ocean meeting an iceberg.
(PointSeven image)

⌃ R.J. MARTIN

Some of the Timascus coloring splashed across the SM-100 blade of the flipper folder in zirconium bolsters and a titanium frame.
(SharpByCoop image)

⌃ BRAD SOUTHARD

The "Flippin' Tanto" is a party favorite for sure, including a Damasteel blade, Timascus frame, and zirconium pivot and back spacer. *(SharpByCoop image)*

Tacti-Turns

Those darn tactical folders, always popular, handy, stealth looking, with pocket clips, thumb studs, flipper mechanisms, frame locks, locking liners—doesn't anyone carry a plain old pocketknife anymore? How about hunting knives in stag handles and drop-point blades, bowie or fillet knives, shouldn't they all be as popular as tactical folders, and why does every other knife need to have a tactical look and feel? What happened to pearl-handle folders with two blades, files and gold bails?

There's room for all of them in the knife industry, and each knife pattern and style is illustrated tenfold within the front and back covers of this book. Yet tactical folders remain the kingpins of the knife industry, the most popular, and as we all know, it's easiest to take potshots at the ones on top.

What resonates with all knife enthusiasts, however, is that innovations, creativity and quality craftsmanship drive the market for custom knives. Nowhere are those qualities more evident than in tactical folders, which have become lighter thanks to high-tech materials, faster because of advancements in bushings, pivots, ball bearings and pivot rings, handier thanks to pocket clip designs and blade opening devises, and more utilitarian as a result of better blade steels, materials and knife patterns.

So curse them all you want, tactical folders, or tacti-turns, are here for the long haul. There are beautiful examples of tactical knives that turn, and no, the makers of such are not taciturn or shy about the popularity of their patterns. They'll let you know all about them if you ask. □

STAN MOIZIS
It's good to see a swing-guard, rocker-release automatic of such fine workmanship, including a K-110 blade, damascus bolsters and dyed moose horn handle scales.
(Roger Marzin image)

LES GEORGE
The stealth, flowing, modern look of the "Harpy" flipper folder is achieved via a CNC-machined titanium frame and a shapely 4-inch stainless damascus blade.

BATTLE HORSE KNIVES
Thumb notches on the spine of the satin-finished, Scandinavian-ground D2 blade combine with the milled and tumbled titanium frame for full hand purchase. *(PointSeven image)*

» TODD HEETER

Thrust needle bearings and a rolling detent screw aid in flipping open the CPM 3V blade of the "Man-O-War" frame-lock folder, complete with anodized titanium frame and an industrial look.

⌄ JARED PRICE

This one's about the lines—a milled titanium handle and Chad Nichols "bacon"-damascus blade—and the color, mostly grey with a touch of orange from the G-10 pivot collar. *(PointSeven image)*

» JASON CLARK

A satin-finished frame-lock dagger is arrow straight, from its "lightning strike" carbon fiber handle to the titanium fittings and all the way to its oh-so-pointy CPM 154 blade tip. *(Ward image)*

⌃ MICHAEL WALKER

Even the 1980s LinerLock® looks modern considering it was fashioned three decades ago, a classic for sure, with a thin profile, sharp blade and thumb indent. *(SharpByCoop image)*

» BOB TERZUOLA

No conversation about tactical folders is complete without mention of Bobby T., progenitor of some original tacti-turns, and maker of the steel, mammoth ivory and meteorite beauty shown here. *(PointSeven image)*

BFF's—Bowie/ Fighters Forever

Sometimes a trend in knives emerges through the melding of two distinct knife forms, as may be the case with bowie/fighters. But are bowies and fighters all that inherently different? For one, there isn't anyone who can pinpoint the exact pattern of the original knife Col. James Bowie used at the Sandbar Fight. Most knife historians agree it was similar to a large butcher knife of the time.

Modern fighters or fighting knives have straight backs like butcher knives and only very slightly curved blades, barely more than daggers or stilettos. A few fighter blades curve up, and others are claw-like in shape. Bowies, on the other hand, exhibit clip-point blades, some with spines that dip only slightly toward the tips. Bowie blades tend to be wider, or deeper from spine to edge, not as skinny. And fighter handles can be slimmer, with bowie grips filling the palm.

Yet the differences between the two types of knives tend to become obscure when makers fashion their own versions of the two. And eventually, like today, bowies and fighters borrow traits from each other and blend into one category— BFF's—Bowie Fighters Forever, and that's just fine, because they should be friends anyway, forever forged in kinship of the fighting blade, and executed flawlessly without regard to differences, like all good BFF's. □

« FRED DUVALL
The brass guard might just suit the top brass, as would the 10-inch CruV blade and Micarta grip of the full-tang straight blade.
(Ward image)

« STUART SMITH
Too pretty to fight, but sharp as hell, the forged damascus dueling bowie dons a damascus clam shell blade catcher, ball guard and a lily white ivory handle.

« MIKE CRADDOCK
Follow the line down the center of the damascus blade straight to the tip of the fixed bowie in a stag and Micarta grip.
(SharpByCoop image)

« JOHN DOYLE

A clamshell double guard protects the fingers from the edge of that incredible 13-inch 1084 blade, allowing the digits to rest on the African blackwood handle.
(SharpByCoop image)

« KEN HALL

Lest we forget the damascus and desert ironwood fighter, this one orchestrated beautifully with a long, subtle swedge and a smooth stainless steel double guard.

« JEFF KNOX

The distressed look of the stonewashed 440C blade goes well with the pointy guard, a look that is softened by the sweet gum handle. *(PointSeven image)*

» CLAUDIO and ARIEL SOBRAL (CAS)

A snake tongue of a san mai steel blade darts out, the serpent coiling its Micarta body and flaring its stainless steel hood. *(Ward image)*

⌃ SCOTT GALLAGHER

A bowie, but with fighter attributes, the 1075 blade displays a wispy temper line complemented by stainless steel fittings and a pommel cap grooved to match the stag grip. *(Ward image)*

STEVE JOHNSON

The maker's rendition of a KA-BAR WW II fighting knife requisitions a CPM 154 blade with a sharpened clip, a hand-ground and polished fuller, a leather handle stabilized by Ernie Grospich, and a stainless guard and pommel.

(Francesco Pachi image)

PAUL LEBATARD

The "Sasquatch Bowie" is a sub-hilt ala a fighter, has lapis lazuli spacers like an art knife, aircraft aluminum fittings (combat knife?), a utilitarian ATS 34 blade and a walnut burl handle.

(PointSeven image)

BEN TENDICK

Slide your hand around the dimpled G-10 handle of the "Skookum Bowie" and brave its 9-inch CPM 3V blade with deep fuller and clip point.

JORDAN LAMOTHE

Olivewood with copper and stainless steel spacers proved an inspired choice for a fighter in a 5-inch, hand-forged 1080 blade.

SCHUYLER LOVESTRAND

A length of fossil walrus artifact like that handle has to inspire a maker to fashion a better blade, and mission accomplished with this CPM 154 beauty.

(PointSeven image)

» DON HANSON III
Some dipsy-doodle damascus bounces its way along the 10-inch clip-point blade, terminating in a point on one end and a fossil walrus artifact handle on the other.
(PointSeven image)

⩔ GARY GROVES
What's black and white and blade all over? That would be an ATS-34 bowie/fighter in a buffalo horn and imitation ivory handle, as well as a stainless steel guard and pommel.
(PointSeven image)

» LIN RHEA
The BFF is a DH III model in a W2 blade, a stag and African blackwood handle and forged stainless fittings, and it's beautiful IMHO.
(PointSeven image)

⩔ SHAYNE CARTER
The blackwood and damascus fighter bends one way, then the other, ingratiating itself into our hearts as it goes along.
(PointSeven image)

⩔ LANDON ROBBINS
A nice blend of the bowie and fighter styles, this one has such a wavy temper line, it makes a splash along the 1084 blade, all anchored by some swell stag.
(PointSeven image)

» ARTHUR LYNN

Crown stag, an oval guard and some impressive damascus, then that neat clip toward the blade point, as much a bowie as a fighter, it's a bargain no matter the price. *(PointSeven image)*

» E. SCOTT MCGHEE

Called the "Cottonmouth Blackout" for its snaking form and black Parkerized 52100 blade, the knife comes in a choice of a Micarta or African blackwood grip.

(SharpByCoop image)

» WILLIAM MILLER

The sub-hilt fighter, in "W's"-pattern damascus and fossil walrus ivory, has a distinct bowie-like clip point.

(PointSeven image)

⌃ SAM LURQUIN

The damascus S-guard and parrying strip on the blade spine are nice touches for a W2 bowie with pronounced clip point and smoky temper line. *(SharpByCoop image)*

« ALAN HUTCHINSON

Hello 16.25-inch fighter, you've got some reach, all in damascus, silver and stag, and a point we thought you'd never get to, but that was ultimately worth the wait. *(Ward image)*

« MARCUS LIN

You have to love the clip point of the Bob Loveless-style sub-hilt fighter in a D2 tool steel blade with a centerline that dips with the clip, not to mention the stag grip. *(SharpByCoop image)*

« STEVE RANDALL

In the "Tactical Bowie" realm is one that stretches over a foot long and includes a black Parkerized 5160 blade and a black Micarta handle. *(Ward image)*

⌃ MICHAEL DEIBERT

The hidden tang of "Big Bowie's" clay-hardened 1095 blade goes all the way through the Oregon maple burl handle and is peened over the damascus pommel. *(Caleb Royer image)*

⌄ GIL HIBBEN

The Rambo III rescue knife, from the maker who designed the knives for the Rambo and Rambo III movies, combines bowie, fighter and survival knife traits, like John Rambo prefers. *(Cory Martin Imaging)*

⌃ TAD LYNCH

That's not a stain but a watery temper line on the 11.5-inch W2 blade of the sub-hilt bowie brought to market in a stabilized Turkish walnut handle. *(Ward image)*

⌃ EDMUND DAVIDSON

Of all integral construction, with the blade, guard and handle frame being one piece of A2 tool steel heat treated by Paul Bos, it is adorned in stag handle slabs. *(PointSeven image)*

» BILL COFFEY

The long, thin, hand-rubbed, hollow-ground CPM 154 blade branches out from a stainless steel guard engraved by Bill Lerma, a popcorn-stag handle and a gold skull crusher pommel.

« NICK WHEELER

The raised clip of the fixed bowie is as handsomely sharp as that smooth wooden handle, complete with thumb rest/indent near the double guard.

(SharpByCoop image)

⌃ DERRICK WULF

The full-tang integral damascus fixed bowie wears only curly koa for covering, and lets its frame show for the knife world to appreciate.

(SharpByCoop image)

Guarded Swords & Daggers

» KEVIN CASHEN
Regal in its makeup and design, this rendition of a 16th-century dagger boasts an iron-wire-wrapped wood handle, a 10-inch damascus blade and a carved guard and pommel.

« BERTIE RIETVELD
Only a bowtie-like guard and arrow-sharp pommel of colored stainless steel could suffice for the lapis-lazuli-handle damascus dagger with titanium ferrules.
(SharpByCoop image)

» LOGAN PEARCE
The guard would deflect sword thrusts, but it's an art dagger, sashaying a damascus blade, and a handle composed of mother-of-pearl and 550-piece silver filigree.
(Ward image)

« VIRGIL ENGLAND
Aptly named the "Thorn" boxed sword, materials include a damascus blade, 22-karat gold and 18-k rose gold, silver, lapis lazuli, mammoth ivory, Madagascar ebony, yellow cedar and leather.

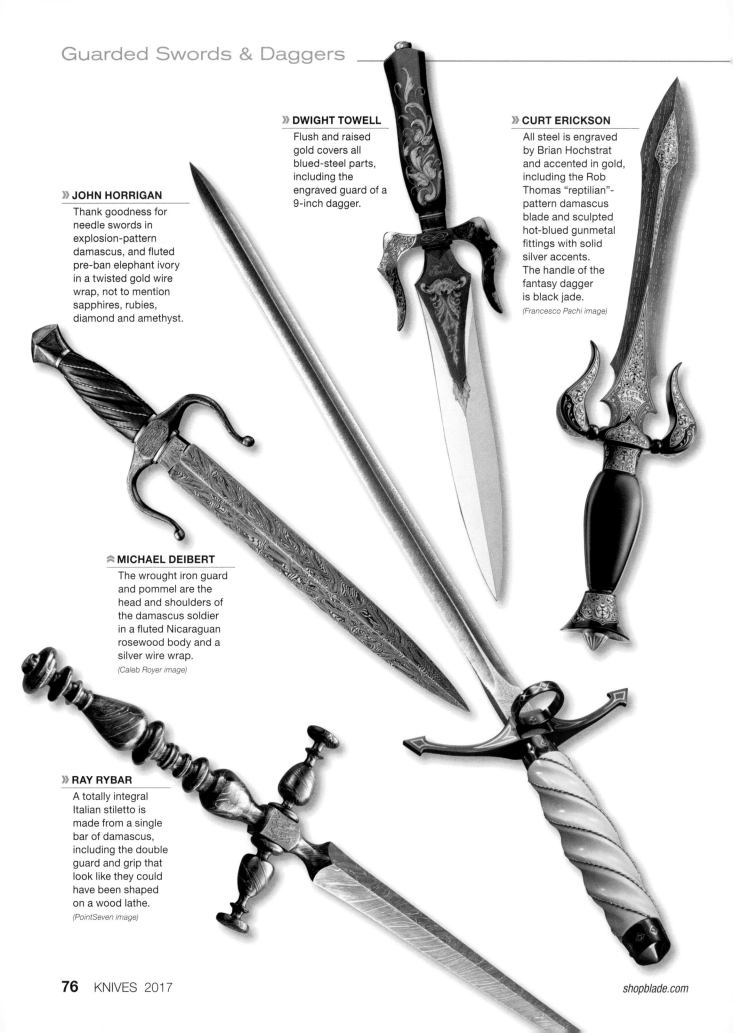

» DWIGHT TOWELL

Flush and raised gold covers all blued-steel parts, including the engraved guard of a 9-inch dagger.

» CURT ERICKSON

All steel is engraved by Brian Hochstrat and accented in gold, including the Rob Thomas "reptilian"- pattern damascus blade and sculpted hot-blued gunmetal fittings with solid silver accents. The handle of the fantasy dagger is black jade.
(Francesco Pachi image)

» JOHN HORRIGAN

Thank goodness for needle swords in explosion-pattern damascus, and fluted pre-ban elephant ivory in a twisted gold wire wrap, not to mention sapphires, rubies, diamond and amethyst.

⌃ MICHAEL DEIBERT

The wrought iron guard and pommel are the head and shoulders of the damascus soldier in a fluted Nicaraguan rosewood body and a silver wire wrap.
(Caleb Royer image)

» RAY RYBAR

A totally integral Italian stiletto is made from a single bar of damascus, including the double guard and grip that look like they could have been shaped on a wood lathe.
(PointSeven image)

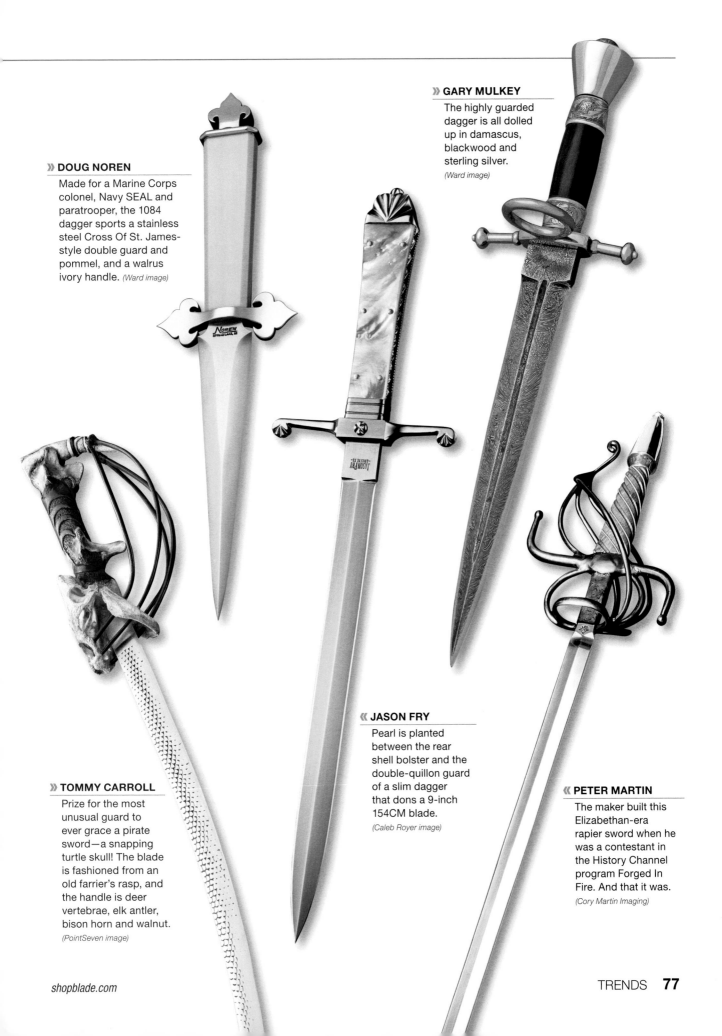

» GARY MULKEY
The highly guarded dagger is all dolled up in damascus, blackwood and sterling silver.
(Ward image)

» DOUG NOREN
Made for a Marine Corps colonel, Navy SEAL and paratrooper, the 1084 dagger sports a stainless steel Cross Of St. James-style double guard and pommel, and a walrus ivory handle. *(Ward image)*

» TOMMY CARROLL
Prize for the most unusual guard to ever grace a pirate sword—a snapping turtle skull! The blade is fashioned from an old farrier's rasp, and the handle is deer vertebrae, elk antler, bison horn and walnut.
(PointSeven image)

« JASON FRY
Pearl is planted between the rear shell bolster and the double-quillon guard of a slim dagger that dons a 9-inch 154CM blade.
(Caleb Royer image)

« PETER MARTIN
The maker built this Elizabethan-era rapier sword when he was a contestant in the History Channel program Forged In Fire. And that it was.
(Cory Martin Imaging)

Folder Fancy

I n the June 2016 issue of *BLADE® Magazine*, Kendall Schorsch, who was featured in the "Knifemaker Showcase" column, is quoted as saying: "I grew up right down the road from where Pat West and Bill Ruple made knives, and I remember seeing Ruple and West custom knives on every farmer's and rancher's hip. Seeing the filework from across the room let me know that it was a custom knife, so I take pride in my filework and that the knives I make are not only tools, but also works of art and time-treasured heirlooms."

Just because they're fancy, doesn't mean they're not tools and "time-treasured heirlooms," as Schorsch noted, and sometimes the extra care that goes into embellishing, jewel inlaying, overlaying, fileworking, carving, etching, sculpting and engraving knives is a sign that they're "custom," or handmade. The filework let Schorsch know, and it inspired him to make knives of his own.

The fancy folders herein could all be used to open letters, tear down boxes, cut threads, trim nails, whittle sticks or cut beef jerky, rope, leather or plastic. Not one of them is delivered dull, and they're all elegant examples. It's OK to let their looks deceive you into thinking they're too pretty to use or that they won't cut. The welcome surprise when they are called to action is all that much better when they slice through a cutting medium like butter. It excites the senses and tickles your folder fancy. □

⌃ LARRY COX

If you fancy folders, the damascus blade and handle of the lock-back folder should fit the bill and cut through other daily distractions. *(Ward image)*

⌃ TOM HEARD

Mokumé bolsters are a perfect match for the mammoth tooth handle scales of a bolster-release auto folder featuring a Rob Thomas stainless damascus blade.

(Tony Derro image)

《 RICHARD ROGERS

The bamboo-like, blue-anodized titanium handle of the damascus frame-lock flipper folder is as brilliant in execution as it is in color and character.

(SharpByCoop image)

⩔ CLIFF PARKER

"Skulls" and "Grim Reaper" mosaic damascus dress the blade and bolsters of a LinerLock® folder with a bog oak grip, gold-plated screws and a black diamond thumb stud.

(Cory Martin Imaging)

⩔ CORY MARTIN

The "reverse"-san-mai-damascus blade provides enough electricity to power the rest of the flipper folder, including a zirconium frame, cherry burl inlays and titanium screws.

⩓ EMMANUEL ESPOSITO

The most skilled tile layers would be hard-pressed to match the mosaic black-lip pearl, black Bakelite and green carbon fiber handle of the "Scorpion." Check out that wild blade grind. *(Francesco Pachi image)*

» BARRY DAVIS

The gent's hunter is outfitted in a 384-layer damascus blade, damascus bolsters, tortoise-shell handle scales and a 14k-gold lanyard ring, pins, blade stop and bolster spacers.

(SharpByCoop image)

⩓ CALVIN ROBINSON

The "Jade G-10" handle scales emit a green/gold hue over the FLF-15 flipper folder, complete with a Sandvik 14C28N blade in a "dark silicon carbide blast finish."

(Caleb Royer image)

Folder Fancy

❯ BRIAN NADEAU

It's amazing what a little anodizing, patterning and styling can do to an otherwise custom but customary CPM S35VN flipper folder. *(SharpByCoop image)*

❮ MURRAY STERLING

Palm the mammoth ivory handle, push your thumb into the Damasteel bolster release and let auto blade pop open with a vengeance.

❮ GLENN WATERS

Two dragons caught in a lightning storm are permanently engraved on the VG-10 blade and Shibuichi Gin silver bolsters of a "flipping tang tab LinerLock" folder.

❮ CHAD NELL

Purple and blue Alpha Knife Supply "Amoeba" Timascus hits its mark, as does the Rob Thomas damascus blade, and the zirconium back spacer and pocket clip. *(Cory Martin Imaging)*

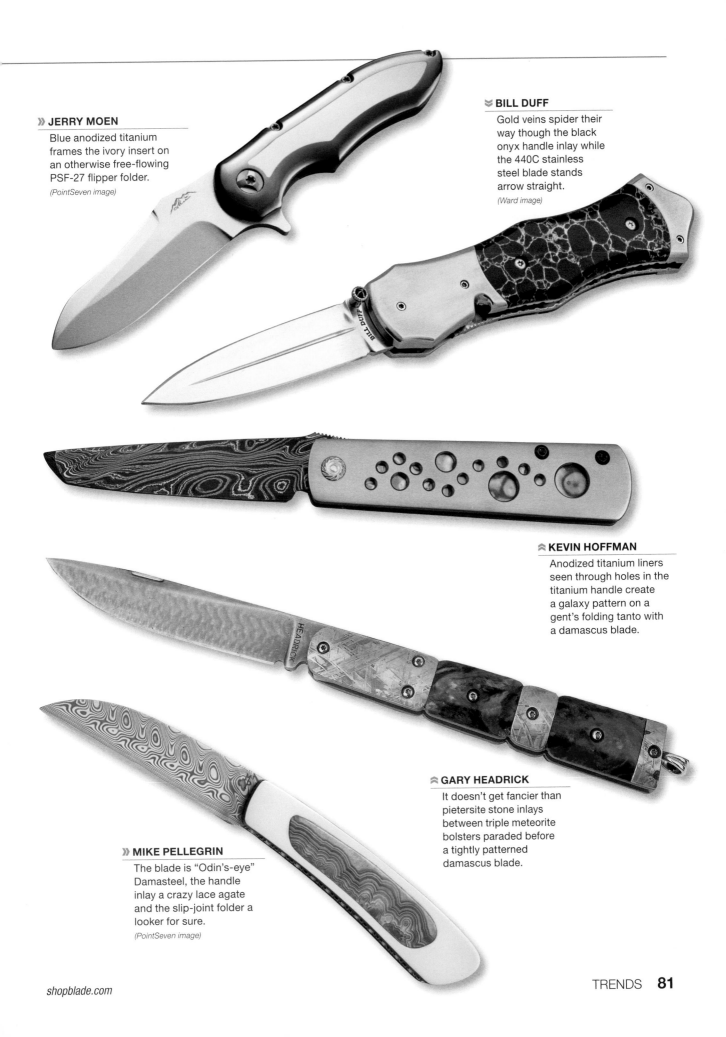

JERRY MOEN

Blue anodized titanium frames the ivory insert on an otherwise free-flowing PSF-27 flipper folder.

(PointSeven image)

BILL DUFF

Gold veins spider their way though the black onyx handle inlay while the 440C stainless steel blade stands arrow straight.

(Ward image)

KEVIN HOFFMAN

Anodized titanium liners seen through holes in the titanium handle create a galaxy pattern on a gent's folding tanto with a damascus blade.

GARY HEADRICK

It doesn't get fancier than pietersite stone inlays between triple meteorite bolsters paraded before a tightly patterned damascus blade.

MIKE PELLEGRIN

The blade is "Odin's-eye" Damasteel, the handle inlay a crazy lace agate and the slip-joint folder a looker for sure.

(PointSeven image)

Folder Fancy

FRANK NIRO

With the damascus blade and Seymchan meteorite bolsters heat colored, the pearl and gold were left natural for some contrast and cutting beauty.

(Custom Knife Gallery Of Colorado image)

STEVE KELLY

The Mokuti handle might draw all the attention, but the Chad Nichols "Starfire" damascus makes an impression, and the titanium and zirconium hardware holds its own. *(SharpByCoop image)*

C. GRAY TAYLOR

Koi fish swim underneath 14k-gold lily pads and flowers (fashioned by Lisa Tomlin) on the exotic handle of an equal-end, lobster-pattern pocketknife. *(Francesco Pachi image)*

SCOT MATSUOKA

That's not ivory, but Kirinite, not an agate but Timascus, and not a mirage, but a handsomely handmade CPM 154 flipper folder.

(PointSeven image)

LARRY NEWTON

Mammoth ivory and gold inlay invigorate a folding dagger in Rob Thomas damascus.

(PointSeven image)

《 GAYLE BRADLEY

A Damasteel blade, gold-plated pins and screws, and an anodized titanium frame further enhance a nice pairing of mammoth tooth and heat-colored Timascus.

(PointSeven image)

≪ JEFF CLAIBORNE

With a gold-lip-pearl handle, two 52100 blades and integral milled bolsters and liners, the peanut pattern pocketknife exhibits just enough snap, crackle and pop.

(Hoffman image)

》 RICK LALA

The carved-titanium dress tactical folder is presented pachyderm style.

(SharpByCoop image)

≪ DAVID KULIS

Some prefer flipper folders in silver blades, others in black, with anodized titanium or damascus bolsters, the decision is theirs. Dyed box elder burl is the grip of choice.

(SharpByCoop image)

» LARRY FUEGEN
Carved mammoth ivory and damascus, along with touches of gold, give a large folding dagger more than enough dimension and depth to delight the senses.
(Francesco Pachi image)

⌃ MATTHEW LERCH
Not every maker can combine Mike Norris damascus and gold-lip pearl into a sculpted knife as smooth and sweet as the "Lancaster." *(Cory Martin Imaging)*

» SEAN O'HARE
Flawlessly fit and finished, the locking liner folder combines lightning-strike carbon fiber, Mike Norris damascus and zirconium as Giorgio Armani would dress a manikin.

« JOHN GRIFFIN
Rough-ground bolsters resemble silver nuggets on either side of the pearl handle of a damascus push-button auto folder.

⌃ RON BEST
If the dress tactical were any dressier it would dine in exclusive company, but there's always a place for a pointedly proper member of the party wearing a coat of many colors.
(SharpByCoop image)

MICHAEL WALKER

Whether it's the deep-etched stainless damascus blade with titanium inlay or the sculpted and gold-inlaid titanium handle, the D-Lock folder walks and talks.

(Francesco Pachi image)

PAUL LUSK

For his "Urban Instinct" LinerLock folder, the maker unearthed mammoth ivory that has sedimentary rock formed into the tusk, adding ladder-pattern damascus, titanium and zirconium.

(SharpByCoop image)

JERRY MCCLURE

To achieve an Art Deco look, the maker employed Damasteel, titanium and nephrite jade, as well as some artistic rendering of the same.

(SharpByCoop image)

MICHAEL RAYMOND

Only the Mediterranean Sea could emit a blue as vibrant as the Timascus handle inlay of a CPM 10V "Starlit" folder.

(SharpByCoop image)

ANDERS HOGSTROM

What one can do with a titanium handle and some copper accents is inspiring, and further driven home by a 1045 blade with soft hamon (temper line). *(SharpByCoop image)*

Crosscut Mammoth & Some Molars

» LARAMIE JACKSON

Did someone dip the mammoth tooth in dye, or did the beast have impacting molars? Either way, a Bob Loveless-style drop-point hunter is the beneficiary of the sweet tooth.

⌃ BILL BEHNKE

A crosscut of mammoth ivory reveals rings expanding outward like a log, while the feather damascus pattern also flares toward the blade edge and spine. *(Cory Martin Imaging)*

⌃ RICHARD TESARIK

The blue glacial ice left its hue among the grains of the mammoth-tooth grip on a damascus LinerLock® folder.

« LOGAN PEARCE

The lines of blue mammoth tooth go one way, and those of the pattern-welded blade steel point another. *(SharpByCoop image)*

⌃ RODNEY WATTS

My, my, the mammoth tooth would make a saber-toothed tiger green with envy. *(SharpByCoop image)*

CORRIE SCHOEMAN
Mammoth tooth highlights the wings of the butterfly knife, complete with Ettore Gianferrari damascus body and wing tips. *(PointSeven image)*

JIM SORNBERGER
The Mike Sakmar mokumé guard and handle wrap bring out the brown hues of the mammoth tooth grip on an ATS-34 California dagger.
(PointSeven image)

SAMUEL STONER JR.
Mammoth tooth makes for a hellacious damascus hunter.
(Cory Martin Imaging)

DAVID BRODZIAK
Fashioning a mammoth tooth handle for the ladder-pattern-damascus bowie was just one step, with Carol Ann O'Connor immortalizing a woolly mammoth on the Western Australia inceana (koa wood) sheath being the other.

ALAIN and JORIS CHOMILIER
Mammoth ivory sliced transversally to resemble what the makers envision as dragon bone accompanies a Mattias Styrefors dragon-pattern damascus blade.

A Synthetic Aesthetic

» D. SCOTT BARRY

The lightning strike carbon fiber handle helps keep the gent's folder at 1.75 ounces, including the modified-drop-point, satin-finished 154CM blade.

(Custom Knife Gallery of Colorado image)

» DON CARLOS ANDRADE

The vision behind the parang-style backpacker was to marry a mustard-finished, forged 52100 blade with a carved Westinghouse linen Micarta handle and bronze and mosaic pins.

⌄ BRAM FRANK

One kinetic-opening folder is pointed, and one blunt, the first in black G-10 and the second orange, and both with indexing indentations on the grips for practice and feel.

(PointSeven image)

⌄ FRED DUVALL

Break out the Micarta-handle 52100 bowie with brass guard, and go trekking through the tundra footloose and fancy free. *(Ward image)*

⩗ DANIEL PICA

A carbon-fiber handle version of the maker's "The Critter" model, this CPM 154 beauty incorporates G-10 liners to further offset the grip, and flared tubes for a final touch.

⩗ AARON FREDERICK

It's the tip-heavy, multi-ground Chad Nichols damascus blade, lightning strike carbon fiber handle and overall shape and style of the folder that sends shivers down the spine.
(SharpByCoop image)

≪ JEFF FREEMAN

The blued and grooved G-10 grip inserts are interchangeable on the D2 button-lock flipper folder with grade 10 bearings, not that you'd want to change them.
(SharpByCoop image)

⩘ ZAC BUCHANAN

"Thunderstorm Kevlar" is a sticky sweet honeycomb of a handle choice for a Dixon Fighter in a CPM 154 blade with extended chute grind. *(SharpByCoop image)*

≪ JEFF HAZE

Removable natural canvas Micarta handle scales sandwich the full tang of the Scandinavian-ground 80CrV2 blade, complete with hand-filed jimping. The "Thornbush" model is prickly hot.

MICHAEL ZIEBA

The titanium handle, finished in copper and black nickel, is as handsome as it is handy, and leads to a 3.5-inch CPM S35VN blade.

(SharpByCoop image)

SHANE SIBERT

A fuller stretches halfway across the tightly patterned Chad Nichols "starfire"-damascus blade, and the lightning strike carbon fiber handle is enhanced by a checkered frame.

(Kris Kandler image)

BEN TENDICK

A natural canvas Micarta haft anchors the "Valkyrie" hammer pole tomahawk, complete with stainless steel flared tubes and a 4140 stainless steel head.

KYLE HANSON

Old Micarta is a traditional choice for the grip of a drop-point hunter dressed up in a damascus blade.

(Cory Martin Imaging)

N.J. "NORM" COHEN

Vine filework climbs along the spine of the combination natural-color and black Micarta handle of a CPM 154 fixed blade with thong tube. *(Glenn Smit image)*

JERRY HOSSOM

The maker wanted to make sure there was enough ivory Micarta handle to hold onto while whittling away with the 2.5-inch blade.

(PointSeven image)

CRAIG CAMERER

The wings of the butterfly knife are combination carbon fiber and superconductor specimens flapping off a W2 blade with distinct temper line.

(PointSeven image)

RICHARD ROGERS

The synthetic aesthetic of the 4F flipper folder includes a damascus blade, Timascus bolster and carbon fiber handle.

(SharpByCoop image)

NEILL SCHUTTE

The Bob Loveless style Big Bear Fighter is the recipient of burgundy Micarta handle scales and a 13-inch Bohler N690 blade that are both to die for, in theory only.

(PointSeven image)

BOB OHLEMANN

Some "shred" carbon fiber with "coffee dust" will perk you up in the morning. Some take theirs with a W2 blade, and a copper bolster and back spacer.

(PointSeven image)

❯❯ STEPHEN NOWACKI

The Templar is built off an 11-layer blade with an L3 core laminated with wrought iron and M3 high-speed tool steel, not to mention sculpted tiger-stripe G-10 handle scales and blue liners.

❯❯ DIETRICH PODMAJERSKY

Engraving on the commercially pure titanium handle makes it an instant collectible, particularly combined with the fine CPM 154 blade. *(SharpByCoop image)*

❯ RICK BARRETT

Even the Mayans couldn't have predicted the "Mayan"-damascus blade, the lightning strike carbon fiber handle scales or the wide tanto blade shape of the flipper folder. *(Cory Martin Imaging)*

❯ KEN ONION

The Armor flipper folder protects the vital organs via a CPM 154 blade, titanium frame and checkered G-10 handle scales. *(PointSeven image)*

❮❮ BILL LUCKETT

When you grind a CPM 154 blade in such a manner, it's a miracle you have enough whereabouts when done to make a solid choice like the blue/black G-10 grip. *(PointSeven image)*

« ERIC OCHS
Custom textured titanium gives a CPM 154 Orca tactical folder a thatched jungle roof look, a little exoticism for the next trip to the supermarket.
(SharpByCoop image)

« DAVID SHARP
Vintage Westinghouse Micarta adds a little mustard to the hotdog of a CPM 154 flipper folder.
(SharpByCoop image)

« JEFF KNOX
So apparently the "Juma" handle material is an "ivory snake" thermoplastic, combined with copper bolsters, hilt and sub-hilt, and a 440C blade, for one that slithers as it slices. *(PointSeven image)*

⩒ RICHARD WRIGHT
Silicon bronze and lightning strike carbon fiber are perfectly paired on a CTS-XHP bolster-release switchblade that works off a ball bearing pivot system.

⩒ MARK KNAPP
The 1911 Combat Survivor is dressed in olive drab, features a black, flat-ground CPM 154 blade and comes with a multi-tool, cord, fish hooks and other gear in a Spec Ops sheath.
(SharpByCoop image)

⩗ SCOTT HALL

Shaping the one-piece 154CM blade with integral guard and frame left just enough room for some 1911 pistol grips to spruce things up a bit.
(Cory Martin Imaging)

« LES GEORGE

Officially adopted as one of the official EOD knives of the U.S. Marine Corps in 2011, the CNC-machined bevels in the G-10 scales and CPM S35VN blade give it a mean albeit utilitarian design.

« BILL DUFF

Ripples flow outward from the center of the brown Micarta grip on a 7.75-inch 440C utility fixed blade. *(Ward image)*

» STEVE MILLER

The Dreamsicle of a knife sports a pink G-10 handle with milky Micarta bolsters and a sharp CPM 154 stick.

« TAKESHI MATSUSAKI

The honeycomb-pattern synthetic handle holds tight to the lock-back folder for fear the damascus blade might bite past the bolster.

Steel-Tipped Boots

BILL BEHNKE

It's rare enough to see a feather-damascus boot knife, much less an engraved one with a mammoth ivory handle, and it's a credit to the maker. *(Cory Martin Imaging)*

BOB LOVELESS

You've gotta include Bob in a boot knife section, his #40 model here in sheep horn and a rare skull crusher pommel. *(Cory Martin Imaging)*

GARY MARTINDALE

In the style of a Bob Loveless "3/4 Boot," the amber stag and 154CM steel model is accurate down to the tapered tang and red liners. *(PointSeven image)*

RICK CLOW

Desert ironwood starts the Loveless 3/4 Boot off before the CPM 154 blade darts away. *(PointSeven image)*

STEPHEN NOWACKI

Aptly named the "Sentinel," the boot dagger stands motionlessly at watch, donned in sculpted canvas Micarta and gun-blued EN45 steel.

Nation Builders

By definition, nation builders are those who take initiative to develop a national community. Mind you, they are usually members of state, and the statesmen build national communities through government programs, the military and schooling. Nation building is the constructing or structuring of a national identity, again, using the power of the state.

These might not be military or state-owned knives, but they sure build national identities, and any member of state would be considered lucky to own such a quality handmade knife that embodies the cultural, natural and physical characteristics, as well as the style, of a nation. Each knife integrates materials available from the country of origin and is designed with the cutting needs in mind of the people who live, work, hunt, play and survive there. The knives are identified with the people, or the people with the knives.

Certain utilitarian knife features and aesthetic elements belong solely to one country, to one people—a community, place and time—and no other blade in the world will embody those same features or aesthetics. The knives are unique in their nationality. They have personality. They are nation builders, and they're building bridges across nations one blade at a time. □

» PHILL HARTSFIELD
One of the last sole-authorship katanas built by Phill, the A2 tool steel piece is double ground and employs an iron tsuba (guard) and cotton ito (hilt wrap).
(SharpByCoop image)

» PAUL JARVIS
The "Oso Raku Bowie" builds bridges across nations using a Doug Ponzio twist-damascus blade, a German silver guard and walrus ivory handle.
(SharpByCoop image)

» ANSSI RUUSUVUORI
The Finnish knifemaker shows us how it's done Laplander style in a hand-forged, zone-tempered 80CrV2 blade, an imbuia (Brazilian walnut) handle and nickel silver furniture.

» DANIEL WATSON

The brilliant take on a Scottish basket-hilt sword showcases a heat-colored blade, bronze guard and steel pommel, with the maker's 18k-gold-leaf inlay and engraving. *(SharpByCoop image)*

» DON CARLOS ANDRADE

The green-hued handle trio of a forged 52100 French tribal knife is curly ash, green G-10 and epoxy-sealed woven cotton linen.

« JASON KNIGHT

One Roman gladius makes it to the handmade knife market in bronze, blackwood and damascus. *(SharpByCoop image)*

» LIAM HOFFMAN

The weight-forward Gurkha kukri in English walnut, German silver and 80CrV2 steel would have excelled in war, the jungle or both. *(SharpByCoop image)*

« GARY ROOT

It took a team to match the skills of a Japanese swordsmith, with Ray Rybar forging the tamagane blade, Scott Irie flat grinding the steel, Christopher Paul offering up the Shakudo (copper and gold) and Shiboichi (copper and silver) decorations, and John Baker inlaying and engraving the tsuba (guard). *(SharpByCoop image)*

» BRION TOMBERLIN

A traditional weapon of the Dayak people of Borneo, the Mandau sports an especially impressive 324-layer "laddered wolf's tooth"-damascus blade and a carved African blackwood grip. *(SharpByCoop image)*

« WALLY HOSTETTER

Wood, stingray skin and wire wrap themselves around a 42-inch 1095 Spanish rapier. En garde!
(PointSeven image)

MICHAEL ZIEBA

Side-by-side are Chinese and French style cleavers in dyed maple and black G-10 grips. Now if we could only get the countries to play so well together.
(SharpByCoop image)

« MARDI MESHEJIAN

The maker's take on a Nepalese kukri features a foot-long, gorgeously ground and shaped damascus blade, a titanium and copper guard, and a fossil walrus ivory handle.
(SharpByCoop image)

» JEREMY SPAKE

The Finnish puukko dons a laminated blade, nickel silver bolster, stabilized bubinga and African blackwood handle, and spacers fashioned from nickel silver and antique ivory piano keys.

Throwback Bowies

No you don't throw them back. You'd better not throw them back. They're way too nice to return, waste or recycle. They're throwback bowies, modern versions of earlier ancestral blades, knives having the features common to those of a former time. They're bowies, born of necessity when a blade was a daily tool and backup weapon, a simpler yet unsettled era when folks moved at a different pace, fended for themselves, knew their enemies as well as their neighbors, labored to eke out a living and were made of sturdy stock.

Speaking of sturdy stock, the throwback bowies on this and the following pages are of thick, long stock ground or forged into wide, clip-point blades that can handle any number of cutting chores. These are whoppers, choppers, whackers and stackers. They work as camp, kitchen, utility or big game knives with a little reach and some wicked curves and points, so weaponry comes immediately to mind.

Throwback bowies embody a period of history when men fought for their right to live long, be free and prosper. They cleared land, built houses and businesses, put up fences yet opened their doors to neighbors. They worked, played, fought and fended. Such bowies are not for the faint of heart, absentminded or those prone to accidents. You don't want to drop or lose your bowie blade. That's not what throwback means. □

⌄ HARVEY DEAN
A replica of an 1835 model, the feather damascus dog-bone bowie parades a 24k-gold-inlaid damascus guard and ferrule, a mammoth ivory handle and 14k-gold studs.

(Francesco Pachi image)

« JOHN DAVIS
Filework extends from the damascus blade spine onto the copper guard and spacer, terminating at the amber stag handle of the S.F. bowie.

(SharpByCoop image)

« PHIL EVANS
The blued S-guard and finial nut look nice next to the stag handle and 5160 blade of the 15.5-inch bowie knife.

(Ward image)

» LIN RHEA
Stag and stacked leather lend brown notes to a nicely ground, clip-point 5160 bowie, nearly 17 inches long, that comes with a pommel cap filed to match the grooves of the handle. *(Ward image)*

⌃ JEAN-LOUIS REGEL
Wootz steel was carefully forged and wrought into the blade of the takedown bowie, along with iron for the guard and frame, and with a fossil walrus ivory grip.
(SharpByCoop image)

» ALAN HUTCHINSON
The coffin-style handle of the 5160 bowie is giraffe bone, perhaps to steady that long neck that comes to an extended clip point.
(Ward image)

» TOM McGINNIS
Such touches as dovetailed bolsters engraved by John Mabry and stag handle slabs highlight the 10-inch California bowie marked with "Sam Elliott" on blade. *(Ward image)*

⌃ MACE VITALE
Winner of the "Antique Bowie Knife Award" as submitted by an ABS journeyman smith at the BLADE Show, considering the stag and 1084 throwback bowie, it was a shoo-in.
(PointSeven image)

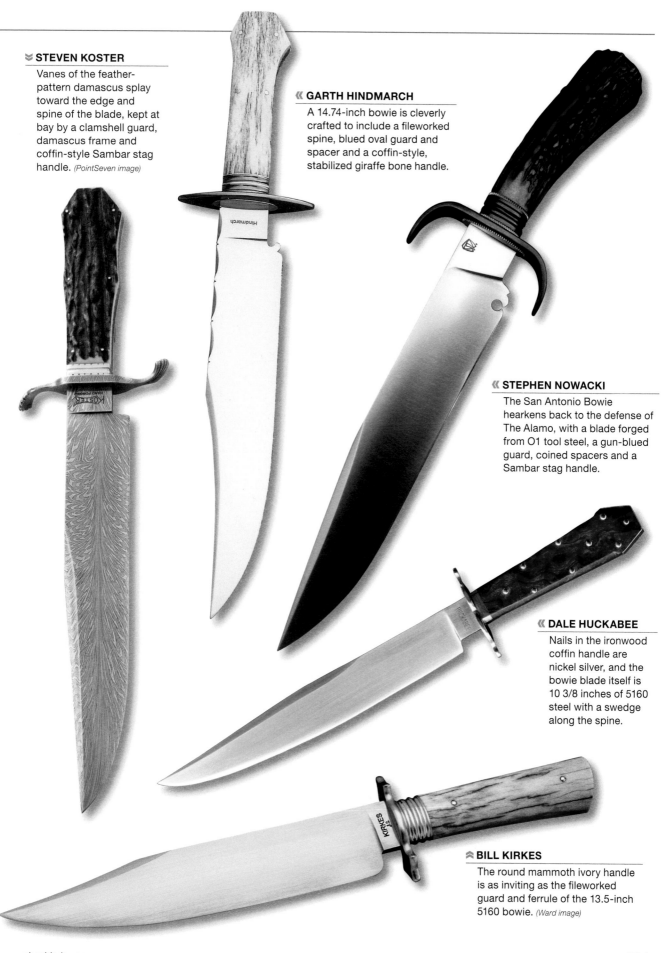

STEVEN KOSTER
Vanes of the feather-pattern damascus splay toward the edge and spine of the blade, kept at bay by a clamshell guard, damascus frame and coffin-style Sambar stag handle. *(PointSeven image)*

GARTH HINDMARCH
A 14.74-inch bowie is cleverly crafted to include a fileworked spine, blued oval guard and spacer and a coffin-style, stabilized giraffe bone handle.

STEPHEN NOWACKI
The San Antonio Bowie hearkens back to the defense of The Alamo, with a blade forged from O1 tool steel, a gun-blued guard, coined spacers and a Sambar stag handle.

DALE HUCKABEE
Nails in the ironwood coffin handle are nickel silver, and the bowie blade itself is 10 3/8 inches of 5160 steel with a swedge along the spine.

BILL KIRKES
The round mammoth ivory handle is as inviting as the fileworked guard and ferrule of the 13.5-inch 5160 bowie. *(Ward image)*

Palpable Pulps

Will wood ever fall out of favor? Year after year, a plethora of knives are built with burly grips, the age and grain lines of the wooden wonders sanded until they stand out like a bodybuilder's pinstriped suit. And like that bodybuilder, the more highly figured, the better. Knifemakers appreciate patterns, whether knife patterns or highly patterned materials. Just like stag, wood remains a perennial favorite.

There are some incredible new synthetic knife handle materials available, everything from lightning strike carbon fiber to old Westinghouse Micarta and glow-in-the-dark acrylics, but nothing can touch wood's natural beauty, character and singularity. A choice slab of burl on the right knife is a match made in a heavenly rainforest canopy, the Sherwood Forest, redwoods of California or among the Giant Sequoias.

Wood is an expression, a touch of exoticism. Few people think of Japanese bamboo, Germany's Black Forest or the Cloud Forest of Costa Rica when contemplating the newest knife handle material, but the wood is out there, already harvested, stabilized and treated, waiting at the knife supplier's house, table or store. These are the ones that feel as good in the hand as they look, true products of Mother Nature, a bounty of beauty, gifts from the forest, offerings in wood, the palpable pulps, and they're still in favor. □

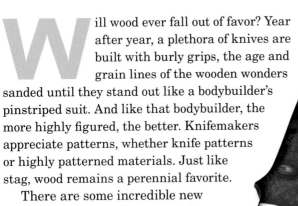

« ROBERT L. APPLEBY JR.
The spots on the blade are damascus patterning, and those of the handle acrylic-filled Banksia pod, the latter attached to the tang via mosaic pins. *(Ward image)*

« JAMES SCROGGS
It's amazing what one can do with a little stabilized spalted maple and some CTS-B75P stainless steel, oh, and talent to spare.

⌃ STEVE MILLER
A perfect melding of patterns, the locking-liner gent's folder integrates a black ash burl handle, African blackwood bolsters and an Alabama Damascus blade.

» JAMES BEHRING
Grooved cocobolo is the palpable pulp that aids in hand purchase on a full-tang "Uplander" model with a hollow-ground S7 blade. *(SharpByCoop image)*

» BILL KIRKES

The long swedge of the 5160 blade attempts to lead the eyes away from the ironwood handle of the hunter/fighter so folks won't spend so much time gawking.

(Ward image)

« KEN CARR

Buckeye burl holds its own against the damascus blade of a hot little drop-point hunter.

(Ward image)

» JEREMY SPAKE

The dense, black ebony hardwood sandwiches two types of stabilized antique whale bone for a tasty treat. The blade of the puukko is another sandwich, with a 52100 core and mild steel sides.

⌃ MARK KNAPP

Black walnut serves admirably as the handle and stand of a convex-ground, AUS-8 Alaskan-style ulu. *(SharpByCoop image)*

» KEVIN CASEY

Tasmanian eucalyptus burl whips up a storm on the grip of a feather-damascus folder, as if the devilish marsupial had been there himself.

(SharpByCoop image)

» JEFF HAINES

Who needs a choice between cherry burl and cocobolo when you can have both on the grip of an ATS-34 fillet knife? I wonder what the fishing creel looks like.

(Cory Martin Imaging)

⩔ DENNIS BRADLEY

Palming the push dagger, fingers wrapped around the cocobolo wood, pointing the mirror-polished, hollow-ground CPM 154 blade outward, the steel gleams.

⩔ MATT GREGORY

The hunter/fighter could handle either job description, outfitted in a sharp 1095 blade and a moabi (African pearwood) handle. Who knew Africa had pear trees?

⩔ ELI JENSEN

We all root for yew root, here on the handle of a differentially hardened and etched 1084 fixed-blade utility knife that also incorporates black G-10 liners and vine filework.

(SharpByCoop image)

⩕ LIAM HOFFMAN

Lignum vitae is the newest country heard from, here on a kukri-like 80CrV2 chopper.

(PointSeven image)

« ERIK FRITZ
The 5160 fighter is handled in buckeye burl so some lucky knife owner can give it a whirl.
(PointSeven image)

⌃ DALE HUCKABEE
There's something about a long fiddleback maple haft—perhaps reminiscent of traditional rifle stock—that takes a tomahawk to a new level. The head has a 5160 cutting edge.

« CHARLES R. HAWKINS JR.
The red and black box elder handle, combined with the fileworked damascus blade, means a-hunting we will go.

⌃ CHRIS BERRY
"Compression growth koa" was allowed to breathe and stretch out across the full tang of a CTS XHP drop-point hunter. *(PointSeven image)*

» GARTH HINDMARCH
Maple burl makes the small 440C utility knife easy to embrace, though it's a likeable little lopper regardless.

» ANDERS HOGSTROM
The maker's interpretation of an Alaskan Nesmuk-style blade is outfitted for the tundra in 1050 high-carbon steel, sculpted bronze and Swedish Masur birch.

⩔ TIM ZOWADA
Bronze accentuates the ends of the koa wood handle, making a damascus utility/hunter presentable for its public debut. *(SharpByCoop image)*

» ZACK JONAS
Ladder-pattern damascus and stabilized curly koa are the rungs that lead carving knife-fork combos like this to new heights.
(SharpByCoop image)

» TOM LEWIS
A mosaic handle of sycamore and cocobolo, highlighted by mosaic pins, of course, are the tiles of a wire-cable-damascus piazza. Bellissimo!

« JORDAN LAMOTHE
Bent like a horse phalanx and hoof, one could certainly saddle up to the hickory wood handle and grab the 1084 hunter by the reins.

» JERRY HOSSOM

The sculpted California buckeye burl handle, attached with mosaic pins, dives right into the bulging yet beguiling PSF-27 blade. *(PointSeven image)*

» RON ROSENBAUGH

Without the stabilized afzalia burl grip, the hot-blued CPM M4 pack knife would have been too scorching for the average hand.

⌃ H.L. HOLBROOK

Box elder burl hugs the tapered tang of a CPM 154 drop-point hunter, set off by red G-10 liners. *(Hoffman image)*

⌃ JEFF KNOX

The target shows you the sweet spot of the amboyna burl handle, while the rest of the savory steel implement speaks for itself. *(PointSeven image)*

⌃ BEN BREDA

Rings of koa climb the grip of a sheath knife, peering over the guard to get a look at the wavy temper line splashing across the re-curved W2 blade. *(PointSeven image)*

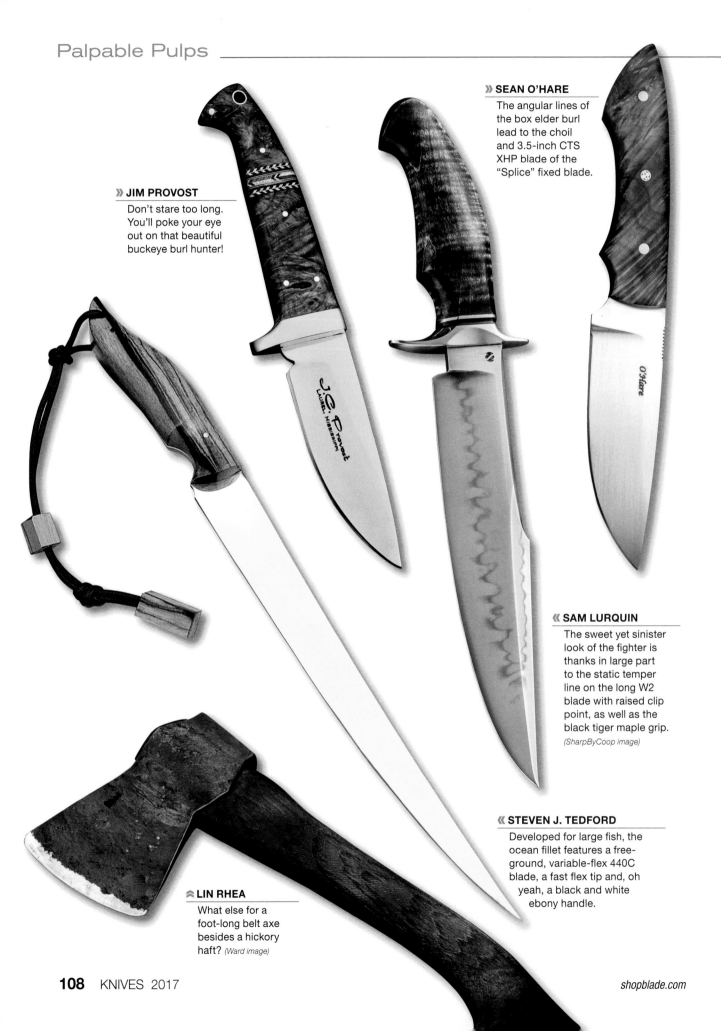

» JIM PROVOST

Don't stare too long. You'll poke your eye out on that beautiful buckeye burl hunter!

» SEAN O'HARE

The angular lines of the box elder burl lead to the choil and 3.5-inch CTS XHP blade of the "Splice" fixed blade.

« SAM LURQUIN

The sweet yet sinister look of the fighter is thanks in large part to the static temper line on the long W2 blade with raised clip point, as well as the black tiger maple grip. *(SharpByCoop image)*

« STEVEN J. TEDFORD

Developed for large fish, the ocean fillet features a free-ground, variable-flex 440C blade, a fast flex tip and, oh yeah, a black and white ebony handle.

⌃ LIN RHEA

What else for a foot-long belt axe besides a hickory haft? *(Ward image)*

« KEVIN CASHEN
The spots are thuya burl and the 4.75-inch fang is O1 tool steel.

« RICK POIRIER
The foliage-like finish of the 7.5-inch O1 blade is an appropriate application considering the rosy redwood burl handle. *(SharpByCoop image)*

« THOMAS HASLINGER
The tang of the hollow-ground CPM S35VN blade tapers into the stabilized curly koa handle, wearing it like a tiger wears stripes.

⌃ JIM MEROLA
Afzalia burl butts up against a bronze guard that partitions it from a frenzied Kevin Casey damascus blade, all the elements somehow coming together in perfect harmony. *(SharpByCoop image)*

» DAVID KURT
An alluring allegiance of box elder burl and old canvas Micarta formed on the handle of a flat-ground 154CM fixed blade. *(SharpByCoop image)*

Straight-Up Daggers

There's another chapter in the Trends section of the book called "Highly Guarded Swords & Daggers" that showcases models with guards that are all over the place, literally, and in a good way. The guards are fashioned to protect, deflect other blades and decorate. That's not the case with the guards of the daggers on this and the following pages. Sure, they're meant to protect, and each serves admirably in that capacity, and could even fend off or deflect blows from other blades. Yet these are straight-up daggers, no fancy stuff, but rather double-edged steel coming to a point. The guards barely interrupt the blade-to-handle flow.

If one were to take up arms, the daggers here would do, and go toe-to-toe, or blow-to-blow, with any other knife models. Many of them are damascus affairs with carved handles, more comfortable in the display cases of knife aficionados who appreciate clean, solid designs when they see them.

It is the ingeniously simple designs of daggers that make them so appealing. While knife wizards around the globe work their magic with multi-ground blades, wild and whacky curves, folding knife mechanisms, gadgets, buttons, locks and levers, the makers of straightforward ones concentrate solely on solid execution and innovative yet utilitarian materials. That's all, no wild stuff, just straight-up daggers. ☐

《 BILL DUFF

A brown Micarta grip gives the 440C dagger a new wrinkle or two.

(Ward image)

》 ANDERS HOGSTROM

From the naturally blue fossil walrus ivory handle to the sterling silver fittings and the double temper line of a 4.5-inch blade, the dagger boasts one amenity after another.

《 JEREMY SPAKE

The dagger plays a sweet tune, assembling a cast of san mai steel, a wrought iron guard from an antique anchor chain, ebony handle, and spacers of antique ivory piano keys.

TRAVIS FRY

A slim dagger born of necessity (the maker and his brother split a bar of steel down the middle and had a contest of who could build the best dagger), this one wows the crowd in a 9-inch 154CM blade, a silver-wire-wrapped, fluted pre-ban elephant ivory handle and a faceted hexagonal pommel.

NATHAN CAROTHERS

An all-integral dagger does the dance in a hollow-ground A2 tool steel blade, guard and tang, the latter of which runs down the center of the G-10 grip. *(SharpByCoop image)*

DAN PETERS

The shiny steel dagger wears an amboyna burl handle and a brass pommel cap. *(Dunfey Pro Photography image)*

BOB CROWDER

Even the fluted buffalo horn doesn't interrupt the straightforward nature of the damascus dagger in a Mokumé guard. *(SharpByCoop image)*

SHANE SIBERT

Clues as to its combat dagger identity include a brass guard and pommel, a contoured G-10 handle with accents and a 7-inch CPM S30V blade.

» LES GEORGE
The turned handle of the maker's first dagger is Chad Nichols stainless steel, while the guard is gun blued and the CPM 154 blade a double-hollow-ground affair.

» JOSHUA STATES
Sixteen inches of damascus, mammoth ivory, some fileworked liners and a quillon guard certainly doesn't disappoint.
(PointSeven image)

» TAN LONG
One of several good things about the "Hitman-47" is that you can see his blued-Damasteel blade from a mile away.
(SharpByCoop image)

» ALAN MITCHELL
The centerline of the blade cuts directly through the middle of the damascus pattern, foreshadowing the quality workmanship of the dagger in an African blackwood handle.

« BILL MILLER
"Twist-W's"-pattern damascus was harnessed and contained within the confines of a dagger blade, the fossil walrus handle providing a pleasant pause. *(PointSeven image)*

GEOFF KEYES

A Tlingit-style dagger is wrought from iron, engraved by Tom Sterling, wrapped with leather and nylon, and adorned in copper.

(PointSeven image)

MIKE ZIEBA

A pair of CPM S60V oyster daggers, in G-10 and maple handles, would shuck their way through the streets of New Orleans. *(SharpByCoop image)*

T.K. STEINGASS

Of the thumbprint dagger ilk, this piece parades a 7.25-inch, double-hollow-ground CPM D2 blade that includes a fuller and a convex tip, and a stabilized koa handle.

(SharpByCoop image)

RON WELLING

A William Scagel-style dagger, the damascus piece is handled in mammoth ivory, ironwood and blood-red spacers.

(Ward image)

AARON WILBURN

There's a perfect temper line running down the center of the hollow-ground W2 blade, a contrast to the silver-wire-wrapped, fluted ancient walrus ivory handle. *(SharpByCoop image)*

Pocket Wares

» MEL FASSIO

The maker guessed right that the blade and bolsters of the wood-handle folder would be sweet spots for some engraving and fancy filework.

⌄ J.T. PALIKKO

The twist-pattern stainless damascus blade of the friction folder, handled in buffalo horn, ends in a curlicue that actually locks the blade in the open position, a design that received a patent in 1998.

⌃ DENNIS BRADLEY

Close the hollow-ground, mirror-polished 440C blade into the camel bone handle and don't ever lose it!

» CHUCK HAWES

With the two-blade, stag-handle damascus folder in the pocket, one would feel rich indeed.

(Cory Martin Imaging)

« JEFF CLAIBORNE

A bone handle pocketknife is chockfull of features like half-stops for the forged 52100 blades, long nail pulls, and integral milled stainless steel bolsters and liners.

(Hoffman image)

CRAIG BREWER

There's a lot in one lock-back whittler package, such as three CPM 154 blades, 416 liners and bolsters, stag handle scales, and a stainless steel shield and pins. *(PointSeven image)*

CALVIN ROBINSON

The folding trapper captured some rose-pattern Damasteel and giraffe bone within its confines, and all who are exposed benefit. *(PointSeven image)*

LEVI MILLER

The bone is jigged just right, the 52100 blades ground, finished and polished, the nail nicks and bolster grooves applied, and the thumb notches placed where needed. *(PointSeven image)*

BILL RUPLE

It's easy to appreciate pocketknife pattern names—"split-back-spring sowbelly whittler"—this one in a stag handle and CPM 154 blades. *(PointSeven image)*

RAYMON HUNT

I think they call the handle material "burnt amber stag," and it's no secret why, a smoking-hot choice for a CPM 154 slip-joint folder. *(Ward image)*

Pocket Wares

DAVID TABER

Of ivory and ATS-34 stainless steel, and incredible workmanship, the three-blade folder is a diamond in the rough. *(Cory Martin Imaging)*

LUKE SWENSON

The large saddle-horn trapper is dressed to the hilt in amber stag and CPM 154 for a trip to town on Saturday. *(PointSeven image)*

TAKESHI MATSUSAKI

If I were a single-blade, pearl-handle, lock-back folder with a nail nick, I'd want to look just like this one.

KEN ERICKSON

The tool steel pruning knife is made old Sheffield, England, style with coined liners and stag covers. *(Cory Martin Imaging)*

JOHN PERRY

Not many can fashion one this clean, precise and pretty, from damascus and mother-of-pearl no less. *(Ward image)*

Forward Tanto Thrust

» PEKKA TUOMINEN

It's easy to love the name of this knife—the Finanto (Finnish tanto)—and its W1 steel blade, antiqued copper habaki (blade collar), antique iron *tsuba* (guard) and curly birch handle.

⩔ DOC HAGEN

Most tantos aren't dual-action CPM 154 autos with polished titanium bolsters, blue-anodized and fileworked liners and a purple Charolite/lavender composite handle, but this one is.

(Custom Knife Gallery Of Colorado image)

⩔ R.W. WILSON

Ivory, brass and stainless steel send the tanto into another hemisphere.

(Cory Martin Imaging)

⩔ JIM PROVOST

Though the tanto is Japanese, the rosewood handle is Honduran, and the CPM 154 blade and nickel silver guard both Mississippian knifemaker style.

(Cory Martin Imaging)

⩔ MATTHEW GREGORY

The chisel-ground A2 Kwaiken has a "zero edge" and a dark grey stingray skin handle under a tsukaito wrap. Yowsers!

"Game On!" Blades

Those that dress out game animals so nicely and perform as if the clock is running out!

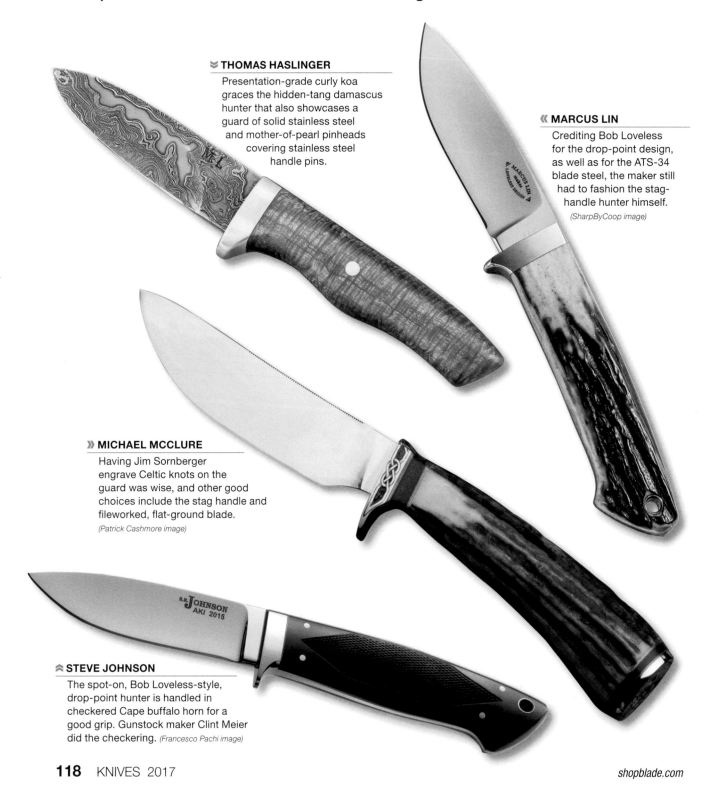

⌄ THOMAS HASLINGER
Presentation-grade curly koa graces the hidden-tang damascus hunter that also showcases a guard of solid stainless steel and mother-of-pearl pinheads covering stainless steel handle pins.

« MARCUS LIN
Crediting Bob Loveless for the drop-point design, as well as for the ATS-34 blade steel, the maker still had to fashion the stag-handle hunter himself.
(SharpByCoop image)

» MICHAEL MCCLURE
Having Jim Sornberger engrave Celtic knots on the guard was wise, and other good choices include the stag handle and fileworked, flat-ground blade.
(Patrick Cashmore image)

⌃ STEVE JOHNSON
The spot-on, Bob Loveless-style, drop-point hunter is handled in checkered Cape buffalo horn for a good grip. Gunstock maker Clint Meier did the checkering. *(Francesco Pachi image)*

» ZAC BUCHANAN

Identified as an "Oregon Hunter," the 4-inch, hollow-ground, drop-point CPM 154 model, with full, tapered tang, blends stag handle scales with super-thin red liners.
(SharpByCoop image)

« JOHN HORRIGAN

You'd have the most exquisite bird-and-trout knife in the marsh if you pulled out the Turkish damascus knife with inlaid 24k-gold guard, keyhole bolster and pre-ban elephant ivory handle.

⌃ BUTCH DEVERAUX

Stag, she oak and brass stack up nicely for the handles and guards of a nice 52100 hunting knife set. *(SharpByCoop image)*

« BILL KIRKES

A hunter/fighter comes in handy many places and for many things, particularly a quality piece like the 5160 high-carbon-steel fixed blade in an ironwood grip.
(Ward image)

MIKE QUESENBERRY

An integral hunter, with 52100 blade, bolsters and tang all one piece of steel, only amboyna burl and black and bronze spacers break up the allied alloy.

(PointSeven image)

HARVEY DEAN

A first for the maker, he built a D.E. Henry-style hunter, forging a trailing-point damascus blade, gold inlaying and engraving the guard and adding a stag handle.

(Francesco Pachi image)

TIMOTHY STEINGASS

Desert ironwood indubitably does handle duty on a full-tang CPM S35VN "Silver Lake Hunter."

(SharpByCoop image)

DENNIS BRADLEY

The gut hook along the spine of the blade is for zipping open animal hide, usually on a brisk day, sun peaking through the leaves of the trees and casting shadows on the elk antler handle.

JOSH FISHER

The large ebony-handle hunter is as clean as a whistle, only sharper.

(Caleb Royer Studio image)

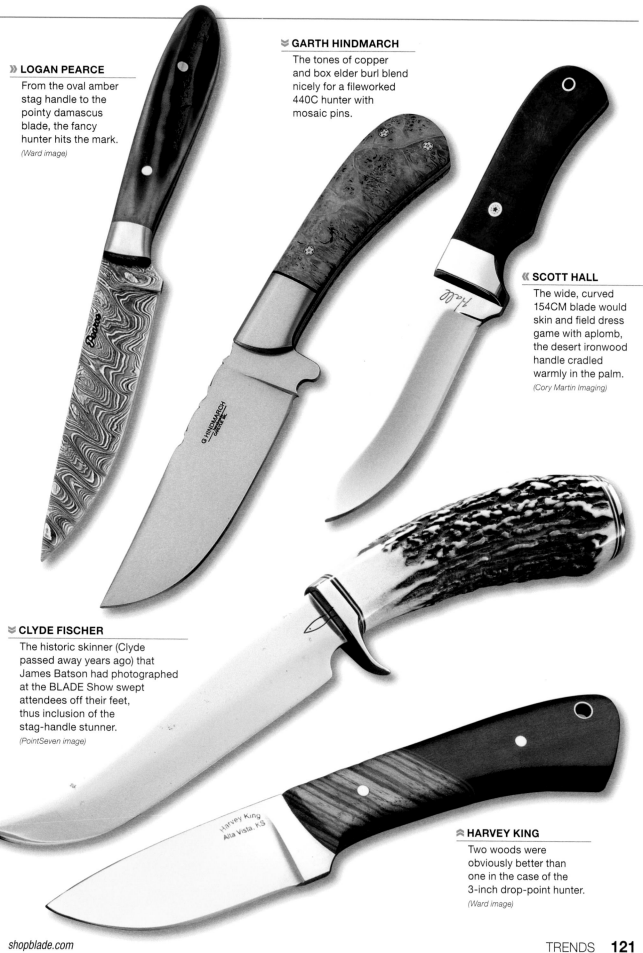

» LOGAN PEARCE

From the oval amber stag handle to the pointy damascus blade, the fancy hunter hits the mark.

(Ward image)

⌄ GARTH HINDMARCH

The tones of copper and box elder burl blend nicely for a fileworked 440C hunter with mosaic pins.

« SCOTT HALL

The wide, curved 154CM blade would skin and field dress game with aplomb, the desert ironwood handle cradled warmly in the palm.

(Cory Martin Imaging)

⌄ CLYDE FISCHER

The historic skinner (Clyde passed away years ago) that James Batson had photographed at the BLADE Show swept attendees off their feet, thus inclusion of the stag-handle stunner.

(PointSeven image)

⌃ HARVEY KING

Two woods were obviously better than one in the case of the 3-inch drop-point hunter.

(Ward image)

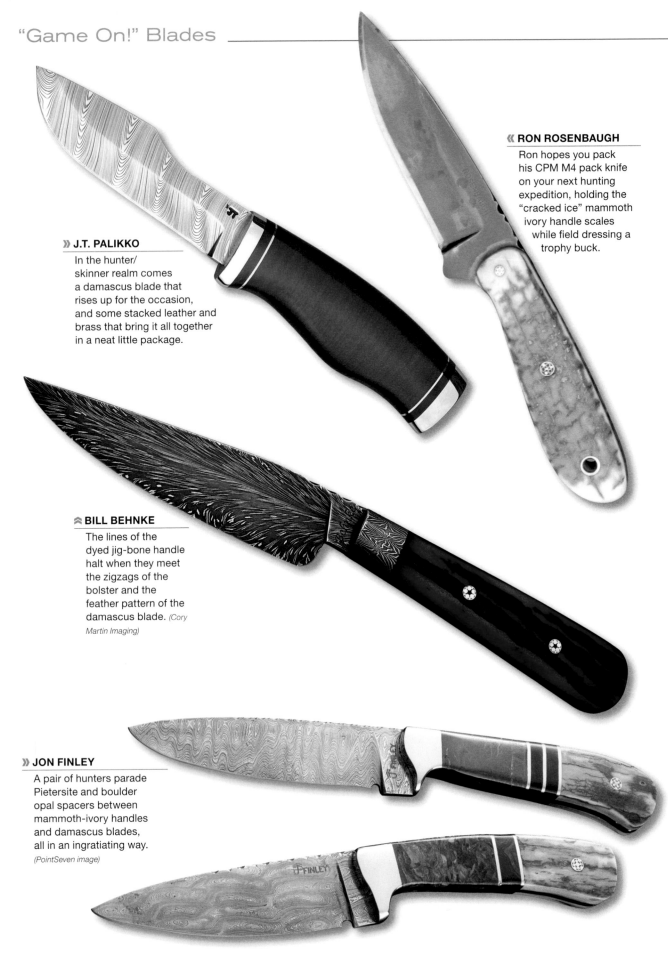

RON ROSENBAUGH

Ron hopes you pack his CPM M4 pack knife on your next hunting expedition, holding the "cracked ice" mammoth ivory handle scales while field dressing a trophy buck.

J.T. PALIKKO

In the hunter/skinner realm comes a damascus blade that rises up for the occasion, and some stacked leather and brass that bring it all together in a neat little package.

BILL BEHNKE

The lines of the dyed jig-bone handle halt when they meet the zigzags of the bolster and the feather pattern of the damascus blade. (Cory Martin Imaging)

JON FINLEY

A pair of hunters parade Pietersite and boulder opal spacers between mammoth-ivory handles and damascus blades, all in an ingratiating way.

(PointSeven image)

CHRIS MONTGOMERY
Hoping the fish is bigger than the usual minnows, 8.25 inches of 15N20 steel stand ready for some fillets, and the Micarta handle won't be slippery when wet. *(Ward image)*

ROBERT L. APPLEBY JR.
In the style of H.H. Heiser, crown stag caps the 11-inch 52100 hunter highlighted by a stacked-leather grip and some spacers.

(Ward image)

DAN LANCE
The grainy goodness of burl wood leads directly into the swirls of the laminated damascus-over-stainless-steel bolsters on a drop-point hunter.

(PointSeven image)

DAVE ARMOUR
The flats of the forge-finished blade lend credence to the name "Rustic Hunter," while the bird's-eye maple handle practically takes flight. *(Cory Martin Imaging)*

JASON FRY
The oosic handle and brown mild steel fittings work well together, practically presenting the W2 blade with distinct temper line to the gathering masses.

(Cory Martin Imaging)

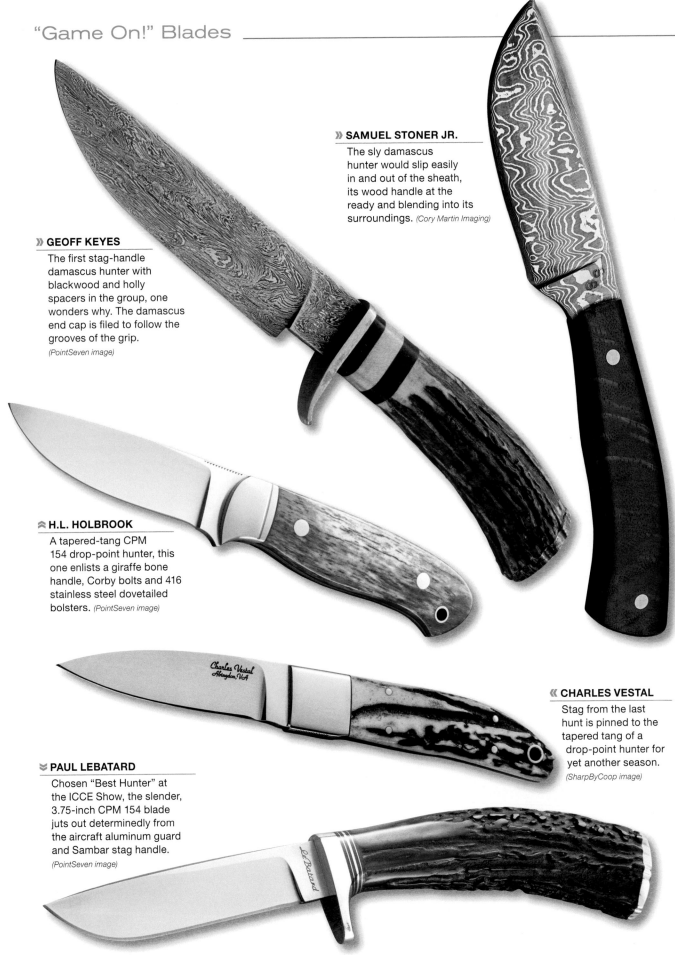

» SAMUEL STONER JR.

The sly damascus hunter would slip easily in and out of the sheath, its wood handle at the ready and blending into its surroundings. *(Cory Martin Imaging)*

» GEOFF KEYES

The first stag-handle damascus hunter with blackwood and holly spacers in the group, one wonders why. The damascus end cap is filed to follow the grooves of the grip.

(PointSeven image)

⌃ H.L. HOLBROOK

A tapered-tang CPM 154 drop-point hunter, this one enlists a giraffe bone handle, Corby bolts and 416 stainless steel dovetailed bolsters. *(PointSeven image)*

« CHARLES VESTAL

Stag from the last hunt is pinned to the tapered tang of a drop-point hunter for yet another season.

(SharpByCoop image)

⌄ PAUL LEBATARD

Chosen "Best Hunter" at the ICCE Show, the slender, 3.75-inch CPM 154 blade juts out determinedly from the aircraft aluminum guard and Sambar stag handle.

(PointSeven image)

» GARY GROVES
A true skinner style in pattern and sweep, the stag-handle ATS-34 fixed blade also includes a little black birch planted above the guard. *(PointSeven image)*

⌄ JERRY FISK
When people talk about high-end hunters 50 years from now, they might reference the mammoth-ivory-handle damascus piece with the gold inlaid and engraved mild steel guard. *(Ward image)*

« DAVID BRODZIAK
Fossil coral is a dynamic handle material, sandwiched by an ebony spacer and pommel, and privy to a "Vinland"-pattern Damasteel blade.

« JIM COFFEE
It's the details—the fileworked spacer of the guard and the way the butt cap is shaped to match the grooves of the stag handle—that provide insight into the quality of the forged W2 hunter.

⌃ MARVIN WINN
The spine of the gentleman's skinner is a continuous arc bending from the tip of the CTS-XHP blade to the end of the green canvas Micarta handle. *(PointSeven image)*

More Love For Loveless

» LIN RHEA

Ah, the standard bearer for all—the drop-point hunter, this one suits up daily in a brown Micarta handle and a 3.75-inch 1084 blade, a handsome soldier. *(Ward image)*

» MARCUS LIN

Of the Loveless New City Knife variety, the Bohler D2 tool steel beauty is done up in some Sambar stag and mirror polished so it shines. *(SharpByCoop image)*

» MAMORU SHIGENO

The maker offers his Loveless-style Big Bear in an ATS-34 blade with a full, tapered tang, and a choice of a fossil walrus ivory, stag or black Micarta handle. *(SharpByCoop image)*

⌃ ALLEN SURLS

One way to make a Loveless Wilderness pattern would be with a "3-D spalted" A2 blade and an ironwood burl handle, and that would be a good manner in which to do it, yes. *(PointSeven image)*

TIM WITHERS

A Bob Loveless-style Baby Bear, the red liners stand out against the pearl handle of the ATS-34 sub-hilt fighter.

(SharpByCoop image)

STEVE JOHNSON

The first Loveless-style Big Bear that Steve made with a carbon fiber handle, the 440C stainless steel sub-hilt fighter is also noteworthy for its overall formation. *(Francesco Pachi image)*

ZAC BUCHANAN

Natural stag seems a nice fit for the 154CM New York Special that snaps into its leather sheath. *(Ben Tendick image)*

MICHAEL MCCLURE

Hold onto the amber stag grip, the flat-ground Loveless-style O1 chute knife is almost too hot to handle.

(Patrick Cashmore image)

JOHN YOUNG

Picasso marble makes a CPM 154 sub-hilt stand out from all the rest.

(PointSeven image)

Keen Campers

amp knives are a conundrum because there are no clear parameters of what defines camp knives. Each knifemaker has his or her own opinions of what constitutes a camp knife, similar to how each camping enthusiast has their own ideas of what exactly camping is. The father of a friend of mine once said, as he stretched out on the picnic table under our camper awning, "So you like this stuff, huh? Camping to me is black and white television."

Though camp knives differ greatly in materials, design and overall makeup, there are similarities in how they're purpose built—for which cutting chores. There seems to be a consensus that camp knives should be able to cut kindling wood, whittle tent stakes, clear brush and prepare meals, whether the latter is cutting steak, chopping vegetables or slicing potatoes. No gent's folders, Japanese wakizashis, daggers, butterfly knives or art knives will do, and many prefer camp knives to be slightly smaller than bowies, though that also varies. To a few, an ideal camp knife would be a bowie or even a bolo, parang or machete.

So next time you awaken to a chill in the air, the sounds of the woods around you, stumble to your feet, reignite the campfire from the night before and fumble for the stainless steel coffee pot, consider what cutting chores will be demanded of your knife that day. Perhaps cutting rope to hang a hammock will be the gist of it, but then what would an ideal hammock-hanging knife look like? ☐

《 MARK KNAPP

The maker's vision of a camp knife was a 1095-and-15N20-damascus blade, a Mokumé guard and a combo black sheep horn and blue amber handle. He saw it clearly.

(SharpByCoop image)

《 DENNIS BRADLEY

The Camper Model carves tent stakes via a 5-inch, flat ground CPM 154 blade anchored by a desert ironwood handle with finger grooves for extra grip.

⌃ KEVIN CASHEN

As fancy as the genre gets, the re-curved camp knife gets the job done in a 10.75-inch damascus blade and a fossil walrus ivory handle. The sheath is tooled leather.

J. NEILSON

The "MTK" (Multi-Task Knife) is a hunter/camper suited for chopping or fine cuts, each involving the hand-rubbed 52100 high carbon steel blade, as well as, of course, the giraffe bone handle.

JEFF HAZE

The name "Krampus" might conjure up visions of a cramped tent, or maybe camping with the Kranks, but regardless one would be well equipped considering the saber-ground 80CrV2 blade.

STEPHAN FOWLER

Here's a hybrid camp/bowie in a W2 blade, blued steel guard and spacers, and a desert ironwood handle.

(SharpByCoop image)

DANIEL WINKLER

A sheath holding a diamond sharpener is included with the WKII Camp Knife in a tan Micarta and rubber handle and a 9.75-inch 80CrV2 blade.

(PointSeven image)

STATE OF THE ART

As if it wasn't enough that knifemakers morph themselves into artists to scrimshaw knife handles, engrave frames and bolsters, sculpt steel, inlay jewels and carve grips, now they've become leatherworkers, as well, fashioning some of the nicest sheaths in some years. See the "Complete Knife/Sheath Packages" section starting on the facing page. And that's just one area where, once again, knifemakers have proven themselves not only incredibly imaginative, but skilled and gifted craftsmen and women who could compete with juried artists across the globe.

These are no hacks. Don't believe me? Look no further than the second chapter of the State Of The Art section of the book, "A Sculpture Park," and decide if it doesn't feel like visiting scenic sculptures, gazing at the creations there. Then have "An Engraving Conversation," watch as "Carvings Come To Knife," see how makers practice the arts of stippling, chasing, jigging, texturing and filigree, and then go on to experience "The Draw Of Scrimshaw."

I've said it before—knife collectors have it made in the shade. Sure, they worked hard for their money, but look at the choices they have of where to spend it. Let's see, do I drop a few Franklins on some "Touches of Turquoise," a little "Uncommon Play In Handle Inlay" or do I visit the "Steel-ustrators" I've come to love so much? Good questions, all, but the individuality doesn't stop there. Others knifemakers gaining entry into the "State Of The Art" chapters are pounding out "Singular San Mai Steel," working "Gold Veins" and forging some "Powerful Pattern Welds." They're going through changes, metamorphosing from talented blade makers into beautiful artists taking wing in a competitive world of creative geniuses. And it's a sight to behold. □

Complete Knife/Sheath Packages 131
A Sculpture Park 136
An Engraving Conversation 138
Carvings Come to Knife 146
Jigged, Filigreed, Stippled, Textured & Chased 148
The Draw of Scrimshaw 150

Touches of Turquoise 153
Uncommon Play in Handle Inlay 154
Steel-ustrators 156
Singular San Mai Steel 160
Gold Veins 162
Powerful Pattern Welds 164

Complete Knife/ Sheath Packages

⌄ KURT SWEARINGEN

The Bill Moran-style Airman's Knife, outfitted in a rosewood handle, bronze fittings and a W2 blade, called for a basketweave-pattern leather sheath and some tooling.

⌄ DAN PETERS

Don't get "Angry Ginger" mad—the kukri comes with 6.5 inches of sharp CPM 3V steel, a stainless steel guard, stabilized spalted pecan handle and a snakeskin-covered sheath.

(PointSeven image)

⌄ LARAMIE JACKSON

A smoky temper line wafts across the 1095 blade of an ironwood-handle bowie/fighter, right into the tooled-leather sheath.

» STEVEN RAMOS

To complement the natural hues of the Stoney Creek brecciated (broken) jasper stone handle, the maker fashioned a tooled leather sheath with some character of its own.

(SharpByCoop image)

▼ TRAVIS PAYNE

It took a long snakeskin-inlaid, tooled-leather sheath from Jack Andress to hold the 16-inch 1095 fixed blade in a koa wood grip, and a copper and damascus guard and butt.

(PointSeven image)

《 JIM KRAUSE

With the 440C push dagger sheathed, the white wildcat on the buffalo horn handle looks wicked above the stingray-skin-inlaid leather holster. *(Ward image)*

》 RON NEWTON

Everything's alive and moving—the feather-pattern damascus blade, bamboo and sheep horn handle, and the tooled and inlaid leather sheath.

(PointSeven image)

》 BILL KENNEDY JR.

Engraving and mosaic pins accent the redwood handle, and a tooled and inlaid leather sheath keeps the 440C fixed blade in pristine condition. *(PointSeven image)*

JOHN COHEA

Primitively styled but modernly executed, the damascus knife with bear jaw handle and copper fittings calls for a fringed leather sheath adorned in beads, braids and more copper. *(Ward image)*

DAVID BRODZIAK

Knowing Carol Ann O'Connor, who painted poppies on Australian Marri wood (eucalyptus), helps in housing the "Vinland"-pattern Damasteel culinary knife with matching burl handle.

JAMES RODEBAUGH

The fine hunter's set—an engraved 5160 hatchet and O1 tool steel knife with curly maple handles and blackwood end caps—carries nicely in basketweave leather.

(PointSeven image)

STEVE MILLER

If I was an oak leaf or an acorn, I'd hang around an Alabama Damascus drop-point hunter in a white Micarta handle and African blackwood bolsters.

⌄ DON HETHCOAT

Picking the cast pinecone handle scales is as inspired as the cowboy cross-draw sheath for the fixed blade.

⟪ PAUL LEBATARD

For his 2,000th knife, the maker enlisted Chad Nichols damascus, impala horn, aluminum and bloodstone, as well as a leather sheath with stud to hook it under a belt.
(PointSeven image)

⟫ KEVIN CASHEN

It would be tough to cover up the slammin' san mai damascus blade by placing it in the tooled leather sheath, but how else to carry the ironwood-handle bowie?

⟪ MARK NEVLING

Boasting a reverse-ladder-pattern damascus blade, Mokumé bolsters and mammoth ivory handle scales, the folding bowie slides inside a leather sheath inlaid with dyed elephant hide.

LEVI GRAHAM

Rawhide covers the sheath and guard of the forged 80CrV2 knife in a mammoth ivory handle, the sheath also featuring quill work, fringes, copper cones, beads and horsehair.

DENIS MURA

The carved leather dragon was a fire breather for sure, lighting up the 3D TechStab handle of a multi-ground 440C fixed blade. *(PointSeven image)*

RUSTY WAIDE

We could wax poetic about the engraved guard, damascus blade, mammoth ivory handle and Steve Brooks carved and inlaid leather sheath, or just let the picture say it all.

(SharpByCoop image)

GABRIEL BELL

Inspired by the coastal Oregon river valley, the tooled leather landscape of the Josh Unruh sheath is a nice companion to a cable-damascus, spear-point bowie in a rosewood handle.

A Sculpture Park

» STEPHEN OLSZEWSKI

The knife artist sculpted the bronze bolster and handle of the "Chinese Dragon Auto," adding a multi-color patina, and forging a Turkish-twist-damascus blade to shape.
(SharpByCoop image)

» ROBERT L. APPLEBY JR.

One solid, integral, sculpted damascus masterwork, with fingers curled around the grip, memories of cane pole fishing with Grandpa are sure to come flooding back.
(Ward image)

⌃ LARRY FUEGEN

The sculpted ladder-pattern damascus blade and rust-browned steel guard, ferrule and pommel of the art dagger coordinate with the carved fossil walrus ivory handle. *(Francesco Pachi image)*

⌄ ELIZABETH LOERCHNER

A true artist can take stainless steel and sculpt it into a natural form, albeit a utilitarian one, adding cloisonné and black-lip-pearl inlays.
(SharpByCoop image)

⌃ JOSEF RUSNAK

Art Deco ceramics sculptor Waylande Desantis Gregory would approve of the highly styled and sculpted carbon fiber, titanium and RWL-34 steel "Waylande" folder.
(SharpByCoop image)

T.R. OVEREYNDER

One must appreciate an Art Nouveau split-tail, pinched-butt (sounds sassy) dagger, this one sculpted from CTS-XHP steel and "snowflake" jade, as only the maker could.

(PointSeven image)

PIERRE REVERDY

Happy or sad, which side of the "poetic damascus" folder are you looking at? The blade and mammoth ivory handle are sculpted, and the bolsters cast in silver.

(Francesco Pachi image)

RICHARD TESARIK

A study in steel and ebony, the "Magnolia" opens and closes like a pretty flower.

WILLIAM TUCH

With just stainless steel, skill, vision and an understanding of form, the artist created a winged knife of wonderful proportions.

(PointSeven image)

RON APPLETON

Molded like clay, there's no sliding contact between the copper handle and A2 blade of the "Vermejo" folder, which works off the maker's Advanced IQ 2.0 mechanism.

(SharpByCoop image)

An Engraving Conversation

I s engraving the most common knife embellishment? Considering the number of engraved versus scrimshawed, sculpted, jewel- or precious-metal-inlaid and carved knives, yes, engraving is likely the most widely used knife enhancing art form, and for good reason. Knives are steel, and engraving is the most logical way to enhance the look and beauty of the blades, bolsters, handles, pinheads and other parts. Couple engraving with a little gold inlay, done by a good hand, and a common knife becomes an exquisite masterpiece.

Those who appreciate and understand art know that only master engravers can create sex appeal and beauty through human forms scratched in steel, ships cutting through water, birds taking wing, lions perched on hillsides or mythological creatures canvassing the area. These are not boxy forms and unintentionally creepy faces, but living, breathing beasts and bohemians birthed in steel and immortalized in lines, curves and shadows.

To engrave a gorgeous knife grip, a beautiful bolster or picturesque blade flat is to put your mark on a tool to be used and admired. It lasts for generations and causes engraving conversations wherever it goes. □

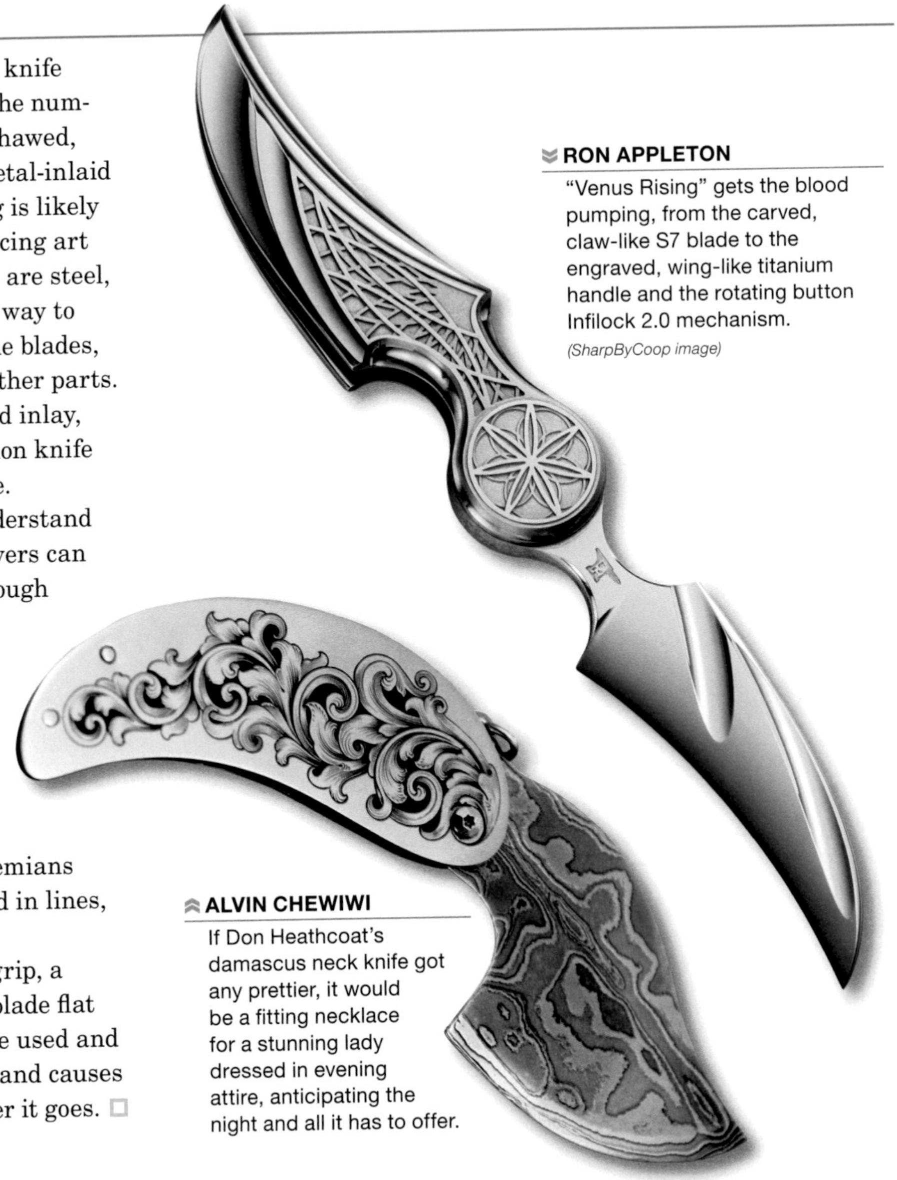

⨠ RON APPLETON

"Venus Rising" gets the blood pumping, from the carved, claw-like S7 blade to the engraved, wing-like titanium handle and the rotating button Infilock 2.0 mechanism. *(SharpByCoop image)*

⨠ ALVIN CHEWIWI

If Don Heathcoat's damascus neck knife got any prettier, it would be a fitting necklace for a stunning lady dressed in evening attire, anticipating the night and all it has to offer.

《 HARRY CALDWELL IV and KATHERINE PLUMER

Use your night vision and you'll spot an owl in a hollowed-out tree, this on the bolster of a mammoth-bark-handle Ray Cover folder. *(SharpByCoop image)*

❯ BILLY ELLIS
Starting with a Bill Coffey window-frame folder, complete with a yellow canyon jasper inlay and damascus blade, the engraver highlighted the good parts via a gold-inlaid leaf motif.

❮ DWIGHT TOWELL
Only a gold border would do for the engraving that adorns the flight-ready handle of a small back-lock folder.

❯ DOUG ASHBY
When you have mammoth ivory, you frame it, in this case with engraved stainless steel bolsters, all of which leads to the 8-inch blade of the long, lean bowie. *(Ward image)*

❯ LUCA BRASCHI
A goddess and nymph adorn the handles of Gus Cecchini's "Styx" set of folders with Chad Nichols san mai damascus blades, the nymphs separating the underworld from the living, of course. *(SharpByCoop image)*

» RAY COVER JR.

A master engraver delves into a pirate ship, cannon, swashbuckler and buried treasure, and doesn't surface until a Joe Kious "double pocket locket" auto folder is completely covered in gold inlay and engraving. Jerry Rados forged the Turkish damascus blade.

(SharpByCoop image)

❯ TAN LONG

The Chinese knifemaker chose a silver handle to illustrate what ancient warriors from his side of the world looked like, complementing it with a forged M4 dagger blade.

(SharpByCoop image)

» VERONIKA TESARIK

Decidedly Art Deco, Richard Tesarik's carved RWL-34 gent's folder is one for the ages.

» BRUCE SHAW

Chevrons and scrolls enliven the bolsters of a pearl-handle Bob Crowder re-curved fixed blade.

(SharpByCoop image)

⌃ STEVE DUNN

The mammoth ivory handle of the John Perry boot knife has nearly as much character as the gold-inlaid and engraved bolsters, nearly.

(Ward image)

« LISA TOMLIN
Golden pedals are planted all around the lapis lazuli handle inlay of Howard Hitchmough's "Blue Velvet" Damasteel folder.
(PointSeven image)

⯆ REINHARD TSCHAGER
An engraved, pearl-handle jewel knife of this magnitude deserves diamond-inlaid gold pins, and a gold chain and pendant, and so it shall have them.
(Francesco Pachi image)

⯆ GORDON ALCORN
Between the dyed maple burl handle of a Peter Pruyn knife and the delightfully dizzying damascus blade are engraved copper bolsters of the most copasetic kind.
(SharpByCoop image)

» JULIE WARENSKI-ERICKSON
The queen of engraving wrapped imperial white jade in twisted gold wire, sculpted and inlaid a double guard and saved some of her finest work for a wicked dagger blade.
(Francesco Pachi image)

« MARK WALDROP
Where the abalone handle inlay ends, the golden scroll engraving begins on a W.D. Pease stainless-damascus back-lock folder.
(PointSeven image)

⟱ LISA TOMLIN

The C. Gray Taylor sportsman's knife showcases engraved bolsters and a quail and Llewellen Setters scene designed, cut out and engraved by Tomlin. The CPM 154 steel implements include two blades, a hoof pick, giblet, corkscrew, manicure blade, buttonhook and awl. *(Francesco Pachi image)*

» JODY MULLER

Turns out skeletons can talk—the engraved bag of bones on the handle of the damascus flipper folder speaking to the art knife enthusiast in those who dare tread near. *(SharpByCoop image)*

» STEPHANIE LEMELIN

The lapis-lazuli-handle dagger wears the gold-inlaid and engraved silver bolsters like a tight-fitting corset, and a sexy one at that. *(SharpByCoop image)*

« MATT LITZ

The only thing more impressive than Travis Payne's damascus folding straight razor with completely engraved silver handle would be to shave with it. *(PointSeven image)*

⩓ AL FRISILLO

A Jon Finley Pietersite-stone-handled damascus hunter benefits from floral and scroll engraving on the bolsters, hilt and sub-hilt. *(Ward image)*

» JULIE WARENSKI-ERICKSON

Playing off the hues of the crackle mammoth ivory, the gold inlay and engraving on a Curt Erickson modern bowie covers and completes the piece.

(Francesco Pachi image)

« LORENZO GAMBA

Golden flowers frame the savannah where lions lie in wait, all within the handle confines of a Scott Sawby mosaic damascus folder.

(Cory Martin Imaging)

⌃ JERE DAVIDSON

With more points than a philosophy professor, Edmund Davidson's fully engraved, all-integral, ivory-handle model is wickedly winsome, and smarter than most profs anyway.

(PointSeven image)

« NATHAN DICKINSON

Gold inlay and engraving are fine go-betweens among the mammoth tooth handles and sharpened steel blades of Jerry Moen's knife set.

(PointSeven image)

RON SKAGGS

The Viking fought so long and hard, all that was left were his skeletal remains, permanently planted on the bolster of a Corbet Sigman ivory-handle fighter.

(SharpByCoop image)

MARIETJIE THORBURN

Giving a skeleton personality is no easy feat, accomplished here on the titanium handle of an Andre Thorburn flipper folder with a Bohler N690 blade.

(SharpByCoop image)

RICK EATON

Combining arabesque "Flowing Vines" with 24k-gold inlay, relief carving and grotesque-styled bulino, the knifemaker elevated his damascus gent's folder to high art.

(Francesco Pachi image)

TOM STERLING

Taking a William Henry B12 damascus spear-point model, the engraver turned it into the "Viper Fish" through some creative gold inlay and engraving. As my teenager would say, "It's savage."

JULIE WARENSKI-ERICKSON

Engraved and gold inlaid, John Young's pearl-handle dagger dances in the moonlight, doesn't it?

(SharpByCoop image)

GLENN WATERS

A tiger and dragon duke it out on the titanium handle of the "Kiba" (fang) frame-lock flipper folder that sports an Elmax stainless steel blade riding on ceramic bearings.

BRAM RAMON

Lounging in the nude, Art Deco style, are lovely ladies gracing the bolsters of an Aad van Ryswyk damascus folder with lock-back mechanism, and inlays of gold and antique turtle shell.

NORIO KOIKE

The Akio Shinozaki stag-handle sub-hilt fighter parades gold inlay and engraving everywhere it can, leaving only a length of re-curved ATS-34 blade unembellished.

(SharpByCoop image)

MICHAEL HENNINGSSON

There's not a straight line on the piece, not the 24k-gold inlays and engraving, the stainless steel frame, RWL-34 blade, not the pivot inlay nor the anodized titanium screw.

TURTLE KLAUSE

The Wayne Spragg bird-and-trout knife was a catch even before the bolster engraving, with the knife also showcasing a stabilized camel leg bone handle and an ATS-34 stainless steel blade.

Carvings Come to Knife

» GARY ROOT

It's nice to have good friends—Ray Rybar who carved the elk antler handle into a dragon (with peridot eyes) and forged a "cat's-eye" damascus blade for the piece. The guard is Robert Eggerling spider web damascus. *(Kris Kandler image)*

» BILL MILLER

The skulls were piling up, so the maker attached them to the tang of the "twisted-W's"- damascus blade on a 13-inch fighter for show and safekeeping. That's a carved stag grip. *(Ward image)*

» WADE COLTER

There's a carved goblin face only a mother could love for each crown stag handle of the damascus friction folders that also showcase damascus fittings and overlays

(PointSeven image)

» JOSEF RUSNAK

Wolves stare and lash out from the bolster of the carved integral RWL-34 fixed blade in a mammoth tusk handle.

» CURT ERICKSON

The handle is carved white marble, gold-lip pearl and abalone with a carved and shadow-engraved gold hummingbird. Julie Warenski-Erickson engraved the 440C dagger, adding precious metal inlays, and there's a carved and sculpted hummingbird on each ring.

(Francesco Pachi image)

⌄ BARRY DAVIS

A favorite subject matter in architecture for its deeply cut leaves, the maker carved a Mediterranean acanthus leaf in gold-lip pearl for his damascus gent's folder. *(SharpByCoop image)*

« VLADIMIR PULIS

Considering the age of the pre-Columbian obsidian blade, an Incan man, complete with pearl collar, carved from buxus (boxwood) seemed an appropriate subject for the handle of the dagger.

« DANIEL WATSON

It took a 48-inch sword to tame the dragon, here cast in magnetite for the pommel and accompanied by a leather and faceted hematite hilt, a steel guard and an S7 blade.

(SharpByCoop image)

⌃ LARRY FUEGEN

That's some carved stag goblin—with opal eyes, fossil walrus ivory teeth, gold tongue and silver cape—on the "Vulcan" forged-damascus scroll friction folder.

(Francesco Pachi image)

» SUCHAT JANGTANONG

It's safe to assume several carving tools were necessary for the mosaic damascus, Mokumé and black-lip pearl of the blued-damascus art knife.

(Cory Martin Imaging)

Jigged, Filigreed, Stippled, Textured & Chased

There's something about indents and dots, honeycomb-looking patterns, textured surfaces, stippling, silver chasing, filigree and jigging that makes for attractive knife handles and bolsters. Maybe it's the 3-D effect of giving an ordinary handmade object more depth, shape and pockets, like the divots inherent in golf balls and in the dents golf balls make in greens and fairways. Such are interrupted, not flat, surfaces, and when associated with knives, they serve a secondary purpose, that of hand purchase. A dimpled or textured surface is easier to hold onto than a smooth one.

Surface manipulation is more than tactical and utilitarian, however, it's aesthetic, using carving, jigging or silver chasing to create pleasing patterns and potholed looks. Jigged-bone handles are as popular today as they were in Grandpa's time, and the art of filigree has been around since the 3rd century B.C., still today practiced by a select few knifemakers who have the necessary skills.

Texturing finds its way onto the handles of tactical and art knives alike, and all types of blades in between. Stippling is a science unto itself, but more of an art than an intellectual activity. Regardless, the knives herein and elsewhere are the benefactors of jigging, filigree, stippling, texturing and chasing, and that's a lot of handcraft to go around. □

⌃ **ERIC OCHS**
Stippling enhances the Moku-Ti handle of a frame-lock flipper folder that also dons a Chad Nichols damascus blade, zirconium spacer and bronze-anodized titanium screws.
(Cory Martin Imaging)

« **ALAIN and JORIS CHOMILIER**
Laminated and textured bronze highlights the art folder, also including a Mike Norris damascus blade, titanium side lock and sapphires set in gold.

» **RICK DUNKERLEY**
A "W's-ladder-pattern-damascus" Persian folder features carved and stippled ancient walrus ivory handle scales and engraving along the back bar. *(Francesco Pachi image)*

» ENRIQUE PENA

The titanium frame of the dress slip-joint folder is jigged to resemble bone and accompanied by a Rob Thomas stainless damascus blade.

(SharpByCoop image)

« LOGAN PEARCE

When working with a "wolf's tooth" damascus blade, it's nice to fashion some silver filigree for the handle and maybe a black-lip-pearl inlay here or there.

(Ward image)

⯆ D. SCOTT BARRY

The carved and anodized copper/niobium/titanium bolsters of the Damasteel gent's folder are carved in a honeycomb pattern and sticky sweet. *(Custom Knife Gallery Of Colorado image)*

» JOHN GRIFFIN

A damascus pushbutton auto, the skinner has Sambar stag handle scales and stainless bolsters carved to resemble "antique bark." Fantabulous!

⯆ JOSEF RUSNAK

His "Handprint" is certainly a one-of-a-kind RWL-34 steel beauty showcasing silver chasing and mammoth tusk, as well as a giraffe bone, Damasteel and silver sheath.

(SharpByCoop image)

The Draw
of Scrimshaw

t draws you in like a crackling fire on a bitterly cold winter night, and it's warm, too.

Whenever ink is stippled into the pores of ivory, good things follow, a wolf or bobcat, skull, an elephant pausing in the forest among exotic birds, an Indian warrior, stoic, proud, a dragon, big horn sheep or naked lady. Images indelibly inked often enliven their hosts, in this case knives, the handles and bolsters of knives, themselves acting as transporters, mobile art, to be taken from one village to the next, shared and admired.

It's not often art is so portable, but scrimshaw is its own animal, a way of depicting scenes and subjects, whether in color or black and white, on natural substances. Most often ivory, bone or horn are the media of choice, where scrimshanders ply their trade, poking pinholes, scratching, etching, painting with pricks, bringing the material back to life and portraying an image, conveying a message.

Art has always been personal, close up and emotional, and scrimshaw is a concentration of marks and manipulations, tight patterns, extremely detailed. It's the draw of scrimshaw, and it brings you into its fold so you can taste the elixir and bask in the afterglow. □

⏷ GARY "GARBO" WILIAMS

From where did the tooth originate that's used on the Gene Baskett damascus folder? The bolsters provide a colossal clue. *(PointSeven image)*

⏶ ANDREA PULISOVA

When the eyes are gold, the stare is cold, or so it is on the ivory handle of Vladimir Pulis's mosaic damascus folder dressed in a tiger motif.

⏶ LINDA KARST STONE

Mammoth ivory is the portal that leads us to Native American lands and the art created therein. John Cohea's bowie also parades a copper bolster and damascus blade. *(Ward image)*

SHERRY SELLERS

Jason Fry requested a bobcat and coyote—prevalent predators in his area—be scrimmed on the mammoth ivory handle of his CPM 154 "Llano" hunter. *(Caleb Royer Studios image)*

LINDA KARST STONE

Man's best friends (Dixie is on one side of the ivory handle, and Lexi on the other) grace the grip of a Jerry Moen folder engraved by Nathan Dickinson. *(PointSeven image)*

DAVID SEMONES

Dragons and tantos go together like the damascus blade and ivory handle of a Lowell Bray Japanese-inspired and flawlessly executed piece.

(PointSeven image)

SMITTY'S DESIGNS

A big horn gets top billing on a Steve Miller LinerLock® folder in an Alabama damascus blade and stabilized, blue "big leaf maple" handle scales.

ERIK NYLUND

The steelhead or rainbow trout is some splashy subject matter for color scrimshaw on the reindeer antler handle of a Bohler N685 model with a nickel silver bolster.

» KURTZ MILLER

For such a royal Robert P. Smith damascus knife with pre-ban-ivory handle, a castle and flying dragon scene seemed appropriate, scrimmed in black and white for effect. *(Ward image)*

» DR. PETER JENSEN

With a thorny necklace and bad intentions, a bound seductress in floral headdress poses for the ivory handle of a Reinhard Tschager dagger. The knife also dons an Ettore Gianferrari damascus blade, Valerio Peli engraving, and gold and diamond inlays.

» DON JENSEN

If the Bob Crowder "Outfitter" model goes everywhere the mountain goats climb, half the fun is the highland hunt. *(SharpByCoop image)*

⌃ TOM HEARD

Skull scrim on bone made a small 1095 neck knife a bit more morbidly alluring. *(Tony Derro image)*

⌃ SANDRA BRADY

A splash of colors starts off the day right on Don Hethcoat's damascus locking-liner folder, the scrimshaw depicting a sunlit nature scene with elephant and exotic birds.

Touches of Turquoise

» LARAMIE JACKSON
Turquoise, ironwood and brass equate to high class, and the drop-point hunter sure alludes to that.

⩖ RON ROSENBAUGH
Red spacers succeed in setting off the turquoise from the buffalo horn bolsters and ironwood handle scales of the CPM M4 drop-point hunter.

⩖ TOM LEWIS
Turquoise in the shape of a Harley-Davidson motorcycle shield is inlaid into the maple burl handle of a fine Harley-motorcycle-chain-damascus fixed blade.

⩓ JON FINLEY
The brown hues within the turquoise spacer lent themselves well to the mammoth tooth handle of the damascus fixed blade.
(PointSeven image)

⩖ ANTONIO BETANCOURT
The maker cut nine turquoise stones to fit the natural openings in the cholla cactus handle of his flint-knapped dagger, this with a Montana jasper blade. It's all wrapped up in deerskin.

Uncommon Play in Handle Inlay

» RON LAKE

A classic inter-frame folder with damascus tab release, it sports geometric black phenolic and ivory celluloid handle inlays, the latter from old organ keys, and gold highlights.

(Francesco Pachi image)

» MICHAEL WALKER

To celebrate 35 years of making knives, Michael created a Champlevé handle—similar to cloisonné, but one piece of metal with integral divisions and pockets, in this case inlaid with opaque enamels. The blade is Devin Thomas stainless damascus.

(SharpByCoop image)

⌄ CHARLES BENNICA

A Bakelite, gold, damascus and Mediterranean red coral handle gives the "Alien" its name, a being equipped with an RWL-34 blade and proprietary locking system.

(Francesco Pachi image)

⌄ OWEN WOOD

A design inspired by an Art Deco lighting fixture, the folder integrates a herringbone pattern as a central element in the blade and handle, the grip having 12 rhomboid-shaped brown-lip-pearl inlays and 18 gold inlays. *(SharpByCoop image)*

⌃ KEVIN CASEY

Forging a feather-damascus blade for the "Rattlesnake Bowie," the maker let the Konstantin Pushkarev handle inlays, within a blackwood grip, speak for themselves.

(SharpByCoop image)

EMMANUEL ESPOSITO

When the "White Fang" was finished, folks gathered around to admire the carbon fiber and gold Mokumé handle inlays, and multi-ground, fang-like blade.

(Francesco Pachi image)

RONALD BEST

The integral, 20-inch D-guard bowie boasts some blue, gold and black inlays of the enlivening kind.

(SharpByCoop image)

JOE OLSON

The maker combines enamel inlay, carving and engraving for the uncommon handle inlay of his guitar knife with a forged and blued guitars-pattern, mosaic-damascus blade.

(Cory Martin Imaging)

KEN STEIGERWALT

In an Art Nouveau style, the tree-leaf-shaped blade is inlaid with 14-karat gold and accompanied by a stainless steel handle parading black-lip-pearl and gold designs.

(Francesco Pachi image)

STEVE JOHNSON and EMMANUEL ESPOSITO

A Bob Loveless-style chute knife features mosaic Bakelite and black-lip-pearl handle inlays within a frame of burgundy Micarta. *(Francesco Pachi image)*

Steel-ustrators

Not many people outside of the knife industry think of mosaic-damascus blades when they envision a blacksmith's forge. Tongs come to mind, hammers, fire, charcoal, black soot and dirty leather aprons, heat, dust, smoke and darkness, but not blued-mosaic damascus blades with images of leaves, reptilian scales, wooly mammoths or bear paw prints forged into the steel.

Yet bladesmiths have delved into and popularized mosaic damascus steel. They've canned it, literally and figuratively, the literal part coming when they use sectioned cans and powdered steel, creating repeating images within the cans, and then forging the powder-filled cans, cutting, folding and cross-sectioning, pounding and heating until desired and planned images spread across steel billets. The billets are shaped, ground, finished and honed into illustrated knife blades. They are Steel-ustrators, and their medium is forged mosaic damascus. It's bladesmith art and it's hot to the touch. □

⋙ RON NEWTON

The "black seaweed" mosaic damascus sprawls across the blade, adding so much depth, character and beauty to the ebony-handle bowie. *(Ward image)*

⟫ PAUL K. BROWN

Multi-color mosaic damascus provides a powerful punch to a 9.5-inch utility knife handled and guarded in ironwood, honey horn and nickel silver. *(Ward image)*

⟪ PAVEL SEVECEK

A frog leaps across steel lily pads, going with the current of the folder blade, one anchored in a white mother-of-pearl handle and black-lip-pearl rear bolster.

⩡ RICK DUNKERLEY

One of the Montana mafia bladesmiths working in mosaic damascus, the smith has obviously mastered his craft to the tune of purple prints and patchworks.

(Francesco Pachi image)

⟪ REINHARD TSCHAGER

Diamonds and gold dress up a dagger in a detailed Ettore Gianferrari mosaic damascus blade and a pure white ivory handle.

⟪ CLIFF PARKER

If the mosaic damascus blade doesn't dazzle the masses, the "grim reaper" bolsters will gain adherents, and the green/brown mammoth ivory should keep them coming. *(Cory Martin Imaging)*

⩘ GLENN WATERS

Across the bolsters and blued "Shaya Forge Nebula Mosaic Damascus" blade is an engraved and gold-inlaid dragon and fireball, and an 18k-green-gold thumb stud. The handle is gold- and silver-inlaid mammoth ivory.

⩡ FRANCO DIONATAM

A micro-mosaic damascus pattern is best examined under a loupe for full effect, while holding the carved ebony grip, of course.

ALAIN and JORIS CHOMILIER

A solitary mammoth stands in a steely landscape forged by the hands of bladesmith Mattias Styrefors. Mammoth ivory makes warm handle scales.

DAVID LISCH

"Dragon thunder" damascus is the fierce fighter blade pattern, softened ever so slightly by an ancient walrus tusk handle. *(SharpByCoop image)*

JEAN-LUIS REGEL

Who knew stag could be fluted and wrapped like ivory, or that mosaic damascus could be forged and finished to the level of artistry the dagger blade exhibits? *(SharpByCoop image)*

GAIL LUNN

Spinning webs while forging steel, the maker fashioned a show-worthy art knife in a cocobolo handle with stippled titanium overlays. *(Cory Martin Imaging)*

JERRY HAINES

The elongated mosaic-damascus pattern gives a lengthy hunter an even more stretched-out look, handled nicely in giraffe bone and engraved by John Mabry. *(Ward image)*

J.W. RANDALL

With a flourish, he pulled out the fleur-de-lis blade and severed the scoundrel's satchel before he got away with the goods. The walrus ivory handle felt good in the hand.

(PointSeven image)

PETER MARTIN

The red damascus fang of the Praying Mantis extends from its mosaic damascus, mammoth ivory and tortoise shell body, its abalone eyes staring dead ahead.

(Cory Martin Imaging)

STEVE HILL

The Joel Davis blade steel is electric, and the combination of the blue mammoth ivory handle and blue opal thumb stud a flash of genius as well.

BRUCE BUMP

One gravitates toward the 10-inch mosaic damascus blade of the ring-guard "Heirloom Bowie" before admiring the engraved handle frame and Turkish walnut inlays. *(PointSeven image)*

SANDRO BOECK

The takedown bowie is named for the ability to disassemble it, not because it'll take down wild boars in a single stab, though it would work, I suspect. *(Adriana Block image)*

Singular San Mai Steel

Meaning "three sheets" in Japanese, modern *san mai* blades have hard steel cores, and thus edges, laminated to and sandwiched between softer outer layers. The outer layers are sometimes stainless steel, but often high-carbon steel, giving the blade a tough exterior with a hard, sharp, cutting inner core. Now that's the way it should be!

And, of course, like damascus, a side benefit to a san mai blade is the pattern that emerges through heat treating and finishing. Just as damascus, which is multiple steels forged together, pounded, folded, forged and folded again and again, then crosscut and etched to bring out a pattern, san mai steel is a lamination, and the divisions between the distinct layers (outer and inner, or core) are visible after heat treating and finishing. Thus san mai blades also exhibit visually pleasing patterns.

Each san mai blade is unique, with no two alike, and there are many ways to laminate blade steels. Even damascus can be laminated with single-alloy steel, so the patterns are limitless. Such is the allure of singular san mai blades, and why knife enthusiasts can't seem to get enough of them. □

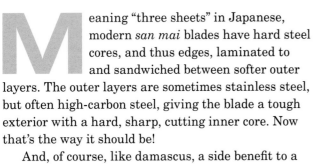

» STEVE RANDALL
The lightning strike-like mark indicates where the sandwiched steels meet on a stag-handle bowie/fighter.
(PointSeven image)

» RICK BARRETT
It's a handsome flipper folder, outfitted in a san mai blade—an Elmax core with Chad Nichols damascus outer layers—and a titanium handle, screws and back bar.
(Cory Martin Imaging)

» PETER PRUYN
Such a tasty sandwich—the blade exhibits an O1 and nickel core with distinct outer layers of 1095 and 15N20 damascus—it's all held together with a brass guard and Alaskan maple burl handle.
(SharpByCoop image)

MICHAEL ZIEBA
Welded in his shop in Brooklyn, New York, the san mai blade has a 52100 core and 410 stainless steel outer layers, and comes with a 24k-gold logo and a stabilized maple burl handle. *(SharpByCoop image)*

PETER MARTIN
Between the san mai damascus blade, super conductor bolsters, anodized titanium liners and carbon fiber handle scales, the flipper folder is dressed to the hilt.
(Cory Martin Imaging)

BILL BURKE
A walrus ivory handle and fire-etched wrought iron guard get close and personal with a san mai blade of 416 stainless and 52100 ball bearing steels.
(PointSeven image)

MILOS KISLINGER
It's a wash as to which one has more waves, the san mai stainless steel blade or the ivory handle of the exceptional locking-liner folder.
(PointSeven image)

KARL ANDERSEN
There was no hiding the fact that it was a san mai steel blade, nor should there have been, complemented nicely here by a blued guard and burly handle.
(PointSeven image)

Gold Veins

⩔ JOHN W. SMITH

Gold emanates out and swirls about from the rising-sun-like pearl inlays of an engraved damascus inter-frame folder.

(Francesco Pachi image)

⩓ MATTHEW LERCH

Visually stunning veins of gold run through the damascus handle inserts of a pair of Zephyr folders, with Brian Hochstrat to credit for inlay and engraving.

(SharpByCoop image)

» AAD VAN RYSWYK

The 24k-gold-inlaid and engraved bolsters bring out the golden hues of the turtle-shell handle on an ATS-34 locking-liner folder.

⩓ JOHN HORRIGAN

Gold leaves and vines crawl up the pearl handle of a "twisted-W's-pattern" damascus bowie with a pronounced clip. The carved, engraved guard is also gold inlaid.

KEN STEIGERWALT

A Bauhaus-style matrix of CPM 154 and stainless steel, and pen shell and 129-piece 14k-gold inlays, the folder is angular in all aspects of design. *(SharpByCoop image)*

GENE BASKETT

The maker wisely asked Mike Norris to forge damascus for the ivory-handle folder, and Paul Markow to plant golden vines along the bolster and blade. *(PointSeven image)*

TORE FOGARIZZU

Like a trellis protecting a garden, rose gold plates the black Bakelite handle inserts of an RWL-34 folding art dagger. *(SharpByCoop image)*

STEVE JOHNSON

The first Bob Loveless-style Big Bear Fighter ever engraved by Barry Lee Hands, the pearl handle, blade, guards and pommel are gilded gorgeously. *(Francesco Pachi image)*

REINHARD TSCHAGER

Gold, diamonds and pearl give the jewel art dagger some swagger and swirl. *(Francesco Pachi image)*

Powerful Pattern Welds

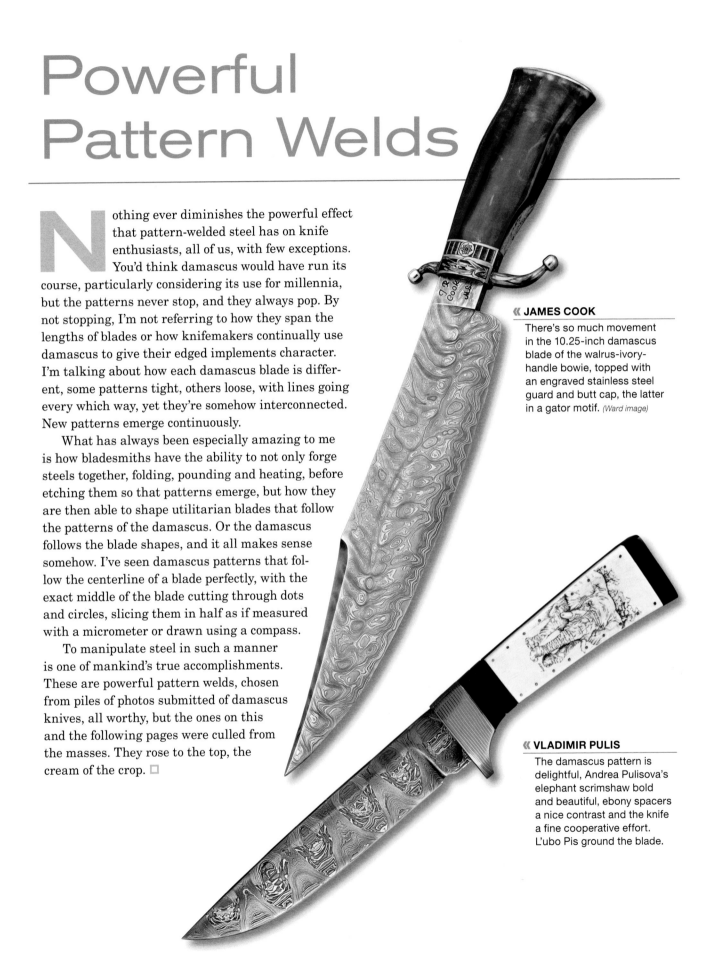

Nothing ever diminishes the powerful effect that pattern-welded steel has on knife enthusiasts, all of us, with few exceptions. You'd think damascus would have run its course, particularly considering its use for millennia, but the patterns never stop, and they always pop. By not stopping, I'm not referring to how they span the lengths of blades or how knifemakers continually use damascus to give their edged implements character. I'm talking about how each damascus blade is different, some patterns tight, others loose, with lines going every which way, yet they're somehow interconnected. New patterns emerge continuously.

What has always been especially amazing to me is how bladesmiths have the ability to not only forge steels together, folding, pounding and heating, before etching them so that patterns emerge, but how they are then able to shape utilitarian blades that follow the patterns of the damascus. Or the damascus follows the blade shapes, and it all makes sense somehow. I've seen damascus patterns that follow the centerline of a blade perfectly, with the exact middle of the blade cutting through dots and circles, slicing them in half as if measured with a micrometer or drawn using a compass.

To manipulate steel in such a manner is one of mankind's true accomplishments. These are powerful pattern welds, chosen from piles of photos submitted of damascus knives, all worthy, but the ones on this and the following pages were culled from the masses. They rose to the top, the cream of the crop. □

《 JAMES COOK

There's so much movement in the 10.25-inch damascus blade of the walrus-ivory-handle bowie, topped with an engraved stainless steel guard and butt cap, the latter in a gator motif. *(Ward image)*

《 VLADIMIR PULIS

The damascus pattern is delightful, Andrea Pulisova's elephant scrimshaw bold and beautiful, ebony spacers a nice contrast and the knife a fine cooperative effort. L'ubo Pis ground the blade.

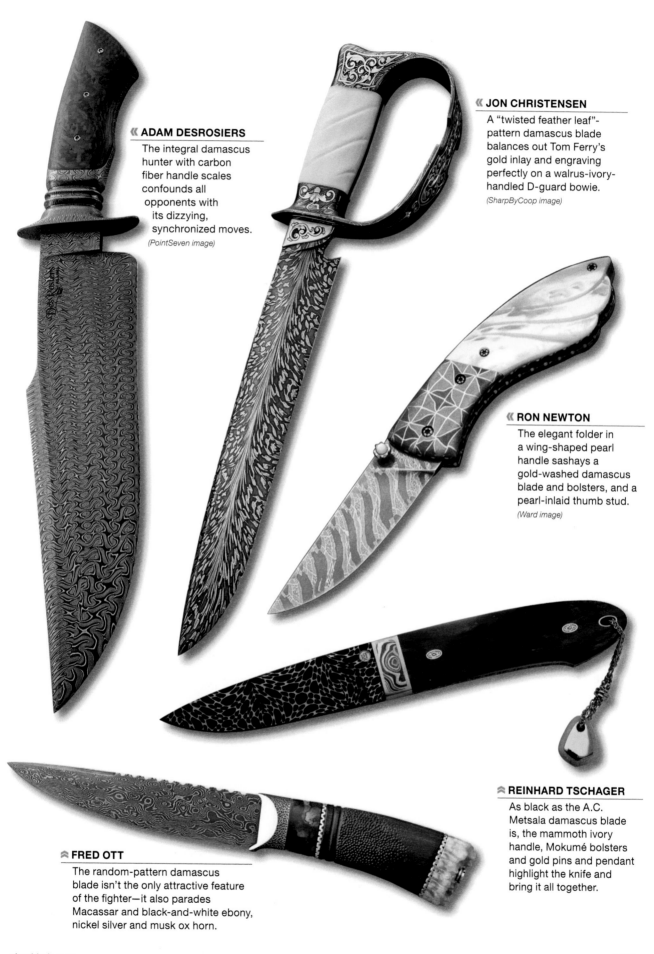

« ADAM DESROSIERS
The integral damascus hunter with carbon fiber handle scales confounds all opponents with its dizzying, synchronized moves.
(PointSeven image)

« JON CHRISTENSEN
A "twisted feather leaf"-pattern damascus blade balances out Tom Ferry's gold inlay and engraving perfectly on a walrus-ivory-handled D-guard bowie.
(SharpByCoop image)

« RON NEWTON
The elegant folder in a wing-shaped pearl handle sashays a gold-washed damascus blade and bolsters, and a pearl-inlaid thumb stud.
(Ward image)

⌃ FRED OTT
The random-pattern damascus blade isn't the only attractive feature of the fighter—it also parades Macassar and black-and-white ebony, nickel silver and musk ox horn.

⌃ REINHARD TSCHAGER
As black as the A.C. Metsala damascus blade is, the mammoth ivory handle, Mokumé bolsters and gold pins and pendant highlight the knife and bring it all together.

» DAVID LISCH

I wonder if he pulled or forged the "W's Taffy" damascus blade, that of a split-ring-guard bowie, complete with ancient walrus tusk handle and domed 14k-gold spacer? Probably both.

» JIM PROVOST

While Damasteel does blade duty, and does it well, a mastodon ivory handle offsets the dagger that is pointed on both ends. *(Cory Martin Imaging)*

⌄ JERRY HAINES

The lines of feather damascus race toward the tip like a fast running stream in the Alaskan wilderness, from where the mammoth ivory handle of the hunter may have come. *(Ward image)*

⌃ STEVEN KOSTER

The bowie boasts a 7-inch feather-pattern-damascus blade, with the shaft of the feather running right down the middle, and a black jigged bone handle. *(PointSeven image)*

« ED SCHEMPP

Turkish and radials damascus did so much dipping and diving, they bent the blade down on a mammoth-ivory-handle folder. And it's a fine one at that. *(PointSeven image)*

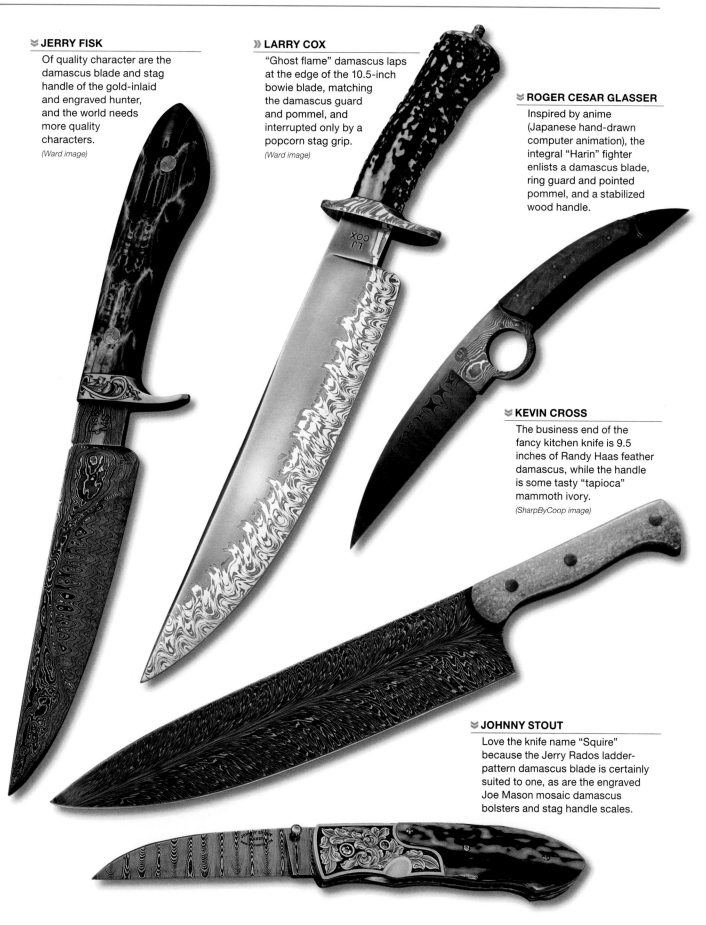

⌄ JERRY FISK

Of quality character are the damascus blade and stag handle of the gold-inlaid and engraved hunter, and the world needs more quality characters.

(Ward image)

⟩⟩ LARRY COX

"Ghost flame" damascus laps at the edge of the 10.5-inch bowie blade, matching the damascus guard and pommel, and interrupted only by a popcorn stag grip.

(Ward image)

⌄ ROGER CESAR GLASSER

Inspired by anime (Japanese hand-drawn computer animation), the integral "Harin" fighter enlists a damascus blade, ring guard and pointed pommel, and a stabilized wood handle.

⌄ KEVIN CROSS

The business end of the fancy kitchen knife is 9.5 inches of Randy Haas feather damascus, while the handle is some tasty "tapioca" mammoth ivory.

(SharpByCoop image)

⌄ JOHNNY STOUT

Love the knife name "Squire" because the Jerry Rados ladder-pattern damascus blade is certainly suited to one, as are the engraved Joe Mason mosaic damascus bolsters and stag handle scales.

» J.T. PALIKKO

The semi-integral hunter has a bubbling hot "Heimskringla"-damascus blade and guard, and a curly birch wood handle for good measure.

⌄ J. NEILSON

Done in a canister weld, the full-tang hunter is forged from 52100 ball bearings and 1095 high-carbon powdered steel for a splendidly spotted pattern, and matched up with mammoth ivory.

» DON HANSON III

A fixed-blade bowie is draped in Don's own damascus and anchored in fossil walrus ivory for a fine effect at that. *(SharpByCoop image)*

⌄ TONY HUGHES

Feather damascus and fossil mastodon ivory tickle all the right fancies. *(PointSeven image)*

⌃ KEN HALL

Dig the damascus blade and the stabilized maple burl handle of the 9 7/8-inch hunter.

DAN PETERSEN
Called "transition damascus," the 10-inch blade certainly does that, and right into a stag handle, and vitreous enamel spacer and butt cap. *(PointSeven image)*

ROBERT P. SMITH
The shape of the mini cleaver is as endearing as the damascus pattern, the pre-ban-ivory handle, opal inlay and filework along the back spacer.
(Ward image)

BRUCE BUMP
The maker wanted a special blade—an accordion-cut 416 dual damascus one—for his "Doc Holiday Bowie," handled in Gary Goudy-checkered Turkish walnut with Jere Davidson-engraved fittings.
(PointSeven image)

KEN STEIGERWALT
The tanto blade and damascus pattern enhance the Art Deco look and feel of the knife that also showcases black-lip-pearl and gold inlays.
(SharpByCoop image)

DAN LANCE
The tight and consistent pattern of the Mike Norris stainless damascus blade preludes the fine fit and finish of the fossilized mammoth ivory handle, stainless guards, mosaic pins and other parts. *(PointSeven image)*

DAVID L. BANKS
Feather shaped, the feather-damascus blade makes the only point needed, handled in stag with an elephant ivory pommel and a silver Concho nut. *(InspirationPoint, L. Elaine M. image)*

JASON KNIGHT
A blade fuller makes the damascus blade of a raised-clip hunter even groovier than it already is, complemented by a Hawaiian curly koa handle for one hot package. *(SharpByCoop image)*

ANDERS HOGSTROM
Don't let the Robert Mattson four-bar-damascus blade—with sharp top edge and hand-carved grooves and scallops—sweep you away before admiring the carved and textured sterling silver fittings and blue fossil walrus ivory handle.

BILL KIRKES
Don't let the damascus bowie with the mammoth ivory handle, S-guard and nickel silver shield fool you, it's not too pretty to fight. *(Ward image)*

JOHN HORRIGAN
Assemble a granite handle, some gold inlay and a damascus blade of explosion and Turkish twist patterns, and call it a dagger.

▼ LARAMIE JACKSON

The flaming-red Kirinite handle contrasts handsomely with the black-as-night Rob Thomas stainless damascus blade and bolsters.

≪ SANDRO BOECK

The damascus is given room to breathe along a multi-ground, swedged and pointy blade, wrapping itself around the natural handle of the "Javali" boar knife. *(Adriana Block image)*

▼ STEVE HILL

The maker says he "saw the blade shape in the billet of Robert Eggerling composite damascus." He also heat colored the bolsters an iridescent color that he calls "parking lot pigeon breast."

≫ E. RUSS ANDREWS II

The "duplex"-damascus blade is worth renting out to new neighbors, who'll also like the damascus fittings and walrus ivory grip of the bowie/fighter with long swedge. *(PointSeven image)*

≫ JON FINLEY

The 416-layer damascus blade is as endearing as the Al Frisillo-engraved guard, the Morrisonite (jasper) handle and the carved pommel of the everyday carry knife. *(Ward image)*

« ROSS MITSUYUKI

The repeating cell- or cube-like pattern of the high-carbon-damascus blade is a nice counterpart to the engraved and anodized bolster and stag handle scales.

« MIKE TYRE

The serpentine feather damascus pattern follows the path of the blade, a coffin-style African blackwood handle holding its own on the other end of a cowboy vest bowie. *(PointSeven image)*

⌃ JERRY VAN EIZENGA and RON WELLING

A foot-long damascus blade dominates the sub-hilt bowie done up in a mammoth ivory handle, and red and silver spacers. *(Ward image)*

⌃ AARON WILBURN

Feather damascus and twist damascus are the featured patterns of a 14-inch bowie that marries the steel with a mammoth ivory handle.
(SharpByCoop image)

⌃ ERIC OCHS

When the Rob Thomas "vines and roses" damascus blade jets open via the flipper mechanism, folks step back to admire the carbon fiber handle inlay and the superconductor pivot collar.

FACTORY TRENDS

Talk, always there's talk. People talk about how jobs are being outsourced to China, Mexico, India and South America. Americans are scared, and sometimes for good reason. The media talks about how manufacturing jobs in the U.S. have disappeared or are disappearing. Images of abandoned buildings and houses in Detroit and Flint, Michigan flash on television screens. Other folks discuss how it used to be, how people took pride in their work, and that products were well made and lasted longer in the good old days. Politicians talk about bringing America back to how it used to be.

Yet there's at least one industry in the world where jobs are being brought back to America, production workers take pride in their work, and the products are solid, well made and last for generations. Sure, there are still knife companies outsourcing work to China, Taiwan, Japan and elsewhere, but there's also a "Made In America" movement underfoot, with many movers and shakers in the industry bringing knife production back to the United States.

With knives being made for soldiers, police, first responders, firefighters, blue collar workers, ranchers, farmers, sailors and extreme sports enthusiasts, quality is often job one. Not always, as there are a good number of "cheap" or "knock-off" knives in the industry, but the majority of knives are manufactured using high standards and quality control. And members of the knife industry tend to take pride in their work, honing blades by hand, whether manufactured on production lines or not, and finely fitting and finishing parts with an eye toward the most minute of details. The knife industry is alive and well, and knife enthusiasts and collectors are the beneficiaries. □

Black Beauty, Not Just Another Horse Story 174

Hawks 'n Hatchets 178

Refined Folders 179

Military Units 180

Black Beauty, Not Just Another Horse Story

Western Cutlery's Black Beauty knife line shows good composition and, well, breeding

By Richard D. White

NOTE: Knives featured herein are from the Richard D. White and Doug Wittich collections.

Many people remember the famous story, *Black Beauty*, written by British author Anna Sewell and published in 1877. To trace the origin of Black Beauty knives and axes, produced by Western Cutlery, originally of Boulder, Colo., one only has to go back as far as the 1950's. Production of hunting or sheath knives by a number of well-known knife companies was in full swing by the '50s. The handle

material of choice for most of these companies was stacked leather, which provided a firm grip, even when wet, and was relatively inexpensive to use.

Western Cutlery offered a full line of hunting knives, from small bird-and-trout fixed blades to larger hunting knives designed to handle even the most difficult skinning tasks. As the preeminent knife company west of the Mississippi River, Western enjoyed success not only with its own branded line, but also as a knife supplier to Montgomery Wards, Sears, Roebuck & Company, Western Auto stores, Coast Cutlery, L.L. Bean and others.

I am not sure just what drove the decision to introduce a new, innovative knife line, but the first mention of Black Beauty knives and axes appears in the 1960 Western Cutlery product catalog, as documented in the biography *Western Cutlery: Knife Makers Who Went West*, by Harvey Platts, the grandson of company founder, H.N. Platts.

Western named Black Beauty knives for their handles, made up of compressed aluminum spacers alternately stacked together with black fiber spacers to give the grips a zebra-like appearance. It was a drastic change for a company that had primarily used stacked-leather knife and axe handles, polished until the leather looked like wood.

According to catalog copy, the black fiber and aluminum handles gave Black Beauty knives "sure-grip performance."

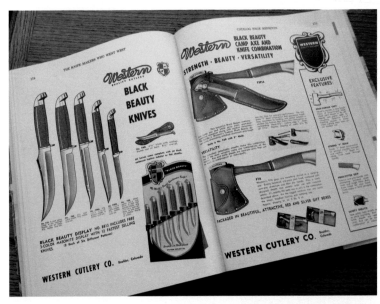

Two pages from a 1960 Western Cutlery catalog, reproduced in Harvey Platts' book, *The Knife Makers Who Went West*, describe the features of Black Beauty hunting knives and axes.

❥ At top-right is the standard Black Beauty Model F40 bearing the Western Boulder, Colo., tang stamp, while the bottom-left knife was made for Coast Cutlery Co. of Portland, Oregon.

⌃ The five Black Beauty hunters are, from left, Models F28, F48A, F40, F66 and F39. The black-fiber-and-aluminum grips were a radical departure from standard stacked-leather handles.

Actually, in evaluating the knives today, the black fiber washers have shrunk over the years, and the aluminum spacers protrude slightly above them, indeed giving the user a non-slip gripping surface.

A SIX-HORSE FIELD

Western offered six knife models in the black fiber and aluminum handles. They included the F39, featuring a 5.25-inch, saber-ground, upswept blade and an overall length of 9.25 inches, and the Model F40, a smaller version of the F39 with a 4.25-inch blade and 8.5 inches overall. Both models sported thumb notches on the blade spines nearest the guards, enabling users to choke up on the blades when undertaking large skinning tasks.

The full-size model F48A and slightly shorter F48B bird-and-trout knives came with 4 3/8-inch and 3 5/8-inch blades, respectively, and stretched 8 and 7 1/8 inches. Each saber-ground blade exhibited *swedges* on the blade spines. The smallest Black Beauty knife was the Model F28, a cute little hunting knife with a 3-inch blade and an overall length of 6 3/8 inches.

The bird-and-trout knives proved the perfect size for skinning out birds and filleting fish, and fit nicely into game bags or fishing creels. Only the smallest model—the F28— had a thong hole in the pommel

for stringing a lanyard through it and around the user's wrist so the knife would not be lost in the freezing waters of mountain streams.

I believe that the "F's" in the model numbers stood for "fiber" handles, as opposed to other knives of the same model designations, but with "L's," which had stacked-leather grips.

Rounding out the six knives in the Black Beauty series was perhaps Western's most popular hunting knife, the Model F66, with a 4.5-inch blade and 8.75 inches overall. An acquaintance who spent over 25 years working for Western told me that the Model 66, at least the leather-handle version and presumably also the Black Beauty variation, was the company's most widely produced model. If you randomly pick up three or four Western knives, it is almost a guarantee that at least one, if not two of them, will be model 66's.

LIGHT & HEAVY STOCK

The Black Beauty series also included a large camp axe or hatchet. Western sold two types of camp axes or hatchets, one a lightweight model, and though it was sold individually, it was most often packaged as one of the company's knife-axe combination sets. Designed to split kindling or cut off small tree branches, the light hatchets were not meant for pounding in metal stakes or chopping large logs.

Two Western axes feature the "I-beam" handle construction, each stamped with the Western logo, the top in the middle of the handle and the bottom on the side of the axe head.

Western's other camp axe, however, made by the Bridgeport Axe Co., was described in company literature as a "drop-forged unit" with strong "I-beam construction" running from the head of the axe through the entire handle. These axes—the F14 models—had nail pullers in the heads for "additional versatility."

Like the Black Beauty knives, the camp axes showcased "sure-grip" handles with alternating polished aluminum and tough, black fiber spacers. An aluminum pommel capped each handle. Unlike the lightweight hatchet, a well-known Western product in its own right, the heavier axes boasted wide heads capable of pounding or hammering without breaking.

These axe handles were generally stamped "Western Cutlery, Boulder, Colorado, USA," while other axes came with the Western name deeply etched on the heads, opposite the cutting edges. The axes themselves were painted black, with polished areas near the cutting edges and around the "Western" stamped areas on the heads.

Western also marketed the Bridgeport axes as "Official Boy Scout" axes. These, however, generally had wood hafts as opposed to aluminum and fiber spacers. The handles on the Boy Scout axes were stained a golden oak color and painted red at the ends.

Western offered the smaller hatchet in a Black Beauty style, and one of these, designated an F10, had a standard aluminum pommel found on most Western Cutlery hunting knives. Some call it a "bird's beak" pommel. Western F10 Black Beauty axes, however, can also be found with another type of pommel generally associated with the larger F14 Bridgeport-produced axe. Dennis Ellingsen, a writer for *Knife World*, once described this pommel as an "animal hoof" style.

RIDING HIGH IN THE LEATHER

Realizing that its knife-axe combinations were great sellers, Western paired up their axes and knives together with leather sheaths attached to each other via keeper straps strung through the bot-

tom of the axe sheaths and long enough
to snap in front of the knives in their own
sheaths. Generally, Western paired up
a Model F39 hunting knife, including a
5-inch, upswept, saber-ground blade, with
a large F14 axe of "I-beam" construction.
Another pairing included the smaller
Western Model F66 hunting knife with a
lightweight F10 hatchet.

I have also seen sets of Western Black
Beauty axes coupled with Model 48 hunting knives. I think, perhaps, that these
sets have been mismatched, with someone
marrying the wrong knife and hatchet.

One striking feature of the Western
Black Beauty knives and knife-axe
combinations was their shiny black
leather sheaths with white stitching and
nickel-plated snaps. The sheaths are
rather impressive, and highlight the aluminum and black handle spacer pattern.
Certainly, these glossy black sheaths complement the
name "Black Beauty."

The sheath for the larger F14 "I-beam"-style axe
had an open back, allowing the axe to be used like a
hammer to pound metal stakes without having to remove it from the sheath. According to the description
in *Knife Makers Who Went West*, such were known as
"safety sheaths."

The knife and axe (or hatchet) sheaths each had
a belt loop so that the pieces could be worn individually. Combined with the striped handles of aluminum
and black spacers, these shiny black sheaths served
to emphasize the innovative Western Cutlery knife
sets within the Black Beauty series.

NEW TO THE BREED

A glance through the 1968 Western catalog un-
covers the Model 40, designated in the Black Beauty
series as an F40. This knife is a smaller version of
the Model F39, with an almost identical upswept
saber-ground blade, but 4 3/8 inches long, and with
an overall knife length of 8 inches.

By the time the 1978 catalog was published, only
one knife in the Black Beauty series remained, that
being the Model F48B bird-and-trout knife with a
3.5-inch blade. It can be assumed that the remaining
Black Beauty knives were discontinued, corresponding with Western's move from Boulder to Longmont,
Colorado. It was also a time when the company
switched from stacked-leather handles to either

The Western knife-axe combination at top is a heavy-duty Bridgeport-
manufactured axe and an F39 hunting knife. Below it is a lightweight
Western axe paired with the F66 hunter.

jigged Delrin™, sometimes mistaken for genuine
stag, or polished Pakkawood™ knife grips. Delrin
and Pakkawood are extremely durable, but signal
the end of an era for Western Cutlery.

Having fashioned its first sheath knife in 1928,
Western ended production in Longmont, in 1992,
going out of business after 66 years and being sold
at auction. The Black Beauty series of knives oc-
cupies only a small piece of the production pie—an
all-too-brief 18 years. Given this short time period,
and considering that most of the Black Beauty series
was made in Boulder and stamped as such, the knife
series remains a unique collectable.

I believe that the Black Beauty Westerns are
currently undervalued, and can still be found in near
mint or even mint condition. The most difficult knife
to find in the series is the smallest bird and trout
knife, the Model F28. For some reason, knife collectors have focused their interests on both ends of the
knife spectrum, in terms of size. The largest hunting
knife of most brands is usually also the most popular,
and the smallest knives have typically appreciated in
value more than standard-length hunters.

It would serve the serious collector well to set
some of the Black Beauty knives aside for later appreciation. Certainly, the innovative handle material
and jet-black embossed sheaths are worthy of a
second look, because Black Beauty isn't, as the name
suggests, just another horse story, or horse trade for
that matter. □

Hawks 'n Hatchets

❧ Designed by Laci Szabo, the Spyderco SzaboHawk is an ergonomic hand axe designed for utility and close combat. The head and haft are made from titanium-carbonitride-coated D2 tool steel, the arcing full-tang haft has smooth G-10 scales, and the chisel-ground butt serves as a pry bar and impact implement.

« Puma hits the tomahawk trail with the Tomahawk XP Puma Green in a 420 stainless steel head that is 15/64-inch thick and sports a 2-inch spike. The haft is a green-and-black co-molded synthetic.

❧ The Wolf pAX 2 combo from TOPS includes not only a hatchet, but also the Wolf Pup small fixed blade. Blade/head steel is 1095 high carbon in a Black Traction Coating and the slabs are tan canvas Micarta.

« The Boker Plus Carnivore features a 6.5-inch head of powder-coated SK5 carbon steel and a contoured haft with shape-matching G-10 scales.

» The Survival Hawk from SOG Specialty Knives & Tools offers a fire starter rod that inserts into the butt of the paracord-wrapped, glass-reinforced nylon haft. The lightweight hawk has a 3-inch head of 2Cr13MoV stainless steel with a nail puller on the opposite end.

≋ The Kershaw Tinder not only serves as a hatchet, but also comes with a bottle opener, pry point, nail remover, hammer and hex tools.

≋ You can attach your choice of a hammer poll, spike or pry bar to the head of the Hogue EX-T01 hatchet. The head is S7 tool steel covered in a KG Gun Kote black finish. The G-Mascus handle slabs come in a choice of black, green, dark earth and red lava.

Refined Folders

» The Aculus from DPx Gear comes in an annual limited edition of 100. The blade is stonewashed Niolox stainless and the titanium handle has a 3D-diamond surface pattern. A quarter-inch hex-base tungsten carbide insert in the handle butt serves as a glass breaker.

» Queen Cutlery's Feathered Buffalo Sleeveboard sports pinched and lined bolsters, D2 blade steel and streaked

≋ Puma Knife Co.'s USA Lonestar 30 lock-back folder takes the venerable sodbuster pattern to a new level. The deep hollow grind is great for getting a keen edge, and the steel is German 440A stainless.

Military Units

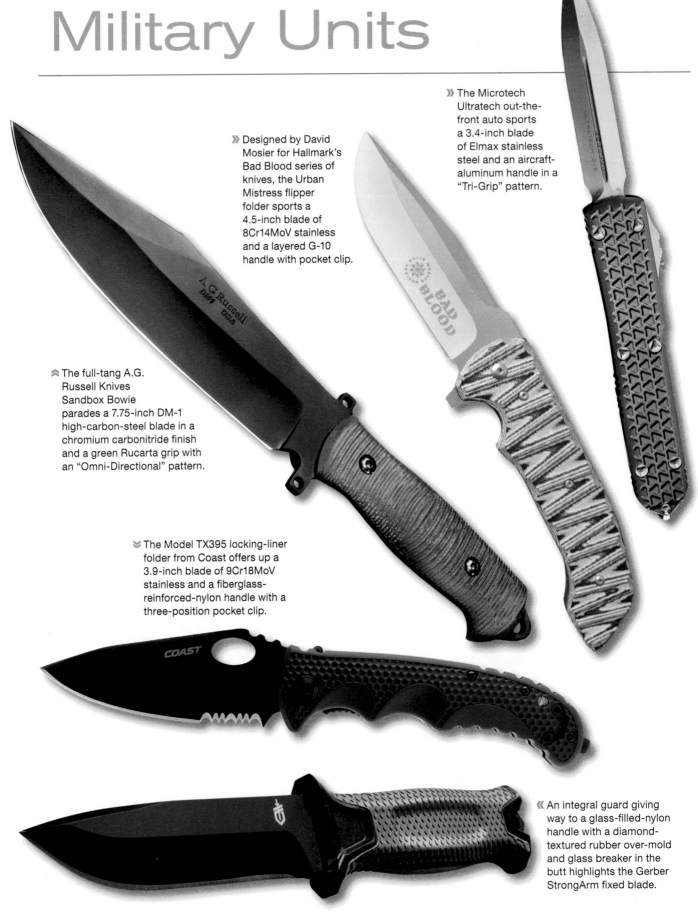

» The Microtech Ultratech out-the-front auto sports a 3.4-inch blade of Elmax stainless steel and an aircraft-aluminum handle in a "Tri-Grip" pattern.

» Designed by David Mosier for Hallmark's Bad Blood series of knives, the Urban Mistress flipper folder sports a 4.5-inch blade of 8Cr14MoV stainless and a layered G-10 handle with pocket clip.

≫ The full-tang A.G. Russell Knives Sandbox Bowie parades a 7.75-inch DM-1 high-carbon-steel blade in a chromium carbonitride finish and a green Rucarta grip with an "Omni-Directional" pattern.

≫ The Model TX395 locking-liner folder from Coast offers up a 3.9-inch blade of 9Cr18MoV stainless and a fiberglass-reinforced-nylon handle with a three-position pocket clip.

« An integral guard giving way to a glass-filled-nylon handle with a diamond-textured rubber over-mold and glass breaker in the butt highlights the Gerber StrongArm fixed blade.

» The ESEE Knives ESEE-5 boasts a 5.25-inch blade of quarter-inch-thick 1095 high-carbon steel with a textured-powder-coat finish in a choice of OD green or black (shown).

⌄ The Praetorian "T" frame-lock folder from Medford Knife & Tool has a 3.75-inch drop-point tanto blade of D2 tool steel in a stonewashed finish. The handle is black-PVD-coated titanium.

« Uddeholm Sleipner stainless steel in a stonewashed finish and a 3D-milled G-10 handle highlight the M5B G10 utility fixed blade from LionSteel.

⌃ KA-BAR has resurrected the Ek Commando brand, and first and foremost in the new line is the Ek Model 4 in a 6.625-inch blade of 1095 Cro-Van high carbon steel. Handle: glass-filled nylon.

⌃ A desert camouflage coated 7.75-inch blade of quarter-inch INFI carbon steel in a flat saber grind and a tan canvas Micarta handle fill out the Busse Combat Team Gemini Desert Crusader.

Knives Marketplace

INTERESTING PRODUCT NEWS FOR BOTH THE CUTLER AND THE KNIFE ENTHUSIAST

The companies and individuals represented on the following pages will be happy to provide additional information — feel free to contact them.

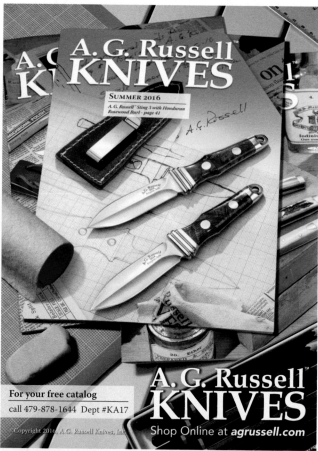
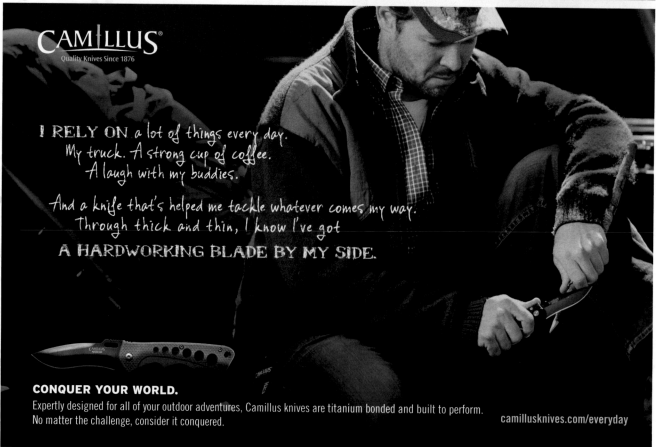

5" CLEAVER

8" CHEF'S KNIFE

6" SANTOKU

6" UTILITY KNIFE

4" PARING KNIFE

- PIECE KITCHEN SET
MICROTECH KNIVES - BORKA BLADES COLLABORATION

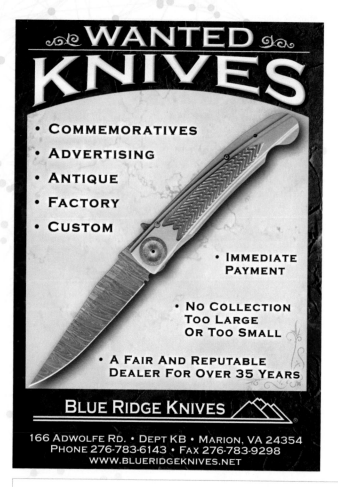

Made for Heroes, Then and Now.

Our truest re-creation of the famous commando knife carried by the First Special Service Force in World War II.

American Walnut display (#21943) *Sold Seperately*

"This isn't just another reproduction, but a real V-42".

– Major John L. Plaster (ret.)
U.S. Army Special Forces Hall of Fame inductee
Author of Secret Commandos

#21994
(Includes Leather Sheath)

V-42

KF

**INTELLIGENT
DISCUSSION FOR THE
KNIFE ENTHUSIAST**

Knifeforums.com

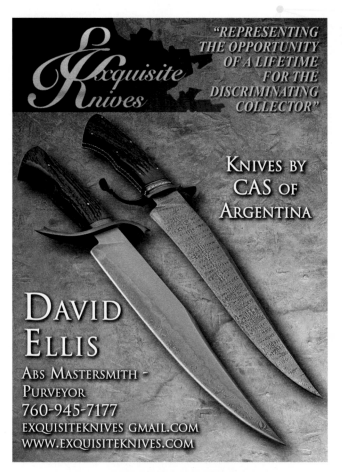

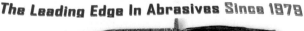

PRO·TECH KNIVES

TR-4
Tactical Response IV
Reporting for Duty!

Full 4" blade • secondary slide safety • hardened glass breaker

pocket clip on reverse • molle compatible sheath included

protechknives.com
Pro-Tech Knives, LLC • 17115 Alburtis Ave.
Artesia, Ca 90701 • 562-860-0678

Knives are life critical edged tools that make adventure possible.

Imagine your life without a knife.

Visit AKTI.org
or call (307) 587-8296

AKTI
AMERICAN
KNIFE & TOOL
INSTITUTE

YOU made BLADE Show 2016 a standout success!

Thank you to our wonderful attendees and exhibitors for being part of BLADE Show's 35th Anniversary celebration—we will see you again next year!

SAVE THE DATE FOR BLADE SHOW 2017!
June 2-4 | Atlanta | Cobb Galleria

Stay connected with BLADE Show

BLADESHOW.COM

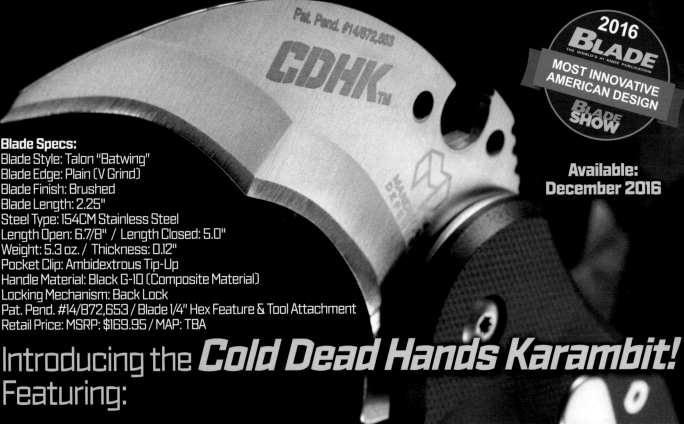

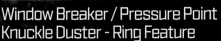

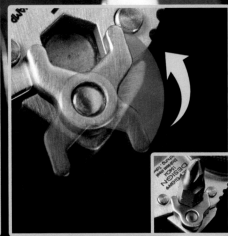

TURN EVERYDAY ITEMS INTO
SURVIVAL ESSENTIALS!

256 pages | 9781440593345 | $16.99

ShopDeerHunting.com

Would you be prepared if you needed to survive in the wilderness?

Bestselling author, Creek Stewart's new rough-and-rugged guide covers everything from small-scale hacks, like using sticks and rope to make a table, to the big stuff, like creating a one-person emergency shelter from a trash bag or purifying dirty water using a plastic bottle and the sun.

CREEK STEWART is an expert survival instructor and author of the bestselling Build the Perfect Bug Out series of books. Stewart hosted two seasons of the show *Fat Guys in the Woods* on the Weather Channel. He's the owner and founder of Willow Haven Outdoor survival training schools in Central Indiana, named one of the "Top 10 Survival Schools" by MSN Travel.

www.adamsmedia.com

DIRECTORY

Custom Knifemakers 202
Knifemakers State-by-State.. 291
Knifemakers Membership Lists 300
Knife Photo Index.. 303
Sporting Cutlers.. 305

Importers... 308
Knifemaking Supplies.. 310
Mail Order Sales... 312
Knife Services 314
Organizations 318
Publications... 319

custom knifemakers

A

ABEGG, ARNIE
5992 Kenwick Cr, Huntington Beach, CA 92648, Phone: 714-848-5697

ABERNATHY, LANCE
Sniper Bladeworks, 1924 Linn Ave., North Kansas City, MO 64116, Phone: 816-585-1595, lanceabernathy@sbcglobal.net; Web: www.sniperbladeworks.com
Specialties: Tactical frame-lock and locking-liner folding knives.

ACCAWI, FUAD
130 Timbercrest Dr., Oak Ridge, TN 37830, Phone: 865-414-4836, gaccawi@comcast.net; Web: www.acremetalworks.com
Specialties: I create one of a kind pieces from small working knives to performance blades and swords. **Patterns:** Styles include, and not limited to hunters, Bowies, daggers, swords, folders and camp knives. **Technical:** I forge primarily 5160, produces own Damascus and does own heat treating. **Prices:** $150 to $3000. **Remarks:** I am a full-time bladesmith. I enjoy producing Persian and historically influenced work. **Mark:** My mark is an eight sided Middle Eastern star with initials in the center.

ACKERSON, ROBIN E
119 W Smith St, Buchanan, MI 49107, Phone: 616-695-2911

ADAMS, JIM
1648 Camille Way, Cordova, TN 38016, Phone: 901-326-0441, jim@JimAdamsKnives.com Web: www.jimadamsknives.com
Specialties: Fixed blades in classic design. **Patterns:** Hunters, fighters, and Bowies. **Technical:** Grinds Damascus, O1, others as requested. **Prices:** Starting at $150. **Remarks:** Full-time maker. **Mark:** J. Adams, Cordova, TN.

ADAMS, LES
3516 S.W. 2nd St., Cape Coral, FL 33991, Phone: 786-999-3060
Specialties: Working straight knives of his design. **Patterns:** Fighters, tactical folders, law enforcing autos. **Technical:** Grinds ATS-34, 440C and D2. **Prices:** $100 to $500. **Remarks:** Part-time maker; first knife sold in 1989. **Mark:** First initial, last name, Custom Knives.

ADDISON, KYLE A
588 Atkins Trail, Hazel, KY 42049-8629, Phone: 270-492-8120, kylest2@yahoo.com
Specialties: Hand forged blades including Bowies, fighters and hunters. **Patterns:** Custom leather sheaths. **Technical:** Forges 5160, 1084, and his own Damascus. **Prices:** $175 to $1500. **Remarks:** Part-time maker, first knife sold in 1996. ABS member. **Mark:** First and middle initial, last name under "Trident" with knife and hammer.

ADKINS, RICHARD L
138 California Ct, Mission Viejo, CA 92692-4079

AIDA, YOSHIHITO
26-7 Narimasu 2-chome, Itabashi-ku, Tokyo, JAPAN 175-0094, Phone: 81-3-3939-0052, Fax: 81-3-3939-0058, Web: http://riverside-land.com/
Specialties: High-tech working straight knives and folders of his design. **Patterns:** Bowies, lockbacks, hunters, fighters, fishing knives, boots. **Technical:** Grinds CV-134, ATS-34; buys Damascus; works in traditional Japanese fashion for some handles and sheaths. **Prices:** $700 to $1200; some higher. **Remarks:** Full-time maker; first knife sold in 1978. **Mark:** Initial logo and Riverside West.

ALBERT, STEFAN
U Lucenecka 434/4, Filakovo 98604, SLOVAKIA, albert@albertknives.com Web: www.albertknives.com
Specialties: Art Knives, Miniatures, Scrimshaw, Bulino. **Prices:** From USD $500 to USD $25000. **Mark:** Albert

ALCORN, DOUGLAS A.
14687 Fordney Rd., Chesaning, MI 48616, Phone: 989-845-6712, daalcornknives@gmail.com
Specialties: Gentleman style military, tactical and presentation knives. **Patterns:** Hunters, miniatures, and military type fixed blade knives and axes. **Technical:** Blades are stock removal and forged using best quality stainless, carbon, and damascus steels. Handle materials are burls, ivory, pearl, leather and other exotics. **Prices:** $200 and up. **Motto:** Simple, Rugged, Elegant, Handcrafted **Remarks:** Knife maker since 1989 and full time since 1999, Knife Makers Guild (voting member), member of the Bladesmith Society. **Mark:** D.A. Alcorn, Maker, Chesaning, MI.

ALDERMAN, ROBERT
2655 Jewel Lake Rd., Sagle, ID 83860, Phone: 208-263-5996
Specialties: Classic and traditional working straight knives in standard patterns or to customer specs and his design; period pieces. **Patterns:** Bowies, fighters, hunters and utility/camp knives. **Technical:** Casts, forges and grinds 1084; forges and grinds L6 and O1. Prefers an old appearance. **Prices:** $100 to $350; some to $700. **Remarks:** Full-time maker; first knife sold in 1975. Doing business as Trackers Forge. Knife-making school. Two-week course for beginners; covers forging, stock removal, hardening, tempering, case making. All materials supplied; $1250. **Mark:** Deer track.

ALEXANDER, EUGENE
Box 540, Ganado, TX 77962-0540, Phone: 512-771-3727
Alexander,, Oleg, and Cossack Blades
15460 Stapleton Way, Wellington, FL 33414, Phone: 443-676-6111, Web: www.cossackblades.com
Technical: All knives are made from hand-forged Damascus (3-4 types of steel are used to create the Damascus) and have a HRC of 60-62. Handle materials are all natural, including various types of wood, horn, bone and leather. Embellishments include the use of precious metals and stones, including gold, silver, diamonds, rubies, sapphires and other unique materials. All knives include hand-made leather sheaths, and some models include wooden presentation boxes and display stands. **Prices:** $395 to over $10,000, depending on design and materials used. **Remarks:** Full-time maker, first knife sold in 1993. **Mark:** Rectangle enclosing a stylized Cyrillic letter "O" overlapping a stylized Cyrillic "K."

ALLAN, TODD
TODD ALLAN KNIVES, 6525 W. Kings Ave., Glendale, AZ 85306, Phone: 623-210-3766, todd@toddallanknives.com; www.toddallanknives.com
Patterns: Fixed-blade hunters and camp knives. **Technical:** Stock-removal method of blade making using 154CM, high-carbon damascus, stainless damascus, 5160 and 1095 blade steels. Handle materials include various Micartas, stabilized woods and mammoth ivory. **Prices:** $175 to $1,000. **Remarks:** Full-time maker.

ALLEN, JIM
Three Sisters Forge, LLC, 18830 Macalpine Loop, Bend, OR 97702, knives@threesistersforge.com; Web: www.threesistersforge.com
Specialties: Folders with titanium frames, and stainless steel blades and fixtures. **Technical:** Stock-removal method of blade making using CPM S35VN steel for now, but always evaluating latest steels. **Prices:** $200 to $300. **Remarks:** Ninety percent of knives go to police and military. Special features such as anodizing and Cerakote coated blades available. **Mark:** The sun setting over the Three Sisters Mountains (the view from the maker's shop).

ALLRED, BRUCE F
1764 N. Alder, Layton, UT 84041, Phone: 801-825-4612, allredbf@msn.com
Specialties: Custom hunting and utility knives. **Patterns:** Custom designs that include a unique grind line, thumb and mosaic pins. **Technical:** ATS-34, 154CM and 440C. **Remarks:** The handle material includes but not limited to Micarta (in various colors), natural woods and reconstituted stone.

ALLRED, ELVAN
31 Spring Terrace Court, St. Charles, MO 63303, Phone: 636-936-8871, allredknives@yahoo.com; Web: www.allredcustomknives.com
Specialties: Innovative sculpted folding knives designed by Elvan's son Scott that are mostly one of a kind. **Patterns:** Mostly folders but some high-end straight knives. **Technical:** ATS-34 SS, 440C SS, stainless Damascus, S30V, 154cm; inlays are mostly natural materials such as pearl, coral, ivory, jade, lapis, and other precious stone. **Prices:** $500 to $4000, some higher. **Remarks:** Started making knives in the shop of Dr. Fred Carter in the early 1990s. Full-time maker since 2006, first knife sold in 1993. Take some orders but work mainly on one-of-a-kind art knives. **Mark:** Small oval with signature Eallred in the center and handmade above.

ALVERSON, TIM (R.V.)
209 Spring Rd. SE, Arab, AL 35016, Phone: 256-224-9620, alvie35@yahoo.com Web: cwknives.blogspot.com
Specialties: Fancy working knives to customer specs; other types on request. **Patterns:** Bowies, daggers, folders and miniatures. **Technical:** Grinds 440C, ATS-34; buys some Damascus. **Prices:** Start at $100. **Remarks:** Full-time maker; first knife sold in 1981. **Mark:** R.V.A. around rosebud.

AMERI, MAURO
Via Riaello No. 20, Trensasco St Olcese, Genova, ITALY 16010, Phone: 010-8357077, mauro.ameri@gmail.com
Specialties: Working and using knives of his design. **Patterns:** Hunters, Bowies and utility/camp knives. **Technical:** Grinds 440C, ATS-34 and 154CM. Handles in wood or Micarta; offers sheaths. **Prices:** $200 to $1200. **Remarks:** Spare-time maker; first knife sold in 1982. **Mark:** Last name, city.

AMMONS, DAVID C
6225 N. Tucson Mtn. Dr, Tucson, AZ 85743, Phone: 520-471-4433, dcammons@msn.com
Specialties: Will build to suit. **Patterns:** Yours or his. **Prices:** $250 to $2000. **Mark:** AMMONS.

AMOS, CHRIS
PO Box 1519, Riverton, WY 82501, Phone: 520-271-9752, caknives@yahoo.com
Specialties: HEPK (High Endurance Performance Knives). **Patterns:** Hunters, fighters, bowies, kitchen knives and camp knives. **Technical:** Hand-forged, high rate of reduction 52100 and 5160 steel. **Prices:** $150 to $1,500. **Remarks:** Part-time maker since 1997, full time since 2012. Coach/instructor at Ed Fowler's Knifemaking School. HEPK mastersmith rating, 2013. **Mark:** Early **mark:** CAK stamped; current **mark:** Amos on right side.

AMOUREUX, A W
PO Box 776, Northport, WA 99157, Phone: 509-732-6292
Specialties: Heavy-duty working straight knives. **Patterns:** Bowies, fighters, camp knives and hunters for world-wide use. **Technical:** Grinds 440C, ATS-34 and 154CM. **Prices:** $80 to $2000. **Remarks:** Full-time maker; first knife sold in 1974. **Mark:** ALSTAR.

ANDERS, DAVID
157 Barnes Dr, Center Ridge, AR 72027, Phone: 501-893-2294
Specialties: Working straight knives of his design. **Patterns:** Bowies, fighters and hunters. **Technical:** Forges 5160, 1080 and Damascus. **Prices:** $225 to $3200. **Remarks:** Part-time maker; first knife sold in 1988. Doing business as Anders Knives. **Mark:** Last name/MS.

ANDERS, JEROME
14560 SW 37th St, Miramar, FL 33027, Phone: 305-613-2990, web:www.andersknives.com
Specialties: Case handles and pin work. **Patterns:** Layered and mosaic steel. **Prices:** $275 and up. **Remarks:** All his knives are truly one-of-a-kind. **Mark:** J. Anders in half moon.

ANDERSEN, HENRIK LEFOLII
Jagtvej 8, Groenholt, Fredensborg, DENMARK 3480, Phone: 0011-45-48483026
Specialties: Hunters and matched pairs for the serious hunter. **Technical:** Grinds A2; uses materials native to Scandinavia. **Prices:** Start at $250. **Remarks:** Part-time maker; first knife sold in 1985. **Mark:** Initials with arrow.

ANDERSEN, KARL B.
20200 TimberLodge Rd., Warba, MN 55793, Phone: 218-398-4270, Karl@andersenforge.com Web: www.andersenforge.com
Specialties: Hunters, bowies, fighters and camp knives forged from high carbon tool steels and Andersen Forge Damascus. **Technical:** All types of materials used. Styles include hidden-tang and full-tang fixed blades, Brut de Forge, integrals and frame-handle construction. **Prices:** Starting at $450 and up. **Remarks:** Full-time maker. ABS journeyman smith. All knives sole authorship. Andersen Forge was instrumental in paving the way for take-down knife construction to be more recognized and broadly accepted in knifemaking today. **Mark:** Andersen in script on obverse. J.S. on either side, depending on knife.

ANDERSON, GARY D
2816 Reservoir Rd, Spring Grove, PA 17362-9802, Phone: 717-229-2665
Specialties: From working knives to collectors quality blades, some folders. **Patterns:** Traditional and classic designs; customer patterns welcome. **Technical:** Forges Damascus carbon and stainless steels. Offers silver inlay, mokume, filework, checkering. **Prices:** $250 and up. **Remarks:** Part-time maker; first knife sold in 1985. Some engraving, scrimshaw and stone work. **Mark:** GAND, MS.

ANDERSON, MEL
29505 P 50 Rd, Hotchkiss, CO 81419-8203, Phone: 970-872-4882, Fax: 970-872-4882, artnedge@tds.net, melsscratchyhand@aol.com; Web: www.scratchyhand.com
Specialties: Full-size, miniature and one-of-a-kind straight knives and folders of his design. **Patterns:** Tantos, Bowies, daggers, fighters, hunters and pressure folders. **Technical:** Grinds 440C, 5160, D2, 1095. **Prices:** Start at $175. **Remarks:** Knifemaker and sculptor, full-time maker; first knife sold in 1987. **Mark:** Scratchy Hand.

ANDERSON, TOM
955 Canal Rd. Extd., Manchester, PA 17345, Phone: 717-266-6475, andersontech1@comcast.net Web: artistryintitanium.com
Specialties: Battle maces and war hammers.

ANDRADE, DON CARLOS
CALIFORNIA CUSTOM KNIVES, 1824 Sunny Hill Ave., Los Osos, CA 93402, Phone: 805-528-8837 or 805-550-2324, andradeartworks@gmail.com; www.californiacustomknives.com
Specialties: Chef knife specialist, also integrally forged personal knives and camp knives. **Technical:** Forges to shape, and a small number of stain-resistant, stock-removal blades. All heat-treating in house. Uses 1095, W2, W1, 1084, 52100, 1065, 1070 and 13C26 blade steels. **Prices:** $250 to $1,650. **Remarks:** Full-time maker; first knife made in 2006 under tutorship of mentor Tai Goo. **Mark:** Initials "DCA" and two circles with a strike running through them (maker's version of infinity/continuity.)

ANDREWS, ERIC
132 Halbert Street, Grand Ledge, MI 48837, Phone: 517-627-7304
Specialties: Traditional working and using straight knives of his design. **Patterns:** Full-tang hunters, skinners and utility knives. **Technical:** Forges carbon steel; heat-treats. All knives come with sheath; most handles are of wood. **Prices:** $80 to $160. **Remarks:** Part-time maker; first knife sold in 1990. Doing business as The Tinkers Bench.

ANDREWS, RUSS
PO Box 7732, Sugar Creek, MO 64054, Phone: 816-252-3344, russandrews@sbcglobal.net; Web:wwwrussandrewsknives.com
Specialties: Hand forged bowies & hunters. **Mark:** E. R. Andrews II. ERAII.

ANGELL, JON
22516 East C R1474, Hawthorne, FL 32640, Phone: 352-475-5380, syrjon@aol.com

ANKROM, W.E.
14 Marquette Dr, Cody, WY 82414, Phone: 307-587-3017, weankrom@hotmail.com
Specialties: Best quality folding knives of his design. Bowies, fighters, chute knives, boots and hunters. **Patterns:** Tacticals, flipper folders, lock backs, LinerLocks and single high art. **Technical:** All high-tech steels, including ATS-34, commercial damascus, CPM 154 steel. **Prices:** $500 and up. **Remarks:** Full-time maker; first knife sold in 1975. **Mark:** Name or name, city, state.

ANSO, JENS
GL. Skanderborgvej 116, Sporup, DENMARK 8472, Phone: 45 86968826, info@ansoknives.com; Web: www.ansoknives.com
Specialties: Working knives of his own design. **Patterns:** Balisongs, swords, folders, drop-points, sheepsfoots, hawkbill, tanto, recurve. **Technical:** Grinds RWL-34 Damasteel S30V, CPM 154CM. Handrubbed or beadblasted finish. **Prices:** $400 to $1200, some up to $3500. **Remarks:** Full-time maker since January 2002. First knife sold 1997. Doing business as ANSOKNIVES. **Mark:** ANSO and/or ANSO with logo.

APELT, STACY E
8076 Moose Ave, Norfolk, VA 23518, Phone: 757-583-5872, sapelt@cox.net
Specialties: Exotic wood and burls, ivories, Bowies, custom made knives to order. **Patterns:** Bowies, hunters, fillet, professional cutlery and Japanese style blades and swords. **Technical:** Hand forging, stock removal, scrimshaw, carbon, stainless and Damascus steels. **Prices:** $65 to $5000. **Remarks:** Professional Goldsmith. **Mark:** Stacy E. Apelt - Norfolk VA.

APLIN, SPENCER
5151 County Rd. 469, Brazoria, TX 77422, Phone: 979-964-4448, spenceraplin@aol.com; Web: www.stacustomknives.com
Specialties: Custom skinners, fillets, bowies and kitchen knives. **Technical:** Stainless steel powder metals, stainless damascus. Handles include stabilized woods, various ivory and Micarta. Guard and butt-cap materials are brass, copper, nickel silver and Mokume. **Prices:** $250 and up. **Remarks:** First knife sold in 1989. Knives made to order only, nothing is pre-made. All blades are hand drawn, then cut from sheet stock. No two are exactly the same. **Mark:** Signature and date completed.

APPLEBY, ROBERT
746 Municipal Rd, Shickshinny, PA 18655, Phone: 570-864-0879, applebyknives@yahoo.com; Web: www.applebyknives.com
Specialties: Working using straight knives and folders of his own and popular and historical designs. **Patterns:** Variety of straight knives and folders. **Technical:** Hand forged or grinds O1, 1084, 5160, 440C, ATS-34, commercial Damascus, makes own sheaths. **Prices:** Starting at $75. **Remarks:** Part-time maker, first knife sold in 1995. **Mark:** APPLEBY over SHICKSHINNY, PA.

APPLETON, RON
315 Glenn St, Bluff Dale, TX 76433, Phone: 254-707-2922; cell: 254-396-9328, ronappleton@hotmail.com; Web: www.appletonknives.com
Specialties: One-of-a-kind folding knives. **Patterns:** Unique folding multi-locks and high-tech patterns. **Technical:** All parts machined, D2, S7, 416, 440C, 6A14V et.al. **Prices:** Start at $27,000 U.S.. **Remarks:** Full-time maker; first knife sold in 1996. **Mark:** Initials in anvil or initials in arrowhead. Usually only shows at the Art Knife Invitational every 2 years in San Diego, CA.

ARBUCKLE, JAMES M
114 Jonathan Jct, Yorktown, VA 23693, Phone: 757-867-9578, a_r_buckle@hotmail.com
Specialties: One-of-a-kind of his design; working knives. **Patterns:** Mostly chef's knives and hunters. **Technical:** Forged and stock removal blades using exotic hardwoods, natural materials, Micarta and stabilized woods. Forge 5160 and 1084; stock removal D2, ATS-34, 440C and 154CM. Makes own pattern welded steel. **Prices:** $195 to $700. **Remarks:** Forge, grind, heat-treat, finish and embellish all knives himself. Does own leatherwork. Part-time maker. ABS Journeyman smith 2007; ASM member. **Mark:** J. Arbuckle or J. ARBUCKLE MAKER.

ARCHER, RAY AND TERRI
4207 South 28 St., Omaha, NE 68107, Phone: 402-505-3084, archerrt@cox.net
Specialties: Basic high-finish working knives. **Patterns:** Hunters, skinners camp knives. **Technical:** Flat grinds various steels like 440C, ATS-34 and CPM-S30V. **Prices:** $75 to $500. **Remarks:** Makes own sheaths; first knife sold 1994. **Mark:** Last name over knives.

ARDWIN, COREY
2117 Cedar Dr., Bryant, AR 72019, Phone: 501-413-1184, ardwinca@gmail.com

ARM-KO KNIVES
PO Box 76280, Marble Ray , KZN, SOUTH AFRICA 4035, Phone: 27 31 5771451, arm-koknives.co.za; Web: www.arm-koknives.co.za
Specialties: They will make what your fastidious taste desires. Be it cool collector or tenacious tactical with handles of mother-of-pearl, fossil & local ivories. Exotic dye/stabilized burls, giraffe bone, horns, carbon fiber, g10, and titanium etc. **Technical:** Via stock removal, grinding Damasteel, carbon & mosaic. Damascus, ATS-34, N690, 440A, 440B, 12C27, RWL34 and high carbon EN 8, 5160 all heat treated in house. **Prices:** From $200 and up. **Remarks:** Father a part-time maker for well over 10 years and member of Knifemakers Guild in SA. Son full-time maker over 3 years. **Mark:** Logo of initials A R M and H A R M "Edged Tools."

ARMOUR, DAVE
61 Sugar Creek Hills, Auburn, IL 62615, Phone: 217-741-0246, dave@armourcutlery.com; Web: www.armourcutlery.com
Specialties: Hunters, utilities and occasional camp and bowie knives. **Technical:** Forges blades from 1084 and 80CrV2, with occasional san mai and damascus steels. **Prices:** $100 to $160 for most knives, up to $250 for dressier pieces. **Remarks:** Part-time maker; knives described as "deliberately casual" with a focus on working knives, performance, individuality and affordability. Field-grade knives usually using copper, stainless or bronze with horn (deer, elk or water buffalo), stabilized wood, Micarta or G-10 handles. Dressier knives often use wrought iron or Mokume with stag or oosic. **Mark:** Armour.

ARMS, ERIC
11153 7 Mile Road, Tustin, MI 49688, Phone: 231-829-3726, ericarms@netonecom.net
Specialties: Working hunters, high performance straight knives. **Patterns:** Variety of hunters, scagel style, Ed Fowler design and drop point. **Technical:** Forge 52100, 5160, 1084 hand grind, heat treat, natural handle, stag horn, elk, big horn, flat grind, convex, all leather sheath work. **Prices:** Starting at $150 **Remarks:** Part-time maker **Mark:** Eric Arms

ARNOLD, JOE
47 Patience Cres, London, ON, CANADA N6E 2K7, Phone: 519-686-2623, arnoldknivesandforge@bell.net

Specialties: Traditional working and using straight knives of his design and to customer specs. **Patterns:** Fighters, hunters and Bowies. **Technical:** Grinds 440C, ATS-34, 5160, and Forges 1084-1085 **Prices:** $75 to $500; some to $2500. **Remarks:** Full-time maker; first knife sold in 1988. **Mark:** Last name, country.

ARROWOOD, DALE
556 Lassetter Rd, Sharpsburg, GA 30277, Phone: 404-253-9672
Specialties: Fancy and traditional straight knives of his design and to customer specs. **Patterns:** Bowies, fighters and hunters. **Technical:** Grinds ATS-34 and 440C; forges high-carbon steel. Engraves and scrimshaws. **Prices:** $125 to $200; some to $245. **Remarks:** Part-time maker; first knife sold in 1989. **Mark:** Anvil with an arrow through it; Old English "Arrowood Knives."

ASHBY, DOUGLAS
10123 Deermont Trail, Dallas, TX 75243, Phone: 214-929-7531, doug@ashbycustomknives.com Web: ashbycustomknives.com
Specialties: Traditional and fancy straight knives and folders of his design or to customer specs. **Patterns:** Skinners, hunters, utility/camp knives, locking liner folders. **Technical:** Grinds ATS-34, commercial Damascus, and other steels on request. **Prices:** $125 to $1000. **Remarks:** Part-time maker; first knife sold in 1990. **Mark:** Name, city.

ASHWORTH, BOYD
1510 Bullard Place, Powder Springs, GA 30127, Phone: 404-583-5652, boydashworthknives@comcast.net; Web: www.boydashworthknives.com
Specialties: Gentlemen's and figurative folders. **Patterns:** Fighters, hunters and gents. **Technical:** Forges own Damascus; offers filework; uses exotic handle materials. **Prices:** $500 to $5,000. **Remarks:** Part-time maker; first knife sold in 1993. **Mark:** Last name.

ATHEY, STEVE
3153 Danube Way, Riverside, CA 92503, Phone: 951-850-8612, stevelonnie@yahoo.com
Specialties: Stock removal. **Patterns:** Hunters & Bowies. **Prices:** $100 to $500. **Remarks:** Part-time maker. **Mark:** Last name with number on blade.

ATKINSON, DICK
General Delivery, Wausau, FL 32463, Phone: 850-638-8524
Specialties: Working straight knives and folders of his design; some fancy. **Patterns:** Hunters, fighters, boots; locking folders in interframes. **Technical:** Grinds A2, 440C and 154CM. Likes filework. **Prices:** $85 to $300; some exceptional knives. **Remarks:** Full-time maker; first knife sold in 1977. **Mark:** Name, city, state.

AYARRAGARAY, CRISTIAN L.
Buenos Aires 250, Parana, Entre Rios, ARGENTINA 3100, Phone: 043-231753
Specialties: Traditional working straight knives of his design. **Patterns:** Fishing and hunting knives. **Technical:** Grinds and forges carbon steel. Uses native Argentine woods and deer antler. **Prices:** $150 to $250; some to $400. **Remarks:** Full-time maker; first knife sold in 1980. **Mark:** Last name, signature.

AYLOR, ERIN LUTZER
10519 Highland School Rd., Myersville, MD 21773, Phone: 240-818-2959, hawkwoodfarm@gmail.com; Web: www.hawkwoodmountainfarm.com
Specialties: Custom knives with an Old World feel using mostly pattern-welded (damascus) steel in ladder, twist and random patterns made from 1084, 1075, 15N20 and 1095 with a core of 5100 or 1095. **Patterns:** Many styles of knives, including hunters, fighters, bowies, Japanese and standard kitchen cutlery, folding knives and woodworking chisels. **Technical:** All blades are coal forged. **Prices:** $300 to $3,500. **Remarks:** Full-time artisan working mostly in metal, wood and silver. Studied at The Appalachian Center for Crafts in Cookeville, Tennessee, where he made his first chisel and knife in 1992. **Mark:** Last name, "AYLOR," with earlier work stamped "ELA."

B

BAARTMAN, GEORGE
PO Box 1116, Bela-Bela, LP, SOUTH AFRICA 0480, Phone: 27 14 736 4036, Fax: 086 636 3408, thabathipa@gmail.com
Specialties: Fancy and working LinerLock® folders of own design and to customers specs. Specialize in pattern filework on liners. **Patterns:** LinerLock® folders. **Technical:** Grinds 12C27, ATS-34, and Damascus, prefer working with stainless damasteel. Hollow grinds to hand-rubbed and polished satin finish. Enjoys working with mammoth, warthog tusk and pearls. **Prices:** Folders from $380 to $1000. **Remarks:** Part-time maker. Member of the Knifemakers Guild of South Africa since 1993. **Mark:** BAARTMAN.

BACHE-WIIG, TOM
N-5966, Eivindvik, NORWAY, Phone: 475-778-4290, Fax: 475-778-1099, tom.bache-wiig@enivest.net; Web: tombachewiig.com
Specialties: High-art and working knives of his design. **Patterns:** Hunters, utility knives, hatchets, axes and art knives. **Technical:** Grinds Uddeholm Elmax, powder metallurgy tool stainless steel. Handles made of rear burls of Nordic woods stabilized with vacuum/high-pressure technique. **Prices:** $430 to $900; some to $2300. **Remarks:** Part-time maker; first knife sold 1988. **Mark:** Etched name and eagle head.

BAGLEY, R. KEITH
OLD PINE FORGE, 4415 Hope Acres Dr, White Plains, MD 20695, Phone: 301-932-0990, keithbagley14@verizon.net; Web: www.oldpineforge.com
Specialties: Folders. **Technical:** Use ATS-34, 5160, 01, 1085 and 1095. **Patterns:** Ladder-wave lightning bolt. **Prices:** $275 to $750. **Remarks:** Farrier for 37 years, blacksmith for 37 years, knifemaker for 25 years. **Mark:** KB inside horseshoe and anvil.

BAILEY, I.R.
Lamorna Cottage, Common End, Colkirk, ENGLAND NR 21 7JD, Phone: 01-328-856-

183, admin@grommitbaileyknives.com; Web: www.grommitbaileyknives.com
Specialties: Hunters, utilities, Bowies, camp knives, fighters. Mainly influenced by Moran, Loveless and Lile. **Technical:** Primarily stock removal using flat ground 1095, 1075, and 80CrV2. Occasionally forges including own basic Damascus. Uses both native and exotic hardwoods, stag, Leather, Micarta and other synthetic handle materials, with brass or 301 stainless fittings. Does some filework and leather tooling. Does own heat treating. **Remarks:** Part-time maker since 2005. All knives and sheaths are sole authorship. **Mark:** Last name stamped.

BAILEY, JOSEPH D.
3213 Jonesboro Dr, Nashville, TN 37214, Phone: 615-889-3172, jbknfemkr@aol.com
Specialties: Working and using straight knives; collector pieces. **Patterns:** Bowies, hunters, tactical, folders. **Technical:** 440C, ATS-34, Damascus and wire Damascus. Offers scrimshaw. **Prices:** $85 to $1200. **Remarks:** Part-time maker; first knife sold in 1988. **Mark:** Joseph D Bailey Nashville Tennessee.

BAIR, MARK
415 E. 700N, Firth, ID 83236, Phone: 208-681-7534, markbair@gmail.com
Specialties: Fixed blades. Hunters, bowies, kitchen, utility, custom orders. **Technical:** High-end damascus, San Mai steel, stainless steel and 52100. Also mammoth ivory and other exotic handles, custom hand filework, and works with high-end custom engravers. **Prices:** $300 to $7,500. **Remarks:** Part-time maker; first knife made in 1988. **Mark:** MB Custom Knives.

BAKER, HERB
14104 NC 87 N, Eden, NC 27288, Phone: 336-627-0338

BAKER, RAY
PO Box 303, Sapulpa, OK 74067, Phone: 918-224-8013
Specialties: High-tech working straight knives. **Patterns:** Hunters, fighters, Bowies, skinners and boots of his design and to customer specs. **Technical:** Grinds 440C, 1095 spring steel or customer request; heat-treats. Custom-made scabbards for any knife. **Prices:** $125 to $500; some to $1000. **Remarks:** Full-time maker; first knife sold in 1981. **Mark:** First initial, last name.

BAKER, TONY
707 Lake Highlands Dr, Allen, TX 75002, Phone: 214-543-1001, tonybakerknives@yahoo.com
Specialties: Hunting knives, integral made **Technical:** 154cm, S30V, and S90V**Prices:** Starting at $500. **Prices:** $200-$1200 **Remarks:** First knife made in 2001

BAKER, WILD BILL
Box 361, Boiceville, NY 12412, Phone: 914-657-8646
Specialties: Primitive knives, buckskinners. **Patterns:** Skinners, camp knives and Bowies. **Technical:** Works with L6, files and rasps. **Prices:** $100 to $350. **Remarks:** Part-time maker; first knife sold in 1989. **Mark:** Wild Bill Baker, Oak Leaf Forge, or both.

BALL, BUTCH
2161 Reedsville Rd., Floyd, VA 24091, Phone: 540-392-3485, ballknives@yahoo.com
Specialties: Fancy and Tactical Folders and Automatics. **Patterns:** Fixed and folders. **Technical:** Use various Damascus and ATS34, 154cm. **Prices:** $300 - $1500. **Remarks:** Part-time maker. Sold first knife in 1990. **Mark:** Ball or BCK with crossed knives.

BALL, KEN
127 Sundown Manor, Mooresville, IN 46158, Phone: 317-834-4803
Specialties: Classic working/using straight knives of his design and to customer specs. **Patterns:** Hunters and utility/camp knives. **Technical:** Flat-grinds ATS-34. Offers filework. **Prices:** $150 to $400. **Remarks:** Part-time maker; first knife sold in 1994. Doing business as Ball Custom Knives. **Mark:** Last name.

BALLESTRA, SANTINO
via D. Tempesta 11/17, Ventimiglia, ITALY 18039, Phone: 0184-215228, ladasin@libero.it
Specialties: Using and collecting straight knives. **Patterns:** Hunting, fighting, skinners, Bowies, medieval daggers and knives. **Technical:** Forges ATS-34, D2, O2, 1060 and his own Damascus. Uses ivory and silver. **Prices:** $500 to $2000; some higher. **Remarks:** Full-time maker; first knife sold in 1979. **Mark:** First initial, last name.

BALLEW, DALE
PO Box 1277, Bowling Green, VA 22427, Phone: 804-633-5701
Specialties: Miniatures only to customer specs. **Patterns:** Bowies, daggers and fighters. **Technical:** Files 440C stainless; uses ivory, abalone, exotic woods and some precious stones. **Prices:** $100 to $800. **Remarks:** Part-time maker; first knife sold in 1988. **Mark:** Initials and last name.

BANAITIS, ROMAS
84 Winthrop St., Medway, MA 02053, Phone: 774-248-5851, rbanaitis@verizon.net
Specialties: Designing art and fantasy knives. **Patterns:** Folders, daggers and fixed blades. **Technical:** Hand-carved blades, handles and fittings in stainless steel, sterling silver and titanium. **Prices:** Moderate to upscale. **Remarks:** First knife sold in 1996. **Mark:** Romas Banaitis.

BANKS, DAVID L.
99 Blackfoot Ave, Riverton, WY 82501, Phone: 307-856-3154/Cell: 307-851-5599, blackfootforge@bresnan.net
Specialties: Heavy-duty working straight knives. **Patterns:** Hunters, Bowies and camp knives. **Technical:** Forges Damascus 1084-15N20, L6-W1 pure nickel, 5160, 52100 and his own Damascus; differential heat treat and tempers. Handles made of horn, antlers and exotic wood. Hand-stitched harness leather sheaths. **Prices:** $300 to $4,000. **Remarks:** Part-time maker. **Mark:** Banks, Blackfoot Forge, Dave Banks.

BAREFOOT, JOE W.
1654 Honey Hill, Wilmington, NC 28442, Phone: 910-641-1143
  Specialties: Working straight knives of his design. **Patterns:** Hunters, fighters and boots; tantos and survival knives. **Technical:** Grinds D2, 440C and ATS-34. Mirror finishes. Uses ivory and stag on customer request only. **Prices:** $50 to $160; some to $500. **Remarks:** Part-time maker; first knife sold in 1980. **Mark:** Bare footprint.

BARKER, JOHN
5725 Boulder Bluff Dr., Cumming, GA 30040, Phone: 678-357-8586, barkerknives@bellsouth.net Web: www.barkerknives.com
  Specialties: Tactical fixed blades and folders. **Technical:** Stock removal method and CPM and Carpenter powdered technology steels. **Prices:** $150 and up. **Remarks:** First knife made 2006. **Mark:** Snarling dog with "Barker" over the top of its head and "Knives" below.

BARKER, REGGIE
40 Columbia Rd. 254, Taylor, AR 71861, Phone: 318-539-2958, rbarker014@gmail.com; Web: www.reggiebarkerknives.com
  Specialties: Pocketknives, fighters, camp knives and bowies. **Technical:** Forges carbon steel, stainless steel for pocketknives and uses own damascus. **Prices:** $300 and up. **Remarks:** Full-time maker. Three-time World Cutting Champion with over 15 wins. Winner of Best Value of Show 2001; Arkansas Knife Show and Journeyman Smith. Border Guard Forge. **Mark:** Barker JS.

BARKER, ROBERT G.
2311 Branch Rd, Bishop, GA 30621, Phone: 706-769-7827
  Specialties: Traditional working/using straight knives of his design. **Patterns:** Bowies, hunters and utility knives, ABS Journeyman Smith. **Technical:** Hand forged carbon and Damascus. Forges to shape high-carbon 5160, cable and chain. Differentially heat-treats. **Prices:** $200 to $500; some to $1000. **Remarks:** Spare-time maker; first knife sold in 1987. **Mark:** BARKER/J.S.

BARKER, STUART
51 Thorpe Dr., Wigston, Leicester, ENGLAND LE18 1LE, Phone: +447887585411, sc_barker@hotmail.com Web: www.barkerknives.co.uk
  Specialties: Fixed blade working knives of his design. **Patterns:** Kitchen, hunter, utility/camp knives. **Technical:** Grinds O1, Rw134 & Damasteel, hand rubbed or shot blast finishes. **Prices:** $150 - $1,000. **Remarks:** Part-time maker; first knife sold 2006. **Mark:** Last initial or last name.

BARKES, TERRY
14844 N. Bluff Rd., Edinburgh, IN 46124, Phone: 812-526-6390, terrybarkes@outlook.comt; Web:http:// my.hsonline.net/wizard/TerryBarkesKnives.htm
  Specialties: Traditional working straight knives of his designs. **Patterns:** Drop point hunters, boot knives, skinning, fighter, utility, all purpose, camp, and grill knives. **Technical:** Grinds 1095 - 1084 - 52100 - 01, Hollow grinds and flat grinds. Hand rubbed finish from 400 to 2000 grit or High polish buff. Hard edge and soft back, heat treat by maker. Likes File work, natural handle material, bone, stag, water buffalo horn, wildbeast bone, ironwood. **Prices:** $200 and up **Remarks:** Full-time maker, first knifge sold in 2005. Doing business as Barkes Knife Shop. **Marks:** Barkes - USA, Barkes Double Arrow - USA

BARLOW, JANA POIRIER
3820 Borland Cir, Anchorage, AK 99517, Phone: 907-243-4581

BARNES, AUBREY G.
11341 Rock Hill Rd, Hagerstown, MD 21740, Phone: 301-223-4587, a.barnes@myactv.net
  Specialties: Classic Moran style reproductions and using knives of his own design. **Patterns:** Bowies, hunters, daggers and utility/camping knives. **Technical:** Forges 5160, 1085, L6 and Damascus, Silver wire inlays. **Prices:** $500 to $5000. **Remarks:** Full-time maker; first knife sold in 1992. Doing business as Falling Waters Forge. **Mark:** First and middle initials, last name, M.S.

BARNES, GARY L.
112 Brandy Ln., Defuniak Springs, FL 32435, Phone: 410-635-6243, Fax: 410-635-6243, glbarnes@glbarnes.com; Web: www.glbarnes.com
  Specialties: Ornate button lock Damascus folders. **Patterns:** Barnes original. **Technical:** Forges own Damascus. **Prices:** Average $2500. **Remarks:** ABS Master Smith since 1983. **Mark:** Hand engraved logo of letter B pierced by dagger.

BARNES, GREGORY
266 W Calaveras St, Altadena, CA 91001, Phone: 626-398-0053, snake@annex.com

BARNES, JACK
PO Box 1315, Whitefish, MT 59937-1315, Phone: 406-862-6078

BARNES, MARLEN R.
904 Crestview Dr S, Atlanta, TX 75551-1854, Phone: 903-796-3668, MRBlives@worldnet.att.net
  Specialties: Hammer forges random and mosaic Damascus. **Patterns:** Hatchets, straight and folding knives. **Technical:** Hammer forges carbon steel using 5160, 1084 and 52100 with 15N20 and 203E nickel. **Prices:** $150 and up. **Remarks:** Part-time maker; first knife sold 1999. **Mark:** Script M.R.B., other side J.S.

BARNES, ROGER
BC Cutlery Co., 314 Rosemarie Pl., Bay Point, CA 94565, Phone: 925-483-6982 or 925-231-4367, bccutlerycompany@gmail.com; Facebook.com/bc cutlery co.
  Mark: BC usa.

BARNES, ROGER
BC Cutlery Co., 314 Rosemarie Pl., Bay Point, CA 94565, bccutlerycompany@gmail.com

Specialties: Various styles of fixed-blade knives with an emphasis on quality in performance and simple aesthetics. **Patterns:** Karambits, Bob Loveless-inspired drop-point hunters and choppers. **Technical:** Uses 52100, 1095, 5160, AEB-L and CPM-3V blade steels, and Micartas, carbon fiber and G-10 handle scales, all USA-made materials. **Prices:** $75 to $500. **Remarks:** Wait time two weeks to one month.

BARNES, WENDELL
PO Box 272, Clinton, MT 59825, Phone: 406-825-0908
  Specialties: Working straight knives. **Patterns:** Hunters, folders, neck knives. **Technical:** Grinds 440C, ATS-34, D2 and Damascus. **Prices:** Start at $75. **Remarks:** Spare-time maker; first knife sold in 1996. **Mark:** First initial, split heart, last name.

BARNES JR., CECIL C.
141 Barnes Dr, Center Ridge, AR 72027, Phone: 501-893-2267

BARNETT, BRUCE
PO Box 447, Mundaring, WA, AUSTRALIA 6073, Phone: 61-4-19243855, bruce@barnettcustomknives.com; web: www.barnettcustomknives.com
  Specialties: Most types of fixed blades, folders, carving sets. **Patterns:** Hunters, Bowies, Camp Knives, Fighters, Lockback and Slipjoint Folders. **Prices:** $200 up **Remarks:** Part time maker. Member Australian Knifemakers Guild and ABS journeyman smith. **Mark:** Barnett + J.S.

BARNETT, VAN
BARNETT INT'L INC, 1135 Terminal Way Ste #209, Reno, NV 89502, Phone: 304-727-5512; 775-513-6969; 775-686-9084, ImATimeMachine@gmail.com & illusionknives@gmail.com; Web: www.VanBarnett.com
  Specialties: Collector grade one-of-a-kind / embellished high art daggers and art folders. **Patterns:** Art daggers and folders. **Technical:** Forges and grinds own Damascus. **Prices:** Upscale. **Remarks:** Designs and makes one-of-a-kind highly embellished art knives using high karat gold, diamonds and other gemstones, pearls, stone and fossil ivories, carved steel guards and blades, all knives are carved and or engraved, does own engraving, carving and other embellishments, sole authorship; full-time maker since 1981. Does one high art collaboration a year with Dellana. Member of ABS. Member Art Knife Invitational Group (AKI) **Mark:** VBARNETT

BARNHILL, WESS
5846 Meadows Run, Spotsylvania, VA 22551, Phone: 540-582-8758, wess.barnhill@gmail.com; Web: www.wessbarnhillknives.com
  Specialties: High-art, collectible and functional straight knives. **Patterns:** Bowies, hunters, camp knives and others. **Technical:** Hand forges high-carbon and damascus steel. Applied art in the forms of engraving, carving and filework. Offers functional leather sheaths in exotic leather. **Prices:** Start at $250. **Remarks:** Sole authorship on all knives, ABS journeyman smith. **Mark:** Last name followed by J.S..

BARR, JUDSON C.
1905 Pickwick Circle, Irving, TX 75060, Phone: 214-724-0564, judsonbarrknives@yahoo.com
  Specialties: Bowies. **Patterns:** Sheffield and Early American. **Technical:** Forged carbon steel and Damascus. Also stock removal. **Remarks:** Journeyman member of ABS. **Mark:** Barr.

BARRETT, RICK L. (TOSHI HISA)
18943 CR 18, Goshen, IN 46528, Phone: 574-533-4297, barrettrick@hotmail.com
  Specialties: Japanese-style blades from sushi knives to katana and fantasy pieces. **Patterns:** Swords, axes, spears/lances, hunter and utility knives. **Technical:** Forges and grinds Damascus and carbon steels, occasionally uses stainless. **Prices:** $250 to $4000+. **Remarks:** Full-time bladesmith, jeweler. **Mark:** Japanese mei on Japanese pieces and stylized initials.

BARRON, BRIAN
123 12th Ave, San Mateo, CA 94402, Phone: 650-341-2683
  Specialties: Traditional straight knives. **Patterns:** Daggers, hunters and swords. **Technical:** Grinds 440C, ATS-34 and 1095. Sculpts bolsters using an S-curve. **Prices:** $130 to $270; some to $1500. **Remarks:** Part-time maker; first knife sold in 1993. **Mark:** Diamond Drag "Barron."

BARRY, SCOTT
Box 354, Laramie, WY 82073, Phone: 307-399-2646, scottyb@uwyo.edu
  Specialties: Currently producing mostly folders, also make fixed blade hunters & fillet knives. **Technical:** Steels used are ATS 34, 154CM, CPM 154, D2, CPM S30V, Damasteel and Devin Thomas stainless damascus. **Prices:** Range from $300 $1000. **Remarks:** Part-time maker. First knife sold in 1972. **Mark:** DSBarry, etched on blade.

BARRY III, JAMES J.
115 Flagler Promenade No., West Palm Beach, FL 33405, Phone: 561-832-4197
  Specialties: High-art working straight knives of his design also high art tomahawks. **Patterns:** Hunters, daggers and fishing knives. **Technical:** Grinds 440C only. Prefers exotic materials for handles. Most knives embellished with filework, carving and scrimshaw. Many pieces designed to stand unassisted. **Prices:** $500 to $10,000. **Remarks:** Part-time maker; first knife sold in 1975. Guild member (Knifemakers) since 1991. **Mark:** Branded initials as a J and B together.

BARTH, J.D.
101 4th St, PO Box 186, Alberton, MT 59820, Phone: 406-722-4557, mtdeerhunter@blackfoot.net; Web: www.jdbarthcustomknives.com
  Specialties: Working and fancy straight knives of his design. LinerLock® folders, stainless and Damascus, fully file worked, nitre bluing. **Technical:** Grinds ATS-34, 440-C, stainless and carbon Damascus. Uses variety of natural handle materials and Micarta.

custom knifemakers

Likes dovetailed bolsters. Filework on most knives, full and tapered tangs. Makes custom fit sheaths for each knife. **Mark:** Name over maker, city and state.

BARTLETT, MARK

102 Finn Cir., Lawrenceburg, TN 38464, Phone: 931-477-5444, moosetrax@live.com
Specialties: Mostly hunters and small bowies, but moving into larger bowies. **Technical:** Forges for the most part, with some stock removal, primarily using 1095, 1084 and 52100 blade steels. Has started damascus recently. Uses hardwoods and Micarta mostly for handles. **Prices:** $200 to $500, with some recent orders booked at $900-$1,000. **Remarks:** Part-time maker; first knife made in September 2013. **Mark:** Last name with a dagger through the middle "T."

BARTLOW, JOHN

14 Red Fox Dr., Sheridan, WY 82801, Phone: 307-673-4941, 2jbartlow@gmail.com
Specialties: Skinner/caper sets, classic working patterns, and known for bird-and-trout classics. **Technical:** ATS-34, CPM-154, damascus available on all LinerLocks. **Prices:** $400 to $2,500. **Remarks:** Full-time maker, Guild member from 1988. **Mark:** Bartlow Sheridan, Wyo.

BASKETT, BARBARA

427 Sutzer Ck Rd, Eastview, KY 42732, Phone: 270-862-5019, bgbaskett@yahoo.com; Web: www.baskettknives.com
Specialties: Hunters and LinerLocks. **Technical:** 440-C, CPM 154, S30V. **Prices:** $250 and up. **Mark:** B. Baskett.

BASKETT, LEE GENE

427 Sutzer Ck. Rd., Eastview, KY 42732, Phone: 270-862-5019, Fax: Cell: 270-766-8724, baskettknives@hotmail.com Web: www.baskettknives.com
Specialties: Fancy working knives and fancy art pieces, often set up in fancy desk stands. **Patterns:** Fighters, Bowies, and Surival Knives; lockback folders and liner locks along with traditional styles. Cutting competition knives. **Technical:** Grinds 01, 440-c, S30V, power CPM154, CPM 4, D2, buys Damascus. Filework provided on most knives. **Prices:** $250 and up. **Remarks:** Part-time maker, first knife sold in 1980. **Mark:** Baskett

BASSETT, DAVID J.

P.O. Box 69-102, Glendene, Auckland, NEW ZEALAND 0645, Phone: 64 9 818 9083, Fax: 64 9 818 9013, david@customknifemaking.co.nz; Web:www.customknifemaking.co.nz
Specialties: Working/using knives. **Patterns:** Hunters, fighters, boot, skinners, tanto. **Technical:** Grinds 440C, 12C27, D2 and some Damascus via stock removal method. **Prices:** $150 to $500. **Remarks:** Part-time maker, first knife sold in 2006. Also carries range of natural and synthetic handle material, pin stock etc. for sale. **Mark:** Name over country in semi-circular design.

BATSON, JAMES

1316 McClung Ave., Huntsville, AL 35801, Phone: 256-971-6860, james.1.batson@gmail.com
Specialties: Forged Damascus blades and fittings in collectible period pieces. **Patterns:** Integral art knives, Bowies, folders, American-styled blades and miniatures. **Technical:** Forges carbon steel and his Damascus. **Prices:** $150 to $1800; some to $4500. **Remarks:** Semi retired full-time maker; first knife sold in 1978. **Mark:** Name, bladesmith with horse's head.

BATSON, RICHARD G.

6591 Waterford Rd, Rixeyville, VA 22737, Phone: 540-937-2318, mbatson6591@comcast.net
Specialties: Military, utility and fighting knives in working and presentation grade. **Patterns:** Daggers, combat and utility knives. **Technical:** Grinds 01, 1095 and 440C. Etches and scrimshaws; offers polished, Parkerized finishes. **Prices:** From $400. **Remarks:** Very limited production to active-dute military and vets only. First knife sold in 1958. **Mark:** Bat in circle, hand-signed and serial numbered.

BATTS, KEITH

500 Manning Rd, Hooks, TX 75561, Phone: 903-277-8466, kbatts@cableone.net
Specialties: Working straight knives of his design or to customer specs. **Patterns:** Bowies, hunters, skinners, camp knives and others. **Technical:** Forges 5160 and his Damascus; offers filework. **Prices:** $245 to $895. **Remarks:** Part-time maker; first knife sold in 1988. **Mark:** Last name.

BAUCHOP, ROBERT

PO Box 330, Munster, KN, SOUTH AFRICA 4278, Phone: +27 39 3192449
Specialties: Fantasy knives; working and using knives of his design and to customer specs. **Patterns:** Hunters, swords, utility/camp knives, diver's knives and large swords. **Technical:** Grinds Sandvick 12C27, D2, 440C. Uses South African hardwoods red ivory, wild olive, African blackwood, etc. on handles. **Prices:** $200 to $800; some to $2000. **Remarks:** Full-time maker; first knife sold in 1986. Doing business as Bauchop Custom Knives and Swords. **Mark:** Viking helmet with Bauchop (bow and chopper) crest.

BAXTER, DALE

291 County Rd 547, Trinity, AL 35673, Phone: 256-355-3626, dale@baxterknives.com
Specialties: Bowies, fighters, and hunters. **Patterns:** No patterns: all unique true customs. **Technical:** Hand forge and hand finish. Steels: 1095 and L6 for carbon blades, 1095/L6 for Damascus. **Remarks:** Full-time bladesmith and sold first knife in 1998. **Mark:** Dale Baxter (script) and J.S. on reverse.

BEAM, JOHN R.

1310 Foothills Rd, Kalispell, MT 59901, Phone: 406-755-2593
Specialties: Classic, high-art and working straight knives of his design. **Patterns:** Bowies and hunters. **Technical:** Grinds 440C, Damascus and scrap. **Prices:** $175 to $600; some

to $3000. **Remarks:** Part-time maker; first knife sold in 1950. Doing business as Beam's Knives. **Mark:** Beam's Knives.

BEATTY, GORDON H.

121 Petty Rd, Seneca, SC 29672, Phone: 867-723-2966
Specialties: Working straight knives, some fancy. **Patterns:** Traditional patterns, mini-skinners and letter openers. **Technical:** Grinds ATS-34; makes knives one-at-a-time. **Prices:** $185 and up. **Remarks:** Part-time maker; first knife sold in 1982. **Mark:** Name.

BEATY, ROBERT B.

CUTLER, 1995 Big Flat Rd, Missoula, MT 59804, Phone: 406-549-1818
Specialties: Plain and fancy working knives and collector pieces; will accept custom orders. **Patterns:** Hunters, Bowies, utility, kitchen and camp knives; locking folders. **Technical:** Grinds D-2, ATS-34, Dendritie D-2, makes all tool steel Damascus, forges 1095, 5160, 52100. **Prices:** $150 to $600, some to $1100. **Remarks:** Full-time maker; first knife sold 1995. **Mark:** Stainless: First name, middle initial, last name, city and state. Carbon: Last name stamped on Ricasso.

BEAUCHAMP, GAETAN

125 de la Rivire, Stoneham, QC, CANADA G3C 0P6, Phone: 418-848-1914, Fax: 418-848-6859, knives@gbeauchamp.ca; Web: www.gbeauchamp.ca
Specialties: Working knives and folders of his design and to customer specs. **Patterns:** Hunters, fighters, fantasy knives. **Technical:** Grinds ATS-34, 440C, Damascus. Scrimshaws on ivory; specializes in buffalo horn and black backgrounds. Offers a variety of handle materials. **Prices:** Start at $250. **Remarks:** Full-time maker; first knife sold in 1992. **Mark:** Signature etched on blade.

BEAVER, DIRK

BEAVER CUSTOM BLADES, Ellijay, GA, Phone: 706-633-7884, dirk@beavercustomblades.com; Web: www.beavercustomblades.com
Specialties: Enjoys doing custom orders and working with his customers, making skinners, tactical fighters, neck knives and folders, anything a customer wants. **Technical:** Uses stock removal and forging methods of blade making, depending on style of knife, and works with high-carbon steel and damascus. **Remarks:** Full-time maker; first knife made in 2009.

BEERS, RAY

2501 Lakefront Dr, Lake Wales, FL 33898, Phone: 443-841-4143, rbknives@copper.net

BEETS, MARTY

390 N 5th Ave, Williams Lake, BC, CANADA V2G 2G4, Phone: 250-392-7199
Specialties: Working and collectable straight knives of his own design. **Patterns:** Hunter, skinners, Bowies and utility knives. **Technical:** Grinds various steels-does all his own work including heat treating. Uses a variety of handle material specializing in exotic hardwoods, antler and horn. **Prices:** $125 to $400. **Remarks:** Wife, Sandy does handmade/hand stitched sheaths. First knife sold in 1988. Business name Beets Handmade Knives.

BEGG, TODD M.

1341 N. McDowell Blvd., Ste. D, Petaluma, CA 94954, Phone: 707-242-1790, info@beggknives.com; Web: http://beggknives.net
Specialties: High-grade tactical folders and fixed blades. **Patterns:** Folders, integrals, fighters. **Technical:** Specializes in flipper folders using "IKBS" (Ikoma Korth Bearing System). **Prices:** $400 - $15,000. **Remarks:** Uses modern designs and materials.

BEHNKE, WILLIAM

8478 Dell Rd, Kingsley, MI 49649, Phone: 231-263-7447, bill@billbehnkeknives.com Web: www.billbehnkeknives.com
Specialties: Fabricates carbide file/grinding guides, LinerLock folders. **Patterns:** Traditional styling in moderate-sized straight and folding knives. **Technical:** Forges own damascus, prefers W-2. **Prices:** $150 to $2,000. **Remarks:** Full-time maker. **Mark:** "Behnke".

BEHRING, JAMES

Behring Made Knives, POB 17317, Missoula, MT 59808, Phone: 406-926-1193, behringmadeknives@gmail.com; Web: www.behringmade.com
Specialties: Custom handmade fixed blades for users and collectors alike. **Patterns:** Include, but are not limited to, hunters, skinners, bird & trout knives, fighters, kitchen cutlery, pocketknives, hatchets, etc. **Technical:** High-carbon steels (01, 5160, 1095), CPM S30V, D2 and 440C stainless steel. Copper, nickel silver and brass fittings. Stag, Micarta, wide variety of wood, various horn (buffalo, musk ox, kudu), fossil and artifact walrus, etc. Open to new mediums upon request. **Prices:** $250 to $1,500. **Mark:** "B" logo with crossed hammer and knife, J. Behring Jr. Montana.

BELL, DON

Box 98, Lincoln, MT 59639, Phone: 406-362-3208, dlb@linctel.net
Patterns: Folders, hunters and custom orders. **Technical:** Carbon steel 52100, 5160, 1095, 1084. Making own Damascus. Flat grinds. Natural handle material including fossil. ivory, pearl, & ironwork. **Remarks:** Full-time maker. First knife sold in 1999. **Mark:** Last name.

BELL, DONALD

2 Division St, Bedford, NS, CANADA B4A 1Y8, Phone: 902-835-2623, donbell@accesswave.ca; Web: www.bellknives.com
Specialties: Fancy knives: carved and pierced folders of his own design. **Patterns:** Locking folders, pendant knives, jewelry knives. **Technical:** Grinds Damascus, pierces and carves blades. **Prices:** $500 to $2000, some to $3000. **Remarks:** Spare-time maker; first knife sold in 1993. **Mark:** Bell symbol with first initial inside.

BELL, GABRIEL

88321 North Bank Lane, Coquille, OR 97423, Phone: 541-396-3605, gabriel@ dragonflyforge.com; Web: www.dragonflyforge.com & tomboyama.com
Specialties: Full line of combat quality Japanese swords. **Patterns:** Traditional tanto to katana. **Technical:** Handmade steel and welded cable. **Prices:** Swords from bare blades to complete high art $1500 to $28,000. **Remarks:** Studied with father Michael Bell. Instruction in sword crafts. Working in partnership with Michael Bell. **Mark:** Dragonfly in shield or kunitoshi.

BELL, MICHAEL

88321 N Bank Lane, Coquille, OR 97423, Phone: 541-396-3605, michael@ dragonflyforge.com; Web: www. Dragonflyforge.com & tomboyama.com
Specialties: Full line of combat quality Japanese swords. **Patterns:** Traditional tanto to katana. **Technical:** Handmade steel and welded cable. **Prices:** Swords from bare blades to complete high art $1500 to $28,000. **Remarks:** Studied with Japanese master Nakajima Muneyoshi. Instruction in sword crafts. Working in partnership with son, Gabriel. **Mark:** Dragonfly in shield or tombo kunimitsu.

BELL, TONY

PO Box 24, Woodland, AL 36280, Phone: 256-449-2655, tbell905@aol.com
Specialties: Hand forged period knives and tomahawks. Art knives and knives made for everyday use. **Technical:** Makes own Damascus. Forges 1095, 5160,1080,L6 steels. Does own heat treating. **Prices:** $75-$1200. **Remarks:** Full time maker. **Mark:** Bell symbol with initial T in the middle.

BENJAMIN JR., GEORGE

3001 Foxy Ln, Kissimmee, FL 34746, Phone: 407-846-7259
Specialties: Fighters in various styles to include Persian, Moro and military. **Patterns:** Daggers, skinners and one-of-a-kind grinds. **Technical:** Forges O1, D2, A2, 5160 and Damascus. Favors Pakkawood, Micarta, and mirror or Parkerized finishes. Makes unique para-military leather sheaths. **Prices:** $150 to $600; some to $1200. **Remarks:** Doing business as The Leather Box. **Mark:** Southern Pride Knives.

BENNETT, BRETT C

420 Adamstown Rd., Reinholds, PA 17569, Phone: 307-220-3919, brett@ bennettknives.com; Web: www.bennettknives.com
Specialties: Hand-rubbed satin finish on all blades. **Patterns:** Mostly fixed-blade patterns. **Technical:** ATS-34, D-2, 1084/15N20 damascus, 1084 forged. **Mark:** "B.C. Bennett" in script or "Bennett" stamped in script.

BENNETT, GLEN C

5821 S Stewart Blvd, Tucson, AZ 85706

BENNETT, PETER

PO Box 143, Engadine, NSW, AUSTRALIA 2233, Phone: 02-520-4975 (home), Fax: 02-528-8219 (work)
Specialties: Fancy and embellished working and using straight knives to customer specs and in standard patterns. **Patterns:** Fighters, hunters, bird/trout and fillet knives. **Technical:** Grinds 440C, ATS-34 and Damascus. Uses rare Australian desert timbers for handles. **Prices:** $90 to $500; some to $1500. **Remarks:** Full-time maker; first knife sold in 1985. **Mark:** First and middle initials, last name; country.

BENNICA, CHARLES

11 Chemin du Salet, Moules et Baucels, FRANCE 34190, Phone: +33 4 67 73 42 40, cbennica@bennica-knives.com; Web: www.bennica-knives.com
Specialties: Fixed blades and folding knives; the latter with slick closing mechanisms with push buttons to unlock blades. Unique handle shapes, signature to the maker. **Technical:** 416 stainless steel frames for folders and ATS-34 blades. Also specializes in Damascus.

BENSINGER, J. W.

583 Jug Brook Rd., Marshfield, VT 05658, Phone: 802-917-1789, jwbensinger@ gmail.com Web: www.vermontbladesmith.com
Specialties: Working hunters, bowies for work and defense, and Finnish patterns. Occasional folders. **Technical:** High performance handforged knives in 5160, 52100, 1080, and in-house damascus. **Prices:** Range from $130 for simple bushcraft knives to $500 for larger knives. Damascus prices on request. **Remarks:** First knife made in 1980 or so. Full-time maker. Customer designs welcome. **Mark:** "JWB" and year in cursive.

BENSON, DON

2505 Jackson St #112, Escalon, CA 95320, Phone: 209-838-7921
Specialties: Working straight knives of his design. **Patterns:** Axes, Bowies, tantos and hunters. **Technical:** Grinds 440C. **Prices:** $100 to $150; some to $400. **Remarks:** Spare-time maker; first knife sold in 1980. **Mark:** Name.

BENTLEY, C L

2405 Hilltop Dr, Albany, GA 31707, Phone: 912-432-6656

BER, DAVE

656 Miller Rd, San Juan Island, WA 98250, Phone: 206-378-7230
Specialties: Working straight and folding knives for the sportsman; welcomes customer designs. **Patterns:** Hunters, skinners, Bowies, kitchen and fishing knives. **Technical:** Forges and grinds saw blade steel, wire Damascus, O1, L6, 5160 and 440C. **Prices:** $100 to $300; some to $500. **Remarks:** Full-time maker; first knife sold in 1985. **Mark:** Last name.

BERG, LEE

PO Box 458, Roseburg, OR 97470, leeandlanny@gmail.com
Specialties: One-of-a-kind and investment-quality straight knives of his own design, incorporating traditional, period, Near East and Asian influence. **Patterns:** Daggers, fighters, hunters, bowies, short swords, full size and miniature. **Technical:** Stock removal with file, damascus, meteorite, O1, D2 and ATS-34. **Prices:** $200 and up. **Remarks:** Part-time maker; first knife sold in 1972. **Mark:** Full name.

BERG, LOTHAR

37 Hillcrest Ln, Kitchener ON, CANADA NZK 1S9, Phone: 519-745-3260; 519-745-3260

BERGER, MAX A.

5716 John Richard Ct, Carmichael, CA 95608, Phone: 916-972-9229, bergerknives@ aol.com
Specialties: Fantasy and working/using straight knives of his design. **Patterns:** Fighters, hunters and utility/camp knives. **Technical:** Grinds ATS-34 and 440C. Offers fileworks and combinations of mirror polish and satin finish blades. **Prices:** $200 to $600; some to $2500. **Remarks:** Part-time maker; first knife sold in 1992. **Mark:** Last name.

BERGH, ROGER

Dalkarlsa 291, Bygdea, SWEDEN 91598, Phone: 469-343-0061, knivroger@hotmail. com; Web: www.rogerbergh.com
Specialties: Collectible all-purpose straight-blade knives. Damascus steel blades, carving and artistic design knives are heavily influenced by nature and have an organic hand crafted feel.

BERGLIN, BRUCE

17441 Lake Terrace Place, Mount Vernon, WA 98274, Phone: 360-333-1217, bruce@ berglins.com
Specialties: Working fixed blades and folders of his own design. **Patterns:** Hunters, boots, bowies, utility, liner locks and slip joints some with vintage finish. **Technical:** Forges carbon steel, grinds carbon steel. Prefers natural handle material. **Prices:** Start at $300. **Remarks:** Part-time maker since 1998. **Mark:** (2 marks) 1. Last name; or 2. First initial, second initial & last name, surrounded with an oval.

BERTOLAMI, JUAN CARLOS

Av San Juan 575, Neuquen, ARGENTINA 8300, fliabertolami@infovia.com.ar
Specialties: Hunting and country labor knives. All of them unique high quality pieces and supplies collectors too. **Technical:** Austrian stainless steel and elephant, hippopotamus and orca ivory, as well as ebony and other fine woods for the handles.

BERTUZZI, ETTORE

Via Partigiani 3, Seriate, Bergamo, ITALY 24068, Phone: 035-294262, Fax: 035-294262
Specialties: Classic straight knives and folders of his design, to customer specs and in standard patterns. **Patterns:** Bowies, hunters and locking folders. **Technical:** Grinds ATS-34, D3, D2 and various Damascus. **Prices:** $300 to $500. **Remarks:** Part-time maker; first knife sold in 1993. **Mark:** Name etched on ricasso.

BESEDICK, FRANK E

1257 Country Club Road, Monongahela, PA 15063-1057, Phone: 724-292-8016, bez32@comcast.net
Specialties: Traditional working and using straight knives of his design. **Patterns:** Hunters, utility/camp knives and miniatures; buckskinner blades and tomahawks. **Technical:** Forges and grinds 5160, O1 and Damascus. Offers filework and scrimshaw. **Prices:** $75 to $300; some to $750. **Remarks:** Part-time maker; first knife sold in 1990. **Mark:** Name or initials.

BESHARA, BRENT (BESH)

PO BOX 557, Holyrood, NL, CANADA A0A 2R0, BESH@beshknives.com Web: www. beshknives.com
Specialties: Fixed blade tools and knives. **Patterns:** BESH Wedge tools and knives. **Technical:** Custom design work, grinds 0-1, D-2, 440C, 154cm. Offers kydex sheathing **Prices:** Start at $250. **Remarks:** Inventor of BESH Wedge geometry, custom maker and designer since 2000. Retired (24yrs) Special Forces, Special Operations Navy bomb disposal diver. Lifelong martial artist. **Mark:** "BESH" stamped.

BEST, RON

1489 Adams Lane, Stokes, NC 27884, Phone: 252-714-1264, ronbestknives@msn. com; Web: www.ronbestknives.com
Specialties: Folders and automatics. **Patterns:** Everything including butterfly knives. **Technical:** Grinds 440C, D-2 and ATS-34. **Prices:** $600 to $8000.

BETANCOURT, ANTONIO L.

5718 Beefwood Ct., St. Louis, MO 63129, Phone: 314-306-1869, bet2001@charter.net
Specialties: One-of-a-kind fixed blades and art knives. **Patterns:** Hunters and Bowies with embellished handles. **Technical:** Uses cast sterling silver and lapidary with fine gemstones, fossil ivory, and scrimshaw. Grinds Damascus and 440C. **Prices:** $100 to $800. **Remarks:** Part-time maker; first knife sold in 1974. **Mark:** Initials in cursive.

BEUKES, TINUS

83 Henry St, Risiville, Vereeniging, GT, SOUTH AFRICA 1939, Phone: 27 16 423 2053
Specialties: Working straight knives. **Patterns:** Hunters, skinners and kitchen knives. **Technical:** Grinds D2, 440C and chain, cable and stainless Damascus. **Prices:** $80 to $180. **Remarks:** Part-time maker; first knife sold in 1993. **Mark:** Full name, city, logo.

BEVERLY II, LARRY H

PO Box 741, Spotsylvania, VA 22553, Phone: 540-846-5426, beverlyknives@aol.com
Specialties: Working straight knives, slip-joints and liner locks. Welcomes customer designs. **Patterns:** Bowies, hunters, guard less fighters and miniatures. **Technical:** Grinds 440C, A2 and O1. **Prices:** $125 to $1000. **Remarks:** Part-time maker; first knife sold in 1986. **Mark:** Initials or last name in script.

BEZUIDENHOUT, BUZZ
PO BOX 28284, Malvern, KZN, SOUTH AFRICA 4055, Phone: 031-4632827, Fax: 031-4632827, buzzbee@mweb.co.za
Specialties: Working and Fancy Folders, my or customer design.**Patterns:** Boots, hunters, kitchen knives and utility/camp knives. **Technical:** Use 12-C-27 + stainless damascus, some carbon damascus. Uses local hardwoods, horn: kudu, impala, buffalo, giraffe bone and ivory for handles.
Prices: $250 to upscale. **Remarks:** Part-time maker; first knife sold in 1985. Member S.A. Knife Makers Guild**Mark:** First name with a bee emblem.

BINGENHEIMER, BRUCE
553 Tiffany Dr., Spring Creek, NV 89815, Phone: 775-934-6295, mbing@citlink.net
Specialties: Forging fixed blade hunters, bowies, fighters. **Technical:** Forges own Damascus. Steel choices 5160, 1084. Damascus steels 15N20, 1080. **Prices:** $300 and up. **Remarks:** ABS Journeyman Smith 2010. Member of Montana Knife Makers Association and Oregon Knife Collector's Association. **Mark:** Bingenheimer (arched over) M B.

BIRDWELL, IRA LEE
PO Box 1448, Congress, AZ 85332, Phone: 928-925-3258, heli.ira@gmail.com
Specialties: Special orders. **Mark:** Engraved signature.

BISH, HAL
9347 Sweetbriar Trace, Jonesboro, GA 30236, Phone: 770-477-2422, hal-bish@hp.com

BISHER, WILLIAM (BILL)
1015 Beck Road, Denton, NC 27239, Phone: 336-859-4686, blackturtleforge@wildblue.net;Web: www.blackturtleforge.com
Specialties: Period pieces, also contemporary belt knives, friction folders. **Patterns:** Own design, hunters, camp/utility, Bowies, belt axes, neck knives, carving sets. **Technical:** Forges straight high carbon steels, and own Damascus, grinds ATS34 and 154CM. Uses natural handle materials (wood, bone, stag horn), micarta and stabilized wood.**Prices:** Starting at $75 - $2500. **Remarks:** Past president of North Carolina Custom Knifemakers Guild, member ABS, Full-time maker as of 2007, first knife made 1989, all work in house, blades and sheaths **Mark:** Last name under crown and turtle

BIZZELL, ROBERT
145 Missoula Ave, Butte, MT 59701, Phone: 406-782-4403, patternweld@yahoo.com
Specialties: Damascus Bowies. **Patterns:** Composite, mosaic and traditional. **Technical:** Fixed blades & LinerLock® folders. **Prices:** Fixed blades start at $275. Folders start at $500. **Remarks:** Currently not taking orders. **Mark:** Hand signed.

BLACK, EARL
3466 South, 700 East, Salt Lake City, UT 84106, Phone: 801-466-8395
Specialties: High-art straight knives and folders; period pieces. **Patterns:** Boots, Bowies and daggers; lockers and gents. **Technical:** Grinds 440C and 154CM. Buys some Damascus. Scrimshaws and engraves. **Prices:** $200 to $1800; some to $2500 and higher. **Remarks:** Full-time maker; first knife sold in 1980. **Mark:** Name, city, state.

BLACK, SCOTT
27100 Leetown Rd, Picayune, MS 39466, Phone: 601-799-5939, copperheadforge@telepak.net
Specialties: Friction folders; fighters. **Patterns:** Bowies, fighters, hunters, smoke hawks, friction folders, daggers. **Technical:** All forged, all work done by him, own hand-stitched leather work; own heat-treating. **Prices:** $100 to $2200. **Remarks:** ABS Journeyman Smith. Cabel / Damascus/ High Carbone. **Mark:** Hot Mark - Copperhead Snake.

BLACK, TOM
921 Grecian NW, Albuquerque, NM 87107, Phone: 505-344-2549, blackknives@comcast.net
Specialties: Working knives to fancy straight knives of his design. **Patterns:** Drop-point skinners, folders, using knives, Bowies and daggers. **Technical:** Grinds 440C, 154CM, ATS-34, A2, D2, CPM-154 and damascus. Offers engraving and scrimshaw. **Prices:** $250 and up; some over $8500. **Remarks:** Full-time maker; first knife sold in 1970. **Mark:** Name, city.

BLACKWELL, ZANE
PO BOX 234, Eden, TX 76837, Phone: 325-869-8821, blackwellknives@hotmail.com; Web: www.blackwellknives.com
Specialties: Hunters, slip-joint folders and kitchen knives. **Patterns:** Drop-point and clip-point hunters, and classic slip-joint patterns like single-blade trappers. **Technical:** CPM 154, ATS-34, 440C and D2 blade steels, and natural handle materials. **Prices:** Single-blade folders start at $400. **Remarks:** Six-month back log. **Mark:** Zane Blackwell Eden Texas.

BLANCHARD, G R (GARY)
PO BOX 292, Dandridge, TN 37725, Phone: 865-397-9515, blanchardcustomknives@yahoo.com; Web: www.blanchardcustomknives.com
Specialties: Fancy folders with patented button blade release and high-art straight knives of his design. **Patterns:** Boots, daggers and locking folders. **Technical:** Grinds 440C and ATS-34 and Damascus. Engraves his knives. **Prices:** $1000 to $15,000 or more. **Remarks:** Full-time maker; first knife sold in 1989. **Mark:** First and middle initials, last name or last name only.

BLAUM, ROY
ROY'S KNIFE & ARCHERY SHOP, 319 N Columbia St, Covington, LA 70433, Phone: 985-893-1060
Specialties: Working straight knives and folders of his design; lightweight easy-open folders. **Patterns:** Hunters, boots, fishing and woodcarving/whittling knives. **Technical:** Grinds A2, D2, O1, 154CM and ATS-34. Offers leatherwork. **Prices:** $40 to $800; some

higher. **Remarks:** Full-time maker; first knife sold in 1976. **Mark:** Engraved signature or etched logo.

Bloodworth Custom Knives
3502 W. Angelica Dr., Meridian, ID 83646, Phone: 208-888-7778
Patterns: Working straight knives, hunters, skinners, bowies, utility knives of his designs or customer specs. Scagel knives. Period knives and traditional frontier knives and sheaths. **Technical:** Grinds D2, ATS34, 154CM, 5160, O1, Damascus, Heat treats, natural and composite handle materials. **Prices:** $185.00 to $1,500. **Remarks:** Roger Smith knife maker. Full-time maker; first knife sold in 1978 **Mark:** Sword over BLOODWORTH.

BLOOMER, ALAN T
PO Box 154, 116 E 6th St, Maquon, IL 61458, Phone: Cell: 309-371-8520, alant.bloomer@winco.net
Specialties: Folders & straight knives & custom pen maker. **Patterns:** All kinds. **Technical:** Does own heat treating. **Prices:** $400 to $1000. **Remarks:** Part-time maker. No orders. **Mark:** Stamp Bloomer.

BLUM, KENNETH
1729 Burleson, Brenham, TX 77833, Phone: 979-836-9577
Specialties: Traditional working straight knives of his design. **Patterns:** Camp knives, hunters and Bowies. **Technical:** Forges 5160; grinds 440C and D2. Uses exotic woods and Micarta for handles. **Prices:** $150 to $300. **Remarks:** Part-time maker; first knife sold in 1978. **Mark:** Last name on ricasso.

BLYSTONE, RONALD L.
231 Bailey Road, Creekside, PA 15732, Phone: 724-397-2671, taxibly@hotmail.com
Specialties: Traditional forged working knives. **Patterns:** Hunting utility and skinners of his own design. **Technical:** Forges his own pattern welded Damascus using carbon steel. **Prices:** Starting at $150. **Remarks:** Spare-time maker.**Mark:** Initials - upsidedown R against the B, inside a circle, over the word FORGE

BOARDMAN, GUY
39 Mountain Ridge R, New Germany, KZN, SOUTH AFRICA 3619, Phone: 031-726-921
Specialties: American and South African-styles. **Patterns:** Bowies, American and South African hunters, plus more. **Technical:** Grinds Bohler steels, some ATS-34. **Prices:** $100 to $600. **Remarks:** Part-time maker; first knife sold in 1986. **Mark:** Name, city, country.

BOCHMAN, BRUCE
183 Howard Place, Grants Pass, OR 97526, Phone: 541-471-1985, 183bab@gmail.com
Specialties: Hunting, fishing, bird and tactical knives. **Patterns:** Hunters, fishing and bird knives. **Technical:** ATS34, 154CM, mirror or satin finish. Damascus. **Prices:** $250 to $350; some to $750. **Remarks:** Part-time maker; first knife sold in 1977. **Mark:** Custom Knives by B. Bochman

BODEN, HARRY
Via Gellia Mill, Bonsall Matlock, Derbyshire, ENGLAND DE4 2AJ, Phone: 0629-825176
Specialties: Traditional working straight knives and folders of his design. **Patterns:** Hunters, locking folders and utility/camp knives. **Technical:** Grinds Sandvik 12C27, D2 and O1. **Prices:** £70 to £150; some to £300. **Remarks:** Full-time maker; first knife sold in 1986. **Mark:** Full name.

BODOLAY, ANTAL
Rua Wilson Soares Fernandes #31, Planalto, Belo Horizonte, MG, BRAZIL MG-31730-700, Phone: 031-494-1885
Specialties: Working folders and fixed blades of his design or to customer specs; some art daggers and period pieces. **Patterns:** Daggers, hunters, locking folders, utility knives and Khukris. **Technical:** Grinds D6, high-carbon steels and 420 stainless. Forges files on request. **Prices:** $30 to $350. **Remarks:** Full-time maker; first knife sold in 1965. **Mark:** Last name in script.

BOECK, SANDRO EDUARDO
St. Eduardo Macedo de Oliveira, 300, Cachoeira do Sul - RS, BRAZIL CEP - 96 505 - 610, Phone: 55-51-99559106, sandroboeck@gmail.com; Web: www.sandroboeck.com.br
Specialties: Fixed blades, integrals, gaucho style, bowies, hunters, dirks and swords. **Technical:** Forges his own damascus, mosaic damascus and high-carbon steel. Constructs integral knives. **Prices:** $500 to $2,000. **Remarks:** Part-time maker, IBO founding member, ABS journeyman smith, SBC lawyer consultant. **Mark:** S.Boeck JS.

BOEHLKE, GUENTER
Parkstrasse 2, 56412 Grobholbach, GERMANY, Phone: (49) 2602-5440, Fax: (49) 2602-5491, Boehlke-Messer@t-online.de; Web: www.boehlke-messer.de
Specialties: Classic working/using straight knives of his design. **Patterns:** Hunters, utility/camp knives and ancient remakes. **Technical:** Grinds Damascus, CPM-T-440V and 440C. Inlays gemstones and ivory. **Prices:** $220 to $700; some to $2000. **Remarks:** Spare-time maker; first knife sold in 1985. **Mark:** Name, address and bow and arrow.

BOHRMANN, BRUCE
61 Portland St, Yarmouth, ME 04096, Phone: 207-846-3385, bbohr@maine.rr.com; Web: Bohrmannknives.com
Specialties: Fixed-blade sporting, camp and hunting knives. **Technical:** Stock-removal maker using 13C26 Sandvik stainless steel hardened to 58-60 Rockwell. **Prices:** $499 for each model. Also, special "Heritage" production using historic certified woods (from Washington's, Jefferson's, Madison's and Henry's Plantations) - $1,250. **Remarks:** Full-time maker; first knife made in 1955. Always developing new models and concepts, such as steak knives, fixed blades and miniatures with special pocket sheaths. All knives serial

#'d and can be personalized by etching initials into blades. **Mark:** The letter "B" connected to and lying beneath deer antlers.

BOJTOS, ARPAD
Dobsinskeho 10, 98403 Lucenec, SLOVAKIA, Phone: 00421-47 4333512; Cell: 00421-91 5875066, bojtos@stonline.sk; Web: www.arpadbojtos.sk
Specialties: Art knives, including over 100 folders. **Patterns:** Daggers, fighters and hunters. **Technical:** Grinds ATS-34 and stainless damascus. Carves on steel, handle materials and sheaths. **Prices:** $5000 to $10,000; some over. **Remarks:** Full-time maker; first knife sold in 1990. **Mark:** AB.

BOLDUC, GARY
1419 Tanglewood Dr., Corona, CA 92882, Phone: 951-739-0137, gary@stillwaterwoods.com; Web: www.bolduckknives.com
Specialties: Fish fillet knives (larger sizes), medium 8" to large 10"-plus. Replica making of primitive Native Alaskan hunting and cutting tools, kitchen cutlery. **Patterns:** Hunters, skinners, fillet, boning, spear points and kitchen cutlery. **Technical:** High-quality stainless steel, mainly CTS-XHP, CPM-154 and CPM-S35VN for improved edge design. **Prices:** $200-$400 and up. **Remarks:** Full-time maker; first knife sold in 2007. **Mark:** First initial, last name with USA under, or grizzly bear with Bolduc Knives underneath.

BOLEWARE, DAVID
PO Box 96, Carson, MS 39427, Phone: 601-943-5372
Specialties: Traditional and working/using straight knives of his design, to customer specs and in standard patterns. **Patterns:** Bowies, hunters and utility/camp knives. **Technical:** Grinds ATS-34, 440C and Damascus. **Prices:** $85 to $350; some to $600. **Remarks:** Part-time maker; first knife sold in 1989. **Mark:** First and last name, city, state.

BOLEY, JAMIE
PO Box 477, Parker, SD 57053, Phone: 605-297-0014, jamie@polarbearforge.com
Specialties: Working knives and historical influenced reproductions. **Patterns:** Hunters, skinners, scramasaxes, and others.**Technical:** Forges 5160, O1, L6, 52100, W1, W2 makes own Damascus. **Prices:** Starts at $125. **Remarks:** Part-time maker. **Mark:** Polar bear paw print with name on the left side and Polar Bear Forge on the right.

BONASSI, FRANCO
Via Nicoletta 4, Pordenone, ITALY 33170, Phone: 0434-550821, frank.bonassi@alice.it
Specialties: Fancy and working one-of-a-kind folder knives of his design. **Patterns:** Folders, linerlocks and back locks. **Technical:** Grinds CPM, ATS-34, 154CM and commercial Damascus. Uses only titanium foreguards and pommels. **Prices:** Start at $350. **Remarks:** Spare-time maker; first knife sold in 1988. Has made cutlery for several celebrities; Gen. Schwarzkopf, Fuzzy Zoeller, etc. **Mark:** FRANK.

BOOCO, GORDON
175 Ash St, PO Box 174, Hayden, CO 81639, Phone: 970-276-3195
Specialties: Fancy working straight knives of his design and to customer specs. **Patterns:** Hunters and Bowies. **Technical:** Grinds 440C, D2 and A2. Heat-treats. **Prices:** $150 to $350; some $600 and higher. **Remarks:** Part-time maker; first knife sold in 1984. **Mark:** Last name with push dagger artwork.

BOOS, RALPH
6018-37A Avenue NW, Edmonton, AB, CANADA T6L 1H4, Phone: 780-463-7094
Specialties: Classic, fancy and fantasy miniature knives and swords of his design or to customer specs. **Patterns:** Bowies, daggers and swords. **Technical:** Hand files O1, stainless and Damascus. Engraves and carves. Does heat bluing and acid etching. **Prices:** $125 to $350; some to $1000. **Remarks:** Part-time maker; first knife sold in 1982. **Mark:** First initials back to back.

BOOTH, PHILIP W
301 S Jeffery Ave, Ithaca, MI 48847, Phone: 989-875-2844, pbooth@charter.net; Web: www.philipbooth.com
Specialties: Folding knives of his design using various mechanisms. **Patterns:** New "Twerp" ball-bearing flipper knife. "Minnow" folding knives, a series of small folding knives started in 1996 and changing yearly. One of a kind hot-rod car themed folding knives. **Technical:** Grinds ATS-34, CPM-154 and commercial damascus. Offers gun blue finishes and file work. **Prices:** $200 and up. **Remarks:** Part-time maker, first knife sold in 1991. **Mark:** Last name or name with city and map logo.

BORGER, WOLF
Benzstrasse 8, Graben-Neudorf, GERMANY 76676, Phone: 07255-72303, Fax: 07255-72304, wolf@messerschmied.de; Web: www.messerschmied.de
Specialties: High-tech working and using straight knives and folders, many with corkscrews or other tools, of his design. **Patterns:** Hunters, Bowies and folders with various locking systems. **Technical:** Grinds 440C, ATS-34 and CPM. Uses stainless Damascus. **Prices:** $250 to $900; some to $1500. **Remarks:** Full-time maker; first knife sold in 1975. **Mark:** Howling wolf and name; first name on Damascus blades.

BOSE, REESE
8810 N. County Rd. 375 E, Shelburn, IN 47879, Phone: 812-397-5114
Specialties: Traditional working and using knives in standard patterns and multi-blade folders. **Patterns:** Multi-blade slip-joints. **Technical:** ATS-34, D2, 154CM and CPM 440V. **Prices:** $600 to $3,000. **Remarks:** Full-time maker; first knife sold in 1992. Photos by Jack Busfield. **Mark:** R. Bose.

BOSE, TONY
7252 N. County Rd, 300 E., Shelburn, IN 47879-9778, Phone: 812-397-5114
Specialties: Traditional working and using knives in standard patterns; multi-blade folders. **Patterns:** Multi-blade slip-joints. **Technical:** Grinds commercial Damascus, ATS-

34 and D2. **Prices:** $400 to $1200. **Remarks:** Full-time maker; first knife sold in 1972. **Mark:** First initial, last name, city, state.

BOSSAERTS, CARL
Rua Albert Einstein 906, Ribeirao Preto, SP, BRAZIL 14051-110, Phone: 016 633 7063
Specialties: Working and using straight knives of his design, to customer specs and in standard patterns. **Patterns:** Hunters, fighters and utility/camp knives. **Technical:** Grinds ATS-34, 440V and 440C; does filework. **Prices:** 60 to $400. **Remarks:** Part-time maker; first knife sold in 1992. **Mark:** Initials joined together.

BOST, ROGER E
30511 Cartier Dr, Palos Verdes, CA 90275-5629, Phone: 310- 541-6833, rogerbost@cox.net
Specialties: Hunters, fighters, boot, utility. **Patterns:** Loveless-style. **Technical:** ATS-34, BG-42, 440C, 59-61RC, stock removal and forge. **Prices:** $300 and up. **Remarks:** First knife sold in 1990. Cal. Knifemakers Assn., ABS. **Mark:** Diamond with initials inside and Palos Verdes California around outside.

BOSWORTH, DEAN
329 Mahogany Dr, Key Largo, FL 33037, Phone: 305-451-1564, DLBOZ@bellsouth.net
Specialties: Free hand hollow ground working knives with hand rubbed satin finish, filework and inlays. **Patterns:** Bird and Trout, hunters, skinners, fillet, Bowies, miniatures. **Technical:** Using 440C, ATS-34, D2, Meier Damascus, custom wet formed sheaths. **Prices:** $250 and up. **Remarks:** Part-time maker; first knife made in 1985. Member Florida Knifemakers Assoc. **Mark:** BOZ stamped in block letters.

BOURBEAU, JEAN YVES
15 Rue Remillard, Notre Dame, Ile Perrot, QC, CANADA J7V 8M9, Phone: 514-453-1069
Specialties: Fancy/embellished and fantasy folders of his design. **Patterns:** Bowies, fighters and locking folders. **Technical:** Grinds 440C, ATS-34 and Damascus. Carves precious wood for handles. **Prices:** $150 to $1000. **Remarks:** Part-time maker; first knife sold in 1994. **Mark:** Interlaced initials.

BOYD, FRANCIS
1811 Prince St, Berkeley, CA 94703, Phone: 510-841-7210
Specialties: Folders and kitchen knives, Japanese swords. **Patterns:** Push-button sturdy locking folders; San Francisco-style chef's knives. **Technical:** Forges and grinds; mostly uses high-carbon steels. **Prices:** Moderate to heavy. **Remarks:** Designer. **Mark:** Name.

BOYE, DAVID
PO Box 1238, Dolan Springs, AZ 86441, Phone: 800-853-1617, Fax: 928-767-4273, boye@cltlink.net; Web: www.boyeknives.com
Specialties: Folders and Boye Basics. Forerunner in the use of dendritic steel and dendritic cobalt for blades. **Patterns:** Lockback folders and fixed blade sheath knives in cobalt. **Technical:** Casts blades in cobalt. **Prices:** From $129 to $360. **Remarks:** Part-time maker; author of Step-by-Step Knifemaking. **Mark:** Name.

BOYES, TOM
2505 Wallace Lake Rd., West Bend, WI 53090, Phone: 262-391-2172
Specialties: Hunters, skinners and fillets. **Technical:** Grinds ATS-34, 440C, O1 tool steel and Damascus. **Prices:** $60 to $1000. **Remarks:** First knife sold in 1998. Doing business as R. Boyes Knives.

BOYSEN, RAYMOND A
125 E St Patrick, Rapid Ciy, SD 57701, Phone: 605-341-7752
Specialties: Hunters and Bowies. **Technical:** High performance blades forged from 52100 and 5160. **Prices:** $200 and up. **Remarks:** American Bladesmith Society Journeyman Smith. Part-time bladesmith. **Mark:** BOYSEN.

BRACH, PAUL
4870 Widgeon Way, Cumming, GA 30028, Phone: 770-595-8952, Web: www.brachknives.com
Specialties: Standard and one-of-a-kind straight knives and locking folders. Nickel silver sheath fittings and gemstone settings used on high-end pieces. **Patterns:** Hunters, bowies, daggers, antique bowies and titanium-frame folders. **Technical:** Grinds CPM-154 and forges high-carbon steel. Usually flat or full convex grinds. **Prices:** $150 to $1,000+. **Remarks:** Part-time maker; first knife sold in 1984. **Mark:** Etched "Paul Brach maker Cumming, GA" or "Brach" stamped.

BRACKETT, JAMIN
PO Box 387, Fallston, NC 28042, Phone: 704-718-3304, jaminbrackett@bellsouth.net; Web: brackettknives.com
Specialties: Hunting, camp, fishing, tactical, and general outdoor use. Handmade of my own design or to customer specs. **Patterns:** Drop point, tanto, fillet, and small EDC the "Tadpole", as well as large camp and tactical knives. **Technical:** Stock removal method, ATS-34 steel cryogenically treated to HRC 59-61. Mirror polish and bead blasted finishes. Handle materials include exotic woods, stag, buffalo horn, colored laminates, Micarta, and G-10. Come hand stitched 8-9 OZ leather sheaths treated in beeswax saddle oil mixture. Tactical models include reinforced tactical nylon sheaths Mollie system compatible. **Prices:** Standard models $150-$325. Personalized engraving available, for gifts and special occasions. **Remarks:** Part-time maker. First knife made in 2009. Member of NC Custom Knifemakers Guild.**Mark:** "Brackett", in bold. Each knife and sheath numbered.

BRADBURN, GARY
BRADBURN CUSTOM CUTLERY, 1714 Park Place, Wichita, KS 67203, Phone: 316-640-5684, gary@bradburnknives.com; Web:www.bradburnknives.com
Specialties: Specialize in clay-tempered Japanese-style knives and swords. **Patterns:** Also Bowies and fighters. **Technical:** Forge and/or grind carbon steel only. **Prices:** $150 to $1200. **Mark:** Initials GB stylized to look like Japanese character.

BRADFORD, GARRICK
582 Guelph St, Kitchener, ON, CANADA N2H-5Y4, Phone: 519-576-9863

BRADLEY, DENNIS
178 Bradley Acres Rd, Blairsville, GA 30512, Phone: 706-745-4364, dbbrad@
windstream.net; Web: www.dennisbradleyknives.com
  Specialties: Working straight knives and folders, some high-art. **Patterns:** Hunters, boots and daggers; slip-joints and two-blades. **Technical:** Grinds CPM 154, CPM S35VN, ATS-34, D2, 440C and commercial damascus. **Prices:** $100 to $500; some to $2000. **Remarks:** Part-time maker; first knife sold in 1973. **Mark:** BRADLEY KNIVES in double heart logo.

BRADLEY, GAYLE
1383 Old Garner Rd., Weatherford, TX 76088-8720, Phone: 817-504-2262, bradleysblades@aol.com; Web: www.bradleysblades.com
  Specialties: High-end folders with wedge locks of maker's own design or lock backs, and work/utility knives. Uses high-end materials, including lapidary work and black-lip-pearl handle inlays. **Technical:** Grinds blades from bar stock, performs own heat treating. **Remarks:** Full-time maker; first knife made in 1988.

BRADLEY, JOHN
PO Box 33, Pomona Park, FL 32181, Phone: 386-649-4739, johnbradleyknives@
yahoo.com
  Specialties: Fixed-blade using and art knives; primitive folders. **Patterns:** Skinners, Bowies, camp knives and primitive knives. **Technical:** Forged and ground 52100, 1095, O1 and Damascus. **Prices:** $250 to $2000. **Remarks:** Full-time maker; first knife sold in 1988. **Mark:** Last name.

BRANDSEY, EDWARD P
4441 Hawkridge Ct, Janesville, WI 53546, Phone: 608-868-9010, ebrandsey@
centurytel.net
  Patterns: Large bowies, hunters, neck knives and buckskinner-styles. Native American influence on some. An occasional tanto, art piece. Does own scrimshaw. See Egnath's second book. Now making locking liner folders. **Technical:** ATS-34, CPM154, 440-C, 0-1 and some damascus. Paul Bos heat treating past 20 years. **Prices:** $350 to $800; some to $4,000. **Remarks:** Full-time maker; first knife sold in 1973. **Mark:** Initials connected.

BRANDT, MARTIN W
833 Kelly Blvd, Springfield, OR 97477, Phone: 541-747-5422, oubob747@aol.com

BRANTON, ROBERT
PO BOX 807, Awendaw, SC 29429, Phone: 843-928-3624, www.brantonknives.com
  Specialties: Working straight knives of his design or to customer specs; throwing knives. **Patterns:** Hunters, fighters and some miniatures. **Technical:** Grinds ATS-34, A2 and 1050; forges 5160, O1. Offers hollow- or convex-grinds. **Prices:** $25 to $400. **Remarks:** Part-time maker; first knife sold in 1985. Doing business as Pro-Flyte, Inc. **Mark:** Last name; or first and last name, city, state.

BRASCHLER, CRAIG W.
HC2 Box 498, Zalma, MO 63787, Phone: 573-495-2203
  Specialties: Art knives, Bowies, utility hunters, slip joints, miniatures, engraving. **Technical:** Flat grinds. Does own selective heat treating. Does own engraving. **Prices:** Starting at $200. **Remarks:** Full-time maker since 2003. **Mark:** Braschler over Martin Oval stamped.

BRATCHER, BRETT
11816 County Rd 302, Plantersville, TX 77363, Phone: 936-894-3788, Fax: (936) 894-3790, brett_bratcher@msn.com
  Specialties: Hunting and skinning knives. **Patterns:** Clip and drop point. Hand forged. **Technical:** Material 5160, D2, 1095 and Damascus. **Prices:** $200 to $500. **Mark:** Bratcher.

BRAY JR., W LOWELL
6931 Manor Beach Rd, New Port Richey, FL 34652, Phone: 727-846-0830, brayknives@aol.com Web: www.brayknives.com
  Specialties: Traditional working and using straight knives and collector pieces. **Patterns:** One of a kind pieces, hunters, fighters and utility knives. **Technical:** Grinds 440C and ATS-34; forges 52100 and Damascus. **Prices:** $125 to $800. **Remarks:** Spare-time maker; first knife sold in 1992. **Mark:** Lowell Bray Knives in shield or Bray Primative in shield.

BREDA, BEN
56 Blueberry Hill Rd., Hope, ME 04847, Phone: 207-701-7777, bredaknives@gmail.com
  Specialties: High-carbon-steel bowies, fighters, hunters chef's knives and LinerLock folders. **Technical:** Forges W2, W1 and 10xx series steels for blades, using natural and stabilized handle materials. **Prices:** Start at $300. **Remarks:** Part-time maker; ABS journeyman smith.

BREED, KIM
733 Jace Dr, Clarksville, TN 37040, Phone: 931-980-4956, sfbreed@yahoo.com
  Specialties: High end through working folders and straight knives. **Patterns:** Hunters, fighters, daggers, Bowies. His design or customers. Likes one-of-a-kind designs. **Technical:** Makes own Mosiac and regular Damascus, but will use stainless steels. Offers filework and sculpted material. **Prices:** $150 to $2000. **Remarks:** Full-time maker. First knife sold in 1990. **Mark:** Last name.

BREND, WALTER
415 County Rd. 782, Etowah, TN 37331, Phone: 256-736-3520, Fax: 256-736-3474, walterbrend@outlook.com or walter@brendknives.com; Web: www.brendknives.com
  Specialties: Tactical-style knives, fighters, automatics. **Technical:** Grinds D-2 and 440C blade steels, 154CM steel. **Prices:** Micarta and titanium handles.

BRENNAN, JUDSON
PO Box 1165, Delta Junction, AK 99737, Phone: 907-895-5153, Fax: 907-895-5404
  Specialties: Period pieces. **Patterns:** All kinds of Bowies, rifle knives, daggers. **Technical:** Forges miscellaneous steels. **Prices:** Upscale, good value. **Remarks:** Muzzle-loading gunsmith; first knife sold in 1978. **Mark:** Name.

BRESHEARS, CLINT
1261 Keats, Manhattan Beach, CA 90266, Phone: 310-372-0739, Fax: 310-372-0739, breshears1@verizon.net; Web: www.clintknives.com
  Specialties: Working straight knives and folders. **Patterns:** Hunters, Bowies and survival knives. Folders are mostly hunters. **Technical:** Grinds 440C, 154CM and ATS-34; prefers mirror finishes. **Prices:** $125 to $750; some to $1800. **Remarks:** Part-time maker; first knife sold in 1978. **Mark:** First name.

BREUER, LONNIE
PO Box 877384, Wasilla, AK 99687-7384
  Specialties: Fancy working straight knives. **Patterns:** Hunters, camp knives and axes, folders and Bowies. **Technical:** Grinds 440C, AEB-L and D2; likes wire inlay, scrimshaw, decorative filing. **Prices:** $60 to $150; some to $300. **Remarks:** Part-time maker; first knife sold in 1977. **Mark:** Signature.

BREWER, CRAIG
425 White Cedar, Killeen, TX 76542, Phone: 254-634-6934, craig6@embarqmail.com
  Specialties: Folders; slip joints, some lock backs and an occasional liner lock. **Patterns:** I like the old traditional patterns. **Technical:** Grinds CPM steels most being CPM-154, 1095 for carbon and some Damascus. **Prices:** $500 and up. **Remarks:** Full-time maker; first knife sold in 2005. **Mark:** BREWER.

BRITTON, TIM
5645 Murray Rd., Winston-Salem, NC 27106, Phone: 336-923-2062, tim@timbritton.com; Web: www.timbritton.com
  Specialties: Small and simple working knives, sgian dubhs, slip joint folders and special tactical designs. **Technical:** Forges and grinds stainless steel. **Prices:** $165 to ???. **Remarks:** Veteran knifemaker. **Mark:** Etched signature.

BROADWELL, DAVID
PO Box 3373, Wichita Falls, TX 76301, Phone: 940-782-4442, david@
broadwellstudios.com; Web: www.broadwellstudios.com
  Specialties: Sculpted high-art straight and folding knives. **Patterns:** Daggers, sub-hilted fighters, folders, sculpted art knives and some Bowies. **Technical:** Grinds mostly Damascus; carves; prefers natural handle materials, including stone. Some embellishment. **Prices:** $500 to $4000; some higher. **Remarks:** Full-time maker since 1989; first knife sold in 1981. **Mark:** Stylized emblem bisecting "B"/with last name below.

BROCK, KENNETH L
PO Box 375, 207 N Skinner Rd, Allenspark, CO 80510, Phone: 303-747-2547, brockknives@nedernet.net
  Specialties: Custom designs, full-tang working knives and button lock folders of his design. **Patterns:** Hunters, miniatures and minis. **Technical:** Flat-grinds D2 and 440C; makes own sheaths; heat-treats. **Prices:** $75 to $800. **Remarks:** Full-time maker; first knife sold in 1978. **Mark:** Last name, city, state and serial number.

BRODZIAK, DAVID
27 Stewart St, PO Box 1130, Albany, WA, AUSTRALIA 6331, Phone: 61 8 9841 3314, brodziak3@bigpond.com; Web: www.brodziakcustomknives.com

BROMLEY, PETER
BROMLEY KNIVES, 1408 S Bettman, Spokane, WA 99212, Phone: 509-534-4235 or 509-710-8365, Fax: 509-536-2666, bromleyknives@q.com
  Specialties: Period Bowies, folder, hunting knives; all sizes and shapes. **Patterns:** Bowies, boot knives, hunters, utility, folder, working knives. **Technical:** High-carbon steel (1084, 1095 and 5160). Stock removal and forge. **Prices:** $85 to $750. **Remarks:** Almost full-time, first knife sold in 1987. A.B.S. Journeyman Smith. **Mark:** Bromley, Spokane, WA.

BROOKER, DENNIS
55858 260th Ave., Chariton, IA 50049, Phone: 641-862-3263, dbrooker@dbrooker.com Web: www.dbrooker.com
  Specialties: Fancy straight knives and folders of his design. Obsidian and glass knives. **Patterns:** Hunters, folders and boots. **Technical:** Forges and grinds. Full-time engraver and designer; instruction available. **Prices:** Moderate to upscale. **Remarks:** Part-time maker. Takes no orders; sells only completed work. **Mark:** Name.

BROOKS, BUZZ
2345 Yosemite Dr, Los Angles, CA 90041, Phone: 323-256-2892

BROOKS, MICHAEL
2811 64th St, Lubbock, TX 79413, Phone: 806-438-3862, chiang@clearwire.net
  Specialties: Working straight knives of his design or to customer specs. **Patterns:** Martial art, Bowies, hunters, and fighters. **Technical:** Grinds 440C, D2 and ATS-34; offers wide variety of handle materials. **Prices:** $75 & up. **Remarks:** Part-time maker; first knife sold in 1985. **Mark:** Initials.

BROOKS, STEVE R
1610 Dunn Ave, Walkerville, MT 59701, Phone: 406-782-5114, Fax: 406-782-5114, steve@brooksmoulds.com; Web: brooksmoulds.com
  Specialties: Working straight knives and folders; period pieces. **Patterns:** Hunters, Bowies and camp knives; folding lockers; axes, tomahawks and buckskinner knives; swords and stilettos. **Technical:** Damascus and mosaic Damascus. Some knives come embellished. **Prices:** $400 to $2000. **Remarks:** Full-time maker; first knife sold in 1982. **Mark:** Lazy initials.

BROOME, THOMAS A

1212 E. Aliak Ave, Kenai, AK 99611-8205, Phone: 907-283-9128, tomlei@ptialaska. ent; Web: www.alaskanknives.com

Specialties: Working hunters and folders **Patterns:** Traditional and custom orders. **Technical:** Grinds ATS-34, BG-42, CPM-S30V. **Prices:** $175 to $350. **Remarks:** Full-time maker; first knife sold in 1979. Doing business as Thom's Custom Knives, Alaskan Man O; Steel Knives. **Mark:** Full name, city, state.

BROTHERS, DENNIS L.

2007 Kent Rd., Oneonta, AL 35121, Phone: 205-466-3276, blademan@ brothersblades.com Web: www.brothersblades.com

Specialties: Fixed blade hunting/working knives of maker's deigns. Works with customer designed specifications. **Patterns:** Hunters, camp knives, kitchen/utility, bird, and trout. Standard patterns and customer designed. **Technical:** Stock removal. Works with stainless and tool steels. SS cryo-treatment. Hollow and flat grinds. **Prices:** $200 - $400. **Remarks:** Sole authorship knives and customer leather sheaths. Part-time maker. Find on facebook "Brothers Blades by D.L. Brothers" **Mark:** "D.L. Brothers, 4B, Oneonta, AL" on obverse side of blade.

BROTHERS, ROBERT L

989 Philpott Rd, Colville, WA 99114, Phone: 509-684-8922

Specialties: Traditional working and using straight knives and folders of his design and to customer specs. **Patterns:** Bowies, fighters and hunters. **Technical:** Grinds D2; forges Damascus. Makes own Damascus from saw steel wire rope and chain; part-time goldsmith and stone-setter. **Prices:** $100 to $400; some higher. **Remarks:** Part-time maker; first knife sold in 1986. **Mark:** Initials and year made.

BROUS, JASON

POB 550, Buellton, CA 93427, Phone: 805-717-7192, jbrous@live.com or brousblades@outlook.com; Web: www.brousblades.com

Patterns: Tactical mid-tech folders, production and customized. **Technical:** Stock removal method using D2 steel. **Prices:** $99 - $700. **Remarks:** Started May 2010.

BROUWER, JERRY

Vennewaard 151, 1824 KD, Alkmaar, NETHERLANDS, Phone: 00-31-618-774146, brouwern1@hotmail.nl; Web: www.brouwerknives.com

Specialties: Tactical fixed blades with epoxy-soaked Japanese wrapped handles, tactical and outdoor knives with Micarta or G-10 handles, tactical frame-lock folders. Fine, embellished knives for the demanding VIP. **Patterns:** Fixed-blade tantos, drop points, either V-ground or chisel ground, hunting knives, outdoor knives, folders, desk knives, pocket tools. **Technical:** Stock removal, only premium powder metallurgy steels and fine stainless damascus. **Prices:** $100 to $1,000. **Remarks:** Part-time maker; first knife sold in 2010. **Mark:** Laser etched "Brouwer" with a jack-o-lantern logo.

BROWER, MAX

2016 Story St, Boone, IA 50036, Phone: 515-432-2938, jmbrower@mchsi.com

Specialties: Hunters. Working/using straight knives. **Patterns:** Hunters. **Technical:** Grinds ATS-34. **Prices:** $300 and up. **Remarks:** Spare-time maker; first knife sold in 1981. **Mark:** Last name.

BROWN, DOUGLAS

1500 Lincolnshire Way, Fort Worth, TX 76134, www.debrownphotography.com

BROWN, HAROLD E

3654 NW Hwy 72, Arcadia, FL 34266, Phone: 863-494-7514, brknives@strato.net

Specialties: Fancy and exotic working knives. **Patterns:** Folders, slip-lock, locking several kinds. **Technical:** Grinds D2 and ATS-34. Embellishment available. **Prices:** $175 to $1000. **Remarks:** Part-time maker; first knife sold in 1976. **Mark:** Name and city with logo.

BROWN, JIM

1097 Fernleigh Cove, Little Rock, AR 72210

BROWN, ROB E

PO Box 15107, Emerald Hill, Port Elizabeth, EC, SOUTH AFRICA 6011, Phone: 27-41-3661086, Fax: 27-41-4511731, rbknives@global.co.za

Specialties: Contemporary-designed straight knives and period pieces. **Patterns:** Utility knives, hunters, boots, fighters and daggers. **Technical:** Grinds 440C, D2, ATS-34 and commercial Damascus. Knives mostly mirror finished; African handle materials. **Prices:** $100 to $1500. **Remarks:** Full-time maker; first knife sold in 1985. **Mark:** Name and country.

BROWNE, RICK

980 West 13th St, Upland, CA 91786, Phone: 909-985-1728

Specialties: Sheffield pattern pocket knives. **Patterns:** Hunters, fighters and daggers. No heavy-duty knives. **Technical:** Grinds ATS-34. **Prices:** Start at $450. **Remarks:** Part-time maker; first knife sold in 1975. **Mark:** R.E. Browne, Upland, CA.

BROWNING, STEVEN W

3400 Harrison Rd, Benton, AR 72015, Phone: 501-316-2450

BRUCE, RICHARD L.

13174 Surcease Mine Road, Yankee Hill, CA 95965, Phone: 530-532-0880, richardkarenbruce@yahoo.com

Specialties: Working straight knives. Prefers natural handle material; stag bone and woods. Admires the classic straight knife look. **Patterns:** Hunters, Fighters, Fishing Knives. **Technical:** Uses 01, 1095, L6, W2 steel. Stock removal method, flat grind, heat treats and tempers own knives. Builds own sheaths; simple but sturdy. **Prices:** $150-$400. **Remarks:** Sold first knife in 2006; part-time maker. **Mark:** RL Bruce.

BRUNCKHORST, LYLE

COUNTRY VILLAGE, 23706 7th Ave SE Ste B, Bothell, WA 98021, Phone: 425-402-

3484, bronks@bronksknifeworks.com; Web: www.bronksknifeworks.com

Specialties: Forges own Damascus with 1084 and 15N20, forges 5160, 52100. Grinds CPM 154 CM, ATS-34, S30V. Hosts Biannual Northwest School of Knifemaking and Northwest Hammer In. Offers online and in-house sharpening services and knife sharpeners. Maker of the Double L Hoofknife. Traditional working and using knives, the new patent pending Xross-Bar Lock folders, tomahawks and irridescent RR spike knives. **Patterns:** Damascus Bowies, hunters, locking folders and featuring the ultra strong locking tactical folding knives. **Prices:** $185 to $1500; some to $3750. **Remarks:** Full-time maker; first knife made in 1976. **Mark:** Bucking horse or bronk.

BRUNER, FRED JR.

BRUNER BLADES, E10910W Hilldale Dr, Fall Creek, WI 54742, Phone: 715-225-8017, fredbruner200@aol.com

Specialties: Tomahawks, pipe tomahawks and period pieces. **Patterns:** Drop point hunters, long knives, French and working knives. **Technical:** Steels used include 1095, 52100, CPM 154 and 5160. **Prices:** $120 to $1,500. **Remarks:** Voting member of the Knifemakers Guild. Made knives for Herters into the 1980s. **Mark:** F.C. Bruner Jr.

BUCHANAN, THAD

THAD BUCHANAN CUSTOM KNIVES, 16401 S.W. Ranchview Rd., Powell Butte, OR 97753, buchananblades@gmail.com; Web: www.buchananblades.com

Specialties: Fixed blades. **Patterns:** Various hunters, trout, bird, utility, boots & fighters, including most Loveless patterns. **Technical:** Stock removal, high polish, variety handle materials. **Prices:** $450 to $2000. **Remarks:** 2005 and 2008 Blade Magazine handmade award for hunter/utility. 2006 Blade West best fixed blade award; 2008 Blade West best hunter/utility. 2010 and 2011 Best Fixed Blade at Plaza Cutlery Show. **Mark:** Thad Buchanan - maker

BUCHANAN, ZAC

168 Chapel Dr., Eugene, OR 97404, Phone: 541-815-6706, zacbuchananknives@ gmail.com; Web: www.zacbuchananknives.com

Specialties: R.W. Loveless-style fixed blades. **Technical:** Stock-removal knifemaker using CPM-154 blade steel, 416 stainless steel fittings and pre-ban elephant ivory, mammoth ivory, buffalo horn, stag and Micarta handles. **Prices:** $500 to $2,000. **Remarks:** Full-time maker; first knife sold in 2009. **Mark:** Zac Buchanan Eugene, Oregon.

BUCHARSKY, EMIL

23 Linkside Pl., Spruce Grove, Alberta, CANADA T7X 3C5, Phone: 587-341-5066, ebuch@telus.net; Web: www.ebuchknives.com

Specialties: Fancy working utility hunters and art folders, usually carved with overlays or inlays of damascus, hidden frames and screws. **Patterns:** Folders, hunters, bowies of maker's own design. **Technical:** Forges own damascus using 1095, 1084, 15N20 and nickel, stock-removal steels from Crucible, CPM alloys and UHB Elmax, natural handle materials of pearl, ancient ivory, bone, stabilized woods and others such as carbon fiber, titanium, stainless steel, mokume gane and gemstones. **Prices:** $400 to $1,000; art knives $1,500 and up. **Remarks:** Full-time maker; first knife made in 1989. **Mark:** Name, city and province in oval on fixed blades. Hand-engraved first name, initial and last name with year, in lower case, on folders.

BUCHNER, BILL

PO Box 73, Idleyld Park, OR 97447, Phone: 541-498-2247, blazinhammer@earthlink. net; Web: www.home.earthlin.net/~blazinghammer

Specialties: Working straight knives, kitchen knives and high-art knives of his design. **Technical:** Uses W1, L6 and his own Damascus. Invented "spectrum metal" for letter openers, folder handles and jewelry. Likes sculpturing and carving in Damascus. **Prices:** $40 to $3000; some higher. **Remarks:** Full-time maker; first knife sold in 1978. **Mark:** Signature.

BUCKNER, JIMMIE H

PO Box 162, Putney, GA 31782, Phone: 229-436-4182

Specialties: Camp knives, Bowies (one-of-a-kind), liner-lock folders, tomahawks, camp axes, neck knives for law enforcement and hide-out knives for body guards and professional people. **Patterns:** Hunters, camp knives, Bowies. **Technical:** Forges 1084, 5160 and Damascus (own), own heat treats. **Prices:** $195 to $795 and up. **Remarks:** Full-time maker; first knife sold in 1980, ABS Master Smith. **Mark:** Name over spade.

BUCKNER, TOM

1842 Overhulse Rd. NW, Olympia, WA 98502, Phone: 360-970-1668, tbuckner1967@gmail.com; Web: www.bucknerknives.com

Specialties: Kitchen knives with custom wooden sayas (sheaths) and folding knives. **Patterns:** Chef's, Santoku, boning, paring and folding knives fashioned using various types of material, all with titanium liners. **Technical:** Blade steels include CPM 154, CPM S30V, CPM S35VN, AEB-L, stainless damascus and high-carbon damascus. Maker heat treats and cryogenically heats and quenches all the listed steels. **Prices:** $200 to $2,000. **Mark:** Tom Buckner Maker Olympia, WA.

BUDELL, MICHAEL

3733 Wieghat Ln., Brenham, TX 77833, Phone: 979-836-3148, mbbudell@att.net

Specialties: Slip Joint Folders. **Technical:** Grinds 01, 440C. File work springs, blades and liners. Natural material scales giraffe, mastadon ivory, elephant ivory, and jigged bone. **Prices:** $175 - $350. **Remarks:** Part-time maker; first knife sold 2006. **Mark:** XA

BUEBENDORF, ROBERT E

108 Lazybrooke Rd, Monroe, CT 06468, Phone: 203-452-1769

Specialties: Traditional and fancy straight knives of his design. **Patterns:** Hand-makes and embellishes belt buckle knives. **Technical:** Forges and grinds 440C, 01, W2, 1095, his own Damascus and 154CM. **Prices:** $200 to $500. **Remarks:** Full-time maker; first knife sold in 1978. **Mark:** First and middle initials, last name and MAKER.

custom knifemakers

BULLARD, BENONI
4416 Jackson 4, Bradford, AR 72020, Phone: 501-344-2672, benandbren@earthlink.net **Specialties:** Bowies and hunters. **Patterns:** Camp knives, bowies, hunters, slip joints, folders, lock blades, miniatures, Hawks Tech. **Technical:** Makes own Damascus. Forges 5160, 1085, 15 N 20. Favorite is 5160. **Prices:** $150 - $1500. **Remarks:** Part-time maker. Sold first knife in 2006. **Mark:** Benoni with a star over the letter i.

BULLARD, RANDALL
7 Mesa Dr., Canyon, TX 79015, Phone: 806-655-0590 **Specialties:** Working/using straight knives and folders of his design or to customer specs. **Patterns:** Hunters, locking folders and slip-joint folders. **Technical:** Grinds O1, ATS-34 and 440C. Does file work. **Prices:** $125 to $300; some to $500. **Remarks:** Part-time maker; first knife sold in 1993. Doing business as Bullard Custom Knives. **Mark:** First and middle initials, last name, maker, city and state.

BULLARD, TOM
117 MC 8068, Flippin, AR 72634, Phone: 870-656-3428, tbullard8@live.com **Specialties:** Traditional folders and hunters. **Patterns:** Bowies, hunters, single and 2-blade trappers, lockback folders. **Technical:** Grinds 440C, A2, D2, ATS-34 and O1. **Prices:** $175 and up. **Remarks:** Offers filework and engraving by Norvell Foster and Terry Thies. Does not make screw-together knives. **Mark:** T Bullard.

BUMP, BRUCE D.
1103 Rex Ln, Walla Walla, WA 99362, Phone: 509-386-8879, brucebump1@gmail.com; Web: www.brucebumpknives.com **Specialties:** Slip joints, bowies and muzzle-loading pistol-knife combinations. **Patterns:** Maker's own damascus patterns including double mosaics. **Technical:** One-of-a-kind pieces. **Prices:** Please email for prices. **Remarks:** Full-time maker, ABS master smith since 2003. **Mark:** Bruce D. Bump "Custom", Bruce D. Bump "MS".

BURDEN, JAMES
405 Kelly St, Burkburnett, TX 76354

BURGER, FRED
Box 436, Munster, KZN, SOUTH AFRICA 4278, Phone: 27 39 3192316, info@swordcane.com; Web: www.swordcane.com **Specialties:** Sword canes, folders, and fixed blades. **Technical:** Double hollow ground and Poniard-style blades. **Prices:** $300 to $3000. **Remarks:** Full-time maker with son, Barry, since 1987. Member South African Guild. **Mark:** Last name in oval pierced by a dagger.

BURGER, PON
12 Glenwood Ave, Woodlands, Bulawayo, ZIMBABWE 75514 **Specialties:** Collector's items. **Patterns:** Fighters, locking folders of traditional styles, buckles. **Technical:** Scrimshaws 440C blade. Uses polished buffalo horn with brass fittings. Cased in buffalo hide book. **Prices:** $450 to $1100. **Remarks:** Full-time maker; first knife sold in 1973. Doing business as Burger Products. **Mark:** Spirit of Africa.

BURGER, TIAAN
69 Annie Botha Ave, Riviera,, Pretoria, GT, SOUTH AFRICA, tiaan_burger@hotmail.com **Specialties:** Sliplock and multi-blade folder. **Technical:** High carbon or stainless with African handle materials **Remarks:** Occasional fixed blade knives.

BURKE, BILL
20 Adams Ranch Rd., Boise, ID 83716, Phone: 208-336-3792, billburke@bladegallery.com **Specialties:** Hand-forged working knives. **Patterns:** Fowler pronghorn, clip point and drop point hunters. **Technical:** Forges 52100 and 5160. Makes own Damascus from 15N20 and 1084. **Prices:** $450 and up. **Remarks:** Dedicated to fixed-blade high-performance knives. ABS Journeyman. Also makes "Ed Fowler" miniatures. **Mark:** Initials connected.

BURNLEY, LUCAS
1005 La Font Rd. SW, Albuquerque, NM 87105, Phone: 505-814-9964, burnleyknives@comcast.net; www.burnleyknives.com **Specialties:** Contemporary tactical fixed blade, and folder designs, some art knives. **Patterns:** Hybrids, neo Japanese, defensive, utility and field knives. **Technical:** Grinds CPM154, A2, D2, BG42, Stainless Damascus as well as titanium and aerospace composites. **Prices:** Most models $225 to $1,500. Some specialty pieces higher. **Remarks:** Full-time maker, first knife sold in 2003. **Mark:** Last name or BRNLY.

BURNS, ROBERT
104 W. 6th St., Carver, MN 55315, Phone: 412-477-4677, wildernessironworks@gmail.com; www.wildernessironworks.org **Specialties:** Utility knives, fighters, axes, pattern-welded axes and Viking swords. **Technical:** Trained as a blacksmith in Colonial style, forges 1095, 1090, 1084, 15N20, 5160, W1, W2, D2, 440C and wrought iron. **Prices:** $135 to $3,000-plus. **Remarks:** Full-time maker; first knife made in 2005. **Mark:** A compass rose with all of the cardinal directions, and underneath, in cursive, "Wilderness Ironworks."

BURRIS, PATRICK R
1263 Cty. Rd. 750, Athens, TN 37303, Phone: 423-336-5715, burrispr@gmail.com **Specialties:** Traditional straight knives and locking-liner folders. **Patterns:** Hunters, bowies, locking-liner folders. **Technical:** Flat grinds high-grade stainless and damascus. **Remarks:** Offers filework, embellishment, exotic materials and damascus **Mark:** Last name in script.

BURROWS, CHUCK
WILD ROSE TRADING CO, 289 La Posta Canyon Rd, Durango, CO 81303, Phone: 970-259-8396, chuck@wrtcleather.com; Web: www.wrtcleather.com **Specialties:** Presentation knives, hawks, and sheaths based on the styles of the American frontier incorporating carving, beadwork, rawhide, braintan, and other period correct materials. Also makes other period style knives such as Scottish Dirks and Moorish jambiyahs. **Patterns:** Bowies, Dags, tomahawks, war clubs, and all other 18th and 19th century frontier style edged weapons and tools. **Technical:** Carbon steel only: 5160, 1080/1084, 1095, O1, Damascus-Our Frontier Shear Steel, plus other styles available on request. Forged knives, hawks, etc. are made in collaborations with bladesmiths. Gib Guignard (under the name of Cactus Rose) and Mark Williams (under the name UB Forged). Blades are usually forge finished and all items are given an aged period look. **Prices:** $500 plus. **Remarks:** Full-time maker, first knife sold in 1973. 40+ years experience working leather. **Mark:** A lazy eight or lazy eight with a capital T at the center. On leather either the lazy eight with T or a WRTC makers stamp.

BURROWS, STEPHEN R
1020 Osage St, Humboldt, KS 66748, Phone: 816-921-1573 **Specialties:** Fantasy straight knives of his design, to customer specs and in standard patterns; period pieces. **Patterns:** Fantasy, bird and trout knives, daggers, fighters and hunters. **Technical:** Forges 5160 and 1095 high-carbon steel, O1 and his Damascus. Offers lost wax casting in bronze or silver of cross guards and pommels. **Prices:** $65 to $600; some to $2000. **Remarks:** Full-time maker; first knife sold in 1983. Doing business as Gypsy Silk. **Mark:** Etched name.

BUSBIE, JEFF
John 316 Knife Works, 170 Towles Rd., Bloomingdale, GA 31302, Phone: 912-656-8238, jbusbie@comcast.net; Web: www.john316knifeworks.com **Specialties:** Working full-tang and hidden-tang fixed blades, locking-liner folders and hard-use knives. **Patterns:** Bowies, skinners, fighters, neck knives, work knives, bird knives, swords, art knives and other creations. **Technical:** Stock-removal maker using Alabama Damascus, CPM stainless steels and D2. Handles from hardwoods, G-10, ivory, bone and exotic materials. **Prices:** $100 to $800 and up. **Remarks:** Part-time maker building 150 to 200 knives a year; first knife sold in 2008. **Mark:** john 316 knife works with a cross in the middle.

BUSCH, STEVE
1989 Old Town Loop, Oakland, OR 97462, Phone: 541-459-2833, steve@buschcustomknives.com; Web: wwwbuschcustomknives.blademakers.com **Specialties:** D/A automatic right and left handed, folders, fixed blade working mainly in Damascus file work, functional art knives, nitrate bluing, heat bluing most all scale materials. **Prices:** $150 to $2000. **Remarks:** Trained under Vallotton family 3 1/2 years on own since 2002. **Mark:** Signature and date of completion on all knives.

BUSFIELD, JOHN
153 Devonshire Circle, Roanoke Rapids, NC 27870, Phone: 252-537-3949, Fax: 252-537-8704, busfield@charter.net **Specialties:** Investor-grade folders; high-grade working straight knives. **Patterns:** Original price-style and trailing-point interframe and sculpted-frame folders, drop-point hunters and semi-skinners. **Technical:** Grinds 154CM and ATS-34. Offers interframes, gold frames and inlays; uses jade, agate and lapis. **Prices:** $275 to $2000. **Remarks:** Full-time maker; first knife sold in 1979. **Mark:** Last name and address.

BUSSE, JERRY
11651 Co Rd 12, Wauseon, OH 43567, Phone: 419-923-6471 **Specialties:** Working straight knives. **Patterns:** Heavy combat knives and camp knives. **Technical:** Grinds D2, A2, INFI. **Prices:** $1100 to $3500. **Remarks:** Full-time maker; first knife sold in 1983. **Mark:** Last name in logo.

BUTLER, BART
822 Seventh St, Ramona, CA 92065, Phone: 760-789-6431

BUTLER, JOHN
777 Tyre Rd, Havana, FL 32333, Phone: 850-539-5742 **Specialties:** Hunters, Bowies, period. **Technical:** Damascus, 52100, 5160, L6 steels. **Prices:** $80 and up. **Remarks:** Making knives since 1986. Journeyman (ABS). **Mark:** JB.

BUTLER, JOHN R
20162 6th Ave N E, Shoreline, WA 98155, Phone: 206-362-3847, rjjjrb@sprynet.com

BUXTON, BILL
155 Oak Bend Rd, Kaiser, MO 65047, Phone: 573-348-3577, camper@yhti.net; Web: www.billbuxtonknives.com **Specialties:** Forged fancy and working straight knives and folders. Mostly one-of-a-kind pieces. **Patterns:** Fighters, daggers, Bowies, hunters, linerlock folders, axes and tomahawks. **Technical:** Forges 52100, 0-1, 1080. Makes own Damascus (mosaic and random patterns) from 1080, 1095, 15n20, and powdered metals 1084 and 4800a. Offers sterling silver inlay, n/s pin patterning and pewter pouring on axe and hawk handles. **Prices:** $300 to $2,500. **Remarks:** Full-time maker, sold first knife in 1998. **Mark:** First initial and last name.

BUZEK, STANLEY
PO Box 731, Waller, TX 77484, Phone: 936-372-1933, stan@sbuzekknives.com; Web: www.sbuzekknives.com **Specialties:** Traditional slip-joint pocketknives, LinerLocks and frame-lock folders, and fixed-blade hunters and skinners. **Technical:** Grinds, heat treats and Rockwell tests CPM-154, and some traditional folders in O1 tool steel. Hand-rubbed finishes. Dyed jigged bone, mammoth ivory and fine stabilized woods. **Prices:** $250 and up. **Remarks:** Serious part-time maker; first knife sold in 2006. **Mark:** S. Buzek on riccasso.

BYBEE, BARRY J
795 Lock Rd. E, Cadiz, KY 42211-8615

Specialties: Working straight knives of his design. **Patterns:** Hunters, fighters, boot knives, tantos and Bowies. **Technical:** Grinds ATS-34, 440C. Likes stag and Micarta for handle materials. **Prices:** $125 to $200; some to $1000. **Remarks:** Part-time maker; first knife sold in 1968. **Mark:** Arrowhead logo with name, city and state.

BYRD, WESLEY L
189 Countryside Dr, Evensville, TN 37332, Phone: 423-775-3826, w.l.byrd@worldnet.att.net
Specialties: Hunters, fighters, Bowies, dirks, sgian dubh, utility, and camp knives. **Patterns:** Wire rope, random patterns. Twists, W's, Ladder, Kite Tail. **Technical:** Uses 52100, 1084, 5160, L6, and 15n20. **Prices:** Starting at $180. **Remarks:** Prefer to work with customer for their design preferences. ABS Journeyman Smith. **Mark:** BYRD, WB <X.

C

CABRERA, SERGIO B
24500 Broad Ave, Wilmington, CA 90744

CAFFREY, EDWARD J
2608 Central Ave West, Great Falls, MT 59404, Phone: 406-727-9102, caffreyknives@gmail.com; Web: www.caffreyknives.net
Specialties: One-of-a-kind using and collector quality pieces. Will accept some customer designs. **Patterns:** Bowies, folders, hunters, fighters, camp/utility, tomahawks and hatchets. **Technical:** Forges all types of Damascus, specializing in Mosaic Damascus, 52100, 5160, 1080/1084 and most other commonly forged steels. **Prices:** Starting at $185; typical hunters start at $400; collector pieces can range into the thousands. **Remarks:** Offers one-on-one basic and advanced bladesmithing classes. ABS Mastersmith. Full-time maker. **Mark:** Stamped last name and MS on straight knives. Etched last name with MS on folders.

CALDWELL, BILL
255 Rebecca, West Monroe, LA 71292, Phone: 318-323-3025
Specialties: Straight knives and folders with machined bolsters and liners. **Patterns:** Fighters, Bowies, survival knives, tomahawks, razors and push knives. **Technical:** Owns and operates a very large, well-equipped blacksmith and bladesmith shop with six large forges and eight power hammers. **Prices:** $400 to $3500; some to $10,000. **Remarks:** Full-time maker and self-styled blacksmith; first knife sold in 1962. **Mark:** Wild Bill and Sons.

CALLAHAN, F TERRY
PO Box 880, Boerne, TX 78006, Phone: 210-260-2378, ftclaw@gvtc.com
Specialties: Custom hand-forged edged knives, collectible and functional. **Patterns:** Bowies, folders, daggers, hunters & camp knives. **Technical:** Forges damascus and 5160. Offers filework, silver inlay and handmade sheaths. **Prices:** $150 to $500. **Remarks:** First knife sold in 1990. ABS/Journeyman Bladesmith. **Mark:** Initial "F" inside a keystone.

CALVERT JR., ROBERT W (BOB)
911 Julia, Rayville, LA 71269, Phone: 318-348-4490, rcalvert1@gmail.com
Specialties: Using and hunting knives; your design or his. Since 1990. **Patterns:** Forges own Damascus; all patterns. **Technical:** 5160, D2, 52100, 1084. Prefers natural handle material. **Prices:** $250 and up. **Remarks:** TOMB Member, ABS. Journeyman Smith. ABS Board of directors **Mark:** Calvert (Block) J S.

CAMBRON, HENRY
169 Severn Way, Dallas, GA 30132-0317, Phone: 770-598-5721, worldclassknives@bellsouth.net; Web: www.worldclassknives.com
Specialties: Everyday carry, working and small neck knives. **Patterns:** Hunters, bowies, camp, utility and combat. **Technical:** Forge, stock removal, filework. Differential quench. Tuff-etched finish. Hand-sewn and Kydex sheaths. **Prices:** $65 to $650. **Remarks:** Full-time maker. **Mark:** First and last name over USA on blades. HC on sheaths.

CAMERER, CRAIG
3766 Rockbridge Rd, Chesterfield, IL 62630, Phone: 618-753-2147, craig@camererknives.com; Web: www.camererknives.com
Specialties: Everyday carry knives, hunters and Bowies. **Patterns:** D-guard, historical recreations and fighters. **Technical:** Most of his knives are forged to shape. **Prices:** $100 and up. **Remarks:** Member of the ABS and PKA. Journeymen Smith ABS.

CAMERON, RON G
PO Box 183, Logandale, NV 89021, Phone: 702-398-3356, rntcameron@mvdsl.com
Specialties: Fancy and embellished working/using straight knives and folders of his design. **Patterns:** Bowies, hunters and utility/camp knives. **Technical:** Grinds ATS-34, AEB-L and Devin Thomas Damascus or own Damascus from 1084 and 15N20. Does filework, fancy pins, mokume fittings. Uses exotic hardwoods, stag and Micarta for handles. Pearl & mammoth ivory. **Prices:** $175 to $850 some to $1000. **Remarks:** Part-time maker; first knife sold in 1994. Doing business as Cameron Handmade Knives. **Mark:** Last name, town, state or last name.

CAMPBELL, DICK
196 Graham Rd, Colville, WA 99114, Phone: 509-684-6080, dicksknives@aol.com
Specialties: Working straight knives, folders and period pieces. **Patterns:** Hunters, fighters, boots and 19th century bowies. **Technical:** Grinds 440C and 154CM. **Prices:** $350 to $4,500. **Remarks:** Full-time maker. First knife sold in 1975. **Mark:** Name.

CAMPBELL, DOUG
46 W Boulder Rd., McLeod, MT 59052, Phone: 406-222-8153, dkcampbl@yahoo.com
Specialties: Sole authorship of fixed blades and folding knives. **Patterns:** Fixed blades, LinerLocks and frame-lock folders. **Technical:** Forged high-carbon, pattern-welded

damascus, Elmax and CPM 154 steels. **Prices:** $300-$1,300. **Remarks:** ABS journeyman smith. **Mark:** Grizzly track surrounded by a "C," or "Campbell" etched on spine.

CAMPOS, IVAN
R.XI de Agosto 107, Tatui, SP, BRAZIL 18270-000, Phone: 00-55-15-997120993, Fax: 00-55-15-2594368, ivan@ivancampos.net; Web: www.ivancampos.net
Specialties: Brazilian handmade and antique knives.

CANDRELLA, JOE
1219 Barness Dr, Warminster, PA 18974, Phone: 215-675-0143
Specialties: Working straight knives, some fancy. **Patterns:** Daggers, boots, Bowies. **Technical:** Grinds 440C and 154CM. **Prices:** $100 to $200; some to $1000. **Remarks:** Part-time maker; first knife sold in 1985. Does business as Franjo. **Mark:** FRANJO with knife as J.

CANTER, RONALD E
96 Bon Air Circle, Jackson, TN 38305, Phone: 731-668-1780, canterr@charter.net
Specialties: Traditional working knives to customer specs. **Patterns:** Beavertail skinners, Bowies, hand axes and folding lockers. **Technical:** Grinds 440C, Micarta & deer antler. **Prices:** $75 and up. **Remarks:** Spare-time maker; first knife sold in 1973. **Mark:** Three last initials intertwined.

CANTRELL, KITTY D
19720 Hwy 78, Ramona, CA 92076, Phone: 760-788-8304

CAPDEPON, RANDY
553 Joli Rd, Carencro, LA 70520, Phone: 318-896-4113, Fax: 318-896-8753
Specialties: Straight knives and folders of his design. **Patterns:** Hunters and locking folders. **Technical:** Grinds ATS-34, 440C and D2. **Prices:** $200 to $600. **Remarks:** Part-time maker; first knife made in 1992. Doing business as Capdepon Knives. **Mark:** Last name.

CAPDEPON, ROBERT
829 Vatican Rd, Carencro, LA 70520, Phone: 337-896-8753, Fax: 318-896-8753
Specialties: Traditional straight knives and folders of his design. **Patterns:** Boots, hunters and locking folders. **Technical:** Grinds ATS-34, 440C and D2. Hand-rubbed finish on blades. Likes natural horn materials for handles, including ivory. Offers engraving. **Prices:** $250 to $750. **Remarks:** Full-time maker; first knife made in 1992. **Mark:** Last name.

CAREY, PETER
P.O. Box 4712, Lago Vista, TX 78645, Phone: 512-358-4839, Web: www.careyblade.com
Specialties: Tactical folders, Every Day Carry to presentation grade. Working straight knives, hunters, and tactical. **Patterns:** High-tech patterns of his own design, Linerlocks, Framelocks, Flippers. **Technical:** Hollow grinds CPM154, CPM S35VN, stainless Damascus, Stellite. Uses titanium, zirconium, carbon fiber, G10, and select natural handle materials. **Prices:** Starting at $450. **Remarks:** Full-time maker, first knife sold in 2002. **Mark:** Last name in diamond.

CARLISLE, JEFF
PO Box 282 12753 Hwy 200, Simms, MT 59477, Phone: 406-264-5693

CARPENTER, RONALD W
Rt. 4 Box 323, Jasper, TX 75951, Phone: 409-384-4087

CARR, JOSEPH E.
W183 N8974 Maryhill Drive, Menomonee Falls, WI 53051, Phone: 920-625-3607, carsmith1@SBCGlobal.net; Web: Hembrook3607@charter.net
Specialties: JC knives. **Patterns:** Hunters, Bowies, fighting knives, every day carries. **Technical:** Grinds ATS-34 and Damascus. **Prices:** $200 to $750. **Remarks:** Full-time maker for 2 years, being taught by Ron Hembrook.

CARR, TIM
3660 Pillon Rd, Muskegon, MI 49445, Phone: 231-766-3582, tim@blackbearforgemi.com Web:www.blackbearforgemi.com
Specialties: Hunters, camp knives. **Patterns:** His or yours. **Technical:** Hand forges 5160, 52100 and Damascus. **Prices:** $125 to $700. **Remarks:** Part-time maker. **Mark:** The letter combined from maker's initials TRC.

CARRILLO, DWAINE
C/O AIRKAT KNIVES, Phone: 405-503-5879, tripwire7@cox.net; Web: www.airkatknives.com

CARROLL, CHAD
12182 McClelland, Grant, MI 49327, Phone: 231-834-9183, CHAD724@msn.com
Specialties: Hunters, Bowies, folders, swords, tomahawks. **Patterns:** Fixed blades, folders. **Prices:** $100 to $2000. **Remarks:** ABS Journeyman May 2002. **Mark:** A backwards C next to a forward C, maker's initials.

CARTER, FRED
5219 Deer Creek Rd, Wichita Falls, TX 76302, Phone: 904-723-4020, fcarter40@live.com
Specialties: High-art investor-class straight knives; some working hunters and fighters. **Patterns:** Classic daggers, Bowies; interframe, stainless and blued steel folders with gold inlay. **Technical:** Grinds a variety of steels. Uses no glue or solder. Engraves and inlays. **Prices:** Generally upscale. **Remarks:** Full-time maker. **Mark:** Signature in oval logo.

CARTER, MIKE
2522 Frankfort Ave, Louisville, KY 40206, Phone: 502-387-4844, mike@cartercrafts.com Web: www.cartercrafts.com
Remarks: Voting Member Knifemakers Guild.

CARTER, MURRAY M
2038 N.W. Aloclek Dr. #225, Hillsboro, OR 97124, Phone: 503-466-1331, murray@

cartercutlery.com; Web: www.cartercutlery.com
Specialties: Traditional Japanese kitchen knives, utilizing San soh ko (three layer) or Kata-ha (two layer) blade construction. Laminated neck knives, traditional Japanese etc. **Patterns:** Works from over 200 standard Japanese and North American designs. **Technical:** Hot forges and cold forges Hitachi white steel #1, Hitachi blue super steel exclusively. **Prices:** $400 to $4,000. **Remarks:** Owns and operates North America's most exclusive traditional Japanese bladesmithing school and Apprentice Program; web site available at which viewers can subscribe to 10 free knife sharpening and maintenance reports. **Mark:** Name in cursive, often appearing with Japanese characters. Other: Offers the world's finest video instruction on sharpening.

CARTER, SHAYNE
5302 Rosewood Cir., Payson, UT 84651, Phone: 801-913-0181, shaynemcarter@hotmail.com
Specialties: Fixed blades. **Patterns:** Hunters, bowies and fighters. **Technical:** Flat grinds, hand finishes, forges blade steel, including own damascus, some 1084, 52100 and 5160. **Remarks:** Part-time maker; first damascus made in 1984.

CASEY, KEVIN
4 Broken Arrow Rd., Lander, WY 82520, Phone: 269-719-7412, kevinvecasey@gmail.com; Web: www.kevincaseycustomknives.com
Specialties: Fixed blades and folders. **Patterns:** Liner lock folders and feather Damascus pattern, mammoth ivory. **Technical:** Forges Damascus and carbon steels. **Prices:** Starting at $500 - $2500. **Remarks:** Member ABS, Knifemakers Guild, Custom Knifemakers Collectors Association.

CASHEN, KEVIN R
Matherton Forge, 5615 Tyler St., Hubbardston, MI 48845, Phone: 989-981-6780, kevin@cashenblades.com; Web: www.cashenblades.com
Specialties: User-oriented straight knives and medieval and renaissance period European swords and daggers. **Patterns:** Hunters and skinners, bowies and camp knives, swords and daggers. **Technical:** Hand forged blades of O1, L6 and maker's own O1-L6-and-O2 damascus, occasionally W2 or 1095, all heat-treated to exacting metallurgical standards. **Prices:** $200 for small hunters to $9,000+ for museum-quality swords, with an average range of $400-$2,000. **Remarks:** Full-time maker, instructor/speaker/consultant; first knife sold in 1985. **Mark:** Gothic "K.C." with master smith stamp. On period pieces, a crowned castle encircled with "Cashen."

CASTEEL, DIANNA
PO Box 63, Monteagle, TN 37356, Phone: 931-212-4341, ddcasteel@charter.net; Web: www.casteelcustomknives.com
Specialties: Small, delicate daggers and miniatures; most knives one-of-a-kind. **Patterns:** Daggers, boot knives, fighters and miniatures. **Technical:** Grinds 440C. Offers stainless Damascus. **Prices:** Start at $350; miniatures start at $250. **Remarks:** Full-time maker. **Mark:** Di in script.

CASTEEL, DOUGLAS
PO Box 63, Monteagle, TN 37356, Phone: 931-212-4341, Fax: 931-723-1856, ddcasteel@charter.net; Web: www.casteelcustomknives.com
Specialties: One-of-a-kind collector-class period pieces. **Patterns:** Daggers, Bowies, swords and folders. **Technical:** Grinds 440C. Offers gold and silver castings.Offers stainless Damascus **Prices:** Upscale. **Remarks:** Full-time maker; first knife sold in 1982. **Mark:** Last name.

CASTELLUCIO, RICH
220 Stairs Rd, Amsterdam, NY 12010, Phone: 518-843-5540, rcastellucio@nycap.rr.com
Patterns: Bowies, push daggers, and fantasy knives. **Technical:** Uses ATS-34, 440C, 154CM. I use stabilized wood, bone for the handles. Guards are made of copper, brass, stainless, nickle, and mokume.

CASTON, DARRIEL
125 Ashcat Way, Folsom, CA 95630, Phone: 916-539-0744, darrielc@gmail.com

CASWELL, JOE
173 S Ventu Park Rd, Newbury, CA 91320, Phone: 805-499-0707, Web:www.caswellknives.com
Specialties: Historic pattern welded knives and swords, hand forged. Also high precision folding and fixed blade "gentleman" and "tactical" knives of his design, period firearms. Inventor of the "In-Line" retractable pocket clip for folding knives. **Patterns:** Hunters, tactical/utility, fighters, bowies, daggers, pattern welded medieval swords, precision folders. **Technical:** Forges own Damascus especially historic forms. Sometimes uses modern stainless steels and Damascus of other makers. Makes some pieces entirely by hand, others using the latest CNC techniques and by hand. Makes sheaths too.**Prices:** $100-$5,500. **Remarks:** Full time makers since 1995. Making mostly historic recreations for exclusive clientele. Recently moving into folding knives and 'modern' designs. **Mark:** CASWELL or CASWELL USA Accompanied by a mounted knight logo.

CATOE, DAVID R
4024 Heutte Dr, Norfolk, VA 23518, Phone: 757-480-3191
Technical: Does own forging, Damascus and heat treatments. **Prices:** $200 to $500; some higher. **Remarks:** Part-time maker; trained by Dan Maragni 1985-1988; first knife sold 1989. **Mark:** Leaf of a camellia.

CECCHINI, GUSTAVO T.
2841 XV Novembro, Sao Jose Rio Preto SP, BRAZIL 15015110, Phone: +55 (17)3222-4267, tomaki@terra.com.br; Web: www.gtcknives.com
Specialties: Tactical and HiTech folders. **Technical:** Stock removal. Stainless steel fixed blades. S30V, S35Vn, S90V, CowryX, Damasteel, Chad Nichols SS damascus, RWL 34, CPM 154 CM, BG 42. **Prices:** $500 - $1500. **Remarks:** Full-time since 2004. **Mark:** Tang Stamp "GTC"

CEPRANO, PETER J.
213 Townsend Brooke Rd., Auburn, ME 04210, Phone: 207-786-5322, bpknives@gmail.com
Specialties: Traditional working/using straight knives; tactical/defense straight knives. Own designs or to a customer's specs. **Patterns:** Hunters, skinners, utility, Bowies, fighters, camp and survival, neck knives. **Technical:** Forges 1095, 5160, W2, 52100 and old files; grinds CPM154cm, ATS-34, 440C, D2, CPMs30v, Damascus from other makes and other tool steels. Hand-sewn and tooled leather and Kydex sheaths. **Prices:** Starting at $125. **Remarks:** Full-time maker, first knife sold in 2001. Doing business as Big Pete Knives. **Mark:** Bold BPK over small BigPeteKnivesUSA.

CHAFFEE, JEFF L
14314 N. Washington St, PO Box 1, Morris, IN 47033, Phone: 812-212-6188
Specialties: Fancy working and utility folders and straight knives. **Patterns:** Fighters, dagger, hunter and locking folders. **Technical:** Grinds commercial Damascus, 440C, ATS-34, D2 and O1. Prefers natural handle materials. **Prices:** $350 to $2000. **Remarks:** Part-time maker; first knife sold in 1988. **Mark:** Last name.

CHAMBERLAIN, JON A
15 S. Lombard, E. Wenatchee, WA 98802, Phone: 509-884-6591
Specialties: Working and kitchen knives to customer specs; exotics on special order. **Patterns:** Over 100 patterns in stock. **Technical:** Prefers ATS-34, D2, L6 and Damascus. **Prices:** Start at $50. **Remarks:** First knife sold in 1986. Doing business as Johnny Custom Knifemakers. **Mark:** Name in oval with city and state enclosing.

CHAMBERLIN, JOHN A
11535 Our Rd., Anchorage, AK 99516, Phone: 907-346-1524, Fax: 907-562-4583
Specialties: Art and working knives. **Patterns:** Daggers and hunters; some folders;. **Technical:** Grinds ATS-34, 440C, A2, D2 and Damascus. Uses Alaskan materials such as oosic, jade, whale jawbone, fossil ivory. **Prices:** Start at $200. **Remarks:** Favorite knives to make are double-edged. Does own heat treating and cryogenic deep freeze. Full-time maker; first knife sold in 1984. **Mark:** Name over English shield and dagger.

CHAMBERS, RONNY
1900 W. Mississippi St., Beebe, AR 72012, Phone: 501-288-1476, chambersronny@yahoo.com; Web: www.chamberscustomknives.net

CHAMBLIN, JOEL
960 New Hebron Church Rd, Concord, GA 30206, Phone: 678-588-6769, chamblinknives@yahoo.com Web: chamblinknives.com
Specialties: Fancy and working folders. **Patterns:** Fancy locking folders, traditional, multi-blades and utility. **Technical:** Uses ATS-34, CPM 154, and commercial Damascus. Offers filework. **Prices:** Start at $400. **Remarks:** Full-time maker; first knife sold in 1989. **Mark:** Last name.

CHAMPION, ROBERT
7001 Red Rock Rd., Amarillo, TX 79118, Phone: 806-622-3970, rchampknives@gmail.com; www.rchampknives.com
Specialties: Traditional working straight knives. **Patterns:** Hunters, skinners, camp knives, bowies and daggers. **Technical:** Grinds 440C, ATS-34, D2 and stainless damascus. **Prices:** $100 to $1,800. **Remarks:** Part-time maker; first knife sold in 1979. Stream-lined hunters. **Mark:** Last name with dagger logo, city and state.

CHAPO, WILLIAM G
45 Wildridge Rd, Wilton, CT 06897, Phone: 203-544-9424
Specialties: Classic straight knives and folders of his design and to customer specs; period pieces. **Patterns:** Boots, Bowies and locking folders. **Technical:** Forges stainless Damascus. Offers filework. **Prices:** $750 and up. **Remarks:** Full-time maker; first knife sold in 1989. **Mark:** First and middle initials, last name, city, state.

CHARD, GORDON R
104 S. Holiday Lane, Iola, KS 66749, Phone: 620-365-2311, Fax: 620-365-2311, gchard@cox.net
Specialties: High tech folding knives in one-of-a-kind styles. **Patterns:** Liner locking folders of own design. Also fixed blade Art Knives. **Technical:** Clean work with attention to fit and finish. Blade steel mostly ATS-34 and 154CM, some CPM440V Vaso Wear and Damascus. **Prices:** $150 to $2500. **Remarks:** First knife sold in 1983. **Mark:** Name, city and state surrounded by wheat on each side.

CHASE, JOHN E
217 Walnut, Aledo, TX 76008, Phone: 817-441-8331, jchaseknives@sbcglobal.net
Specialties: Straight working knives in standard patterns or to customer specs. **Patterns:** Hunters, fighters, daggers and Bowies. **Technical:** Grinds D2 and O1; offers mostly satin finishes. **Prices:** Start at $325. **Remarks:** Part-time maker; first knife sold in 1974. **Mark:** Last name in logo.

CHAUVIN, JOHN
200 Anna St, Scott, LA 70583, Phone: 337-237-6138, Fax: 337-230-7980
Specialties: Traditional working and using straight knives of his design, to customer specs and in standard patterns. **Patterns:** Bowies, fighters, and hunters. **Technical:** Grinds ATS-34, 440C and O1 high-carbon. Paul Bos heat treating. Uses ivory, stag, oosic and stabilized Louisiana swamp maple for handle materials. Makes sheaths using alligator and ostrich. **Prices:** $200 and up. Bowies start at $500. **Remarks:** Part-time maker; first knife sold in 1995. **Mark:** Full name, city, state.

CHAVEZ, RAMON
314 N. 5th St., Belen, NM 87002, Phone: 505-453-6008, ramon@chavesknives.com; Web: www.chavesknives.com
Specialties: Frame-lock folding knives and fixed blades. **Patterns:** Hunters, skinners, bushcraft, tactical, neck knives and utility. **Technical:** Grind/stock removal of CPM D2, D2 and CPM 3V. Handles are mostly titanium and Micarta. Thermal molding plastic for sheaths. **Prices:** Start at $225. **Remarks:** Full-time maker; first knife made in 1993, first knife sold in 2010. **Mark:** CHAVES USA with skeleton key.

CHEATHAM, BILL
PO Box 636, Laveen, AZ 85339, Phone: 602-237-2786, blademan76@aol.com
Specialties: Working straight knives and folders. **Patterns:** Hunters, fighters, boots and axes; locking folders. **Technical:** Grinds 440C. **Prices:** $150 to $350; exceptional knives to $600. **Remarks:** Full-time maker; first knife sold in 1976. **Mark:** Name, city, state.

CHERRY, FRANK J
3412 Tiley N.E., Albuquerque, NM 87110, Phone: 505-883-8643

CHEW, LARRY
3025 De leon Dr., Weatherford, TX 76087, Phone: 817-573-8035, chewman@swbell.net; Web: www.voodooinside.com
Specialties: High-tech folding knives. **Patterns:** Double action automatic and manual folding patterns of his design. **Technical:** CAD designed folders utilizing roller bearing pivot design known as "VooDoo." Double action automatic folders with a variety of obvious and disguised release mechanisms, some with lock-outs. **Prices:** Manual folders start at $475, double action autos start at $750. **Remarks:** Made and sold first knife in 1988, first folder in 1989. Full-time maker since 1997. **Mark:** Name and location etched in blade, Damascus autos marked on spring inside frame. Earliest knives stamped LC.

CHILDERS, DAVID
15575 Marina Dr., Unit 227, Montgomery, TX 77356, childersdavid@att.net; Web: www.davidchildersknives.com

CHINNOCK, DANIEL T.
380 River Ridge Dr., Union, MO 63084, Phone: 314-276-6936, Web: www.DanChinnock.com; email: Sueanddanc@cs.com
Specialties: One of a kind folders in Damascus and Mammoth Ivory. Performs intricate pearl inlays into snake wood and giraffe bone. Makes matchingt ivory pistol grips for colt 1911's and Colt SAA. **Patterns:** New folder designs each year, thin ground and delicate gentleman's folders, large "hunting" folders in stainless Damascus and CPM154. Several standard models carried by Internet dealers. **Prices:** $500-$1500 **Remarks:** Full-time maker in 2005 and a voting member of the Knifemakers Guild. Performs intricate file work on all areas of knife. **Mark:** Signature on inside of backbar, starting in 2009 blades are stamped with a large "C" and "Dan" buried inside the "C".

CHOMILIER, ALAIN AND JORIS
20 rue des Hauts de Chanturgue, Clermont-Ferrand, FRANCE 63100, Phone: + 33 4 73 25 64 47, jo_chomilier@yahoo.fr
Specialties: One-of-a-kind knives; exclusive designs; art knives in carved patinated bronze, mainly folders, some straight knives and art daggers. **Patterns:** Liner-lock, side-lock, button-lock, lockback folders. **Technical:** Grind carbon and stainless damascus; also carve and patinate bronze. **Prices:** $400 to $3000, some to $4000. **Remarks:** Spare-time makers; first knife sold in 1995; Use fossil stone and ivory, mother-of-pearl, (fossil) coral, meteorite, bronze, gemstones, high karat gold. **Mark:** A. J. Chomilier in italics.

CHRISTENSEN, JON P
516 Blue Grouse, Stevensville, MT 59870, Phone: 406-697-8377, jpcknives@gmail.com; Web: www.jonchristensenknives.com
Specialties: Hunting/utility knives, folders, art knives. **Patterns:** Mosaic damascus**Technical:** Sole authorship, forges 01, 1084, 52100, 5160, Damascus from 1084/15N20. **Prices:** $220 and up. **Remarks:** ABS Mastersmith, first knife sold in 1999. **Mark:** First and middle initial surrounded by last initial.

CHURCHMAN, T W (TIM)
475 Saddle Horn Drive, Bandera, TX 78003, Phone: 210-240-0317, tim.churchman@nustarenergy.com
Specialties: Fancy and traditional straight knives. Bird/trout knives of his design and to customer specs. **Patterns:** Bird/trout knives, Bowies, daggers, fighters, boot knives, some miniatures. **Technical:** Grinds 440C, D2 and 154CM. Offers stainless fittings, fancy filework, exotic and stabilized woods, elk and other antler, and hand sewed lined sheaths. Also flower pins as a style. **Prices:** $350 to $450; some to $2,250. **Remarks:** Part-time maker; first knife made in 1981 after reading "KNIVES '81." Doing business as "Custom Knives Churchman Made." **Mark:** "Churchman" over Texas outline, "Bandera" under.

CIMMS, GREG
Kayne Custom Knife Works, 2297 Rt. 44, Ste. B, Pleasant Valley, NY 12569, Phone: 845-475-7220, cimms1@aol.com
Patterns: Kitchen knives, hunters, bowies, fighters, small swords, bird-and-trout knives, tactical pieces, tomahawks, axes and bushcraft blades. **Technical:** Damascus and straight-carbon-steel cutlery, with some mosaic-damascus and powder-metal pieces. **Prices:** $300 to $4,000. **Remarks:** Full-time maker since 2014; first knife made in 2013. **Mark:** A compass with a "K" in the middle.

CLAIBORNE, JEFF
1470 Roberts Rd, Franklin, IN 46131, Phone: 317-736-7443, jeff@claiborneknives.com; Web: www.claiborneknives.com
Specialties: Multi blade slip joint folders. All one-of-a-kind by hand, no jigs or fixtures, swords, straight knives, period pieces, camp knives, hunters, fighters, ethnic swords

all periods. Handle: uses stag, pearl, oosic, bone ivory, mastadon-mammoth, elephant or exotic woods. **Technical:** Forges high-carbon steel, makes Damascus, forges cable grinds, O1, 1095, 5160, 52100, L6. **Prices:** $250 and up. **Remarks:** Full-time maker; first knife sold in 1989. **Mark:** Stylized initials in an oval.

CLAIBORNE, RON
2918 Ellistown Rd, Knox, TN 37924, Phone: 615-524-2054, Bowie@icy.net
Specialties: Multi-blade slip joints, swords, straight knives. **Patterns:** Hunters, daggers, folders. **Technical:** Forges Damascus: mosaic, powder mosaic. Prefers bone and natural handle materials; some exotic woods. **Prices:** $125 to $2500. **Remarks:** Part-time maker; first knife sold in 1979. Doing business as Thunder Mountain Forge Claiborne Knives. **Mark:** Claiborne.

CLARK, D E (LUCKY)
413 Lyman Lane, Johnstown, PA 15909-1409
Specialties: Working straight knives and folders to customer specs. **Patterns:** Customer designs. **Technical:** Grinds D2, 440C, 154CM. **Prices:** $100 to $200; some higher. **Remarks:** Part-time maker; first knife sold in 1975. **Mark:** Name on one side; "Lucky" on other.

CLARK, HOWARD F
115 35th Pl, Runnells, IA 50237, Phone: 515-966-2126, howard@mvforge.com; Web: mvforge.com
Specialties: Currently Japanese-style swords. **Patterns:** Katana. **Technical:** Forges L6 and 1086. **Prices:** $1200 to 5000. **Remarks:** Full-time maker; first knife sold in 1979. Doing business as Morgan Valley Forge. Prior **Mark:** Block letters and serial number on folders; anvil/initials logo on straight knives. Current **Mark:** Two character kanji "Big Ear."

CLARK, JASON
24896 77th Rd., O'Brien, FL 32071, Phone: 386-935-2922, jclark@clarkcustomknives.com; Web: www.clarkcustomknives.com
Specialties: Frame-lock and LinerLock folders. **Patterns:** Drop points, tantos, Persians, clip points, razors and wharncliffes. **Technical:** Sole authorship of knives, constructing 100 percent in house, including designing, cutting, shaping, grinding, heat treating, fitting and finishing. Top quality materials and components, as well as hand-rubbed finishes, media blasting, stonewashing, anodizing and polishing. Licensed to use IKBS (Ikoma Korth Bearing System). **Remarks:** Part-time maker. **Mark:** Cross with initials incorporated.

CLEVELAND, MIKE
Half Life Knives, 329 W. Strasburg Way, Mustang, OK 73064, Phone: 405-627-6097, lawdawg3006@yahoo.com
Specialties: Stock removal fixed-blade knives, multi-ground tactical, hunting, chef's knives and tactical 'hawks. **Patterns:** Multi-ground tactical, hunting, kitchen knives and 'hawks. **Technical:** Stock-removal method of blade making, including 80CrV2, 1095, 1084, 1075, 5160, 52100, CPM M4 REX and damascus steels. **Remarks:** Full-time maker, 'hawk maker. **Mark:** Half skull with half Life Knives circling it.

CLINCO, MARCUS
821 Appelby Street, Venice, CA 90291, Phone: 818-610-9640, marcus@clincoknives.com; Web: www.clincoknives.com
Specialties: I make mostly fixed blade knives with an emphasis on everyday working and tactical models. Most of my knives are stock removal with the exception of my sole authored damascus blades. I have several integral models including a one piece tactical model named the viper. **Technical:** Most working knife models in ATS 34. Integrals in O-1, D-2 and 440 C. Damascus in 1080 and 15 N 20. Large camp and Bowie models in 5160 and D-2. Handle materials used include micarta, stabilized wood, G-10 and occasionally stag and ivory. **Prices:** $200 - $600.

COATS, KEN
317 5th Ave, Stevens Point, WI 54481, Phone: 715-544-0115
Specialties: Does own jigged bone scales **Patterns:** Traditional slip joints - shadow patterns **Technical:** ATS-34 Blades and springs. Milled frames. Grinds ATS-34, 440C. Stainless blades and backsprings. Does all own heat treating and freeze cycle. Blades are drawn to 60RC. Nickel silver or brass bolsters on folders are soldered, neutralized and pinned. Handles are jigged bone, hardwoods antler, and Micarta. Cuts and jigs own bone, usually shades of brown or green. **Prices:** $300 and up

COCKERHAM, LLOYD
1717 Carolyn Ave, Denham Springs, IA 70726, Phone: 225-665-1565

Coffee, Jim
2785 Rush Rd., Norton, OH 44203, Phone: 330-631-3355, jcoffee735@aol.com
Specialties: Stock Removal, hunters, skinners, fighters. **Technical:** Bowie handle material - stabilized wood, micarta, mammoth ivory, stag. Full tang and hidden tang. Steels - 0-1, d-2, 5160, damascus **Prices:** $150 to $500 and up. **Remarks:** Part-time maker since 2008.**Mark:** full name in a football etch.

COFFEY, BILL
68 Joshua Ave, Clovis, CA 93611, Phone: 559-299-4259, williamccoffey@comcast.net
Specialties: Working and fancy straight knives and folders of his design. **Patterns:** Hunters, fighters, utility, LinerLock® folders and fantasy knives. **Technical:** Grinds 440C, ATS-34, A-Z and commercial Damascus. **Prices:** $250 to $1000; some to $2500. **Remarks:** Full-time maker. First knife sold in 1993. **Mark:** First and last name, city, state.

COFFMAN, DANNY
541 Angel Dr S, Jacksonville, AL 36265-5787, Phone: 256-435-1619
Specialties: Straight knives and folders of his design. Now making liner locks for $650 to $1200 with natural handles and contrasting Damascus blades and bolsters. **Patterns:** Hunters, locking and slip-joint folders. **Technical:** Grinds Damascus, 440C and D2.

custom knifemakers

COHEA—COOMBS JR.

Offers filework and engraving. **Prices:** $100 to $400; some to $800. **Remarks:** Spare-time maker; first knife sold in 1992. Doing business as Customs by Coffman. **Mark:** Last name stamped or engraved.

COHEA, JOHN M
114 Rogers Dr., Nettleton, MS 38855, Phone: 662-322-5916, jhncohea@hotmail.com
Web: http://jmcknives.blademakers.com
Specialties: Frontier style knives, hawks, and leather. **Patterns:** Bowies, hunters, patch/neck knives, tomahawks, and friction folders. **Technical:** Makes both forged and stock removal knives using high carbon steels and damascus. Uses natural handle materials that include antler, bone, ivory, horn, and figured hardwoods. Also makes rawhide covered sheaths that include fringe, tacks, antique trade beads, and other period correct materials. **Prices:** $100 - $1500, some higher. **Remarks:** Part-time maker, first knife sold in 1999. **Mark:** COHEA stamped on riccasso.

COHEN, N J (NORM)
2408 Sugarcone Rd, Baltimore, MD 21209, Phone: 410-484-3841, inquiry@njcknives.com; Web: www.njcknives.com
Specialties: Working class knives. **Patterns:** Hunters, skinners, bird knives, push daggers, boots, kitchen and practical customer designs. **Technical:** Stock removal 440C, ATS-34, CPM 154 and D2. Handles of Micarta, Corian and stabilized woods. **Prices:** $50 to $250. **Remarks:** Part-time maker; first knife sold in 1982. **Mark:** NJC engraved.

COLE, JAMES M
505 Stonewood Blvd, Bartonville, TX 76226, Phone: 817-430-0302, dogcole@swbell.net

COLEMAN, JOHN A
7325 Bonita Way, Citrus Heights, CA 95610-3003, Phone: 916-335-1568, slimsknifes@yahoo.com
Specialties: Minis, hunters, bowies of his design or yours. **Patterns:** Plain to fancy file back working knives. **Technical:** Grinds 440C, ATS-34, 145CM, D2, 1095, 5160, 01. Some hand-forged blades. Exotic woods bone, antler and some ivory. **Prices:** $100 to $500. **Remarks:** Does some carving in handles. Part-time maker. First knife sold in 1989. OKCA 2010 Award winner for best mini of show. **Mark:** Cowboy setting on log whittling Slim's Custom Knives above cowboy and name and state under cowboy.

COLLINS, LYNN M
138 Berkley Dr, Elyria, OH 44035, Phone: 440-366-7101
Specialties: Working straight knives. **Patterns:** Field knives, boots and fighters. **Technical:** Grinds D2, 154CM and 440C. **Prices:** Start at $200. **Remarks:** Spare-time maker; first knife sold in 1980. **Mark:** Initials, asterisks.

COLTER, WADE
PO Box 2340, Colstrip, MT 59323, Phone: Shop: 406-748-2010, Fax: Cell: 406-740-1554
Specialties: Fancy and embellished straight knives, folders and swords of his design; historical and period pieces. **Patterns:** Bowies, swords and folders. **Technical:** Hand forges 52100 ball bearing steel and L6, 1090, cable and chain Damascus from 5N20 and 1084. Carves and makes sheaths. **Prices:** $250 to $3500. **Remarks:** SemiRetired; first knife sold in 1990. Doing business as "Colter's Hell" Forge. **Mark:** Initials on left side ricasso.

COLWELL, KEVIN
Professor's Forge, 15 Stony Hill Rd., Cheshire, CA 06410, Phone: 203-439-2223, colwellk2@southernct.edu
Specialties: Swords (Dao, jian, seax, messer, baurnwehr, etc.) and knives (puukko, Viking-style, hunters, skinners, bowies, fighters and chef's knives). **Technical:** Forges blades, vivid pattern welding or subtle pattern welding with beautiful hamon and grain structure. **Prices:** $175 to $500, swords $900 and up, depending upon what customer wants in adornment. **Remarks:** Associate professor of psychology.

CONKLIN, GEORGE L
Box 902, Ft. Benton, MT 59442, Phone: 406-622-3268, Fax: 406-622-3410, 7bbgrus@3rivers.net
Specialties: Designer and manufacturer of the "Brisket Breaker." **Patterns:** Hunters, utility/camp knives and hatchets. **Technical:** Grinds 440C, ATS-34, D2, 1095, 154CM and 5160. Offers some forging and heat-treats for others. Offers some jewelling. **Prices:** $65 to $200; some to $1000. **Remarks:** Full-time maker. Doing business as Rocky Mountain Knives. **Mark:** Last name in script.

CONLEY, BOB
1013 Creasy Rd, Jonesboro, TN 37659, Phone: 423-753-3302
Specialties: Working straight knives and folders. **Patterns:** Lockers, two-blades, gents, hunters, traditional-styles, straight hunters. **Technical:** Grinds 440C, 154CM and ATS-34. Engraves. **Prices:** $250 to $450; some to $600. **Remarks:** Full-time maker; first knife sold in 1979. **Mark:** Full name, city, state.

CONN JR., C T
206 Highland Ave, Attalla, AL 35954, Phone: 205-538-7688
Specialties: Working folders, some fancy. **Patterns:** Full range of folding knives. **Technical:** Grinds 02, 440C and 154CM. **Prices:** $125 to $300; some to $600. **Remarks:** Part-time maker; first knife sold in 1982. **Mark:** Name.

CONNOLLY, JAMES
2486 Oro-Quincy Hwy, Oroville, CA 95966, Phone: 530-534-5363, rjconnolly@sbcglobal.net
Specialties: Classic working and using knives of his design. **Patterns:** Boots, Bowies, daggers and swords. **Technical:** Grinds ATS-34, BG42, A2, 01. **Prices:** $100 to $500; some to $1500. **Remarks:** Part-time maker; first knife sold in 1980. Doing business as Gold Rush Designs. **Mark:** First initial, last name, Handmade.

CONNOR, JOHN W
PO Box 12981, Odessa, TX 79768-2981, Phone: 915-362-6901

CONNOR, MICHAEL
Box 502, Winters, TX 79567, Phone: 915-754-5602
Specialties: Straight knives, period pieces, some folders. **Patterns:** Hunters to camp knives to traditional locking folders to Bowies. **Technical:** Forges 5160, O1, 1084 steels and his own Damascus. **Prices:** Moderate to upscale. **Remarks:** Spare-time maker; first knife sold in 1974. ABS Master Smith 1983. **Mark:** Last name, M.S.

CONTI, JEFFREY D
POB 16, Judith Gap, MT 59453, Phone: 253-569-6303, Web: FaceBook at JL Knives
Specialties: Working straight knives. **Patterns:** Tactical, survival, hunting, campting, fishing and kitchen knives. **Technical:** Grinds D2, 154CM, 440C and O1. Engraves. **Prices:** Start at $150. **Remarks:** Part-time maker; first knife sold in 1980. Does own heat treating. **Mark:** Electrical etch: "JG Knives."

CONWAY, JOHN
13301 100th Place NE, Kirkland, WA 98034, Phone: 425-823-2821, jcknives@Frontier.com
Specialties: Folders; working and Damascus. Straight knives, camp, utility and fighting knives. **Patterns:** LinerLock® folders of own design. Hidden tang straight knives of own design. **Technical:** Flat grinds forged carbon steels and own Damascus steel, including mosaic. **Prices:** $300 to $850. **Remarks:** Part-time maker since 1999. **Mark:** Oval with stylized initials J C inset.

COOGAN, ROBERT
1560 Craft Center Dr, Smithville, TN 37166, Phone: 615-597-6801, http://iweb.tntech.edu/rcoogan/
Specialties: One-of-a-kind knives. **Patterns:** Unique items like ulu-style Appalachian herb knives. **Technical:** Forges; his Damascus is made from nickel steel and W1. **Prices:** Start at $100. **Remarks:** Part-time maker; first knife sold in 1979. **Mark:** Initials or last name in script.

COOK, JAMES R
455 Anderson Rd, Nashville, AR 71852, Phone: 870 845 5173, jr@jrcookknives.com; Web: www.jrcookknives.com
Specialties: Working straight knives and folders of his design or to customer specs. **Patterns:** Bowies, hunters and camp knives. **Technical:** Forges 1084 and high-carbon Damascus. **Prices:** $800 to $20,000. **Remarks:** Full-time maker; first knife sold in 1986. **Mark:** First and middle initials, last name.

COOK, LOUISE
475 Robinson Ln, Ozark, IL 62972, Phone: 618-777-2932
Specialties: Working and using straight knives of her design and to customer specs; period pieces. **Patterns:** Bowies, hunters and utility/camp knives. **Technical:** Forges 5160. Filework; pin work; silver wire inlay. **Prices:** Start at $50/inch. **Remarks:** Part-time maker; first knife sold in 1990. Doing business as Panther Creek Forge. **Mark:** First name and Journeyman stamp on one side; panther head on the other.

COOK, MIKE
475 Robinson Ln, Ozark, IL 62972, Phone: 618-777-2932
Specialties: Traditional working and using straight knives of his design and to customer specs. **Patterns:** Bowies, hunters and utility/camp knives. **Technical:** Forges 5160. Filework; pin work. **Prices:** Start at $50/inch. **Remarks:** Spare-time maker; first knife sold in 1991. **Mark:** First initial, last name and Journeyman stamp on one side; panther head on the other.

COOK, MIKE A
10927 Shilton Rd, Portland, MI 48875, Phone: 517-242-1352, macook@hughes.net
Web: www.artofishi.com
Specialties: Fancy/embellished and period pieces of his design. **Patterns:** Daggers, fighters and hunters. **Technical:** Stone bladed knives in agate, obsidian and jasper. Scrimshaws; opal inlays. **Prices:** $60 to $300; some to $800. **Remarks:** Part-time maker; first knife sold in 1988. Doing business as Art of Ishi. **Mark:** Initials and year.

COOKE, MARK
LongDog Forge, 21619 Slippery Creek Ln., Spring, TX 77388, markcooke5@gmail.com; Web: www.longdogforge.com
Specialties: One-off handforged blades featuring bold design, technical processes, sole authorship and an emphasis on a clean, complete package. **Technical:** Presently working with mono steel blades via W2, 1084, 80CrV2, as well as others upon request. **Remarks:** Enjoys challenging commissions that push the boundaries of the maker's skill set. All work done under the same roof, from initial forging of the blade to stitching of the sheath to ensure quality and adherence to the original design. Combines Old World techniques with modern design elements to achieve balance between form and function. **Mark:** Dachshund (LongDog) mark typically located on the spine of the blade.

COOMBS JR., LAMONT
546 State Rt 46, Bucksport, ME 04416, Phone: 207-469-3057, Fax: 207-469-3057, theknifemaker@hotmail.com; Web: www.knivesby.com/coombs-knives.html
Specialties: Classic fancy and embellished straight knives; traditional working and using straight knives. Knives of his design and to customer specs. **Patterns:** Hunters, folders and utility/camp knives. **Technical:** Hollow- and flat-grinds ATS-34, 440C, A2, D2 and O1; grinds Damascus from other makers. **Prices:** $100 to $500; some to $3500. **Remarks:** Full-time maker; first knife sold in 1988. **Mark:** Last name on banner, handmade underneath.

COON, RAYMOND C

21135 S.E. Tillstrom Rd, Damascus, OR 97089, Phone: 503-658-2252, Raymond@damascusknife.com; Web: Damascusknife.com

Specialties: Working straight knives in standard patterns. **Patterns:** Hunters, Bowies, daggers, boots and axes. **Technical:** Forges high-carbon steel and Damascus or 97089. **Prices:** Start at $235. **Remarks:** Full-time maker; does own leatherwork, makes own Damascus, daggers; first knife sold in 1995. **Mark:** First initial, last name.

COOPER, PAUL

9 Woods St., Woburn, MA 01801, Phone: 781-938-0519, byksm@yahoo.com

Specialties: Forged, embellished, hand finished fixed-blade knives. **Patterns:** One of a kind designs, often inspired by traditional and historic pieces. **Technical:** Works in tool steel, damascus and natural materials. **Prices:** $500 - $2000. **Remarks:** Part-time maker, formally apprenticed under J.D. Smith. Sold first piece in 2006. **Mark:** Letter C inside bleeding heart.

COPELAND, THOM

136 Blue Bayou Ests., Nashville, AR 71852, tcope@cswnet.com

Specialties: Hand forged fixed blades; hunters, Bowies and camp knives. **Remarks:** Member of ABS and AKA (Arkansas Knifemakers Association). **Mark:** Copeland.

COPPINS, DANIEL

700 S. 9th St., Cambridge, OH 43725, Phone: 740-995-9009, info@battlehorseknives.com; Web: www.battlehorseknives.com

Specialties: Bushcraft knives, tacticals, hunting. **Technical:** Grinds 440C, D2. Antler handles. **Patterns:** Many. **Prices:** $40 to $600. **Remarks:** Sold first knife in 2002; formerly Blind Horse Knives. **Mark:** Horse-Kicking Donkey.

CORBY, HAROLD

218 Brandonwood Dr, Johnson City, TN 37604, Phone: 423-926-9781

Specialties: Large fighters and Bowies; self-protection knives; art knives. Along with art knives and combat knives, Corby now has a all new automatic MO.PB1, also side lock MO LL-1 with titanium liners G-10 handles. **Patterns:** Sub-hilt fighters and hunters. **Technical:** Grinds 154CM, ATS-34 and 440C. **Prices:** $200 to $6000. **Remarks:** Full-time maker; first knife sold in 1969. Doing business as Knives by Corby. **Mark:** Last name.

CORDOVA, JOEY

1594 S. Hill Rd., Bernalillo, NM 87004, Phone: 505-410-3809, joeyscordova@gmail.com; www.joelouiknives.com

Patterns: High-carbon full-tang knives and hidden-tang bowies, as well as small neck knives. **Technical:** Differentially heat-treats blades producing hamons (temper lines). **Prices:** $120 and up. **Remarks:** Full-time knifemaker and part-time ring maker.

CORDOVA, JOSEPH G

1450 Lillie Dr, Bosque Farms, NM 87068, Phone: 505-869-3912, kcordova@rt66.com

Specialties: One-of-a-kind designs, some to customer specs. **Patterns:** Fighter called the 'Gladiator', hunters, boots and cutlery. **Technical:** Forges 1095, 5160; grinds ATS-34, 440C and 154CM. **Prices:** Moderate to upscale. **Remarks:** Full-time maker; first knife sold in 1953. Past chairman of American Bladesmith Society. **Mark:** Cordova made.

CORICH, VANCE

POB 97, Morrison, CO 80465, Phone: 303-999-1553, vancecorichcutlery@gmail.com; https://sites.google.com/site/vancesproject/

Specialties: Fixed blades, usually 2 to 7 inches, recurved blades, locking-liner folders and friction folders. **Technical:** Differential heat treating on high-carbon steels. **Prices:** $150 to $1,000. **Remarks:** Part-time maker working on going full time. **Mark:** Stamped "VCC" or VANCE.

CORKUM, STEVE

34 Basehoar School Rd, Littlestown, PA 17340, Phone: 717-359-9563, sco7129849@aol.com; Web: www.hawknives.com

CORNETT, BRIAN

1511 N. College St., McKinney, TX 75069, Phone: 972-310-7289, devildogdesign@tx.rr.com; www.d3devildogdesigns.com

Patterns: Tactical, hunting, neck knives and personal-defense tools. **Technical:** Stock removal of 1095, O1 tool steel, 52100, D2, CPM 154 and damascus. **Prices:** $50 to $300. **Remarks:** Full-time maker; first knife made in 2011. **Mark:** D3.

CORNWELL, JEFFREY

Treasure Art Blades, PO Box 244014, Anchorage, AK 99524, Phone: 907-887-1661, cornwellsjej@alaska.net

Specialties: Organic, sculptural shapes of original design from damascus steel and mokume gane. **Technical:** Blade creations from Robert Eggerling damascus and Mike Sakmar mokume. **Remarks:** Free-time maker. **Mark:** Stylized J inside a circle.

COSTA, SCOTT

409 Coventry Rd, Spicewood, TX 78669, Phone: 830-693-3431

Specialties: Working straight knives. **Patterns:** Hunters, skinners, axes, trophy sets, custom boxed steak sets, carving sets and bar sets. **Technical:** Grinds D2, ATS-34, 440 and Damascus. Heat-treats. **Prices:** $225 to $2000. **Remarks:** Full-time maker; first knife sold in 1985. **Mark:** Initials connected.

COTTRILL, JAMES I

1776 Ransburg Ave, Columbus, OH 43223, Phone: 614-274-0020

Specialties: Working straight knives of his design. **Patterns:** Caters to the boating and hunting crowd; cutlery. **Technical:** Grinds O1, D2 and 440C. Likes filework. **Prices:** $95 to $250; some to $500. **Remarks:** Full-time maker; first knife sold in 1977. **Mark:** Name, city, state, in oval logo.

COUSINO, GEORGE

7818 Norfolk, Onsted, MI 49265, Phone: 517-467-4911, cousinoknives@yahoo.com; Web: www.cousinoknives.com

Specialties: Hunters, Bowies using knives. **Patterns:** Hunters, Bowies, buckskinners, folders and daggers. **Technical:** Grinds 440C. **Prices:** $95 to $300. **Remarks:** Part-time maker; first knife sold in 1981. **Mark:** Last name.

COVER, JEFF

11355 Allen Rd, Potosi, MO 63664, Phone: 573-749-0008, jeffcovercustomknives@hotmail.com

Specialties: Folders and straight knives. **Patterns: Technical:** Various knife steels and handle materials. **Prices:** $70 to $500. **Mark:** Jeff Cover J.C. Custom Knives.

COVER, RAYMOND A

16235 State Hwy. U, Mineral Point, MO 63660, Phone: 573-749-3783

Specialties: High-tech working straight knives and folders in working patterns. **Patterns:** Slip joints, lockbacks, multi-blade folders. **Technical:** Various knife steels and handle materials. **Prices:** Swords from bare blades to complete high art $200 to $600. **Mark:** "R Cover"

COWLES, DON

1026 Lawndale Dr, Royal Oak, MI 48067, Phone: 248-541-4619, don@cowlesknives.com; Web: www.cowlesknives.com

Specialties: Straight, non-folding pocket knives of his design. **Patterns:** Gentlemen's pocket knives. **Technical:** Grinds CPM154, S30V, Damascus, Talonite. Engraves; pearl inlays in some handles. **Prices:** Start at $300. **Remarks:** Full-time maker; first knife sold in 1994. **Mark:** Full name with oak leaf.

COX, LARRY

701 W. 13th St, Murfreesboro, AR 71958, Phone: 870-258-2429, Fax: Cell: 870-557-8062, cox870@windstream.net

Specialties: Forges his own "ghost flame" damascus. **Patterns:** Skinners, hunters, camp knives and bowies. **Technical:** Forges 5160, 1084, and L6 with 1084 and 5160 for damascus, as well as doing own heat treating. **Prices:** $300 and up. **Remarks:** Sole ownership of knives. Part-time maker; first knife sold in 2007. Member ABS and Arkansas Knifemakers Association. **Mark:** "L U" over "COX."

COX, SAM

1756 Love Springs Rd, Gaffney, SC 29341, Phone: 864-489-1892, Web: www.coxworks.com

Remarks: Started making knives in 1981 for another maker. 1st knife sold under own name in 1983. Full-time maker 1985-2009. Retired in 2010. Now part time. **Mark:** Different logo each year.

COYE, BILL

PO Box 470684, Tulsa, OK 74147, Phone: 918-232-5721, info@coyeknives.com; Web: www.coyeknives.com

Specialties: Tactical and utility knives. **Patterns:** Fighters and utility. **Technical:** Grinds CPM154CM, 154CM, CTS-XHP and Elmax stainless steels. **Prices:** $210 to $320. **Remarks:** Part-time maker. First knife sold in 2009. **Mark:** COYE.

CRADDOCK, MIKE

300 Blythe Dr., Thomasville, NC 27360, Phone: 336-382-8461, ncbladesmith@gmail.com

Specialties: Fighters, bowies. **Patterns:** Hunters and working knives. **Technical:** Forges and grinds high-carbon steel, and does own damascus. **Prices:** $350 to $1,500. **Mark:** CRADDOCK.

CRAIG, ROGER L

2617 SW Seabrook Ave, Topeka, KS 66614, Phone: 785-249-4109

Specialties: Working and camp knives, some fantasy; all his design. **Patterns:** Fighters, hunter. **Technical:** Grinds 1095 and 5160. Most knives have file work. **Prices:** $50 to $250. **Remarks:** Part-time maker; first knife sold in 1991. Doing business as Craig Knives. **Mark:** Last name-Craig.

CRAIN, JACK W

PO Box 212, Granbury, TX 76048, jack@jackcrainknives.com Web: www.jackcrainknives.com

Specialties: Fantasy and period knives; combat and survival knives. **Patterns:** One-of-a-kind art or fantasy daggers, swords and Bowies; survival knives. **Technical:** Forges Damascus; grinds stainless steel. Carves. **Prices:** $350 to $2500; some to $20,000. **Remarks:** Full-time maker; first knife sold in 1969. Designer and maker of the knives seen in the films Dracula 2000, Executive Decision, Demolition Man, Predator I and II, Commando, Die Hard I and II, Road House, Ford Fairlane and Action Jackson, and television shows War of the Worlds, Air Wolf, Kung Fu: The Legend Cont. and Tales of the Crypt. **Mark:** Stylized crane.

CRAMER, BRENT

PO BOX 99, Wheatland, IN 47597, Phone: 812-881-9961, Bdcramer@juno.com Web: BDCramerKnives.com

Specialties: Traditional and custom working and using knives. **Patterns:** Traditional single blade slip-joint folders and standard fixed blades. **Technical:** Stock removal only. Pivot bushing construction on folders. Steel: D-2, 154 CM, ATS-34, CPM-D2, CPM-154CM, O-1, 52100, A-2. All steels heat treated in shop with LN Cryo. Handle Material: Stag, Bone, Wood, Ivory, and Micarta. **Prices:** $150 - $550. **Remarks:** Part-time maker. First fixed blade sold in 2003. First folder sold in 2007. **Mark:** BDC and B.D.Cramer.

CRAWFORD, PAT AND WES

205 N. Center, West Memphis, AR 72301, Phone: 870-732-2452, patcrawford1@

earthlink.com; Web: www.crawfordknives.com
Specialties: Stainless steel Damascus. High-tech working self-defense and combat types and folders. **Patterns:** Tactical-more fancy knives now. **Technical:** Grinds S30V. **Prices:** $400 to $2000. **Remarks:** Full-time maker; first knife sold in 1973. **Mark:** Last name.

CRAWLEY, BRUCE R
16 Binbrook Dr, Croydon, VIC, AUSTRALIA 3136
Specialties: Folders. **Patterns:** Hunters, lockback folders and Bowies. **Technical:** Grinds 440C, ATS-34 and commercial Damascus. Offers filework and mirror polish. **Prices:** $160 to $3500. **Remarks:** Part-time maker; first knife sold in 1990. **Mark:** Initials.

CRENSHAW, AL
Rt 1 Box 717, Eufaula, OK 74432, Phone: 918-452-2128
Specialties: Folders of his design and in standard patterns. **Patterns:** Hunters, locking folders, slip-joint folders, multi blade folders. **Technical:** Grinds 440C, D2 and ATS-34. Does filework on back springs and blades; offers scrimshaw on some handles. **Prices:** $150 to $300; some higher. **Remarks:** Full-time maker; first knife sold in 1981. Doing business as A. Crenshaw Knives. **Mark:** First initial, last name, Lake Eufaula, state stamped; first initial last name in rainbow; Lake Eufaula across bottom with Okla. in middle.

CREWS, RANDY
627 Cricket Trail Rd., Patriot, OH 45658, Phone: 740-379-2329, randy.crews@sbcglobal.net
Specialties: Fixed blades, bowies and hunters. **Technical:** 440C, Alabama Damascus, 1095 with file work. Stock removal method. **Prices:** Start at $150. **Remarks:** Collected knives for 30 years. Part-time maker; first knife made in 2002. **Mark:** Crews Patriot OH.

CRIST, ZOE
2274 Deep Gap Rd., Flat Rock, NC 28731, Phone: 828-275-6689, zoe@zoecristknives.com Web: www.zoecristknives.com
Specialties: San mai and stainless steel. Custom damascus and traditional damascus working and art knives. Also makes Mokume. Works to customer specs. **Patterns:** All damascus hunters, bowies, fighters, neck, boot and high-end art knives. **Technical:** Makes all his own damascus steel from 1095, L6, 15n20. Forges all knives, heat treats, filework, differential heat treating. **Prices:** $150 - $2500. **Remarks:** Full-time maker, has been making knives since 1988, went full-time 2009. Also makes own leather sheaths. **Mark:** Small "z" with long tail on left side of blade at ricasso.

CROCKFORD, JACK
1859 Harts Mill Rd, Chamblee, GA 30341, Phone: 770-457-4680
Specialties: Lockback folders. **Patterns:** Hunters, fishing and camp knives, traditional folders. **Technical:** Grinds A2, D2, ATS-34 and 440C. Engraves and scrimshaws. **Prices:** Start at $175. **Remarks:** Part-time maker; first knife sold in 1975. **Mark:** Name.

CROSS, KEVIN
5 Pear Orchard Rd., Portland, CT 06480, Phone: 860-894-2385, kevincross@comcast.net; Web: www.kevincrossknives.com
Specialties: Working/using and presentation grade fixed-blade knives and custom kitchen knives. **Patterns:** Hunters, skinners, fighters. Bowies, camp knives. **Technical:** Stock removal maker. Uses O1, 1095, 154 CPM as well as Damascus from Eggerling, Ealy, Donnelly, Nichols, Thomas and others. Most handles are natural materials such as burled and spalted woods, stag and ancient ivory. **Prices:** $200 - $1,200. **Remarks:** Part-time maker. First knife sold around 1997. **Mark:** Name.

CROSS, ROBERT
RMB 200B, Manilla Rd, Tamworth, NSW, AUSTRALIA 2340, Phone: 067-618385

CROTTS, DAN
PO Box 68, Elm Springs, AR 72728, Phone: 479-422-7874, dancrottsknives@yahoo.com Web: www.facebook.com/dancrottsknives
Specialties: User grade, hunting, tactical and folders. **Technical:** High-end tool steel. **Prices:** $2200. **Remarks:** Specializes in making performance blades. **Mark:** Crotts.

CROUCH, BUBBA
POB 461, Pleasanton, TX 78064, Phone: 210-846-6890, tommycrouch69@gmail.com; Web: FaceBook Crouch Custom Knives
Specialties: Slip joints, straight blades. **Patterns:** Case style. Offers filework. **Technical:** ATS-34, CPM 154 and commercial damascus. Using stag, bone and mammoth ivory handle material. **Prices:** $250 to $1,200. **Remarks:** Part-time maker, first knife sold in 2010. **Mark:** Crouch.

CROWDER, GARY L
112480 S. 4614 Rd., Sallisaw, OK 74955, Phone: 918-775-9009, gcrowder99@yahoo.com
Specialties: Folders, multi-blades. **Patterns:** Traditional with a few sheath knives. **Technical:** Flat grinds ATS-34, D2 and others, as well as Damascus via stock-removal. **Prices:** $150 to $600. **Remarks:** Retired, part-time maker. First knife sold in 1994. **Mark:** small acid-etched "Crowder" on blade.

CROWDER, ROBERT
Box 1374, Thompson Falls, MT 59873, Phone: 406-827-4754
Specialties: Traditional working knives to customer specs. **Patterns:** Hunters, Bowies, fighters and fillets. **Technical:** Grinds ATS-34, 154CM, 440C, Vascowear and commercial Damascus. **Prices:** $225 to $500; some to $2500. **Remarks:** Full-time maker; first knife sold in 1985. **Mark:** R Crowder signature & Montana.

CROWELL, JAMES L
676 Newnata Cutoff, Mtn. View, AR 72560, Phone: 870-746-4215, crowellknives@yahoo.com; Web: www.crowellknives.com

Specialties: Bowie knives; fighters and working knives. **Patterns:** Hunters, fighters, Bowies, daggers and folders. Period pieces: War hammers, Japanese and European. **Technical:** Forges 10 series carbon steels as well as O1, L6, W2 and his own damascus. "Flame painted" hamons (temper lines). **Prices:** $525 to $5,500; some to $8,500. **Remarks:** Full-time maker; first knife sold in 1980. Earned ABS Master Bladesmith in 1986. 2016 Marked 30 years as an ABS master smith. **Mark:** A shooting star.

CROWL, PETER
5786 County Road 10, Waterloo, IN 46793, Phone: 260-488-2532, pete@petecrowlknives.com; Web: www.petecrowlknives.com
Specialties: Bowie, hunters. **Technical:** Forges 5160, 1080, W2, 52100. **Prices:** $200 and up. **Remarks:** ABS Journeyman smith. **Mark:** Last name in script.

CROWNER, JEFF
2621 Windsor Pl., Plano, TX 75075, Phone: 541-201-3182, Fax: 541-579-3762
Specialties: Custom knife maker. I make some of the following: wilderness survival blades, martial art weapons, hunting blades. **Technical:** I differentially heat treat every knife. I use various steels like 5160, L-6, Cable Damascus, 52100, 6150, and some stainless types. I use the following for handle materials: TeroTuf by Columbia Industrial products and exotic hardwoods and horn. I make my own custom sheaths as well with either kydex or leather.

CROWTHERS, MARK F
PO Box 4641, Rolling Bay, WA 98061-0641, Phone: 206-842-7501

CUCCHIARA, MATT
387 W. Hagler, Fresno, CA 93711, Phone: 559-917-2328, matt@cucchiaraknives.com Web: www.cucchiaraknives.com
Specialties: I make large and small, plain or hand carved Ti handled Tactical framelock folders. All decoration and carving work done by maker. Also known for my hand carved Ti pocket clips. **Prices:** Start at around $400 and go as high as $1500 or so.

CULHANE, SEAN K.
8 Ranskroon Dr., Horizon, Roodepoort, 1740, SOUTH AFRICA, Phone: +27 82 453-1741, sculhane@wbs.co.za; www.culhaneknives.co.za
Specialties: Traditional working straight knives and folders in standard patterns and to customer specifications. **Patterns:** Fighters, hunters, kitchen cutlery, utility and Scottish dirks and sgian dubhs. **Technical:** Hollow grinding Sandvik 12C27 and commercial damascus. Full process, including heat treating and sheaths done by maker. **Prices:** From $180 up, depending on design and materials. **Remarks:** Part-time maker; first knife sold in 1988. **Mark:** First and surname in Gothic script curved over the word "Maker."

CULVER, STEVE
5682 94th St, Meriden, KS 66512, Phone: 785-230-2505, Web: www.culverart.com; Facebook: Steve Culver Knives; YouTube: SteveCulverMS1
Specialties: Edged weapons. Spiral-welded damascus gun barrels, collectible and functional. **Patterns:** Bowies, daggers, hunters, folders and combination weapons. **Technical:** Forges carbon steels and his own damascus. Stock removal of stainless steel for some folders. **Prices:** $500 to $50,000. **Remarks:** Full-time maker; also builds muzzle-loading pistols. **Mark:** Last name, MS.

CUMMING, BOB
CUMMING KNIVES, 35 Manana Dr, Cedar Crest, NM 87008, Phone: 505-286-0509, cumming@comcast.net; Web: www.cummingknives.com
Specialties: One-of-a-kind exhibition grade custom Bowie knives, exhibition grade and working hunters, bird & trout knives, salt and fresh water fillet knives. Low country oyster knives, custom tanto's plains Indian style sheaths & custom leather, all types of exotic handle materials, scrimshaw and engraving. Added folders in 2006. Custom oyster knives. **Prices:** $95 to $3500 and up. **Remarks:** Mentored by the late Jim Nolen, sold first knife in 1978 in Denmark. Retired U.S. Foreign Service Officer. Member NCCKG. **Mark:** Stylized CUMMING.

CURTISS, DAVID
Curtiss Knives, PO Box 902, Granger, IN 46530, Phone: 574-651-2158, david@curtissknives.com; Web: www.curtissknives.com
Specialties: Specialize in custom tactical-style folders and flipper folders, with some of the best sellers being in the Nano and Cruze series. The Nano is now being produced by Boker Knives. Many new knife designs coming soon.

CURTISS, STEVE L
PO Box 448, Eureka, MT 59914, Phone: 406-889-5510, Fax: 406-889-5510, slc@bladerigger.com; Web: http://www.bladerigger.com
Specialties: True custom and semi-custom production (SCP), specialized concealment blades; advanced sheaths and tailored body harnessing systems. **Patterns:** Tactical/personal defense fighters, swords, utility and custom patterns. **Technical:** Grinds A2 and Talonite®; heat-treats. Sheaths: Kydex or Kydex-lined leather laminated or Kydex-lined with Rigger Coat™. Exotic materials available. **Prices:** $50 to $10,000. **Remarks:** Full-time maker. Doing business as Blade Rigger L.L.C. Martial artist and unique defense industry tools and equipment. **Mark:** For true custom: Initials and for SCP: Blade Rigger.

D

DAILEY, G E
577 Lincoln St, Seekonk, MA 02771, Phone: 508-336-5088, gedailey@msn.com; Web: www.gedailey.com
Specialties: One-of-a-kind exotic designed edged weapons. **Patterns:** Folders, daggers and swords. **Technical:** Reforges and grinds Damascus; prefers hollow-grinding. Engraves, carves, offers filework and sets stones and uses exotic gems and gold. **Prices:**

Start at $1100. **Remarks:** Full-time maker. First knife sold in 1982. **Mark:** Last name or stylized initialed logo.

DAKE, C M
19759 Chef Menteur Hwy, New Orleans, LA 70129-9602, Phone: 504-254-0357, Fax: 504-254-9501
Specialties: Fancy working folders. **Patterns:** Front-lock lockbacks, button-lock folders. **Technical:** Grinds ATS-34 and Damascus. **Prices:** $500 to $2500; some higher. **Remarks:** Full-time maker; first knife sold in 1988. Doing business as Bayou Custom Cutlery. **Mark:** Last name.

DAKE, MARY H
Rt 5 Box 287A, New Orleans, LA 70129, Phone: 504-254-0357

DALEY, MARK
P.O. Box 427, Waubaushene, Ontario, CANADA L0K 2C0, Phone: 705-543-1080, mark@markdaleyknives.com
Specialties: Art knives with handles made of stainless steel, bronze, gold, silver, pearl and Shibuichi. Many of the maker's knives are also textured and/or carved. **Mark:** Engraved "Mark Daley" or chiseled initials "MD."

DALLYN, KELLY
124 Deerbrook Place S.E., Calgary, AB, CANADA T2J 6J5, Phone: 403-475-3056, info@dallyn-knives.com Web: dallyn-knives.com
Specialties: Kitchen, utility, and hunting knives

DALY, MICHAEL
9728 3rd Ave., Brooklyn, NY 11209, Phone: 718-748-7796, sifubayridge@aol.com
Specialties: Tactical/utility and EDC (everyday carry) fixed blades. **Technical:** Stock removal method of blade making using ATS-34 and 154CM steels, and linen and paper Micarta handles. **Remarks:** Began making knives as a hobby in 2009 under the guidance of Marcus Clinco and Bill Herndon. Member of the California Knifemakers Association. **Mark:** Last name in a Chinese seal.

DAMLOVAC, SAVA
10292 Bradbury Dr, Indianapolis, IN 46231, Phone: 317-839-4952
Specialties: Period pieces, fantasy, Viking, Moran type all Damascus daggers. **Patterns:** Bowies, fighters, daggers, Persian-style knives. **Technical:** Uses own Damascus, mostly hand forges. **Prices:** $150 to $2500; some higher. **Remarks:** Full-time maker; first knife sold in 1993. Specialty, Bill Moran all Damascus dagger sets, in Moran-style wood case. **Mark:** "Sava" stamped in Damascus or etched in stainless.

D'ANDREA, JOHN
8517 N Linwood Loop, Citrus Springs, FL 34433-5045, Phone: 352-489-2803, shootist1@tampabay.rr.com
Specialties: Fancy working straight knives and folders with filework and distinctive leatherwork. **Patterns:** Hunters, fighters, daggers, folders and an occasional sword. **Technical:** Grinds ATS-34, 154CM, 440C and D2. **Prices:** $220 to $1000. **Remarks:** Part-time maker; first knife sold in 1986. **Mark:** First name, last initial imposed on samurai sword.

D'ANGELO, LAURENCE
14703 NE 17th Ave, Vancouver, WA 98686, Phone: 360-573-0546
Specialties: Straight knives of his design. **Patterns:** Bowies, hunters and locking folders. **Technical:** Grinds D2, ATS-34 and 440C. Hand makes all sheaths. **Prices:** $100 to $200. **Remarks:** Full-time maker; first knife sold in 1987. **Mark:** Football logo—first and middle initials, last name, city, state, Maker.

DANIEL, TRAVIS E
PO Box 1223, Thomaston, GA 30286, Phone: 706-601-6418, dtravis405@gmail.com
Specialties: Traditional working straight knives of his design or to customer specs. **Patterns:** Hunters, fighters and utility/camp knives. **Technical:** Grinds ATS-34, 440-C, 154CM, forges his own Damascus. Stock removal. **Prices:** $125 to $500. **Remarks:** Full-time maker; first knife sold in 1976. **Mark:** TED.

DANIELS, ALEX
1416 County Rd 415, Town Creek, AL 35672, Phone: 256-685-0943, akdknives@gmail.com; Web: http://alexdanielscustomknives.com
Specialties: Working and using straight knives and folders; period pieces, reproduction Bowies. **Patterns:** Mostly reproduction Bowies but offers full line of knives. **Technical:** BG-42, 440C, 1095, 52100 forged blades. **Prices:** $350 to $5500. **Remarks:** Full-time maker; first knife sold in 1963. **Mark:** First and middle initials, last name, city and state.

DARBY, DAVID T
30652 S 533 Rd, Cookson, OK 74427, Phone: 918-457-4868, knfmkr@fullnet.net
Specialties: Forged blades only, all styles. **Prices:** $350 and up. **Remarks:** ABS Journeyman Smith. **Mark:** Stylized quillion dagger incorporates last name (Darby).

DARBY, JED
7878 E Co Rd 50 N, Greensburg, IN 47240, Phone: 812-663-2696
Specialties: Traditional working/using straight knives of his design and to customer specs. **Patterns:** Bowies, hunters and utility/camp knives. **Technical:** Grinds 440C, ATS-34 and Damascus. **Prices:** $70 to $550; some to $1000. **Remarks:** Full-time maker; first knife sold in 1992. Doing business as Darby Knives. **Mark:** Last name and year.

DARBY, RICK
71 Nestingrock Ln, Levittown, PA 19054
Specialties: Working straight knives. **Patterns:** Boots, fighters and hunters with mirror finish. **Technical:** Grinds 440C and CPM440V. **Prices:** $125 to $300. **Remarks:** Part-time maker; first knife sold in 1974. **Mark:** First and middle initials, last name.

DARCEY, CHESTER L
1608 Dominik Dr, College Station, TX 77840, Phone: 979-696-1656, DarceyKnives@yahoo.com
Specialties: Lockback, LinerLock® and scale release folders. **Patterns:** Bowies, hunters and utilities. **Technical:** Stock removal on carbon and stainless steels, forge own Damascus. **Prices:** $200 to $1000. **Remarks:** Part-time maker, first knife sold in 1999. **Mark:** Last name in script.

DARK, ROBERT
2218 Huntington Court, Oxford, AL 36203, Phone: 256-831-4645, dark@darkknives.com; Web: www.darkknives.com
Specialties: Fixed blade working knives of maker's designs. Works with customer designed specifications. **Patterns:** Hunters, Bowies, camp knives, kitchen/utility, bird and trout. Standard patterns and customer designed. **Technical:** Forged and stock removal. Works with high carbon, stainless and Damascus steels. Hollow and flat grinds. **Prices:** $175 to $750. **Remarks:** Sole authorship knives and custom leather sheaths. Full-time maker. **Mark:** "R Dark" on left side of blade.

DARPINIAN, DAVE
PO Box 2643, Olathe, KS 66063, Phone: 913-244-7114, darpo1956@yahoo.com Web: www.kansasknives.org
Specialties: Hunters and Persian fighters with natural handle materials. **Patterns:** Full range of straight knives including art daggers. **Technical:** Art grinds own damascus and purchased damascus. Creates clay-tempered hamon on 1095 blade steel. **Prices:** $300 to $1000. **Remarks:** First knife made in 1986, part-time maker, member of ABS and KCKA. **Mark:** Last name on the spline.

DAVIDSON, EDMUND
3345 Virginia Ave, Goshen, VA 24439, Phone: 540-997-5651, davidson.edmund@gmail.com; Web: www.edmunddavidson.com
Specialties: High class art integrals. **Patterns:** Many hunters and art models. **Technical:** CPM 154-CM. **Prices:** $100 to infinity. **Remarks:** Full-time maker; first knife sold in 1986. **Mark:** Name in deer head or custom logos.

DAVIDSON, SCOTT
SOLID ROCK KNIVES, 149 Pless Cir., Alto, GA 30510, Phone: 678-316-1318, Fax: 770-869-0882, solidrockknives@bellsouth.net
Specialties: Tactical knives, some hunters, skinners, bird-and-trout and neck knives. **Technical:** Stock-removal method of blade making, using CPM S30V, 440C and ATS-34 steels, also O1 and 1095HC tool steels. **Prices:** $100 to $1,200, depending on materials used. **Remarks:** Part-time maker; first knife made in 1996. **Mark:** "Ichthys," the Christian fish, with maker's name and address in or around the fish.

DAVIS, BARRY L
4262 US 20, Castleton, NY 12033, Phone: 518-477-5036, daviscustomknives@yahoo.com
Specialties: Collector grade Damascus folders. Traditional designs with focus on turn-of-the-century techniques employed. Sole authorship. Forges own Damascus, does all carving, filework, gold work and piquet. Uses only natural handle material. Enjoys doing multi-blade as well as single blade folders and daggers. **Prices:** Prices range from $2000 to $7000. **Remarks:** First knife sold in 1980.

DAVIS, CHARLIE
ANZA KNIVES, PO Box 457, Lakeside, CA 92040-9998, Phone: 619-561-9445, Fax: 619-390-6283, sales@anzaknives.com; Web: www.anzaknives.com
Specialties: Fancy and embellished working straight knives of his design. **Patterns:** Hunters, camp and utility knives. **Technical:** Grinds high-carbon files. **Prices:** $20 to $185, custom depends. **Remarks:** Full-time maker; first knife sold in 1980. Now offers custom. **Mark:** ANZA U.S.A.

DAVIS, DON
8415 Coyote Run, Loveland, CO 80537-9665, Phone: 970-669-9016, Fax: 970-669-8072
Specialties: Working straight knives in standard patterns or to customer specs. **Patterns:** Hunters, utility knives, skinners and survival knives. **Technical:** Grinds 440C, ATS-34. **Prices:** $75 to $250. **Remarks:** Full-time maker; first knife sold in 1985. **Mark:** Signature, city and state.

DAVIS, JESSE W
3853 Peyton Rd., Coldwater, MS 38618, Phone: 901-849-7250, jessewdavis@yahoo.com
Specialties: Working straight knives and boots in standard patterns and to customer specs. **Patterns:** Boot knives, daggers, fighters, subhilts & Bowies. **Technical:** Grinds A2, D2, 440C and commercial Damascus. **Prices:** $125 to $1000. **Remarks:** Full-time maker; first knife sold in 1977. Former member Knifemakers Guild (in good standing). **Mark:** Name or initials.

DAVIS, JOEL
74538 165th, Albert Lea, MN 56007, Phone: 507-377-0808, joelknives@yahoo.com
Specialties: Complete sole authorship presentation grade highly complex pattern-welded mosaic Damascus blade and bolster stock. **Patterns:** To date Joel has executed over 900 different mosaic Damascus patterns in the past four years. Anything conceived by maker's imagination. **Technical:** Uses various heat colorable "high vibrancy" steels, nickel 200 and some powdered metal for bolster stock only. Uses 1095, 1075 and 15N20. High carbon steels for cutting edge blade stock only. **Prices:** 15 to $50 per square inch and up depending on complexity of pattern. **Remarks:** Full-time mosaic Damascus metal smith focusing strictly on never-before-seen mosaic patterns. Most of maker's work is used for art knives ranging between $1500 to $4500.

custom knifemakers

DAVIS, JOHN
235 Lampe Rd, Selah, WA 98942, Phone: 509-697-3845, 509-945-4570, jdwelds@charter.net
Specialties: Damascus and mosaic Damascus, working knives, working folders, art knives and art folders. **Technical:** Some ATS-34 and stainless Damascus. Embellishes with fancy stabilized wood, mammoth and walrus ivory. **Prices:** Start at $150. **Remarks:** Part-time maker; first knife sold in 1996. **Mark:** Name city and state on Damascus stamp initials; name inside back RFR.

DAVIS, JOHN H.
33842 Picciola Dr., Fruitland Park, FL 34731, Phone: 209-740-7125, jdavis@custom-knifemaker.com; Web: www.custom-knifemaker.com
Patterns: Daggers, bowies, drop-point hunters, bird & trout knives, folding knives and custom orders. **Technical:** Forged knives primarily, but does some stock removal, makes own damascus steel using 1095 and 15N20, and also uses 52100, W2, CPM 154 stainless steel and 440C. **Prices:** $250 and up. **Remarks:** Part-time maker; first knife made in high school in 1977. Voting member of the Knifemakers' Guild and an ABS member, also president and treasurer for the Florida Knifemakers' Association. **Mark:** JD with a cross bar for the "H" between the "JD" and "Davis" under it.

DAVIS, STEVE
3370 Chatsworth Way, Powder Springs, GA 30127, Phone: 770-427-5740, bsdavis@bellsouth.net
Specialties: Gents and ladies folders. **Patterns:** Straight knives, slip-joint folders, locking-liner folders. **Technical:** Grinds ATS-34 forges own Damascus. Offers filework; prefers hand-rubbed finishes and natural handle materials. Uses pearl, ivory, stag and exotic woods. **Prices:** $250 to $800; some to $1500. **Remarks:** Full-time maker; first knife sold in 1988. Doing business as Custom Knives by Steve Davis. **Mark:** Name engraved on blade.

DAVIS JR., JIM
5129 Ridge St, Zephyrhills, FL 33541, Phone: 813-779-9213 813-469-4241 Cell, jimdavisknives@aol.com
Specialties: Presentation-grade fixed blade knives w/composite hidden tang handles. Employs a variety of ancient and contemporary ivories. **Patterns:** One-of-a-kind gents, personal, and executive knives and hunters w/unique cam-lock pouch sheaths and display stands. **Technical:** Flat grinds ATS-34 and stainless Damascus w/most work by hand w/assorted files. **Prices:** $300 and up. **Remarks:** Full-time maker, first knives sold in 2000. **Mark:** Signature w/printed name over "HANDCRAFTED."

DAVISON, TODD A.
230 S. Wells St., Kosciusko, MS 39090, Phone: 662-739-7440, crazyknifeblade@yahoo.com; Web: www.tadscustomknives.com
Specialties: Making working/using and collector folders of his design. All knives are truly made one of a kind. Each knife has a serial number inside the liner. **Patterns:** Single and double blade traditional slip-joint pocket knives. **Technical:** Free hand hollow ground blades, hand finished. Using only the very best materials possible. Holding the highest standards to fit & finish and detail. Does his own heat treating. ATS34 and D2 steel. **Prices:** $450 to $900, some higher. **Remarks:** Full time maker, first knife sold in 1981. **Mark:** T.A. DAVISON USA.

DAWKINS, DUDLEY L
221 NW Broadmoor Ave., Topeka, KS 66606-1254, Phone: 785-817-9343, dawkind@reagan.com or dawkind@sbcglobal.net
Specialties: Stylized old or "Dawkins Forged" with anvil in center. New tang stamps. **Patterns:** Straight knives. **Technical:** Mostly carbon steel; some Damascus-all knives forged. **Prices:** Knives: $275 and up; Sheaths: $95 and up. **Remarks:** All knives supplied with wood-lined sheaths. ABS Member, sole authorship. **Mark:** Stylized "DLD or Dawkins Forged with anvil in center.

DAWSON, BARRY
7760 E Hwy 69, Prescott Valley, AZ 86314, Phone: 928-255-9830, dawsonknives@yahoo.com; Web: www.dawsonknives.com
Specialties: Samurai swords, combat knives, collector daggers, tactical, folding and hunting knives. **Patterns:** Offers over 60 different models. **Technical:** Grinds 440C, ATS-34, own heat-treatment. **Prices:** $75 to $1500; some to $5000. **Remarks:** Full-time maker; first knife sold in 1975. **Mark:** Last name, USA in print or last name in script.

DAWSON, LYNN
7760 E Hwy 69 #C-5 157, Prescott Valley, AZ 86314, Phone: 928-713-2812, lynnknives@yahoo.com; Web: www.lynnknives.com
Specialties: Swords, hunters, utility, and art pieces. **Patterns:** Over 25 patterns to choose from. **Technical:** Grinds 440C, ATS-34, own heat treating. **Prices:** $80 to $1000. **Remarks:** Custom work and her own designs. **Mark:** The name "Lynn" in print or script.

DE BRAGA, JOSE C.
1341 9e Rue, Trois Rivieres, QC, CANADA G8Y 2Z2, Phone: 418-948-5864, josedebraga@cgocable.ca
Specialties: Art knives, fantasy pieces and working knives of his design or to customer specs. **Patterns:** Knives with sculptured or carved handles, from miniatures to full-size working knives. **Technical:** Grinds and hand-files 440C and ATS-34. A variety of steels and handle materials available. Offers lost wax casting. **Prices:** Start at $300. **Remarks:** Full-time maker; wax modeler, sculptor and knifemaker; first knife sold in 1984. **Mark:** Initials in stylized script and serial number.

DE MARIA JR., ANGELO
12 Boronda Rd, Carmel Valley, CA 93924, Phone: 831-659-3381, Fax: 831-659-1315, angelodemaria1@mac.com
Specialties: Damascus, fixed and folders, sheaths. **Patterns:** Mosaic and random. **Technical:** Forging 5160, 1084 and 15N20. **Prices:** $200+. **Remarks:** Part-time maker. **Mark:** Angelo de Maria Carmel Valley, CA etch or AdM stamp.

DE MESA, JOHN
1565 W. Main St., STE. 208 #229, Lewisville, TX 75057, Phone: 972-310-3877, TogiArts@me.com; Web: http://togiarts.com/ and http://togiarts.com/CSC/index.html
Specialties: Japanese sword polishing. **Technical:** Traditional sword polishing of Japanese swords made by sword makers in Japan and U.S.**Prices:** Starting at $75 per inch. **Remarks:** Custom Swords Collaborations IN collaboration with Jose De Braga, we can mount Japanese style sword with custom carved handles, sword fittings and scabbards to customer specs.

DE WET, KOBUS
2601 River Road, Yakima, WA 98902, Phone: 509-728-3736, kobus@moderndamascus.com, Web: www.moderndamascus.com
Specialties: Working and art knives **Patterns:** Every knife is unique. Fixed blades and folders. Hunting, Bowie, Tactical and Utility knives. **Technical:** I enjoy forging my own damascus steel, mainly from 15N20 and 1084. I also use stock removal and stainless steels.**Prices:** Starting at $200**Remarks:** Part time maker, started in 2007**Mark:** Circled "K" / Modern Damascus - Kobus de Wet

DEAN, HARVEY J
3266 CR 232, Rockdale, TX 76567, Phone: 512-446-3111, Fax: 512-446-5060, dean@tex1.net; Web: www.harveydean.com
Specialties: Collectible, functional knives. **Patterns:** Bowies, hunters, folders, daggers, swords, battle axes, camp and combat knives. **Technical:** Forges 1095, O1 and his Damascus. **Prices:** $350 to $10,000. **Remarks:** Full-time maker; first knife sold in 1981. **Mark:** Last name and MS.

DEBAUD, JAKE
1309 Glyndon Dr., Plano, TX 75034, Phone: 972-741-6280, jake@debaudblades.com; Web: www.debaudknives.com
Specialties: Custom damascus art knives, hunting knives and tactical knives. **Technical:** A2, D2, O1, 1095 and some stainless if requested ATS-34 or 154CM and S30V. **Remarks:** Full-time maker. Have been making knives for three years.

DEBRAGA, JOVAN
141 Notre Dame des Victoir, Quebec, CANADA G2G 1J3, Phone: 418-997-0819/418-877-1915, jovancdebraga@msn.com
Specialties: Art knives, fantasy pieces and working knives of his design or to customer specs. **Patterns:** Knives with sculptured or carved handles, from miniatures to full-sized working knives. **Technical:** Grinds and hand-files 440C, and ATS-34. A variety of steels and handle materials available. **Prices:** Start at $300. **Remarks:** Full time maker. Sculptor and knifemaker. First knife sold in 2003. **Mark:** Initials in stylized script and serial number.

DEIBERT, MICHAEL
7570 Happy Hollow Rd., Trussville, AL 35173, Phone: 205-612-2359, mike@deibertknives.com; Web: deibertknives.com
Specialties: Working straight knives in full or hidden tangs, in mono or damascus steel. **Patterns:** Choppers, bowies, hunters and bird-and-trout knives. **Technical:** Makes own damascus, forges all blades and does own heat treating. **Remarks:** ABS journeyman smith, part-time maker. **Mark:** Flaming "D" over an anvil.

DEL RASO, PETER
28 Mayfield Dr, Mt. Waverly, VIC, AUSTRALIA 3149, Phone: 613 98060644, delraso@optusnet.com.au
Specialties: Fixed blades, some folders, art knives. **Patterns:** Daggers, Bowies, tactical, boot, personal and working knives. **Technical:** Grinds ATS-34, commercial Damascus and any other type of steel on request. **Prices:** $100 to $1500. **Remarks:** Part-time maker, first show in 1993. **Mark:** Maker's surname stamped.

DELAROSA, JIM
502 Fairview Cir., Waterford, WI 53185, Phone: 262-422-8604, D-knife@hotmail.com
Specialties: Working straight knives and folders of his design or customer specs. **Patterns:** Hunters, skinners, fillets, utility and locking folders. **Technical:** Grinds ATS-34, 440-C, D2, O1 and commercial Damascus. **Prices:** $100 to $500; some higher. **Remarks:** Part-time maker. **Mark:** First and last name.

DELL, WOLFGANG
Am Alten Berg 9, Owen-Teck, GERMANY D-73277, Phone: 49-7021-81802, wolfgang@dell-knives.de; Web: www.dell-knives.de
Specialties: Fancy high-art straight of his design and to customer specs. **Patterns:** Fighters, hunters, Bowies and utility/camp knives. **Technical:** Grinds ATS-34, RWL-34, Elmax, Damascus (Fritz Schneider). Offers high gloss finish and engraving. **Prices:** $500 to $1000; some to $1600. **Remarks:** Full-time maker; first knife sold in 1992. **Mark:** Hopi hand of peace.

DELLANA
STARLANI INT'L INC, 1135 Terminal Way Ste #209, Reno, NV 89502, Phone: 304-727-5512; 702-569-7827, 1dellana@gmail.com; Web: www.dellana.cc
Specialties: Collector grade fancy/embellished high art folders and art daggers. **Patterns:** Locking folders and art daggers. **Technical:** Forges her own Damascus and W-2. Engraves, does stone setting, filework, carving and gold/platinum fabrication. Prefers exotic, high karat gold, platinum, silver, gemstone and mother-of-pearl handle materials. **Prices:** Upscale. **Remarks:** Sole authorship, full-time maker, first knife sold in 1994. Also does one high art collaboration a year with Van Barnett. **Member:** Art Knife Invitational and ABS. **Mark:** First name.

DELONG, DICK
PO Box 1024, Centerville, TX 75833-1024, Phone: 903-536-1454
Specialties: Fancy working knives and fantasy pieces. **Patterns:** Hunters and small skinners. **Technical:** Grinds and files O1, D2, 440C and Damascus. Offers cocobolo and Osage orange for handles. **Prices:** Start at $50. **Remarks:** Part-time maker. Member of Art Knife Invitational. Voting member of Knifemakers Guild. Member of ABS. **Mark:** Last name; some unmarked.

DEMENT, LARRY
PO Box 1807, Prince Fredrick, MD 20678, Phone: 410-586-9011
Specialties: Fixed blades. **Technical:** Forged and stock removal. **Prices:** $75 to $200. **Remarks:** Affordable, good feelin', quality knives. Part-time maker.

DENNEHY, JOHN D
1142 52 Ave. Ct., Greeley, CO 80634, Phone: 970-218-7128, jddennehy@yahoo.com; Web: www.thewildirishrose.com
Specialties: Working straight knives, throwers, and leatherworker's knives. **Technical:** 440C, & O1, heat treats own blades, part-time maker, first knife sold in 1989. **Patterns:** Small hunting to presentation Bowies, leatherworks round and head knives. **Prices:** $200 and up. **Remarks:** Custom sheath maker, sheath making seminars at the Blade Show.

DENNING, GENO
CAVEMAN ENGINEERING, 135 Allenvalley Rd, Gaston, SC 29053, Phone: 803-794-6067, cden101656@aol.com; Web: www.cavemanengineering.com
Specialties: Mirror finish. **Patterns:** Hunters, fighters, folders. **Technical:** ATS-34, 440V, S-30-V D2. **Prices:** $100 and up. **Remarks:** Full-time maker since 1996. Sole income since 1999. Instructor at Montgomery Community College (Grinding Blades). A director of SCAK: South Carolina Association of Knifemakers. **Mark:** Troy NC.

DERESPINA, RICHARD
derespinaknives@yahoo.com; Web: www.derespinaknives.com
Specialties: Custom fixed blades and folders, Kris and Karambit. **Technical:** I use the stock removal method. Steels I use are S30V, 154CM, D2, 440C, BG42. Handles made of G10 particularly Micarta, etc. **Prices:** $150 to $550 depending on model. **Remarks:** Full-time maker. **Mark:** My etched logos are two, my last name and Brooklyn NY mark as well as the Star/Yin Yang logo. The star being both representative of various angles of attack common in combat as well as being three triangles, each points to levels of metaphysical understanding. The Yin and Yang have my company initials on each side D & K. Yin and Yang shows the ever present physics of life.

DERINGER, CHRISTOPH
625 Chemin Lower, Cookshire, QC, CANADA J0B 1M0, Phone: 819-345-4260, cdsab@sympatico.ca
Specialties: Traditional working/using straight knives and folders of his design and to customer specs. **Patterns:** Boots, hunters, folders, art knives, kitchen knives and utility/camp knives. **Technical:** Forges 5160, O1 and Damascus. Offers a variety of filework. **Prices:** Start at $250. **Remarks:** Full-time maker; first knife sold in 1989. **Mark:** Last name stamped/engraved.

DERR, HERBERT
413 Woodland Dr, St. Albans, WV 25177, Phone: 304-727-3866
Specialties: Damascus one-of-a-kind knives, carbon steels also. **Patterns:** Birdseye, ladder back, mosaics. **Technical:** All styles functional as well as artistically pleasing. **Prices:** $90 to $175 carbon, Damascus $250 to $800. **Remarks:** All Damascus made by maker. **Mark:** H.K. Derr.

DESAULNIERS, ALAIN
100 Pope Street, Cookshire, QC, CANADA J0B 1M0, pinklaperez@sympatico.ca Web: www.desoknives.com
Specialties: Mostly Loveless style knives. **Patterns:** Double grind fighters, hunters, daggers, etc. **Technical:** Stock removal, ATS-34, CPM. High-polished blades, tapered tangs, high-quality handles. **Remarks:** Full-time. Collaboration with John Young. **Prices:** $425 and up. **Mark:** Name and city in logo.

DESROSIERS, ADAM
PO Box 1954, Petersburg, AK 99833, Phone: 907-518-4570, adam@alaskablades.com Web: www.alaskablades.com
Specialties: High performance, forged, carbon steel and damascus camp choppers, and hunting knives. Hidden tang, full tang, and full integral construction. High performance heat treating. Knife designs inspired by life in Alaskan bush. **Technical:** Hand forges tool steels and damascus. Sole authorship. Full range of handle materials, micarta to Ivory. Preferred steels: W-2, O-1, L-6, 15n20, 1095. **Prices:** $200 - $3000. **Remarks:** ABS member. Has trained with Masters around the world. **Mark:** DrsRosiers over Alaska, underlined with a rose.

DESROSIERS, HALEY
PO Box 1954, Petersburg, AK 99833, Phone: 907-518-1416, haley@alaskablades.com Web: www.alaskablades.com
Specialties: Hunting knives, integrals and a few choppers, high performance.**Technical:** Hand forged blades designed for hard use, exotic wood, antler and ivory handles. **Prices:** $300 - $1500. **Remarks:** Forged first knife in 2001. Part-time bladesmith all year except for commercial fishing season. **Mark:** Capital HD.

DETMER, PHILLIP
14140 Bluff Rd, Breese, IL 62230, Phone: 618-526-4834, jpdetmer@att.net
Specialties: Working knives. **Patterns:** Bowies, daggers and hunters. **Technical:** Grinds ATS-34 and D2. **Prices:** $60 to $400. **Remarks:** Part-time maker; first knife sold in 1977. **Mark:** Last name with dagger.

DEUBEL, CHESTER J.
6211 N. Van Ark Rd., Tucson, AZ 85743, Phone: 520-440-7255, cjdeubel@yahoo.com; Web: www.cjdeubel.com
Specialties: Fancy working straight knives and folders of his or customer design, with intricate file work. **Patterns:** Fighters, Bowies, daggers, hunters, camp knives, and cowboy. **Technical:** Flat guard, hollow grind, antiqued, all types Damascus, 154cpm Stainsteel, high carbon steel, 440c Stainsteel. **Prices:** From $250 to $3500. **Remarks:** Started making part-time in 1980; went to full-time in 2000. Don Patch is my engraver. **Mark:** C.J. Deubel.

DEVERAUX, BUTCH
PO Box 1356, Riverton, WY 82501, Phone: 307-851-0601, bdeveraux@wyoming.com; Web: www.deverauxknives.com
Specialties: High-performance working straight knives. **Patterns:** Hunters, fighters, EDC's, miniatures and camp knives. **Technical:** Forged 52100 blade steel, brass guards, sheep-horn handles, as well as stag, cocobolo, she-oak and ironwood. **Prices:** $400 to $3,000. **Remarks:** Part-time maker; first knife sold in 2005. **Mark:** Deveraux on right ricasso.

DEYONG, CLARENCE
8716 Camelot Trace, Sturtevant, WI 53177, Phone: 630-465-6761, cmdeyong@yahoo.com; Web: www.deyongknives.com
Patterns: Mainly creates full-tang hunters, skinners and fighters. **Technical:** Stock removal with some forging, using rasps and files for blade stock with an emphasis on natural handle materials. **Prices:** $150 to $300 with custom sheaths. **Remarks:** Making knives since 1981. **Mark:** DeYong and blade # engraved on the blade.

DIAZ, JOSE
409 W. 12th Ave, Ellensburg, WA 98926, jose@diaztools.com Web: www.diaztools.com
Specialties: Affordable custom user-grade utility and camp knives. Also makes competition cutting knives. **Patterns:** Mas. **Technical:** Blade materials range from high carbon steels and Damascus to high performance tool and stainless steels. Uses both forge and stock removal methods in shaping the steel. Handle materials include Tero Tuf, Black Butyl Burl, Micarta, natural woods and G10. **Prices:** $65-$700. **Remarks:** Part-time knife maker; made first knife in 2008. **Mark:** Reclining tree frog with a smile, and "Diaz Tools."

DICK, DAN
P.O. Box 2303, Hutchinson, KS 67504-2303, Phone: 620-669-6805, Dan@DanDickKnives.com; Web: www.dandickknives.com
Specialties: Traditional working/using fixed bladed knives of maker's design. **Patterns:** Hunters, skinners and utility knives. **Technical:** Stock removal maker using CTS-XHP and D2. Prefers such materials as exotic and fancy burl woods. Makes his own sheaths, all leather with tooling. **Prices:** $150 and up. **Remarks:** Part-time maker since 2006. **Marks:** Name in outline border of Kansas.

DICKERSON, GAVIN
PO Box 7672, Petit, GT, SOUTH AFRICA 1512, Phone: +27 011-965-0988, Fax: +27 011-965-0988
Specialties: Straight knives of his design or to customer specs. **Patterns:** Hunters, skinners, fighters and Bowies. **Technical:** Hollow-grinds D2, 440C, ATS-34, 12C27 and Damascus upon request. Prefers natural handle materials; offers synthetic handle materials. **Prices:** $190 to $2500. **Remarks:** Part-time maker; first knife sold in 1982. **Mark:** Name in full.

DICKISON, SCOTT S
179 Taylor Rd, Portsmouth, RI 02871, Phone: 401-847-7398, squared22@cox .net; Web: http://sqauredknives.com
Specialties: Straight knives, locking folders and slip joints of his design. **Patterns:** Sgain dubh, bird and trout knives. **Technical:** Forges and grinds commercial Damascus, D2, O1 and sandvik stainless. **Prices:** $400 to $1000; some higher. **Remarks:** Part-time maker; first knife sold in 1989. **Mark:** Stylized initials.

DICRISTOFANO, ANTHONY P
10519 Nevada Ave., Melrose Park, IL 60164, Phone: 847-845-9598, sukemitsu@sbcglobal.net Web: www.namahagesword.com or www.sukemitsu.com
Specialties: Japanese-style swords. **Patterns:** Katana, Wakizashi, Otanto, Kozuka. **Technical:** Tradition and some modern steels. All clay tempered and traditionally hand polished using Japanese wet stones. **Remarks:** Part-time maker. **Prices:** Varied, available on request. **Mark:** Blade tang signed in "SUKEMITSU."

DIETZ, HOWARD
421 Range Rd, New Braunfels, TX 78132, Phone: 830-885-4662
Specialties: Lock-back folders, working straight knives. **Patterns:** Folding hunters, high-grade pocket knives. ATS-34, 440C, CPM 440V, D2 and stainless Damascus. **Prices:** $300 to $1000. **Remarks:** Full-time gun and knifemaker; first knife sold in 1995. **Mark:** Name, city, and state.

DIETZEL, BILL
779 Baycove Ct., Middleburg, FL 32068, Phone: 904-282-1091, wdms97@bellsouth.net
Specialties: Forged straight knives and folders. **Patterns:** His interpretations. **Technical:** Forges his Damascus and other steels. **Prices:** Middle ranges. **Remarks:** Likes natural materials; uses titanium in folder liners. Master Smith (1997). **Mark:** Name.

DIGANGI, JOSEPH M
PO Box 257, Los Ojos, NM 87551, Phone: 505-929-2987, Fax: 505-753-8144, Web: www.digangidesigns.com
Specialties: Kitchen and table cutlery. **Patterns:** French chef's knives, carving sets, steak knife sets, some camp knives and hunters. Holds patents and trademarks for "System

II" kitchen cutlery set. **Technical:** Grinds ATS-34. **Prices:** $150 to $595; some to $1200. **Remarks:** Full-time maker; first knife sold in 1983. **Mark:** DiGangi Designs.

DILL, ROBERT
1812 Van Buren, Loveland, CO 80538, Phone: 970-667-5144, Fax: 970-667-5144, dillcustomknives@msn.com
Specialties: Fancy and working knives of his design. **Patterns:** Hunters, Bowies and fighters. **Technical:** Grinds 440C and D2. **Prices:** $100 to $800. **Remarks:** Full-time maker; first knife sold in 1984. **Mark:** Logo stamped into blade.

DINTRUFF, CHUCK
306 East S.R. 60, Plant City, FL 33567, Phone: 813-381-6916, DINTRUFFKNIVES@aol.com; Web: dintruffknives.com and spinwellfab.com

DION, GREG
3032 S Jackson St, Oxnard, CA 93033, Phone: 519-981-1033
Specialties: Working straight knives, some fancy. Welcomes special orders. **Patterns:** Hunters, fighters, camp knives, Bowies and tantos. **Technical:** Grinds ATS-34, 154CM and 440C. **Prices:** $85 to $300; some to $600. **Remarks:** Part-time maker; first knife sold in 1985. **Mark:** Name.

DIONATAM, FRANCO
Sebastiao Jacinto de Amorim goncalves n 277, Filadelfia, Ibitinga-SP, BRAZIL 14940-000, francofacasartesanais@hotmail.com
Patterns: Bowies, hunters, camp knives, utilitarian and chef's knives. **Technical:** Uses 5160, 1070, 52100 and several damascus steel patterns. Knife handle materials include stabilized wood, natural wood, mammoth ivory, deer horn and exotic materials. **Prices:** $700 to $6,000. **Remarks:** ABS journeyman smith who prefers working from orders. **Mark:** Franco.

DIOTTE, JEFF
DIOTTE KNIVES, 159 Laurier Dr, LaSalle, ON, CANADA N9J 1L4, Phone: 519-978-2764

DIPPOLD, AL
90 Damascus Ln, Perryville, MO 63775, Phone: 573-547-1119, adippold@midwest.net
Specialties: Fancy one-of-a-kind locking folders. **Patterns:** Locking folders. **Technical:** Forges and grinds mosaic and pattern welded Damascus. Offers filework on all folders. **Prices:** $500 to $3500; some higher. **Remarks:** Full-time maker; first knife sold in 1980. **Mark:** Last name in logo inside of liner.

DISKIN, MATT
PO Box 653, Freeland, WA 98249, Phone: 360-730-0451, info@volcanknives.com; Web: www.volcanknives.com
Specialties: Damascus autos. **Patterns:** Dirks and daggers. **Technical:** Forges mosaic Damascus using 15N20, 1084, 02, 06, L6; pure nickel. **Prices:** Start at $500. Remarks; Full-time maker. **Mark:** Last name.

DIXON JR., IRA E
PO Box 26, Cave Junction, OR 97523, irasknives@yahoo.com
Specialties: Straight knives of his design. **Patterns:** All patterns include art knives. **Technical:** Grinds CPM materials, Damascus and some tool steels. **Prices:** $275 to $2000. **Remarks:** Full-time maker; first knife sold in 1993. **Mark:** First name, Handmade.

DOBRATZ, ERIC
25371 Hillary Lane, Laguna Hills, CA 92653, Phone: 949-233-5170, knifesmith@gmail.com
Specialties: Differentially quenched blades with Hamon of his design or with customer input. **Patterns:** Hunting, camp, kitchen, fighters, bowies, traditional tanto, and unique fixed blade designs. **Technical:** Hand-forged high carbon and damascus. Prefers natural material for handles; rare/exotic woods and stag, but also uses micarta and homemade synthetic materials. **Prices:** $150 - $1500. **Remarks:** Part-time maker; first knife made in 1995. **Mark:** Stylized Scarab beetle.

DODD, ROBERT F
4340 E Canyon Dr, Camp Verde, AZ 86322, Phone: 928-567-3333, rfdknives@commspeed.net; Web: www.rfdoddknives.com
Specialties: Folders, fixed blade hunter/skinners, Bowies, daggers. **Patterns:** Drop point. **Technical:** ATS-34 and Damascus. **Prices:** $250 and up. **Remarks:** Hand tooled leather sheaths. **Mark:** R. F. Dodd, Camp Verde AZ.

DOIRON, DONALD
6 Chemin Petit Lac des Ced, Messines, QC, CANADA J0X-2J0, Phone: 819-465-2489

DOMINY, CHUCK
PO Box 593, Colleyville, TX 76034, Phone: 817-498-4527
Specialties: Titanium LinerLock® folders. **Patterns:** Hunters, utility/camp knives and LinerLock® folders. **Technical:** Grinds 440C and ATS-34. **Prices:** $250 to $3000. **Remarks:** Full-time maker; first knife sold in 1976. **Mark:** Last name.

DOOLITTLE, MIKE
13 Denise Ct, Novato, CA 94947, Phone: 415-897-3246
Specialties: Working straight knives in standard patterns. **Patterns:** Hunters and fishing knives. **Technical:** Grinds 440C, 154CM and ATS-34. **Prices:** $125 to $200; some to $750. **Remarks:** Part-time maker; first knife sold in 1981. **Mark:** Name, city and state.

DORNELES, DAVE
7404 NW 30th St, Bethany, OK 73008, Phone: 405-789-0750
Specialties: Folders of his design. **Patterns:** Various patterns. **Technical:** Hand-grinds 440C, ATS-34. Offers engraving and filework on all folders. **Prices:** Starting at $450. **Remarks:** Full-time maker; first knife sold in 1987. **Mark:** First initial, last name.

DORNELES, LUCIANO OLIVEIRIA
Rua 15 De Novembro 2222, Nova Petropolis, RS, BRAZIL 95150-000, Phone: 011-55-54-303-303-90, tchebufalo@hotmail.com
Specialties: Traditional "true" Brazilian-style working knives and to customer specs. **Patterns:** Brazilian hunters, utility and camp knives, Bowies, Dirk. A master at the making of the true "Faca Campeira Gaucha," the true camp knife of the famous Brazilian Gauchos. A Dorneles knife is 100 percent hand-forged with sledge hammers only. Can make spectacular Damascus hunters/daggers. **Technical:** Forges only 52100 and his own Damascus, can put silver wire inlay on customer design handles on special orders; uses only natural handle materials. **Prices:** $250 to $1000. **Mark:** Symbol with L. Dorneles.

DOTSON, TRACY
1280 Hwy C-4A, Baker, FL 32531, Phone: 850-537-2407
Specialties: Folding fighters and small folders. **Patterns:** LinerLock® and lockback folders. **Technical:** Hollow-grinds ATS-34 and commercial Damascus. **Prices:** Start at $250. **Remarks:** Part-time maker; first knife sold in 1995. **Mark:** Last name.

DOUCETTE, R
CUSTOM KNIVES, 19 Evelyn St., Brantford, ON, CANADA N3R 3G8, Phone: 519-756-9040, randy@randydoucetteknives.com; Web: www.randydoucetteknives.com
Specialties: High-end tactical folders with filework and multiple grinds. **Patterns:** Tactical folders. **Technical:** All knives are handmade. The only outsourcing is heat treatment. **Prices:** $900 to $2,500. **Remarks:** Full-time knifemaker; 2-year waiting list. Maker is proud to produce original knife designs every year!lm **Mark:** R. Doucette

DOURSIN, GERARD
Chemin des Croutoules, Pernes les Fontaines, FRANCE 84210
Specialties: Period pieces. **Patterns:** Liner locks and daggers. **Technical:** Forges mosaic Damascus. **Prices:** $600 to $4000. **Remarks:** First knife sold in 1983. **Mark:** First initial, last name and I stop the lion.

DOUSSOT, LAURENT
1008 Montarville, St. Bruno, QC, CANADA J3V 3T1, Phone: 450-441-3298, doussot@skalja.com; Web: www.skalja.com, www.doussot-knives.com
Specialties: Fancy and embellished folders and fantasy knives. **Patterns:** Fighters and locking folders. **Technical:** Grinds ATS-34 and commercial Damascus. Scale carvings on all knives; most bolsters are carved titanium. **Prices:** $350 to $3000. **Remarks:** Part-time maker; first knife was sold in 1992. **Mark:** Stylized initials inside circle.

DOWNIE, JAMES T
1295 Sandy Ln., Apt. 1208, Sarnia, Ontario, CANADA N7V 4K5, Phone: 519-491-8234
Specialties: Serviceable straight knives and folders; period pieces. **Patterns:** Hunters, Bowies, camp knives, fillet and miniatures. **Technical:** Grinds D2, 440C and ATS-34, Damasteel, stainless steel Damascus. **Prices:** $195 and up. **Remarks:** Full-time maker; first knife sold in 1978. **Mark:** Signature of first and middle initials, last name.

DOWNING, LARRY
12268 State Route 181 N, Bremen, KY 42325, Phone: 270-525-3523, larrydowning@bellsouth.net; Web: www.downingknives.com
Specialties: Working straight knives and folders. **Patterns:** From mini-knives to daggers, folding lockers to interframes. **Technical:** Forges and grinds 154CM, ATS-34 and his own Damascus. **Prices:** $195 to $950; some higher. **Remarks:** Part-time maker; first knife sold in 1979. **Mark:** Name in arrowhead.

DOWNING, TOM
2675 12th St, Cuyahoga Falls, OH 44223, Phone: 330-923-7464
Specialties: Working straight knives; period pieces. **Patterns:** Hunters, fighters and tantos. **Technical:** Grinds 440C, ATs-34 and CPM-T-440V. Prefers natural handle materials. **Prices:** $150 to $900, some to $1500. **Remarks:** Part-time maker; first knife sold in 1979. **Mark:** First and middle initials, last name.

DOWNS, JAMES F
2247 Summit View Rd, Powell, OH 43065, Phone: 614-766-5350, jfdowns1@yahoo.com; Web: www.downshandmadeknives.com
Specialties: Working straight knives of his design or to customer specs. **Patterns:** Folders, Bowies, boot, hunters, utility. **Technical:** Grinds 440C and other steels. Prefers mastodon ivory, all pearls, stabilized wood and elephant ivory. **Prices:** $75 to $1200. **Remarks:** Full-time maker; first knife sold in 1980. **Mark:** Last name.

DOX, JAN
Zwanebloemlaan 27, Schoten, BELGIUM B 2900, Phone: 32 3 658 77 43, jan.dox@scarlet.be; Web: doxblades.weebly.com
Specialties: Working/using knives, from kitchen to battlefield. **Patterns:** Own designs, some based on traditional ethnic patterns (Scots, Celtic, Scandinavian and Japanese) or to customer specs. **Technical:** Grinds D2/A2 and stainless, forges carbon steels, convex edges. Handles: Wrapped in modern or traditional patterns, resin impregnated if desired. Natural or synthetic materials, some carved. **Prices:** $50 and up. **Remarks:** Spare-time maker, first knife sold 2001. **Mark:** Name or stylized initials.

DOYLE, JOHN
4779 W. M-61, Gladwin, MI 48624, Phone: 989-802-9470, jdoyleknives@gmail.com
Specialties: Hunters, camp knives and bowies. **Technical:** Forges 1075, 1080, 1084, 1095 and 5160. Will practice stock-removal method of blademaking on small knives at times. **Remarks:** Full-time maker; first knife made in 2009. **Mark:** J. Doyle in "Invitation" style print font

DOZIER, BOB
Dozier Knives and Arkansas Made Dozier, PO Box 1941, Springdale, AR 72765, Phone: 888-823-0023/479-756-0023, Fax: 479-756-9139, info@dozierknives.com;

Web www.dozierknives.com
Specialties: Folding knives and collector-grade knives (Dozier Knives) and hunting and tactical fixed blades (Arkansas Dozier Made). **Technical:** Uses D2. **Prices:** Start at $205 (Arkansas Made Dozier) or $500 (Dozier Knives). **Remarks:** Full-time maker; first knife sold in 1965. **Mark:** Dozier with an arrow through the D and year over arrow for foldiers, or R.L. Dozier, maker, St. Paul, AR in an oval for the collector-grad knives (Dozier Knives); and Arkansas, Made, Dozier in a circle (Arkansas Dozier Made).

DRAPER, AUDRA
#10 Creek Dr, Riverton, WY 82501, Phone: 307-856-6807 or 307-851-0426 cell, adraper@wyoming.com; Web: www.draperknives.com
Specialties: One-of-a-kind straight and folding knives. Also pendants, earring and bracelets of Damascus. **Patterns:** Design custom knives, using, Bowies, and minis. **Technical:** Forge Damascus; heat-treats all knives. **Prices:** Vary depending on item. **Remarks:** Full-time maker; master bladesmith in the ABS. Member of the PKA; first knife sold in 1995. **Mark:** Audra.

DRAPER, MIKE
#10 Creek Dr, Riverton, WY 82501, Phone: 307-856-6807, adraper@wyoming.com
Specialties: Mainly folding knives in tactical fashion, occasonal fixed blade. **Patterns:** Hunters, Bowies and camp knives, tactical survival. **Technical:** Grinds S30V stainless steel. **Prices:** Starting at $250+. **Remarks:** Full-time maker; first knife sold in 1996. **Mark:** Initials M.J.D. or name, city and state.

DREW, GERALD
213 Hawk Ridge Dr, Mill Spring, NC 28756, Phone: 828-713-4762
Specialties: Blade ATS-34 blades. Straight knives. **Patterns:** Hunters, camp knives, some Bowies and tactical. **Technical:** ATS-34 preferred. **Prices:** $65 to $400. **Mark:** GL DREW.

DRISCOLL, MARK
4115 Avoyer Pl, La Mesa, CA 91941, Phone: 619-670-0695, markdriscoll91941@yahoo.com
Specialties: High-art, period pieces and working/using knives of his design or to customer specs; some fancy. **Patterns:** Swords, Bowies, fighters, daggers, hunters and primitive (mountain man-styles). **Technical:** Forges 52100, 5160, O1, L6, 1095, 15n20, W-2 steel and makes his own Damascus and mokume; also does multiple quench heat treating. Uses exotic hardwoods, ivory and horn, offers fancy file work, carving, scrimshaws. **Prices:** $150 to $550; some to $1500. **Remarks:** Part-time maker; first knife sold in 1986. Doing business as Mountain Man Knives. **Mark:** Double "M."

DROST, JASON D
Rt 2 Box 49, French Creek, WV 26218, Phone: 304-472-7901
Specialties: Working/using straight knives of his design. **Patterns:** Hunters and utility/camp knives. **Technical:** Grinds 154CM and D2. **Prices:** $125 to $5000. **Remarks:** Spare-time maker; first knife sold in 1995. **Mark:** First and middle initials, last name, maker, city and state.

DROST, MICHAEL B
Rt 2 Box 49, French Creek, WV 26218, Phone: 304-472-7901
Specialties: Working/using straight knives and folders of all designs. **Patterns:** Hunters, locking folders and utility/camp knives. **Technical:** Grinds ATS-34, D2 and CPM-T-440V. Offers dove-tailed bolsters and spacers, filework and scrimshaw. **Prices:** $125 to $400; some to $740. **Remarks:** Full-time maker; first knife sold in 1990. Doing business as Drost Custom Knives. **Mark:** Name, city and state.

DRUMM, ARMIN
Lichtensteinstrasse 33, Dornstadt, GERMANY 89160, Phone: 49-163-632-2842, armin@drumm-knives.de; Web: www.drumm-knives.de
Specialties: One-of-a-kind forged and Damascus fixed blade knives and folders. **Patterns:** Classic Bowie knives, daggers, fighters, hunters, folders, swords. **Technical:** Forges own Damascus and carbon steels, filework, carved handles. **Prices:** $250 to $800, some higher. **Remarks:** First knife sold in 2001, member of the German Knifemakers Guild. **Mark:** First initial, last name.

DUCKER, BRIAN
Lamorna Cottage, Common End, Colkirk, ENGLAND NR21 7JD, Phone: 01-328-856-183, admin@grommitbaileyknives.com; Web: www.grommitbaileyknives.com
Specialties: Hunters, utility pieces, bowies, camp knives, fighters and folders. **Technical:** Stock removal and forged 1095, 1075 and 80CrV2. Forging own damascus, using exotic and native hardwoods, stag, leather, Micarta and other synthetic materials, with brass and 301 stainless steel fittings. Own leatherwork and heat treating. **Remarks:** Part-time maker since 2009, full time Dec. 2013. All knives and sheaths are sole authorship. **Mark:** GROMMIT UK MAKER & BAILEY GROMMIT MAKERS.

DUFF, BILL
2801 Ash St, Poteau, OK 74953, Phone: 918-647-4458
Specialties: Straight knives and folders, some fancy. **Patterns:** Hunters, folders and miniatures. **Technical:** Grinds 440-C and commercial Damascus. **Prices:** $250 and up. **Remarks:** First knife sold in 1976. **Mark:** Bill Duff.

DUFOUR, ARTHUR J
8120 De Armoun Rd, Anchorage, AK 99516, Phone: 907-345-1701
Specialties: Working straight knives from standard patterns. **Patterns:** Hunters, Bowies, camp and fishing knives—grinded thin and pointed. **Technical:** Grinds 440C, ATS-34, AEB-L. Tempers 57-58R; hollow-grinds. **Prices:** $135; some to $250. **Remarks:** Part-time maker; first knife sold in 1970. **Mark:** Prospector logo.

DUGDALE, DANIEL J.
11 Eleanor Road, Walpole, MA 02081, Phone: 508-404-6509, dlpdugdale@comcast.net

Specialties: Button-lock and straight knives of his design. **Patterns:** Utilities, hunters, skinners, and tactical. **Technical:** Falt grinds D-2 and 440C, aluminum handles with anodized finishes. **Prices:** $150 to $500. **Remarks:** Part-time maker since 1977. **Mark:** Deer track with last name, town and state.

DUNCAN, RON
5090 N. Hwy. 63, Cairo, MO 65239, Phone: 660-263-8949, www.duncanmadeknives.com
Remarks: Duncan Made Knives

DUNKERLEY, RICK
PO Box 601, Lincoln, MT 59639, Phone: 406-210-4101, dunkerleyknives@gmail.com Web: www.dunkerleyknives.com
Specialties: Mosaic Damascus folders and carbon steel utility knives. **Patterns:** One-of-a-kind folders, standard hunters and utility designs. **Technical:** Forges 52100, Damascus and mosaic Damascus. Prefers natural handle materials. **Prices:** $200 and up. **Remarks:** Full-time maker; first knife sold in 1984, ABS Master Smith. Doing business as Dunkerley Custom Knives. Dunkerley handmade knives, sole authorship. **Mark:** Dunkerley, MS.

DUNLAP, JIM
800 E. Badger Lee Rd., Sallisaw, OK 74955, Phone: 918-774-2700, dunlapknives@gmail.com
Specialties: Traditional slip-joint folders. **Patterns:** Single- and multi-blade traditional slip joints. **Technical:** Grinds ATS-34, CPM-154 and damascus. **Prices:** $250 and up. **Remarks:** Part-time maker; first knife sold in 2009. **Mark:** Dunlap.

DUNN, STEVE
376 Biggerstaff Rd, Smiths Grove, KY 42171, Phone: 270-563-9830, dunnknives@windstream.net; Web: www.stevedunnknives.com
Specialties: Working and using straight knives of his design; period pieces. Offers engraving and gold inlay. **Patterns:** Hunters, skinners, Bowies, fighters, camp knives, folders, swords and battle axes. **Technical:** Forges own Damascus, 1075, 15N20, 52100, 1084, L6. **Prices:** Moderate to upscale. **Remarks:** Full-time maker; first knife sold in 1990. **Mark:** Last name and MS.

DURAN, JERRY T
PO Box 9753, Albuquerque, NM 87119, Phone: 505-873-4676, jtdknives@hotmail.com; Web: http://www.google.com/profiles/jtdknivesLLC
Specialties: Tactical folders, Bowies, fighters, liner locks, autopsy and hunters. **Patterns:** Folders, Bowies, hunters and tactical knives. **Technical:** Forges own Damascus and forges carbon steel. **Prices:** Moderate to upscale. **Remarks:** Full-time maker; first knife sold in 1978. **Mark:** Initials in elk rack logo.

DURHAM, KENNETH
BUZZARD ROOST FORGE, 10495 White Pike, Cherokee, AL 35616, Phone: 256-359-4287, www.home.hiwaay.net/~jamesd/
Specialties: Bowies, dirks, hunters. **Patterns:** Traditional patterns. **Technical:** Forges 1095, 5160, 52100 and makes own Damascus. **Prices:** $85 to $1600. **Remarks:** Began making knives about 1995. Received Journeyman stamp 1999. Got Master Smith stamp in 2004. **Mark:** Bull's head with Ken Durham above and Cherokee AL below.

DURIO, FRED
144 Gulino St, Opelousas, LA 70570, Phone: 337-948-4831/cell 337-351-2652, fdurio@yahoo.com
Specialties: Folders. **Patterns:** Liner locks; plain and fancy. **Technical:** Makes own Damascus. **Prices:** Moderate to upscale. **Remarks:** Full-time maker. **Mark:** Last name-Durio.

DUVALL, FRED
10715 Hwy 190, Benton, AR 72015, Phone: 501-778-9360
Specialties: Working straight knives and folders. **Patterns:** Locking folders, slip joints, hunters, fighters and Bowies. **Technical:** Grinds D2 and CPM440V; forges 5160. **Prices:** $100 to $400; some to $800. **Remarks:** Part-time maker; first knife sold in 1973. **Mark:** Last name.

DWYER, DUANE
565 Country Club Dr., Escondido, CA 92029, Phone: 760-471-8275, striderguys@striderknives.com; Web: www.striderknives.com
Specialties: Primarily tactical. **Patterns:** Fixed and folders. **Technical:** Primarily stock removal specializing in highly technical materials. **Prices:** $100 and up, based on the obvious variables. **Remarks:** Full-time maker since 1996.

DYER, DAVID
4531 Hunters Glen, Granbury, TX 76048, Phone: 817-573-1198
Specialties: Working skinners and early period knives. **Patterns:** Customer designs, his own patterns. **Technical:** Coal forged blades; 5160 and 52100 steels. Grinds D2, 1095, L6. **Prices:** $150 for neck knives and small (3" to 3-1/2"). To $600 for large blades and specialty blades. **Mark:** Last name DYER electro etched.

DYESS, EDDIE
1005 Hamilton, Roswell, NM 88201, Phone: 505-623-5599, eddyess@msn.com
Specialties: Working and using straight knives in standard patterns. **Patterns:** Hunters and fighters. **Technical:** Grinds 440C, 154CM and D2 on request. **Prices:** $150 to $300, some higher. **Remarks:** Spare-time maker; first knife sold in 1980. **Mark:** Last name.

E

EAKER, ALLEN L
416 Clinton Ave Dept KI, Paris, IL 61944, Phone: 217-466-5160
Specialties: Traditional straight knives and folders of his design. **Patterns:** Hunters, locking folders and slip-joint folders. **Technical:** Grinds 440C; inlays. **Prices:** $200 to

$500. **Remarks:** Spare-time maker; first knife sold in 1994. **Mark:** Initials in tankard logo stamped on tang, serial number and surname on back.

EALY, DELBERT
PO Box 121, Indian River, MI 49749, Phone: 231-238-4705

EATON, FRANK L JR
5365 W. Meyer Rd., Farmington, MO 63640, Phone: 703-314-8708, eatontactical@ me.com; Web: www.frankeatonknives.com
Specialties: Full tang/hidden tang fixed working and art knives of his own design. **Patterns:** Hunters, skinners, fighters, Bowies, tacticals and daggers. **Technical:** Stock removal maker, prefer using natural materials. **Prices:** $175 to $400. **Remarks:** Part-time maker - Active Duty Airborn Ranger-Making 4 years. **Mark:** Name over 75th Ranger Regimental Crest.

EATON, RICK
313 Dailey Rd, Broadview, MT 59015, Phone: 406-667-2405, rick@eatonknives.com; Web: www.eatonknives.com
Specialties: Interframe folders and one-hand-opening side locks. **Patterns:** Bowies, daggers, fighters and folders. **Technical:** Grinds 154CM, ATS-34, 440C and other maker's Damascus. Makes own mosaic Damascus. Offers high-quality hand engraving, Bulino and gold inlay. **Prices:** Upscale. **Remarks:** Full-time maker; first knife sold in 1982. **Mark:** Full name and/or full name and address.

EBISU, HIDESAKU
3-39-7 Koi Osako, Nishi Ku, Hiroshima, JAPAN 733 0816

ECHOLS, RODGER
2853 Highway 371 W, Nashville, AR 71852-7577, Phone: 870-845-9173 or 870-845-0400, blademanechols@aol.com; Web: www.echolsknives.com
Specialties: Liner locks, auto-scale release, lock backs. **Patterns:** His or yours. **Technical:** Autos. **Prices:** $500 to $1700. **Remarks:** Likes to use pearl, ivory and Damascus the most. Made first knife in 1984. Part-time maker; tool and die maker by trade. **Mark:** Name.

EDDY, HUGH E
211 E Oak St, Caldwell, ID 83605, Phone: 208-459-0536

EDGE, TOMMY
1244 County Road 157, Cash, AR 72421, Phone: 870-897-6150, tedge@tex.net
Specialties: Fancy/embellished working knives of his design. **Patterns:** Bowies, hunters and utility/camping knives. **Technical:** Grinds 440C, ATS-34 and D2. Makes own cable Damascus; offers filework. **Prices:** $70 to $250; some to $1500. **Remarks:** Part-time maker; first knife sold in 1973. **Mark:** Stamped first initial, last name and stenciled name, city and state in oval shape.

EDMONDS, WARRICK
Adelaide Hills, SOUTH AUSTRALIA, Phone: 61-8-83900339, warrick@riflebirdknives. com Web: www.riflebirdknives.com
Specialties: Fixed blade knives with select and highly figured exotic or unique Australian wood handles. Themed collectors knives to individually designed working knives from Damascus, RWL34, 440C or high carbon steels. **Patterns:** Hunters, utilities and workshop knives, cooks knives with a Deco to Modern flavour. Hand sewn individual leather sheaths. **Technical:** Stock removal using only steel from well known and reliable sources. **Prices:** $250Aust to $1000Aust. **Remarks:** Part-time maker since 2004. **Mark:** Name stamped into sheath.

EDWARDS, MITCH
303 New Salem Rd, Glasgow, KY 42141, Phone: 270-404-0758 / 270-404-0758, medwards@glasgow-ky.com; Web: www.traditionalknives.com
Specialties: Period pieces. **Patterns:** Neck knives, camp, rifleman and Bowie knives. **Technical:** All hand forged, forges own Damascus O1, 1084, 1095, L6, 15N20. **Prices:** $200 to $1000. **Remarks:** Journeyman Smith. **Mark:** Broken heart.

EHRENBERGER, DANIEL ROBERT
1213 S Washington St, Mexico, MO 65265, Phone: 573-633-2010
Specialties: Affordable working/using straight knives of his design and to custom specs. **Patterns:** 10" western Bowie, fighters, hunting and skinning knives. **Technical:** Forges 1085, 1095, his own Damascus and cable Damascus. **Prices:** $80 to $500. **Remarks:** Full-time maker, first knife sold 1994. **Mark:** Ehrenberger JS.

EKLUND, MAIHKEL
Fone Stam V9, Farila, SWEDEN 82041, info@art-knives.com; Web: www.art-knives. com
Specialties: Collector-grade working straight knives. **Patterns:** Hunters, Bowies and fighters. **Technical:** Grinds ATS-34, Uddeholm and Dama steel. Engraves and scrimshaws. **Prices:** $200 to $2000. **Remarks:** Full-time maker; first knife sold in 1983. **Mark:** Initials or name.

ELDRIDGE, ALLAN
7731 Four Winds Dr, Ft. Worth, TX 76133, Phone: 817-370-7778; Cell: 817-296-3528
Specialties: Fancy classic straight knives in standard patterns. **Patterns:** Hunters, Bowies, fighters, folders and miniatures. **Technical:** Grinds O1 and Damascus. Engraves silver-wire inlays, pearl inlays, scrimshaws and offers filework. **Prices:** $50 to $500; some to $1200. **Remarks:** Spare-time maker; first knife sold in 1965. **Mark:** Initials.

ELISHEWITZ, ALLEN
875 Hwy. 321 N, Ste. 600, #212, Lenoir City, TN 37771, Phone: 865-816-3309, allen@elishewitzknives.com; Web: elishewitzknives.com
Specialties: Collectible high-tech working straight knives and folders of his design. **Patterns:** Working, utility and tactical knives. **Technical:** Designs and uses innovative locking mechanisms. All designs drafted and field-tested. **Prices:** $600 to $1000. **Remarks:** Full-time maker; first knife sold in 1989. **Mark:** Gold medallion inlaid in blade.

ELLEFSON, JOEL
PO Box 1016, 310 S 1st St, Manhattan, MT 59741, Phone: 406-284-3111
Specialties: Working straight knives, fancy daggers and one-of-a-kinds. **Patterns:** Hunters, daggers and some folders. **Technical:** Grinds A2, 440C and ATS-34. Makes own mokume in bronze, brass, silver and shibuishi; makes brass/steel blades. **Prices:** $100 to $500; some to $2000. **Remarks:** Part-time maker; first knife sold in 1978. **Mark:** Stylized last initial.

ELLERBE, W B
3871 Osceola Rd, Geneva, FL 32732, Phone: 407-349-5818
Specialties: Period and primitive knives and sheaths. **Patterns:** Bowies to patch knives, some tomahawks. **Technical:** Grinds Sheffield O1 and files. **Prices:** Start at $35. **Remarks:** Full-time maker; first knife sold in 1971. Doing business as Cypress Bend Custom Knives. **Mark:** Last name or initials.

ELLIOTT, JERRY
4507 Kanawha Ave, Charleston, WV 25304, Phone: 304-925-5045, elliottknives@ gmail.com
Specialties: Classic and traditional straight knives and folders of his design and to customer specs. **Patterns:** Hunters, locking folders and Bowies. **Technical:** Grinds ATS-34, 154CM, O1, D2 and T-440-V. All guards silver-soldered; bolsters are pinned on straight knives, spot-welded on folders. **Prices:** $80 to $265; some to $1000. **Remarks:** Full-time maker; first knife sold in 1972. **Mark:** First and middle initials, last name, knife maker, city, state.

ELLIS, WILLIAM DEAN
2767 Edgar Ave, Sanger, CA 93657, Phone: 559-314-4459, urleebird@comcast.net; Web: www.billysblades.com
Specialties: Classic and fancy knives of his design. **Patterns:** Boots, fighters and utility knives. **Technical:** Grinds ATS-34, D2 and Damascus. Offers tapered tangs and six patterns of filework; tooled multi-colored sheaths. **Prices:** $250 to $1500 **Remarks:** Part-time maker; first knife sold in 1991. Doing business as Billy's Blades. Also make shave-ready straight razors for actual use. **Mark:** "B" in a five-point star next to "Billy," city and state within a rounded-corner rectangle.

ELLIS, WILLY B
1025 Hamilton Ave., Tarpon Springs, FL 34689, Phone: 727-942-6420, Web: www. willyb.com
Specialties: One-of-a-kind high art and fantasy knives of his design. Occasional customs full size and miniatures. **Patterns:** Bowies, fighters, hunters and others. **Technical:** Grinds 440C, ATS-34, 1095, carbon Damascus, ivory bone, stone and metal carving. **Prices:** $175 to $15,000. **Remarks:** Full-time maker, first knife made in 1973. Member Knifemakers Guild and FEGA. Jewel setting inlays. **Mark:** Willy B. or WB'S C etched or carved.

ELROD, ROGER R
58 Dale Ave, Enterprise, AL 36330, Phone: 334-347-1863

EMBRETSEN, KAJ
FALUVAGEN 67, Edsbyn, SWEDEN 82830, Phone: 46-271-21057, Fax: 46-271-22961, kay.embretsen@telia.com Web:www.embretsenknives.com
Specialties: Damascus folding knives. **Patterns:** Uses mammoth ivory and some pearl. **Technical:** Uses own Damascus steel. **Remarks:** Full time since 1983. **Prices:** $2500 to $8000. **Mark:** Name inside the folder.

EMERSON, ERNEST R
1234 W. 254th, Harbor City, CA 90710, Phone: 310-539-5633, info@emersonknives. com; Web: www.emersonknives.com
Specialties: High-tech folders and combat fighters. **Patterns:** Fighters, LinerLock® combat folders and SPECWAR combat knives. **Technical:** Grinds 154CM and Damascus. Makes folders with titanium fittings, liners and locks. Chisel grind specialist. **Prices:** $550 to $850; some to $10,000. **Remarks:** Full-time maker; first knife sold in 1983. **Mark:** Last name and Specwar knives.

EMMERLING, JOHN
POB 2080, Gearheart, OR 97138, Phone: 503-738-5434, gearhartironwerks@gmail. com; Web: www.gearhartironwerks.com

ENCE, JIM
145 S 200 East, Richfield, UT 84701, Phone: 435-896-6206
Specialties: High-art period pieces (spec in California knives) art knives. **Patterns:** Art, boot knives, fighters, Bowies and occasional folders. **Technical:** Grinds 440C for polish and beauty boys; makes own Damascus. **Prices:** Upscale. **Remarks:** Full-time maker; first knife sold in 1977. Does own engraving, gold work and stone work. Guild member since 1977. Founding member of the AKI. **Mark:** Ence, usually engraved.

ENGLAND, VIRGIL
1340 Birchwood St, Anchorage, AK 99508, Phone: 907-274-9494, hardfistdown@ gmail.com; Web: www.virgilenglandshetlandarmory.com
Specialties: Edged weapons and equipage, one-of-a-kind only. **Patterns:** Axes, swords, lances and body armor. **Technical:** Forges and grinds as pieces dictate. Offers stainless and Damascus. **Prices:** Upscale. **Remarks:** A veteran knifemaker. No commissions. **Mark:** Stylized initials.

ENGLE, WILLIAM
16608 Oak Ridge Rd, Boonville, MO 65233, Phone: 816-882-6277
Specialties: Traditional working and using straight knives of his design. **Patterns:** Hunters, Bowies and fighters. **Technical:** Grinds 440C, ATS-34 and 154 CM. **Prices:** $250

to $500; some higher. **Remarks:** Part-time maker; first knife sold in 1982. All knives come with certificate of authenticity. **Mark:** Last name in block lettering.

ENGLISH, JIM

14586 Olive Vista Dr, Jamul, CA 91935, Phone: 619-669-0833
Specialties: Traditional working straight knives to customer specs. **Patterns:** Hunters, bowies, fighters, tantos, daggers, boot and utility/camp knives. **Technical:** Grinds 440C, ATS-34, commercial Damascus and customer choice. **Prices:** $130 to $350. **Remarks:** Part-time maker; first knife sold in 1985. In addition to custom line, also does business as Mountain Home Knives. **Mark:** Double "A," Double "J" logo.

ENNIS, RAY

1220S 775E, Ogden, UT 84404, Phone: 800-410-7603, Fax: 501-621-2683, nifmakr@hotmail.com; Web:www.ennis-entrekusa.com

ENOS III, THOMAS M

12302 State Rd 535, Orlando, FL 32836, Phone: 407-239-6205, tmenos3@att.net
Specialties: Heavy-duty working straight knives; unusual designs. **Patterns:** Swords, machetes, daggers, skinners, filleting, period pieces. **Technical:** Grinds 440C. **Prices:** $75 to $1500. **Remarks:** Full-time maker; first knife sold in 1972. No longer accepting custom requests. Will be making his own designs. Send SASE for listing of items for sale. **Mark:** Name in knife logo and year, type of steel and serial number.

EPTING, RICHARD

4976 Drake Dr., College Station, TX 77845-7176, Phone: 979-255-2161, rgeknives@hotmail.com; Web: www.eptingknives.com
Specialties: Folders and working straight knives. **Patterns:** Hunters, Bowies, and locking folders. **Technical:** Forges high-carbon steel and his own Damascus. **Prices:** $200 to $800; some to $1800. **Remarks:** Part-time maker, first knife sold 1996. **Mark:** Name in arch logo.

ERICKSON, DANIEL

Ring Of Fire Forge, 20011 Welch Rd., Snohomish, WA 98296, Phone: 206-355-1793, Web: www.ringoffireforge.com
Specialties: Likes to fuse traditional and functional with creative concepts. **Patterns:** Hunters, fighters, bowies, folders, slip joints, art knives, the Phalanx. **Technical:** Forges own pattern-welded damascus blades (1080/15N20), 5160, CruForgeV, 52100 and W2. Uses figured burls, stabilized woods, fossil ivories and natural and unique materials for handles. Custom stands and sheaths. **Prices:** $250 to $1,500. **Remarks:** Sole authorship, designer and inventor. Started making in 2003; first knife sold in 2004. ABS journeyman smith. **Mark:** "Ring of Fire" with Erickson moving through it.

ERICKSON, L.M.

1379 Black Mountain Cir, Ogden, UT 84404, Phone: 801-737-1930
Specialties: Straight knives; period pieces. **Patterns:** Bowies, fighters, boots and hunters. **Technical:** Grinds 440C, 154CM and commercial Damascus. **Prices:** $200 to $900; some to $5000. **Remarks:** Part-time maker; first knife sold in 1981. **Mark:** Name, city, state.

ERICKSON, WALTER E.

22280 Shelton Tr, Atlanta, MI 49709, Phone: 989-785-5262, wberic@src-milp.com
Specialties: Unusual survival knives and high-tech working knives. **Patterns:** Butterflies, hunters, tantos. **Technical:** Grinds ATS-34 or customer choice. **Prices:** $150 to $500; some to $1500. **Remarks:** Full-time maker; first knife sold in 1981. **Mark:** Using pantograph with assorted fonts (no longer stamping).

ERIKSEN, JAMES THORLIEF

dba VIKING KNIVES, 3830 Dividend Dr, Garland, TX 75042, Phone: 972-494-3667, Fax: 972-235-4932, VikingKnives@aol.com
Specialties: Heavy-duty working and using straight knives and folders utilizing traditional, Viking original and customer specification patterns. Some high-tech and fancy/embellished knives available. **Patterns:** Bowies, hunters, skinners, boot and belt knives, utility/camp knives, fighters, daggers, locking folders, slip-joint folders and kitchen knives. **Technical:** Hollow-grinds 440C, D2, ASP-23, ATS-34, 154CM, Vascowear. **Prices:** $150 to $300; some to $600. **Remarks:** Full-time maker; first knife sold in 1985. Doing business as Viking Knives. For a color catalog showing 50 different models, mail $5 to above address. **Mark:** VIKING or VIKING USA for export.

ERNEST, PHIL (PJ)

PO Box 5240, Whittier, CA 90607-5240, Phone: 562-556-2324, hugger883562@yahoo.com; Web:www.ernestcustomknives.com
Specialties: Fixed blades. **Patterns:** Wide range. Many original as well as hunters, camp, fighters, daggers, bowies and tactical. Specialzin in Wharncliff's of all sizes. **Technical:** Grinds commercial Damascus, Mosaid Damascus. ATS-34, and 440C. Full Tangs with bolsters. Handle material includes all types of exotic hardwood, abalone, peal mammoth tooth, mammoth ivory, Damascus steel and Mosaic Damascus. **Remarks:** Full time maker. First knife sold in 1999. **Prices:** $200 to $1800. Some to $2500. **Mark:** Owl logo with PJ Ernest Whittier CA or PJ Ernest.

ESPOSITO, EMMANUEL

Via Reano 70, Buttigliera Alta TO, ITALY 10090, Phone: 39-011932-16-21, www.emmanuelmaker.it
Specialties: Folding knife with his patent system lock mechanism with mosaic inlay.

ESSEGIAN, RICHARD

7387 E Tulare St, Fresno, CA 93727, Phone: 309-255-5950
Specialties: Fancy working knives of his design; art knives. **Patterns:** Bowies and some small hunters. **Technical:** Grinds A2, D2, 440C and 154CM. Engraves and inlays. **Prices:** Start at $600. **Remarks:** Part-time maker; first knife sold in 1986. **Mark:** Last name, city and state.

ESTABROOK, ROBBIE

1014 Madge Ct., Conway, SC 29526, Phone: 843-489-2331, r1956e@hotmail.com
Specialties: Traditional working straight knives. **Patterns:** Hunters and fishing knives. **Technical:** Hand grinds ATS 34 and D2. **Prices:** $100 and up. **Remarks:** Part-time maker. **Mark:** ESTABROOK.

ETZLER, JOHN

11200 N Island, Grafton, OH 44044, Phone: 440-748-2460, jetzler@bright.net; Web: members.tripod.com/~etzlerknives/
Specialties: High-art and fantasy straight knives and folders of his design and to customer specs. **Patterns:** Folders, daggers, fighters, utility knives. **Technical:** Forges and grinds nickel Damascus and tool steel; grinds stainless steels. Prefers exotic, natural materials. **Prices:** $250 to $1200; some to $6500. **Remarks:** Full-time maker; first knife sold in 1992. **Mark:** Name or initials.

EVANS, BRUCE A

409 CR 1371, Booneville, MS 38829, Phone: 662-720-0193, beknives@avsia.com; Web: www.bruceevans.homestead.com/open.html
Specialties: Forges blades. **Patterns:** Hunters, Bowies, or will work with customer. **Technical:** 5160, cable Damascus, pattern welded Damascus. **Prices:** $200 and up. **Mark:** Bruce A. Evans Same with JS on reverse of blade.

EVANS, CARLTON

PO Box 72, Fort Davis, TX 79734, Phone: 817-223-8556, carlton@carltonevans.com; Web: www.carltonevans.com
Specialties: High end folders and fixed blades. **Technical:** Uses the stock removal methods. The materials used are of the highest quality. **Remarks:** Full-time knifemaker, voting member of Knifemakers Guild, member of the Texas Knifemakers and Collectors Association.

EVANS, PHIL

594 SE 40th, Columbus, KS 66725, Phone: 620-249-0639, phil@glenviewforge.com; Web: www.glenviewforge.com
Specialties: Working knives, hunters, skinners, also enjoys making Bowies and fighters, high carbon or Damascus. **Technical:** Forges own blades and makes own Damascus. Uses all kinds of ancient Ivory and bone. Stabilizes own native hardwoods. **Prices:** $150 - $1,500. **Remarks:** Part-time maker. Made first knife in 1995. **Mark:** EVANS.

EVANS, RONALD B

209 Hoffer St, Middleton, PA 17057-2723, Phone: 717-944-5464

EVANS, VINCENT K AND GRACE

HC 1 Box 5275, Keaau, HI 96749-9517, Phone: 808-966-8978, evansvk@gmail.com
Web: www.picturetrail.com/vevans
Specialties: Period pieces; swords. **Patterns:** Scottish, Viking, central Asian. **Technical:** Forges 5160 and his own Damascus. **Prices:** $700 to $4000; some to $8000. **Remarks:** Full-time maker; first knife sold in 1983. **Mark:** Last initial with fish logo.

EWING, JOHN H

3276 Dutch Valley Rd, Clinton, TN 37716, Phone: 865-457-5757, johnja@comcast.net
Specialties: Working straight knives, hunters, camp knives. **Patterns:** Hunters. **Technical:** Grinds 440-D2. Forges 5160, 1095 prefers forging. **Prices:** $150 and up. **Remarks:** Part-time maker; first knife sold in 1985. **Mark:** First initial, last name, some embellishing done on knives.

F

FAIRLY, DANIEL

2209 Bear Creek Canyon Rd, Bayfield, CO 81122, danielfairlyknives@gmail.com; Web: www.danielfairlyknives.com
Specialties: "Craftsmanship without compromise. **Patterns:** Ultralight titanium utilities, everyday carry, folders, kitchen knives, Japanese-influenced design. **Technical:** Grinds mostly tool steel and carbidized titanium in .050" to .360" thick material. Uses heavy duty handle materials and flared test tube fasteners or epoxy soaked wrapped handles. Most grinds are chisel; flat convex and hollow grinds used. **Prices:** $85 to $1,850. **Remarks:** Full-time maker since first knife sold in Feb. 2011. **Mark:** Fairly written in all capitals with larger F.

FANT JR., GEORGE

1983 CR 3214, Atlanta, TX 75551-6515, Phone: (903) 846-2938

FARID, MEHR R

8 Sidney Close, Tunbridge Wells, Kent, ENGLAND TN2 5QQ, Phone: 011-44-1892 520345, farid@faridknives.com; Web: www.faridknives.com
Specialties: Hollow handle survival knives. High tech folders. **Patterns:** Flat grind blades & chisel ground LinerLock® folders. **Technical:** Grinds 440C, CPMT-440V, CPM-420V, CPM-15V, CPM5125V, and T-1 high speed steel. **Prices:** $550 to $5000. **Remarks:** Full-time maker; first knife sold in 1991. **Mark:** First name stamped.

FARR, DAN

6531 E. Poleline Ave., Post Falls, ID 83854, Phone: 585-721-1388
Specialties: Hunting, camping, fighting and utility. **Patterns:** Fixed blades. **Technical:** Forged or stock removal. **Prices:** $150 to $750.

FASSIO, MELVIN G

420 Tyler Way, Lolo, MT 59847, Phone: 406-544-1391, fassiocustomknives@gmail.com; Web: www.fassiocustomknives.com
Specialties: Working folders to customer specs. **Patterns:** Locking folders, hunters and traditional-style knives. **Technical:** Grinds 440C. **Prices:** $125 to $350. **Remarks:** Part-time maker; first knife sold in 1975. **Mark:** Name and city, dove logo.

FAUCHEAUX, HOWARD J
PO Box 206, Loreauville, LA 70552, Phone: 318-229-6467
    Specialties: Working straight knives and folders; period pieces. Also a hatchet with capping knife in the handle. **Patterns:** Traditional locking folders, hunters, fighters and Bowies. **Technical:** Forges W2, 1095 and his own Damascus; stock removal D2. **Prices:** Start at $200. **Remarks:** Full-time maker; first knife sold in 1969. **Mark:** Last name.

FAUST, JOACHIM
Kirchgasse 10, Goldkronach, GERMANY 95497

FELIX, ALEXANDER
PO Box 4036, Torrance, CA 90510, Phone: 310-320-1836, sgiandubh@dslextreme.com
    Specialties: Straight working knives, fancy ethnic designs. **Patterns:** Hunters, Bowies, daggers, period pieces. **Technical:** Forges carbon steel and Damascus; forged stainless and titanium jewelry, gold and silver casting. **Prices:** $110 and up. **Remarks:** Jeweler, ABS Journeyman Smith. **Mark:** Last name.

FELLOWS, MIKE
P.O. Box 184, Riversdale 6670, SOUTH AFRICA, Phone: 27 82 960 3868, karatshin@gmail.com
    Specialties: Miniatures, art knives and folders with occasional hunters and skinners. **Patterns:** Own designs. **Technical:** Uses own damascus. **Prices:** Upon request. **Remarks:** Uses only indigenous materials. Exotic hardwoods, horn and ivory. Does all own embellishments. **Mark:** "SHIN" letter from Hebrew alphabet over Hebrew word "Karat." Other: Member of Knifemakers Guild of South Africa.

FERGUSON, JIM
4652 Hackett St., Lakewood, CA 90713, Phone: 562-342-4890, jim@twistednickel.com; Web: www.twistednickel.com, www.howtomakeaknife.net
    Specialties: Bowies and push blades. **Patterns:** All styles. **Technical:** Flat and hollow grinds. Sells in U.S. and Canada. **Prices:** $100 to $1,200. **Mark:** Push blade with "Ferguson-USA." Also makes swords, battle axes and utilities.

FERGUSON, JIM
3543 Shadyhill Dr, San Angelo, TX 76904, Phone: 325-655-1061
    Specialties: Straight working knives and folders. **Patterns:** Working belt knives, hunters, Bowies and some folders. **Technical:** Grinds ATS-34, D2 and Vascowear. Flat-grinds hunting knives. **Prices:** $200 to $600; some to $1000. **Remarks:** Full-time maker; first knife sold in 1987. **Mark:** First and middle initials, last name.

FERGUSON, LEE
1993 Madison 7580, Hindsville, AR 72738, Phone: 479-443-0084, info@fergusonknives.com; Web: www.fergusonknives.com
    Specialties: Straight working knives and folders, some fancy. **Patterns:** Hunters, daggers, swords, locking folders and slip-joints. **Technical:** Grinds D2, 440C and ATS-34; heat-treats. **Prices:** $50 to $600; some to $4000. **Remarks:** Full-time maker; first knife sold in 1977. **Mark:** Full name.

FERRIER, GREGORY K
3119 Simpson Dr, Rapid City, SD 57702, Phone: 605-342-9280

FERRY, TOM
16005 SE 322nd St, Auburn, WA 98092, Phone: 253-939-4468, tomferryknives@Q.com; Web: tomferryknives.com
    Specialties: Presentation grade knives. **Patterns:** Folders and fixed blades. **Technical:** Specialize in Damascus and engraving. **Prices:** $500 and up. **Remarks:** DBA: Soos Creek Ironworks. ABS Master Smith. **Mark:** Combined T and F in a circle and/or last name.

FINCH, RICKY D
1179 Hwy 844, West Liberty, KY 41472, Phone: 606-743-7151, finchknives@mrtc.com; Web: www.finchknives.com
    Specialties: Traditional working/using straight knives of his design or to customer spec. **Patterns:** Hunters, skinners and utility/camp knives. LinerLock® of his design. **Technical:** Grinds 440C, ATS-34 and CPM154, hand rubbed stain finish, use Micarta, stabilized wood, natural and exotic. **Prices:** $85 to $225. **Remarks:** Part-time maker, first knife made 1994. Doing business as Finch Knives. **Mark:** Last name inside outline of state of Kentucky.

FINLEY, JON M.
3921 W. 142nd Dr., Leawood, KS 66224, Phone: 913-707-0016, jon66224@hotmail.com
    Specialties: Fancy hunters with mosaic handles and channel inlays, with much use of exotic woods, mammoth ivory and gemstones. **Technical:** Stock-removal method of blade making using high-carbon damascus steel. **Prices:** $200 to $1,000. **Remarks:** Part-time maker; first knife made in 2012. **Mark:** Logo and last name.

FINNEY, GARETT
7181 Marcob Way, Loomis, CA 95650, Phone: 650-678-7332, garett@finneyknives.com; Web: www.finneyknives.com
    Specialties: Customizes knives utilizing materials that couldn't be used for handle materials until the maker casts them into acrylic. He then combines the cast items with exotic natural materials via inlays in order to create unique, one-of-a-kind works of art. **Technical:** Most knives are mirror polished with fileworked blade spines and engraved bolsters. **Prices:** $80 to $900, depending on knife and materials. **Remarks:** Full-time maker. **Mark:** Maker signs his name via engraving, and also uses a stamp for stock-removal or forged pieces.

FISHER, JAY
1405 Edwards, Clovis, NM 88101, jayfisher@jayfisher.com Web: www.JayFisher.com
    Specialties: High-art, working and collector's knives of his design and client's designs. Military working and commemoratives. Gemstone handles, Locking combat sheaths. **Patterns:** Hunters, daggers, folding knives, museum pieces and high-art sculptures. **Technical:** 440C, ATS-34, CPMS30V, D2, O1, CPM154CM, CPMS35VN. Prolific maker of stone-handled knives and swords. **Prices:** $850 to $150,000. **Remarks:** Full-time maker; first knife sold in 1980. High resolution etching, computer and manual engraving. **Mark:** Signature "JaFisher"

FISHER, JOSH
JN Fisher Knives, 8419 CR 3615, Murchison, TX 75778, Phone: 903-203-2130, fisherknives@aol.com; Web: www.jnfisherknives.com
    Specialties: Frame-handle fighters. **Technical:** Forge 5160 and 1084 blade steels. **Prices:** $125 to $1,000. **Remarks:** Part-time maker; first knife made in 2007. ABS journeyman smith. **Mark:** Josh Fisher etched. "JS" also etched on the reverse.

FISHER, LANCE
9 Woodlawn Ave., Pompton Lakes, NJ 07442, Phone: 973-248-8447, lance.fisher@sandvik.com
    Specialties: Wedding cake knives and servers, forks, etc. Including velvet lined wood display cases. **Patterns:** Drop points, upswept skinners, Bowies, daggers, fantasy, medieval, San Francisco style, chef or kitchen cutlery. **Technical:** Stock removal method only. Steels include but are not limited to CPM 154, D2, CPM S35VN, CPM S90V and Sandvik 13C26. Handle materials include stag, sheep horn, exotic woods, micarta, and G10 as well as reconstituted stone. **Prices:** $350 - $2000. **Remarks:** Part-time maker, will become full-time on retirement. Made and sold first knife in 1981 and has never looked back. **Mark:** Tang stamp.

FISK, JERRY
10095 Hwy 278 W, Nashville, AR 71852, Phone: 870-845-4456, jerry@jerryfisk.com; Web: www.jerryfisk.com or Facebook: Jerry Fisk, MS Custom Knives
    Specialties: Edged weapons, collectible and functional. **Patterns:** Bowies, daggers, swords, hunters, camp knives and others. **Technical:** Forges carbon steels and his own pattern welded steels. **Prices:** $1100 to $20,000. **Remarks:** National living treasure. **Mark:** Name, MS.

FISTER, JIM
PO Box 307, Simpsonville, KY 40067
    Specialties: One-of-a-kind collectibles and period pieces. **Patterns:** Bowies, camp knives, hunters, buckskinners, and daggers. **Technical:** Forges, 1085, 5160, 52100, his own Damascus, pattern and turkish. **Prices:** $150 to $2500. **Remarks:** Part-time maker; first knife sold in 1982. **Mark:** Name and MS.

FITCH, JOHN S
45 Halbrook Rd, Clinton, AR 72031-8910, Phone: 501-893-2020

FITZ, ANDREW A. SR. AND JR.
63 Bradford Hwy., Milan, TN 38358, Phone: 731-420-0139, fitzknives@yahoo.com
    Specialties: Tactical utility flipper folders and fixed blades of the makers' designs. **Patterns:** High-tech utility/defense folders and fixed blades. **Technical:** Grinds CPM 154, CTS B75P, PSF27, Elmax and CTS XHP. Titanium and carbon fiber handles, or G-10 on tactical utility folders. **Prices:** $600 to $1,300 (Andrew Sr.) and $200 to $500 (Andrew Jr.). **Remarks:** Fitz Sr. made and sold first knife in 2002. Fitz Jr. made first knife in 2013 and sold first knife in 2014. **Mark:** Fitz Sr.: Last name Fitz; and Fitz Jr.: Last name with Jr. in the Z.

FITZGERALD, DENNIS M
4219 Alverado Dr, Fort Wayne, IN 46816-2847, Phone: 219-447-1081
    Specialties: One-of-a-kind collectibles and period pieces. **Patterns:** Skinners, fighters, camp and utility knives; period pieces. **Technical:** Forges 1085, 1095, L6, 5160, 52100, his own pattern and Turkish Damascus. **Prices:** $100 to $500. **Remarks:** Part-time maker; first knife sold in 1985. Doing business as The Ringing Circle. **Mark:** Name and circle logo.

FLINT, ROBERT
2902 Aspen, Anchorage, AK 99517, Phone: 907-243-6706
    Specialties: Working straight knives and folders. **Patterns:** Utility, hunters, fighters and gents. **Technical:** Grinds ATS-34, BG-42, D2 and Damascus. **Prices:** $150 and up. **Remarks:** Part-time maker, first knife sold in 1998. **Mark:** Last name; stylized initials.

FLOURNOY, JOE
5750 Lisbon Rd, El Dorado, AR 71730, Phone: 870-863-7208, flournoy@ipa.net
    Specialties: Working straight knives and folders. **Patterns:** Hunters, Bowies, camp knives, folders and daggers. **Technical:** Forges only high-carbon steel, steel cable and his own Damascus. **Prices:** $350 Plus. **Remarks:** First knife sold in 1977. **Mark:** Last name and MS in script.

FLUDDER, KEITH
3 Olive Ln., Tahmoor, New South Wales, AUSTRALIA 2573, Phone: 612 46843236 or 61 412687868, keith@knifemaker.com.au; Web: www.bladesmith.com.au
    Specialties: Damascus and carbon steel fixed blades and art knives. **Patterns:** Bowies, fighters, hunters, tantos, wakizashis, katanas and kitchen knives. **Technical:** Forges and makes own damascus, including mosaics and multi-bars from 1075 and 15N20. Also uses 1084, W2, O1, 52100 and 5160. **Prices:** $275 to $3,000. **Remarks:** Full-time maker since 2000; ABS journeyman smith since 2014; first knife made in 1989. **Mark:** Reverse K on F centered in Southern Cross constellation. Fludder on spine.

FLYNT, ROBERT G
15173 Christy Lane, Gulfport, MS 39503, Phone: 228-832-3378 or cell: 228-265-0410, robertflynt@cableone.net; Web: www.flyntstoneknifeworks.com
    Specialties: All types of fixed blades: drop point, clip point, trailing point, bull-nose

hunters, tactical, fighters and bowies. LinerLock, slip-joint and lockback folders. **Technical:** Using 154CM, CPM-154, ATS-34, 440C, CPM-3V and 52100 steels. Most blades made by stock removal, hollow and flat grind methods. Forges some cable damascus and uses numerous types of damascus purchased in billets from various makers. All filework and bluing done by the maker. Various wood handles, bone and horn materials, including some with wire inlay and other embellishments. Most knives sold with custom-fit leather sheaths, most include exotic skin inlay when appropriate. **Prices:** $150 and up, depending on embellishments on blade and sheath. **Remarks:** Full-time maker; first knife made in 1966. Knifemakers' Guild member. **Mark:** Last name in cursive letters or a knife striking a flint stone.

FOGARIZZU, BOITEDDU
via Crispi 6, Pattada, ITALY 07016
Specialties: Traditional Italian straight knives and folders. **Patterns:** Collectible folders. **Technical:** forges and grinds 12C27, ATS-34 and his Damascus. **Prices:** $200 to $3000. **Remarks:** Full-time maker; first knife sold in 1958. **Mark:** Full name and registered logo.

FONTENOT, GERALD J
901 Maple Ave, Mamou, LA 70554, Phone: 318-468-3180

FORREST, BRIAN
FORREST KNIVES, PO Box 611, Descanso, CA 91916, Phone: 619-445-6343, forrestforge@gmail.com; Web: www.forrestforge.biz
Specialties: Forged tomahawks, working knives, big Bowies. **Patterns:** Traditional and extra large Bowies. **Technical:** Hollow grinds: 440C, 1095, S160 Damascus. **Prices:** $125 and up. **Remarks:** Member of California Knifemakers Association. Full-time maker. First knife sold in 1971. **Mark:** Forrest USA/Tomahawks marked FF (Forrest Forge).

FORTHOFER, PETE
5535 Hwy 93S, Whitefish, MT 59937, Phone: 406-862-2674
Specialties: Interframes with checkered wood inlays; working straight knives. **Patterns:** Traditional-style hunting knives. **Technical:** Grinds D2, 440C, 154CM and ATS-34, and prefers mammoth ivory handles and mokume guards. **Prices:** $650 to $850. **Remarks:** Part-time maker; full-time gunsmith. First knife sold in 1979. **Mark:** Name and logo.

FOSTER, AL
118 Woodway Dr, Magnolia, TX 77355, Phone: 936-372-9297
Specialties: Straight knives and folders. **Patterns:** Hunting, fishing, folders and Bowies. **Technical:** Grinds 440-C, ATS-34 and D2. **Prices:** $100 to $1000. **Remarks:** Full-time maker; first knife sold in 1981. **Mark:** Scorpion logo and name.

FOSTER, BURT
23697 Archery Range Rd, Bristol, VA 24202, Phone: 276-669-0121, burt@burtfoster.com; Web:www.burtfoster.com
Specialties: Working straight knives, laminated blades, and some art knives of his design. **Patterns:** Bowies, hunters, daggers. **Technical:** Forges 52100, W-2 and makes own Damascus. Does own heat treating. **Remarks:** ABS MasterSmith. Full-time maker, believes in sole authorship. **Mark:** Signed "BF" initials.

FOSTER, NORVELL C
7945 Youngsford Rd, Marion, TX 78124-1713, Phone: 830-914-2078
Specialties: Engraving; ivory handle carving. **Patterns:** American-large and small scroll-oak leaf and acorns. **Prices:** $25 to $400. **Remarks:** Have been engraving since 1957. **Mark:** N.C. Foster - Marion - Tex and current year.

FOSTER, RONNIE E
95 Riverview Rd., Morrilton, AR 72110, Phone: 501-354-5389
Specialties: Working, using knives, some period pieces, work with customer specs. **Patterns:** Hunters, fighters, Bowies, liner-lock folders, camp knives. **Technical:** Forge-5160, 1084, O1, 15N20-makes own Damascus. **Prices:** $200 (start). **Remarks:** Part-time maker. First knife sold 1994. **Mark:** Ronnie Foster MS.

FOSTER, TIMOTHY L
723 Sweet Gum Acres Rd, El Dorado, AR 71730, Phone: 870-863-6188

FOWLER, CHARLES R
226 National Forest Rd 48, Ft McCoy, FL 32134-9624, Phone: 904-467-3215

FOWLER, ED A.
Willow Bow Ranch, PO Box 1519, Riverton, WY 82501, Phone: 307-856-9815
Specialties: High-performance working and using straight knives. **Patterns:** Hunter, camp, bird, and trout knives and Bowies. New model, the gentleman's Pronghorn. **Technical:** Low temperature forged 52100 from virgin 5-1/2 round bars, multiple quench heat treating, engraves all knives, all handles domestic sheep horn processed and aged at least 5 years. Makes heavy duty hand-stitched waxed harness leather pouch type sheaths. **Prices:** $800 to $7000. **Remarks:** Full-time maker. First knife sold in 1962. **Mark:** Initials connected.

FOWLER, STEPHAN
1142 Reading Dr. NW, Acworth, GA 30102, Phone: 770-726-9706, stephan@fowlerblades.com; Web: www.fowlerblades.com
Specialties: Bowies. **Patterns:** Bowies, hunters, chef's knives (American and Japanese style). **Technical:** Primarily W2 blade steel, also 52100, 1084, 1095 and various damascus patterns. **Prices:** $200 and up. **Remarks:** Part-time maker since 2004. **Mark:** Fowler.

FRALEY, D B
1355 Fairbanks Ct, Dixon, CA 95620, Phone: 707-678-0393, dbtfnives@sbcglobal.net; Web:www.dbfraleyknives.com
Specialties: Usable gentleman's fixed blades and folders. **Patterns:** Four locking-liner and frame-lock folders in four different sizes. **Technical:** Grinds CPM S30V, 154CM and

6K Stellite. **Prices:** $250 and up. **Remarks:** Part-time maker. First knife sold in 1990. **Mark:** First and middle initials, last name over a buffalo.

FRAMSKI, WALTER P
24 Rek Ln, Prospect, CT 06712, Phone: 203-758-5634

FRANCE, DAN
Box 218, Cawood, KY 40815, Phone: 606-573-6104
Specialties: Traditional working and using straight knives of his design. **Patterns:** Hunters, Bowies and utility/camp knives. **Technical:** Forges and grinds O1, 5160 and L6. **Prices:** $35 to $125; some to $350. **Remarks:** Spare-time maker; first knife sold in 1985. **Mark:** First name.

FRANCIS, JOHN D
FRANCIS KNIVES, 18 Miami St., Ft. Loramie, OH 45845, Phone: 937-295-3941, jdfrancis72@gmail.com
Specialties: Utility and hunting-style fixed bladed knives of 440 C and ATS-34 steel; Micarta, exotic woods, and other types of handle materials. **Prices:** $90 to $150 range. **Remarks:** Exceptional quality and value at factory prices. **Mark:** Francis-Ft. Loramie, OH stamped on tang.

FRANK, HEINRICH H
3323 N.E. Avery St., Newport, OR 97365, Phone: 541-265-8683
Specialties: High-art investor-class folders, handmade and engraved. **Patterns:** Folding daggers, hunter-size folders and gents. **Technical:** Grinds 07 and O1. **Prices:** $2,100 to $16,000. **Remarks:** Full-time maker; first knife sold in 1965. Doing business as H.H. Frank Knives. **Mark:** Name, address and date.

FRANKLIN, LARRY
Mya Knives, 418 S. 7th St., Stoughton, WI 53589, Phone: 608-719-2758
Specialties: Fixed-blade hunters, kitchen knives and bird-and-trout knives. **Technical:** Forges 20 percent of blades and uses stock-removal method of blade making on the other 80 percent, with favorite steels being 1095, D2, 440C and 14-4 CrMo steels. **Prices:** $85 to $500. **Remarks:** Started making knives around 2005. **Mark:** Daughter's name with a leaf for her favorite season.

FRANKLIN, MIKE
12040 Garnet Dr., Clermont, FL 34711, Phone: 606-407-0029, mikefranklin2013@gmail.com
Specialties: Hunters of all sizes, neck knives and tacticals ranging from small to fighter size. **Patterns:** Hunters with all blade shapes, lots of tactical tanto blades, some radical. **Technical:** Mostly full-tang knives, some with tapered tangs and others narrow tangs. **Prices:** $150 to $1,000+. **Remarks:** Retired to Florida and makes knives he desires to make on a limited basis. **Mark:** Franklin made (with an Old English "F.")

FRAPS, JOHN R
3810 Wyandotte Tr, Indianapolis, IN 46240-3422, Phone: 317-849-9419, jfraps@att.net; Web: www.frapsknives.com
Specialties: Working and collector grade LinerLock® and slip joint folders. **Patterns:** One-of-a kind linerlocks and traditional slip joints. **Technical:** Flat and hollow grinds ATS-34, Damascus, Talonite, CPM S30V, 154Cm, Stellite 6K; hand rubbed or mirror finish. **Prices:** $200 to $1500, some higher. **Remarks:** Voting member of the Knifemaker's Guild; Full-time maker; first knife sold in 1997. **Mark:** Cougar Creek Knives and/or name.

FRAZIER, JIM
6315 Wagener Rd., Wagener, SC 29164, Phone: 803-564-6467, jbfrazierknives@gmail.com; Web: www.jbfrazierknives.com
Specialties: Hunters, semi skinners, oyster roast knives, bird and trout, folders, many patterns of own design with George Herron/Geno Denning influence. **Technical:** Stock removal maker using CPM-154, ATS-34, CPM-S30V and D2. Hollow grind, mainly mirror finish, some satin finish. Prefer to use natural handle material such as stag, horn, mammoth ivory, highly figured woods, some Micarta, others on request. Makes own leather sheaths on 1958 straight needle stitcher. **Prices:** $125 to $600. **Remarks:** Part-time maker since 1989. **Mark:** JB Frazier in arch with Knives under it. Stamp on sheath is outline of state of SC, JB Frazier Knives Wagener SC inside outline.

FRED, REED WYLE
3149 X S, Sacramento, CA 95817, Phone: 916-739-0237
Specialties: Working using straight knives of his design. **Patterns:** Hunting and camp knives. **Technical:** Forges any 10 series, old files and carbon steels. Offers initialing upon request; prefers natural handle materials. **Prices:** $30 to $300. **Remarks:** Part-time maker; first knife sold in 1994. Doing business as R.W. Fred Knifemaker. **Mark:** Engraved first and last initials.

FREDEEN, GRAHAM
5121 Finadene Ct., Colorado Springs, CO 80916, Phone: 719-331-5665, fredeenblades@hotmail.com Web: www.fredeenblades.com
Specialties: Working class knives to high-end custom knives. Traditional pattern welding and mosaic Damascus blades. **Patterns:** All types: Bowies, fighters, hunters, skinners, bird and trout, camp knives, utility knives, daggers, etc. Occasionally swords, both European and Asian. **Technical:** Differential heat treatment and Hamon. Damascus steel rings and jewelry. Hand forged blades and Damascus steel. High carbon blade steels: 1050, 1075/1080, 1084, 1095, 5160, 52100, W1, W2, O1, 15n20 **Prices:** $100 - $2,000. **Remarks:** Sole authorship. Part-time maker. First blade produced in 2005. Member of American Bladesmith Society and Professional Knifemaker's Association **Mark:** "Fredeen" etched on the ricasso or on/along the spine of the blade.

FREDERICK, AARON
272 Brooks Ln, West Liberty, KY 41472-8961, Phone: 606-743-2015, aaronf@mrtc.com; Web: www.frederickknives.com

Specialties: Makes most types of knives, but as for now specializes in the Damascus folder. Does all own Damascus and forging of the steel. Also prefers natural material such as ivory and pearl. Also offer several types of file work on blades, spacers, and liners. Has just recently started doing carving and can do a limited amount of engraving.

FREEMAN, MATT
Fresno, CA 93720, Phone: 559-375-4408, cmftwknives@gmail.com; Web: www.youtube.com/cmftwknives
Specialties: Fixed blades and butterfly knives. **Technical:** Using mostly 1084, 154CM, D2 and file steel, works in any requested materials via stock removal. Also does knife modifications and leather/Kydex work. Three months or less waiting list. **Prices:** $75+. **Mark:** CMFTW.

FREER, RALPH
114 12th St, Seal Beach, CA 90740, Phone: 562-493-4925, Fax: same, ralphfreer@adelphia.net
Specialties: Exotic folders, liner locks, folding daggers, fixed blades. **Patters:** All original. **Technical:** Lots of Damascus, ivory, pearl, jeweled, thumb studs, carving ATS-34, 420V, 530V. **Prices:** $400 to $2500 and up. **Mark:** Freer in German-style text, also Freer shield.

FREY JR., W FREDERICK
305 Walnut St, Milton, PA 17847, Phone: 570-742-9576, wffrey@ptd.net
Specialties: Working straight knives and folders, some fancy. **Patterns:** Wide range miniatures, boot knives and lock back folders. **Technical:** Grinds A2, O1 and D2; vaseo wear, cru-wear and CPM S90V. **Prices:** $100 to $250; some to $1200. **Remarks:** Spare-time maker; first knife sold in 1983. All knives include quality hand stitched leather sheaths. **Mark:** Last name in script.

FRIEDLY, DENNIS E
12 Cottontail Lane E, Cody, WY 82414, Phone: 307-527-6811, friedlyknives@hotmail.com Web: www.friedlyknives.com
Specialties: Fancy working straight knives and daggers, lock back folders and liner locks. Also embellished bowies. **Patterns:** Hunters, fighters, short swords, minis and miniatures; new line of full-tang hunters/boots. **Technical:** Grinds 440C, commercial Damascus, mosaic Damascus and ATS-34 blades; prefers hidden tangs and full tangs. Both flat and hollow grinds. **Prices:** $350 to $2500. Some to $10,000. **Remarks:** Full-time maker; first knife sold in 1972. **Mark:** D.E. Friedly-Cody, WY. Friedly Knives

FRIESEN, DAVE J
Qualicum Beach, British Columbia, CANADA, Phone: 250-927-4113, info@islandblacksmith.ca; Web: www.islandblacksmith.ca
Specialties: Charcoal-forged classical tanto and fusion-style takedown knives crafted by hand from reclaimed and natural materials using traditional techniques.

FRIGAULT, RICK
1189 Royal Pines Rd, Golden Lake, ON, CANADA K0J 1X0, Phone: 613-401-2869, Web: www.rfrigaultknives.ca
Specialties: Fixed blades. **Patterns:** Hunting, tactical and large Bowies. **Technical:** Grinds ATS-34, 440-C, D-2, CPMS30V, CPMS60V, CPMS90V, BG42 and Damascus. Use G-10, Micarta, ivory, antler, ironwood and other stabilized woods for carbon fiber handle material. Makes leather sheaths by hand. Tactical blades include a Concealex sheath made by "On Scene Tactical." **Remarks:** Sold first knife in 1997. Member of Canadian Knifemakers Guild. **Mark:** RFRIGAULT.

FRITZ, ERIK L
837 River St Box 1203, Forsyth, MT 59327, Phone: 406-351-1101, tacmedic45@yahoo.com
Specialties: Forges carbon steel 1084, 5160, 52100 and Damascus. **Patterns:** Hunters, camp knives, bowies and folders as well as forged tactical. **Technical:** Forges own Mosaic and pattern welded Damascus as well as doing own heat treat. **Prices:** A$200 and up. **Remarks:** Sole authorship knives and sheaths. Part time maker first knife sold in 2004. ABS member. **Mark:** E. Fritz in arc on left side ricasso.

FRITZ, JESSE
900 S. 13th St, Slaton, TX 79364, Phone: 806-828-5083
Specialties: Working and using straight knives in standard patterns. **Patterns:** Hunters, utility/camp knives and skinners with gut hook, Bowie knives, kitchen carving sets by request. **Technical:** Grinds 440C, O1 and 1095. Uses 1095 steel. Fline-napped steel design, blued blades, filework and machine jewelling. Inlays handles with turquoise, coral and mother-of-pearl. Makes sheaths. **Prices:** $85 to $275; some to $500. **Mark:** Last name only (FRITZ).

FRIZZELL, TED
14056 Low Gap Rd, West Fork, AR 72774, Phone: 501-839-2516, mmhwaxes@aol.com Web: www.mineralmountain.com
Specialties: Swords, axes and self-defense weapons. **Patterns:** Small skeleton knives to large swords. **Technical:** Grinds 5160 almost exclusively—1/4" to 1/2"— bars some O1 and A2 on request. All knives come with Kydex sheaths. **Prices:** $45 to $1200. **Remarks:** Full-time maker; first knife sold in 1984. Doing business as Mineral Mountain Hatchet Works. Wholesale orders welcome. **Mark:** A circle with line in the middle; MM and HW within the circle.

FRIZZI, LEONARDO
Via Kyoto 31, Firenze, ITALY 50126, Phone: 335-344750, postmaster@frizzi-knives.com; Web: www.frizzi-knives.com
Specialties: Fancy handmade one-of-a kind folders of his own design, some fixed blade and dagger. **Patterns:** Folders liner loch and back locks. **Technical:** Grinds rwl 34, cpm 154, cpm s30v, stainless damascus and the best craft damascus, own heat treating. I

usually prefer satin finish the flat of the blade and mirror polish the hollow grind; special 18k gold, filework. **Prices:** $600 to $4,000. **Remarks:** Part-time maker, first knife sold in 2003. **Mark:** Full name, city, country, or initial, last name and city, or initial in square logo.

FRONEFIELD, DANIEL
20270 Warriors Path, Peyton, CO 80831, Phone: 719-749-0226, dfronfld@hiwaay.com
Specialties: Fixed and folding knives featuring meteorites and other exotic materials. **Patterns:** San-mai Damascus, custom Damascus. **Prices:** $500 to $3000.

FROST, DEWAYNE
1016 Van Buren Rd, Barnesville, GA 30204, Phone: 770-358-1426, lbrtyhill@aol.com
Specialties: Working straight knives and period knives. **Patterns:** Hunters, Bowies and utility knives. **Technical:** Forges own Damascus, cable, etc. as well as stock removal. **Prices:** $150 to $500. **Remarks:** Part-time maker ABS Journeyman Smith. **Mark:** Liberty Hill Forge Dewayne Frost w/liberty bell.

FRUHMANN, LUDWIG
Stegerwaldstr 8, Burghausen, GERMANY 84489
Specialties: High-tech and working straight knives of his design. **Patterns:** Hunters, fighters and boots. **Technical:** Grinds ATS-34, CPM-T-440V and Schneider Damascus. Prefers natural handle materials. **Prices:** $200 to $1500. **Remarks:** Spare-time maker; first knife sold in 1990. **Mark:** First initial and last name.

FRY, DEAN
1569 Balsam Rd., Wellsboro, PA 16901, Phone: 570-948-9019, fireflycollection@yahoo.com; Web: www.balsamridgeknives.com
Specialties: User-type fixed blades, including hunters, bird & trout, neck knives, drop points and everyday carry pieces. **Technical:** Hollow, Scandi and flat grinds using CPM 154 and Alabama Damascus steels. Exotic wood, antler and composite handles, and leather and Kydex sheaths made in house. **Prices:** $95 to $250. **Remarks:** Part-time maker; first knife sold in 2007. **Mark:** Initials in script stamped on blade.

FRY, JASON
7310 County Rd. 324, Hawley, TX 79525, Phone: 325-669-4805, frycustomknives@gmail.com; Web: www.frycustomknives.com
Specialties: Traditional hunting patterns in native Texas materials. **Patterns:** Primarily EDC and hunting/skinning knives under 8 inches, slip-joint folders and art knives. **Technical:** Stock removal and forging of 1080 carbon steel, D2 tool steel and 154CM stainless. **Prices:** $150 to $3,000. **Remarks:** Part-time maker since July 2008, and 2015 voting member of the Knifemakers' Guild. 2015 president of the Texas Knifemakers Guild. **Mark:** Jason Fry over Abilene, TX (2015 and prior), and Jason Fry over Hawley, TX (2015 and forward).

FUEGEN, LARRY
617 N Coulter Circle, Prescott, AZ 86303, Phone: 928-776-8777, fuegen@cableone.net; Web: www.larryfuegen.com
Specialties: High-art folders and classic and working straight knives. **Patterns:** Forged scroll folders, lockback folders and classic straight knives. **Technical:** Forges 5160, 1095 and his own Damascus. Works in exotic leather; offers elaborate filework and carving; likes natural handle materials, now offers own engraving. **Prices:** $1,200 to $26,000. **Remarks:** Full-time maker; first knife sold in 1975. Sole authorship on all knives. ABS Mastersmith. **Mark:** Initials connected or last name engraved.

FUJIKAWA, SHUN
Sawa 1157, Kaizuka, Osaka, JAPAN 597 0062, Phone: 81-724-23-4032, Fax: 81-726-23-9229
Specialties: Folders of his design and to customer specs. **Patterns:** Locking folders. **Technical:** Grinds his own steel. **Prices:** $450 to $2500; some to $3000. **Remarks:** Part-time maker.

FUKUTA, TAK
38-Umeagae-cho, Seki-City, Gifu, JAPAN, Phone: 0575-22-0264
Specialties: Bench-made fancy straight knives and folders. **Patterns:** Sheffield-type folders, Bowies and fighters. **Technical:** Grinds commercial Damascus. **Prices:** Start at $300. **Remarks:** Full-time maker. **Mark:** Name in knife logo.

FULLER, BRUCE A
3366 Ranch Rd. 32, Blanco, TX 78606, Phone: 832-262-0529, fullcoforg@aol.com
Specialties: One-of-a-kind working/using straight knives and folders of his designs. **Patterns:** Bowies, hunters, folders, and utility/camp knives. **Technical:** Forges high-carbon steel and his own Damascus. Prefers El Solo Mesquite and natural materials. Offers filework. **Prices:** $200 to $500; some to $1800. **Remarks:** Spare-time maker; first knife sold in 1991. Doing business as Fullco Forge. **Mark:** Fullco, M.S.

FULLER, JACK A
7103 Stretch Ct, New Market, MD 21774, Phone: 719-395-3374, coloradojack2003@yahoo.com
Specialties: Straight working knives of his design and to customer specs. **Patterns:** Fighters, camp knives, hunters, tomahawks and art knives. **Technical:** Forges 5160, O1, W2 and his own Damascus. Does silver wire inlay and own leather work, wood lined sheaths for big camp knives. **Prices:** $400 and up. **Remarks:** Part-time maker. Master Smith in ABS; first knife sold in 1979. **Mark:** Fuller's Forge, MS.

FULTON, MICKEY
406 S Shasta St, Willows, CA 95988, Phone: 530-934-5780
Specialties: Working straight knives and folders of his design. **Patterns:** Hunters, Bowies, lockback folders and steak knife sets. **Technical:** Hand-filed, sanded, buffed ATS-34, 440C and A2. **Prices:** $65 to $600; some to $1200. **Remarks:** Full-time maker; first knife sold in 1979. **Mark:** Signature.

G

GADBERRY, EMMET
82 Purple Plum Dr, Hattieville, AR 72063, Phone: 501-354-4842

GADDY, GARY LEE
205 Ridgewood Lane, Washington, NC 27889, Phone: 252-946-4359
Specialties: Working/using straight knives of his design; period pieces. **Patterns:** Bowies, hunters, utility/camp knives, oyster knives. **Technical:** Grinds ATS-34, O1; forges 1095. **Prices:** $175+ **Remarks:** Spare-time maker; first knife sold in 1991. No longer accepts orders. **Mark:** Quarter moon stamp.

GAETA, ANGELO
Rua: Saldanha Marinho, 1281, Centro Jau, SP-CEP: 14.201310, BRAZIL 17201-310, e.a.gaeta@gmail.com; Facebook: cutelaria.a.gaeta@gmail.com
Specialties: Straight using knives to customers' specs. **Patterns:** Hunters, fighters, daggers, belt push daggers. **Technical:** Grinds ATS-34 and 440C stainless steel. All knives are unique pieces. **Prices:** $400 and up. **Remarks:** Full-time maker; first knife sold in 1992. **Mark:** First initial, last name.

GAHAGAN, KYLE
200 Preachers Bottom Dr., Moravian Falls, NC 28654, Phone: 919-359-9220, kylegahagan78@yahoo.com; Web: www.gahaganknives.com
Specialties: Bowies and fighters. **Patterns:** Custom designs from maker or customer. **Technical:** Forges 1095, W2, 1075, 1084 and damascus blade steels. **Prices:** $200 and up. **Remarks:** Full-time bladesmith; sold first knife in 2011. **Mark:** Gahagan crest with Gahagan underneath.

GAINES, BUDDY
GAINES KNIVES, 155 Red Hill Rd., Commerce, GA 30530, Web: www.gainesknives.com
Specialties: Collectible and working folders and straight knives. **Patterns:** Folders, hunters, Bowies, tactical knives. **Technical:** Forges own Damascus, grinds ATS-34, D2, commercial Damascus. Prefers mother-of-pearl and stag. **Prices:** Start at $200. **Remarks:** Part-time maker, sold first knife in 1985. **Mark:** Last name.

GAINEY, HAL
904 Bucklevel Rd, Greenwood, SC 29649, Phone: 864-223-0225, Web: www.scak.org
Specialties: Traditional working and using straight knives and folders. **Patterns:** Hunters, slip-joint folders and utility/camp knives. **Technical:** Hollow-grinds ATS-34 and D2; makes sheaths. **Prices:** $95 to $145; some to $500. **Remarks:** Full-time maker; first knife sold in 1975. **Mark:** Eagle head and last name.

GALLAGHER, BARRY
POB 892, 130 Main St., Lincoln, MT 59639, Phone: 406-366-6248, Web: www.gallagherknives.com
Specialties: One-of-a-kind Damascus folders. **Patterns:** Folders, utility to high art, some straight knives, hunter, Bowies, and art pieces. **Technical:** Forges own mosaic Damascus and carbon steel, some stainless. **Prices:** $400 to $5000+. **Remarks:** Full-time maker; first knife sold in 1993. Doing business as Gallagher Custom Knives. **Mark:** Last name.

GALLAGHER, SCOTT
335 Winston Manor Rd., Santa Rosa Beach, FL 32459, Phone: 850-865-8264, scottgallagher04@gmail.com; Facebook: SGallagherKnives
Specialties: Traditional hunters, bowies, fighters and camp knives. **Technical:** Forged-to-shape 1075, 80CrV2, 5160 and W2 blade steels. **Prices:** $300 to $1,500. **Remarks:** Serious part-time maker; first knife sold in 2014. **Mark:** S. Gallagher (with Anvil & Hammer).

GAMBLE, ROGER
18515 N.W. 28th Pl., Newberry, FL 32669, ROGERLGAMBLE@COX.NET
Specialties: Traditional working/using straight knives and folders of his design. **Patterns:** Liner locks and hunters. **Technical:** Grinds ATS-34 and Damascus. **Prices:** $150 to $2000. **Remarks:** Part-time maker; first knife sold in 1982. Doing business as Gamble Knives. **Mark:** First name in a fan of cards over last name.

GANN, TOMMY
2876 State Hwy. 198, Canton, TX 75103, Phone: 903-848-9375
Specialties: Art and working straight knives of my design or customer preferences/design. **Patterns:** Bowie, fighters, hunters, daggers. **Technical:** Forges Damascus 52100 and grinds ATS-34 and D2. **Prices:** $200 to $2500. **Remarks:** Full-time knifemaker, first knife sold in 2002. ABS journey bladesmith. **Mark:** TGANN.

GANSHORN, CAL
123 Rogers Rd., Regina, SK, CANADA S4S 6T7, Phone: 306-584-0524, cganshorn@accesscomm.ca or cganshorn@myaccess.ca
Specialties: Working and fancy fixed blade knives. **Patterns:** Bowies, hunters, daggers, and filleting. **Technical:** Makes own forged Damascus billets, ATS, salt heat treating, and custom forges and burners. **Prices:** $250 to $1500. **Remarks:** Part-time maker. **Mark:** Last name etched in ricasso area.

GARAU, MARCELLO
Via Alagon 42, Oristano, ITALY 09170, Phone: 00393479073454, marcellogarau@ibero.it Web: www.knifecreator.com
Specialties: Mostly lock back folders with interframe. **Technical:** Forges own damascus for both blades and frames. **Prices:** 200 - 2,700 Euros. **Remarks:** Full-time maker; first knife made in 1995. Attends Milano Knife Show and ECCKSHOW yearly. **Mark:** M.Garau inside handle.

GARCIA, MARIO EIRAS
Rua Edmundo Scannapieco 300, Caxingui, SP, BRAZIL 05516-070, Phone: 011-37218304, Fax: 011-37214528
Specialties: Fantasy knives of his design; one-of-a-kind only. **Patterns:** Fighters, daggers, boots and two-bladed knives. **Technical:** Forges car leaf springs. Uses only natural handle material. **Prices:** $100 to $200. **Remarks:** Part-time maker; first knife sold in 1976. **Mark:** Two "B"s, one opposite the other.

GARDNER, ROBERT
13462 78th Pl. N, West Palm Beach, FL 33412
Specialties: Straight blades, forged and clay hardened or differentialy heat treated. Kydex and leather sheath maker. **Patterns:** Working/using knives, some to customer specs, and high-end knives, daggers, bowies, ethnic knives, and Steelhead and Lil' Chub woodland survival/bushcraft knife set with an elaborate, versatile sheath system. Affordable hard-use production line of everyday carry belt knives, and less-expensive forged knives, neck knives and "wrench" knives. **Technical:** Grinds, forges and heat treats high-carbon 1084, 1095, 1075, W1, W2, 5160 and 52100 steels, some natural handle materials and Micarta for full-tang knives. **Prices:** $60 and up; sheaths $30 and up. **Remarks:** Full-time maker since 2010; first knife sold in 1986. **Mark:** Initials in angular script, stamped, engraved or etched.

GARNER, GEORGE
7527 Calhoun Dr. NE, Albuquerque, NM 87109, Phone: 505-797-9317, razorbackblades@msn.com Web: www.razorbackblades.com
Specialties: High art locking liner folders and Daggers of his own design. Working and high art straight knives. **Patterns:** Bowies, daggers, fighters and locking liner folders. **Technical:** Grinds 440C, CPM-154, ATS34 and others. Damascus, Mosaic Damascus and Mokume. Makes own custom leather sheaths. **Prices:** $150 - $2,500. **Remarks:** Part-time maker since 1993. Full-time maker as of 2011. Company name is Razorback Blades. **Mark:** GEORGE GARNER.

GARNER, LARRY W
13069 FM 14, Tyler, TX 75706, Phone: 903-597-6045, lwgarner@classicnet.net
Specialties: Fixed blade hunters and Bowies. **Patterns:** His designs or yours. **Technical:** Hand forges 5160. **Prices:** $200 to $500. **Remarks:** Apprentice bladesmith. **Mark:** Last name.

GARVOCK, MARK W
RR 1, Balderson, ON, CANADA K1G 1A0, Phone: 613-833-2545, Fax: 613-833-2208, garvock@travel-net.com
Specialties: Hunters, Bowies, Japanese, daggers and swords. **Patterns:** Cable Damascus, random pattern welded or to suit. **Technical:** Forged blades; hi-carbon. **Prices:** $250 to $900. **Remarks:** CKG member and ABS member. Shipping and taxes extra. **Mark:** Big G with M in middle.

GATLIN, STEVE
3812 Arroyo Seco, Schwartz, TX 78154, Phone: 229-328-5074, stevegatlinknives@hotmail.com; Web: www.stevegatlinknives.com
Specialties: Loveless-style knives, double-ground fighters and traditional hunters. Some tactical models of maker's design. Fixed blades only. **Technical:** Grinds CPM-154, ATS-34 and 154CM. **Prices:** $450 to $1,500 on base models. **Remarks:** Voting member of Knifemakers' Guild since 2009; first knife sold in 2008. **Mark:** Typical football shape with name on top and city below.

GEDRAITIS, CHARLES J
GEDRAITIS HAND CRAFTED KNIVES, 444 Shrewsbury St, Holden, MA 01520, Phone: 508-963-1861, gedraitisknives@yahoo.com; Web: www.gedraitisknives.com
Specialties: One-of-a-kind folders & automatics of his own design. **Patterns:** One-of-a-kind. **Technical:** Forges to shape mostly stock removal. **Prices:** $300 to $2500. **Remarks:** Full-time maker. **Mark:** 3 scallop shells with an initial inside each one: CJG.

GENOVESE, RICK
PO Box 226, 182 Purtill Tr., Tonto Basin, AZ 85553, Phone: 916-693-3979, genoveseknives@hotmail.com; Web: www.rickgenoveseknives.com
Specialties: Interframe-style folders. **Patterns:** Sleek folders in gentleman's designs. Also folding dirks and daggers. **Technical:** Main blade material is CPM 154. Also uses damascus by Devin Thomas and Jerry Rados. Inlays gemstones such as lapis lazuli, jade, opal, dinosaur bone, tiger eye, jasper, agate, malachite, petrified wood, as well as various pearls. **Prices:** $1,500-$10,000. **Remarks:** Full-time maker; first knife sold in 1975. **Mark:** Genovese in stylized letters.

GEORGE, HARRY
3137 Old Camp Long Rd, Aiken, SC 29805, Phone: 803-649-1963, hdkk-george@scescape.net
Specialties: Working straight knives of his design or to customer specs. **Patterns:** Hunters, skinners and utility knives. **Technical:** Grinds ATS-34. Prefers natural handle materials, hollow-grinds and mirror finishes. **Prices:** Start at $70. **Remarks:** Part-time maker; first knife sold in 1985. Trained under George Herron. Member SCAK. Member Knifemakers Guild. **Mark:** Name, city, state.

GEORGE, LES
6537 S. Staples St., Ste. 125 #406, Corpus Christi, TX 78413, Phone: 361-288-9777, les@georgeknives.com; Web: www.georgeknives.com
Specialties: Tactical frame locks and fixed blades. **Patterns:** Folders, balisongs, and fixed blades. **Technical:** CPM154, S30V, Chad Nichols Damascus. **Prices:** $200 to $800. **Remarks:** Full-time maker, first knife sold in 1992. Doing business as www.georgeknives.com. **Mark:** Last name over logo.

custom knifemakers

GEORGE, TOM
550 Aldbury Dr, Henderson, NV 89014, tagmaker@aol.com
Specialties: Working straight knives, display knives, custom meat cleavers, and folders of his design. **Patterns:** Hunters, Bowies, daggers, buckskinners, swords and folders. **Technical:** Uses D2, 440C, ATS-34 and 154CM. **Prices:** $500 to $13,500. **Remarks:** Custom orders not accepted "at this time". Full-time maker. First knife 1982; first 350 knives were numbered; after that no numbers. Almost all his knives today are Bowies and swords. Creator and maker of the "Past Glories" series of knives. **Mark:** Tom George maker.

GEPNER, DON
2615 E Tecumseh, Norman, OK 73071, Phone: 405-364-2750
Specialties: Traditional working and using straight knives of his design. **Patterns:** Bowies and daggers. **Technical:** Forges his Damascus, 1095 and 5160. **Prices:** $100 to $400; some to $1000. **Remarks:** Spare-time maker; first knife sold in 1991. Has been forging since 1954; first edged weapon made at 9 years old. **Mark:** Last initial.

GERNER, THOMAS
PO Box 301, Walpole, WA, AUSTRALIA 6398, gerner@bordernet.com.au; Web: www. deepriverforge.com
Specialties: Forged working knives; plain steel and pattern welded. **Patterns:** Tries most patterns heard or read about. **Technical:** 5160, L6, O1, 52100 steels; Australian hardwood handles. **Prices:** $220 and up. **Remarks:** Achieved ABS Master Smith rating in 2001. **Mark:** Like a standing arrow and a leaning cross, T.G. in the Runic (Viking) alphabet.

GHIO, PAOLO
4330 Costa Mesa, Pensacola, FL 32504-7849, Phone: 850-393-0135, paologhio@ hotmail.com
Specialties: Folders, fillet knives and skinners. **Patterns:** Maker's own design, or will work from a customer's pattern. **Technical:** Stock removal, all work in house, including heat treat. **Prices:** $200 to $500. **Mark:** PKG.

GIAGU, SALVATORE AND DEROMA MARIA ROSARIA
Via V Emanuele 64, Pattada (SS), ITALY 07016, Phone: 079-755918, Fax: 079-755918, coltelligiagupattada@tiscali.it Web: www.culterpattada.it
Specialties: Using and collecting traditional and new folders from Sardegna. **Patterns:** Folding, hunting, utility, skinners and kitchen knives. **Technical:** Forges ATS-34, 440, D2 and Damascus. **Prices:** $200 to $2000; some higher. **Mark:** First initial, last name and name of town and muflon's head.

GIBERT, PEDRO
Los Alamos 410, San Martin de los Andes, Neuquen, ARGENTINA 8370, Phone: 054-2972-410868, rosademayo@infovia.com.ar
Specialties: Hand forges: Stock removal and integral. High quality artistic knives of his design and to customer specifications. **Patterns:** Country (Argentine gaucho-style), knives, folders, Bowies, daggers, hunters. Others upon request. **Technical:** Blade: Bohler k110 Austrian steel (high resistance to waste). Handles: (Natural materials) ivory elephant, killer whale, hippo, walrus tooth, deer antler, goat, ram, buffalo horn, bone, rhea, sheep, cow, exotic woods (South America native woods) hand carved and engraved guards and blades. Stainless steel guards, finely polished: semi-matte or shiny finish. Sheaths: Raw or tanned leather, hand-stitched; rawhide or cotton yarn embroidered. Box: One wood piece, hand carved. Wooden hinges and locks. **Prices:** $600 and up. **Remarks:** Full-time maker. Made first knife in 1987. **Mark:** Only a rose logo. Buyers initials upon request.

GIBO, GEORGE
PO Box 4304, Hilo, HI 96720, Phone: 808-987-7002, geogibo@hilo808.net
Specialties: Straight knives and folders. **Patterns:** Hunters, bird and trout, utility, gentlemen and tactical folders. **Technical:** Grinds ATS-34, BG-42, Talonite, Stainless Steel Damascus. **Prices:** $250 to $1000. **Remarks:** Spare-time maker; first knife sold in 1995. **Mark:** Name, city and state around Hawaiian "Shaka" sign.

GILBERT, CHANTAL
291 Rue Christophe-Colomb est #105, Quebec City, QC, CANADA G1K 3T1, Phone: 418-525-6961, Fax: 418-525-4666, gilbertc@medion.qc.ca; Web:www.chantalgilbert. com
Specialties: Straight art knives that may resemble creatures, often with wings, shells and antennae, always with a beak of some sort, fixed blades in a feminine style. **Technical:** ATS-34 and Damascus. Handle materials usually silver that she forms to shape via special molds and a press; ebony and fossil ivory. **Prices:** Range from $500 to $4000. **Remarks:** Often embellishes her art knives with rubies, meteorite, 18k gold and similar elements.

GILBREATH, RANDALL
55 Crauswell Rd, Dora, AL 35062, Phone: 205-648-3902
Specialties: Damascus folders and fighters. **Patterns:** Folders and fixed blades. **Technical:** Forges Damascus and high-carbon; stock removal stainless steel. **Prices:** $300 to $1500. **Remarks:** Full-time maker; first knife sold in 1979. **Mark:** Name in ribbon.

GILJEVIC, BRANKO
35 Hayley Crescent, Queanbeyan 2620, New South Wales, AUSTRALIA 0262977613
Specialties: Classic working straight knives and folders of his design. **Patterns:** Hunters, Bowies, skinners and locking folders. **Technical:** Grinds 440C. Offers acid etching, scrimshaw and leather carving. **Prices:** $150 to $1500. **Remarks:** Part-time maker; first knife sold in 1987. Doing business as Sambar Custom Knives. **Mark:** Company name in logo.

GINGRICH, JUSTIN
5329 Anna Belle Ln., Wade, NC 28395, Phone: 507-230-0398, justin@ gingrichtactical.com Web: www.gingrichtactical.com
Specialties: Anything from bushcraft to tactical, heavy on the tactical. **Patterns:** Fixed blades and folders. **Technical:** Uses all types of steel and handle material, method is stock-removal. **Prices:** $30 - $1000. **Remarks:** Full-time maker. **Mark:** Tang stamp is the old Ranger Knives logo.

GIRTNER, JOE
409 Catalpa Ave, Brea, CA 92821, Phone: 714-529-2388, conceptsinknives@aol.com
Specialties: Art knives and miniatures. **Patterns:** Mainly Damascus (some carved). **Technical:** Many techniques and materials combined. Wood carving knives and tools, hunters, custom orders. **Prices:** $55 to $3000. **Mark:** Name.

GITTINGER, RAYMOND
6940 S Rt 100, Tiffin, OH 44883, Phone: 419-397-2517

GLASSER, ROGER CESAR
Av. Ceci, 679 - Sao Paulo - SP, BRAZIL 04065-001, Phone: +55-11-974615357, roger.glasser@gmail.com; Web: www.mostrainternacionaldecutelaria.com
Specialties: Fixed blades, military knives, fighters and hunters. **Prices:** $300 to $1,000. **Remarks:** Part-time maker, IBO founder, ABS member, SBC member and CKCA member. Creator and manager of the biggest knife show in Latin America: Mostra Internacional de Cutelaria, a.k.a. Brazil Knife Show. **Mark:** R.Glasser.

GLOVER, RON
5896 Thornhill Ave., Cincinnati, OH 45224, Phone: 513-404-7107, r.glover@ zoomtown.com
Specialties: High-tech working straight knives and folders. **Patterns:** Hunters to Bowies; some interchangeable blade models; unique locking mechanisms. **Technical:** Grinds 440C, 154CM; buys Damascus. **Prices:** $70 to $500; some to $800. **Remarks:** Part-time maker; first knife in 1981. **Mark:** Name in script.

GLOVER, WARREN D
dba BUBBA KNIVES, PO Box 475, Cleveland, GA 30528, Phone: 706-865-3998, Fax: 706-348-7176, warren@bubbaknives.net; Web: www.bubbaknives.net
Specialties: Traditional and custom working and using straight knives of his design and to customer request. **Patterns:** Hunters, skinners, bird and fish, utility and kitchen knives. **Technical:** Grinds 440, ATS-34 and stainless steel Damascus. **Prices:** $75 to $400 and up. **Remarks:** Full-time maker; sold first knife in 1995. **Mark:** Bubba, year, name, state.

GODDARD, WAYNE
473 Durham Ave, Eugene, OR 97404, Phone: 541-689-8098, wgoddard44@comcast.net
Specialties: Working/using straight knives and folders. **Patterns:** Hunters and folders. **Technical:** Works exclusively with wire Damascus and his own-pattern welded material. **Prices:** $250 to $4000. **Remarks:** Full-time maker; first knife sold in 1963. **Mark:** Blocked initials on forged blades; regular capital initials on stock removal.

GODLESKY, BRUCE F.
1002 School Rd., Apollo, PA 15613, Phone: 724-840-5786, brucegodlesky@yahoo. com; Web: www.birdforge.com
Specialties: Working/using straight knives and tomahawks, mostly forged. **Patterns:** Hunters, birds and trout, fighters and tomahawks. **Technical:** Most forged, some stock removal. Carbon steel only. 5160, O-1, W2, 10xx series. Makes own Damascus and welded cable. **Prices:** Starting at $75. **Mark:** BIRDOG FORGE.

GOERS, BRUCE
3423 Royal Ct S, Lakeland, FL 33813, Phone: 941-646-0984
Specialties: Fancy working and using straight knives of his design and to customer specs. **Patterns:** Hunters, fighters, Bowies and fantasy knives. **Technical:** Grinds ATS-34, some Damascus. **Prices:** $195 to $600; some to $1300. **Remarks:** Part-time maker; first knife sold in 1990. Doing business as Vulture Cutlery. **Mark:** Buzzard with initials.

GOLDBERG, DAVID
321 Morris Rd, Ft Washington, PA 19034, Phone: 215-654-7117, david@ goldmountainforge.com; Web: www.goldmountainforge.com
Specialties: Japanese-style designs, will work with special themes in Japanese genre. **Patterns:** Kozuka, Tanto, Wakazashi, Katana, Tachi, Sword canes, Yari and Naginata. **Technical:** Forges his own Damascus and makes his own handmade tamehagane steel from straw ash, iron, carbon and clay. Uses traditional materials, carves fittings handles and cases. Hardens all blades in traditional Japanese clay differential technique. **Remarks:** Full-time maker; first knife sold in 1987. Japanese swordsmanship teacher (jaido) and Japanese self-defense teach (aikido). **Mark:** Name (kinzan) in Japanese Kanji on Tang under handle.

GOLDEN, RANDY
6492 Eastwood Glen Dr, Montgomery, AL 36117, Phone: 334-271-6429, rgolden1@ mindspring.com
Specialties: Collectable quality hand rubbed finish, hunter, camp, Bowie straight knives, custom leather sheaths with exotic skin inlays and tooling. **Technical:** Stock removal ATS-34, CPM154, S30V and BG-42. Natural handle materials primarily stag and ivory. **Prices:** $500 to $1500. **Remarks:** Full-time maker, member Knifemakers Guild, first knife sold in 2000. **Mark:** R. R. Golden Montgomery, AL.

GONCALVES, LUIZ GUSTAVO
R Alberto Gebara, 124A -Sao Paulo - SP, BRAZIL 04611-060, Phone: +55-11-98336-0001, lgustavo@lgustavo.com; Web: www.lgustavo.com
Specialties: Most types of fixed blades of his own designs or to customer specs. **Patterns:** Hunters, fighters, bowies, gaucho, utility, camp and kitchen knives. **Technical:** Forges and grinds carbon steel (5160, 52100, O1) and his own damascus in random, ladder, raindrop, W's and other patterns. Heat treatment in electronically controlled kiln to obtain maximum control. Natural handle materials, including hardwood, stabilized wood, giraffe bone, deer stag, merino horn and others. Flat and hollow grinds. **Prices:** $400

to $1,300. **Remarks:** Part-time maker, ABS apprentice; first knife sold in 2012. **Mark:** LGustavo.

GONZALEZ, LEONARDO WILLIAMS
Ituzaingo 473, Maldonado, URUGUAY 20000, Phone: 598 4222 1617, Fax: 598 4222 1617, willyknives@hotmail.com; Web: www.willyknives.com
Specialties: Classic high-art and fantasy straight knives; traditional working and using knives of his design, in standard patterns or to customer specs. **Patterns:** Hunters, Bowies, daggers, fighters, boots, swords and utility/camp knives. **Technical:** Forges and grinds high-carbon and stainless Bohler steels. **Prices:** $100 to $2500. **Remarks:** Full-time maker; first knife sold in 1985. **Mark:** Willy, whale, R.O.U.

GOO, TAI
5920 W Windy Lou Ln, Tucson, AZ 85742, Phone: 520-744-9777, taigoo@msn.com; Web: www.taigoo.com
Specialties: High art, neo-tribal, bush and fantasy. **Technical:** Hand forges, does own heat treating, makes own Damascus. **Prices:** $150 to $500 some to $10,000. **Remarks:** Full-time maker; first knife sold in 1978. **Mark:** Chiseled signature.

GOOD, D.R.
Custom Knives and Weaponry, 6125 W. 100 S., Tipton, IN 46072, Phone: 765-963-6971, drntammigood@bluemarble.net
Specialties: Working knives, own design, Scagel style, "critter" knives, carved handles. **Patterns:** Bowies, large and small, neck knives and miniatures. Offers carved handles, snake heads, eagles, wolves, bear, skulls. **Technical:** Damascus, some stelite, 6K, pearl, ivory, moose. **Prices:** $150 - $1500. **Remarks:** Full-time maker. First knife was Bowie made from a 2-1/2 truck bumper in military. **Mark:** D.R. Good in oval and for minis, DR with a buffalo skull.

GOODE, BEAR
BEAR KNIVES, PO Box 6474, Navajo Dam, NM 87419, Phone: 505-632-8184, beargood58@gmail.com
Specialties: Working/using straight knives of his design and in standard patterns. **Patterns:** Bowies, hunters and utility/camp knives. **Technical:** Grinds 440C, ATS-34, 154-CM; forges and grinds 1095, 5160 and other steels on request; uses Damascus. **Prices:** $150 and up. **Remarks:** Full-time maker since 2010; first knife made in 1975 and first knife sold in 1993. Doing business as Bear Knives. **Mark:** First and last name with a three-toed paw print.

GOODE, BRIAN
203 Gordon Ave, Shelby, NC 28152, Phone: 704-434-6496, web:www.bgoodeknives.com
Specialties: Flat ground working knives with etched/antique or brushed finish. **Patterns:** Field, camp, hunters, skinners, survival, kitchen, maker's design or yours. Currently full tang only with supplied leather sheath. **Technical:** O-1, D2 and other ground flat stock. Stock removal and differential heat treat preferred. Etched antique/etched satin working finish preferred. Micarta and hardwoods for strength. **Prices:** $150 to $700. **Remarks:** Part-time maker and full-time knife lover. First knife in 2004. **Mark:** B. Goode with NC separated by a feather.

GOODPASTURE, TOM
13432 Farrington Road, Ashland, VA 23005, Phone: 804-752-8363, rtg007@aol.com; web: goodpastureknives.com
Specialties: Working/using straight knives of his own design, or customer specs. File knives and primative reproductions. **Patterns:** Hunters, bowies, small double-edge daggers, kitchen, custom miniatures and camp/utility. **Technical:** Stock removal, D-2, 0-1, 12C27, 420 HC, 52100. Forged blades of W-2, 1084, and 1095. Flat grinds only. **Prices:** $60 - $300. **Remarks:** Part-time maker, first knife sold at Blade Show 2005. Lifetime guarantee and sharpening. **Mark:** Early mark were initials RTG, current **mark:** Goodpasture.

GORDON, LARRY B
23555 Newell Cir W, Farmington Hills, MI 48336, Phone: 248-477-5483, lbgordon1@aol.com
Specialties: Folders, small fixed blades. New design rotating scale release automatic. **Patterns:** Rotating handle locker. Ambidextrous fire (R&L) **Prices:** $450 minimum. **Remarks:** High line materials preferred. **Mark:** Gordon.

GORENFLO, JAMES T (JT)
9145 Sullivan Rd, Baton Rouge, LA 70818, Phone: 225-261-5868
Specialties: Traditional working and using straight knives of his design. **Patterns:** Bowies, hunters and utility/camp knives. **Technical:** Forges 5160, 1095, 52100 and his own Damascus. **Prices:** Start at $200. **Remarks:** Part-time maker; first knife sold in 1992. **Mark:** Last name or initials, J.S. on reverse.

GOSHOVSKYY, VASYL
BL.4, C. San Jaime 65, Torreblanca 12596, Castellon de la Plana, SPAIN, Phone: +34-664-838-882, baz_knife@mail.ru; Web: www.goshovskyy-knives.com
Specialties: Presentation and working fixed-blade knives. **Patterns:** R.W. Loveless-pattern knives, primarily hunters and skinners. **Technical:** Stock-removal method. Prefers natural materials for handle scales. Uses primarily RWL-34, CPM-154, N690 or similar blade steel. **Remarks:** Full-time maker.

GOSSMAN, SCOTT
PO Box 41, Whiteford, MD 21160, Phone: 443-617-2444, scogos@peoplepc.com; Web:www.gossmanknives.com
Specialties: Heavy duty knives for big-game hunting and survival. **Patterns:** Modified clip-point/spear-point blades, bowies, hunters and bushcraft. **Technical:** Grinds A2, O1, CPM-154, CPM-3V, S7, flat/convex grinds and convex micro-bevel edges. **Prices:** $65 to

$500. **Remarks:** Full-time maker doing business as Gossman Knives. **Mark:** Gossman and steel type.

GOTTAGE, DANTE
43227 Brooks Dr, Clinton Twp., MI 48038-5323, Phone: 586-286-7275
Specialties: Working knives of his design or to customer specs. **Patterns:** Large and small skinners, fighters, Bowies and fillet knives. **Technical:** Grinds O1, 440C and 154CM and ATS-34. **Prices:** $150 to $600. **Remarks:** Part-time maker; first knife sold in 1975. **Mark:** Full name in script letters.

GOTTAGE, JUDY
43227 Brooks Dr, Clinton Twp., MI 48038-5323, Phone: 810-343-4662, jgottage@remaxmetropolitan.com
Specialties: Custom folders of her design or to customer specs. **Patterns:** Interframes or integral. **Technical:** Stock removal. **Prices:** $300 to $3000. **Remarks:** Full-time maker; first knife sold in 1980. **Mark:** Full name, maker in script.

GOTTSCHALK, GREGORY J
12 First St. (Ft. Pitt), Carnegie, PA 15106, Phone: 412-279-6692
Specialties: Fancy working straight knives and folders to customer specs. **Patterns:** Hunters to tantos, locking folders to minis. **Technical:** Grinds 440C, 154CM, ATS-34. Now making own Damascus. Most knives have mirror finishes. **Prices:** Start at $150. **Remarks:** Part-time maker; first knife sold in 1977. **Mark:** Full name in crescent.

GOUKER, GARY B
PO Box 955, Sitka, AK 99835, Phone: 907-747-3476
Specialties: Hunting knives for hard use. **Patterns:** Skinners, semi-skinners, and such. **Technical:** Likes natural materials, inlays, stainless steel. **Prices:** Moderate. **Remarks:** New Alaskan maker. **Mark:** Name.

GRAHAM, GORDON
3145 CR 4008, New Boston, TX 75570, Phone: 903-293-2610, Web: www.grahamknives.com
Prices: $325 to $850. **Mark:** Graham.

GRAHAM, LEVI
6296 W. 3rd St., Greeley, CO 80634, Phone: 970-371-0477, lgknives@hotmail.com; www.levigrahamknives.com
Specialties: Forged frontier/period/Western knives. **Patterns:** Hunters, patch knives, skinners, camp, belt and bowies. **Technical:** Forges high-carbon steels and some stock removal in 1095, 1084, 5160, L6, 80CRV2 and 52100. Handle materials include antler, bone, ivory, horn, hardwoods, Micarta and G-10. Rawhide-covered, vegetable-tanned sheaths decorated with deer fringe, quill work for a band or medicine wheel, beads, cones, horse hair, etc. Custom orders welcome. **Prices:** $300 and up. **Remarks:** Member of ABS and PKA. **Mark:** "lg" stamped in lower case letters.

GRANGER, PAUL J
704 13th Ct. SW, Largo, FL 33770-4471, Phone: 727-953-3249, grangerknives@live.com Web: http://palehorsefighters.blogspot.com
Specialties: Working straight knives of his own design and a few folders. **Patterns:** 2.75" to 4" work knives, tactical knives and Bowies from 5"-9." **Technical:** Grinds CPM154-CM, ATS-34 and forges 52100 and 1084. Offers filework. **Prices:** $95 to $500. **Remarks:** Part-time maker since 1997. Sold first knife in 1997. Doing business as Granger Knives and Pale Horse Fighters. Member of ABS and Florida Knifemakers Association. **Mark:** "Granger" or "Palehorse Fighters."

GRANGETTE, ALAIN
7, Erenas, 23210 Azat-Chatenet, FRANCE, Phone: 05-55-81-32-64, alain.grangette@gmail.com; Web: www.alaingrangette.com
Specialties: Art knives and folders with precise, complex folding mechanisms and tight fits and finishes. **Patterns:** Art folders, fixed blades and cutlery. **Technical:** Uses Pantograph and includes mirror finishing, engraving and contemporary materials. Every knife realized is a unique piece, and every blade, mechanism, screw and all other parts are handmade.

GRAVELINE, PASCAL AND ISABELLE
38 Rue de Kerbrezillic, Moelan-sur-Mer, FRANCE 29350, Phone: 33 2 98 39 73 33, atelier.graveline@wanadoo.fr; Web: www.graveline-couteliers.com
Specialties: French replicas from the 17th, 18th and 19th centuries. **Patterns:** Traditional folders and multi-blade pocket knives; traveling knives, fruit knives and fork sets; puzzle knives and friend's knives; rivet less knives. **Technical:** Grind 12C27, ATS-34, Damascus and carbon steel. **Prices:** $500 to $5000. **Remarks:** Full-time makers; first knife sold in 1992. **Mark:** Last name over head of ram.

GRAVES, DAN
4887 Dixie Garden Loop, Shreveport, LA 71105, Phone: 318-865-8166, Web: wwwtheknifemaker.com
Specialties: Traditional forged blades and Damascus. **Patterns:** Bowies (D guard also), fighters, hunters, large and small daggers. **Remarks:** Full-time maker. **Mark:** Initials with circle around them.

GRAY, BOB
8206 N Lucia Court, Spokane, WA 99208, Phone: 509-468-3924
Specialties: Straight working knives of his own design or to customer specs. **Patterns:** Hunter, fillet and carving knives. **Technical:** Forges 5160, L6 and some 52100; grinds 440C. **Prices:** $100 to $600. **Remarks:** Part-time knifemaker; first knife sold in 1991. Doing business as Hi-Land Knives. **Mark:** HI-L.

GRAY, DANIEL
GRAY KNIVES, POB 718, Brownville, ME 04414, Phone: 207-965-2191, mail@grayknives.com; Web: www.grayknives.com
Specialties: Straight knives, fantasy, folders, automatics and traditional of his own design. **Patterns:** Automatics, fighters, hunters. **Technical:** Grinds O1, 154CM and D2. **Prices:** From $155 to $750. **Remarks:** Full-time maker; first knife sold in 1974. **Mark:** Gray Knives.

GRAY, ROBB
6026 46th Ave. SW, Seattle, WA 98136, Phone: 206-280-7622, robb.gray@graycloud-designs.com; Web: www.graycloud-designs.com
Specialties: Hunting, fishing and leather-workers' knives, along with daggers and utility ranch knives. **Technical:** Stock-removal maker using 440C, CPM-S30V, CPM-154, CPM-12C27, CPM-13C26 and CPM-19C27 stainless steels. Also engraves knives in Sheridan, single point and Western bright cut styles. Owner of "Resinwood," a certified wood fiber product sold to knifemaker supply companies for handle material. **Remarks:** Full-time artist/maker; first knife made in 2009. **Mark:** A rain cloud with name "Graycloud" next to it, surrounded by an oval.

GRAYMAN, MIKE
GRAYMAN KNIVES, POB 50, PMB 132, Lake Arrowhead, CA 92352, info@graymanknives.com; Web: www.graymanknives.com
Specialties: Single-bevel fixed blades and hard-use frame-lock folders. **Technical:** Hand grinds fixed blades using 1095 steel with GunKote finishes, G-10 handles, Cordura sheaths and free personalized hand engraving on blade spines. Precision-machined folders include CPM 20CV and CPM S30V blade steels with titanium handles. **Prices:** $160 to $425. **Remarks:** Started making knives in 2004. **Mark:** "Grayman" hand engraved on the spine of each knife.

GRECO, JOHN
100 Mattie Jones Rd, Greensburg, KY 42743, Phone: 270-932-3335
Specialties: Folders. **Patterns:** Tactical, fighters, camp knives, short swords. **Technical:** Stock removal carbon steel. **Prices:** Affordable. **Remarks:** Full-time maker since 1979. First knife sold in 1979. **Mark:** GRECO

GREEN, BILL
6621 Eastview Dr, Sachse, TX 75048, Phone: 972-463-3147
Specialties: High-art and working straight knives and folders of his design and to customer specs. **Patterns:** Bowies, hunters, kitchen knives and locking folders. **Technical:** Grinds ATS-34, D2 and 440V. Hand-tooled custom sheaths. **Prices:** $70 to $350; some to $750. **Remarks:** Part-time maker; first knife sold in 1990. **Mark:** Last name.

GREEN, WILLIAM (BILL)
46 Warren Rd, View Bank, VIC, AUSTRALIA 3084, Fax: 03-9459-1529
Specialties: Traditional high-tech straight knives and folders. **Patterns:** Japanese-influenced designs, hunters, Bowies, folders and miniatures. **Technical:** Forges O1, D2 and his own Damascus. Offers lost wax castings for bolsters and pommels. Likes natural handle materials, gems, silver and gold. **Prices:** $400 to $750; some to $1200. **Remarks:** Full-time maker. **Mark:** Initials.

GREENAWAY, DON
3325 Dinsmore Tr, Fayetteville, AR 72704, Phone: 501-521-0323
Specialties: Liner locks and bowies. **Prices:** $150 to $1500. **Remarks:** 20 years experience. **Mark:** Greenaway over Fayetteville, Ark.

GREENE, CHRIS
707 Cherry Lane, Shelby, NC 28150, Phone: 704-434-5620

GREENE, DAVID
570 Malcom Rd, Covington, GA 30209, Phone: 770-784-0657
Specialties: Straight working using knives. **Patterns:** Hunters. **Technical:** Forges mosaic and twist Damascus. Prefers stag and desert ironwood for handle material.

GREENE, STEVE
DUNN KNIVES INC, PO Box 307 1449 Nocatee St., Intercession City, FL 33848, Phone: 800-245-6483, s.greene@earthlink.net; Web: www.dunnknives.com
Specialties: Skinning & fillet knives. **Patterns:** Skinners, drop points, clip points and fillets. **Technical:** CPM-S30V powdered metal steel manufactured by Niagara Specialty Metals. **Prices:** $100 to $350. **Mark:** Dunn by Greene and year. **Remarks:** Full-time knifemaker. First knife sold in 1972. Each knife is handcrafted and includes holster-grade leather sheath.

GREENFIELD, G O
2605 15th St #310, Everett, WA 98201, Phone: 425-232-6011, garyg1946@yahoo.com
Specialties: High-tech and working straight knives and folders of his design. **Patterns:** Boots, daggers, hunters and one-of-a-kinds. **Technical:** Grinds ATS-34, D2, 440C and T-440V. Makes sheaths for each knife. **Prices:** $100 to $800; some to $10,000. **Remarks:** Part-time maker; first knife sold in 1978. **Mark:** Springfield®, serial number.

GREGORY, MATTHEW M.
74 Tarn Tr., Glenwood, NY 14069, Phone: 716-863-1215, mgregoryknives@yahoo.com; Web: www.mgregoryknives.com
Patterns: Wide variation of styles, as I make what I like to make. Bowies, fighters, Neo-American/Japanese-inspired blades, occasionally kitchen knives. **Technical:** Forging and stock removal, using forging steels such as 1084, 1095, W2 and CruForgeV, as well as high-alloy steels like CPM-3V and CPM-S110V. Hamon (blade temper line) development and polishing. **Prices:** $350 and up. **Remarks:** Part-time maker since 2005. **Mark:** M. Gregory.

GREGORY, MICHAEL
211 Calhoun Rd, Belton, SC 29627, Phone: 864-338-8898, gregom.123@charter.net
Specialties: Interframe folding knives, working hunters and period pieces. Hand rubbed finish, engraving by maker. **Patterns:** Hunters, bowies, daggers and folding knives. **Technical:** Grinds ATS-34 and other makers' damascus. **Prices:** $200 and up. **Remarks:** Full-time maker; first knife sold in 1980. **Mark:** Name, city in logo.

GREINER, RICHARD
1073 E County Rd 32, Green Springs, OH 44836, Phone: 419-483-4613, rgreiner7295@yahoo.com
Specialties: High-carbon steels, edge hardened. **Patterns:** Most. **Technical:** Hand forged. **Prices:** $125 and up. **Remarks:** Have made knives for 30 years. **Mark:** Maple leaf.

GREISS, JOCKL
Herrenwald 15, Schenkenzell, GERMANY 77773, Phone: +49 7836 95 71 69 or +49 7836 95 55 76, www.jocklgreiss@yahoo.com
Specialties: Classic and working using straight knives of his design. **Patterns:** Bowies, daggers and hunters. **Technical:** Uses only Jerry Rados Damascus. All knives are one-of-a-kind made by hand; no machines are used. **Prices:** $700 to $2000; some to $3000. **Remarks:** Full-time maker; first knife sold in 1984. **Mark:** An "X" with a long vertical line through it.

GREY, PIET
PO Box 363, Naboomspruit, LP, SOUTH AFRICA 0560, Phone: 014-743-3613
Specialties: Fancy working and using straight knives of his design. **Patterns:** Fighters, hunters and utility/camp knives. **Technical:** Grinds ATS-34 and AEB-L; forges and grinds Damascus. Solder less fitting of guards. Engraves and scrimshaws. **Prices:** $125 to $750; some to $1500. **Remarks:** Part-time maker; first knife sold in 1970. **Mark:** Last name.

GRIFFIN, JOHN
26101 Pine Shadows, Hockley, TX 77447, Phone: 281-414-7111, griff6363@yahoo.com; Web: www.griffinknives.us
Specialties: Push button automatics. **Patterns:** All patterns, including custom-designed pieces. **Technical:** Stainless and damascus blade steels with differing textured designs on stainless steel bolsters. **Prices:** Start at $800. **Remarks:** Guaranteed for life, very durable and unique designs.

GRIFFIN JR., HOWARD A
14299 SW 31st Ct, Davie, FL 33330, Phone: 954-474-5406, mgriffin18@aol.com
Specialties: Working straight knives and folders. **Patterns:** Hunters, Bowies, locking folders with his own push-button lock design. **Technical:** Grinds 440C. **Prices:** $100 to $200; some to $500. **Remarks:** Part-time maker; first knife sold in 1983. **Mark:** Initials.

GRIMES, MARK
PO BOX 1293, Bedford, TX 76095, Phone: 817-320-7274, ticktock107@gmail.com
Specialties: Qs. **Patterns:** Hunters, fighters, bowies. **Technical:** Custom hand forged 1084 steel blades full and hidden tang, heat treating, sheathes. **Prices:** $150-$400. **Remarks:** Part-time maker, first knife sold in 2009. **Mark:** Last name.

GRIZZARD, JIM
3626 Gunnels Ln., Oxford, AL 36203, Phone: 256-403-1232, grizzardforgiven@aol.com
Specialties: Hand carved art knives inspired by sole authorship. **Patterns:** Fixedblades, folders, and swords. **Technical:** Carving handles, artgrinding, forged and stock removal. **Prices:** Vary. **Remarks:** Uses knives mostly as a ministry to bless others. **Mark:** FOR HIS GLORY CUSTOM KNIVES OR j grizzard in a grizzly bear.

GROSPITCH, ERNIE
18440 Amityville Dr, Orlando, FL 32820, Phone: 407-568-5438, shrpknife@aol.com; Web: www.erniesknives.com
Specialties: Bowies, hunting, fishing, kitchen, lockback folders, leather craft and knifemaker logo stenciling/blue lightning stencil. **Patterns:** My design or customer's. **Technical:** Stock removal using most available steels. **Prices:** Vary. **Remarks:** Full-time maker, sold first knife in 1990. Blue Lightning stencils. **Mark:** Etched name over Thunderbird image.

GROSS, W W
109 Dylan Scott Dr, Archdale, NC 27263-3858
Specialties: Working knives. **Patterns:** Hunters, boots, fighters. **Technical:** Grinds **Prices:** Moderate. **Remarks:** Full-time maker. **Mark:** Name.

GROSSMAN, STEWART
24 Water St #419, Clinton, MA 01510, Phone: 508-365-2291; 800-mysword
Specialties: Miniatures and full-size knives and swords. **Patterns:** One-of-a-kind miniatures—jewelry, replicas—and wire-wrapped figures. Full-size art, fantasy and combat knives, daggers and modular systems. **Technical:** Forges and grinds most metals and Damascus. Uses gems, crystals, electronics and motorized mechanisms. **Prices:** $20 to $300; some to $4500 and higher. **Remarks:** Full-time maker; first knife sold in 1985. **Mark:** G1.

GROVES, GARY
P.O. Box 101, Canvas, WV 26662, ggroves51@gmail.com
Specialties: Fixed blades and hidden-tang knives. **Patterns:** Hunters, skinners and bowies. **Technical:** Stock-removal method using ATS 34 and 154CM steels. Handles are mainly natural materials such as bone, horn, stag and wood, with filework on just about all knives. Every knife comes with a made-to-fit sheath. **Prices:** $350 to $1,200. **Remarks:** Full-time knifemaker; first knife sold in 2007. **Mark:** Last name over an anvil and a capital G in the middle of the anvil.

GRUSSENMEYER, PAUL G

310 Kresson Rd, Cherry Hill, NJ 08034, Phone: 856-428-1088, pgrussentne@ comcast.net; Web: www.pgcarvings.com
Specialties: Assembling fancy and fantasy straight knives with his own carved handles. **Patterns:** Bowies, daggers, folders, swords, hunters and miniatures. **Technical:** Uses forged steel and Damascus, stock removal and knapped obsidian blades. **Prices:** $250 to $4000. **Remarks:** Spare-time maker; first knife sold in 1991. **Mark:** First and last initial hooked together on handle.

GUARNERA, ANTHONY R

42034 Quail Creek Dr, Quartzhill, CA 93536, Phone: 661-722-4032
Patterns: Hunters, camp, Bowies, kitchen, fighter knives. **Technical:** Forged and stock removal. **Prices:** $100 and up.

GUINN, TERRY

13026 Hwy 6 South, Eastland, TX 76448, Phone: 254-629-8603, Web: www. terryguinn.com
Specialties: Working fixed blades and balisongs. **Patterns:** Almost all types of folding and fixed blades, from patterns and "one of a kind". **Technical:** Stock removal all types of blade steel with preference for air hardening steel. Does own heat treating, all knives Rockwell tested in shop. **Prices:** $200 to $2,000. **Remarks:** Part time maker since 1982, sold first knife 1990. **Mark:** Full name with cross in the middle.

GUNTER, BRAD

13 Imnaha Rd., Tijeras, NM 87059, Phone: 505-281-8080

GUNTHER, EDDIE

11 Nedlands Pl Burswood, Auckland, NEW ZEALAND 2013, Phone: 006492722373, eddit.gunther49@gmail.com
Specialties: Drop point hunters, boot, Bowies. All mirror finished. **Technical:** Grinds D2, 440C, 12c27. **Prices:** $250 to $800. **Remarks:** Part-time maker, first knife sold in 1986. **Mark:** Name, city, country.

H

HAAS, RANDY

HHH Knives, 3875 Vandyke Rd., Marlette, MI 48453, Phone: 989-635-7059, Web: www.hhhcustomknives.com
Specialties: Handmade custom kitchen and culinary knives, hunters, fighters, folders and art knives. **Technical:** Damascus maker and sales. **Remarks:** Full-time maker for 10 years. **Mark:** Three H's with a knife behind the HHH.

HACKNEY, DANA A.

787 Mountain Meadows Rd., Naples, ID 83847-5044, Phone: 719-481-3940; Cell: 719-651-5634, danahackneyknives@gmail.com and dshackney@Q.com
Specialties: Hunters, bowies and everyday carry knives, and some kitchen cutlery. **Technical:** ABS journeyman smith who forges 1080 series, 5160, 52100, 01, W2 and his own damascus. Uses CPM-154 mostly for stainless knives. **Prices:** $150 and up. **Remarks:** Sole ownership knives and sheaths. Full-time maker as of July 2012. Sold first knife in 2005. ABS, MKA and PKA member. **Mark:** Last name, HACKNEY on left-side ricasso.

HAGEN, DOC

POB 58, 702 5th St. SE, Pelican Rapids, MN 56572, Phone: 218-863-8503, dochagen@gmail.com; Web: www.dochagencustomknives.com
Specialties: Folders. Autos:bolster release-dual action. Slipjoint folders**Patterns:** Defense-related straight knives; wide variety of folders. **Technical:** Dual action release, bolster release autos. **Prices:** $300 to $800; some to $3000. **Remarks:** Full-time maker; first knife sold in 1975. Makes his own Damascus. **Mark:** DOC HAGEN in shield, knife, banner logo; or DOC.

HAGGERTY, GEORGE S

PO Box 88, Jacksonville, VT 05342, Phone: 802-368-7437, swewater@sover.net
Specialties: Working straight knives and folders. **Patterns:** Hunters, claws, camp and fishing knives, locking folders and backpackers. **Technical:** Forges and grinds W2, 440C and 154CM. **Prices:** $85 to $300. **Remarks:** Part-time maker; first knife sold in 1981. **Mark:** Initials or last name.

HAGUE, GEOFF

Unit 5, Project Workshops, Lains Farm, Quarley, Hampshire, UNITED KINGDOM SP11 8PX, Phone: (+44) 01672-870212, Fax: (+44) 01672 870212, geoff@ hagueknives.com; Web: www.hagueknives.com
Specialties: Fixed blade and folding knives. **Patterns:** Back lock, locking liner, slip joint, and friction folders. **Technical:** Grinds D2, RWL-34 and damascus. Mainly natural handle materials. **Prices:** $500 to $2,000. **Remarks:** Full-time maker. **Mark:** Last name.

HAINES, JEFF

Haines Custom Knives, W3678 Bay View Rd., Mayville, WI 53050, Phone: 920-387-0212, knifeguy95@gmail.com; Web: www.hainescustom.com
Patterns: Hunters, skinners, camp knives, customer designs welcome. **Technical:** Forges 1095, 5160, and Damascus, grinds A2. **Prices:** $75 and up. **Remarks:** Part-time maker since 1995. **Mark:** Last name.

HALE, LLOYD

7593 Beech Hill Rd., Pulaski, TN 38478, Phone: 931-424-5846, lloydahale@gmail.com
Specialties: Museum-grade, one-of-a-kind daggers, folders and sub-hilt fighting knives. **Remarks:** Full-time maker for 44+ years. Spent 20+ years creating a one-of-a-kind knife collection for Owsley Brown Frazier of Louisville, KY. I don't accept orders anymore.

HALFRICH, JERRY

340 Briarwood, San Marcos, TX 78666, Phone: 512-353-2582, jerryhalfrich@ grandecom.net; Web: www.halfrichknives.com
Specialties: Working knives and specialty utility knives for the professional and serious hunter. Uses proven designs in both straight and folding knives. Pays close attention to fit and finish. Art knives on special request. **Patterns:** Hunters, skinners, and lockback, LinerLock and slip-joint folders. **Technical:** Grinds both flat and hollow D2, Damasteel and CPM 154, makes high precision folders. **Prices:** $450 to $1,500. **Remarks:** Full-time maker since 2000. DBA Halfrich Custom Knives. **Mark:** HALFRICH.

HALL, JEFF

179 Niblick Rd., # 180, Paso Robles, CA 93446, Phone: 562-594-4740, info@ nemesis-knives.com; Web: nemesis-knives.com
Specialties: Collectible and working folders and fixed blades of his design. **Technical:** Grinds CPM-S35VN, CPM-154, and various makers' damascus. **Patterns:** Fighters, gentleman's, hunters and utility knives. **Prices:** $100 and up. **Remarks:** Full-time maker. First knife sold 1998. **Mark:** Last name.

HALL, KEN

606 Stevenson Cove Rd., Waynesville, NC 28785, Phone: 828-627-2135, khall@ hallenergyconsulting.com; Web: www.kenhallknives.com
Specialties: Standard and one-of-a-kind fixed-blade knives with leather sheaths. **Patterns:** Hunters, bowies, fighters, chef's knives and tantos. **Technical:** Forges high-carbon steel, flat grinds. **Prices:** $300 to $1,500. **Remarks:** Part-time maker; first knives sold in 2010. **Mark:** Etched "Ken Hall" or "KHall JS."

HALL, SCOTT M.

5 Hickory Hts., Geneseo, IL 61254, Phone: 309-945-2184, smhall@theinter.com; www.hallcustomknives.com
Specialties: Fixed-blade, hollow-ground working knives of his own design and to customer specs. **Patterns:** Designs catering to soldiers and outdoorsmen, including variations of hunters, bowies, fighters and occasionally fillet and kitchen knives. **Technical:** Usually grinds CPM S30V and 154CM, but uses other steels upon request. Handle materials include G-10, Micarta, stag, horn and exotic woods. Most knives are offered with hand-tooled and stitched leather sheaths or Spec Ops sheaths. **Prices:** $150 to $350+. **Remarks:** Part-time maker; first knife sold in 2000. **Mark:** Last name.

HAMLET JR., JOHNNY

300 Billington, Clute, TX 77531, Phone: 979-265-6929, nifeman@swbell.net; Web: www.hamlets-handmade-knives.com
Specialties: Working straight knives and folders. **Patterns:** Hunters, fighters, fillet and kitchen knives, locking folders. Likes upswept knives and trailing-points. **Technical:** Grinds 440C, D2, ATS-34. Makes sheaths. **Prices:** $125 and up. **Remarks:** Full-time maker; sold first knife in 1988. **Mark:** Hamlet's Handmade in script.

HAMMOND, HANK

189 Springlake Dr, Leesburg, GA 31763, Phone: 229-434-1295, godogs57@ bellsouth.net
Specialties: Traditional hunting and utility knives of his design. Will also design and produce knives to customer's specifications. **Patterns:** Straight or sheath knives, hunters skinners as well as Bowies and fighters. **Technical:** Grinds (hollow and flat grinds) CPM 154CM, ATS-34. Also uses Damascus and forges 52100. Offers filework on blades. Handle materials include all exotic woods, red stag, sambar stag, deer, elk, oosic, bone, fossil ivory, Micarta, etc. All knives come with sheath handmade for that individual knife. **Prices:** $100 up to $500. **Remarks:** Part-time maker. Sold first knife in 1981. Doing business as Double H Knives. **Mark:** "HH" inside 8 point deer rack.

HAMMOND, JIM

104 Owens Parkway, Ste. M, Birmingham, AL 35244, Phone: 256-651-1376, jim@ jimhammondknives.com; Web: www.jimhammondknives.com
Specialties: High-tech fighters and folders. **Patterns:** Proven-design fighters. **Technical:** Grinds 440C, 440V, S30V and other specialty steels. **Prices:** $385 to $1200; some to $9200. **Remarks:** Full-time maker; first knife sold in 1977. Designer for Columbia River Knife and Tool. **Mark:** Full name, city, state in shield logo.

HAMMOND, RAY

Hammond Knives, LLC, 3750 Quail Creek Dr., Buford, GA 30519, Phone: 678-300-2883, rayhammond01@yahoo.com; Web: www.biggamehuntingblades.com
Specialties: Fixed blades, primarily hunting knives, utility knives and bowies. **Technical:** Stock removal and forged blades, including 5160, 1095, CPM-154 and damascus blade steels. **Prices:** Start at $300. **Remarks:** Part-time maker; first knife built in 2008. **Mark:** Capital letters RH surrounded by a broken circle, pierced by a knife silhouette, atop the circle is my name, and below the circle the words "custom knives." Will soon alter this to simply my last name.

HANCOCK, TIM

29125 N. 153rd St., Scottsdale, AZ 85262, Phone: 480-998-8849, westernbladesmith@gmail.com
Specialties: High-art and working straight knives and folders of his design and to customer preferences. **Patterns:** Bowies, fighters, daggers, tantos, swords, folders. **Technical:** Forges damascus and 52100; grinds ATS-34. Makes damascus. Silver-wire inlays; offers carved fittings and file work. **Prices:** $1,000 to $50,000. **Remarks:** Full-time maker; first knife sold in 1988. ABS master smith and AKI member. No longer taking orders. **Mark:** Last name or heart.

HAND, BILL

PO Box 717, 1103 W. 7th St., Spearman, TX 79081, Phone: 806-659-2967, Fax: 806-

custom knifemakers

659-5139, klinker43@yahoo.com
Specialties: Traditional working and using straight knives and folders of his design or to customer specs. **Patterns:** Hunters, Bowies, folders and fighters. **Technical:** Forges 5160, 52100 and Damascus. **Prices:** Start at $150. **Remarks:** Part-time maker; Journeyman Smith. Current delivery time 12 to 16 months. **Mark:** Stylized initials.

HANKALA, JUKKA
Tuhkurintie 225, 39580 Riitiala, FINLAND, Phone: +358-400-684-625, jukka@hankala.com; www.hankala.com
Specialties: Traditional puukkos and maker's own knife models. **Patterns:** Maker's own puukko models, hunters, folders and ART-knives. **Technical:** Forges Silversteel, Bohler K510, Damasteel stainless damascus and RWL-34 blade steels, as well as his own 15N20-and-1.2842 damascus, mosaic damascus and color damascus. **Prices:** Start at $300. **Remarks:** Full-time maker since 1985. **Mark:** J. Hankala.

HANSEN, LONNIE
PO Box 4956, Spanaway, WA 98387, Phone: 253-847-4632, lonniehansen@msn.com; Web: lchansen.com
Specialties: Working straight knives of his design. **Patterns:** Tomahawks, tantos, hunters, fillet. **Technical:** Forges 1086, 52100, grinds 440V, BG-42. **Prices:** Starting at $300. **Remarks:** Part-time maker since 1989. **Mark:** First initial and last name. Also first and last initial.

HANSEN, ROBERT W
405 357th Ave. NE, Cambridge, MN 55008, Phone: 763-689-3242
Specialties: Working straight knives, folders and integrals. **Patterns:** From hunters to minis, camp knives to miniatures; folding lockers and slip-joints in original styles. **Technical:** Grinds O1, 440C and 154CM; likes filework. **Prices:** $100 to $450; some to $600. **Remarks:** Part-time maker; first knife sold in 1983. **Mark:** Fish w/h inside surrounded by Bob Hansen maker.

HANSON, KYLE S.
POB 12, Success, MO 65570, Phone: 573-674-3045, khansonknives@gmail.com; https://kylehansonknives.wordpress.com/
Specialties: W2 fixed blades with striking hamons and one-of-a-kind, handforged damascus, as well as damascus bolsters and guards on many knives. **Patterns:** Utility knives, hunters, fighters, bowies and the occasional tactical piece. Fixed blades only, with full or hidden tangs. **Technical:** Forges his own damascus, though he can't help dig into his father, Don Hanson III's, stash once in a while, and is particularly fond of intricate hamons on W2 blades. Also fond of walrus ivory, mother-of-pearl, curly koa and desert ironwood handles. **Remarks:** Full-time maker, first knife sold in 2012. Learned everything he knows from his father and couldn't ask for a better teacher in the world of custom knives. **Mark:** KYLE HANSON.

HANSON III, DON L.
Sunfish Forge, PO Box 13, Success, MO 65570-0013, Phone: 573-674-3045, Web: www.sunfishforge.com; www.donhansonknives.com
Specialties: One-of-a-kind damascus folders, slip joints and forged fixed blades. **Patterns:** Small, fancy pocket knives, large folding fighters and Bowies. **Technical:** Forges own pattern welded Damascus, file work and carving also carbon steel blades with hamons. **Prices:** $800 and up. **Remarks:** Full-time maker, first knife sold in 1984. ABS mastersmith. **Mark:** Sunfish.

HARA, KOJI
292-2 Osugi, Seki-City, Gifu, JAPAN 501-3922, Phone: 0575-24-7569, Fax: 0575-24-7569, info@knifehousehara.com; Web: www.knifehousehara.com
Specialties: High-tech and working straight knives of his design; some folders. **Patterns:** Hunters, locking folders and utility/camp knives. **Technical:** Grinds Cowry X, Cowry Y and ATS-34. Prefers high mirror polish; pearl handle inlay. **Prices:** $400 to $2500. **Remarks:** Full-time maker; first knife sold in 1980. Doing business as Knife House "Hara." **Mark:** First initial, last name in fish.

HARDING, CHAD
12365 Richland Ln, Solsberry, IN 47459, hardingknives@yahoo.com; www.hardingknives.net
Specialties: Hunters and camp knives, occasional fighters or bowies. No folders. **Technical:** Hand forge 90% of work. Prefer 10XX steels and tool steels. Makes own damascus and cable and chainsaw chain damascus. 100% sole authorship on knives and sheaths. Mostly natural handle material, prefer wood and stag. **Prices:** $150 to $1,000. **Remarks:** Part-time maker, member of ABS. First knife sold in 2005. **Mark:** Last name.

HARDING, JACOB
POB 10451, Fairbanks, AK 99710, Phone: 907-347-2961, harding-jake@hotmail.com, www.etsy.com/shop/hardingjm9, Facebook at Walking Stick Arts
Specialties: Blacksmith making handforged blades, including hunting and camp knives, black powder patch knives and collector pieces. **Technical:** Forges high-carbon 5160 steel, and likes to use recycled materials whenever possible, including leaf springs, files, railroad spikes, ammo casings for brass work and handle parts. **Prices:** $80 to $500. **Mark:** Harding, and location: ALASKA.

HARDY, DOUGLAS E
114 Cypress Rd, Franklin, GA 30217, Phone: 706-675-6305

HARDY, SCOTT
639 Myrtle Ave, Placerville, CA 95667, Phone: 530-622-5780, Web: www.innercite.com/~shardy
Specialties: Traditional working and using straight knives of his design. **Patterns:** Most anything with an edge. **Technical:** Forges carbon steels. Japanese stone polish. Offers

mirror finish; differentially tempers. **Prices:** $100 to $1000. **Remarks:** Part-time maker; first knife sold in 1982. **Mark:** First initial, last name and Handmade with bird logo.

HARKINS, J A
PO Box 218, Conner, MT 59827, Phone: 406-821-1060, kutter@customknives.net; Web: customknives.net
Specialties: OTFs, Automatics, Folders. **Technical:** Grinds ATS-34. Engraves; offers gem work. **Prices:** $1500 and up. **Remarks:** Celebrating 20th year as full-time maker. **Mark:** First and middle initials, last name.

HARLEY, LARRY W
348 Deerfield Dr, Bristol, TN 37620, Phone: 423-878-5368 (shop); cell: 423-530-1133, Web: www.lonesomepineknives.com
Specialties: One-of-a-kind Persian in one-of-a-kind Damascus. Working knives, period pieces. **Technical:** Forges and grinds ATS-34, 440c, L6, 15, 20, 1084, and 52100. **Patterns:** Full range of straight knives, tomahawks, razors, buck skinners and hog spears. **Prices:** $200 and up. **Mark:** Pine tree.

HARLEY, RICHARD
609 Navaho Trl., Bristol, VA 24201, Phone: 423-878-5368; cell: 423-408-5720
Specialties: Hunting knives, Bowies, friction folders, one-of-a-kind. **Technical:** Forges 1084, S160, 52100, Lg. **Prices:** $150 to $1000. **Mark:** Pine tree with name.

HARM, PAUL W
818 N. Young Rd, Attica, MI 48412, Phone: 810-724-5582, harm@blclinks.net
Specialties: Early American working knives. **Patterns:** Hunters, skinners, patch knives, fighters, folders. **Technical:** Forges and grinds 1084, O1, 52100 and own Damascus. **Prices:** $75 to $1000. **Remarks:** First knife sold in 1990. **Mark:** Connected initials.

HARNER III, "BUTCH" LLOYD R.
745 Kindig Rd., Littlestown, PA 17340, butch@harnerknives.com; Web: www.harnerknives.com
Specialties: Kitchen knives and straight razors. **Technical:** CPM-3V, CPM-154 and various Carpenter powdered steel alloys. **Remarks:** Full-time maker since 2007. **Mark:** L.R. Harner (2005-Sept. 2012) and Harner III (after Oct. 2012)

HARRINGTON, ROGER
P.O. Box 157, Battle, East Sussex, ENGLAND TN 33 3 DD, Phone: 0854-838-7062, info@bisonbushcraft.co.uk; Web: www.bisonbushcraft.co.uk
Specialties: Working straight knives to his or customer's designs, flat saber Scandinavia-style grinds on full tang knives, also hollow and convex grinds. **Technical:** Grinds O1, D2, Damascus. **Prices:** $200 to $800. **Remarks:** First knife made by hand in 1997 whilst traveling around the world. **Mark:** Bison with bison written under.

HARRIS, CASS
19855 Fraiser Hill Ln, Bluemont, VA 20135, Phone: 540-554-8774, Web: www.tdogforge.com
Prices: $160 to $500.

HARRIS, JAY
991 Johnson St, Redwood City, CA 94061, Phone: 415-366-6077
Specialties: Traditional high-tech straight knives and folders of his design. **Patterns:** Daggers, fighters and locking folders. **Technical:** Uses 440C, ATS-34 and CPM. **Prices:** $250 to $850. **Remarks:** Spare-time maker; first knife sold in 1980.

HARRIS, JOHN
PO Box 2466, Quartzsite, AZ 85346, Phone: 951-653-2755, johnharrisknives@yahoo.com; Web: www.johnharrisknives.com
Specialties: Hunters, daggers, Bowies, bird and trout, period pieces, Damascus and carbon steel knives, forged and stock removal. **Prices:** $200 to $1000.

HARRISON, BRIAN
BFH KNIVES, 2359 E Swede Rd, Cedarville, MI 49719, Phone: 906-430-0720, bfh_knives@yahoo.com
Specialties: High grade fixed blade knives. **Patterns:** Many sizes & variety of patterns from small pocket carries to large combat and camp knives. Mirror and bead blast finishes. All handles of high grade materials from ivory to highly figured stabilized woods to stag, deer & moose horn and Micarta. Hand sewn fancy sheaths for pocket or belt. **Technical:** Flat & hollow grinds usually ATS-34 but some O1, L6 and stellite 6K. **Prices:** $150 to $1200. **Remarks:** Full-time maker, sole authorship. Made first knife in 1980, sold first knife in 1999. Received much knowledge from the following makers: George Young, Eric Erickson, Webster Wood, Ed Kalfayan who are all generous men. **Mark:** Engraved blade outline w/ BFH Knives over the top edge, signature across middle & Cedarville, MI underneath.

HARRISON, JIM (SEAMUS)
721 Fairington View Dr, St. Louis, MO 63129, Phone: 314-791-6350, jrh@seamusknives.com; Web: www.seamusknives.com
Specialties: "Crossover" folders, liner-locks and frame-locks. **Patterns:** Uber, Author, Skyyy Folders, Ryan, Landon, Connor and flipper folders. **Technical:** Uses CPM S30V and 154, Stellite 6k and stainless damascus by Norris, Thomas, Nichols and Damasteel. **Prices:** Folders $550 to $1,400. **Remarks:** Full-time maker since 2008, maker since 1999. **Mark:** Seamus

HARSEY, WILLIAM H
82710 N. Howe Ln, Creswell, OR 97426, Phone: 541-510-8707, billharsey@gmail.com
Specialties: High-tech kitchen and outdoor knives. **Patterns:** Folding hunters, trout and bird folders; straight hunters, camp knives and axes. **Technical:** Grinds; etches. **Prices:** $125 to $300; some to $1500. Folders start at $350. **Remarks:** Full-time maker; first knife sold in 1979. **Mark:** Full name, state, U.S.A.

HART, BILL

647 Cedar Dr, Pasadena, MD 21122, Phone: 410-255-4981
Specialties: Fur-trade era working straight knives and folders. **Patterns:** Springback folders, skinners, Bowies and patch knives. **Technical:** Forges and stock removes 1095 and 5160 wire Damascus. **Prices:** $100 to $600. **Remarks:** Part-time maker; first knife sold in 1986. **Mark:** Name.

HARTMAN, ARLAN (LANNY)

6102 S Hamlin Cir, Baldwin, MI 49304, Phone: 231-745-4029
Specialties: Working straight knives and folders. **Patterns:** Drop-point hunters, coil spring lockers, slip-joints. **Technical:** Flat-grinds D2, 440C and ATS-34. **Prices:** $300 to $2000. **Remarks:** Part-time maker; first knife sold in 1982. **Mark:** Last name.

HARTMAN, TIM

3812 Pedroncelli Rd NW, Albuquerque, NM 87107, Phone: 505-385-6924, tbonz1@comcast.net
Specialties: Exotic wood scales, sambar stag, filework, hunters. **Patterns:** Fixed blade hunters, skinners, utility and hiking. **Technical:** 154CM, Ats-34 and D2. Mirror finish and contoured scales. **Prices:** Start at $200-$450. **Remarks:** Started making knives in 2004. **Mark:** 3 lines Ti Hartman, Maker, Albuquerque NM

HARVEY, KEVIN

HEAVIN FORGE, PO Box 768, Belfast, LP, SOUTH AFRICA 1100, Phone: 27-13-253-0914, info@heavinforge.co.za Web: www.heavinforge.co.za
Specialties: Large knives of presentation quality and creative art knives. **Patterns:** Fixed blades of Bowie, dagger and fighter-styles, occasionally folders and swords. **Technical:** Stock removal of stainless and forging of carbon steel and own Damascus. Indigenous African handle materials preferred. Own engraving Often collaborate with wife, Heather (ABS MS) under the logo "Heavin." **Prices:** $500 to $5000 average $1500. **Remarks:** Full-time maker and knifemaking instructor. Master bladesmith with ABS. First knife sold in 1984. **Mark:** First name and surname, oval with "M S" in the middle.

HARVEY, MAX

6 Winchester Way, Leeming, Perth, Western Australia 6149, AUSTRALIA, Phone: 61 (8) 93101103 or 61-478-633-356, mcharveyknives@outlook.com; http://mcharveycustomknives.com/wordpress/?page_id=84
Specialties: Fixed-blade knives of all styles. **Patterns:** Camp knives, skinners, bowies, daggers and high-end art knives. **Technical:** Stock-removal using ATS-34, 154CM, 440C and damascus. Do all my own faceting of gem stones in the high-end knives. **Prices:** $250 to $5,000. **Remarks:** Full-time maker; first knife sold in 1981, and founding member of the Australian Knife Makers Guild. **Mark:** First and middle initials, and surname (M C Harvey).

HARVEY, MEL

P.O. Box 176, Nenana, AK 99760, Phone: 907-832-5660, tinker1mh@gmail.com
Specialties: Fixed blade knives for hunting and fishing. **Patterns:** Hunters, skinners. **Technical:** Stock removal on ATS-34, 440C, 01, 1095; Damascus blades using 1095 and 15N20. **Prices:** Starting at $350. **Remarks:** ABS member, attended Bill Moran School; 50+ knives sold since 2007. **Mark:** Mel Harvey over serial number over Nenana, AK.

HASLINGER, THOMAS

6460 Woodland Dr., British Columbia V1B 3G7, CANADA, Phone: 778-212-6300, Web: www.haslinger-knives.com / www.haslinger-culinary.com
Specialties: One-of-a-kind using, working and art knives HCK signature sweeping grind lines. Maker of New Generation and Evolution Chef series. Differential heat treated stainless steel. **Patterns:** Likes to work with customers on design. **Technical:** Grinds various specialty alloys, including Damascus, High end satin finish. Prefers natural handle materials e.g. ancient ivory stag, pearl, abalone, stone and exotic woods. Does inlay work with stone, uses sterling silver, niobium and gold wire work. Custom sheaths using matching woods or hand stitched with unique leather. Offers engraving. **Prices:** $300 and up. **Remarks:** Full-time maker; first knife sold in 1994. Doing business as Haslinger Custom Knives. **Mark:** Two marks used, high end work uses stylized initials, other uses elk antler with Thomas Haslinger, Canada, handcrafted above.

HAWES, CHUCK

HAWES FORGE, PO Box 176, Weldon, IL 61882, Phone: 217-736-2479
Specialties: 95 percent of all work in own Damascus. **Patterns:** Slip-joints liner locks, hunters, Bowie's, swords, anything in between. **Technical:** Forges everything, uses all high-carbon steels, no stainless. **Prices:** $150 to $4000. **Remarks:** Like to do custom orders, his style or yours. Sells Damascus. Full-time maker since 1995. **Mark:** Small football shape. Chuck Hawes maker Weldon, IL.

HAWK, GRANT AND GAVIN

Box 401, Idaho City, ID 83631, Phone: 208-392-4911, blademaker25@msn.com; www.hawkknifedesigns.com, @hawkknives on Instagram
Specialties: Grant and Gavin Hawk make custom knives, mid-tech knives and have had designs with Kershaw, CRKT, Boker, Buck, Camillus, Chris Reeve Knives, Mantis Knives, Millit Knives and Quartermaster. Specialize in folders with innovative locking systems, such as their new Deadlock OTF, the first OTF (out the front auto) with zero blade play. **Technical:** Grind 204P, Elmax, CPM S35VN, CPM 530V, ATS-34, BG-42 and XHP, and use titanium and carbon fiber folder parts. **Prices:** $450 and up. **Remarks:** Full-time makers. **Mark:** G&G Hawk, Hawk Designs.

HAWKINS, BUDDY

PO Box 5969, Texarkana, TX 75505-5969, Phone: 903-838-7917, buddyhawkins@cableone.net

HAWKINS JR., CHARLES R.

2764 Eunice, San Angelo, TX 76901, Phone: 325-947-7875, chawk12354@aol.com;

Web: www.hawkcustomknives.com
Specialties: Custom knives, fixed blades, railroad spike knives and rasp file knives. **Technical:** Stock removal and some forging, using 1095 and 440C steel. **Prices:** $135 and up. **Remarks:** Part-time maker; first knife sold in 2008. **Mark:** Full name, city and state.

HAWLEY, TROY G.

THAWLEY KNIVES, 226 CR 2036, Ivanhoe, TX 75447, Phone: 903-664-4568, thawley123@gmail.com
Specialties: Hunting and fishing knives, kitchen cutlery, tacticals, fighters, tactical machetes and art knives of his own design. **Technical:** Stock removal method of blade making primarily working with 440C, CPM 154 and damascus, with other steels upon request. Forges high-carbon steels, such as 5160 spring steel, to create one-of-a-kind bowies, sabers and hunting knives. **Prices:** Start at $180 and up. **Remarks:** First knife sold in 2014. Member of the Texas Knifemakers Guild. **Mark:** "T."

HAYES, WALLY

9960, 9th Concession, RR#1, Essex, ON, CANADA N8M-2X5, Phone: 226-787-4289, hayesknives@hayesknives.com; Web: www.hayesknives.com
Specialties: Classic and fancy straight knives and folders. **Patterns:** Daggers, Bowies, fighters, tantos. **Technical:** Forges own Damascus and O1; engraves. **Prices:** $150 to $14,000. **Mark:** Last name, M.S. and serial number.

HAYNES, JERRY

260 Forest Meadow Dr, Gunter, TX 75058, Phone: 903-433-1424, jhaynes@arrow-head.com; Web: http://www.arrow-head.com
Specialties: Working straight knives and folders of his design, also historical blades. **Patterns:** Hunters, skinners, carving knives, fighters, renaissance daggers, locking folders and kitchen knives. **Technical:** Grinds ATS-34, CPM, Stellite 6K, D2 and acquired Damascus. Prefers exotic handle materials. Has B.A. in design. Studied with R. Buckminster Fuller. **Prices:** $200 to $1200. **Remarks:** Part-time maker. First knife sold in 1953. **Mark:** Arrowhead and last name.

HAYS, MARK

HAYS HANDMADE KNIVES, 1008 Kavanagh Dr., Austin, TX 78748, Phone: 512-292-4410, markhays@austin.rr.com
Specialties: Working straight knives and folders. Patterns inspired by Randall and Stone. **Patterns:** Bowies, hunters and slip-joint folders. **Technical:** 440C stock removal. Repairs and restores Stone knives. **Prices:** Start at $200. **Remarks:** Part-time maker, brochure available, with Stone knives 1974-1983, 1990-1991. **Mark:** First initial, last name, state and serial number.

HAZE, JEFF

JEFF HAZE CUSTOM KNIVES, 1703 E. 168th St. N, Skiatook, OK 74070, Phone: 918-855-5330, jeffhaze@rocketmail.com; facebook.com/jeffhazecustoms
Specialties: Bushcraft, hunting and everyday carry (EDC) knives. **Technical:** Scandi, saber and flat grinds using the stock-removal method of blade making, and with 1084 high-carbon and 80CrV2 steels. **Prices:** $100 to $250. **Remarks:** Full-time maker; first knife made in 2013. **Mark:** HAZE.

HEADRICK, GARY

122 Wilson Blvd, Juan Les Pins, FRANCE 06160, Phone: 033 610282885, headrick-gary@wanadoo.fr; Web: garyheadrick.free.fr
Specialties: Hi-tech folders with natural furnishings. Back lock & back spring. **Patterns:** Damascus and mokumes. **Technical:** Forges damascus using all steel (no nickel). All frames are titanium, and has a new tactical flipper folder model. **Prices:** $500 to $2,000. **Remarks:** Full-time maker for last eight years, active maker for the past 18 years. German Guild-French Federation, 10 years active, member of the ABS and Italian Corporation. **Mark:** HEADRICK on ricosso is new marking.

HEANEY, JOHN D

9 Lefe Court, Haines City, FL 33844, Phone: 863-422-5823, jdh199@msn.com; Web: www.heaneyknives.com
Specialties: Forged 5160, O1 and Damascus. Prefers using natural handle material such as bone, stag and oosic. Plans on using some of the various ivories on future knives. **Prices:** $250 and up. **Remarks:** ABS member. Received journeyman smith stamp in June. **Mark:** Heaney JS.

HEARD, TOM

Turning Point Knives, 2240 Westwood Dr., Waldorf, MD 20601, Phone: 301-843-8626; cell: 301-752-1944, turningpointknives@comcast.net
Specialties: Gent's working/using LinerLocks, automatics and flipper folders of his design. **Patterns:** Fixed blades of varying styles, folders and neck knives. **Technical:** Flat grinds 1095, O1, damascus and 154CM. Offers acid-etched blade embellishments, scrimshaw and hand-tooled custom leather sheaths. Does own heat-treating. **Prices:** $100 to $700. **Remarks:** Full-time maker since retiring; first knife sold in 2012. **Mark:** TH over last name.

HEATH, WILLIAM

PO Box 131, Bondville, IL 61815, Phone: 217-863-2576
Specialties: Classic and working straight knives, folders. **Patterns:** Hunters and Bowies LinerLock® folders. **Technical:** Grinds ATS-34, 440C, 154CM, Damascus, handle materials Micarta, woods to exotic materials snake skins cobra, rattle snake, African flower snake. Does own heat treating. **Prices:** $75 to $300 some $1000. **Remarks:** Full-time maker. First knife sold in 1979. **Mark:** W. D. HEATH.

HEBEISEN, JEFF

310 19th Ave N, Hopkins, MN 55343, Phone: 952-935-4506, jhebeisen@peoplepc.com
Specialties: One of a kind fixed blade of any size up to 16". **Patterns:** Miniature, Hunters,

Skinners, Daggers, Bowies, Fighters and Neck knives. **Technical:** Stock removal using CPM-154, D2, 440C. Handle mterial varies depending on intended use, mostly natural materials such as bone, horn, antler, and wood. Filework on many. Heavy duty sheaths made to fit. **Prices:** From $100 to $750. **Remarks:** Full-time maker. First knife sold in 2007. **Mark:** Started new mark in 2012: J. Hebeisen, Hopkins, MN. Older **mark:** arched name over buffalo skull.

HEDGES, DEE
192 Carradine Rd., Bedfordale, WA, AUSTRALIA 6112, dark_woods_forge@yahoo.com.au; Web: www.darkwoodsforge.com
Patterns: Makes any and all patterns and style of blades from working blades to swords to Japanese inspired. Favors exotic and artistic variations and unique one-off pieces. **Technical:** Forges all blades from a range of steels, favoring 1084, W2, 52100, 5160 and Damascus steels she makes from a 1084/15n20 mix. **Prices:** Start at $200. **Remarks:** Full-time bladesmith and jeweller. Started making blades professionally in 1999, earning my Journeyman Smith rating in 2010. **Mark:** "Dark Woods" atop an ivy leaf, with "Forge" underneath.

HEDLUND, ANDERS
Samstad 400, Brastad, SWEDEN 45491, Phone: 46-523-139 48, anderskniv@passagen.se; Web: http://hem.passagen.se/anderskniv
Specialties: Fancy high-end collectible folders, high-end collectible Nordic hunters with leather carvings on the sheath. Carvings combine traditional designs with own designs. **Patterns:** Own designs. **Technical:** Grinds most steels, but prefers mosaic Damascus and RWL-34. Prefers mother-of-pearl, mammoth, and mosaic steel for folders. Prefers desert ironwood, mammoth, stabilized arctic birch, willow burl, and Damascus steel or RWL-34 for stick tang knives. **Prices:** Starting at $750 for stick tang knives and staring at $1500 for folders. **Remarks:** Part-time maker, first knife sold in 1988. Nordic champion (five countries) several times and Swedish champion 20 times in different classes. **Mark:** Stylized initials or last name.

HEDRICK, DON
131 Beechwood Hills, Newport News, VA 23608, Phone: 757-877-8100, donaldhedrick@cox.net; Web: www.donhedrickknives.com
Specialties: Working straight knives; period pieces and fantasy knives. **Patterns:** Hunters, boots, Bowies and miniatures. **Technical:** Grinds 440C and commercial Damascus. Also makes micro-mini Randall replicas. **Prices:** $150 to $550; some to $1200. **Remarks:** Part-time maker; first knife sold in 1982. **Mark:** First initial, last name in oval logo.

HEETER, TODD S.
9569 Polo Place N., Mobile, AL 36695, Phone: 251-490-5107, toddheeter78@yahoo.com; Web: www.heeterknifeworks.com
Specialties: Complete range of handforged knives, one-of-a-kind custom pieces. **Patterns:** Military-style frame-lock folders, neck knives, railroad spike folders. **Technical:** Handforged blades, including 1095 and D2, stainless steel, Alabama Damascus, doing one-sided chisel grinds and all ranges of flat grinds. Specializes in war-torn look, hand-hammered copper, pattern etching, antique copper and brass handle scales. **Prices:** $150 to $950. **Remarks:** Part-time maker, full-time fabricator and machinist, tool and die maker; first knife sold in 2009. **Mark:** Stamped first initial, middle initial and full last name, logo: HK with a dagger crossing letters.

HEGE, JOHN B.
P.O. Box 316, Danbury, NC 27106, Phone: 336-593-8324, jbhege@embarqmail.com; www.jbhegecustomknives.com
Specialties: Period-style knives and traditional bowies, utility hunters and fancy pieces. **Technical:** Forges larger pieces and often uses stock removal for knives 6 inches and smaller. **Remarks:** ABS journeyman smith since 2013.

HEGWALD, J L
1106 Charles, Humboldt, KS 66748, Phone: 316-473-3523
Specialties: Working straight knives. **Patterns:** Makes Bowies, miniatures. **Technical:** Forges or grinds O1, L6, 440C; mixes materials in handles. **Prices:** $35 to $200; some higher. **Remarks:** Part-time maker; first knife sold in 1983. **Mark:** First and middle initials.

HEHN, RICHARD KARL
Lehnmuehler Str 1, Dorrebach, GERMANY 55444, Phone: 06724 3152
Specialties: High-tech, full integral working knives. **Patterns:** Hunters, fighters and daggers. **Technical:** Grinds CPM T-440V, CPM T-420V, forges his own stainless Damascus. **Prices:** $1000 to $10,000. **Remarks:** Full-time maker; first knife sold in 1963. **Mark:** Runic last initial in logo.

HEIMDALE, J E
7749 E 28 CT, Tulsa, OK 74129, Phone: 918-640-0784, heimdale@sbcglobal.net
Specialties: Art knives **Patterns:** Bowies, daggers **Technical:** Makes allcomponents and handles - exotic woods and sheaths. Uses Damascus blades by other Blademakers, notably R.W. Wilson. **Prices:** $300 and up. **Remarks:** Part-time maker. First knife sold in 1999. Marks: JEHCO

HEINZ, JOHN
611 Cafferty Rd, Upper Black Eddy, PA 18972, Phone: 610-847-8535, Web: www.herugrim.com
Specialties: Historical pieces / copies. **Technical:** Makes his own steel. **Prices:** $150 to $800. **Mark:** "H."

HEITLER, HENRY
8106 N Albany, Tampa, FL 33604, Phone: 813-933-1645
Specialties: Traditional working and using straight knives of his design and to customer specs. **Patterns:** Fighters, hunters, utility/camp knives and fillet knives. **Technical:** Flat-grinds ATS-34; offers tapered tangs. **Prices:** $135 to $450; some to $600. **Remarks:** Part-time maker; first knife sold in 1990. **Mark:** First initial, last name, city, state circling double H's.

HELSCHER, JOHN W
2645 Highway 1, Washington, IA 52353, Phone: 319-653-7310

HELTON, ROY
HELTON KNIVES, 2941 Comstock St., San Diego, CA 92111, Phone: 858-277-5024

HEMPERLEY, GLEN
13322 Country Run Rd, Willis, TX 77318, Phone: 936-228-5048, hemperley.com
Specialties: Specializes in hunting knives, does fixed and folding knives.

HENDRICKS, SAMUEL J
2162 Van Buren Rd, Maurertown, VA 22644, Phone: 703-436-3305
Specialties: Integral hunters and skinners of thin design. **Patterns:** Boots, hunters and locking folders. **Technical:** Grinds ATS-34, 440C and D2. Integral liners and bolsters of N-S and 7075 T6 aircraft aluminum. Does leatherwork. **Prices:** $50 to $250; some to $500. **Remarks:** Full-time maker; first knife sold in 1992. **Mark:** First and middle initials, last name, city and state in football-style logo.

HENDRICKSON, E JAY
4204 Ballenger Creek Pike, Frederick, MD 21703, Phone: 301-663-6923, Fax: 301-663-6923, ejayhendrickson@comcast.net
Specialties: Specializes in silver wire inlay. **Patterns:** Bowies, Kukri's, camp, hunters, and fighters. **Technical:** Forges 06, 1084, 5160, 52100, D2, L6 and W2; makes Damascus. Moran-styles on order. **Prices:** $400 to $8,000. **Remarks:** Full-time maker; first knife made in 1972; first knife sold in 1974. **Mark:** Last name, M.S.

HENDRICKSON, SHAWN
2327 Kaetzel Rd, Knoxville, MD 21758, Phone: 301-432-4306
Specialties: Hunting knives. **Patterns:** Clip points, drop points and trailing point hunters. **Technical:** Forges 5160, 1084 and L6. **Prices:** $175 to $400.

HENDRIX, JERRY
HENDRIX CUSTOM KNIVES, 17 Skyland Dr. Ext., Clinton, SC 29325, Phone: 864-833-2659
Specialties: Traditional working straight knives of all designs. **Patterns:** Hunters, utility, boot, bird and fishing. **Technical:** Grinds ATS-34 and 440C. **Prices:** $85 to $275. **Remarks:** Full-time maker. Hand stitched, waxed leather sheaths. **Mark:** Full name in shape of knife.

HENDRIX, WAYNE
9636 Burton's Ferry Hwy, Allendale, SC 29810, Phone: 803-584-3825, Fax: 803-584-3825, whendrixknives@gmail.com Web: www.hendrixknives.com
Specialties: Working/using knives of his design. **Patterns:** Hunters and fillet knives. **Technical:** Grinds ATS-34, D2 and 440C. **Prices:** $100 and up. **Remarks:** Full-time maker; first knife sold in 1985. **Mark:** Last name.

HENNINGSSON, MICHAEL
Klingkarrsvagen 8, 430 83 Vrango (Gothenburg), SWEDEN, Phone: +46 76 626 06 51, michael.henningsson@gmail.com; Web: henningssonknives.com
Specialties: Handmade folding knives, mostly tactical linerlocks and framelocks. **Patterns:** Own design in both engravings and knife models. **Technical:** All kinds of stee; such as Damascus, but prefer clean RWL-43. Tweaking a lot with hand engraving and therefore leaves clean steel mostly. Work a lot with inlays of various materials. **Prices:** Starting at $1200 and up, depending on decoration and engravings. **Remarks:** Part-time maker, first knife sold in 2010. **Mark:** Hand engraved name or a Viking sail with initials in runes

HENSLEY, WAYNE
PO Box 904, Conyers, GA 30012, Phone: 770-483-8938, rebwayhe@bellsouth.net
Specialties: Period pieces and fancy working knives. **Patterns:** Boots to bowies, locking folders to miniatures. Large variety of straight knives. **Technical:** Grinds ATS-34, 440C, D2 and commercial damascus. **Prices:** $175 and up. **Remarks:** Full-time maker; first knife sold in 1974. **Mark:** Hensley USA.

HERBST, GAWIE
PO Box 59158, Karenpark, Akasia, GT, SOUTH AFRICA 0118, Phone: +27 72 060 3687, Fax: +27 12 549 1876, gawie@herbst.co.za Web: www.herbst.co.za
Specialties: Hunters, Utility knives, Art knives and Liner lock folders.

HERBST, PETER
Komotauer Strasse 26, Lauf a.d. Pegn., GERMANY 91207, Phone: 09123-13315, Fax: 09123-13379
Specialties: Working/using knives and folders of his design. **Patterns:** Hunters, fighters and daggers; interframe and integral. **Technical:** Grinds CPM-T-440V, UHB-Elmax, ATS-34 and stainless Damascus. **Prices:** $300 to $3000; some to $8000. **Remarks:** Full-time maker; first knife sold in 1981. **Mark:** First initial, last name.

HERBST, THINUS
PO Box 59158, Karenpark, Akasia, GT, SOUTH AFRICA 0118, Phone: +27 82 254 8016, thinus@herbst.co.za; Web: www.herbst.co.za
Specialties: Plain and fancy working straight knives of own design and liner lock folders. **Patterns:** Hunters, utility knives, art knives, and liner lock folders. **Technical:** Prefer exotic materials for handles. Most knives embellished with file work, carving and scrimshaw. **Prices:** $200 to $2000. **Remarks:** Full-time maker, member of the Knifemakers Guild of South Africa.

HERMAN, TIM

517 E. 126 Terrace, Olathe, KS 66061-2731, Phone: 913-839-1924, HermanKnives@comcast.net

Specialties: Investment-grade folders of his design; interframes and bolster frames. **Patterns:** Interframes and new designs in carved stainless. **Technical:** Grinds ATS-34 and damasteel Damascus. Engraves and gold inlays with pearl, jade, lapis and Australian opal. **Prices:** $1500 to $20,000 and up. **Remarks:** Full-time maker; first knife sold in 1978. Inventor of full-color bulino engraving since 1993. **Mark:** Etched signature.

HERNDON, WM R "BILL"

32520 Michigan St, Acton, CA 93510, Phone: 661-269-5860, bherndons1@roadrunner.com

Specialties: Straight knives, plain and fancy. **Technical:** Carbon steel (white and blued), Damascus, stainless steels. **Prices:** Start at $175. **Remarks:** Full-time maker; first knife sold in 1972. American Bladesmith Society journeyman smith. **Mark:** Signature and/or helm logo.

HERRING, MORRIS

Box 85 721 W Line St, Dyer, AR 72935, Phone: 501-997-8861, morrish@ipa.com

HETHCOAT, DON

Box 1764, Clovis, NM 88101, Phone: 575-762-5721, dhethcoat@plateautel.net; Web: www.donhethcoat.com

Specialties: Liner locks, lock backs and multi-blade folder patterns. **Patterns:** Hunters, Bowies. **Technical:** Grinds stainless; forges Damascus. **Prices:** Moderate to upscale. **Remarks:** Full-time maker; first knife sold in 1969. **Mark:** Last name on all.

HEWITT, RONALD "COTTON"

P.O. Box 326, Adel, GA 31620, Phone: 229-896-6366 or 229-237-4378, gobbler12@msn.com; www.hewittknives.com

Specialties: LinerLock folders and assisted flippers. **Technical:** Grinds CPM 154, CPM S35VN, CPM 3V and 52100 blade steels. Assisted flippers all have thrust bearings. **Prices:** $350 and up. **Remarks:** Full-time maker; first knife sold in 1975. **Mark:** Last name.

HIBBEN, DARYL

PO Box 172, LaGrange, KY 40031-0172, Phone: 502-222-0983, dhibben1@bellsouth.net

Specialties: Working straight knives, some fancy to customer specs. **Patterns:** Hunters, fighters, Bowies, short sword, art and fantasy. **Technical:** Grinds 440C, ATS-34, 154CM, Damascus; prefers hollow-grinds. **Prices:** $275 and up. **Remarks:** Full-time maker; first knife sold in 1979. Retired, part time. **Mark:** Etched full name in script.

HIBBEN, GIL

PO Box 13, LaGrange, KY 40031, Phone: 502-222-1397, Fax: 502-222-2676, gil@hibbenknives.com Web: www.hibbenknives.com

Specialties: Working knives and fantasy pieces to customer specs. **Patterns:** Full range of straight knives, including swords, axes and miniatures; some locking folders. **Technical:** Grinds ATS-34, 440C and D2. **Prices:** $300 to some $10,000. **Remarks:** Full-time maker; first knife sold in 1957. Maker and designer of Rambo III knife; made swords for movie Marked for Death and throwing knife for movie Under Seige; made belt buckle knife and knives for movie Perfect Weapon; made knives featured in movie Star Trek the Next Generation , Star Trek Nemesis. 1990 inductee Cutlery Hall of Fame; designer for United Cutlery. Official klingon armourer for Star Trek. Knives also for movies of the Expendables and the Expendables sequel. Over 37 movies and TV productions. Past president of the Knifemakers' Guild. Celebrating 59 years since first knife sold. **Mark:** Hibben Knives. City and state, or signature.

HIBBEN, WESTLEY G

14101 Sunview Dr, Anchorage, AK 99515

Specialties: Working straight knives of his design or to customer specs. **Patterns:** Hunters, fighters, daggers, combat knives and some fantasy pieces. **Technical:** Grinds 440C mostly. Filework available. **Prices:** $200 to $400; some to $3000. **Remarks:** Part-time maker; first knife sold in 1988. **Mark:** Signature.

HICKS, GARY

341 CR 275, Tuscola, TX 79562, Phone: 325-554-9762

Hielscher, Guy

PO Box 992, 6550 Otoe Rd., Alliance, NE 69301, Phone: 308-762-4318, g-hielsc@bbcwb.net Web: www.ghknives.com

Specialties: Working Damascus fixed blade knives. **Patterns:** Hunters, fighters, capers, skinners, bowie, drop point. **Technical:** Forges own Damascus using 1018 and 0-1 tool steels. **Prices:** $285 and up. **Remarks:** Member of PKA. Part-time maker; sold first knife in 1988. **Mark:** Arrowhead with GH inside.

HIGH, TOM

5474 S 1128 Rd, Alamosa, CO 81101, Phone: 719-589-2108, www.rockymountainscrimshaw.com

Specialties: Hunters, some fancy. **Patterns:** Drop-points in several shapes; some semi-skinners. Knives designed by and for top outfitters and guides. **Technical:** Grinds ATS-34; likes hollow-grinds, mirror finishes; prefers scrimable handles. **Prices:** $300 to $8000.. **Remarks:** Full-time maker; first knife sold in 1965. Limited edition wildlife series knives. **Mark:** Initials connected; arrow through last name.

HILL, RICK

20 Nassau, Maryville, IL 62062-5618, Phone: 618-288-4370

Specialties: Working knives and period pieces to customer specs. **Patterns:** Hunters, locking folders, fighters and daggers. **Technical:** Grinds D2, 440C and 154CM; forges his own Damascus. **Prices:** $75 to $500; some to $3000. **Remarks:** Part-time maker; first knife sold in 1983. **Mark:** Full name in hill shape logo.

HILL, STEVE E

217 Twin Lake Tr., Spring Branch, TX 78070, Phone: 830-624-6258 (cell) or 830-885-6108 (home), kingpirateboy2@juno.com or kingpirateboy2@gvtc.com; Web: www.stevehillknives.com

Specialties: Fancy manual and automatic LinerLock folders, small fixed blades and classic bowie knives. **Patterns:** Classic to cool folding and fixed blade designs. **Technical:** Grinds damascus fabricated in the U.S.A. and occasional high-carbon 1095, etc. Prefers natural handle materials, and offers elaborate filework, carving and inlays. **Prices:** $250 to $6,000, some higher. **Remarks:** Knifemaker to rock stars, Hollywood celebrities and occasional riff raff. Full-time maker; first knife sold in 1978. **Mark:** S. Hill Spring Branch Texas hand inscribed on inside of folder handle, spine or on a fixed blade spine.

HILLMAN, CHARLES

225 Waldoboro Rd, Friendship, ME 04547, Phone: 207-832-4634

Specialties: Working knives of his own or custom design. Heavy Scagel influence. **Patterns:** Hunters, fishing, camp and general utility. Occasional folders. **Technical:** Grinds D2 and 440C. File work, blade and handle carving, engraving. Natural handle materials-antler, bone, leather, wood, horn. Sheaths made to order. **Prices:** $60 to $500. **Remarks:** Part-time maker; first knife sold 1986. **Mark:** Last name in oak leaf.

HINDERER, RICK

5373 Columbus Rd., Shreve, OH 44676, Phone: 330-317-2964, rhind64@earthlink.net; Web: www.rickhindererknives.com

Specialties: Working tactical knives, and some one-of-a kind. **Patterns:** Makes his own. **Technical:** Grinds Duratech 20 CV and CPM S30V. **Prices:** $150 to $4000. **Remarks:** Full-time maker doing business as Rick Hinderer Knives, first knife sold in 1988. **Mark:** R. Hinderer.

HINDMARCH, GARTH

PO Box 135, Carlyle, SK, CANADA S0C 0R0, Phone: 306-453-2568

Specialties: Working and fancy straight knives, bowies. **Patterns:** Hunters, skinners, bowies. **Technical:** Grinds 440C, ATS 34, some damascus. **Prices:** $250 to $1,100. **Remarks:** Part-time maker; first knife sold 1994. All knives satin finished. Does filework, offers engraving, stabilized wood, giraffe bone, some Micarta. **Mark:** First initial, last name, city, province.

HINK III, LES

1599 Aptos Lane, Stockton, CA 95206, Phone: 209-547-1292

Specialties: Working straight knives and traditional folders in standard patterns or to customer specs. **Patterns:** Hunting and utility/camp knives; others on request. **Technical:** Grinds carbon and stainless steels. **Prices:** $80 to $200; some higher. **Remarks:** Part-time maker; first knife sold in 1980. **Mark:** Last name, or last name 3.

HINMAN, THEODORE

186 Petty Plain Road, Greenfield, MA 01301, Phone: 413-773-0448, armenemargosian@verizon.net

Specialties: Tomahawks and axes. Offers classes in bladesmithing and toolmaking.

HINSON AND SON, R

2419 Edgewood Rd, Columbus, GA 31906, Phone: 706-327-6801

Specialties: Working straight knives and folders. **Patterns:** Locking folders, liner locks, combat knives and swords. **Technical:** Grinds 440C and commercial Damascus. **Prices:** $200 to $450; some to $1500. **Remarks:** Part-time maker; first knife sold in 1983. Son Bob is co-worker. **Mark:** HINSON, city and state.

HINTZ, GERALD M

5402 Sahara Ct, Helena, MT 59602, Phone: 406-458-5412

Specialties: Fancy, high-art, working/using knives of his design. **Patterns:** Bowies, hunters, daggers, fish fillet and utility/camp knives. **Technical:** Forges ATS-34, 440C and D2. Animal art in horn handles or in the blade. **Prices:** $75 to $400; some to $1000. **Remarks:** Part-time maker; first knife sold in 1980. Doing business as Big Joe's Custom Knives. Will take custom orders. **Mark:** F.S. or W.S. with first and middle initials and last name.

HIRAYAMA, HARUMI

4-5-13 Kitamachi, Warabi City, Saitama, JAPAN 335-0001, Phone: 048-443-2248, Fax: 048-443-2248, swanbird3@gmail.com; Web: www.ne.jp/asahi/harumi/knives

Specialties: High-tech working knives of her design. **Patterns:** Locking folders, interframes, straight gents and slip-joints. **Technical:** Grinds 440C or equivalent; uses natural handle materials and gold. **Prices:** Start at $2500. **Remarks:** Part-time maker; first knife sold in 1985. **Mark:** First initial, last name.

HIROTO, FUJIHARA

2-34-7 Koioosako, Nishi-ku, Hiroshima, JAPAN, Phone: 082-271-8389, fjhr8363@crest.ocn.ne.jp

HOBART, GENE

100 Shedd Rd, Windsor, NY 13865, Phone: 607-655-1345

HOCKENSMITH, DAN

104 North Country Rd 23, Berthoud, CO 80513, Phone: 970-231-6506, blademan@skybeam.com; Web: www.dhockensmithknives.com

Specialties: Traditional working and using straight knives of his design. **Patterns:** Hunters, Bowies, folders and utility/camp knives. **Technical:** Uses his Damascus, 5160, carbon steel, 52100 steel and 1084 steel. Hand forged. **Prices:** $250 to $1500. **Remarks:** Part-time maker; first knife sold in 1987. **Mark:** Last name or stylized "D" with H inside.

HODGE III, JOHN

422 S 15th St, Palatka, FL 32177, Phone: 904-328-3897

Specialties: Fancy straight knives and folders. **Patterns:** Various. **Technical:** Pattern-

custom knifemakers

welded Damascus—"Southern-style." **Prices:** To $1000. **Remarks:** Part-time maker; first knife sold in 1981. **Mark:** JH3 logo.

HOEL, STEVE
PO Box 283, Pine, AZ 85544-0283, Phone: 928-476-6523

Specialties: Investor-class folders, straight knives and period pieces of his design. **Patterns:** Folding interframes lockers and slip-joints; straight Bowies, boots and daggers. **Technical:** Grinds 154CM, ATS-34 and commercial Damascus. **Prices:** $600 to $1200; some to $7500. **Remarks:** Full-time maker. **Mark:** Initial logo with name and address.

HOFER, LOUIS
BOX 125, Rose Prairie, BC, CANADA V0C 2H0, Phone: 250-827-3999, anvil_needles@hotmail.cq; www.anvilandneedles.com

Specialties: Damascus knives, working knives, fixed blade bowies, daggers. **Patterns:** Hunting, skinning, custom. **Technical:** Wild damascus, random damascus. **Prices:** $450 and up. **Remarks:** Part-time maker since 1995. **Mark:** Logo of initials.

HOFFMAN, JAY
Hoffman Haus + Heraldic Device, 911 W Superior St., Munising, MI 49862, Phone: 906-387-3440, hoffmanhaus1@yahoo.com; Web: www.hoffmanhausknives.com

Technical: Scrimshaw, metal carving, own casting of hilts and pommels, etc. Most if not all leather work for sheaths. **Remarks:** Has been making knives for 50 + years. Professionally since 1991. **Mark:** Early knives marked "Hoffman Haus" and year. Now marks "Hoffman Haus Knives" on the blades. Starting in 2010 uses heraldic device. Will build to your specs. Lag time 1-2 months.

HOFFMAN, JESS
W7089 Curt Black Rd., Shawano, WI 54166, Phone: 715-584-2466, mooseyard@gmail.com; Web: www.jhoffmanknives.com

Specialties: Working fixed blades. **Technical:** Stock removal of carbon, stainless and damascus steels. Handles range from paper Micarta to exotic hardwoods. **Prices:** Start at $75. **Remarks:** Part-time knifemaker. **Mark:** Ancestral lower-case "h" and/or J. Hoffman.

HOFFMAN, KEVIN L
28 Hopeland Dr, Savannah, GA 31419, Phone: 912-920-3579, Fax: 912-920-3579, kevh052475@aol.com; Web: www.KLHoffman.com

Specialties: Distinctive folders and fixed blades. **Patterns:** Titanium frame lock folders. **Technical:** Sculpted guards and fittings cast in sterling silver and 14k gold. Grinds ATS-34, CPM S30V damascus. Makes kydex sheaths for his fixed blade working knives. **Prices:** $400 and up. **Remarks:** Full-time maker since 1981. **Mark:** KLH.

HOFFMAN, LIAM
POB 1584, Newland, NC 28657, Phone: 828-260-4593, liam@hoffmanblacksmithing.com; Web: www.hoffmanblacksmithing.com

Specialties: Handforged one-off knives and axes. **Technical:** Full-tang knives and integral knives out of high-carbon steel or damascus, generally preferring to use wood handles. Also utilitarian-type working axes. **Prices:** $170 to $400 (axes) and $400 to $1,500 (knives). **Remarks:** Full-time 19-year-old maker who made his first knife at 13 years old, a bladesmith by trade. Axes are some of the finest in the world, in comparison with known smiths Autine, John Neeman and Gansfors bruk, working axes with functionality over aesthetics in mind, and quality over quantity. Nearly all knives are one of a kind, preferring to make integral knives. Everything made in the U.S.A. **Mark:** Knife touch mark is a Japanese hammer with "Hoffman" underneath, and the axe touch mark reads NC, LH, USA.

HOGAN, THOMAS R
2802 S. Heritage Ave, Boise, ID 83709, Phone: 208-362-7848

HOGSTROM, ANDERS T
P.O. Box 72, 37011 Backaryd, SWEDEN, Phone: 46 702 674 574, andershogstrom@hotmail.com or info@andershogstrom.com; Web: www.andershogstrom.com

Specialties: Short and long daggers, fighters and swords For select pieces makes wooden display stands. **Patterns:** Daggers, fighters, short knives and swords and an occasional sword. **Technical:** Grinds 1050 High Carbon, Damascus and stainless, forges own Damasus on occasion, fossil ivories. Does clay tempering and uses exotic hardwoods. **Prices:** Start at $850. **Marks:** Last name in maker's own signature.

HOKE, THOMAS M
3103 Smith Ln, LaGrange, KY 40031, Phone: 502-222-0350

Specialties: Working/using knives, straight knives. Own designs and customer specs. **Patterns:** Daggers, Bowies, hunters, fighters, short swords. **Technical:** Grind 440C, Damascus and ATS-34. Filework on all knives. Tooling on sheaths (custom fit on all knives). Any handle material, mostly exotic. **Prices:** $100 to $700; some to $1500. **Remarks:** Full-time maker, first knife sold in 1986. **Mark:** Dragon on banner which says T.M. Hoke.

HOLBROOK, H L
PO Box 483, Sandy Hook, KY 41171, Phone: Cell: 606-794-1497, hhknives@mrtc.com

Specialties: Traditional working using straight knives of his design, to customer specs and in standard patterns. Stabilized wood. **Patterns:** Hunters, mild tacticals and neck knives with kydex sheaths. **Technical:** Grinds CPM154CM, 154CM. Blades have hand-rubbed satin finish. Uses exotic woods, stag, G-10 and Micarta. Hand-sewn sheath with each straight knife. **Prices:** $165 to $485. **Remarks:** Part-time maker; first knife sold in 1983. Doing business as Holbrook Knives. **Mark:** Name, city, state.

HOLDER, D'ALTON
18910 McNeil Rd., Wickenburg, AZ 85390, Phone: 928-684-2025, Fax: 623-878-3964, dholderknives@commspeed.net; Web: dholder.com

Specialties: Deluxe working knives and high-art hunters. **Patterns:** Drop-point hunters, fighters, Bowies. **Technical:** Grinds ATS-34; uses amber and other materials in combination on stick tangs. **Prices:** $400 to $1000; some to $2000. **Remarks:** Full-time maker; first knife sold in 1966. **Mark:** D'HOLDER, city and state.

HOLLOWAY, PAUL
714 Burksdale Rd, Norfolk, VA 23518, Phone: 757-547-6025, houdini969@yahoo.com

Specialties: Working straight knives and folders to customer specs. **Patterns:** Lockers, fighters and boots, push knives, from swords to miniatures. **Technical:** Grinds A2, D2, 154CM, 440C and ATS-34. **Prices:** $210 to $1,200; some to $1,500, higher. **Remarks:** Retired; first knife sold in 1981. USN 28 years, deputy sheriff 16 years. **Mark:** Name and city in logo.

HOOK, BOB
3247 Wyatt Rd, North Pole, AK 99705, Phone: 907-488-8886, grayling@alaska.net; Web: www.alaskaknifeandforge.com

Specialties: Forged carbon steel. Damascus blades. **Patterns:** Pronghorns, bowies, drop point hunters and knives for the kitchen. **Technical:** 5160, 52100, carbon steel and 1084 and 15N20 pattern welded steel blades are hand forged. Heat treated and ground by maker. Handles are natural materials from Alaska. I favor sole authorship of each piece. **Prices:** $300-$1000. **Remarks:** Journeyman smith with ABS. I have attended the Bill Moran School of Bladesmithing. Knife maker since 2000. **Mark:** Hook.

HORN, DES
PO Box 322, Onrusrivier, WC, SOUTH AFRICA 7201, Phone: 27283161795, Fax: +27866280824, deshorn@usa.net

Specialties: Folding knives. **Patterns:** Ball release side lock mechanism and interframe automatics. **Technical:** Prefers working in totally stainless materials. **Prices:** $800 to $7500. **Remarks:** Full-time maker. Enjoys working in gold, titanium, meteorite, pearl and mammoth. **Mark:** Des Horn.

HORN, JESS
2526 Lansdown Rd, Eugene, OR 97404, Phone: 541-463-1510, jandahorn@earthlink.net

Specialties: Investor-class working folders; period pieces; collectibles. **Patterns:** High-tech design and finish in folders; liner locks, traditional slip-joints and featherweight models. **Technical:** Grinds ATS-34, 154CM. **Prices:** Start at $1000. **Remarks:** Full-time maker; first knife sold in 1968. **Mark:** Full name or last name.

HORNE, GRACE
The Old Public Convenience, 469 Fulwood Road, Sheffield, UNITED KINGDOM S10 3QA, gracehorne@hotmail.co.uk Web: www.gracehorn.co.uk

Specialties: Knives of own design, mainly slip-joint folders. **Technical:** Grinds RWL34, Damasteel and own Damascus for blades. Scale materials vary from traditional (coral, wood, precious metals, etc) to unusual (wool, fabric, felt, etc), **Prices:** $500 - $1500**Remarks:** Part-time maker. **Mark:** 'gH' and 'Sheffield'.

HORRIGAN, JOHN
433 C.R. 200 D, Burnet, TX 78611, Phone: 512-756-7545 or 512-636-6562, jhorrigan@yahoo.com Web: www.eliteknives.com

Specialties: High-end custom knives. **Prices:** $450 - $12,500. **Remarks:** Part-time maker. Obtained Mastersmith stamp 2005. First knife made in 1982. **Mark:** Horrigan M.S.

HORTON, SCOT
PO Box 451, Buhl, ID 83316, Phone: 208-543-4222

Specialties: Traditional working stiff knives and folders. **Patterns:** Hunters, skinners, utility, hatchets and show knives. **Technical:** Grinds ATS-34 and D-2 tool steel. **Prices:** $400 to $2500. **Remarks:** First knife sold in 1990. **Mark:** Full name in arch underlined with arrow, city, state.

HOSSOM, JERRY
3585 Schilling Ridge, Duluth, GA 30096, Phone: 770-449-7809, jerry@hossom.com; Web: www.hossom.com

Specialties: Working straight knives of his own design. **Patterns:** Fighters, combat knives, modern Bowies and daggers, modern swords, concealment knives for military and LE uses. **Technical:** Grinds 154CM, S30V, CPM-3V, CPM-154 and stainless Damascus. Uses natural and synthetic handle materials. **Prices:** $350-1500, some higher. **Remarks:** Full-time maker since 1997. First knife sold in 1983. **Mark:** First initial and last name, includes city and state since 2002.

HOSTETLER, LARRY
10626 Pine Needle Dr., Fort Pierce, FL 34945, Phone: 772-465-8352, hossknives@bellsouth.net Web: www.hoss-knives.com

Specialties: EDC working knives and custom collector knives. Utilizing own designs and customer designed creations. Maker uses a wide variety of exotic materials. **Patterns:** Bowies, hunters and folders. **Technical:** Stock removal, grinds ATS-34, carbon and stainless Damascus, embellishes most pieces with file work. **Prices:** $200 - $1500. Some custom orders higher. **Remarks: Motto:** "EDC doesn't have to be ugly." First knife made in 2001, part-time maker, voting member in the Knife Maker's Guild. Doing business as "Hoss Knives." **Mark:** "Hoss" etched into blade with a turn of the century fused bomb in place of the "O" in Hoss.

HOSTETTER, WALLY
P.O. Box 404, San Mateo, FL 32187, Phone: 386-649-0731, shiningmoon_13@yahoo.com; www.shiningmoon13.com

Specialties: Japanese swords and pole arms, and all their mountings from different time periods, other sword styles. **Technical:** Hand forges 1075 on up to 1095 steels, some with vanadium alloys. **Prices:** $1,200 to $6,500. **Remarks:** Full-time maker; first sword was a katana in 1999. **Mark:** Signature on tang in Japanese kanji is Wally San.

HOUSE, CAMERON
2001 Delaney Rd Se, Salem, OR 97306, Phone: 503-585-3286, chouse357@aol.com
Specialties: Working straight knives. **Patterns:** Hunters, Bowies, fighters. **Technical:** Grinds ATS-34, 530V, 154CM. **Remarks:** Part-time maker, first knife sold in 1993. **Prices:** $150 and up. **Mark:** HOUSE.

HOUSE, GARY
2851 Pierce Rd, Ephrata, WA 98823, Phone: 509-754-3272, spindry101@aol.com
Specialties: Bowies, hunters, daggers and some swords. **Patterns:** Unlimited, SW Indian designs, geometric patterns, bowies, hunters and daggers. **Technical:** Mosaic damascus bar stock, forged blades, using 1084, 15N20 and some nickel. Forged company logos and customer designs in mosaic damascus. **Prices:** $500 & up. **Remarks:** Some of the finest and most unique patterns available. ABS master smith. Marks: Initials GTH, G hanging T, H.

HOWARD, DURVYN M.
4220 McLain St S, Hokes Bluff, AL 35903, Phone: 256-504-1853
Specialties: Collectible upscale folders; one-of-a-kind, gentlemen's folders. Unique mechanisms and multiple patents. **Patterns:** Conceptual designs; each unique and different. **Technical:** Uses natural and exotic materials and precious metals. **Prices:** $7,500 to $35,000. **Remarks:** Full-time maker; 52 years experience. **Mark:** Howard.

HOWE, TORI
30020 N Stampede Rd, Athol, ID 83801, Phone: 208-449-1509, wapiti@knifescales.com; Web:www.knifescales.com
Specialties: Custom knives, knife scales & Damascus blades. **Remarks:** Carry James Luman polymer clay knife scales.

HOWELL, JASON G
1112 Sycamore, Lake Jackson, TX 77566, Phone: 979-297-9454, tinyknives@yahoo.com; Web:www.howellbladesmith.com
Specialties: Fixed blades and LinerLock® folders. Makes own Damascus. **Patterns:** Clip and drop point. **Prices:** $150 to $750. **Remarks:** Likes making Mosaic Damascus out of the ordinary stuff. Member of TX Knifemakers and Collectors Association; apprentice in ABS; working towards Journeyman Stamp. **Mark:** Name, city, state.

HOWELL, KEITH A.
67 Hidden Oaks Dr., Oxford, AL 36203, Phone: 256-283-3269, keith@howellcutlery.com; Web: www.howellcutlery.com
Specialties: Working straight knives and folders of his design or to customer specs. **Patterns:** Hunters, utility pieces, neck knives, everyday carry knives and friction folders. **Technical:** Grinds damascus, 1095 and 154CM. **Prices:** $100 to $250. **Remarks:** Part-time maker; first knife sold in 2007. **Mark:** Last name.

HOWELL, LEN
550 Lee Rd 169, Opelika, AL 36804, Phone: 334-749-1942
Specialties: Traditional and working knives of his design and to customer specs. **Patterns:** Buckskinner, hunters and utility/camp knives. **Technical:** Forges cable Damascus, 1085 and 5160; makes own Damascus. **Mark:** Engraved last name.

HOWELL, TED
1294 Wilson Rd, Wetumpka, AL 36092, Phone: 205-569-2281, Fax: 205-569-1764
Specialties: Working/using straight knives and folders of his design; period pieces. **Patterns:** Bowies, fighters, hunters. **Technical:** Forges 5160, 1085 and cable. Offers light engraving and scrimshaw; filework. **Prices:** $75 to $250; some to $450. **Remarks:** Part-time maker; first knife sold in 1991. Doing business as Howell Co. **Mark:** Last name, Slapout AL.

HOY, KEN
54744 Pinchot Dr, North Fork, CA 93643, Phone: 209-877-7805

HRISOULAS, JIM
SALAMANDER ARMOURY, 284-C Lake Mead Pkwy #157, Henderson, NV 89105, Phone: 702-566-8551, www.atar.com
Specialties: Working straight knives; period pieces. **Patterns:** Swords, daggers and sgian dubhs. **Technical:** Double-edged differential heat treating. **Prices:** $85 to $175; some to $600 and higher. **Remarks:** Full-time maker; first knife sold in 1973. Author of The Complete Bladesmith, The Pattern Welded Blade and The Master Bladesmith. Doing business as Salamander Armory. **Mark:** 8R logo and sword and salamander.

HUCKABEE, DALE
254 Hwy 260, Maylene, AL 35114, Phone: 205-664-2544, huckabeeknives@hotmail.com; Web: http://dalehuckabeeknives.weebly.com
Specialties: Fixed-blade knives and tomahawks of his design. **Technical:** Steel used: 5160, 1084, and Damascus. **Prices:** $225 and up, depending on materials used. **Remarks:** Hand forged. Journeyman Smith. Part-time maker. **Mark:** Stamped Huckabee J.S.

HUCKS, JERRY
KNIVES BY HUCKS, 1807 Perch Road, Moncks Corner, SC 29461, Phone: 843-761-6481, Fax: Cell: 843-708-1649, knivesbyhucks@gmail.com
Specialties: Drop points, bowies and oyster knives. **Patterns:** To customer specs or maker's own design. **Technical:** CPM-154, ATS-34, 5160, 15N20, D2 and 1095 mostly for damascus billets. **Prices:** $200 and up. **Remarks:** Full-time maker, retired as a machinist in 1990. Makes sheaths sewn by hand with some carving. Will custom make to order or by sketch. Will also make a miniature bowie on request. Thirty years making knives. **Mark:** Robin Hood hat with Moncks Corner under.

HUDSON, C ROBBIN
116 Hansonville Rd., Rochester, NH 03839, Phone: 603-786-9944, bladesmith8@gmail.com
Specialties: High-art working knives. **Patterns:** Hunters, Bowies, fighters and kitchen knives. **Technical:** Forges W2, nickel steel, pure nickel steel, composite and mosaic Damascus; makes knives one-at-a-time. **Prices:** 500 to $1200; some to $5000. **Remarks:** Full-time maker; first knife sold in 1970. **Mark:** Last name and MS.

HUDSON, ROBERT
3802 Black Cricket Ct, Humble, TX 77396, Phone: 713-454-7207
Specialties: Working straight knives of his design. **Patterns:** Bowies, hunters, skinners, fighters and utility knives. **Technical:** Grinds D2, 440C, 154CM and commercial Damascus. **Prices:** $85 to $350; some to $1500. **Remarks:** Part-time maker; first knife sold in 1980. **Mark:** Full name, handmade, city and state.

HUGHES, DAN
301 Grandview Bluff Rd, Spencer, TN 38585, Phone: 931-946-3044
Specialties: Working straight knives to customer specs. **Patterns:** Hunters, fighters, fillet knives. **Technical:** Grinds 440C and ATS-34. **Prices:** $55 to $175; some to $300. **Remarks:** Part-time maker; first knife sold in 1984. **Mark:** Initials.

HUGHES, DARYLE
10979 Leonard, Nunica, MI 49448, Phone: 616-837-6623, hughes.builders@verizon.net
Specialties: Working knives. **Patterns:** Buckskinners, hunters, camp knives, kitchen and fishing knives. **Technical:** Forges and grinds 52100 and Damascus. **Prices:** $125 to $1000. **Remarks:** Part-time maker; first knife sold in 1979. **Mark:** Name and city in logo.

HUGHES, ED
280 1/2 Holly Lane, Grand Junction, CO 81503, Phone: 970-243-8547, edhughes26@msn.com
Specialties: Working and art folders. **Patterns:** Buys Damascus. **Technical:** Grinds stainless steels. Engraves. **Prices:** $300 and up. **Remarks:** Full-time maker; first knife sold in 1978. **Mark:** Name or initials.

HUGHES, LAWRENCE
207 W Crestway, Plainview, TX 79072, Phone: 806-293-5406
Specialties: Working and display knives. **Patterns:** Bowies, daggers, hunters, buckskinners. **Technical:** Grinds D2, 440C and 154CM. **Prices:** $125 to $300; some to $2000. **Remarks:** Full-time maker; first knife sold in 1979. **Mark:** Name with buffalo skull in center.

HUGHES, TONY
Tony Hughes Forged Blades, 7536 Trail North Dr., Littleton, CO 80125, Phone: 303-941-1092, tonhug@msn.com
Specialties: Fixed blades, bowies/fighters and hunters of maker's own damascus steel. **Technical:** Forges damascus and mosaic-damascus blades. Fittings are 416 stainless steel, 1095-and-nickel damascus, 1080-and-15N20 damascus or silicon bronze. Prefers ivory, desert ironwood, blackwood, ebony and other burls. **Prices:** $450 and up. **Remarks:** Full-time ABS journeyman smith forging knives for 20 years. **Mark:** Tony Hughes and JS on the other side.

HULETT, STEVE
115 Yellowstone Ave, West Yellowstone, MT 59758-0131, Phone: 406-646-4116, blade1231@msn.com; Web: www.seldomseenknives.com
Specialties: Classic, working/using knives, straight knives, folders. Your design, custom specs. **Patterns:** Utility/camp knives, hunters, and LinerLock folders, lock back pocket knives. **Technical:** Grinds 440C stainless steel, 01 Carbon, 1095. Shop is retail and knife shop; people watch their knives being made. We do everything in house: "all but smelt the ore, or tan the hide." **Prices:** Strarting $250 to $7000. **Remarks:** Full-time maker; first knife sold in 1994. **Mark:** Seldom seen knives/West Yellowstone Montana.

HULSEY, HOYT
379 Shiloh, Attalla, AL 35954, Phone: 256-538-6765
Specialties: Traditional working straight knives and folders of his design. **Patterns:** Hunters and utility/camp knives. **Technical:** Grinds 440C, ATS-34, O1 and A2. **Prices:** $75 to $250. **Remarks:** Part-time maker; first knife sold in 1989. **Mark:** Hoyt Hulsey Attalla AL.

HUMENICK, ROY
PO Box 55, Rescue, CA 95672, rhknives@gmail.com; Web: www.humenick.com
Specialties: Traditional multiblades and tactical slipjoints. **Patterns:** Original folder and fixed blade designs, also traditional patterns. **Technical:** Grinds premium steels and Damascus. **Prices:** $350 and up; some to $1500. **Remarks:** First knife sold in 1984. **Mark:** Last name in ARC.

HUMPHREY, LON
4 Western Ave., Newark, OH 43055, Phone: 740-644-1137, lonhumphrey@gmail.com
Specialties: Hunters, tacticals, and bowie knives. **Prices:** I make knives that start in the $150 range and go up to $1000 for a large bowie. **Remarks:** Has been blacksmithing since age 13 and progressed to the forged blade.

HUMPHREYS, JOEL
90 Boots Rd, Lake Placid, FL 33852, Phone: 863-773-0439
Specialties: Traditional working/using straight knives and folders of his design and in standard patterns. **Patterns:** Hunters, folders and utility/camp knives. **Technical:** Grinds ATS-34, D2, 440C. All knives have tapered tangs, mitered bolster/handle joints, handles of horn or bone fitted sheaths. **Prices:** $135 to $225; some to $350. **Remarks:** Part-time maker; first knife sold in 1990. Doing business as Sovereign Knives. **Mark:** First name or "H" pierced by arrow.

HUNT, RAYMON E.
3H's KNIVES, LLC, 600 Milam Ct., Irving, TX 75038, Phone: 214-507-0896, Fax: 972-887-9931, Web: www.3hsknives.com

Specialties: Forged and stock removal for both using and collector-grade knives. **Patterns:** Kitchen cutlery, bowies, daggers, hunters, tactical, utility, slip joints and straight razors. **Technical:** Steels include 5160, 1075, 1084, 1095, O1, CPM 154, CTS XHP and damascus. Heat treating in-house using oven and torch edge hardening. Uses his own damascus of 1095 and 15N20 and purchases damascus. Engraving and gold inlay by Steve Dunn, filework, peined and polished pins of sterling silver and gold, fire and niter bluing. **Remarks:** American Bladesmith Society, apprentice. **Mark:** 3Hs on left side of blade near the grind line.

HUNTER, HYRUM
285 N 300 W, PO Box 179, Aurora, UT 84620, Phone: 435-529-7244
Specialties: Working straight knives of his design or to customer specs. **Patterns:** Drop and clip, fighters dagger, some folders. **Technical:** Forged from two-piece Damascus. **Prices:** Prices are adjusted according to size, complexity and material used. **Remarks:** Will consider any design you have. Part-time maker; first knife sold in 1990. **Mark:** Initials encircled with first initial and last name and city, then state. Some patterns are numbered.

HUNTER, RICHARD D
7230 NW 200th Ter, Alachua, FL 32615, Phone: 386-462-3150
Specialties: Traditional working/using knives of his design or customer suggestions; filework. **Patterns:** Folders of various types, Bowies, hunters, daggers. **Technical:** Traditional blacksmith; hand forges high-carbon steel (5160, 1084, 52100) and makes own Damascus; grinds 440C and ATS-34. **Prices:** $200 and up. **Remarks:** Part-time maker; first knife sold in 1992. **Mark:** Last name in capital letters.

HURST, JEFF
PO Box 247, Rutledge, TN 37861, Phone: 865-828-5729, jhurst@esper.com
Specialties: Working straight knives and folders of his design. **Patterns:** Tomahawks, hunters, boots, folders and fighters. **Technical:** Forges W2, O1 and his own Damascus. Makes mokume. **Prices:** $250 to $600. **Remarks:** Full-time maker; first knife sold in 1984. Doing business as Buzzard's Knob Forge. **Mark:** Last name; partnered knives are marked with Newman L. Smith, handle artisan, and SH in script.

HUSE, JAMES D. II
P.O. Box 1753, Buda, TX 78610, Phone: 512-296-9888, huseknives@gmail.com; Web: www.huseknives.com
Specialties: Texas-legal carry knives, hunters and utility knives, and large camp knives and bowies on request. **Patterns:** Clip points, drop points, Puma-style trailing points and fighter styles. **Technical:** Makes most knives using the stock-removal method of blade making with A2 tool steel, hardening and tempering it to 60-61 HRC on the Rockwell Hardness Scale. Does forge some knives, and when forging, uses 1084, 52100, 1095 and 15N20 damascus, as well as CruForge V. **Prices:** $150 to $700. **Remarks:** Part-time maker; first knife made in 2001. Member of Texas Knifemakers' Guild (secretary) and American Bladesmith Society (apprentice).

HUSIAK, MYRON
PO Box 238, Altona, VIC, AUSTRALIA 3018, Phone: 03-315-6752
Specialties: Straight knives and folders of his design or to customer specs. **Patterns:** Hunters, fighters, lock-back folders, skinners and boots. **Technical:** Forges and grinds his own Damascus, 440C and ATS-34. **Prices:** $200 to $900. **Remarks:** Part-time maker; first knife sold in 1974. **Mark:** First initial, last name in logo and serial number.

HUTCHESON, JOHN
SURSUM KNIFE WORKS, 1237 Brown's Ferry Rd., Chattanooga, TN 37419, Phone: 423-667-6193, sursum5071@aol.com; Web: www.sursumknife.com
Specialties: Straight working knives, hunters. **Patterns:** Customer designs, hunting, speciality working knives. **Technical:** Grinds D2, S7, O1 and 5160, ATS-34 on request. **Prices:** $100 to $300, some to $600. **Remarks:** First knife sold 1985, also produces a mid-tech line. Doing business as Sursum Knife Works. **Mark:** Family crest boar's head over 3 arrows.

HUTCHINSON, ALAN
315 Scenic Hill Road, Conway, AR 72034, Phone: 501-470-9653, hutchinsonblades@yahoo.com
Specialties: Hunters, bowies, fighters, combat/survival knives. **Patterns:** Traditional edged weapons and tomahawks, custom patterns. **Technical:** Forges 10 series, 5160, L6, O1, CruForge V, damascus and his own patterns. **Prices:** $250 and up. **Remarks:** Prefers natural handle materials, part-time maker. **Mark:** Last name.

HYTOVICK, JOE "HY"
14872 SW 111th St, Dunnellon, FL 34432, Phone: 800-749-5339, Fax: 352-489-3732, hyclassknives@aol.com
Specialties: Straight, folder and miniature. **Technical:** Blades from Wootz, Damascus and Alloy steel. **Prices:** To $5000. **Mark:** HY.

I

IKOMA, FLAVIO
R Manoel Rainho Teixeira 108, Presidente Prudente, SP, BRAZIL 19031-220, Phone: 0182-22-0115, fikoma@itelesonica.com.br
Specialties: Tactical fixed blade knives, LinerLock® folders and balisongs. **Patterns:** Utility and defense tactical knives built with hi-tech materials. **Technical:** Grinds S30V and Damasteel. **Prices:** $500 to $1000. **Mark:** Ikoma hand made beside Samurai

IMBODEN II, HOWARD L.
620 Deauville Dr, Dayton, OH 45429, Phone: 513-439-1536
Specialties: One-of-a-kind hunting, flint, steel and art knives. **Technical:** Forges and grinds stainless, high-carbon and Damascus. Uses obsidian, cast sterling silver, 14K and 18K gold guards. Carves ivory animals and more. **Prices:** $65 to $25,000. **Remarks:** Full-time maker; first knife sold in 1986. Doing business as Hill Originals. **Mark:** First and last initials, II.

IMEL, BILLY MACE
1616 Bundy Ave, New Castle, IN 47362, Phone: 765-529-1651
Specialties: High-art working knives, period pieces and personal cutlery. **Patterns:** Daggers, fighters, hunters; locking folders and slip-joints with interframes. **Technical:** Grinds D2, 440C and 154CM. **Prices:** $300 to $2000; some to $6000. **Remarks:** Part-time maker; first knife sold in 1973. **Mark:** Name in monogram.

IOANNIS-MINAS, FILIPPOU
5, Krinis Str, Nea Smyrni, Athens, GREECE 171 22, Phone: (1) 210-9352093, kamami53@yahoo.gr

IRIE, MICHAEL L
MIKE IRIE HANDCRAFT, 1606 Auburn Dr., Colorado Springs, CO 80909, Phone: 719-572-5330, mikeirie@aol.com
Specialties: Working fixed blade knives and handcrafted blades for the do-it-yourselfer. **Patterns:** Twenty standard designs along with custom. **Technical:** Blades are ATS-34, BG-43, 440C with some outside Damascus. **Prices:** Fixed blades $95 and up, blade work $45 and up. **Remarks:** Formerly dba Wood, Irie and Co. with Barry Wood. Full-time maker since 1991. **Mark:** Name.

ISAO, OHBUCHI
702-1 Nouso, Yame-City, Fukuoka, JAPAN, Phone: 0943-23-4439, www.5d.biglobe. ne.jp/~ohisao/

ISHIHARA, HANK
86-18 Motomachi, Sakura City, Chiba, JAPAN, Phone: 043-485-3208, Fax: 043-485-3208
Specialties: Fantasy working straight knives and folders of his design. **Patterns:** Boots, Bowies, daggers, fighters, hunters, fishing, locking folders and utility camp knives. **Technical:** Grinds ATS-34, 440C, D2, 440V, CV-134, COS25 and Damascus. Engraves. **Prices:** $250 to $1000; some to $10,000. **Remarks:** Full-time maker; first knife sold in 1987. **Mark:** HANK.

J

JACKS, JIM
344 S. Hollenbeck Ave, Covina, CA 91723-2513, Phone: 626-331-5665
Specialties: Working straight knives in standard patterns. **Patterns:** Bowies, hunters, fighters, fishing and camp knives, miniatures. **Technical:** Grinds Stellite 6K, 440C and ATS-34. **Prices:** Start at $100. **Remarks:** Spare-time maker; first knife sold in 1980. **Mark:** Initials in diamond logo.

JACKSON, CHARLTON R
6811 Leyland Dr, San Antonio, TX 78239, Phone: 210-601-5112

JACKSON, DAVID
214 Oleander Ave, Lemoore, CA 93245, Phone: 559-925-8247, jnbcrea@lemoorenet. com
Specialties: Forged steel. **Patterns:** Hunters, camp knives and bowies. **Prices:** $300 and up. **Mark:** G.D. Jackson - Maker - Lemoore CA.

JACKSON, LARAMIE
POB 442, Claysprings, AZ 85923, Phone: 480-747-3804, ljacksonknives@yahoo.com
Specialties: Traditional hunting and working knives and folders, chef's knives. **Patterns:** Bowies, fighters, hunters, daggers and skinners. **Technical:** Grinds 440C, CPM D2, CPM S30V, W2, O1, 52100, 5160, L6, 1095, damascus and whatever customer wants. Offers sheaths. **Prices:** $100-$450+. **Remarks:** Full-time maker; first knife sold in 2010. **Mark:** First initial and last name.

JACQUES, ALEX
332 Williams St., Warwick, RI 02906, Phone: 617-771-4441, customrazors@gmail. com Web: www.customrazors.com
Specialties: One-of-a-kind, heirloom quality straight razors … functional art. **Technical:** Damascus, O1, CPM154, and various other high-carbon and stainless steels. **Prices:** $450 and up. **Remarks:** First knife sold in 2008. **Mark:** Jack-O-Lantern logo with "A. Jacques" underneath.

JAKSIK JR., MICHAEL
427 Marschall Creek Rd, Fredericksburg, TX 78624, Phone: 830-997-1119
Mark: MJ or M. Jaksik.

JANGTANONG, SUCHAT
10901 W. Cave Blvd., Dripping Springs, TX 78620, Phone: 512-264-1501, shakeallpoints@yahoo.com; Web: www.mrdamascusknives.com
Specialties: One-of-a-kind handmade art knives, carving pearl and titanium. **Patterns:** Folders (lock back and LinerLock), some fixed blades and butterfly knives. **Technical:** Grinds ATS-34 and damascus steels. **Prices:** $500 to $3,000. **Remarks:** Third-generation, began making knives in 1982; full-time maker who lives in Uthai Thani Province of Thailand. **Mark:** Name (Suchat) on blade.

JANSEN VAN VUUREN, LUDWIG
311 Brighton Rd., Waldronville 9018, Dunedin, NEW ZEALAND, Phone: 64-3-7421012, ludwig@nzhandmadeknives.co.nz; Web: www.nzhandmadeknives.co.nz
Specialties: Fixed-blade knives of his design or custom specifications. **Patterns:** Hunting, fishing, bird-and-trout and chef's knives. **Technical:** Stock-removal maker, Elmax, Sandvik 12C27 and other blade steels on request. Handle material includes

Micarta, antler and a wide selection of woods. **Prices:** Starting at $250. **Remarks:** Part-time maker since 2008. **Mark:** L J van Vuuren.

JARVIS, PAUL M
30 Chalk St, Cambridge, MA 02139, Phone: 617-547-4355 or 617-661-3015
Specialties: High-art knives and period pieces of his design. **Patterns:** Japanese and Mid-Eastern knives. **Technical:** Grinds Myer Damascus, ATS-34, D2 and O1. Specializes in height-relief Japanese-style carving. Works with silver, gold and gems. **Prices:** $200 to $17,000. **Remarks:** Part-time maker; first knife sold in 1978.

JEAN, GERRY
25B Cliffside Dr, Manchester, CT 06040, Phone: 860-649-6449
Specialties: Historic replicas. **Patterns:** Survival and camp knives. **Technical:** Grinds A2, 440C and 154CM. Handle slabs applied in unique tongue-and-groove method. **Prices:** $125 to $250; some to $1000. **Remarks:** Spare-time maker; first knife sold in 1973. **Mark:** Initials and serial number.

JEFFRIES, MIKE
1015 Highland Ave., Louisville, KY 40204, Phone: 502-592-4240, 2birdsmetalworks@gmail.com; Facebook.com/2BirdsMetalWorks, Instagram @2BirdsMetalworks
Specialties: Handmade custom knives, mostly drop-point and wharncliffe-style blades. **Patterns:** Outdoor, camping, hiking, hunting and bushcraft knives. **Technical:** Stock removal of high-carbon and tool steels, as well as damascus. Prefers stabilized wood and synthetic handles, the latter including G-10, carbon fiber and Thunderstorm Kevlar. **Prices:** $150 to $800. **Remarks:** Three years making knives, two years full time. **Mark:** MJK.

JEFFRIES, ROBERT W
Route 2 Box 227, Red House, WV 25168, Phone: 304-586-9780, wvknifeman@hotmail.com; Web: www.jeffriesknieswv.tripod.com
Specialties: Hunters, Bowies, daggers, lockback folders and LinerLock push buttons. **Patterns:** Skinning types, drop points, typical working hunters, folders one-of-a-kind. **Technical:** Grinds all types of steel. Makes his own Damascus. **Prices:** $125 to $600. Private collector pieces to $3000. **Remarks:** Starting engraving. Custom folders of his design. Part-time maker since 1988. **Mark:** Name etched or on plate pinned to blade.

JENKINS, MITCH
194 East 500 South, Manti, Utah 84642, Phone: 435-813-2532, mitch.jenkins@gmail.com Web: MitchJenkinsKnives.com
Specialties: Hunters, working knives. **Patterns:** Johnson and Loveless Style. Drop points, skinners and semi-skinners, Capers and utilities. **Technical:** 154CM and ATS-34. Experimenting with S30V and love working with Damascus on occasion. **Prices:** $150 and up. **Remarks:** Slowly transitioning to full-time maker; first knife made in 2008. **Mark:** Jenkins Manti, Utah and M. Jenkins, Utah.

JENSEN, ELI
525 Shalimar Dr., Prescott, AZ 86303, Phone: 928-606-0373, ej89@nau.edu
Specialties: Fixed blades, mostly small and mid-size drop-points. **Technical:** Stock-removal method of blade making, preferring interesting natural materials, including burls, roots and uncommon species. **Prices:** $400 and up. **Remarks:** Part-time maker; first knife made in 2010. **Mark:** First and last name in cursive.

JENSEN, JOHN LEWIS
JENSEN KNIVES, 146 W. Bellevue Dr. #7, Pasadena, CA 91105, Phone: 626-773-0296, john@jensenknives.com; Web: www.jensenknives.com
Specialties: Designer and fabricator of modern, original one-of-a-kind, hand crafted, custom ornamental edged weaponry. Combines skill, precision, distinction and the finest materials, geared toward the discriminating art collector. **Patterns:** Folding knives and fixed blades, daggers, fighters and swords. **Technical:** High embellishment, BFA 96 Rhode Island School of Design: jewelry and metalsmithing. Grinds carbon and stainless, and carbon/stainless damascus. Works with custom made Damascus to his specs. Uses gold, silver, gemstones, pearl, titanium, fossil mastodon and walrus ivories. Carving, file work, soldering, deep etches Damascus, engraving, layers, bevels, blood grooves. Also forges his own Damascus. **Prices:** Start at $10,000. **Remarks:** Available on a first come basis and via commission based on his designs. **Mark:** Maltese cross/butterfly shield.

JERNIGAN, STEVE
3082 Tunnel Rd., Milton, FL 32571, Phone: 850-994-0802, Fax: 850-994-0802, jerniganknives@att.net
Specialties: Investor-class folders and various theme pieces. **Patterns:** Array of models and sizes in side plate locking interframes and conventional liner construction, including tactical and automatics. **Technical:** Grinds ATS-34, CPM-T-440V and damascus. Inlays mokume (and minerals) in blades and sculpts marble cases. **Prices:** $650 to $1,800; some to $6,000. **Remarks:** Full-time maker, first knife sold in 1982. **Mark:** Last name.

JOBIN, JACQUES
46 St Dominique, Levis, QC, CANADA G6V 2M7, Phone: 418-833-0283, Fax: 418-833-8378
Specialties: Fancy and working straight knives and folders; miniatures. **Patterns:** Minis, fantasy knives, fighters and some hunters. **Technical:** ATS-34, some Damascus and titanium. Likes native snake wood. Heat-treats. **Prices:** Start at $250. **Remarks:** Full-time maker; first knife sold in 1986. **Mark:** Signature on blade.

JOEHNK, BERND
Posadowskystrasse 22, Kiel, GERMANY 24148, Phone: 0431-7297705, Fax: 0431-7297705
Specialties: One-of-a-kind fancy/embellished and traditional straight knives of his design and from customer drawing. **Patterns:** Daggers, fighters, hunters and letter openers.

Technical: Grinds and file 440C, ATS-34, powder metal orgical, commercial Damascus and various stainless and corrosion-resistant steels. **Prices:** Upscale. **Remarks:** Likes filework. Leather sheaths. Offers engraving. Part-time maker; first knife sold in1990. Doing business as metal design kiel. All knives made by hand. **Mark:** From 2005 full name and city, with certificate.

JOHANNING CUSTOM KNIVES, TOM
1735 Apex Rd, Sarasota, FL 34240 9386, Phone: 941-371-2104, Fax: 941-378-9427, Web: www.survivalknives.com
Specialties: Survival knives. **Prices:** $375 to $775.

JOHANSSON, ANDERS
Konstvartarevagen 9, Grangesberg, SWEDEN 77240, Phone: 46 240 23204, Fax: +46 21 358778, www.scrimart.u.se
Specialties: Scandinavian traditional and modern straight knives. **Patterns:** Hunters, fighters and fantasy knives. **Technical:** Grinds stainless steel and makes own Damascus. Prefers water buffalo and mammoth for handle material. **Prices:** Start at $100. **Remarks:** Spare-time maker; first knife sold in 1994. Works together with scrimshander Viveca Sahlin. **Mark:** Stylized initials.

JOHNSON, C E GENE
1240 Coan Street, Chesterton, IN 46304, Phone: 219-787-8324, ddjlady55@aol.com
Specialties: Lock-back folders and springers of his design or to customer specs. **Patterns:** Hunters, Bowies, survival lock-back folders. **Technical:** Grinds D2, 440C, A18, O1, Damascus; likes filework. **Prices:** $100 to $2000. **Remarks:** Full-time maker; first knife sold in 1975. **Mark:** Gene.

JOHNSON, DAVID A
1791 Defeated Creek Rd, Pleasant Shade, TN 37145, Phone: 615-774-3596, artsmith@mwsi.net

JOHNSON, GORDON A.
981 New Hope Rd, Choudrant, LA 71227, Phone: 318-768-2613
Specialties: Using straight knives and folders of my design, or customers. Offering filework and hand stitched sheaths. **Patterns:** Hunters, bowies, folders and miniatures. **Technical:** Forges 5160, 1084, 52100 and my own Damascus. Some stock removal on working knives and miniatures. **Prices:** Mid range. **Remarks:** First knife sold in 1990. ABS apprentice smith. **Mark:** Interlocking initials G.J. or G. A. J.

JOHNSON, JERRY
PO Box 491, Spring City, Utah 84662, Phone: 435-851-3604 or 435-462-3688, Web: sanpetesilver.com
Specialties: Hunter, fighters, camp. **Patterns:** Multiple. **Prices:** $225 - $3000. **Mark:** Jerry E. Johnson Spring City, UT in several fonts.

JOHNSON, JERRY L
29847 260th St, Worthington, MN 56187, Phone: 507-376-9253; Cell: 507-370-3523, doctorj55@yahoo.com
Specialties: Straight knives, hunters, bowies, and fighting knives. **Patterns:** Drop points, trailing points, bowies, and some favorite Loveless patterns. **Technical:** Grinds ATS 34, 440C, S30V, forges own damascus, mirror finish, satin finish, file work and engraving done by self. **Prices:** $250 to $1500. **Remarks:** Part-time maker since 1991, member of knifemakers guild since 2009. **Mark:** Name over a sheep head or elk head with custom knives under the head.

JOHNSON, JOHN R
PO Box 246, New Buffalo, PA 17069, Phone: 717-834-6265, jrj@jrjknives.com; Web: www.jrjknives.com
Specialties: Working hunting and tactical fixed blade sheath knives. **Patterns:** Hunters, tacticals, Bowies, daggers, neck knives and primitives. **Technical:** Flat, convex and hollow grinds. ATS-34, CPM154CM, L6, O1, D2, 5160, 1095 and Damascus. **Prices:** $60 to $700. **Remarks:** Full-time maker, first knife sold in 1996. Doing business as JRJ Knives. Custom sheath made by maker for every knife, **Mark:** Initials connected.

JOHNSON, JOHN R
5535 Bob Smith Ave, Plant City, FL 33565, Phone: 813-986-4478, rottyjohn@msn.com
Specialties: Hand forged and stock removal. **Technical:** High tech. Folders. **Mark:** J.R. Johnson Plant City, FL.

JOHNSON, KEITH R.
9179 Beltrami Line Rd. SW, Bemidji, MN 56601, Phone: 218-368-7482, keith@greatriverforge.com; www.greatriverforge.com
Specialties: Slip-joint and lockback folders. **Patterns:** Mostly traditional patterns but with customer preferences, some of maker's own patterns. **Technical:** Mainly uses CTS XHP, sometimes other high-quality stainless steels, Damasteel. Variety of handle materials, including bone, mammoth ivory, Micarta, G-10 and carbon fiber. **Remarks:** Full-time maker; first knife sold in 1986. **Mark:** K.R. JOHNSON (arched) over BEMIDJI.

JOHNSON, MIKE
38200 Main Rd, Orient, NY 11957, Phone: 631-323-3509, mjohnsoncustomknives@hotmail.com
Specialties: Large Bowie knives and cutters, fighters and working knives to customer specs. **Technical:** Forges 5160, O1. **Prices:** $325 to $1200. **Remarks:** Full-time bladesmith. **Mark:** Johnson.

JOHNSON, R B
Box 11, Clearwater, MN 55320, Phone: 320-558-6128, Fax: 320-558-6128, rb@rbjohnsonknives.com; Web: rbjohnsonknives.com
Specialties: Liner locks with titanium, mosaic Damascus. **Patterns:** LinerLock® folders,

custom knifemakers

skeleton hunters, frontier Bowies. **Technical:** Damascus, mosaic Damascus, A-2, O1, 1095. **Prices:** $200 and up. **Remarks:** Full-time maker since 1973. Not accepting orders. **Mark:** R B Johnson (signature).

JOHNSON, RANDY
2575 E Canal Dr, Turlock, CA 95380, Phone: 209-632-5401
Specialties: Folders. **Patterns:** Locking folders. **Technical:** Grinds Damascus. **Prices:** $200 to $400. **Remarks:** Spare-time maker; first knife sold in 1989. Doing business as Puedo Knifeworks. **Mark:** PUEDO.

JOHNSON, RICHARD
W165 N10196 Wagon Trail, Germantown, WI 53022, Phone: 262-251-5772, rlj@execpc.com; Web: http://www.execpc.com/~rlj/index.html
Specialties: Custom knives and knife repair.

JOHNSON, RYAN M
3103 Excelsior Ave., Signal Mountain, TN 37377, Phone: 866-779-6922, contact@rmjtactical.com; Web: www.rmjforge.com www.rmjtactical.com
Specialties: Historical and Tactical Tomahawks. Some period knives and folders. **Technical:** Forges a variety of steels including own Damascus. **Prices:** $500 - $1200 **Remarks:** Full-time maker began forging in 1986. **Mark:** Sledge-hammer with halo.

JOHNSON, STEVEN R
202 E 200 N, PO Box 5, Manti, UT 84642, Phone: 435-835-7941, srj@mail.manti.com; Web: www.srjknives.com
Specialties: Investor-class working knives. **Patterns:** Hunters, fighters, boots. **Technical:** Grinds CPM-154CM and CTS-XHP. **Prices:** $1,500 to $20,000. Engraved knives up to $50,000. **Remarks:** Full-time maker; first knife sold in 1972. Also see SR Johnson forum on www.knifenetwork.com. **Mark:** Registered trademark, including name, city, state, and optional signature mark.

JOHNSON, TIMOTHY A.
Worcester, MA, tim@blackstoneknife.com
Specialties: Custom kitchen knives. **Technical:** Stock removal of stainless, high carbon, san mai and damascus blade steels. **Prices:** $250 to $800. **Remarks:** Part-time maker, first knife made around 1994. **Mark:** Stylized initials TAJ.

JOHNSON, TOMMY
144 Poole Rd., Troy, NC 27371, Phone: 910-975-1817, tommy@tjohnsonknives.com Web: www.tjohnsonknives.com
Specialties: Straight knives for hunting, fishing, utility, and linerlock and slip joint folders since 1982.

JOHNSON, WM. C. "BILL"
225 Fairfield Pike, Enon, OH 45323, Phone: 937-864-7802, wjohnson64@woh.RR.com
Patterns: From hunters to art knives as well as custom canes, some with blades. **Technical:** Stock removal method utilizing 440C, ATS34, 154CPM, and custom Damascus. **Prices:** $175 to over $2500, depending on design, materials, and embellishments. **Remarks:** Full-time maker. First knife made in 1978. Member of the Knifemakers Guild since 1982. **Mark:** Crescent shaped WM. C. "BILL" JOHNSON, ENON OHIO. Also uses an engraved or electro signature on some art knives and on Damascus blades.

JOHNSTON, DR. ROBT
PO Box 9887 1 Lomb Mem Dr, Rochester, NY 14623

JOKERST, CHARLES
9312 Spaulding, Omaha, NE 68134, Phone: 402-571-2536
Specialties: Working knives in standard patterns. **Patterns:** Hunters, fighters and pocketknives. **Technical:** Grinds 440C, ATS-34. **Prices:** $90 to $170. **Remarks:** Spare-time maker; first knife sold in 1984. **Mark:** Early work marked RCJ; current work marked with last name and city.

JONAS, ZACHARY
204 Village Rd., Wilmot, NH 03287, Phone: 603-877-0128, zack@jonasblade.com; www.jonasblade.com
Specialties: Custom high-carbon damascus, sporting knives, kitchen knives and art knives. Always interested in adding to the repertoire. **Patterns:** Kitchen and bowie knives, hunters, daggers, push daggers, tantos, boot knives, all custom. **Technical:** Forges all damascus blades, works with high-carbon steels to suit the client's individual tastes and needs. **Remarks:** Full-time maker, ABS journeyman smith trained by ABS master smith J.D. Smith, juried member of League of New Hampshire Craftsmen. **Mark:** Sytlized "Z" symbol on one side, "JS" on other, either stamped, engraved or etched.

JONES, BARRY M AND PHILLIP G
221 North Ave, Danville, VA 24540, Phone: 804-793-5282
Specialties: Working and using straight knives and folders of their design and to customer specs; combat and self-defense knives. **Patterns:** Bowies, fighters, daggers, swords, hunters and LinerLock® folders. **Technical:** Grinds 440C, ATS-34 and D2; flat-grinds only. All blades hand polished. **Prices:** $100 to $1000, some higher. **Remarks:** Part-time makers; first knife sold in 1989. **Mark:** Jones Knives, city, state.

JONES, ENOCH
7278 Moss Ln, Warrenton, VA 20187, Phone: 540-341-0292
Specialties: Fancy working straight knives. **Patterns:** Hunters, fighters, boots and Bowies. **Technical:** Forges and grinds O1, W2, 440C and Damascus. **Prices:** $100 to $350; some to $1000. **Remarks:** Part-time maker; first knife sold in 1982. **Mark:** First name.

JONES, JACK P.
17670 Hwy. 2 East, Ripley, MS 38663, Phone: 662-837-3882, jacjones@ripleycable.net
Specialties: Working knives in classic design. **Patterns:** Hunters, fighters, and Bowies.

Technical: Grinds D2, A2, CPM-154, CTS-XHP and ATS-34. **Prices:** $200 and up. **Remarks:** Full-time maker since retirement in 2005, first knife sold in 1976. **Mark:** J.P. Jones, Ripley, MS.

JONES, ROGER MUDBONE
GREENMAN WORKSHOP, 320 Prussia Rd, Waverly, OH 45690, Phone: 740-739-4562, greenmanworkshop@yahoo.com
Specialties: Working in cutlery to suit working woodsman and fine collector. **Patterns:** Bowies, hunters, folders, hatchets in both period and modern style, scale miniatures a specialty. **Technical:** All cutlery hand forged to shape with traditional methods; multiple quench and draws, limited Damascus production hand carves wildlife and historic themes in stag/antler/ivory, full line of functional and high art leather. All work sole authorship. **Prices:** $50 to $5000 **Remarks:** Full-time maker/first knife sold in 1979. **Mark:** Stamped R. Jones hand made or hand engraved sig. W/Bowie knife mark.

JORGENSEN, CARSON
1805 W Hwy 116, Mt Pleasant, UT 84647, tcjorgensenknife@gmail.com; Web: tcjknives.com
Specialties: Stock removal, Loveless Johnson and young styles. **Prices:** Most $100 to $800.

K

K B S, KNIVES
RSD 181, North Castlemaine, VIC, AUSTRALIA 3450, Phone: 0011 61 3 54 705864
Specialties: Historically inspired bowies, and restoration of fixed and folding knives. **Patterns:** Bowies and folders. **Technical:** Flat and hollow grinds, filework. **Prices:** $500 and up. **Remarks:** First knife sold in 1983, foundation member of Australian Knife Guild. **Mark:** Initials and address within Southern cross.

KACZOR, TOM
375 Wharncliffe Rd N, Upper London, ON, CANADA N6G 1E4, Phone: 519-645-7640

KAGAWA, KOICHI
1556 Horiyamashita, Hatano-Shi, Kanagawa, JAPAN
Specialties: Fancy high-tech straight knives and folders to customer specs. **Patterns:** Hunters, locking folders and slip-joints. **Technical:** Uses 440C and ATS-34. **Prices:** $500 to $2000; some to $20,000. **Remarks:** Part-time maker; first knife sold in 1986. **Mark:** First initial, last name-YOKOHAMA.

KAIN, CHARLES
KAIN DESIGNS, 1736 E. Maynard Dr., Indianapolis, IN 46227, Phone: 317-781-9549, Fax: 317-781-8521, charles@kaincustomknives.com; Web: www.kaincustomknives.com
Specialties: Unique Damascus art folders. **Patterns:** Any. **Technical:** Specialized & patented mechanisms. **Remarks:** Unique knife & knife mechanism design. **Mark:** Kain and Signet stamp for unique pieces.

KANKI, IWAO
691-2 Tenjincho, Ono-City, Hyogo, JAPAN 675-1316, Phone: 07948-3-2555, Web: www.chiyozurusadahide.jp
Specialties: Plane, knife. **Prices:** Not determined yet. **Remarks:** Masters of traditional crafts designated by the Minister of International Trade and Industry (Japan). **Mark:** Chiyozuru Sadahide.

KANSEI, MATSUNO
109-8 Uenomachi, Nishikaiden, Gifu, JAPAN 501-1168, Phone: 81-58-234-8643
Specialties: Folders of original design. **Patterns:** LinerLock® folder. **Technical:** Grinds VG-10, Damascus. **Prices:** $350 to $2000. **Remarks:** Full-time maker. First knife sold in 1993. **Mark:** Name.

KANTER, MICHAEL
ADAM MICHAEL KNIVES, 14550 West Honey Ln., New Berlin, WI 53151, Phone: 262-860-1136, mike@adammichaelknives.com; Web: www.adammichaelknives.com
Specialties: Fixed blades and folders. **Patterns:** Drop point hunters, Bowies and fighters. **Technical:** Jerry Rados Damascus, BG42, CPM, S60V and S30V. **Prices:** $375 and up. Remarls: Ivory, mammoth ivory, stabilized woods, and pearl handles. **Mark:** Engraved Adam Michael.

KARP, BOB
PO Box 47304, Phoenix, AZ 85068, Phone: 602 870-1234
602 870-1234, Fax: 602-331-0283
Remarks: Bob Karp "Master of the Blade."

KATO, SHINICHI
Rainbow Amalke 402, Moriyama-ku Nagoya, Aichi, JAPAN 463-0002, Phone: 81-52-736-6032, skato-402@u0l.gate01.com
Specialties: Flat grind and hand finish. **Patterns:** Bowie, fighter. Hunting and folding knives. **Technical:** Hand forged,flat grind. **Prices:** $100 to $2000. **Remarks:** Part-time maker. **Mark:** Name.

KATSUMARO, SHISHIDO
2-6-11 Kamiseno, Aki-ku, Hiroshima, JAPAN, Phone: 090-3634-9054, Fax: 082-227-4438, shishido@d8.dion.ne.jp

KAUFFMAN, DAVE
158 Jackson Creek Rd., Clancy, MT 59634, Phone: 406-431-8435
Specialties: Field grade and exhibition grade hunting knives and ultra light folders. **Patterns:** Fighters, Bowies and drop-point hunters. **Technical:** S30V and SS Damascus. **Prices:** $155 to $1200. **Remarks:** Full-time maker; first knife sold in 1989. On the cover of Knives '94. **Mark:** First and last name, city and state.

KAY, J WALLACE
332 Slab Bridge Rd, Liberty, SC 29657

KAZSUK, DAVID
27789 Ethanac Rd., Menifee, CA 92585, Phone: 951-216-0883, ddkaz@hotmail.com
Specialties: Hand forged. Prices: $150+. Mark: Last name.

KEARNEY, JAROD
1505 Parkersburg Turnpike, Swoope, VA 24479, jarodkearney@gmail.com Web: www.jarodkearney.com
Patterns: Bowies, skinners, hunters, Japanese blades, Sgian Dubhs

KEESLAR, JOSEPH F
391 Radio Rd, Almo, KY 42020, Phone: 270-753-7919, Fax: 270-753-7919, suzjoe.kees@gmail.com
Specialties: Classic and contemporary Bowies, combat, hunters, daggers and folders. Patterns: Decorative filework, engraving and custom leather sheaths available. Technical: Forges 5160, 52100 and his own Damascus steel. Prices: $300 to $3000. Remarks: Full-time maker; first knife sold in 1976. ABS Master Smith, and 50 years as a bladesmith (1962-2012). Mark: First and middle initials, last name in hammer, knife and anvil logo, M.S.

KEESLAR, STEVEN C
115 Lane 216 Hamilton Lake, Hamilton, IN 46742, Phone: 260-488-3161, sskeeslar@hotmail.com
Specialties: Traditional working/using straight knives of his design and to customer specs. Patterns: Bowies, hunters, utility/camp knives. Technical: Forges 5160, files 52100 Damascus. Prices: $100 to $600; some to $1500. Remarks: Part-time maker; first knife sold in 1976. ABS member. Mark: Fox head in flames over Steven C. Keeslar.

KEETON, WILLIAM L
6095 Rehobeth Rd SE, Laconia, IN 47135-9550, Phone: 812-969-2836, wlkeeton@hughes.net, Web: www.keetoncustomknives.com
Specialties: Plain and fancy working knives. Patterns: Hunters and fighters; locking folders and slip-joints. Names patterns after Kentucky Derby winners. Technical: Grinds any of the popular alloy steels. Prices: $250 to $8,000. Remarks: Full-time maker; first knife sold in 1971. Mark: Logo of key.

KEHIAYAN, ALFREDO
Cuzco 1455 Ing., Maschwitz, Buenos Aires, ARGENTINA B1623GXU, Phone: 540-348-4442212, Fax: 54-077-75-4493-5359, alfredo@kehiayan.com.ar; Web: www.kehiayan.com.ar
Specialties: Functional straight knives. Patterns: Utility knives, skinners, hunters and boots. Technical: Forges and grinds SAE 52.100, SAE 6180, SAE 9260, SAE 5160, 440C and ATS-34, titanium with nitride. All blades mirror-polished; makes leather sheath and wood cases. Prices: From $350 up. Remarks: Full-time maker; first knife sold in 1983. Some knives are satin finish (utility knives). Mark: Name.

KEISUKE, GOTOH
105 Cosumo-City Otozu 202, Oita-city, Oita, JAPAN, Phone: 097-523-0750, k-u-an@ki.rim.or.jp

KELLER, BILL
12211 Las Nubes, San Antonio, TX 78233, Phone: 210-653-6609
Specialties: Primarily folders, some fixed blades. Patterns: Autos, liner locks and hunters. Technical: Grinds stainless and Damascus. Prices: $400 to $1000, some to $4000. Remarks: Part-time maker, first knife sold 1995. Mark: Last name inside outline of Alamo.

KELLEY, GARY
17485 SW Pheasant Lane, Aloha, OR 97006, Phone: 503-649-7867, garykelley@thebladmaker.com; Web: wwwthebladmaker.com
Specialties: Primitive knives and blades. Patterns: Fur trade era rifleman's knives, tomahawks, and hunting knives. Technical: Hand-forges and precision investment casts. Prices: $35 to $125. Remarks: Family business. Doing business as The Blademaker. Mark: Fir tree logo.

KELLY, DAVE
865 S. Shenandoah St., Los Angeles, CA 90035, Phone: 310-657-7121, dakcon@sbcglobal.net
Specialties: Collector and user one-of-a-kind (his design) fixed blades, liner lock folders, and leather sheaths. Patterns: Utility and hunting fixed blade knives with hand-sewn leather sheaths, Gentleman liner lock folders. Technical: Grinds carbon steels, hollow, convex, and flat. Offers clay differentially hardened blades, etched and polished. Uses Sambar stag, mammoth ivory, and high-grade burl woods. Hand-sewn leather sheaths for fixed blades and leather pouch sheaths for folders. Prices: $250 to $750, some higher. Remarks: Full-time maker, first knife made in 2003. Mark: First initial, last name with large K.

KELLY, STEVEN
11407 Spotted Fawn Ln., Bigfork, MT 59911, Phone: 406-212-2195, steve@skknives.com; Web: www.skknives.com
Specialties: Tactical-style folders. Technical: Damascus from 1084 or 1080 and 15n20. 52100.

KELSEY, NATE
3867 N. Forestwood Dr., Palmer, AK 99645, Phone: 907-360-4469, edgealaska@mac.com; Web: www.edgealaska.com
Specialties: Forges high-performance 52100, stock removal on 154CM for Extreme Duty Worldwide. Patterns: Hunters, fighters, bowies and neck knives. Technical: Forges own damascus, 52100 and W2 blade steels, and stock removal of XHP and 154CM. Prices: $250 to $5,000. Remarks: Maker since 1990, member ABS. Mark: EDGE ALASKA or last name and Palmer AK.

KELSO, JIM
577 Collar Hill Rd, Worcester, VT 05682, Phone: 802-229-4254, Fax: 802-229-0595, kelsomaker@gmail.com; Web:www.jimkelso.com
Specialties: Fancy high-art straight knives and folders that mix Eastern and Western influences. Only uses own designs. Patterns: Daggers, swords and locking folders. Technical: Works with top bladesmiths. Prices: $15,000 to $60,000 . Remarks: Full-time maker; first knife sold in 1980. Mark: Stylized initials.

KEMP, LAWRENCE
8503 Water Tower Rd, Ooltewah, TN 37363, Phone: 423-344-2357, larry@kempknives.com Web: www.kempknives.com
Specialties: Bowies, hunters and working knives. Patterns: Bowies, camp knives, hunters and skinners. Technical: Forges carbon steel, and his own Damascus. Prices: $250 to $1500. Remarks: Part-time maker, first knife sold in 1991. ABS Journeyman Smith since 2006. Mark: L.A. Kemp.

KENNEDY JR., BILL
PO Box 850431, Yukon, OK 73085, Phone: 405-354-9150, bkfish1@gmail.com; www.billkennedyjrknives.com
Specialties: Working straight knives and folders. Patterns: Hunters, minis, fishing, and pocket knives. Technical: Grinds D2, 440C, ATS-34, BG42. Prices: $110 and up. Remarks: Part-time maker; first knife sold in 1980. Mark: Last name and year made.

KERANEN, PAUL
4122 S. E. Shiloh Ct., Tacumseh, KS 66542, Phone: 785-220-2141, pk6269@yahoo.com
Specialties: Specializes in Japanese style knives and swords. Most clay tempered with hamon. Patterns: Does bowies, fighters and hunters. Technical: Forges and grinds carbons steel only. Make my own Damascus. Prices: $75 to $800. Mark: Keranen arched over anvil.

KEYES, DAN
6688 King St, Chino, CA 91710, Phone: 909-628-8329

KEYES, GEOFF P.
13027 Odell Rd NE, Duvall, WA 98019, Phone: 425-844-0758, 5ef@polarisfarm.com; Web: www5elementsforge.com
Specialties: Working grade fixed blades, 19th century style gents knives. Patterns: Fixed blades, your design or mine. Technical: Hnad-forged 5160, 1084, and own Damascus. Prices: $200 and up. Remarks: Geoff Keyes DBA 5 Elements Forge, ABS Journeyman Smith. Mark: Early mark KEYES etched in script. New mark as of 2009: pressed GPKeyes.

KHALSA, JOT SINGH
368 Village St, Millis, MA 02054, Phone: 508-376-8162, Fax: 508-532-0517, jotkhalsa@comcast.net; Web: www.khalsakirpans.com, www.lifeknives.com, and www.thekhalsaraj.com
Specialties: Liner locks, one-of-a-kind daggers, swords, and kirpans (Sikh daggers) all original designs. Technical: Forges own Damascus, uses others high quality Damascus including stainless, and grinds stainless steels. Uses natural handle materials frequently unusual minerals. Pieces are frequently engraved and more recently carved. Prices: Start at $700.

KHARLAMOV, YURI
Oboronnay 46, Tula, RUSSIA 300007
Specialties: Classic, fancy and traditional knives of his design. Patterns: Daggers and hunters. Technical: Forges only Damascus with nickel. Uses natural handle materials; engraves on metal, carves on nut-tree; silver and pearl inlays. Prices: $600 to $2380; some to $4000. Remarks: Full-time maker; first knife sold in 1988. Mark: Initials.

KI, SHIVA
5222 Ritterman Ave, Baton Rouge, LA 70805, Phone: 225-356-7274, shivakicustomknives@netzero.net; Web: www.shivakicustomknives.com
Specialties: Working straight knives and folders. Patterns: Emphasis on personal defense knives, martial arts weapons. Technical: Forges and grinds; makes own Damascus; prefers natural handle materials. Prices: $550 to $10,000.Remarks: Full-time maker; first knife sold in 1981. Mark: Name with logo.

KIEFER, TONY
112 Chateaugay Dr, Pataskala, OH 43062, Phone: 740-927-6910
Specialties: Traditional working and using straight knives in standard patterns. Patterns: Bowies, fighters and hunters. Technical: Grinds 440C and D2; forges D2. Flat-grinds Bowies; hollow-grinds drop-point and trailing-point hunters. Prices: $110 to $300; some to $200. Remarks: Spare-time maker; first knife sold in 1988. Mark: Last name.

KILBY, KEITH
1902 29th St, Cody, WY 82414, Phone: 307-587-2732
Specialties: Works with all designs. Patterns: Mostly Bowies, camp knives and hunters of his design. Technical: Forges 52100, 5160, 1095, Damascus and mosaic Damascus. Prices: $250 to $3500. Remarks: Part-time maker; first knife sold in 1974. Doing business as Foxwood Forge. Mark: Name.

KILEY, MIKE AND JANDY
ROCKING K KNIVES, 1325 Florida, Chino Valley, AZ 86323, Phone: 928-910-2647
Specialties: Period knives for cowboy action shooters and mountain men. Patterns: Bowies, drop-point hunters, skinners, sheepsfoot blades and spear points. Technical: Steels are 1095, 0-1, Damascus and others upon request. Handles include all types of wood, with cocobolo, ironwood, rosewood, maple and bacote being favorites as well as

buffalo horn, stag, elk antler, mammoth ivory, giraffe boon, sheep horn and camel bone. **Prices:** $100 to $500 depending on style and materials. Hand-tooled leather sheaths by Jan and Mike. **Mark:** Stylized K on one side; Kiley on the other.

KILPATRICK, CHRISTIAN A
6925 Mitchell Ct, Citrus Heights, CA 95610, Phone: 916-729-0733, crimsonkil@gmail.com; Web:www.crimsonknives.com

Specialties: All forged weapons (no firearms) from ancient to modern. All blades produced are first and foremost useable tools, and secondly but no less importantly, artistic expressions. **Patterns:** Hunters, bowies, daggers, swords, axes, spears, boot knives, bird knives, ethnic blades and historical reproductions. Customer designs welcome. **Technical:** Forges and grinds, makes own Damascus. Does file work. **Prices:** $125 to $3200. **Remarks:** 26 year part time maker. First knife sold in 2002.

KILROY, KYLE
POB 24655, Knoxville, TN 37933, Phone: 843-729-5141, kylekilroy@yahoo.com; Web: www.kylekilroy.com

Specialties: Traditional forged knives in a mixture of traditional and modern materials. Professional chemical engineering background in polymers allows the exclusive use of many unique handle materials. **Patterns:** Bowie/fighting knife patterns, hunting knives, chef's knives and modern bearing flipper folders. **Technical:** Forges D2, 1090, 1095 and several other carbon steels depending on application. Forges own damascus and can produce stainless blades via stock removal. **Prices:** $80 and up. **Remarks:** Professional engineer; first knife sold in 1996. **Mark:** Name above Charleston SC, with earlier stamp being "Chicora Gun Works" in three lines.

KIMBERLEY, RICHARD L.
86-B Arroyo Hondo Rd, Santa Fe, NM 87508, Phone: 505-820-2727

Specialties: Fixed-blade and period knives. **Technical:** 01, 52100, 9260 steels. **Remarks:** Member ABS. Marketed under "Kimberleys of Santa Fe." **Mark:** "By D. KIMBERLEY SANTA FE NM."

KIMSEY, KEVIN
198 Cass White Rd. NW, Cartersville, GA 30121, Phone: 770-387-0779 and 770-655-8879

Specialties: Tactical fixed blades and folders. **Patterns:** Fighters, folders, hunters and utility knives. **Technical:** Grinds 440C, ATS-34 and D2 carbon. **Prices:** $100 to $400; some to $600. **Remarks:** Three-time Blade magazine award winner, knifemaker since 1983. **Mark:** Rafter and stylized KK.

KING, BILL
14830 Shaw Rd, Tampa, FL 33625, Phone: 813-961-3455, billkingknives@yahoo.com

Specialties: Folders, lockbacks, liner locks, automatics and stud openers. **Patterns:** Wide varieties; folders. **Technical:** ATS-34 and some Damascus; single and double grinds. Offers filework and jewel embellishment; nickel-silver Damascus and mokume bolsters. **Prices:** $150 to $475; some to $850. **Remarks:** Full-time maker; first knife sold in 1976. All titanium fitting on liner-locks; screw or rivet construction on lock-backs. **Mark:** Last name in crown.

KING, FRED
430 Grassdale Rd, Cartersville, GA 30120, Phone: 770-382-8478, Web: http://www.fking83264@aol.com

Specialties: Fancy and embellished working straight knives and folders. **Patterns:** Hunters, Bowies and fighters. **Technical:** Grinds ATS-34 and D2: forges 5160 and Damascus. Offers filework. **Prices:** $100 to $3500. **Remarks:** Spare-time maker; first knife sold in 1984. **Mark:** Kings Edge.

KING JR., HARVEY G
32170 Hwy K4, Alta Vista, KS 66834, Phone: 785-499-5207, Web: www.harveykingknives.com

Specialties: Traditional working and using straight knives of his design and to customer specs. **Patterns:** Hunters, Bowies and fillet knives. **Technical:** Grinds 01, A2 and D2. Prefers natural handle materials; offers leatherwork. **Prices:** Start at $150. **Remarks:** Full-time maker; first knife sold in 1988. **Mark:** Name, city, state, and serial number.

KINKER, MIKE
8755 E County Rd 50 N, Greensburg, IN 47240, Phone: 812-663-5277, kinkercustomknives@gmail.com

Specialties: Working/using knives, straight knives. Starting to make folders. Your design. **Patterns:** Boots, daggers, hunters, skinners, hatchets. **Technical:** Grind 440C and ATS-34, others if required. Damascus, dovetail bolsters, jeweled blade. **Prices:** $125 to 375; some to $1000. **Remarks:** Part-time maker; first knife sold in 1991. Doing business as Kinker Custom Knives. **Mark:** Kinker

KINNIKIN, TODD
EUREKA FORGE, 7 Capper Dr., Pacific, MO 63069-3603, Phone: 314-938-6248

Specialties: Mosaic Damascus. **Patterns:** Hunters, fighters, folders and automatics. **Technical:** Forges own mosaic Damascus with tool steel Damascus edge. Prefers natural, fossil and artifact handle materials. **Prices:** $1200 to $2400. **Remarks:** Full-time maker; first knife sold in 1994. **Mark:** Initials connected.

KIRK, RAY
PO Box 1445, Tahlequah, OK 74465, Phone: 918-207-8076, ray@rakerknives.com; Web: www.rakerknives.com

Specialties: Folders, skinners fighters, and Bowies. **Patterns:** Neck knives and small hunters and skinners. Full and hidden-tang integrals from 52100 round bar. **Technical:** Forges all knives from 52100 and own damascus. **Prices:** $65 to $3000. **Remarks:** Started forging in 1989; makes own Damascus. **Mark:** Stamped "Raker" on blade.

KIRKES, BILL
235 Oaklawn Cir., Little Rock, AR 72206, Phone: 501-551-0135, bill@kirkesknives.com; Web: www.kirkesknives.com

Specialties: Handforged fixed blades. **Technical:** High-carbon 5160 and 1084 blade steels. Will build to customer's specs, prefers to use natural handle material. **Remarks:** ABS Journeyman smith. **Mark:** Kirkes.

KISLINGER, MILOS
KISLINGER KNIVES, Dobronin 314 58812, CZECH REPUBLIC, Phone: +420724570451, kislinger.milos@centrum.cz; Web: http://kislingerknives.blogspot.cz/ or Facebook.com/KislingerKnives

Specialties: Fine folders, daggers, automatic knives, flipper folders and bowies. **Technical:** Forges own damascus steel, and uses ivory, pearl and more luxurious handle materials. **Prices:** $400 and up. **Remarks:** Knifemaker and blacksmith since 2005, with first knife made eight years ago.

KISTNER, DEE
107 Whitecrest Dr., Crossville, TN 38571, Phone: 931-200-1233, dkknives@gmail.com; Web: www.kistnerknives.com

Specialties: Working knives. **Patterns:** Everyday carry, hunting and outdoor knives, military knives. **Technical:** Flat grinds 1075 steel, differentially heat treated. **Prices:** $100 and up. **Remarks:** Full-time maker, sole authorship. **Mark:** KISTNER.

KITSMILLER, JERRY
67277 Las Vegas Dr, Montrose, CO 81401, Phone: 970-249-4290

Specialties: Working straight knives in standard patterns. **Patterns:** Hunters, boots. **Technical:** Grinds ATS-34 and 440C only. **Prices:** $75 to $200; some to $300. **Remarks:** Spare-time maker; first knife sold in 1984. **Mark:** JandS Knives.

KLAASEE, TINUS
PO Box 10221, George, WC, SOUTH AFRICA 6530

Specialties: Hunters, skinners and utility knives. **Patterns:** Uses own designs and client specs. **Technical:** N690 stainless steel 440C Damascus. **Prices:** $700 and up. **Remarks:** Use only indigenous materials. Hardwood, horns and ivory. Makes his own sheaths and boxes. **Mark:** Initials and sur name over warthog.

KLEIN, KEVIN
129 Cedar St., Apt. 2, Boston, MA 02119, Phone: 609-937-8949, kevin.a.klein779@gmail.com

Specialties: Forged damascus blades using 15N20 and 1084. **Remarks:** Full-time maker; first knife made in 2012. Apprentice to J.D. Smith starting in 2012. **Mark:** KAK? or ?, depending on piece.

KLEIN, KIERAN
2436 Stonewall Rd. NE, Check, VA 24072, Phone: 540-651-2454, hammerdownkjk@gmail.com; Web: www.hammerdownforge.com

Specialties: Large chopping blades as well as camping and EDC (everyday carry) styles. **Patterns:** Custom khukuri styles, drop points, sheepsfoot, etc. **Technical:** Stock removal method of blade making using 80CrV2, 52100, 1075, W2 and CPM 3V blade steels, and high-quality stabilized burl wood, carbon fiber, G-10 and Micarta handles. **Prices:** $125 to $1,200. **Remarks:** Full-time maker since 2013; first knife made in 2012. **Mark:** Mountain range profile over HDF initials with Virginia, USA under that.

KNAPP, MARK
Mark Knapp Custom Knives, 1971 Fox Ave, Fairbanks, AK 99701, Phone: 907-452-7477, info@markknappcustomknives.com; Web: www.markknappcustomknives.com

Specialties: Mosaic handles of exotic natural materials from Alaska and around the world. Folders, fixed blades, full and hidden tangs. **Patterns:** Folders, hunters, skinners, and camp knives. **Technical:** Forges own Damascus, uses both forging and stock removal with ATS-34, 154CM, stainless Damascus, carbon steel and carbon Damascus. **Prices:** $800-$3000. **Remarks:** Full time maker, sold first knife in 2000. **Mark:** Mark Knapp Custom Knives Fairbanks, AK.

KNAPTON, CHRIS C.
76 Summerland Dr., Henderson, Aukland, NEW ZEALAND, Phone: 09-835-3598, knaptch76@gmail.com; Web: www.knappoknives.com

Specialties: Working and fancy straight and folding knives of his own design. **Patterns:** Tactical, utility, hunting fixed and folding knives. **Technical:** Predominate knife steels are Elmax, CPM-154 and D2. All blades made via the stock removal method. **Prices:** $120 - $500. **Remarks:** Part-time maker. **Mark:** Stylized letter K, country name and Haast eagle.

KNICKMEYER, HANK
6300 Crosscreek, Cedar Hill, MO 63016, Phone: 636-285-3210

Specialties: Complex mosaic Damascus constructions. **Patterns:** Fixed blades, swords, folders and automatics. **Technical:** Mosaic Damascus with all tool steel Damascus edges. **Prices:** $500 to $2000; some $3000 and higher. **Remarks:** Part-time maker; first knife sold in 1989. Doing business as Dutch Creek Forge and Foundry. **Mark:** Initials connected.

KNICKMEYER, KURT
6344 Crosscreek, Cedar Hill, MO 63016, Phone: 314-274-0481

KNIGHT, JASON
110 Paradise Pond Ln, Harleyville, SC 29448, Phone: 843-452-1163, jasonknightknives.com

Specialties: Bowies. **Patterns:** Bowies and anything from history or his own design. **Technical:** 1084, 5160, O1, 52102, Damascus/forged blades. **Prices:** $200 and up. **Remarks:** Bladesmith. **Mark:** KNIGHT.

KNIPSCHIELD, TERRY
808 12th Ave NE, Rochester, MN 55906, Phone: 507-288-7829, terry@knipknives.com; Web: www.knipknives.com
Specialties: Folders and fixed blades and leather working knives. **Patterns:** Variations of traditional patterns and his own new designs. **Technical:** Stock removal. Grinds CPM-154CM, ATS-34, stainless Damascus, 01. **Prices:** $60 to $1200 and higher for upscale folders. **Mark:** Etchd logo on blade, KNIP with shield image.

KNOTT, STEVE
KNOTT KNIVES, 203 Wild Rose, Guyton, GA 31312, Phone: 912-536-7651, knottknives@yahoo.com; FaceBook: Knott Knives/Steve Knott
Technical: Uses ATS-34/440C and some commercial Damascus, single and double grinds with mirror or satin finishes. **Patterns:** Hunters, boot knives, bowies, and tantos, slip joint, LinerLock and lock-back folders. Uses a wide variety of handle materials to include ironwood, coca-bola and colored stabilized wood, also horn, bone and ivory upon customer request. **Remarks:** First knife sold in 1991. Part-time maker.

KNOWLES, SHAWN
750 Townsbury Rd, Great Meadows, NJ 07838, Phone: 973-670-3307, skcustomknives@gmail.com Web: shawnknowlescustomknives.com

KOHLS, JERRY
N4725 Oak Rd, Princeton, WI 54968, Phone: 920-295-3648
Specialties: Working knives and period pieces. **Patterns:** Hunters-boots and Bowies, your designs or his. **Technical:** Grinds, ATS-34 440c 154CM and 1095 and commercial Damascus. **Remarks:** Part-time maker. **Mark:** Last name.

KOJETIN, W
20 Bapaume Rd Delville, Germiston, GT, SOUTH AFRICA 1401, Phone: 27118733305/mobile 27836256208
Specialties: High-art and working straight knives of all designs. **Patterns:** Daggers, hunters and his own Man hunter Bowie. **Technical:** Grinds D2 and ATS-34; forges and grinds 440B/C. Offers "wrap-around" pava and abalone handles, scrolled wood or ivory, stacked filework and setting of faceted semi-precious stones. **Prices:** $185 to $600; some to $11,000. **Remarks:** Spare-time maker; first knife sold in 1962. **Mark:** Billy K.

KOLENKO, VLADIMIR
505 Newell Dr., Huntingdon Valley, PA 19006, Phone: 617-501-8366, kolenkv@yahoo.com; Web: www.kolenko.com
Specialties: Daggers and fighters. **Patterns:** Art knives. **Technical:** Typically uses custom mosaic damascus blades forged by various bladesmiths and commercial damascus makers. **Prices:** $1,000 to $2,500. **Remarks:** Making jewelry and fashioning knives have been longstanding hobbies, so the maker combined them and says he enjoys the whole process, not just the end product. He guesses that makes the difference between a hobby and business.

KOLITZ, ROBERT
W9342 Canary Rd, Beaver Dam, WI 53916, Phone: 920-887-1287
Specialties: Working straight knives to customer specs. **Patterns:** Bowies, hunters, bird and trout knives, boots. **Technical:** Grinds O1, 440C; commercial Damascus. **Prices:** $50 to $100; some to $500. **Remarks:** Spare-time maker; first knife sold in 1979. **Mark:** Last initial.

KOMMER, RUSS
4609 35th Ave N, Fargo, ND 58102, Phone: 701-281-1826, russkommer@yahoo.com Web: www.russkommerknives.com
Specialties: Working straight knives with the outdoorsman in mind. **Patterns:** Hunters, semi-skinners, fighters, folders and utility knives, art knives. **Technical:** Hollow-grinds ATS-34, 440C and 440V. **Prices:** $125 to $850; some to $3000. **Remarks:** Full-time maker; first knife sold in 1995. **Mark:** Bear paw—full name, city and state or full name and state.

KOPP, TODD M
PO Box 3474, Apache Jct., AZ 85217, Phone: 480-983-6143, tmkopp@msn.com
Specialties: Classic and traditional straight knives. Fluted handled daggers. **Patterns:** Bowies, boots, daggers, fighters, hunters, swords and folders. **Technical:** Grinds 5160, 440C, ATS-34. All Damascus steels, or customers choice. Some engraving and filework. **Prices:** $200 to $1200; some to $4000. **Remarks:** Part-time maker; first knife sold in 1989. **Mark:** Last name in Old English, some others name, city and state.

KOSTER, DANIEL
KOSTER KNIVES, 1711 Beverly Ct., Bentonville, AR 72712, Phone: 479-366-7794, dan@kosterknives.com Web: www.kosterknives.com
Patterns: Bushcraft, survival, outdoor and utility knives. **Technical:** Stock-removal method of blade making, using CPM 3V steel. **Prices:** $150 to $300. **Remarks:** Full-time knifemaker in business since 2005. **Mark:** "K" in a circle, negative shape.

KOSTER, STEVEN C
16261 Gentry Ln, Huntington Beach, CA 92647, Phone: 714-907-7250, kosterknives@verizon.net Web: www.kosterhandforgedknives.com
Specialties: Walking sticks, hand axes, tomahawks, Damascus. **Patterns:** Ladder, twists, round horn. **Technical:** Use 5160, 52100, 1084, 1095 steels. Ladder, twists, **Prices:** $200 to $1000. **Remarks:** Wood and leather sheaths with silver furniture. ABS Journeyman 2003. California knifemakers member. **Mark:** Koster squeezed between lines.

KOVACIK, ROBERT
Zavadska 122, Tomasovce 98401, SLOVAKIA, Phone: Mobil: 00421907644800, kovacikart@gmail.com Web: www.robertkovacik.com
Specialties: Engraved hunting knives, guns engraved; Knifemakers. **Technical:** Fixed blades, folder knives, miniatures. **Prices:** $350 to $10,000 U.S. **Mark:** R.

KOVAR, EUGENE
2626 W 98th St., Evergreen Park, IL 60642, Phone: 708-636-3724/708-790-4115, baldemaster333@aol.com
Specialties: One-of-a-kind miniature knives only. **Patterns:** Fancy to fantasy miniature knives; knife pendants and tie tacks. **Technical:** Files and grinds nails, nickel-silver and sterling silver. **Prices:** $5 to $35; some to $100. **Mark:** GK.

KOYAMA, CAPTAIN BUNSHICHI
3-23 Shirako-cho, Nakamura-ku, Nagoya, Aichi, JAPAN City 453-0817, Phone: 052-461-7070, Fax: 052-461-7070
Specialties: Innovative folding knife. **Patterns:** General purpose one hand. **Technical:** Grinds ATS-34 and Damascus. **Prices:** $400 to $900; some to $1500. **Remarks:** Part-time maker; first knife sold in 1994. **Mark:** Captain B. Koyama and the shoulder straps of CAPTAIN.

KRAFT, STEVE
408 NE 11th St, Abilene, KS 67410, Phone: 785-263-1411
Specialties: Folders, lockbacks, scale release auto, push button auto. **Patterns:** Hunters, boot knives and fighters. **Technical:** Grinds ATS-34, Damascus; uses titanium, pearl, ivory etc. **Prices:** $500 to $2500. **Remarks:** Part-time maker; first knife sold in 1984. **Mark:** Kraft.

KRAMMES, JEREMY
138 W. Penn St., Schuylkill Haven, PA 17972, Phone: 570-617-5753, blade@jkknives.com; Web: www.jkknives.com
Specialties: Working folders and collectible art knives. **Technical:** Stock removal, hollow grinding, carving and engraving. **Prices:** $550+ for working knives, and $1,000+ for art knives. **Remarks:** Part-time maker; first knife sold in 2004. **Mark:** Stylized JK on blade.

KRAPP, DENNY
1826 Windsor Oak Dr, Apopka, FL 32703, Phone: 407-880-7115
Specialties: Fantasy and working straight knives of his design. **Patterns:** Hunters, fighters and utility/camp knives. **Technical:** Grinds ATS-34 and 440C. **Prices:** $85 to $300; some to $800. **Remarks:** Spare-time maker; first knife sold in 1988. **Mark:** Last name.

KRAUSE, JIM
3272 Hwy H, Farmington, MO 63640, Phone: 573-756-7388 or 573-701-7047, james_krause@sbcglobal.net
Specialties: Folders, fixed blades and neck knives. **Patterns:** New pattern for each knife. **Technical:** CPM steels or high-carbon steel on request. **Prices:** $125 and up for neck knives, $250 and up for fixed blades and $250 to $1,000 for folders and damascus pieces. **Remarks:** Full-time maker; first knife made in 2000. Makes one knife at a time with the best materials the maker can find. **Mark:** Krause Handmade with Christian fish.

KREGER, THOMAS
1996 Dry Branch Rd., Lugoff, SC 29078, Phone: 803-438-4221, tdkreger@bellsouth.net
Specialties: South Carolina/George Herron style working/using knives. Customer designs considered. **Patterns:** Hunters, skinners, fillet, liner lock folders, kitchen, and camp knives. **Technical:** Hollow and flat grinds of ATS-34, CPM154CM, and 5160. **Prices:** $100 and up. **Remarks:** Full-time maker. President of the South Carolina Association of Knifemakers 2002-2006, and current president since 2013. **Mark:** TDKreger.

KREH, LEFTY
210 Wichersham Way, "Cockeysville", MD 21030

KREIBICH, DONALD L.
1638 Commonwealth Circle, Reno, NV 89503, Phone: 775-746-0533, dmkreno@sbcglobal.net
Specialties: Working straight knives in standard patterns. **Patterns:** Bowies, boots and daggers; camp and fishing knives. **Technical:** Grinds 440C, 154CM and ATS-34; likes integrals. **Prices:** $100 to $200; some to $500. **Remarks:** Part-time maker; first knife sold in 1980. **Mark:** First and middle initials, last name.

KREIN, TOM
P.O. Box 994, 337 E. Main St., Gentry, AR 72734, Phone: 479-233-0508, kreinknives@gmail.com; www.kreinknives.net
Specialties: LinerLock folders and fixed blades designed to be carried and used. **Technical:** Stock removal using D2, A2, CPM 3V, CPM 154, CPM M4, Stellite 6K and damascus, and makes his own sheaths. **Prices:** $250 to $500 and up. **Remarks:** Full-time maker; first knife made in 1993. **Mark:** Last name and the year the knife was made in the shape of a circle, with a bulldog in the middle.

KRESSLER, D F
Mittelweg 31 i, D-28832 Achim, GERMANY 28832, Phone: +49 (0) 42 02/76-5742, Fax: +49 (0) 42 02/7657 41, info@kresslerknives.com; Web: www.kresslerknives.com
Specialties: High-tech integral and interframe knives. **Patterns:** Hunters, fighters, daggers. **Technical:** Grinds new state-of-the-art steels; prefers natural handle materials. **Prices:** Upscale. **Mark:** Name in logo.

KUBASEK, JOHN A
74 Northhampton St, Easthampton, MA 01027, Phone: 413-527-7917, jaknife01@yahoo.com
Specialties: Left- and right-handed LinerLock® folders of his design or to customer specs. Also new knives made with Ripcord patent. **Patterns:** Fighters, tantos, drop points, survival knives, neck knives and belt buckle knives. **Technical:** Grinds 154CM, S30 and Damascus. **Prices:** $395 to $1500. **Remarks:** Part-time maker; first knife sold in 1985. **Mark:** Name and address etched.

KULIS, DAVID S.
10741 S. Albany Ave., Chicago, IL 60655, windycitywoodworks@hotmail.com
Patterns: Folding LinerLocks, frame locks, straight hunters, fighters and kitchen knives. **Technical:** Stock removal method of making blades with hollow grinds and using CPM S30V, CPM 154, O1 and damascus steels. Handle materials include everything from stabilized wood to carbon fiber. **Prices:** $150 to $1,000. **Remarks:** Part-time maker; first knife sold in 2015. **Mark:** Stylized "DK" etched into blade.

KURT, DAVID
POB 1377, Molalla, OR 97038, Phone: 503-871-5420, dkurtknives@aol.com; Web: www.dkurtknives.com
Specialties: Fixed blades. **Patterns:** Tactical, utility and hunting knives. **Technical:** Stock removal method of blade making using primarily 154CM steel or to customers' preferences. **Remarks:** Full-time maker. **Mark:** Bear skull with maker's full name.

L

LAINSON, TONY
114 Park Ave, Council Bluffs, IA 51503, Phone: 712-322-5222
Specialties: Working straight knives, liner locking folders. **Technical:** Grinds 154CM, ATS-34, 440C buys Damascus. Handle materials include Micarta, carbon fiber G-10 ivory pearl and bone. **Prices:** $95 to $600. **Remarks:** Part-time maker; first knife sold in 1987. **Mark:** Name and state.

LAIRSON SR., JERRY
H C 68 Box 970, Ringold, OK 74754, Phone: 580-876-3426, bladesmt@brightok.net; Web: www.lairson-custom-knives.net
Specialties: Damascus collector grade knives & high performance field grade hunters & cutting competition knives. **Patterns:** Damascus, random, raindrop, ladder, twist and others. **Technical:** All knives hammer forged. Mar Tempering**Prices:** Field grade knives $300. Collector grade $400 & up. **Mark:** Lairson. **Remarks:** Makes any style knife but prefer fighters and hunters. ABS Mastersmith, AKA member, KGA member. Cutting competition competitor.

LAKE, RON
3360 Bendix Ave, Eugene, OR 97401, Phone: 541-484-2683
Specialties: High-tech working knives; inventor of the modern interframe folder. **Patterns:** Hunters, boots, etc.; locking folders. **Technical:** Grinds 154CM and ATS-34. Patented interframe with special lock release tab. **Prices:** $2200 to $3000; some higher. **Remarks:** Full-time maker; first knife sold in 1966. **Mark:** Last name.

LALA, PAULO RICARDO P AND LALA, ROBERTO P.
R Daniel Martins 636, Presidente Prudente, SP, BRAZIL 19031-260, Phone: 0182-210125, korthknives@terra.com.br; Web: www.ikbsknifetech.com
Specialties: Straight knives and folders of all designs to customer specs. **Patterns:** Bowies, daggers fighters, hunters and utility knives. **Technical:** Grinds and forges D6, 440C, high-carbon steels and Damascus. **Prices:** $60 to $400; some higher. **Remarks:** Full-time makers; first knife sold in 1991. All stainless steel blades are ultra sub-zero quenched. **Mark:** Sword carved on top of anvil under KORTH.

LAMB, CURTIS J
3336 Louisiana Ter, Ottawa, KS 66067-8996, Phone: 785-242-6657

LAMBERT, KIRBY
2131 Edgar St, Regina, SK, CANADA S4N 3K8, kirby@lambertknives.com; Web: www.lambertknives.com
Specialties: Tactical/utility folders. Tactical/utility Japanese style fixed blades. **Prices:** $200 to $1500 U.S. **Remarks:** Full-time maker since 2002. **Mark:** Black widow spider and last name Lambert.

LAMEY, ROBERT M
15800 Lamey Dr, Biloxi, MS 39532, Phone: 228-396-9066, Fax: 228-396-9022, rmlamey@ametro.net; Web: www.lameyknives.com
Specialties: Bowies, fighters, hard use knives. **Patterns:** Bowies, fighters, hunters and camp knives. **Technical:** Forged and stock removal. **Prices:** $125 to $350. **Remarks:** Lifetime reconditioning; will build to customer designs, specializing in hard use, affordable knives. **Mark:** LAMEY.

LAMOTHE, JORDAN
1317 County Rte. 31, Granville, NY 12832, Phone: 518-368-5147, jgl2@williams.edu; Web: www.jordanlamothe.com
Specialties: Handforged fixed blades and stock-removal folders. **Patterns:** Chef's, utility, paring, boning, fillet, hunting and camp knives, fighters and lockback folders. **Technical:** Forges W1, W2, 1084, 1095 and 1075 blade steels, grinding folder blades from 154CM and 440C. **Prices:** $100 to $600. **Remarks:** Part-time maker; first knife sold in 2014. **Mark:** Stamped JL.

LANCASTER, C G
No 2 Schoonwinkel St, Parys, Free State, SOUTH AFRICA, Phone: 0568112090
Specialties: High-tech working and using knives of his design and to customer specs. **Patterns:** Hunters, locking folders and utility/camp knives. **Technical:** Grinds Sandvik 12C27, 440C and D2. Offers anodized titanium bolsters. **Prices:** $450 to $750; some to $1500. **Remarks:** Part-time maker; first knife sold in 1990. **Mark:** Etched logo.

LANCE, BILL
12820 E. Scott Rd., Palmer, AK 99645-8863, Phone: 907-694-1487, Web: www.lanceknives.com
Specialties: Ulu sets and working straight knives; limited issue sets. **Patterns:** Several ulu patterns, drop-point skinners. **Technical:** Uses ATS-34 and AEBL; ivory, horn and high-class wood handles. **Prices:** $145 to $500; art sets to $7,500. **Remarks:** First knife sold in 1981. **Mark:** Last name over a lance.

LANCE, DAN
889 Pamela Kay Ln., Weatherford, TX 76088, Phone: 940-682-5381, dan@danlanceknives.com; Web: www.danlanceknives.com
Specialties: High-end locking folders of maker's own designs. **Patterns:** Locking folders, fighters, skinners, hunting and camp knives. **Technical:** Stock removal using stainless damascus, CPM 154 and PSF-27 primarily. Performs own heat treating. Handle materials consist of mammoth ivory, stag, exotic woods, Kirinite, carbon fiber and various bones and horns. **Prices:** $250 to $1,250, some higher. **Remarks:** Full-time maker; first knife made and sold in 2014. Member of the ABS and Knifemakers' Guild. **Mark:** Dan Lance over a lance with a broken shaft.

LANCE, LUCAS
3600 N. Charley, Wasilla, AK 99654, Phone: 907-357-0349, lucas@lanceknives.com; Web: www.lanceknives.com
Specialties: Working with materials native to Alaska such as fossilized ivory, bone, musk ox bone, sheep horn, moose antler, all combined with exotic materials from around the world. **Patterns:** Fully functional knives of my own design. **Technical:** Mainly stock removal, flat grinds in ATS-34, 440C, 5160 and various makes of American-made damascus. **Prices:** $165 to $850. **Remarks:** Second-generation knifemaker who grew up and trained in father, Bill Lance's, shop. First knife designed and made in 1994. **Mark:** Last name over a lance.

LANDERS, JOHN
758 Welcome Rd, Newnan, GA 30263, Phone: 404-253-5719
Specialties: High-art working straight knives and folders of his design. **Patterns:** Hunters, fighters and slip-joint folders. **Technical:** Grinds 440C, ATS-34, 154CM and commercial Damascus. **Prices:** $85 to $250; some to $500. **Remarks:** Part-time maker; first knife sold in 1989. **Mark:** Last name.

LANDIS, DAVID E. SR.
4544 County Rd. 29, Galion, OH 44833, Phone: 419-946-3145, del@redbird.net
Specialties: Damascus knives in ladder, twist, double-twist and "W's" patterns. Makes leather sheaths and forges his own damascus. **Prices:** $250 to $500. **Remarks:** Retiree who says knifemaking keeps him learning with new challenges and meeting a lot of great people. **Mark:** DEL.

LANG, DAVID
6153 Cumulus Circle, Kearns, UT 84118, Phone: 801-809-1241, dknifeguy@msn.com
Specialties: Art knives, metal sheaths, push daggers, fighting knives, hunting knives, camp knives, skinning knives, pocketknives, utility knives and three-finger knives. **Patterns:** Prefers to work with own patterns, but will consider other designs. **Technical:** Flat grinds, hollow grinds, hand carving on the blades and handles, and gold and silver casting. **Remarks:** Will work from his designs or to customer specifications. Has been making knives for over 20 years and has learned from some of the best. **Prices:** $250 to $3,000, with most work ranging from $750 to $1,500. **Mark:** Dlang over UTAH.

LANGLEY, GENE H
1022 N. Price Rd, Florence, SC 29506, Phone: 843-669-3150
Specialties: Working knives in standard patterns. **Patterns:** Hunters, boots, fighters, locking folders and slip-joints. **Technical:** Grinds 440C, 154CM and ATS-34. **Prices:** $125 to $450; some to $1000. **Remarks:** Part-time maker; first knife sold in 1979. **Mark:** Name.

LANGLEY, MICK
1015 Centre Crescent, Qualicum Beach, BC, CANADA V9K 2G6, Phone: 250-752-4261
Specialties: Period pieces and working knives. **Patterns:** Bowies, push daggers, fighters, boots. Some folding lockers. **Technical:** Forges 5160, 1084, W2 and his own Damascus. **Prices:** $250 to $2500; some to $4500. **Remarks:** Full-time maker, first knife sold in 1977. **Mark:** Langley with M.S. (for ABS Master Smith)

LANKTON, SCOTT
8065 Jackson Rd. R-11, Ann Arbor, MI 48103, Phone: 313-426-3735
Specialties: Pattern welded swords, krisses and Viking period pieces. **Patterns:** One-of-a-kind. **Technical:** Forges W2, L6 nickel and other steels. **Prices:** $600 to $12,000. **Remarks:** Part-time bladesmith, full-time smith; first knife sold in 1976. **Mark:** Last name logo.

LAPEN, CHARLES
Box 529, W. Brookfield, MA 01585
Specialties: Chef's knives for the culinary artist. **Patterns:** Camp knives, Japanese-style swords and wood working tools, hunters. **Technical:** Forges 1075, car spring and his own Damascus. Favors narrow and Japanese tangs. **Prices:** $200 to $400; some to $2000. **Remarks:** Part-time maker; first knife sold in 1972. **Mark:** Last name.

LAPLANTE, BRETT
4545 CR412, McKinney, TX 75071, Phone: 972-838-9191, blap007@aol.com
Specialties: Working straight knives and folders to customer specs. **Patterns:** Survival knives, Bowies, skinners, hunters. **Technical:** Grinds D2 and 440C. Heat-treats. **Prices:** $200 to $800. **Remarks:** Part-time maker; first knife sold in 1987. **Mark:** Last name in Canadian maple leaf logo.

LARGIN, KEN
KELGIN Knifemakers Co-Op, 2001 S. State Rd. 1, Connersville, IN 47331, Phone: 765-969-5012, kelginfinecutlery@gmail.com; Web: www.kelgin.com
Specialties: Retired from general knifemaking. Only take limited orders in meteorite damascus or solid meteorite blades. **Patterns:** Any. **Technical:** Stock removal or forged. **Prices:** $500 & up. **Remarks:** Travels the U.S. full time teaching hands-on "History Of

Cutting Tools" to Scouts and any interested group. Participants flint knap, forge and keep three tools they make! **Mark:** K.C. Largin (Kelgin mark retired in 2004).

LARK, DAVID
6641 Schneider Rd., Kingsley, MI 49649, Phone: 231-342-1076, dblark58@yahoo.com **Specialties:** Traditional straight knives, art knives, folders. **Patterns:** All types. **Technical:** Grinds all types of knife making steel and makes damascus. **Prices:** $600 and up. **Remarks:** Full-time maker, custom riflemaker, and engraver. **Mark:** Lark in script and DBL on engraving.

LAROCHE, JEAN-MARC
16 rue Alexandre Dumas, 78160 Marly le Roi, FRANCE, Phone: +33 1 39 16 16 58, infojmlaroche@orange.fr; Web: www.jmlaroche.com **Specialties:** Fantasy pieces to customer specs. **Patterns:** Straight knives and folding knives. **Technical:** Stainless or damascus blade steels. **Prices:** $800 to $4,000, some to $10,000. **Remarks:** Full-time sculptor; full-time knifemaker for 12 years from 1992 to 2004. Awards won include BLADEhandmade "Best In Show" Award in 1997 and "Best Fantasy Knife" at the 1998 BLADE Show West. Artistic design knives are influenced by fantasy movies and comics with handles in bronze, silver or resin, including animal skulls, bones and natural stones. Collaborations with Gil Hibben and Roger Bergh. Recently created a knife capable of mechanical movement: "The Living Knife" with a blade by Bergh. **Mark:** Logo, + name sometimes.

LARSON, RICHARD
549 E Hawkeye Ave, Turlock, CA 95380, Phone: 209-668-1615, lebatardknives@aol.com **Specialties:** Sound working knives, lightweight folders, practical tactical knives. **Patterns:** Hunters, trout and bird knives, fish fillet knives, Bowies, tactical sheath knives, one- and two-blade folders. **Technical:** Grinds ATS-34, A2, D2, CPM 3V and commercial. Damascus; forges and grinds 52100, O1 and 1095. Machines folder frames from aircraft aluminum. **Prices:** $40 to $650. **Remarks:** Full-time maker. First knife made in 1974. Offers knife repair, restoration and sharpening. All knives are serial numbered and registered in the name of original purchaser. **Mark:** Stamped last name or etched logo of last name, city, and state.

LARY, ED
951 Rangeline Rd., Mosinee, WI 54455, Phone: 715-630-6202, laryblades@hotmail.com **Specialties:** Upscale hunters and art knives with display presentations. **Patterns:** Hunters, period pieces. **Technical:** Grinds all steels, heat treats, fancy filework and engraving. **Prices:** Upscale. **Remarks:** Full-time maker since 1974. **Mark:** Hand engraved "Ed Lary" in script.

LAURENT, KERMIT
1812 Acadia Dr, LaPlace, LA 70068, Phone: 504-652-5629 **Specialties:** Traditional and working straight knives and folders of his design. **Patterns:** Bowies, hunters, utilities and folders. **Technical:** Forges own Damascus, plus uses most tool steels and stainless. Specializes in altering cable patterns. Uses stabilized handle materials, especially select exotic woods. **Prices:** $100 to $2500; some to $50,000. **Remarks:** Full-time maker; first knife sold in 1982. Doing business as Kermit's Knife Works. Favorite material is meteorite Damascus. **Mark:** First name.

LAURENT, VERONIQUE
Avenue du Capricorne, 53, 1200 Brussels, BELGIUM, Phone: 0032 477 48 66 73, whatsonthebench@gmail.com **Specialties:** Fixed blades and friction folders. **Patterns:** Bowies, camp knives, "ladies knives" and maker's own designs. **Technical:** Makes own san mai steel with the edges in blue paper steel and the sides in pure nickel and O2, called "Nickwich," meaning nickel in a sandwich. Makes own damascus, numerical milling embellishment, inlays and sheaths. **Prices:** Start at $350. **Remarks:** Part-time knifemaker since 2005 and ABS journeyman smith since 2013.

LAWRENCE, ALTON
201 W Stillwell, De Queen, AR 71832, Phone: 870-642-7643, Fax: 870-642-4023, uncle21@riversidemachine.net; Web: riversidemachine.net **Specialties:** Classic straight knives and folders to customer specs. **Patterns:** Bowies, hunters, folders and utility/camp knives. **Technical:** Forges 5160, 1095, 1084, Damascus and railroad spikes. **Prices:** Start at $100. **Remarks:** Part-time maker; first knife sold in 1988. **Mark:** Last name inside fish symbol.

LAY, L J
602 Mimosa Dr, Burkburnett, TX 76354, Phone: 940-569-1329 **Specialties:** Working straight knives in standard patterns; some period pieces. **Patterns:** Drop-point hunters, Bowies and fighters. **Technical:** Grinds ATS-34 to mirror finish; likes Micarta handles. **Prices:** Moderate. **Remarks:** Full-time maker; first knife sold in 1985. **Mark:** Name or name with ram head and city or stamp L J Lay.

LAY, R J (BOB)
Box 1225, Logan Lake, BC, CANADA V0K 1W0, Phone: 250-523-9923, rjlay@telus.net **Specialties:** Traditional-styled, fancy straight knifes of his design. Specializing in hunters. **Patterns:** Bowies, fighters and hunters. **Technical:** Grinds high-performance stainless and tool steels. Uses exotic handle and spacer material. File cut, prefers narrow tang. Sheaths available. **Prices:** $200 to $500, some to $5000. **Remarks:** Full-time maker, first knife in 1976. Doing business as Lay's Custom Knives. **Mark:** Signature acid etched.

LEAVITT JR., EARL F
Pleasant Cove Rd Box 306, E. Boothbay, ME 04544, Phone: 207-633-3210 **Specialties:** 1500-1870 working straight knives and fighters; pole arms. **Patterns:** Historically significant knives, classic/modern custom designs. **Technical:** Flat-grinds O1; heat-treats. Filework available. **Prices:** $90 to $350; some to $1000. **Remarks:** Full-

time maker; first knife sold in 1981. Doing business as Old Colony Manufactory. **Mark:** Initials in oval.

LEBATARD, PAUL M
14700 Old River Rd, Vancleave, MS 39565, Phone: 228-826-4137, Fax: Cell phone: 228-238-7461, lebatardknives@aol.com **Specialties:** Sound working hunting and fillet knives, folding knives, practical tactical knives. **Patterns:** Hunters, trout and bird knives, fish fillet knives, kitchen knives, Bowies, tactical sheath knives, one- and two-blade folders. **Technical:** Grinds ATS-34, D-2, CPM 3-V, CPM-154CM, and commercial Damascus; forges and grinds 1095, O1, and 52100. **Prices:** $75 to $850; some to $1,200. **Remarks:** Full-time maker, first knife made in 1974. Charter member Gulf Coast Custom Knifemakers; Voting member Knifemaker's Guild. **Mark:** Stamped last name, or etched logo of last name, city, and state. **Other:** All knives are serial numbered and registered in the name of the original purchaser.

LEBER, HEINZ
Box 446, Hudson's Hope, BC, CANADA V0C 1V0, Phone: 250-783-5304 **Specialties:** Working straight knives of his design. **Patterns:** 20 models, from capers to Bowies. **Technical:** Hollow-grinds D2 and M2 steel; mirror-finishes and full tang only. Likes moose, elk, stone sheep for handles. **Prices:** $175 to $1000. **Remarks:** Full-time maker; first knife sold in 1975. **Mark:** Initials connected.

LEBLANC, GARY E
1403 Fairview Ln., Little Falls, MN 56345, Phone: 320-232-0245, butternutcove@ hotmail.com **Specialties:** Hunting and fishing, some kitchen knives and the Air Assualt tactical knife. Does own leather and Kydex work. **Patterns:** Stock removal. **Technical:** Mostly ATS34 for spec knives--orders, whatever the customer desires. **Prices:** Full range; $85 for parring knife, up $4000 plus fro collector grade hunter and fillet set. **Remarks:** First knife in 1998. **Mark:** Circular with star in center and LEBLANC on upper curve and KNIFEWORKS on lower curve.

LECK, DAL
Box 1054, Hayden, CO 81639, Phone: 970-276-3663 **Specialties:** Classic, traditional and working knives of his design and in standard patterns; period pieces. **Patterns:** Boots, daggers, fighters, hunters and push daggers. **Technical:** Forges O1 and 5160; makes his own Damascus. **Prices:** $175 to $700; some to $1500. **Remarks:** Part-time maker; first knife sold in 1990. Doing business as The Moonlight Smithy. **Mark:** Stamped: hammer and anvil with initials.

LEE, ETHAN
17200 N. Tucker School Rd., Sturgeon, MO 65284, Phone: 573-682-4364, elee4364@aol.com; Facebook page: ELEE Knives **Specialties:** Practical, usable, quality-crafted custom knives. **Technical:** Primarily damascus and hand-forged high-carbon steel, as well as 440C or 154CM stainless. **Prices:** $200-$500. **Remarks:** Part-time knifemaker; first knife made in 2007. **Mark:** ELEE.

LEE, RANDY
PO Box 1873, St. Johns, AZ 85936, Phone: 928-337-2594, randylee.knives@yahoo. com; Web.www.randyleeknives.com **Specialties:** Traditional working and using straight knives of his design. **Patterns:** Bowies, fighters, hunters, daggers. **Technical:** Grinds ATS-34, 440C Damascus, and 154CPM. Offers sheaths. **Prices:** $325 to $2500. **Remarks:** Full-time maker; first knife sold in 1979. **Mark:** Full name, city, state.

LEEPER, DAN
10344 Carney Dr. SE, Olympia, WA 98501, Phone: 360-250-2130, leeperd@ymail. com; Web: www.leeperknives.com **Specialties:** Hunters, fighters, bowies and chef's knives. **Technical:** Forges 52100, W2, 1084 and 5160 blade steels. Stock removal using CPM 154 stainless and other modern alloy steels. Does own heat treating and leather work. **Prices:** Start at $200. **Remarks:** ABS member. **Mark:** Dan Leeper Olympia WA.

LELAND, STEVE
2300 Sir Francis Drake Blvd, Fairfax, CA 94930-1118, Phone: 415-457-0318, Fax: 415-457-0995, Web: www.stephenleland@comcast.net **Specialties:** Traditional and working straight knives and folders of his design. **Patterns:** Hunters, fighters, Bowies, chefs. **Technical:** Grinds O1, ATS-34 and 440C. Does own heat treat. Makes nickel silver sheaths. **Prices:** $150 to $750; some to $1500. **Remarks:** Part-time maker; first knife sold in 1987. Doing business as Leland Handmade Knives. **Mark:** Last name.

LEMAIRE, RYAN M.
14045 Leon Rd., Abbeville, LA 70510, Phone: 337-893-1937, ryanlemaire@yahoo.com **Specialties:** All styles. Enjoys early American and frontier styles. Also, office desk sets for hunters and fishermen. **Patterns:** Hunters, camp knives, miniatures and period styles. **Technical:** Stock removal, carbon steel, stainless steel and damascus. Some forging of guards. Leather and wooden sheaths. **Prices:** Vary. **Remarks:** Member of American Bladesmith Society and Louisiana Craft Guild. **Mark:** First name, city and state in oval.

LEMCKE, JIM L
10649 Haddington Ste 180, Houston, TX 77043, Phone: 888-461-8632, Fax: 713-461-8221, jimll@hal-pc.org; Web: www.texasknife.com **Specialties:** Large supply of custom ground and factory finished blades; knife kits; leather sheaths; in-house heat treating and cryogenic tempering; exotic handle material (wood, ivory, oosik, horn, stabilized woods); machines and supplies for knifemaking; polishing and finishing supplies; heat treat ovens; etching equipment; bar, sheet and rod material (brass, stainless steel, nickel silver); titanium sheet material. Catalog. $4.

LEMELIN, STEPHANIE
3495 Olivier St., Brossard, CANADA J4Y 2J9, Phone: 514-462-1322, stephlemelin@hotmail.com
Specialties: Art knives, mostly ornate. **Patterns:** Knives with sculptured or carved handles. Straight knives and folders. **Technical:** Grinds 440C, CPM 154 and ATS-34, all knives hand filed and flat ground. **Remarks:** Part-time maker, jeweler and knifemaker; first knife sold in 2013. **Mark:** Lemelin.

LEMOINE, DAVID C
239 County Rd. 637, Mountain Home, AR 72653, Phone: 870-656-4730, dlemoine@davidlemoineknives.com; Web: davidlemoineknives.com
Specialties: Superior edge geometry on high performance custom classic and tactical straight blades and liner lock folders. **Patterns:** Hunters, skinners, bird and trout, fillet, camp, tactical, and military knives. Some miniatures. **Technical:** Flat and hollow grinds, CPMS90V, CPMS35V, CPMS30V, D2, A2, O1, 440C, ATS34, 154cm,Damasteel, Chad Nichols, Devin Thomas, and Robert Eggerling Damascus. Hidden and full tapered tangs, ultra-smooth folding mechanisms. File work, will use most all handle materials, does own professional in-house heat treatment and Rockwell testing. Hot blueing. **Prices:** $250 and up. **Remarks:** Part-time maker, giving and selling knives since 1986. Each patron receives a NIV Sportsman's Field Bible. **Mark:** Name, city and state in full oval with cross in the center. Reverse image on other side. The cross never changes.

LENNON, DALE
459 County Rd 1554, Alba, TX 75410, Phone: 903-765-2392, devildaddy1@netzero.net
Specialties: Working / using knives. **Patterns:** Hunters, fighters and Bowies. **Technical:** Grinds high carbon steels, ATS-34, forges some. **Prices:** Starts at $120. **Remarks:** Part-time maker, first knife sold in 2000. **Mark:** Last name.

LEONARD, RANDY JOE
188 Newton Rd, Sarepta, LA 71071, Phone: 318-994-2712

LEONE, NICK
9 Georgetown Dr, Pontoon Beach, IL 62040, Phone: 618-792-0734, nickleone@sbcglobal.net
Specialties: 18th century period straight knives. **Patterns:** Fighters, daggers, bowies. Besides period pieces makes modern designs. **Technical:** Forges 5160, W2, O1, 1098, 52100 and his own Damascus. **Prices:** $100 to $1000; some to $3500. **Remarks:** Full-time maker; first knife sold in 1987. Doing business as Anvil Head Forge. **Mark:** AHF, Leone, NL.

LERCH, MATTHEW
N88 W23462 North Lisbon Rd, Sussex, WI 53089, Phone: 262-246-6362, Web: www.lerchcustomknives.com
Specialties: Folders and folders with special mechanisms. **Patterns:** Interframe and integral folders; lock backs, assisted openers, side locks, button locks and liner locks. **Technical:** Grinds ATS-34, 1095, 440 and Damascus. Offers filework and embellished bolsters. **Prices:** $900 and up. **Remarks:** Full-time maker; first knife made in 1986. **Mark:** Last name.

LESSWING, KEVIN
29A East 34th St, Bayonne, NJ 07002, Phone: 551-221-1841, klesswing@excite.com
Specialties: Traditonal working and using straight knives of his design or to customer specs. A few folders. Makes own leather sheaths. **Patterns:** Hunters, daggers, bowies, bird and trout. **Technical:** Forges high carbon and tool steels, makes own Damascus, grinds CPM154CM, Damasteel, and other stainless steels. Does own heat treating. **Remarks:** Voting member of Knifemakers Guild, part-time maker. **Mark:** KL on early knives, LESSWING on Current knives.

LEU, POHAN
PO BOX 15423, Rio Rancho, NM 87174, Phone: 949-300-6412, pohanleu@hotmail.com Web: www.leucustom.com
Specialties: Japanese influenced fixed blades made to your custom specifications. Knives and swords. A2 tool steel, Stock Removal. **Prices:** $180 and up. **Remarks:** Full-time; first knife sold in 2003. **Mark:** LEU or PL.

LEVENGOOD, BILL
15011 Otto Rd, Tampa, FL 33624, Phone: 813-961-5688, bill.levengood@verison.net; Web: www.levengoodknives.com
Specialties: Working straight knives and folders. **Patterns:** Hunters, Bowies, folders and collector pieces. **Technical:** Grinds ATS-34, S-30V, CPM-154 and Damascus. **Prices:** $175 to $1500. **Remarks:** Full time maker; first knife sold in 1983. **Mark:** Last name, city, state.

LEVIN, JACK
201 Brighton 1st Road, Suite 3R, Brooklyn, NY 11235, Phone: 718-415-7911, jacklevin1@yahoo.com
Specialties: Folders with mechanisms.

LEVINE, BOB
101 Westwood Dr, Tullahoma, TN 37388, Phone: 931-454-9943, levineknives@msn.com
Specialties: Working left- and right-handed LinerLock® folders. **Patterns:** Hunters and folders. **Technical:** Grinds ATS-34, 440C, D2, O1 and some Damascus; hollow and some flat grinds. Uses fossil ivory, Micarta and exotic woods. Provides custom leather sheath with each fixed knife. **Prices:** Starting at $135. **Remarks:** Full-time maker; first knife sold in 1984. Voting member Knifemakers Guild, German Messermaher Guild. **Mark:** Name and logo.

LEWIS, BILL
PO Box 63, Riverside, IA 52327, Phone: 319-461-1609, kalewis52@exede.net
Specialties: Folders of all kinds including those made from one-piece of white tail antler with or without the crown. **Patterns:** Hunters, folding hunters, fillet, Bowies, push daggers, etc. **Prices:** $20 to $200. **Remarks:** Full-time maker; first knife sold in 1978. **Mark:** W.E.L.

LEWIS, MIKE
94134 Covey Ln., Coquille, OR 97423-6736, Phone: 386-753-0936, mikeswords@outlook.com
Specialties: Traditional straight knives. **Patterns:** Swords and daggers. **Technical:** Grinds 440C, ATS-34 and 5160. Frequently uses cast bronze and cast nickel guards and pommels. **Prices:** $100 to $750. **Remarks:** Part-time maker; first knife sold in 1988. **Mark:** Mike Lewis.

LEWIS, TOM R
1613 Standpipe Rd, Carlsbad, NM 88220, Phone: 575-885-3616, lewisknives@gmail.com
Specialties: Traditional working straight knives. **Patterns:** Outdoor knives, hunting knives and Bowies. **Technical:** Grinds ATS-34 and CPM-154, forges 5168, W2, 1084 and O1. Makes wire, pattern welded and chainsaw Damascus. **Prices:** $140 to $1500. **Remarks:** Full-time maker; first knife sold in 1980. Doing business as TR Lewis Handmade Knives. **Mark:** Lewis family crest.

LICATA, STEVEN
LICATA CUSTOM KNIVES, 146 Wilson St. 1st Floor, Boonton, NJ 07005, Phone: 973-588-4909, kniveslicata@aol.com; Web: www.licataknives.com
Specialties: Fantasy swords and knives. One-of-a-kind sculptures in steel. **Prices:** $200 to $25,000.

LIEBENBERG, ANDRE
8 Hilma Rd, Bordeaux, Randburg, GT, SOUTH AFRICA 2196, Phone: 011-787-2303
Specialties: High-art straight knives of his design. **Patterns:** Daggers, fighters and swords. **Technical:** Grinds 440C and 12C27. **Prices:** $250 to $500; some $4000 and higher. Giraffe bone handles with semi-precious stones. **Remarks:** Spare-time maker; first knife sold in 1990. **Mark:** Initials.

LIEGEY, KENNETH R
288 Carney Dr, Millwood, WV 25262, Phone: 304-273-9545
Specialties: Traditional working/using straight knives of his design and to customer specs. **Patterns:** Hunters, utility/camp knives, miniatures. **Technical:** Grinds 440C. **Prices:** $125 and up. **Remarks:** Spare-time maker; first knife sold in 1977. **Mark:** First and middle initials, last name.

LIGHTFOOT, GREG
RR #2, Kitscoty, AB, CANADA T0B 2P0, Phone: 780-846-2812; 780-800-1061, Pitbull@lightfootknives.com; Web: www.lightfootknives.com
Specialties: Stainless steel and Damascus. **Patterns:** Boots, fighters and locking folders. **Technical:** Grinds BG-42, 440C, D2, CPM steels, Stellite 6K. Offers engraving. **Prices:** $500 to $2000. **Remarks:** Full-time maker; first knife sold in 1988. Doing business as Lightfoot Knives. **Mark:** Shark with Lightfoot Knives below.

LIN, MARCUS
26825 Morena Dr., Mission Viejo, CA 92691, Phone: 310-720-4368, marcuslin7@gmail.com; Web: www.linknives.com
Specialties: Working knives in the Loveless tradition. **Patterns:** Original patterns direct from the Loveless Shop, designed by R.W. Loveless and, on special request, maker's own patterns. **Technical:** Main blade material is Hitachi's ATS-34; other steels available. Please inquire. **Prices:** $550 to $1,750. **Remarks:** Part-time maker since 2004. Mentored by R.W. Loveless and Jim Merritt. Sole authorship work: knives and sheaths, except for heat treat (which goes to Paul Bos Heat Treat). **Mark:** Main logo is "Marcus Lin, maker, Loveless Design."

LINKLATER, STEVE
8 Cossar Dr, Aurora, ON, CANADA L4G 3N8, Phone: 905-727-8929, knifman@sympatico.ca
Specialties: Traditional working/using straight knives and folders of his design. **Patterns:** Fighters, hunters and locking folders. **Technical:** Grinds ATS-34, 440V and D2. **Prices:** $125 to $350; some to $600. **Remarks:** Part-time maker; first knife sold in 1987. Doing business as Links Knives. **Mark:** LINKS.

LISCH, DAVID K
16948 Longmire Rd., Yelm, WA 98597, Phone: 206-919-5431, Web: www.davidlisch.com
Specialties: One-of-a-kind collectibles, straight knives and custom kitchen knives of own design and to customer specs. **Patterns:** Hunters, bowies and fighters. **Technical:** Forges all his own Damascus under 360-pound air hammer. Forges and chisels wrought iron, pure iron, and bronze butt caps. **Prices:** Starting at $1,000. **Remarks:** Full-time blacksmith, part-time bladesmith. **Mark:** D. Lisch M.S.

LISTER JR., WELDON E
116 Juniper Ln, Boerne, TX 78006, Phone: 210-269-0102, wlister@grtc.com; Web: www.weldonlister.com
Specialties: One-of-a-kind fancy and embellished folders. **Patterns:** Locking and slip-joint folders. **Technical:** Commercial Damascus and O1. All knives embellished. Engraves, inlays, carves and scrimshaws. **Prices:** Upscale. **Remarks:** Spare-time maker; first knife sold in 1991. **Mark:** Last name.

LITTLE, GARY M
94716 Conklin Meadows Ln, PO Box 156, Broadbent, OR 97414, Phone: 503-572-2656
Specialties: Fancy working knives. **Patterns:** Hunters, tantos, Bowies, axes and buckskinners; locking folders and interframes. **Technical:** Forges and grinds O1, L6m,

1095, and 15N20; makes his own Damascus; bronze fittings. **Prices:** $120 to $1500. **Remarks:** Full-time maker; first knife sold in 1979. Doing business as Conklin Meadows Forge. **Mark:** Name, city and state.

LITTLE, LARRY

1A Cranberry Ln, Spencer, MA 01562, Phone: 508-885-2301, littcran@aol.com
Specialties: Working straight knives of his design or to customer specs. Likes Scagel-style. **Patterns:** Hunters, fighters, Bowies, folders. **Technical:** Grinds and forges L6, O1, 5160, 1095, 1080. Prefers natural handle material especially antler. Uses nickel silver. Makes own heavy duty leather sheath. **Prices:** Start at $125. **Remarks:** Part-time maker. First knife sold in 1985. Offers knife repairs. **Mark:** Little on one side, LL brand on the other.

LIVESAY, NEWT

3306 S. Dogwood St, Siloam Springs, AR 72761, Phone: 479-549-3356, Fax: 479-549-3357, newt@newtlivesay.com; Web:www.newtlivesay.com
Specialties: Combat utility knives, hunting knives, titanium knives, swords, axes, KYDWX sheaths for knives and pistols, custom orders.

LIVINGSTON, ROBERT C

PO Box 6, Murphy, NC 28906, Phone: 704-837-4155
Specialties: Art letter openers to working straight knives. **Patterns:** Minis to machetes. **Technical:** Forges and grinds most steels. **Prices:** Start at $20. **Remarks:** Full-time maker; first knife sold in 1988. Doing business as Mystik Knifeworks. **Mark:** MYSTIK.

LOCKETT, LOWELL C.

344 Spring Hill Dr., Canton, GA 30115, Phone: 770-846-8114, lcl1932@gmail.com or spur1932@windstream.net
Technical: Forges 5160, 1095 and other blade steels, and uses desert ironwood, ivory and other handle materials. **Prices:** $150 to $1,500. **Remarks:** ABS journeyman smith.

LOCKETT, STERLING

527 E Amherst Dr, Burbank, CA 91504, Phone: 818-846-5799
Specialties: Working straight knives and folders to customer specs. **Patterns:** Hunters and fighters. **Technical:** Grinds. **Prices:** Moderate. **Remarks:** Spare-time maker. **Mark:** Name, city with hearts.

LOERCHNER, WOLFGANG

WOLFE FINE KNIVES, PO Box 255, Bayfield, ON, CANADA N0M 1G0, Phone: 519-565-2196
Specialties: Traditional straight knives, mostly ornate. **Patterns:** Small swords, daggers and stilettos; locking folders and miniatures. **Technical:** Grinds D2, 440C and 154CM; all knives hand-filed and flat-ground. **Prices:** Vary. **Remarks:** Full-time maker; first knife sold in 1983. Doing business as Wolfe Fine Knives. **Mark:** WOLFE.

LOGAN, IRON JOHN

4260 Covert, Leslie, MI 49251, ironjohnlogan@gmail.com; www.ironjohnlogan.com
Patterns: Hunting, camping, outdoor sheath knives, folding knives, axes, tomahawks, historical knives. swords, working chef's knives, and woodwork and leather work knives. **Technical:** Forges low-alloy steels, wrought iron, bloom and hearth materials, or high-alloy steel as the job insists. Makes own damascus and San Mai seel, modern materials and stainlesses. Vegetable-tanned leather sheaths, and American hardwood handles like hickory, walnut and cherry. **Prices:** $200 to $2,000. **Remarks:** Full-time bladesmith; first knife made in 1998. **Mark:** Two horizontal lines crossed by one vertical line and an angle off the bottom to creat a "J."

LONEWOLF, J AGUIRRE

481 Hwy 105, Demorest, GA 30535, Phone: 706-754-4660, Fax: 706-754-8470, lonewolfandsons@windstream.net, Web: www.knivesbylonewolf.com www.eagleswinggallery.com
Specialties: High-art working and using straight knives of his design. **Patterns:** Bowies, hunters, utility/camp knives and fine steel blades. **Technical:** Forges Damascus and high-carbon steel. Most knives have hand-carved moose antler handles. **Prices:** $55 to $500; some to $2000. **Remarks:** Full-time maker; first knife sold in 1980. Doing business as Lonewolf and Sons LLC. **Mark:** Stamp.

LONG, GLENN A

10090 SW 186th Ave, Dunnellon, FL 34432, Phone: 352-489-4272, galong99@att.net
Specialties: Classic working and using straight knives of his design and to customer specs. **Patterns:** Hunters, Bowies, utility. **Technical:** Grinds 440C D2 and 440V. **Prices:** $85 to $300; some to $800. **Remarks:** Part-time maker; first knife sold in 1990. **Mark:** Last name inside diamond.

LONGWORTH, DAVE

1200 Red Oak Ridge, Felicity, OH 45120, Phone: 513-876-2372
Specialties: High-tech working knives. **Patterns:** Locking folders, hunters, fighters and elaborate daggers. **Technical:** Grinds O1, ATS-34, 440C; buys Damascus. **Prices:** $125 to $600; some higher. **Remarks:** Part-time maker; first knife sold in 1980. **Mark:** Last name.

LOOS, HENRY C

210 Ingraham, New Hyde Park, NY 11040, Phone: 516-354-1943, hcloos@optonline.net
Specialties: Miniature fancy knives and period pieces of his design. **Patterns:** Bowies, daggers and swords. **Technical:** Grinds O1 and 440C. Uses sterling, 18K, rubies and emeralds. All knives come with handmade hardwood cases. **Prices:** $90 to $195; some to $250. **Remarks:** Spare-time maker; first knife sold in 1990. **Mark:** Script last initial.

LOUKIDES, DAVID E

76 Crescent Circle, Cheshire, CT 06410, Phone: 203-271-3023, Loussharp1@sbcglobal.net; Web: www.prayerknives.com
Specialties: Hand forged working blades and collectible pieces. **Patterns:** Chef knives, bowies, and hunting knives. . **Technical:** Uses 1084, 1095, 5160, W2, O1 and 1084-and-

15N20 damascus. **Prices:** Normally $200 to $1,000. **Remarks:** part-time maker, Journeyman Bladesmith, Full-time Journeyman Toolmaker. **Mark:** Loukides JS.

LOVE, ED

19443 Mill Oak, San Antonio, TX 78258, Phone: 210-497-1021, Fax: 210-497-1021, annaedlove@sbcglobal.net
Specialties: Hunting, working knives and some art pieces. **Technical:** Grinds ATS-34, and 440C. **Prices:** $150 and up. **Remarks:** Part-time maker. First knife sold in 1980. **Mark:** Name in a weeping heart.

LOVESTRAND, SCHUYLER

1136 19th St SW, Vero Beach, FL 32962, Phone: 772-778-0282, Fax: 772-466-1126, lovestranded@aol.com
Specialties: Fancy working straight knives of his design and to customer specs; unusual fossil ivories. **Patterns:** Hunters, fighters, Bowies and fishing knives. **Technical:** Grinds stainless steel. **Prices:** $550 to $2,500. **Remarks:** Part-time maker; first knife sold in 1982. **Mark:** Name in logo.

LOVETT, MICHAEL

PO Box 121, Mound, TX 76558, Phone: 254-865-9956, michaellovett@embarqmail.com
Specialties: The Loveless Connection Knives as per R.W. Loveless-Jim Merritt. **Patterns:** All Loveless Patterns and Original Lovett Patterns. **Technical:** Complicated double grinds and premium fit and finish. **Prices:** $1000 and up. **Remarks:** High degree of fit and finish - Authorized collection by R. W. Loveless **Mark:** Loveless Authorized football or double nude.

LOZIER, DON

5394 SE 168th Ave, Ocklawaha, FL 32179, Phone: 352-625-3576
Specialties: Tactical folders, collaborative art pieces and sole authorship fixed blades. **Patterns:** Various. **Technical:** Grinds CPM 154, 440C and stainless damascus. **Prices:** $350 to $15,000. **Remarks:** Full-time maker and dealer. **Mark:** Name or DLFF.

LUCHAK, BOB

15705 Woodforest Blvd, Channelview, TX 77530, Phone: 281-452-1779
Specialties: Presentation knives; start of The Survivor series. **Patterns:** Skinners, Bowies, camp axes, steak knife sets and fillet knives. **Technical:** Grinds 440C. Offers electronic etching; filework. **Prices:** $50 to $1500. **Remarks:** Full-time maker; first knife sold in 1983. Doing business as Teddybear Knives. **Mark:** Full name, city and state with Teddybear logo.

LUCHINI, BOB

1220 Dana Ave, Palo Alto, CA 94301, Phone: 650-321-8095, rwluchin@bechtel.com

LUCIE, JAMES R

9100 Calera Dr., Unit 9, Austin, TX 78735, Phone: 512-436-9202 or 231-557-3084, scagel@netonecom.net
Specialties: William Scagel-style knives. **Patterns:** Authentic scagel-style knives and miniatures. **Technical:** Forges 1084 steel. **Prices:** $1,200 and up. **Remarks:** Full-time maker; first knife sold in 1975. Believes in sole authorship of his work. ABS Journeyman Smith. **Mark:** Scagel-style Kris stamp and maker's name and address.

LUCKETT, BILL

108 Amantes Ln, Weatherford, TX 76088, Phone: 817-320-1568, luckettknives@gmail.com Web: www.billluckettcustomknives.com
Specialties: Uniquely patterned robust straight knives. **Patterns:** Fighters, Bowies, hunters. **Technical:** 154CM stainless.**Prices:** $550 to $1500. **Remarks:** Part-time maker; first knife sold in 1975. Knifemakers Guild Member. **Mark:** Last name over Bowie logo.

LUDWIG, RICHARD O

57-63 65 St, Maspeth, NY 11378, Phone: 718-497-5969
Specialties: Traditional working/using knives. **Patterns:** Boots, hunters and utility/camp knives folders. **Technical:** Grinds 440C, ATS-34 and BG42. File work on guards and handles; silver spacers. Offers scrimshaw. **Prices:** $325 to $400; some to $2000. **Remarks:** Full-time maker. **Mark:** Stamped first initial, last name, state.

LUI, RONALD M

4042 Harding Ave, Honolulu, HI 96816, Phone: 808-734-7746
Specialties: Working straight knives and folders in standard patterns. **Patterns:** Hunters, boots and liner locks. **Technical:** Grinds 440C and ATS-34. **Prices:** $100 to $700. **Remarks:** Spare-time maker; first knife sold in 1988. **Mark:** Initials connected.

LUNDSTROM, JAN-AKE

Mastmostigen 8, Dals-Langed, SWEDEN 66010, Phone: 0531-40270
Specialties: Viking swords, axes and knives in cooperation with handle makers. **Patterns:** All traditional-styles, especially swords and inlaid blades. **Technical:** Forges his own Damascus and laminated steel. **Prices:** $200 to $1000. **Remarks:** Full-time maker; first knife sold in 1985; collaborates with museums. **Mark:** Runic.

LUNDSTROM, TORBJORN (TOBBE)

Norrskenet 4, Are, SWEDEN 83013, 9lundstrm@telia.com Web: http://tobbeiare.se/site/
Specialties: Hunters and collectible knives. **Patterns:** Nordic-style hunters and art knives with unique materials such as mammoth and fossil walrus ivory. **Technical:** Uses forged blades by other makers, particularly Mattias Styrefors who mostly uses 15N20 and 20C steels and is a mosaic blacksmith. **Remarks:** First knife made in 1986.

LUNN, GAIL

434 CR 1422, Mountain Home, AR 72653, Phone: 870-424-2662, gail@lunnknives.com; Web: www.lunnknives.com
Specialties: Fancy folders and double action autos, some straight blades. **Patterns:** One-of-a-kind, all types. **Technical:** Stock removal, hand made. **Prices:** $300 and up. **Remarks:** Fancy file work, exotic materials, inlays, stone etc. **Mark:** Name in script.

LUNN, LARRY A
434 CR 1422, Mountain Home, AR 72653, Phone: 870-424-2662, larry@lunnknives.com; Web: www.lunnknives.com
Specialties: Fancy folders and double action autos; some straight blades. **Patterns:** All types; his own designs. **Technical:** Stock removal; commercial Damascus. **Prices:** $125 and up. **Remarks:** File work inlays and exotic materials. **Mark:** Name in script.

LUPOLE, JAMIE G
KUMA KNIVES, 285 Main St., Kirkwood, NY 13795, Phone: 607-775-9368, jlupole@stny.rr.com
Specialties: Working and collector grade fixed blades, ethnic-styled blades. **Patterns:** Fighters, Bowies, tacticals, hunters, camp, utility, personal carry knives, some swords. **Technical:** Forges and grinds 10XX series and other high-carbon steels, grinds ATS-34 and 440C, will use just about every handle material available. **Prices:** $100 to $500 and up. **Remarks:** Part-time maker since 1999. **Mark:** "KUMA" and/or name, city, state etched, or "Daiqoma saku" in Kanji.

LURQUIN, SAMUEL
Hameau Du Bois, Hoyaux 10, 7133 Buvrinnes Belgique, Binches, BELGIUM, Phone: 0032-478-349-051, knifespirit@hotmail.com; Web: www.samuel-lurquin.com
Specialties: Forged bowies, fighters, hunters and working knives. **Technical:** Uses, but is not limited to, W1, W2 and L6 blade steels, creates own pattern-welded steel. Commonly uses wood, walrus ivory, mammoth ivory and stag for handles. **Prices:** $500 and up. **Remarks:** Full-time maker beginning in 2014, ABS master smith as of 2015.

LUTZ, GREG
127 Crescent Rd, Greenwood, SC 29646, Phone: 864-229-7340
Specialties: Working and using knives and period pieces of his design and to customer specs. **Patterns:** Fighters, hunters and swords. **Technical:** Forges 1095 and O1; grinds ATS-34. Differentially heat-treats forged blades; uses cryogenic treatment on ATS-34. **Prices:** $50 to $350; some to $1200. **Remarks:** Part-time maker; first knife sold in 1986. Doing business as Scorpion Forge. **Mark:** First initial, last name.

LYLE III, ERNEST L
LYLE KNIVES, PO Box 1755, Chiefland, FL 32644, Phone: 352-490-6693, ernestlyle@msn.com
Specialties: Fancy period pieces; one-of-a-kind and limited editions. **Patterns:** Arabian/Persian influenced fighters, military knives, Bowies and Roman short swords; several styles of hunters. **Technical:** Grinds 440C, D2 and 154 CM. Engraves. **Prices:** $200 - $7500. **Remarks:** Full-time maker; first knife sold in 1972. **Mark:** Lyle Knives over Chiefland, Fla.

LYNCH, TAD
140 Timberline Dr., Beebe, AR 72012, Phone: 501-626-1647, lynchknives@yahoo.com Web: lynchknives.com
Specialties: Forged fixed blades. **Patterns:** Bowies, choppers, fighters, hunters. **Technical:** Hand-forged W-2, 1084, 1095 clay quenched 52100, 5160. **Prices:** Starting at $250. **Remarks:** Part-time maker, also offers custom leather work via wife Amy Lynch. **Mark:** T.D. Lynch over anvil.

LYNN, ARTHUR
29 Camino San Cristobal, Galisteo, NM 87540, Phone: 505-466-3541, amyandarthur@aol.com
Specialties: Handforged Damascus knives. **Patterns:** Folders, hunters, Bowies, fighters, kitchen. **Technical:** Forges own Damascus. **Prices:** Moderate.

LYONS, WILLIAM R. (BILL)
7287 Ave. 354, Palisade, NE 69040, Phone: 970-219-1600, wrlyons@lyonsknives.com; Web: www.lyonsknives.com
Specialties: Scrimshaw, ivory inlay, silver wire inlay, hand-carved wood handles and leather handles. **Patterns:** Fighters, bowies, camp knives, integrals, and Moran and Scagel styles. **Technical:** Heat treating to very precise levels, makes own damascus and forges O1, O6, W2, 5160, 1084, 1095, 15N20 and L6. **Prices:** $250 to $3,000. **Remarks:** Full-time maker; member of ABS since 1990. Antique reproductions, all natural handle material, leather sheaths. **Mark:** LYONS.

M

MACCAUGHTRY, SCOTT F.
Fullerton Forge, 1824 Sorrel St, Camarillo, CA 93010, Phone: 805-750-2137, smack308@hotmail.com
Specialties: Fixed blades and folders. **Technical:** Forges 5160, 52100, W2 and his own damascus using 1084 and 15N20 steels. **Prices:** $275 and up. **Remarks:** ABS journeyman smith. **Mark:** S. MacCaughtry in script, and J.S. on the back side.

MACDONALD, DAVID
2824 Hwy 47, Los Lunas, NM 87031, Phone: 505-866-5866

MACKIE, JOHN
13653 Lanning, Whittier, CA 90605, Phone: 562-945-6104
Specialties: Forged. **Patterns:** Bowie and camp knives. **Technical:** Attended ABS Bladesmith School. **Prices:** $75 to $500. **Mark:** Oval JOHN MACKIE over FORGED with an anvil and thistle in the middle.

MACKRILL, STEPHEN
PO Box 1580, Pinegowrie, Johannesburg, GT, SOUTH AFRICA 2123, Phone: 27-11-474-7139, Fax: 27-11-474-7139, info@mackrill.co.za; Web: www.mackrill.net
Specialties: Art fancy, historical, collectors and corporate gifts cutlery. **Patterns:** Fighters, hunters, camp, custom lock back and LinerLock® folders. **Technical:** N690, 12C27, ATS-34, silver and gold inlay on handles; wooden and silver sheaths. **Prices:** $330 and upwards. **Remarks:** First knife sold in 1978. **Mark:** Mackrill fish with country of origin.

MADRULLI, MME JOELLE
Residence Ste Catherine B1, Salon De Provence, FRANCE 13330

MAESTRI, PETER A
S11251 Fairview Rd, Spring Green, WI 53588, Phone: 608-546-4481
Specialties: Working straight knives in standard patterns. **Patterns:** Camp and fishing knives, utility green-river-styled. **Technical:** Grinds 440C, 154CM and 440A. **Prices:** $15 to $45; some to $150. **Remarks:** Full-time maker; first knife sold in 1981. Provides professional cutler service to professional cutters. **Mark:** CARISOLO, MAESTRI BROS., or signature.

MAGEE, JIM
741 S. Ohio St., Salina, KS 67401, Phone: 785-820-6928, jimmagee@cox.net
Specialties: Working and fancy folding knives. **Patterns:** Liner locking folders, favorite is his Persian. **Technical:** Grinds ATS-34, Devin Thomas & Eggerling Damascus, titanium. Liners Prefer mother-of-pearl handles. **Prices:** Start at $225 to $1200. **Remarks:** Part-time maker, first knife sold in 2001. Purveyor since 1982. Past president of the Professional Knifemakers Association **Mark:** Last name.

MAGRUDER, JASON
3700 Bellinger Ln. #13, Medford, OR 97501, Phone: 719-210-1579, jason@magruderknives.com; web: MagruderKnives.com
Specialties: Unique and innovative designs combining the latest modern materials with traditional hand craftsmanship. **Patterns:** Fancy neck knives. Tactical gents folders. Working straight knives. **Technical:** Flats grinds CPM3v, CPM154, ATS34, 1080, and his own forged damascus. Hand carves carbon fiber, titanium, wood, ivory, and pearl handles. Filework and carving on blades. **Prices:** $150 and up. **Remarks:** Part-time maker; first knife sold in 2000. **Mark:** Last name.

MAHOMEDY, A R
PO Box 76280, Marble Ray, KZN, SOUTH AFRICA 4035, Phone: +27 31 577 1451, arm-koknives@mweb.co.za; Web: www.arm-koknives.co.za
Specialties: Daggers and elegant folders of own design finished with finest exotic materials currently available. **Technical:** Via stock removal, grinds Damasteel, Damascus and the famous hardenable stainless steels. **Prices:** U.S. $650 and up. **Remarks:** Part-time maker. First knife sold in 1995. Voting member knifemakers guild of SA, FEGA member starting out Engraving. **Mark:** Initials A R M crowned with a "Minaret."

MAHOMEDY, HUMAYD A.R.
PO BOX 76280, Marble Ray, KZN, SOUTH AFRICA 4035, Phone: +27 31 577 1451, arm-koknives@mweb.co.za
Specialties: Tactical folding and fixed blade knives. **Patterns:** Fighters, utilities, tacticals, folders and fixed blades, daggers, modern interpretation of Bowies. **Technical:** Stock-removal knives of Bohler N690, Bohler K110, Bohler K460, Sandvik 12C27, Sandvik RWL 34. Handle materials used are G10, Micarta, Cape Buffalo horn, Water Buffalo horn, Kudu horn, Gemsbok horn, Giraffe bone, Elephant ivory, Mammoth ivory, Arizona desert ironwood, stabilised and dyed burls. **Prices:** $250 - $1000. **Remarks:** First knife sold in 2002. Full-time knifemaker since 2002. First person of color making knives full-time in South Africa. Doing business as HARM EDGED TOOLS. **Mark:** HARM and arrow over EDGED TOOLS.

MAIENKNECHT, STANLEY
38648 S R 800, Sardis, OH 43946

MAINES, JAY
SUNRISE RIVER CUSTOM KNIVES, 5584 266th St., Wyoming, MN 55092, Phone: 651-462-5301, jaymaines@fronternet.net; Web: http://www.sunrisecustomknives.com
Specialties: Heavy duty working, classic and traditional fixed blades. Some high-tech and fancy embellished knives available. **Patterns:** Hunters, including wild boar hunting knives and spears, skinners, fillet knives, bowies tantos, boot daggers, barbecue implements and cutlery sets. **Technical:** Hollow ground, stock removal blades of 440C, ATS-34 and CPM S-90V. Prefers natural handle materials, exotic hard woods, and stag, rams and buffalo horns. Offers dovetailed bolsters in brass, stainless steel and nickel silver. Custom sheaths from matching wood or hand-stitched from heavy duty water buffalo hide. **Prices:** Moderate to up-scale. **Remarks:** Part-time maker; first knife sold in 1992. Doing business as Sunrise River Custom Knives. Offers fixed blade knife repair and handle conversions, and custom leather sheaths. **Mark:** Full name under a Rising Sun logo.

MAINOLFI, DR. RICCARDO
Via Pastiniello, 6-84017, Positano (SA), ITALY, Phone: +39 3338128775 OR +39 3493586416, riccardomainolfi@gmail.com; Web: www.mainolfiknife.com, Instagram @ riccardomainolfi, Facebook @ Riccardo Mainolfi
Specialties: Handmade hunting and tactical knives, as well as art knives and collaborative pieces with famous engravers. **Technical:** Stock removal method of blade making using RWL-34, CPM 154 and Elmax steel, and occasionally CPM S30V, CPM S35V or Sleipner steels. Heat treats own blades in furnace with electronically controlled temperature. Uses AISI 416 and AISI 304 for bolsters and pins. **Prices:** $200 and up. **Remarks:** Part-time maker; first knife made in 2003, purchasing his first belt sander in 2004. **Mark:** Stylized blade in which is written the maker's name, with the beautiful city in which he resides.

MAISEY, ALAN
PO Box 197, Vincentia, NSW, AUSTRALIA 2540, Phone: 2-4443 7829, tosanaji@excite.com
Specialties: Daggers, especially krisses; period pieces. **Technical:** Offers knives and finished blades in Damascus and nickel Damascus. **Prices:** $75 to $2000; some higher.

Remarks: Part-time maker; provides complete restoration service for krisses. Trained by a Japanese Kris smith. **Mark:** None, triangle in a box, or three peaks.

MAJORS, CHARLIE

1911 King Richards Ct, Montgomery, TX 77316, Phone: 713-826-3135, charliemajors@sbcglobal.net

Specialties: Fixed-blade hunters and slip-joint and lock-back folders. **Technical:** Practices stock removal method, preferring CPM154 steel and natural handle materials such as ironwood, stag, and mammoth ivory. Also takes customer requests. Does own heat treating and cryogenic quenching. **Remarks:** First knife made in 1980.

MAKOTO, KUNITOMO

3-3-18 Imazu-cho, Fukuyama-city, Hiroshima, JAPAN, Phone: 084-933-5874, kunitomo@po.iijnet.or.jp

MALABY, RAYMOND J

835 Calhoun Ave, Juneau, AK 99801, Phone: 907-586-6981, Fax: 907-523-8031, malaby@gci.net

Specialties: Straight working knives. **Patterns:** Hunters, skiners, Bowies, and camp knives. **Technical:** Hand forged 1084, 5160, O1 and grinds ATS-34 stainless. **Prices:** $195 to $400. **Remarks:** First knife sold in 1994. **Mark:** First initial, last name, city, and state.

MALLOY, JOE

1039 Schwabe St, Freeland, PA 18224, Phone: 570-436-6416, jdmalloy@msn.com

Specialties: Working straight knives of his own design or to customers' specs. **Patterns:** Full-tang hunters, bird & trout knives, neck knives, folders (plain or fancy), fighters, camp knives, khukuris and tomahawks. DEA specs. Each knife comes with a custom leather or Kydex sheath. **Technical:** Hollow or flat grinds CPM 154, D2, A2, 440C and damascus. Titanium on fancy folders with multi-color anodizing and filework. **Prices:** $200 to $1,800. **Remarks:** Part-time maker; first knife sold in 1982. Voting member of the Knifemakers' Guild since 1990. **Mark:** First and middle initials and last name, city and state.

MANARO, SAL

10 Peri Ave., Holbrook, NY 11741, Phone: 631-737-1180, maker@manaroknives.com

Specialties: Tactical folders, bolstered titanium LinerLocks, handmade folders, and fixed blades with hand-checkered components. **Technical:** Compound grinds, hidden fasteners and welded components, with blade steels including CPM-154, damascus, Stellite, D2, S30V and O-1 by the stock-removal method of blade making. **Prices:** $500 and up. **Remarks:** Part-time maker, made first knife in 2001. **Mark:** Last name with arrowhead underline.

MANDT, JOE

3735 Overlook Dr. NE, St. Petersburg, FL 33703, Phone: 813-244-3816, jmforge@mac.com

Specialties: Forged Bowies, camp knives, hunters, skinners, fighters, boot knives, military style field knives. **Technical:** Forges plain carbon steel and high carbon tool steels, including W2, 1084, 5160, O1, 9260, 15N20, cable Damascus, pattern welded Damascus, flat and convex grinds. Prefers natural handle materials, hand-rubbed finishes, and stainless low carbon steel, Damascus and wright iron fittings. Does own heat treat. **Prices:** $150 to $750. **Remarks:** Part-time maker, first knife sold in 206. **Mark:** "MANDT".

MANEKER, KENNETH

RR 2, Galiano Island, BC, CANADA V0N 1P0, Phone: 604-539-2084

Specialties: Working straight knives; period pieces. **Patterns:** Camp knives and hunters; French chef knives. **Technical:** Grinds 440C, 154CM and Vascowear. **Prices:** $50 to $200; some to $300. **Remarks:** Part-time maker; first knife sold in 1981. Doing business as Water Mountain Knives. **Mark:** Japanese Kanji of initials, plus glyph.

MANLEY, DAVID W

3270 Six Mile Hwy, Central, SC 29630, Phone: 864-654-1125, dmanleyknives@bellsouth.net

Specialties: Working straight knives of his design or to custom specs. **Patterns:** Hunters, boot and fighters. **Technical:** Grinds 440C and ATS-34. **Prices:** $80 to $400. **Remarks:** Part-time maker; first knife sold in 1994. **Mark:** First initial, last name, year and serial number.

MANN, MICHAEL L

IDAHO KNIFE WORKS, PO Box 144, Spirit Lake, ID 83869, Phone: 509 994-9394, Web: www.idahoknifeworks.com

Specialties: Good working blades, historical reproductions, modern or custom designs. **Patterns:** Cowboy bowies, mountain man period blades, old-style folders, designer and maker of "The Cliff Knife," hunting and fillet knives. **Technical:** Forges 5160 high-carbon steel blades. Stock removal of 15N20. **Prices:** $200 to $730. **Remarks:** Made first knife in 1965. Full-time making knives as Idaho Knife Works since 1989. Functional as well as collectible. Each knife is truly unique! **Mark:** Four mountain peaks are his initials MM.

MANN, TIM

BLADEWORKS, PO Box 1196, Honokaa, HI 96727, Phone: 808-775-0949, Fax: 808-775-0949, birdman@shaka.com

Specialties: Hand-forged knives and swords. **Patterns:** Bowies, tantos, pesh kabz, daggers. **Technical:** Use 5160, 1050, 1075, 1095 and ATS-34 steels, cable Damascus. **Prices:** $200 to $800. **Remarks:** Just learning to forge Damascus. **Mark:** None yet.

MARAGNI, DAN

RD 1 Box 106, Georgetown, NY 13072, Phone: 315-662-7490

Specialties: Heavy-duty working knives, some investor class. **Patterns:** Hunters, fighters and camp knives, some Scottish types. **Technical:** Forges W2 and his own Damascus; toughness and edge-holding a high priority. **Prices:** $125 to $500; some to $1000.

Remarks: Full-time maker; first knife sold in 1975. **Mark:** Celtic initials in circle.

MARCHAND, RICK

Wildertools, 69 Maple Ave., POB 1635, Lunenburg, Nova Scotia, CANADA B0J 2C0, Phone: 226-783-8771, rickmarchand@wildertools.com; Web: www.wildertools.com

Specialties: Specializing in multicultural, period stylized blades and accoutrements. **Technical:** Hand forged from 1070/84/95, L6 and 52100 steel. **Prices:** $175 - $1,500. **Remarks:** Maker since 2007. ABS apprentice smith. **Mark:** Tang stamp: "MARCHAND" along with two Japanese-style characters resembling "W" and "M."

MARINGER, TOM

2692 Powell St., Springdale, AR 72764, maringer@arkansas.net; Web: shirepost.com/cutlery.

Specialties: Working straight and curved blades with stainless steel furniture and wire-wrapped handles. **Patterns:** Subhilts, daggers, boots, swords. **Technical:** Grinds D-2, A-2, ATS-34. May be safely disassembled by the owner via pommel screw or pegged construction. **Prices:** $2000 to $3000, some to $20,000. **Remarks:** Former full-time maker, now part-time. First knife sold in 1975. **Mark:** Full name, year, and serial number etched on tang under handle.

MARKLEY, KEN

7651 Cabin Creek Lane, Sparta, IL 62286, Phone: 618-443-5284

Specialties: Traditional working and using knives of his design and to customer specs. **Patterns:** Fighters, hunters and utility/camp knives. **Technical:** Forges 5160, 1095 and L6; makes his own Damascus; does file work. **Prices:** $150 to $800; some to $2000. **Remarks:** Part-time maker; first knife sold in 1991. Doing business as Cabin Creek Forge. **Mark:** Last name, JS.

MARLOWE, CHARLES

10822 Poppleton Ave, Omaha, NE 68144, Phone: 402-933-5065, cmarlowe1@cox.net; Web: www.marloweknives.com

Specialties: Folding knives and balisong. **Patterns:** Tactical pattern folders. **Technical:** Grind ATS-34, S30V, CPM154, 154CM, Damasteel, others on request. Forges/grinds 1095 on occasion. **Prices:** Start at $450. **Remarks:** First knife sold in 1993. Full-time since 1999. **Mark:** Turtle logo with Marlowe above, year below.

MARLOWE, DONALD

2554 Oakland Rd, Dover, PA 17315, Phone: 717-764-6055

Specialties: Working straight knives in standard patterns. **Patterns:** Bowies, fighters, boots and utility knives. **Technical:** Grinds D2 and 440C. Integral design hunter models. **Prices:** $130 to $850. **Remarks:** Spare-time maker; first knife sold in 1977. **Mark:** Last name.

MARSH, JEREMY

6169 3 Mile NE, Ada, MI 49301, Phone: 616-889-1945, steelbean@hotmail.com; Web: www.marshcustomknives.com

Specialties: Locking liner folders, dressed-up gents knives, tactical knives, and dress tacticals. **Technical:** CPM S30V stainless and Damascus blade steels using the stock-removal method of bladesmithing. **Prices:** $450 to $1500. **Remarks:** Self-taught, part-time knifemaker; first knife made in 2004. **Mark:** Maker's last name and large, stylized M.

MARSHALL, REX

1115 State Rte. 380, Wilmington, OH 45177, Phone: 937-604-8430, rexmarshall@hotmail.com; www.rexmarshallcustomknives.com

Specialties: Handforged fixed-blade traditional hunters, bowies and fighters. **Technical:** Forges and stock removal, using 5160, 1080, 1095 and 52100 high carbon steels, with stainless steels on request. Will custom build to customer's specifications. **Prices:** $125 and up. **Remarks:** Offers custom plain and lined sheaths, decorative filework. First knife made in 2011. **Mark:** Rex Marshall over eagle.

MARTIN, CORY

4249 Taylor Harbor #7, Racine, WI 53403, Phone: 262-352-5392, info@corymartinimaging.com; Web: www.corymartinimaging.com, Facebook: Cory Martin Imaging, Instagram: corymartinimaging

Specialties: Unique high-tech folders using a wide variety of materials. CNC skills used to create inlays, textures and patterns. **Technical:** Forges own damascus as well as his own unique "reverse san mai damascus." **Prices:** Moderate. **Remarks:** Part-time maker and son of Peter Martin, Cory is establishing his own unique style with creative designs and unmatched fit and finish. **Mark:** "CMD" and "C. Martin."

MARTIN, GENE

PO Box 396, Williams, OR 97544, Phone: 541-846-6755, bladesmith@customknife.com

Specialties: Straight knives and folders. **Patterns:** Fighters, hunters, skinners, boot knives, spring back and lock back folders. **Technical:** Grinds ATS-34, 440C, Damascus and 154CM. Forges; makes own Damascus; scrimshaws. **Prices:** $150 to $2500. **Remarks:** Full-time maker; first knife sold in 1993. Doing business as Provision Forge. **Mark:** Name and/or crossed staff and sword.

MARTIN, HAL W

781 Hwy 95, Morrilton, AR 72110, Phone: 501-354-1682, hal.martin@sbcglobal.net

Specialties: Hunters, Bowies and fighters. **Prices:** $250 and up. **Mark:** MARTIN.

MARTIN, HERB

2500 Starwood Dr, Richmond, VA 23229, Phone: 804-747-1675, hamjlm@hotmail.com

Specialties: Working straight knives. **Patterns:** Skinners, hunters and utility. **Technical:** Hollow grinds ATS-34, and Micarta handles. **Prices:** $125 to $200. **Remarks:** Part-time Maker. First knife sold in 2001. **Mark:** HA MARTIN.

MARTIN, MICHAEL W

Box 572, Jefferson St, Beckville, TX 75631, Phone: 903-678-2161

Specialties: Classic working/using straight knives of his design and in standard patterns.

Patterns: Hunters. **Technical:** Grinds ATS-34, 440C, O1 and A2. Bead blasted, Parkerized, high polish and satin finishes. Sheaths are handmade. Also hand forges cable Damascus. **Prices:** $185 to $280 some higher. **Remarks:** Part-time maker; first knife sold in 1995. Doing business as Michael W. Martin Knives. **Mark:** Name and city, state in arch.

MARTIN, PETER
28220 N. Lake Dr, Waterford, WI 53185, Phone: 262-706-3076, Web: www.petermartinknives.com
Specialties: Fancy, fantasy and working straight knives and folders of his design and in standard patterns. **Patterns:** Bowies, fighters, hunters, locking folders and liner locks. **Technical:** Forges own Mosaic Damascus, powdered steel and his own Damascus. Prefers natural handle material; offers file work and carved handles. **Prices:** Moderate. **Remarks:** Full-time maker; first knife sold in 1988. Doing business as Martin Custom Products. **Mark:** Martin Knives.

MARTIN, RANDALL J
51 Bramblewood St, Bridgewater, MA 02324, Phone: 508-279-0682
Specialties: High tech folding and fixed blade tactical knives employing the latest blade steels and exotic materials. Employs a unique combination of 3d-CNC machining and hand work on both blades and handles. All knives are designed for hard use. Clean, radical grinds and ergonomic handles are hallmarks of RJ's work, as is his reputation for producing "Scary Sharp" knives. **Technical:** Grinds CPM30V, CPM 3V, CPM154CM, A2 and stainless Damascus. Other CPM alloys used on request. Performs all heat treating and cryogenic processing in-house. **Remarks:** Full-time maker since 2001 and materials engineer. Former helicopter designer. First knife sold in 1976.

MARTIN, TONY
PO Box 10, Arcadia, MO 63621, Phone: 573-546-2254, arcadian@charter.net; Web: www.arcadianforge.com
Specialties: Specializes in historical designs, esp. puukko, skean dhu. **Remarks:** Premium quality blades, exotic wood handles, unmatched fit and finish. **Mark:** AF.

MARTIN, JOHN ALEXANDER
821 N Grand Ave, Okmulgee, OK 74447, Phone: 918-758-1099, jam@jamblades.com; Web: www.jamblades.com
Specialties: Inlaid and engraved handles. **Patterns:** Bowies, fighters, hunters and traditional patterns. Swords, fixed blade knives, folders and axes. **Technical:** Forges 5160, 1084, 10XX, O1, L6 and his own Damascus. **Prices:** Start at $300. **Remarks:** Part-time maker. **Mark:** Two initials with last name and MS or 5 pointed star.

MARZITELLI, PETER
19929 35A Ave, Langley, BC, CANADA V3A 2R1, Phone: 604-532-8899, info@marzknives.com; Web: www.marzknives.com
Specialties: Specializes in unique functional knife shapes and designs using natural and synthetic handle materials. **Patterns:** Fixed blades: hunting, tactical, utility and art knives. **Technical:** Grinds 154CM, CPM steels, damascus and more. **Prices:** $220 to $1000 (average $375). **Remarks:** Full-time maker; first knife sold in 1984. **Mark:** Stylized logo reads "Marz."

MASON, BILL
9306 S.E. Venns St., Hobe Sound, FL 33455, Phone: 772-545-3649
Specialties: Combat knives; some folders. **Patterns:** Fighters to match knife types in book Cold Steel. **Technical:** Grinds O1, 440C and ATS-34. **Prices:** $115 to $250; some to $350. **Remarks:** Spare-time maker; first knife sold in 1979. **Mark:** Initials connected.

MASSEY, AL
Box 14 Site 15 RR#2, Mount Uniacke, NS, CANADA B0N 1Z0, Phone: 902-866-4754, armjan@eastlink.ca
Specialties: Working knives and period pieces. **Patterns:** Swords and daggers of Celtic to medieval design, Bowies. **Technical:** Forges 5160, 1084 and 1095. Makes own Damascus. **Prices:** $200 to $500, damascus $300-$1000. **Remarks:** Part-time maker, first blade sold in 1988. **Mark:** Initials and JS on Ricasso.

MASSEY, ROGER
4928 Union Rd, Texarkana, AR 71854, Phone: 870-779-1018, rmassey668@aol.com
Specialties: Traditional and working straight knives and folders of his design and to customer specs. **Patterns:** Bowies, hunters, daggers and utility knives. **Technical:** Forges 1084 and 52100, makes his own Damascus. Offers filework and silver wire inlay in handles. **Prices:** $200 to $1500; some to $2500. **Remarks:** Part-time maker; first knife sold in 1991. **Mark:** Last name, M.S.

MASSEY, RON
61638 El Reposo St., Joshua Tree, CA 92252, Phone: 760-366-9239 after 5 p.m., Fax: 763-366-4620
Specialties: Classic, traditional, fancy/embellished, high art, period pieces, working/using knives, straight knives, folders, and automatics. Your design, customer specs, about 175 standard patterns. **Patterns:** Automatics, hunters and fighters. All folders are side-locking folders. Unless requested as lock books slip joint he specializes or custom designs. **Technical:** ATS-34, 440C, D-2 upon request. Engraving, filework, scrimshaw, most of the exotic handle materials. All aspects are performed by him: inlay work in pearls or stone, handmade Pem' work. **Prices:** $110 to $2500; some to $6000. **Remarks:** Part-time maker; first knife sold in 1976.

MATA, LEONARD
3583 Arruza St, San Diego, CA 92154, Phone: 619-690-6935

MATHEWS, CHARLIE AND HARRY
TWIN BLADES, 121 Mt Pisgah Church Rd., Statesboro, GA 30458, Phone: 912-865-9098, twinblades@bulloch.net; Web: www.twinxblades.com

Specialties: Working straight knives, carved stag handles. **Patterns:** Hunters, fighters, bowies and period pieces. **Technical:** Grinds D2, CPM S30V, CPM 3V, ATS-34 and commercial damascus; handmade sheaths some with exotic leather, filework. **Prices:** Starting at $200. **Remarks:** Twin brothers making knives full-time under the label of Twin Blades. Charter members Georgia Custom Knifemakers Guild. Members of The Knifemakers Guild. Charlie is secretary/treasurer of the Knifemakers' Guild. **Mark:** Twin Blades over crossed knives, reverse side steel type.

MATSUNO, KANSEI
109-8 Uenomachi, Nishikaiden, Gifu-City, JAPAN 501-1168, Phone: 81 58 234 8643

MATSUOKA, SCOT
94-415 Ukalialii Place, Mililani, HI 96789, Phone: 808-625-6658, Fax: 808-625-6658, scottym@hawaii.rr.com; Web: www.matsuokaknives.com
Specialties: Folders, fixed blades with custom hand-stitched sheaths. **Patterns:** Gentleman's knives, hunters, tactical folders. **Technical:** CPM 154CM, 440C, 154, BG42, bolsters, file work, and engraving. **Prices:** Starting price $350. **Remarks:** Part-time maker, first knife sold in 2002. **Mark:** Logo, name and state.

MATSUSAKI, TAKESHI
MATSUSAKI KNIVES, 151 Ono-Cho, Sasebo-shi, Nagasaki, JAPAN, Phone: 0956-47-2938, Fax: 0956-47-2938
Specialties: Working and collector grade front look and slip joint. **Patterns:** Sheffield type folders. **Technical:** Grinds ATS-34 k-120. **Prices:** $250 to $1000, some to $8000. **Remarks:** Part-time maker, first knife sold in 1990. **Mark:** Name and initials.

MAXEN, MICK
2 Huggins Welham Green, Hatfield, Herts, UNITED KINGDOM AL97LR, Phone: 01707 261213, mmaxen@aol.com
Specialties: Damascus and Mosaic. **Patterns:** Medieval-style daggers and Bowies. **Technical:** Forges CS75 and 15N20 / nickel Damascus. **Mark:** Last name with axe above.

MAXFIELD, LYNN
382 Colonial Ave, Layton, UT 84041, Phone: 801-544-4176, lcmaxfield@msn.com
Specialties: Sporting knives, some fancy. **Patterns:** Hunters, fishing, fillet, special purpose: some locking folders. **Technical:** Grinds 440-C, 154-CM, CPM154, D2, CPM S30V, and Damascus. **Prices:** $125 to $400; some to $900. **Remarks:** Part-time maker; first knife sold in 1979. **Mark:** Name, city and state.

MAXWELL, DON
1484 Celeste Ave, Clovis, CA 93611, Phone: 559-299-2197, maxwellknives@aol.com; Web: maxwellknives.com
Specialties: Fancy folding knives and fixed blades of his design. **Patterns:** Hunters, fighters, utility/camp knives, LinerLock® folders, flippers and fantasy knives. **Technical:** Grinds 440C, ATS-34, D2, CPM 154, and commercial Damascus. **Prices:** $250 to $1000; some to $2500. **Remarks:** Full-time maker; first knife sold in 1987. **Mark:** Last name only or Maxwell MAX-TAC.

MAY, CHARLES
10024 McDonald Rd., Aberdeen, MS 39730, Phone: 662-369-0404, charlesmayknives@yahoo.com; Web: charlesmayknives.blademakers.com
Specialties: Fixed-blade sheath knives. **Patterns:** Hunters and fillet knives. **Technical:** Scandinavian-ground D2 and S30V blades, black micarta and wood handles, nickel steel pins with maker's own pocket carry or belt-loop pouches. **Prices:** $215 to $495. **Mark:** "Charles May Knives" and a knife in a circle.

MAYNARD, LARRY JOE
PO Box 493, Crab Orchard, WV 25827
Specialties: Fancy and fantasy straight knives. **Patterns:** Big knives; a Bowie with a full false edge; fighting knives. **Technical:** Grinds standard steels. **Prices:** $350 to $500; some to $1000. **Remarks:** Full-time maker; first knife sold in 1986. **Mark:** Middle and last initials.

MAYNARD, WILLIAM N.
2677 John Smith Rd, Fayetteville, NC 28306, Phone: 910-425-1615
Specialties: Traditional and working straight knives of all designs. **Patterns:** Combat, Bowies, fighters, hunters and utility knives. **Technical:** Grinds 440C, ATS-34 and commercial Damascus. Offers fancy filework; handmade sheaths. **Prices:** $100 to $300; some to $750. **Remarks:** Full-time maker; first knife sold in 1988. **Mark:** Last name.

MAYO JR., HOMER
18036 Three Rivers Rd., Biloxi, MS 39532, Phone: 228-326-8298
Specialties: Traditional working straight knives, folders and tactical. **Patterns:** Hunters, fighters, tactical, bird, Bowies, fish fillet knives and lightweight folders. **Technical:** Grinds 440C, ATS-34, D-2, Damascus, forges and grinds 52100 and custom makes sheaths. **Prices:** $100 to $1000. **Remarks:** Part-time maker **Mark:** All knives are serial number and registered in the name of the original purchaser, stamped last name or etched.

MAYO JR., TOM
67 412 Alahaka St, Waialua, HI 96791, Phone: 808-637-6560, mayot001@hawaii.rr.com; Web: www.mayoknives.com
Specialties: Framelocks/tactical knives. **Patterns:** Combat knives, hunters, Bowies and folders. **Technical:** Titanium/stellite/S30V. **Prices:** $500 to $1000. **Remarks:** Full-time maker; first knife sold in 1982. **Mark:** Volcano logo with name and state.

MAYVILLE, OSCAR L
2130 E. County Rd 910S, Marengo, IN 47140, Phone: 812-338-4159
Specialties: Working straight knives; period pieces. **Patterns:** Kitchen cutlery, Bowies camp knives and hunters. **Technical:** Grinds A2, O1 and 440C. **Prices:** $50 to $350; some to $500. **Remarks:** Full-time maker; first knife sold in 1984. **Mark:** Initials over knife logo.

MCABEE, WILLIAM
27275 Norton Grade, Colfax, CA 95713, Phone: 530-389-8163
Specialties: Working/using knives. **Patterns:** Fighters, Bowies, Hunters. **Technical:** Grinds ATS-34. **Prices:** $75 to $200; some to $350. **Remarks:** Part-time maker; first knife sold in 1990. **Mark:** Stylized WM stamped.

MCCALLEN JR., HOWARD H
110 Anchor Dr, So Seaside Park, NJ 08752

MCCARLEY, JOHN
4165 Harney Rd, Taneytown, MD 21787
Specialties: Working straight knives; period pieces. **Patterns:** Hunters, Bowies, camp knives, miniatures, throwing knives. **Technical:** Forges W2, O1 and his own Damascus. **Prices:** $150 to $300; some to $1000. **Remarks:** Part-time maker; first knife sold in 1977. **Mark:** Initials in script.

MCCARTY, HARRY
1479 Indian Ridge Rd, Blaine, TN 37709, harry@indianridgeforge.com; Web: www.indianridgeforge.com
Specialties: Period pieces. **Patterns:** Trade knives, Bowies, 18th and 19th century folders and hunting swords. **Technical:** Forges and grinds high-carbon steel. **Prices:** $75 to $1300. **Remarks:** Full-time maker; first knife sold in 1977. Doing business as Indian Ridge Forge.**Mark:** Stylized initials inside a shamrock.

MCCLURE, JERRY
3052 Isim Rd, Norman, OK 73026, Phone: 405-321-3614, jerry@jmcclureknives.net; Web: www.jmcclureknives.net
Specialties: Gentleman's folder, linerlock with my jeweled pivot system of eight rubies, forged one-of-a-kind Damascus Bowies, and a line of hunting/camp knives. **Patterns:** Folders, Bowie, and hunting/camp **Technical:** Forges own Damascus, also uses Damasteel and does own heat treating. **Prices:** $500 to $3,000 and up **Remarks:** Full-time maker, made first knife in 1965. **Mark:** J.MCCLURE

MCCLURE, MICHAEL
803 17th Ave, Menlo Park, CA 94025, Phone: 650-323-2596, mikesknives@att.net; Web: www.customknivesbymike.com
Specialties: Working/using straight knives of his design and to customer specs. **Patterns:** Bowies, hunters, skinners, utility/camp, tantos, fillets and boot knives. **Technical:** Forges high-carbon and Damascus; also grinds stainless, all grades. **Prices:** Start at $300. **Remarks:** Part-time maker; first knife sold in 1991. ABS Journeyman Smith. **Mark:** Mike McClure.

MCCONNELL JR., LOYD A
309 County Road 144-B, Marble Falls, TX 78654, Phone: 830-596-3488, ccknives@ccknives.com; Web: www.ccknives.com
Specialties: Working straight knives and folders, some fancy. **Patterns:** Hunters, boots, Bowies, locking folders and slip-joints. **Technical:** Grinds CPM Steels, ATS-34 and BG-42 and commercial Damascus. **Prices:** $450 to $10,000. **Remarks:** Full-time maker; first knife sold in 1975. Doing business as Cactus Custom Knives. Markets product knives under name: Lone Star Knives. **Mark:** Name, city and state in cactus logo.

MCCORNOCK, CRAIG
MCC MTN OUTFITTERS, 4775 Rt. 212/PO 162, Willow, NY 12495, Phone: 845-679-9758, Mccmtn@aol.com; Web: www.mccmtn.com
Specialties: Carry, utility, hunters, defense type knives and functional swords. **Patterns:** Drop points, hawkbills, tantos, waklizashis, katanas **Technical:** Stock removal, forged and Damascus, (yes, he still flints knap). **Prices:** $200 to $2000. **Mark:** McM.

MCCOUN, MARK
14212 Pine Dr, DeWitt, VA 23840, Phone: 804-469-7631, mccounandsons@live.com
Specialties: Working/using straight knives of his design and in standard patterns; custom miniatures. **Patterns:** Locking liners, integrals. **Technical:** Grinds Damascus, ATS-34 and 440C. **Prices:** $150 to $500. **Remarks:** Part-time maker; first knife sold in 1989. **Mark:** Name, city and state.

MCCRACKIN, KEVIN
3720 Hess Rd, House Spings, MO 63051, Phone: 636-677-6066

MCCRACKIN AND SON, V J
3720 Hess Rd, House Springs, MO 63051, Phone: 636-677-6066
Specialties: Working straight knives in standard patterns. **Patterns:** Hunters, Bowies and camp knives. **Technical:** Forges L6, 5160, his own Damascus, cable Damascus. **Prices:** $125 to $700; some to $1500. **Remarks:** Part-time maker; first knife sold in 1983. Son Kevin helps make the knives. **Mark:** Last name, M.S.

MCCULLOUGH, JERRY
274 West Pettibone Rd, Georgiana, AL 36033, Phone: 334-382-7644, ke4er@alaweb.com
Specialties: Standard patterns or custom designs. **Technical:** Forge and grind scrap-tool and Damascus steels. Use natural handle materials and turquoise trim on some. Filework on others. **Prices:** $65 to $250 and up. **Remarks:** Part-time maker. **Mark:** Initials (JM) combined.

MCDONALD, RICH
5010 Carmel Rd., Hillboro, OH 45133, Phone: 937-466-2071, rmclongknives@aol.com; Web: www.longknivesandleather.com
Specialties: Traditional working/using and art knives of his design. **Patterns:** Bowies, hunters, folders, primitives and tomahawks. **Technical:** Forges 5160, 1084, 1095, 52100 and his own Damascus. Fancy filework. **Prices:** $200 to $1500. **Remarks:** Full-time maker; first knife sold in 1994. **Mark:** First and last initials connected.

MCDONALD, ROBERT J
14730 61 Court N, Loxahatchee, FL 33470, Phone: 561-790-1470
Specialties: Traditional working straight knives to customer specs. **Patterns:** Fighters, swords and folders. **Technical:** Grinds 440C, ATS-34 and forges own Damascus. **Prices:** $150 to $1000. **Remarks:** Part-time maker; first knife sold in 1988. **Mark:** Electro-etched name.

MCDONALD, W.J. "JERRY"
7173 Wickshire Cove E, Germantown, TN 38138, Phone: 901-756-9924, wjmcdonaldknives@msn.com; Web: www.mcdonaldknives.com
Specialties: Classic and working/using straight knives of his design and in standard patterns. **Patterns:** Bowies, hunters kitchen and traditional spring back pocket knives. **Technical:** Grinds ATS-34, 154CM, D2, 440V, BG42 and 440C. **Prices:** $125 to $1000. **Remarks:** Full-time maker; first knife sold in 1989. **Mark:** First and middle initials, last name, maker, city and state. Some of his knives are stamped McDonald in script.

MCFALL, KEN
PO Box 458, Lakeside, AZ 85929, Phone: 928-537-2026, Fax: 928-537-8066, knives@citlink.net
Specialties: Fancy working straight knives and some folders. **Patterns:** Daggers, boots, tantos, Bowies; some miniatures. **Technical:** Grinds D2, ATS-34 and 440C. Forges his own Damascus. **Prices:** $200 to $1200. **Remarks:** Part-time maker; first knife sold in 1984. **Mark:** Name, city and state.

MCFARLIN, ERIC E
PO Box 2188, Kodiak, AK 99615, Phone: 907-486-4799, e2mc@reagan.com
Specialties: Working knives of his design. **Patterns:** Bowies, skinners, camp knives and hunters. **Technical:** Flat and convex grinds 440C, A2 and AEB-L. **Prices:** Start at $350. **Remarks:** Part-time maker; first knife sold in 1989. **Mark:** Name and city and Old Goat logo.

MCFARLIN, J W
3331 Pocohantas Dr, Lake Havasu City, AZ 86404, Phone: 928-453-7612, Fax: 928-453-7612, aztheedge@NPGcable.com
Technical: Flat grinds, D2, ATS-34, 440C, Thomas and Peterson Damascus. **Remarks:** From working knives to investment. Customer designs always welcome. 100 percent handmade. Made first knife in 1972. **Prices:** $150 to $3000. **Mark:** Hand written in the blade.

MCGHEE, E. SCOTT
7136 Lisbon Rd., Clarkton, NC 28433, Phone: 910-448-2224, guineahogforge@gmail.com; Web: www.guineahogforge.com
Specialties: Hunting knives, kitchen blades, presentation blades, tactical knives and sword canes. **Technical:** Forge and stock removal, all flat-ground blades, including 1080-and-15N20 damascus, 1084, O1 and W2. **Prices:** $200 to $3,500. **Remarks:** Full-time maker; first knife sold in 2009. Currently an ABS journeyman smith. **Mark:** E. Scott McGhee (large print) above Guinea Hog Forge (small print).

MCGILL, JOHN
PO Box 302, Blairsville, GA 30512, Phone: 404-745-4686
Specialties: Working knives. **Patterns:** Traditional patterns; camp knives. **Technical:** Forges L6 and 9260; makes Damascus. **Prices:** $50 to $250; some to $500. **Remarks:** Full-time maker; first knife sold in 1982. **Mark:** XYLO.

MCGOWAN, FRANK E
12629 Howard Lodge Rd., Sykesville, MD 21784, Phone: 443-745-2611, lizmcgowan31@gmail.com
Specialties: Fancy working knives and folders to customer specs. **Patterns:** Survivor knives, fighters, fishing knives, folders and hunters. **Technical:** Grinds and forges O1, 440C, 5160, ATS-34, 52100, or customer choice. **Prices:** $100 to $1000; some more. **Remarks:** Full-time maker; first knife sold in 1986. **Mark:** Last name.

MCGRATH, PATRICK T
8343 Kenyon Ave, Westchester, CA 90045, Phone: 310-338-8764, hidinginLA@excite.com

MCGRODER, PATRICK J
5725 Chapin Rd, Madison, OH 44057, Phone: 216-298-3405, Fax: 216-298-3405
Specialties: Traditional working/using knives of his design. **Patterns:** Bowies, hunters and utility/camp knives. **Technical:** Grinds ATS-34, D2 and customer requests. Does reverse etching; heat-treats; prefers natural handle materials; custom made sheath with each knife. **Prices:** $125 to $250. **Remarks:** Part-time maker. **Mark:** First and middle initials, last name, maker, city and state.

MCGUANE IV, THOMAS F
410 South 3rd Ave, Bozeman, MT 59715, Phone: 406-586-0248, Web: http://www.thomasmcguane.com
Specialties: Multi metal inlaid knives of handmade steel. **Patterns:** Lock back and LinerLock® folders, fancy straight knives. **Technical:** 1084/1SN20 Damascus and Mosaic steel by maker. **Prices:** $1000 and up. **Mark:** Surname or name and city, state.

MCHENRY, WILLIAM JAMES
Box 67, Wyoming, RI 02898, Phone: 401-539-8353
Specialties: Fancy high-tech folders of his design. **Patterns:** Locking folders with various mechanisms. **Technical:** One-of-a-kind only, no duplicates. Inventor of the Axis Lock. Most pieces disassemble and feature top-shelf materials including gold, silver and gems. **Prices:** Upscale. **Remarks:** Full-time maker; first knife sold in 1988. Former goldsmith. **Mark:** Last name or name and last initials.

MCINTYRE, SHAWN
71 Leura Grove, Hawthornm, E VIC, AUSTRALIA 3123, Phone: 61 3 9813 2049/Cell 61 412 041 062, macpower@netspace.net.au; Web: www.mcintyreknives.com

custom knifemakers

Specialties: Damascus & CS fixed blades and art knives. **Patterns:** Bowies, hunters, fighters, kukris, integrals. **Technical:** Forges, makes own Damascus including pattern weld, mosaic, and composite multi-bars form O1 & 15N20 Also uses 1084, W2, and 52100. **Prices:** $275 to $2000. **Remarks:** Full-time maker since 1999. **Mark:** Mcintyre in script.

MCKEE, NEIL
674 Porter Hill Rd., Stevensville, MT 59870, Phone: 406-777-3507, mckeenh@wildblue.net
Specialties: Early American. **Patterns:** Nessmuk, DeWeese, French folders, art pieces. **Technical:** Engraver. **Prices:** $150 to $1000. **Mark:** Oval with initials.

MCKENZIE, DAVID BRIAN
2311 B Ida Rd, Campbell River, BC, CANADA V9W-4V7

MCKIERNAN, STAN
11751 300th St, Lamoni, IA 50140, Phone: 641-784-6873/641-781-0368, slmck@hotmailc.om
Specialties: Self-sheathed knives and miniatures. **Patterns:** Daggers, ethnic designs and individual styles. **Technical:** Grinds Damascus and 440C. **Prices:** $200 to $500, some to $1500. **Mark:** "River's Bend" inside two concentric circles.

MCLUIN, TOM
36 Fourth St, Dracut, MA 01826, Phone: 978-957-4899, tmcluin@comcast.net
Specialties: Working straight knives and folders of his design. **Patterns:** Boots, hunters and folders. **Technical:** Grinds ATS-34, 440C, O1 and Damascus; makes his own mokume. **Prices:** $100 to $400; some to $700. **Remarks:** Part-time maker; first knife sold in 1991. **Mark:** Last name.

MCLURKIN, ANDREW
2112 Windy Woods Dr, Raleigh, NC 27607, Phone: 919-834-4693, mclurkincustomknives.com
Specialties: Collector grade folders, working folders, fixed blades, and miniatures. Knives made to order and to his design. **Patterns:** Locking liner and lock back folders, hunter, working and tactical designs. **Technical:** Using patterned Damascus, Mosaic Damascus, ATS-34, BG-42, and CPM steels. Prefers natural handle materials such as pearl, ancient ivory and stabilized wood. Also using synthetic materials such as carbon fiber, titanium, and G10. **Prices:** $250 and up. **Mark:** Last name. Mark is often on inside of folders.

MCNABB, TOMMY
CAROLINA CUSTOM KNIVES, PO Box 327, Bethania, NC 27010, Phone: 336-924-6053, tommy@tmcnabb.com; Web: carolinaknives.com
Specialties: Classic and working knives of his own design or to customer's specs. **Patterns:** Traditional bowies. Tomahawks, hunters and customer designs. **Technical:** Forges his own Damascus steel, hand forges or grinds ATS-34 and other hi-tech steels. Prefers mirror finish or satin finish on working knives. Uses exotic or natural handle material and stabilized woods. **Prices:** $300-$3500. **Remarks:** Full time maker. Made first knife in 1982. **Mark:** "Carolina Custom Knives" on stock removal blades "T. McNabb" on custom orders and Damascus knives.

MCNEES, JONATHAN
15203 Starboard Pl, Northport, AL 35475, Phone: 205-391-8383, jmackusmc@yahoo.com; Web: www.mcneescustomknives.com
Specialties: Tactical, outdoors, utility. **Technical:** Stock removal method utilizing carbon and stainless steels to include 1095, cpm154, A2, cpms35v. **Remarks:** Part-time maker, first knife made in 2007. **Mark:** Jmcnees

MCRAE, J MICHAEL
6100 Lake Rd, Mint Hill, NC 28227, Phone: 704-545-2929, scotia@carolina.rr.com; Web: www.scotiametalwork.com
Specialties: Scottish dirks, sgian dubhs, broadswords. **Patterns:** Traditional blade styles with traditional and slightly non-traditional handle treatments. **Technical:** Forges 5160 and his own Damascus. Prefers stag and exotic hardwoods for handles, many intricately carved. **Prices:** Starting at $125, some to $3500. **Remarks:** Journeyman Smith in ABS, member of ABANA. Full-time maker, first knife made in 1982. Doing business as Scotia Metalwork. **Mark:** Last name underlined with a claymore.

MCWILLIAMS, SEAN
PO Box 1685, Carbondale, CO 81623, Phone: 970-618-0198, info@seanmcwilliamsforge.com; Web: www.seanmcwilliamsforge.com
Specialties: Tactical, survival and working knives in Kydex-and-nylon sheaths. **Patterns:** Fighters, bowies, hunters and sports knives, period pieces, swords, martial arts blades and some folders, including Panama Folder linerlocks. **Technical:** Forges only CPM T440V, CPM S90V and CPM S35VN. **Prices:** $230 to $2,500. **Remarks:** Full-time maker; first knife sold in 1972. **Mark:** Stylized bear paw.

MEERDINK, KURT
248 Yulan Barryville Rd., Barryville, NY 12719-5305, Phone: 845-557-0783
Specialties: Working straight knives. **Patterns:** Hunters, Bowies, tactical and neck knives. **Technical:** Grinds ATS-34, 440C, D2, Damascus. **Prices:** $95 to $1100. **Remarks:** Full-time maker, first knife sold in 1994. **Mark:** Meerdink Maker, Rio NY.

MEERS, ANDREW
1100 S Normal Ave., Allyn Bldg MC 4301, Carbondale, IL 62901, Phone: 774-217-3574, namsuechool@gmail.com
Specialties: Pattern welded blades, in the New England style. **Patterns:** Can do open or closed welding and fancies middle eastern style blades. **Technical:** 1095, 1084, 15n20, 5160, w1, w2 steels **Remarks:** Part-time maker attending graduate school at SIUC; looking to become full-time in the future as well as earn ABS Journeyman status. **Mark:** Korean character for south.

MEIER, DARYL
75 Forge Rd, Carbondale, IL 62903, Phone: 618-549-3234, Web: www.meiersteel.com
Specialties: One-of-a-kind knives and swords. **Patterns:** Collaborates on blades. **Technical:** Forges his own Damascus, W1 and A203E, 440C, 431, nickel 200 and clad steel. **Prices:** $500 and up. **Remarks:** Full-time smith and researcher since 1974; first knife sold in 1974. **Mark:** Name.

MELIN, GORDON C
14207 Coolbank Dr, La Mirada, CA 90638, Phone: 562-946-5753

MELOY, SEAN
7148 Rosemary Lane, Lemon Grove, CA 91945-2105, Phone: 619-465-7173
Specialties: Traditional working straight knives of his design. **Patterns:** Bowies, fighters and utility/camp knives. **Technical:** Grinds 440C, ATS-34 and D2. **Prices:** $125 to $300. **Remarks:** Part-time maker; first knife sold in 1985. **Mark:** Broz Knives.

MENEFEE, RICKY BOB
2440 County Road 1322, Blanchard, OK 73010, rmenefee@pldi.net; Web: www.menefeeknives.com
Specialties: Working straight knives and pocket knives. **Patterns:** Hunters, fighters, minis & Bowies. **Technical:** Grinds 154CM, A2 and CPM S90V. **Prices:** $200 to $2,000. **Remarks:** Part-time maker, first knife sold in 1996. Member of KGA of Oklahoma, also Knifemakers Guild. **Mark:** Menefee made or Menefee stamped in blade.

MENSCH, LARRY C
Larry's Knife Shop, 578 Madison Ave, Milton, PA 17847, Phone: 570-742-9554
Specialties: Custom orders. **Patterns:** Bowies, daggers, hunters, tantos, short swords and miniatures. **Technical:** Grinds ATS-34, stainless steel Damascus; blade grinds hollow, flat and slack. Filework; bending guards and fluting handles with finger grooves. **Prices:** $200 and up. **Remarks:** Full-time maker; first knife sold in 1993. Doing business as Larry's Knife Shop. **Mark:** Connected capital "L" and small "m" in script.

MERCER, MIKE
149 N. Waynesville Rd, Lebanon, OH 45036, Phone: 513-932-2837, mmercer08445@roadrunner.com
Specialties: Miniatures and autos. **Patterns:** All folder patterns. **Technical:** Diamonds and gold, one-of-a-kind, Damascus, O1, stainless steel blades. **Prices:** $500 to $5000. **Remarks:** Carved wax - lost wax casting. **Mark:** Stamp - Mercer.

MERCHANT, TED
7 Old Garrett Ct, White Hall, MD 21161, Phone: 410-343-0380
Specialties: Traditional and classic working knives. **Patterns:** Bowies, hunters, camp knives, fighters, daggers and skinners. **Technical:** Forges W2 and 5160; makes own Damascus. Makes handles with wood, stag, horn, silver and gem stone inlay; fancy filework. **Prices:** $125 to $600; some to $1500. **Remarks:** Full-time maker; first knife sold in 1985. **Mark:** Last name.

MEROLA, JIM
6648 Ridge Blvd., Brooklyn, NY 11220, Phone: 347-342-6923, jimolds@earthlink.net; Web: www.jimmerola.com
Specialties: Folders and fixed blades, including antique bowie reproductions, all in stainless steel and damascus. **Technical:** Stock removal method of blade making, using the finest steels and handle materials. **Prices:** $400 to $1,500. **Remarks:** Part-time maker since 1998.

MERZ III, ROBERT L
1447 Winding Canyon, Katy, TX 77493, Phone: 281-391-2897, bobmerz@consolidated.net; Web: www.merzknives.com
Specialties: Folders. **Prices:** $400 to $2,000. **Remarks:** Full-time maker; first knife sold in 1974. **Mark:** MERZ.

MESENBOURG, NICK
2545 Upper 64th Ct. E, Inver Grove Heights, MN 55076, Phone: 651-457-2753 or 651-775-7505, mesenbourg_nicholas@hotmail.com; www.ndmknives.com
Specialties: Working straight knives of his design or to customer specs, also sport-themed knives. **Patterns:** Hunters, skinners, bowies, fighters, utility and fillet knives. **Technical:** Grinds 440C stainless steel and commercial damascus. **Prices:** $175-$450, special knives higher. **Remarks:** Part-time maker; first knife sold in 2008. **Mark:** Encircled N D M capital letters.

MESHEJIAN, MARDI
5 Bisbee Court 109 PMB 230, Santa Fe, NM 87508, Phone: 505-310-7441, toothandnail13@yahoo.com
Specialties: One-of-a-kind art knives, folders and kitchen knives. **Patterns:** Swords, daggers, folders and other weapons. **Technical:** Forged steel Damascus and titanium Damascus. **Prices:** $300 to $5000 some to $7000. **Mark:** Stamped stylized "M."

METHENY, H A "WHITEY"
7750 Waterford Dr, Spotsylvania, VA 22551, Phone: 540842-1440, Fax: 540-582-3095, hametheny@aol.com; Web: www metheny knives.com
Specialties: Working and using straight knives of his design and to customer specs. **Patterns:** Hunters and kitchen knives. **Technical:** Grinds 440C and ATS-34. Offers filework; tooled custom sheaths. **Prices:** $350 to $450. **Remarks:** Spare-time maker; first knife sold in 1990. **Mark:** Initials/full name football logo.

METSALA, ANTHONY
30557 103rd St. NW, Princeton, MN 55371, Phone: 763-389-2628, acmetsala@izoom.net; Web: www.metsalacustomknives.com
Specialties: Sole authorship one-off mosaic Damascus liner locking folders, sales of makers finished one-off mosaic Damascus blades. **Patterns:** Except for a couple EDC

folding knives, maker does not use patterns. **Technical:** Forges own mosaic Damascus carbon blade and bolster material. All stainless steel blades are heat treated by Paul Bos. **Prices:** $250 to $1500. **Remarks:** Full-time knifemaker and Damascus steel maker, first knife sold in 2005. **Mark:** A.C. Metsala or Metsala.

METZ, GREG T
c/o Yellow Pine Bar HC 83, BOX 8080, Cascade, ID 83611, Phone: 208-382-4336, metzenterprise@yahoo.com
Specialties: Hunting and utility knives. **Prices:** $350 and up. **Remarks:** Natural handle materials; hand forged blades; 1084 and 1095. **Mark:** METZ (last name).

MEYER, CHRISTOPHER J
737 Shenipsit Lake Rd, Tolland, CT 06084, Phone: 860-875-1826, shenipsitforge.cjm@gmail.com
Specialties: Handforged tool steels. **Technical:** Forges tool steels, grinds stainless. **Remarks:** Spare-time maker; sold first knife in 2003. **Mark:** Name and/or "Shenipsit Forge."

MICHINAKA, TOSHIAKI
I-679 Koyamacho-nishi, Tottori-shi, Tottori, JAPAN 680-0947, Phone: 0857-28-5911
Specialties: Art miniature knives. **Patterns:** Bowies, hunters, fishing, camp knives & miniatures. **Technical:** Grinds ATS-34 and 440C. **Prices:** $300 to $900 some higher. **Remarks:** Part-time maker. First knife sold in 1982. **Mark:** First initial, last name.

MICKLEY, TRACY
42112 Kerns Dr, North Mankato, MN 56003, Phone: 507-947-3760, tracy@mickleyknives.com; Web: www.mickleyknives.com
Specialties: Working and collectable straight knives using mammoth ivory or burl woods, LinerLock® folders. **Patterns:** Custom and classic hunters, utility, fighters and Bowies. **Technical:** Grinding 154-CM, BG-42 forging O1 and 52100. **Prices:** Starting at $325 **Remarks:** Part-time since 1999. **Mark:** Last name.

MIDGLEY, BEN
PO Box 577, Wister, OK 74966, Phone: 918-655-6701, mauricemidgley@windstream.net
Specialties: Multi-blade folders, slip-joints, some lock-backs and hunters. File work, engraving and scrimshaw. **Patterns:** Reproduce old patterns, trappers, muskrats, stockman, whittlers, lockbacks an hunters. **Technical:** Grinds ATS-34, 440C, 12-C-27, CPM-154, some carbon steel, and commercial Damascus. **Prices:** $385 to $1875. **Remarks:** Full-time maker, first knife sold in 2002. **Mark:** Name, city, and state stamped on blade.

MIKOLAJCZYK, GLEN
4650 W. 7 Mile Rd., Caledonia, WI 53108, Phone: 414-791-0424, Fax: 262-835-9697, glenmikol@aol.com Web: www.customtomahawk.com
Specialties: Pipe hawks, fancy folders, bowies, long blades, hunting knives, all of his own design. **Technical:** Sole-author, forges own Damascus and powdered steel. Works with ivory, bone, tortoise, horn and antlers, tiger maple, pearl for handle materials. Designs and does intricate file work and custom sheaths. Enjoys exotic handle materials. **Prices:** Moderate. **Remarks:** Founded Weg Von Wennig Forge in 2003, first knife sold in 2004. Also, designs and builds mini-forges. Will build upon request. International sales accepted. **Mark:** Tomahawk and name.

MILES JR., C R "IRON DOCTOR"
1541 Porter Crossroad, Lugoff, SC 29078, Phone: 803-600-9397
Specialties: Traditional working straight knives of his design or made to custom specs. **Patterns:** Hunters, fighters, utility camp knives and hatches. **Technical:** Grinds O1, D2, ATS-34, 440C, 1095, and 154 CPM. Forges 18th century style cutlery of high carbon steels. Also forges and grinds old files and farrier's rasps to make knives. Custom leather sheaths. **Prices:** $100 and up. **Remarks:** Part-time maker, first knife sold in 1997. **Mark:** Iron doctor plus name and serial number.

MILITANO, TOM
CUSTOM KNIVES, 77 Jason Rd., Jacksonville, AL 36265-6655, Phone: 256-435-7132, jeffkin57@aol.com
Specialties: Fixed blade, one-of-a-kind knives. **Patterns:** Bowies, fighters, hunters and tactical knives. **Technical:** Grinds 440C, CPM 154CM, A2, and Damascus. Hollow grinds, flat grinds, and decorative filework. **Prices:** $150 plus. **Remarks:** Part-time maker. Sold first knives in the mid-to-late 1980s. **Mark:** Name engraved in ricasso area - type of steel on reverse side.

MILLARD, FRED G
27627 Kopezyk Ln, Richland Center, WI 53581, Phone: 608-647-5376
Specialties: Working/using straight knives of his design or to customer specs. **Patterns:** Bowies, hunters, utility/camp knives, kitchen/steak knives. **Technical:** Grinds ATS-34, O1, D2 and 440C. Makes sheaths. **Prices:** $110 to $300. **Remarks:** Full-time maker; first knife sold in 1993. Doing business as Millard Knives. **Mark:** Mallard duck in flight with serial number.

MILLER, CHELSEA GRACE
0 Ainslie St., Brooklyn, NY 11211, Phone: 917-623-7804, chelsea@chelseamillerknives.com; Web: www.chelseamillerknives.com
Specialties: Selection of rustic cheese knives and kitchen knives. **Technical:** Uses recycled tool steel, such as mechanic's files, wood files and rasps. Forges cheese and smaller kitchen knives, using stock removal to preserve the rasp pattern on large kitchen knives. All the wood for handles is collected from the maker's family farm in Vermont, including spalted maple, apple and walnut. **Prices:** $200 to $500. **Remarks:** Full-time maker; first knife made in 2011. Maker often examines that first knife and admires its simplicity, though it lacks functionality, and uses it as inspiration to remain as imaginative as possible.

MILLER, HANFORD J
1751 Mountain Ranch Rd., Lakspur, CO 80118, Phone: 719-999-2551, hanford.miller@gmail.com
Specialties: Working knives in Moran styles, Bowie, period pieces, Cinquedea. **Patterns:** Daggers, Bowies, working knives. **Technical:** All work forged: W2, 1095, 5160 and Damascus. ABS methods; offers fine silver repousse, scabbard mountings and wire inlay, oak presentation cases. **Prices:** $400 to $1000; some to $3000 and up. **Remarks:** Full-time maker; first knife sold in 1968. **Mark:** Initials or name within Bowie logo.

MILLER, JAMES P
9024 Goeller Rd, RR 2, Box 28, Fairbank, IA 50629, Phone: 319-635-2294, Web: www.damascusknives.biz
Specialties: All tool steel Damascus; working knives and period pieces. **Patterns:** Hunters, Bowies, camp knives and daggers. **Technical:** Forges and grinds 1095, 52100, 440C and his own Damascus. **Prices:** $175 to $500; some to $1500. **Remarks:** Full-time maker; first knife sold in 1970. **Mark:** First and middle initials, last name with knife logo.

MILLER, LEVI
8065 N. 450 West, Howe, IN 46746, Phone: 260-562-2724, lmcustomknives@gmail.com; Facebook.com/Lmknives
Specialties: Traditional knives. **Patterns:** Slip joints, hunters, camp knives and hoof knives. **Technical:** Forges 52100 and 80CrV2. **Prices:** $200 and up. **Remarks:** Part-time maker; first knife sold in 2009. ABS journeyman smith. **Mark:** LRMiller Howe IN JS.

MILLER, M A
11625 Community Center Dr, Unit #1531, Northglenn, CO 80233, Phone: 303-280-3816
Specialties: Using knives for hunting. 3-1/2"-4" Loveless drop-point. Made to customer specs. **Patterns:** Skinners and camp knives. **Technical:** Grinds 440C, D2, O1 and ATS-34 Damascus miniatures. **Prices:** $225 to $350; miniatures $75 to $150. **Remarks:** Part-time maker; first knife sold in 1988. **Mark:** Last name stamped in block letters or first and middle initials, last name, maker, city and state with triangles on either side etched.

MILLER, MICHAEL
3030 E Calle Cedral, Kingman, AZ 86401, Phone: 928-757-1359, mike@mmilleroriginals.com
Specialties: Hunters, Bowies, and skinners with exotic burl wood, stag, ivory and gemstone handles. **Patterns:** High carbon steel knives. **Technical:** High carbon and nickel alloy Damascus and high carbon and meteorite Damascus. Also mosaic Damascus. **Prices:** $235 to $4500. **Remarks:** Full-time maker since 2002, first knife sold 2000; doing business as M Miller Originals. **Mark:** First initial and last name with 'handmade' underneath.

MILLER, MICHAEL E
910146 S. 3500 Rd., Chandler, OK 74834, Phone: 918-377-2411, mimiller1@cotc.net
Specialties: Traditional working/using knives of his design. **Patterns:** Bowies, hunters and kitchen knives. **Technical:** Grinds ATS-34, CPM 440V; forges Damascus and cable Damascus and 52100. Prefers scrimshaw, fancy pins, basket weave and embellished sheaths. **Prices:** $130 to $500. **Remarks:** Part-time maker; first knife sold in 1984. Doing business as Miller Custom Knives. Member of Knife Group Of Oklahoma. **Mark:** First and middle initials, last name, maker.

MILLER, NATE
Sportsman's Edge, 1075 Old Steese Hwy N, Fairbanks, AK 99712, Phone: 907-460-4718, sportsmansedge@gci.net Web: www.alaskasportsmansedge.com
Specialties: Fixed blade knives for hunting, fishing, kitchen and collector pieces. **Patterns:** Hunters, skinners, utility, tactical, fishing, camp knives-your pattern or mine. **Technical:** Stock removal maker, ATS-34, 154CM, 440C, D2, 1095, other steels on request. Handle material includes micarta, horn, antler, fossilized ivory and bone, wide selection of woods. **Prices:** $225-$800. **Remarks:** Full time maker since 2002. **Mark:** Nate Miller, Fairbanks, AK.

MILLER, RICK
516 Kanaul Rd, Rockwood, PA 15557, Phone: 814-926-2059
Specialties: Working/using straight knives of his design and in standard patterns. **Patterns:** Bowies, daggers, hunters and friction folders. **Technical:** Grinds L6. Forges 5160, L6 and Damascus. Patterns for Damascus are random, twist, rose or ladder. **Prices:** $75 to $250; some to $400. **Remarks:** Part-time maker; first knife sold in 1982. **Mark:** Script stamp "R.D.M."

MILLER, RONALD T
12922 127th Ave N, Largo, FL 34644, Phone: 813-595-0378 (after 5 p.m.)
Specialties: Working straight knives in standard patterns. **Patterns:** Combat knives, camp knives, kitchen cutlery, fillet knives, locking folders and butterflies. **Technical:** Grinds D2, 440C and ATS-34; offers brass inlays and scrimshaw. **Prices:** $45 to $325; some to $750. **Remarks:** Part-time maker; first knife sold in 1984. **Mark:** Name, city and state in palm tree logo.

MILLER, STEVE
1376 Pine St., Clearwater, FL 33756, Phone: 727-461-4180, millknives@aol.com; Web: www.millerknives.com
Patterns: Bowies, hunters, skinners, folders. **Technical:** Primarily uses CPM 154, 440C, ATS-34, CPM S30V, damascus and Sandvik stainless steels. Exotic hardwoods, bone, horn, antler, ivory, synthetics. All leather work and sheaths made by me and handstitched. **Remarks:** Have been making custom knives for sale since 1990. Part-time maker, hope to go full time in about five and a half years (after retirement from full-time job). **Mark:** Last name inside a pentagram.

MILLER, TERRY
P.O. Box 262, Healy, AK 99743, Phone: 907-683-1239, terry@denalidomehome.com
Specialties: Alaskan ulus with wood or horn. **Remarks:** New to knifemaking (7 years).

MILLER, WILLIAM (BILL)
21937 Holiday Ln., Warsaw, MO 65355, Phone: 660-723-1866, wmknives@hotmail.com
Specialties: Uses own handforged high-carbon damascus for bowies, daggers, push daggers and hunters. **Patterns:** All different styles. **Prices:** $250 to $3,000. **Remarks:** Uses exotic hardwood, stag, fossil ivory and fossil bone as handle materials. **Mark:** "W" over "M" in an oval.

MILLS, LOUIS G
9450 Waters Rd, Ann Arbor, MI 48103, Phone: 734-668-1839
Specialties: High-art Japanese-style period pieces. **Patterns:** Traditional tantos, daggers and swords. **Technical:** Makes steel from iron; makes his own Damascus by traditional Japanese techniques. **Prices:** $900 to $2000; some to $8000. **Remarks:** Spare-time maker. **Mark:** Yasutomo in Japanese Kanji.

MILLS, MICHAEL
151 Blackwell Rd, Colonial Beach, VA 22443-5054, Phone: 804-224-0265
Specialties: Working knives, hunters, skinners, utility and Bowies. **Technical:** Forge 5160 differential heat-treats. **Prices:** $300 and up. **Remarks:** Part-time maker, ABS Journeyman. **Mark:** Last name in script.

MINCHEW, RYAN
2101 Evans Ln., Midland, TX 79705, Phone: 806-752-0223, ryan@minchewknives.com Web: www.minchewknives.com
Specialties: Hunters and folders. **Patterns:** Standard hunters and bird-and-trout knives. **Prices:** $150 to $500. **Mark:** Minchew.

MINNICK, JIM & JOYCE
144 North 7th St, Middletown, IN 47356, Phone: 765-354-4108, jmjknives@aol.com; Web: www.minnickknives@aol.com
Specialties: Lever-lock folding art knives, liner-locks. **Patterns:** Stilettos, Persian and one-of-a-kind folders. **Technical:** Grinds and carves Damascus, stainless, and high-carbon. **Prices:** $950 to $7000. **Remarks:** Part-time maker; first knife sold in 1976. Husband and wife team. **Mark:** Minnick and JMJ.

MIRABILE, DAVID
PO BOX 20417, Juneau, AK 99802, Phone: 907-321-1103, dmirabile02@gmail.com; Web: www.mirabileknives.com
Specialties: Elegant edged weapons and hard use Alaskan knives. **Patterns:** Fighters, personal carry knives, special studies of the Tlinget dagger. **Technical:** Uses W-2, 1080, 15n20, 1095, 5160, and his own Damascus, and stainless/high carbon San Mai.

MITCHELL, ALAN
133 Standard Dr., Blairgowrie, Randburg, Gauteng, SOUTH AFRICA, Phone: +27(83) 501 0944, alspostbox@hotmail.com; Facebook.com/mitchellhandmade
Specialties: Forged working and using knives. **Patterns:** Hunters, utility knives and bowies. **Technical:** Forges high-carbon steels with flat and hollow grinds and hamons (temper lines). **Prices:** $100 to $1,000. **Remarks:** Member of Knife Makers Guild of South Africa. **Mark:** Mitchell.

MITCHELL, JAMES A
PO Box 4646, Columbus, GA 31904, Phone: 404-322-8582
Specialties: Fancy working knives. **Patterns:** Hunters, fighters, Bowies and locking folders. **Technical:** Grinds D2, 440C and commercial Damascus. **Prices:** $100 to $400; some to $900. **Remarks:** Part-time maker; first knife sold in 1976. Sells knives in sets. **Mark:** Signature and city.

MITCHELL, MAX DEAN AND BEN
3803 VFW Rd, Leesville, LA 71440, Phone: 318-239-6416
Specialties: Hatchet and knife sets with folder and belt and holster all match. **Patterns:** Hunters, 200 L6 steel. **Technical:** L6 steel; soft back, hand edge. **Prices:** $300 to $500. **Remarks:** Part-time makers; first knife sold in 1965. Custom orders only; no stock. **Mark:** First names.

MITCHELL, WM DEAN
2405 County Rd. 1550, Warren, TX 77664, Phone: 409-547-0420, wmdeanmitchell@gmail.com
Specialties: Functional and collectable cutlery. **Patterns:** Personal and collector's designs. **Technical:** Forges own Damascus and carbon steels. **Prices:** Determined by the buyer. **Remarks:** Gentleman knifemaker. ABS Master Smith 1994.**Mark:** Full name with anvil and MS or WDM and MS.

MITSUYUKI, ROSS
PO Box 29577, Honolulu, HI 96820, Phone: 808-778-5907, Fax: 808-671-3335, r.p.mitsuyuki@gmail.com; Web:www.picturetrail.com/homepage/mrbing
Specialties: Working straight knives and folders/engraving titanium & 416 S.S. **Patterns:** Hunting, fighters, utility knives and boot knives. **Technical:** 440C, BG42, ATS-34, S30V, CPM154, and Damascus. **Prices:** $150 and up. **Remarks:** Spare-time maker, first knife sold in 1998. **Mark:** (Honu) Hawaiian sea turtle.

MIVILLE-DESCHENES, ALAIN
1952 Charles A Parent, Quebec, CANADA G2B 4B2, Phone: 418-845-0950, Fax: 418-845-0950, amd@miville-deschenes.com; Web: www.miville-deschenes.com
Specialties: Working knives of his design or to customer specs and art knives. **Patterns:** Bowies, skinner, hunter, utility, camp knives, fighters, art knives. **Technical:** Grinds ATS-34, CPMS30V, 0-1, D2, and sometime forge carbon steel. **Prices:** $250 to $700; some

higher. **Remarks:** Part-time maker; first knife sold in 2001. **Mark:** Logo (small hand) and initials (AMD).

MOELLER, HARALD
#17-493 Pioneer Crescent, Parksville, BC, CANADA V9P 1V2, Phone: 250-248-0391, moeknif@shaw.ca; Web: www.collectiblecustomknives.com
Specialties: Collector grade San Fransisco Dagger; small fighters, Fantasy Axes, Bowies, Survival Knives. Special design award winning liner lock folders; Viper throwing knives. **Technical:** Steels - 440-C, ATS34, damascus, etc. Materials: mammoth, Abalone, MOP, Black Water Buffalo, 14K Gold, rubies, diamonds, etc. **Prices:** Throwing knives - $80 to $350; Fighters - $400 to $600; Axe - $3200; Folders - $600 to $3400; Dagger - Up to $9,000 **Remarks:** Now part time maker, first knife sold in 1979. member Southern California Blades; Member Oregon Knife Collectors Assoc.**Mark:** Moeller

MOEN, JERRY
4478 Spring Valley Rd., Dallas, TX 75244, Phone: 972-839-1609, jmoen@moencustomknives.com Web: moencustomknives.com
Specialties: Hunting, pocket knives, fighters tactical, and exotic. **Prices:** $500 to $5,000.

MOIZIS, STAN
8213 109B St., Delta, British Columbia (BC), CANADA V4C 4G9, Phone: 604-597-8929, moizis@telus.net
Specialties: Automatic and spring-assist folding knives and soon to come out-the-fronts. **Patterns:** Well-made carry knives with some upper-end materials available for steel and handles. All patterns are freehand, and thus each knife is unique. **Marks:** "SM" on blade with date and place of manufacture on inside of spacer. On knives with professionally out-of-house machined parts, mark is "BRNO BORN."

MOJZIS, JULIUS
B S Timravy 6, 98511 Halic, SLOVAKIA, julius.mojzis@gmail.com; Web: www.juliusmojzis.com
Specialties: Art Knives. **Prices:** USD 2000. **Mark:** MOJZIS.

MONCUS, MICHAEL STEVEN
1803 US 19 N, Smithville, GA 31787, Phone: 912-846-2408

MONTANO, GUS A
P.O. Box 501264, San Diego, CA 92150, Phone: 619-273-5357
Specialties: Traditional working/using straight knives of his design. **Patterns:** Boots, Bowies and fighters. **Technical:** Grinds 1095 and 5160; grinds and forges cable. Double or triple hardened and triple drawn; hand-rubbed finish. Prefers natural handle materials. **Prices:** $200 to $400; some to $600. **Remarks:** Spare-time maker; first knife sold in 1997. **Mark:** First initial and last name.

MONTEIRO, VICTOR
31 Rue D'Opprebais, Maleves Ste Marie, BELGIUM 1360, Phone: 010 88 0441, victor.monteiro@skynet.be
Specialties: Working and fancy straight knives, folders and integrals of his design. **Patterns:** Fighters, hunters and kitchen knives. **Technical:** Grinds ATS-34, 440C, D2, Damasteel and other commercial Damascus, embellishment, filework and domed pins. **Prices:** $300 to $1000, some higher. **Remarks:** Part-time maker; first knife sold in 1989. **Mark:** Logo with initials connected.

MONTELL, TY
PO BOX 1312, Thatcher, AZ 85552, Phone: 575-538-1610, Fax: Cell: 575-313-4373, montellfamily@aol.com
Specialties: Automatics, slip-joint folders, hunting and miniatures.**Technical:** Stock removal. Steel of choice is CPM-154, Devin Thomas Damascus. **Prices:** $250 and up. **Remarks:** First knife made in 1980. **Mark:** Tang stamp - Montell.

MONTENEGRO, FACUNDO
777 Jorge L. Borges St., Merlo (5881) San Luis, ARGENTINA, Phone: 005492664759472, faca32@yahoo.com.ar; Web: www.montenegroknives.com.ar
Specialties: Bowies, hunters, gaucho knives and integrals. **Technical:** Forges own damascus and O1, specializing in Turkish and mosaic damascus on gaucho knives and hunting swords. **Prices:** $400 and up, with most pieces around $850 to $2,000. **Remarks:** First ABS journeyman smith from Argentina, and considered one of the best knifemakers of Argentina. **Mark:** Montenegro JS.

MONTGOMERY, STEPHEN R.
4621 Crescent Rd., Madison, WI 53711, Phone: 608-658-2623, smontgomery2211@gmail.com
Specialties: Working hunters, bowies and Scottish knives. **Patterns:** Small hunters of the maker's design. **Technical:** Forges and grinds 1095, CVR 80 and 154CM steels. **Prices:** $65 to $300. **Remarks:** Uses what he makes, as he is a hunter, archer and armored combat fighter. **Mark:** sm.

MOONEY, MIKE
19432 E. Cloud Rd., Queen Creek, AZ 85142, Phone: 480-244-7768, mike@moonblades.com; Web: www.moonblades.com
Specialties: Hand-crafted high-performing straight knives of his or customer's design. **Patterns:** Bowies, fighters, hunting, camp and kitchen users or collectible. **Technical:** Flat-grind, hand-rubbed finish, S30V, CPM 154, Damascus, any steel. **Prices:** $300 to $3000. **Remarks:** Doing business as moonblades.com. Commissions are welcome. **Mark:** M. Mooney followed by crescent moon.

MOORE, DAVY
Moyriesk, Quin, Co Clare, IRELAND, Phone: 353 (0)65 6825975, davy@mooreireland.com; Web: http://www.mooreireland.com

Specialties: Traditional and Celtic outdoor hunting and utility knives. **Patterns:** Traditional hunters and skinners, Celtic pattern hunting knives, Bushcrafting, fishing, utility/camp knives. **Technical:** Stock removal knives 01, D2, RWL 34, ATS 34, CPM 154, Damasteel (various).**Prices:** 250-1700 Euros.**Remarks:** Full-time maker, first knife sold in 2004. **Mark:** Three stars over rampant lion / MOORE over Ireland.

MOORE, JAMES B
1707 N Gillis, Ft. Stockton, TX 79735, Phone: 915-336-2113
Specialties: Classic working straight knives and folders of his design. **Patterns:** Hunters, Bowies, daggers, fighters, boots, utility/camp knives, locking folders and slip-joint folders. **Technical:** Grinds 440C, ATS-34, D2, L6, CPM and commercial Damascus. **Prices:** $85 to $700; exceptional knives to $1500. **Remarks:** Full-time maker; first knife sold in 1972. **Mark:** Name, city and state.

MOORE, JON P
304 South N Rd, Aurora, NE 68818, Phone: 402-849-2616, Web: www.sharpdecisionknives.com
Specialties: Working and fancy straight knives using antler, exotic bone, wood and Micarta. Will use customers' antlers on request. **Patterns:** Hunters, skinners, camp and bowies. **Technical:** Hand-forged high carbon steel. Makes his own damascus. **Prices:** Start at $125. **Remarks:** Full-time maker, sold first knife in 2003. Does on-location knife forging demonstrations. **Mark:** Sword through anvil with name.

MOORE, MARVE
HC 89 Box 393, Willow, AK 99688, Phone: 907-232-0478, marvemoore@aol.com
Specialties: Fixed blades forged and stock removal. **Patterns:** Hunter, skinners, fighter, short swords. **Technical:** 100 percent of his work is done by hand. **Prices:** $100 to $500. **Remarks:** Also makes his own sheaths. **Mark:** -MM-.

MOORE, MICHAEL ROBERT
70 Beauliew St, Lowell, MA 01850, Phone: 978-479-0589, Fax: 978-441-1819

MOORE, TED
340 E Willow St, Elizabethtown, PA 17022, Phone: 717-367-3939, tedmoore@tedmooreknives.com; Web: www.tedmooreknives.com
Specialties: Damascus folders, cigar cutters, high art. **Patterns:** Slip joints, linerlock, cigar cutters. **Technical:** Grinds Damascus and stainless steels. **Prices:** $250 and up. **Remarks:** Part-time maker; first knife sold 1993. **Mark:** Moore U.S.A.

MORALES, RAMON
LP-114, Managua, NICARAGUA, Phone: 011-505-824-8950, nicaraguabladesmith@gmail.com
Specialties: Forges knives and enjoys making brut de forge pieces. **Patterns:** Choppers, bowies and hunters. **Technical:** Does all his own blade heat treating in house and makes his own damascus. **Remarks:** Only ABS journeyman smith in Central America. **Mark:** Initials "RM" inside the outline of Nicaragua.

MORETT, DONALD
116 Woodcrest Dr, Lancaster, PA 17602-1300, Phone: 717-746-4888

MORGAN, JEFF
9200 Arnaz Way, Santee, CA 92071, Phone: 619-448-8430
Specialties: Early American style knives. **Patterns:** Hunters, bowies, etc. **Technical:** Carbon steel and carbon steel damascus. **Prices:** $60 to $400

MORGAN, TOM
14689 Ellett Rd, Beloit, OH 44609, Phone: 330-537-2023
Specialties: Working straight knives and period pieces. **Patterns:** Hunters, boots and presentation tomahawks. **Technical:** Grinds 01, 440C and 154CM. **Prices:** Knives, $65 to $200; tomahawks, $100 to $325. **Remarks:** Full-time maker; first knife sold in 1977. **Mark:** Last name and type of steel used.

MORO, CORRADO
Via Omegna, 22 - Rivoli 10098, Torino, ITALY, Phone: +39 3472451255, info@moroknives.com; Web: www.moroknives.com
Specialties: High-end folders of his own design and to customer specs, unique locking and pivoting systems. **Patterns:** Inspired by nature and technology. **Technical:** Uses ATS 34, 916 and 904L blade steels, and titanium, carbon-lip inlays, precious metals and diamonds. **Prices:** $3,500 to $11,000 and above. **Remarks:** Full-time maker; first knife sold in 2011. **Mark:** MORO on blade.

MORRIS, C H
1590 Old Salem Rd, Frisco City, AL 36445, Phone: 334-575-7425
Specialties: LinerLock® folders. **Patterns:** Interframe liner locks. **Technical:** Grinds 440C and ATS-34. **Prices:** Start at $350. **Remarks:** Full-time maker; first knife sold in 1973. Doing business as Custom Knives. **Mark:** First and middle initials, last name.

MORRIS, ERIC
306 Ewart Ave, Beckley, WV 25801, Phone: 304-255-3951

MORRIS, MICHAEL S.
609 S. Main St., Yale, MI 48097, Phone: 810-887-7817, michaelmorrisknives@gmail.com
Specialties: Hunting and Tactical fixed blade knives of his design made from files. **Technical:** All knives hollow ground on 16" wheel. Hand stitches his own sheaths also. **Prices:** From $60 to $350 with most in the $90 to $125 range. **Remarks:** Machinist since 1980, made his first knife in 1984, sold his first knife in 2004. Now full-time maker. **Mark:** Last name with date of manufacture.

MOSES, STEVEN
1610 W Hemlock Way, Santa Ana, CA 92704

MOSIER, DAVID
1725 Millburn Ave., Independence, MO 64056, Phone: 816-796-3479, dmknives@aol.com Web: www.dmknives.com
Specialties: Tactical folders and fixed blades. **Patterns:** Fighters and concealment blades. **Technical:** Uses S35VN, CPM 154, S30V, 154CM, ATS-34, 440C, A2, D2, Stainless damascus, and Damasteel. Fixed blades come with Kydex sheaths made by maker. **Prices:** $150 to $1000. **Remarks:** Full-time maker, business name is DM Knives. **Mark:** David Mosier Knives encircling sun.

MOULTON, DUSTY
135 Hillview Lane, Loudon, TN 37774, Phone: 865-408-9779, Web: www.moultonknives.com
Specialties: Fancy and working straight knives. **Patterns:** Hunters, fighters, fantasy and miniatures. **Technical:** Grinds ATS-34 and Damascus. **Prices:** $300 to $2000. **Remarks:** Full-time maker; first knife sold in 1991. Now doing engraving on own knives as well as other makers. **Mark:** Last name.

MOYER, RUSS
1266 RD 425 So, Havre, MT 59501, Phone: 406-395-4423
Specialties: Working knives to customer specs. **Patterns:** Hunters, Bowies and survival knives. **Technical:** Forges W2 & 5160. **Prices:** $150 to $350. **Remarks:** Part-time maker; first knife sold in 1976. **Mark:** Initials in logo.

MULKEY, GARY
533 Breckenridge Rd, Branson, MO 65616, Phone: 417-335-0123, gary@mulkeyknives.com; Web: www.mulkeyknives.com
Specialties: Sole authorship damascus and high-carbon steel hunters, bowies and fighters. **Patterns:** Fixed blades (hunters, bowies, and fighters). **Prices:** $450 and up. **Remarks:** Full-time maker since 1997. **Mark:** MUL above skeleton key.

MULLER, JODY
3359 S. 225th Rd., Goodson, MO 65663, Phone: 417-752-3260, mullerforge2@hotmail.com; Web: www.mullerforge.com
Specialties: Hand engraving, carving and inlays, fancy folders and oriental styles. **Patterns:** One-of-a-kind fixed blades and folders in all styles. **Technical:** Forges own Damascus and high carbon steel. **Prices:** $300 and up. **Remarks:** Full-time knifemaker, does hand engraving, carving and inlay. All work done by maker. **Mark:** Muller

MUNJAS, BOB
600 Beebe Rd., Waterford, OH 45786, Phone: 740-336-5538, Web: hairofthebear.com
Specialties: Damascus and carbon steel sheath knives. **Patterns:** Hunters and neck knives. **Technical:** My own Damascus, 5160, 1095, 1984, L6, and W2. Forge and stock removal. Does own heat treating and makes own sheaths. **Prices:** $100 to $500. **Remarks:** Part-time maker. **Mark:** Moon Munjas.

MURA, DENIS
Via Pesciule 15 56021, Cascina (Pi), ITALY, Phone: +39 3388365277, zeb1d@libero.it; Web: www.denismura.com
Specialties: Straight knives. **Patterns:** Hunters, bowies, camp knives and everyday carry (EDC) knives. **Technical:** Grinds A2, D2, W2; 440C, RWL 34; CPM 154, Sleipner, Niolox, 1095, 1084, 1070, C145SC, Becut, damascus and san mai steels. **Prices:** Start at $250. **Remarks:** Part-time maker; first knife made in 2006. **Mark:** MD.

MURSKI, RAY
12129 Captiva Ct, Reston, VA 22091-1204, Phone: 703-264-1102, rmurski@gmail.com
Specialties: Fancy working/using folders of his design. **Patterns:** Hunters, slip-joint folders and utility/camp knives. **Technical:** Grinds CPM-3V **Prices:** $125 to $500. **Remarks:** Spare-time maker; first knife sold in 1996. **Mark:** Engraved name with serial number under name.

MUTZ, JEFF
8210 Rancheria Dr. Unit 7, Rancho Cucamonga, CA 91730, Phone: 909-559-7129, jmutzknives@hotmail.com; Web: www.jmutzknives.com
Specialties: Traditional working/using fixed blade and slip-jointed knives of own design and customer specs. **Patterns:** Hunters, skinners, and folders. **Technical:** Forges and grinds all steels Offers scrimshaw. **Prices:** $225 to $800. **Remarks:** Full-time maker, first knife sold in 1998. **Mark:** First initial, last name over "maker."

MYERS, PAUL
644 Maurice St, Wood River, IL 62095, Phone: 618-258-1707
Specialties: Fancy working straight knives and folders. **Patterns:** Full range of folders, straight hunters and Bowies; tie tacks; knife and fork sets. **Technical:** Grinds D2, 440C, ATS-34 and 154CM. **Prices:** $100 to $350; some to $3000. **Remarks:** Full-time maker; first knife sold in 1974. **Mark:** Initials with setting sun on front; name and number on back.

MYERS, STEVE
1045 Marshall St., Carlinville, IL 62626-1048, Phone: 217-416-0800, myersknives@ymail.com
Specialties: Working straight knives and integrals. **Patterns:** Camp knives, hunters, skinners, Bowies, and boot knives.**Technical:** Forges own Damascus and high carbon steels. **Prices:** $250 to $1,000. **Remarks:** Full-time maker, first knife sold in 1985. **Mark:** Last name in logo.

N

NADEAU, BRIAN
SHARPBYDESIGN LLC, 8 Sand Hill Rd., Stanhope, NJ 07874, Phone: 862-258-0792, nadeau@sharpbydesign.com; Web: www.sharpbydesign.com
Specialties: High-quality tactical fixed blades and folders, collector and working blades.

custom knifemakers

All blades and sheaths of maker's own design. Designs, writes programs and machines all components on CNC equipment, nothing water jet, everything hand finished. **Technical:** Works with new CPM steels, but loves to get an order for a W2 blade with a nice hamon or temper line. **Prices:** $100 and up. **Remarks:** Part-time maker. **Mark:** Name in script, or initials "BN" skewed on top of one another.

NARASADA, MAMORU
9115-8 Nakaminowa, Minowa-machi, Kamiina-gun, NAGANO, JAPAN 399-4601, Phone: 81-265-79-3960, Fax: 81-265-79-3960
Specialties: Utility working straight knife. **Patterns:** Hunting, fishing, and camping knife. **Technical:** Grind and forges / ATS34, VG10, 440C, CRM07. **Prices:** $150 to $500, some higher. **Remarks:** First knife sold in 2003. **Mark:** M.NARASADA with initial logo.

NATEN, GREG
1804 Shamrock Way, Bakersfield, CA 93304-3921
Specialties: Fancy and working/using folders of his design. **Patterns:** Fighters, hunters and locking folders. **Technical:** Grinds 440C, ATS-34 and CPM440V. Heat-treats; prefers desert ironwood, stag and mother-of-pearl. Designs and sews leather sheaths for straight knives. **Prices:** $175 to $600; some to $950. **Remarks:** Spare-time maker; first knife sold in 1992. **Mark:** Last name above battle-ax, handmade.

NAUDE, LOUIS
P.O. Box 1103, Okahandja, Namibia, AFRICA 7560, Phone: +264 (0)81-38-36-285, info@louisnaude.co.za Web: www.louisnaude.co.za
Specialties: Folders, Hunters, Custom.. **Patterns:** See Website. **Technical:** Stock removal, African materials. **Prices:** See website. **Remarks:** Still the tool! **Mark:** Louis Naude Knives with family crest.

NAZZ, THEO "ROCK"
159 2nd Ave., Apt. 12, New York, NY 10003, Phone: 917-532-7291, theorocknazz@gmail.com; Web: www.theorocknazz.com
Specialties: Knives, daggers and swords with 3-D-printed cast metal components that increase the ability to grip while offering extensive customization. **Technical:** Monosteel blades are CruForgeV, 80CrV2 and W2; san mai is typically one of the aforementioned steels with a stainless, pattern-welded or wrought iron shell. Pattern-welded blades are 1080, W2, 80CrV2 and/or 15N20 for the cutting edge, and wrought iron, pure nickel, stainless and/or 15N20 for the shell/spine if applicable. Does own heat treat to form a variety of hamons (temper lines). **Prices:** $400 to $1,500, or $1,000 to $8,000 for swords. **Remarks:** Part-time maker since 2007. **Mark:** "N" fileworked on the spine, or "N" incorporated in a 3-D printed metal component.

NEALY, BUD
125 Raccoon Way, Stroudsburg, PA 18360, Phone: 570-402-1018, Fax: 570-402-1018, bnealy@ptd.net; Web: www.budnealyknifemaker.com
Specialties: Original design concealment knives with designer multi-concealment sheath system. **Patterns:** Fixed Blades and Folders **Technical:** Grinds CPM 154, XHP, and Damascus. **Prices:** $200 to $2500. **Remarks:** Full-time maker; first knife sold in 1980. **Mark:** Name, city, state or signature.

NEASE, WILLIAM
2336 Front Rd., LaSalle, ON, CANADA Canada N9J 2C4, wnease@hotmail.com Web: www.unsubtleblades.com
Specialties: Hatchets, choppers, and Japanese-influenced designs. **Technical:** Stock removal. Works A-2, D-2, S-7, O-1, powder stainless alloys, composite laminate blades with steel edges. **Prices:** $125 to $2200. **Remarks:** Part-time maker since 1994. **Mark:** Initials W.M.N. engraved in cursive on exposed tangs or on the spine of blades.

NEDVED, DAN
206 Park Dr, Kalispell, MT 59901, bushido2222@yahoo.com
Specialties: Slip joint folders, liner locks, straight knives. **Patterns:** Mostly traditional or modern blend with traditional lines. **Technical:** Grinds ATS-34, 440C, 1095 and uses other makers Damascus. **Prices:** $95 and up. Mostly in the $150 to $200 range. **Remarks:** Part-time maker, averages 2 a month. **Mark:** Dan Nedved or Nedved with serial # on opposite side.

NEELY, GREG
5419 Pine St, Bellaire, TX 77401, Phone: 713-991-2677, gtneely64@comcast.net
Specialties: Traditional patterns and his own patterns for work and/or collecting. **Patterns:** Hunters, Bowies and utility/camp knives. **Technical:** Forges own Damascus, 1084, 5160 and some tool steels. Differentially tempers. **Prices:** $225 to $5000. **Remarks:** Part-time maker; first knife sold in 1987. **Mark:** Last name or interlocked initials, MS.

NEELY, JONATHAN
JAECO KNIVES, 2401 N. Beech Ln., Greensboro, NC 27455, Phone: 336-540-4925, jaecoknives@gmail.com; Web: http://www.jaecoknives.com
Specialties: Fixed-blade hunters, EDC (everyday carry) and utility-style knives. **Technical:** Stock removal maker using 1084 steel. **Prices:** Start at $25 to $30 per inch. **Remarks:** Part-time maker and full-time stay-at-home dad who feels confident he will be making knives for the rest of his life; first knife made in 2014. **Mark:** "Jaeco" (Jon and Erin's Company) with a mountain range logo.

NEILSON, J
187 Cistern Ln., Towanda, PA 18848, Phone: 570-721-0470, Web: www.mountainhollow.net
Specialties: Working and collectable fixed blade knives. **Patterns:** Hunter/fighters, Bowies, neck knives and daggers. **Technical:** Multiple high-carbon steels as well as maker's own damascus. **Prices:** $100 to $7,500. **Remarks:** ABS Master Smith, full-time maker, judge on History Channel's "Forged In Fire" program, doing business as Neilson's Mountain Hollow. Each knife comes with a sheath. **Mark:** J. Neilson MS.

NELL, CHAD
2424 E. 2070 S, St. George, UT 84790, Phone: 435-229-6442, chad@nellknives.com; Web: www.nellknives.com
Specialties: Frame-lock folders and fixed blades. **Patterns:** Templar, ESG, Hybrid and Loveless patterns. **Technical:** Grinds CPM-154, ATS-34. **Prices:** Starting at $300. **Remarks:** Full-time maker since Sep 2011, First knife made in May 2010. **Mark:** C. Nell Utah, USA or C. Nell Kona, Hawaii.

NELSON, KEN
2712 17th St., Racine, WI 53405, Phone: 262-456-7519 or 262-664-5293, ken@ironwolfonline.com Web: www.ironwolfonline.com
Specialties: Working straight knives, period pieces. **Patterns:** Utility, hunters, dirks, daggers, throwers, hawks, axes, swords, pole arms and blade blanks as well. **Technical:** Forges 5160, 52100, W2, 10xx, L6, carbon steels and own Damascus. Does his own heat treating. **Prices:** $50 to $350, some to $3000. **Remarks:** Part-time maker. First knife sold in 1995. Doing business as Iron Wolf Forge. **Mark:** Stylized wolf paw print.

NETO JR.,, NELSON AND DE CARVALHO, HENRIQUE M.
R. Joao Margarido No 20-V, Braganca Paulista, SP, BRAZIL 12900-000, Phone: 011-7843-6889, Fax: 011-7843-6889
Specialties: Straight knives and folders. **Patterns:** Bowies, katanas, jambyias and others. **Technical:** Forges high-carbon steels. **Prices:** $70 to $3000. **Remarks:** Full-time makers; first knife sold in 1990. **Mark:** HandN.

NEVLING, MARK
BURR OAK KNIVES, 3567 N. M52, Owosso, MI 48867, Phone: 989-472-3167, burroakknives@aol.com; Web: www.burroakknives.com
Specialties: Tactical folders using stainless over high-carbon San Mai. **Patterns:** Hunters, fighters, bowies, folders and small executive knives. **Technical:** Convex grinds, forges, uses only high-carbon and damascus. **Prices:** $200 to $4,000. **Remarks:** Full-time maker, first knife sold 1988. Apprentice damascus smith to George Werth and Doug Ponzio.

NEWBERRY, ALLEN
PO BOX 301, Lowell, AR 72745, Phone: 479-530-6439, newberry@newberryknives.com Web: www.newberryknives.com
Specialties: Fixed blade knives both forged and stock removal. **Patterns:** Traditional patterns as well as newer designs inspired by historical and international blades. **Technical:** Uses 1095, W2, 5160, 154-CM, other steels by request. **Prices:** $150 to $450+. **Remarks:** Many of the knives feature hamons. **Mark:** Newberry with a capital N for forged pieces and newberry with a lower case n for stock removal pieces.

NEWCOMB, CORBIN
628 Woodland Ave, Moberly, MO 65270, Phone: 660-263-4639
Specialties: Working straight knives and folders; period pieces. **Patterns:** Hunters, axes, Bowies, folders, buckskinned blades and boots. **Technical:** Hollow-grinds D2, 440C and 154CM; prefers natural handle materials. Makes own Damascus; offers cable Damascus. **Prices:** $100 to $500. **Remarks:** Full-time maker; first knife sold in 1982. Doing business as Corbin Knives. **Mark:** First name and serial number.

NEWHALL, TOM
3602 E 42nd Stravenue, Tucson, AZ 85713, Phone: 520-721-0562, gggaz@aol.com

NEWTON, LARRY
1758 Pronghorn Ct, Jacksonville, FL 32225, Phone: 904-537-2066, lnewton1@comcast.net; Web: larrynewtonknives.com
Specialties: Traditional and slender high-grade gentlemen's automatic folders, locking liner type tactical, and working straight knives. **Patterns:** Front release locking folders, interframes, hunters, and skinners. **Technical:** Grinds Damascus, ATS-34, 440C and D2. **Prices:** Folders start at $350, straights start at $150. **Remarks:** Retired teacher. Full-time maker. First knife sold in 1989. Won Best Folder for 2008 - Blade Magazine. **Mark:** Last name.

NEWTON, RON
223 Ridge Ln, London, AR 72847, Phone: 479-293-3001, rnewton@centurylink.net
Specialties: All types of folders and fixed blades. Blackpowder gun knife combos. **Patterns:** Traditional slip joint, multi-blade patterns, antique bowie repros. **Technical:** Forges traditional and mosaid damascus. Performs engraving and gold inlay. **Prices:** $500 and up. **Remarks:** Creates hidden mechanisms in assisted opening folders. **Mark:** NEWTON M.S. in a western invitation font."

NGUYEN, MIKE
213 Fawn Ct., Pittsburgh, PA 15239, Phone: 949-812-2749, mike12_nguyen@yahoo.com; Instagram.com: mike12_nguyen
Patterns: Folders, flipper folders and fixed blades. **Technical:** Stock-removal maker using no smart-controlled machines, sole authorship, in-house heat-treating and custom one-off designs. Uses all types of stainless steels such as CPM 154, CTS-XHP, CPM S90V, as well as high-carbon and damascus. Any materials available, such as carbon fiber, Micarta, copper, zirconium and titanium. **Prices:** $850 to $1,300 and up. **Remarks:** Part-time maker working on one knife at a time. Does not have bookings, but rather holds a lotto for the next build spot at the end of his current build. **Mark:** "M" with extended horizontal lines at end, but maker never puts mark on the blade or anywhere visible.

NICHOLS, CALVIN
710 Colleton Rd., Raleigh, NC 27610, Phone: 919-523-4841, calvin.nichols@nicholsknives.com; Web: http://nicholsknives.com
Specialties: Flame-colored high carbon damascus. **Patterns:** Fixed blades or folders, bowies and daggers. **Technical:** Stock removal. **Prices:** Start at $200. **Remarks:** Full-time maker, 22 years experience, own heat treating, 2012 Best Custom and High Art winner National and North Carolina Knifemakers Guild member. **Mark:** First, last name--city, state

NICHOLS, CHAD
1125 Cr 185, Blue Springs, MS 38828, Phone: 662-538-5966, chadn28@hotmail.com Web: chadnicholsdamascus.com
Specialties: Gents folders and everyday tactical/utility style knives and fixed hunters. **Technical:** Makes own stainless damascus, mosaic damascus, and high carbon damascus. **Prices:** $450 - $1000. **Mark:** Name and Blue Springs.

NICHOLSON, R. KENT
16502 Garfield Ave., Monkton, MD 21111, Phone: 410-323-6925
Specialties: Large using knives. **Patterns:** Bowies and camp knives in the Moran-style. **Technical:** Forges W2, 9260, 5160; makes Damascus. **Prices:** $150 to $995. **Remarks:** Part-time maker; first knife sold in 1984. **Mark:** Name.

NIELSON, JEFF V
1060 S Jones Rd, Monroe, UT 84754, Phone: 435-527-4242, jvn1u205@hotmail.com
Specialties: Classic knives of his design and to customer specs. **Patterns:** Fighters, hunters; miniatures. **Technical:** Grinds 440C stainless and Damascus. **Prices:** $100 to $1200. **Remarks:** Part-time maker; first knife sold in 1991. **Mark:** Name, location.

NIEMUTH, TROY
3143 North Ave, Sheboygan, WI 53083, Phone: 414-452-2927
Specialties: Period pieces and working/using straight knives of his design and to customer specs. **Patterns:** Hunters and utility/camp knives. **Technical:** Grinds 440C, 1095 and A2. **Prices:** $85 to $350; some to $500. **Remarks:** Full-time maker; first knife sold in 1995. **Mark:** Etched last name.

NILSSON, JONNY WALKER
Akkavare 16, 93391 Arvidsjaur, SWEDEN, Phone: +46 702144207, 0960.13048@telia.com; Web: www.jwnknives.com
Specialties: High-end collectible Nordic hunters, engraved reindeer antler. World class freehand engravings. Matching engraved sheaths in leather, bone and Arctic wood with inlays. Combines traditional techniques and design with his own innovations. Master Bladesmith who specializes in forging mosaic Damascus. Sells unique mosaic Damascus bar stock to folder makers. **Patterns:** Own designs and traditional Sami designs. **Technical:** Mosaic Damascus of UHB 20 C 15N20 with pure nickel, hardness HRC 58-60. **Prices:** $1500 to $6000. **Remarks:** Full-time maker since 1988. Nordic Champion (5 countries) numerous times, 50 first prizes in Scandinavian shows. Yearly award in his name in Nordic Championship. Knives inspired by 10,000 year old indigenous Sami culture. **Mark:** JN on sheath, handle, custom wood box. JWN on blade.

NIRO, FRANK
1948 Gloaming Dr, Kamloops, B.C., CANADA V1S1P8, Phone: 250-372-8332, niro@telus.net
Specialties: Liner locking folding knives in his designs in what might be called standard patterns. **Technical:** Enjoys grinding mosaic Damascus with pure nickel of the make up for blades that are often double ground; as well as meteorite for bolsters which are then etched and heat colored. Uses 416 stainless for spacers with inlays of natural materials, gem stones with also file work. Liners are made from titanium are most often fully file worked and anodized. Only uses natural materials particularly mammoth ivory for scales. **Prices:** $500 to $1500 **Remarks:** Full time maker. Has been selling knives for over thirty years. **Mark:** Last name on the inside of the spacer.

NISHIUCHI, MELVIN S
6121 Forest Park Dr, Las Vegas, NV 89156, Phone: 702-501-3724, msnknives@yahoo.com
Specialties: Collectable quality using/working knives. **Patterns:** Locking liner folders, fighters, hunters and fancy personal knives. **Technical:** Grinds ATS-34 and Devin Thomas Damascus; prefers semi-precious stone and exotic natural handle materials. **Prices:** $375 to $2000. **Remarks:** Part-time maker; first knife sold in 1985. **Mark:** Circle with a line above it.

NOLEN, STEVE
3325 Teton, Longmont, CO 80504-6251, Phone: 720-334-1801, stevenolen1@msn.com; Web: www.nolenknives.org
Specialties: Working knives and hunters. **Patterns:** Wide variety of straight knives and neck knives. **Technical:** Grinds D2, ATS-34 and 440C. Offers filework and makes exotic handles. **Prices:** $75 to $1,000, some higher. **Remarks:** Part-time maker, third generation, and still has quite a few of R.D. Nolen's collection. **Mark:** NK in oval logo and NOLEN-Steve Nolen knives have hardness and steel engraved by logo.

NOLTE, BARBIE
10801 Gram B Cir., Lowell, AR 72745, Phone: 479-283-2095, barbie.b@gmail.com
Specialties: Collector-grade high art knives. **Technical:** Hollow grinds high-carbon, mosaic-damascus blades. Limited supply. **Prices:** Start at $600. All prices include handmade exotic leather sheaths. **Mark:** B Bell and B Nolte.

NOLTE, STEVE
10801 Gram B Cir., Lowell, AR 72745, Phone: 479-629-1676, snolte@alertalarmsys.com; Web: www.snolteknives.com
Specialties: Fancy hunters and skinners, a few fighters, some collector-grade, high-art knives. One-of-a-kind mosaic handle creations including exotic stone work. **Technical:** Mostly high-carbon damascus, some stainless damascus with very few straight stainless blades. Hollow grinds. **Prices:** Start at $400. All prices include handmade sheaths, mostly exotic leathers. **Mark:** S.Nolte.

NORDELL, INGEMAR
Skarp Œvagen 5, FŠrila, SWEDEN 82041, Phone: 0651-23347, ingi@ingemarnordell.se; Web: www.ingemarnordell.se

Specialties: Classic working and using straight knives and fighters. **Technical:** Forges and grinds ATS-34, D2 and Sandvik. **Prices:** $300 to $3,000. **Remarks:** Part-time maker; first knife sold in 1985. **Mark:** Initials or name.

NOREN, DOUGLAS E
14676 Boom Rd, Springlake, MI 49456, Phone: 616-842-4247, gnoren@icsworldmail.com
Specialties: Hand forged blades, custom built and made to order. Hand filework, carving and casting. Stag and stacked handles. Replicas of Scagel and Joseph Rogers pieces, as well as American bowies. Hand-tooled custom made sheaths. **Technical:** Master smith, 5160, 52100 and 1084 steel. **Prices:** $400 and up. **Remarks:** Sole authorship, works in all mediums, ABS Mastersmith, all knives come with a custom hand-tooled sheath. Enjoys the challenge and meeting people.

NORFLEET, ROSS W
4110 N Courthouse Rd, Providence Forge, VA 23140-3420, Phone: 804-966-2596, rossknife@aol.com
Specialties: Classic, traditional and working/using knives of his design or in standard patterns. **Patterns:** Hunters and folders. **Technical:** Hollow-grinds 440C and ATS-34. **Prices:** $150 to $550. **Remarks:** Part-time maker; first knife sold in 1992. **Mark:** Last name.

NORTON, DON
95N Wilkison Ave, Port Townsend, WA 98368-2534, Phone: 306-385-1978
Specialties: Fancy and plain straight knives. **Patterns:** Hunters, small Bowies, tantos, boot knives, fillets. **Technical:** Prefers 440C, Micarta, exotic woods and other natural handle materials. Hollow-grinds all knives except fillet knives. **Prices:** $185 to $2800; average is $200. **Remarks:** Full-time maker; first knife sold in 1980. **Mark:** Full name, Hsi Shuai, city, state.

NOWACKI, STEPHEN R.
167 King Georges Ave, Regents Park, Southampton, Hampshire, ENGLAND SO154LD, Phone: 023 81 785 630 or 079 29 737 872, forgesmith9@gmail.com; Web: www.whitetigerknives.com
Specialties: Hand-forged, bowies, daggers, tactical blades, hunters and mountain-man style folders. **Technical:** Hitachi white paper steel and stainless carbon San Mai. Heat treats and uses natural handle materials. **Prices:** $200 - $1500. **Remarks:** Full-time maker. First knife sold in 2000. Doing business as White Tiger Knives. **Mark:** Stylized W T.

NOWLAND, RICK
3677 E Bonnie Rd, Waltonville, IL 62894, Phone: 618-279-3170, ricknowland@frontiernet.net
Specialties: Slip joint folders in traditional patterns. **Patterns:** Trapper, whittler, sowbelly, toothpick and copperhead. **Technical:** Uses ATS-34, bolsters and liners have integral construction. **Prices:** $225 to $1000. **Remarks:** Part-time maker. **Mark:** Last name.

NUCKELS, STEPHEN J
1105 Potomac Ave, Hagerstown, MD 21742, Phone: 301-739-1287, sgnucks@myactv.net
Specialties: Traditional using/working/everyday carry knives and small neck knives. **Patterns:** Hunters, bowies, Drop and trailing point knives, frontier styles. **Technical:** Hammer forges carbon steels, stock removal. Modest silver wire inlay and file work. Sheath work. **Remarks:** Spare-time maker forging under Potomac Forge, first knife made in 2008. Member W.F. Moran Jr. Foundation, American Bladesmith Society. **Mark:** Initials.

NUNN, GREGORY
HC64 Box 2107, Castle Valley, UT 84532, Phone: 435-259-8607
Specialties: High-art working and using knives of his design; new edition knife with handle made from anatomized dinosaur bone, first ever made. **Patterns:** Flaked stone knives. **Technical:** Uses gem-quality agates, jaspers and obsidians for blades. **Prices:** $250 to $2300. **Remarks:** Full-time maker; first knife sold in 1989. **Mark:** Name, knife and edition numbers, year made.

NYLUND, ERIK
Kyrontie 31, 65320 Vaasa, FINLAND, Phone: +358456349392, erik.nylund@pp2.inet.fi; Web: http://personal.inet.fi/koti/erik.nylund/
Specialties: Art knives. **Patterns:** Art knives, hunters and leuku knives. **Technical:** Forges Silversteel and 52100, and grinds RWL-34, Damasteel and 13C26. **Prices:** Start at $250. **Remarks:** Part-time maker. **Mark:** Erik Nylund, or earlier knives marked EN.

O

OATES, LEE
PO BOX 214, Bethpage, TN 37022, Phone: 281-838-0480 or 281-838-0468, bearoates89@comcast.net; Web: www.bearclawknives.com
Specialties: Friction folders, period correct replicas, traditional, working and primitive knives of my design or to customer specs. **Patterns:** Bowies, teflon-coated fighters, daggers, hunters, fillet and kitchen cutlery. **Technical:** Heat treating service for other makers. Teaches blacksmithing/bladesmithing classes. Forges carbon, 440C, D2, and makes own Damascus, stock removal on SS and kitchen cutlery, Teflon coatings available on custom hunters/fighters, makes own sheaths. **Prices:** $150 to $2500. **Remarks:** Full-time maker and heat treater since 1996. First knive sold in 1988. **Mark:** Harmony (yin/yang) symbol with two bear tracks inside all forged blades; etched "Commanche Cutlery" on SS kitchen cutlery.

O'BRIEN, MIKE J.
3807 War Bow, San Antonio, TX 78238, Phone: 210-256-0673, obrien8700@att.net
Specialties: Quality straight knives of his design. **Patterns:** Mostly daggers (safe queens), some hunters. **Technical:** Grinds 440c, ATS-34, and CPM-154. Emphasis on

clean workmanship and solid design. Likes hand-rubbed blades and fittings, exotic woods. **Prices:** $300 to $700 and up. **Remarks:** Part-time maker, made first knife in 1988. **Mark:** O'BRIEN in semi-circle.

OCHS, CHARLES F
124 Emerald Lane, Largo, FL 33771, Phone: 727-536-3827, Fax: 727-536-3827, charlesox@oxforge.com; Web: www.oxforge.com
Specialties: Working knives; period pieces. **Patterns:** Hunters, fighters, Bowies, buck skinners and folders. **Technical:** Forges 52100, 5160 and his own Damascus. **Prices:** $150 to $1800; some to $2500. **Remarks:** Full-time maker; first knife sold in 1978. **Mark:** OX Forge.

OCHS, ERIC
PO BOX 1311, Sherwood, OR 97140, Phone: 503-925-9790, Fax: 503-925-9790, eric@ochs.com Web: www.ochssherworx.com
Specialties: Tactical folders and flippers, as well as fixed blades for tactical, hunting and camping. **Patterns:** Tactical liner- and frame-lock folders with texture in various synthetic and natural materials. **Technical:** Focus on powder metals, including CPM-S30V, Elmax, CPM-154, CPM-3V and CPM-S35VN, as well as damascus steels. Flat, hollow, compound and Loveless-style grinds. **Prices:** $300 - $2,500. **Remarks:** Full-time maker; made first knife in 2008 and started selling knives in mid-2009. **Mark:** The words "Ochs Sherworx" separated by an eight point compass insignia was used through 2013. Beginning in January 2014, "Ochs Worx" separated by navigation star compass insignia.

ODOM JR., VICTOR L.
PO Box 572, North, SC 29112, Phone: 803-247-2749, cell 803-608-0829, vlodom3@tds.net; Web: www.odomforge.com
Specialties: Forged knives and tomahawks; stock removal knives. **Patterns:** Hunters, Bowies, George Herron patterns, and folders. **Technical:** Use 1095, 5160, 52100 high carbon and alloy steels, ATS-34, and 154 CM. **Prices:** Straight knives $60 and up. Folders $250 and up. **Remarks:** Student of Mr. George Herron. SCAK.ORG. **Mark:** Steel stamp "ODOM" and etched "Odom Forge North, SC" plus year.

OELOFSE, TINUS
P.O. Box 33879, Glenstantia, Pretoria, SOUTH AFRICA 0100, Phone: +27-82-3225090, tinusoelofseknives@gmail.com
Specialties: Top-class folders, mainly LinerLocks, and practical fixed blades. **Technical:** Using damascus, mostly Damasteel, and blade billets. Mammoth ivory, mammoth tooth, mother-of-pearl, gold and black-lip-pearl handles for folders. Giraffe bone, warthog ivory, horn and African hardwoods for hunters. Deep relief engraving, mostly leaf and scroll, and daughter Mariscke's scrimshaw. Likes to work on themed knives and special projects. Hand-stitched sheaths by Kitty. **Prices:** $350 to $1,500. **Mark:** Tinus Oelofse in an oval logo with a dagger outline used for the "T."

OGDEN, BILL
OGDEN KNIVES, PO Box 52, Avis
AVIS, PA 17721, Phone: 570-974-9114
Specialties: One-of-a-kind, liner-lock folders, hunters, skinners, minis. **Technical:** Grinds ATS-34, 440-C, D2, 52100, Damascus, natural and unnatural handle materials, hand-stitched custom sheaths. **Prices:** $50 and up. **Remarks:** Part-time maker since 1992. Marks: Last name or "OK" stamp (Ogden Knives).

OGLETREE JR., BEN R
2815 Israel Rd, Livingston, TX 77351, Phone: 409-327-8315
Specialties: Working/using straight knives of his design. **Patterns:** Hunters, kitchen and utility/camp knives. **Technical:** Grinds ATS-34, W1 and 1075; heat-treats. **Prices:** $200 to $400. **Remarks:** Part-time maker; first knife sold in 1955. **Mark:** Last name, city and state in oval with a tree on either side.

O'HARE, SEAN
1831 Rte. 776, Grand Manan, NB, CANADA E5G 2H9, Phone: 506-662-8524, sean@oharecustomknives.com; Web: www.oharecustomknives.com
Specialties: Fixed blade hunters and folders. **Patterns:** Fixed and folding knives, daily carry to collectible art. **Technical:** Stock removal, flat ground. **Prices:** $250 USD to $2,000 USD. **Remarks:** Strives to balance aesthetics, functionality and durability. **Mark:** O'Hare.

OHLEMANN, BOB
RANGERMADE KNIVES, Phone: 832-549-7218, ohlemannr@hotmail.com; Web: www.rangermadeknives.com, Facebook.com/rangermadeknives
Specialties: Texas-based maker of custom LinerLocks and fixed blades. **Technical:** Forges and stock removal working primarily in W2, CPM 154 and damascus, with other materials including zirconium, meteorite, Timascus, stag, mammoth ivory and precious metals and gems. **Prices:** Fixed blades start at $350 and folders start at $700. **Remarks:** Full-time maker who has been making knives since 2014.

OLIVE, MICHAEL E
6388 Angora Mt Rd, Leslie, AR 72645, Phone: 870-363-4668
Specialties: Fixed blades. **Patterns:** Bowies, camp knives, fighters and hunters. **Technical:** Forged blades of 1084, W2, 5160, Damascus of 1084, and1572. **Prices:** $250 and up. **Remarks:** Received J.S. stamp in 2005. **Mark:** Olive.

OLIVER, TODD D
OLIVER CUSTOM BLADES, 7430 Beckle Rd., Cheyenne, WY 82009, Phone: 812-821-5928, tdblues7@aol.com
Specialties: Damascus hunters and daggers. High-carbon as well. **Patterns:** Ladder, twist random. **Technical:** Sole author of all his blades. **Prices:** $350 and up. **Remarks:** Learned bladesmithing from Jim Batson at the ABS school and Damascus from Billy Merritt in Indiana. **Mark:** T.D. Oliver Spencer IN. Two crossed swords and a battle ax.

OLSON, DARROLD E
PO Box 1182, McMinnville, OR 97128, Phone: 541-285-1412
Specialties: Straight knives and folders of his design and to customer specs. **Patterns:** Hunters, liner locks and slip joints. **Technical:** Grinds ATS-34, 154CM and 440C. Uses anodized titanium; sheaths wet-molded. **Prices:** $125 to $550 and up. **Remarks:** Part-time maker; first knife sold in 1989. **Mark:** Name, type of steel and year.

OLSON, JOE
2008 4th Ave., #8, Great Falls, MT 59405, Phone: 406-735-4404, olsonhandmade@hotmail.com; Web: www.olsonhandmade.com
Specialties: Theme based art knives specializing in mosaic Damascus autos, folders, and straight knives, all sole authorship. **Patterns:** Mas. **Technical:** Foix. **Prices:** $300 to $5000 with most in the $3500 range. **Remarks:** Full-time maker for 15 years. **Mark:** Folders marked OLSON relief carved into back bar. Carbon steel straight knives stamped OLSON, forged hunters also stamped JS on reverse side.

OLSON, ROD
Box 373, Nanton, AB, CANADA T0L 1R0, Phone: 403-646-5838, rod.olson@hotmail.com
Patterns: Button lock folders. **Technical:** Grinds RWL 34 blade steel, titanium frames. **Prices:** Mid range. **Remarks:** Part-time maker; first knife sold in 1979. **Mark:** Last name.

OLSZEWSKI, STEPHEN
1820 Harkney Hill Rd, Coventry, RI 02816, Phone: 401-397-4774, blade5377@yahoo.com; Web: www.olszewskiknives.com
Specialties: Lock back, liner locks, automatics (art knives). **Patterns:** One-of-a-kind art knives specializing in figurals. **Technical:** Damascus steel, titanium file worked liners, fossil ivory and pearl. Double actions. **Prices:** $400 to $20,000. **Remarks:** Will custom build to your specifications. Quality work with guarantee. **Mark:** SCO inside fish symbol. Also "Olszewski."

O'MACHEARLEY, MICHAEL
129 Lawnview Dr., Wilmington, OH 45177, Phone: 937-728-2818, omachearleycustomknives@yahoo.com
Specialties: Forged and Stock removal; hunters, skinners, bowies, plain to fancy. **Technical:** ATS-34 and 5160, forges own Damascus. **Prices:** $180-$1000 and up. **Remarks:** Full-time maker, first knife made in 1999. **Mark:** Last name and shamrock.

O'MALLEY, DANIEL
4338 Evanston Ave N, Seattle, WA 98103, Phone: 206-261-1735
Specialties: Custom chef's knives. **Remarks:** Making knives since 1997.

ONION, KENNETH J
47-501 Hui Kelu St, Kaneohe, HI 96744, Phone: 808-239-1300, shopjunky@aol.com; Web: www.kenonionknives.com
Specialties: Folders featuring speed safe as well as other invention gadgets. **Patterns:** Hybrid, art, fighter, utility. **Technical:** S30V, CPM 154V, Cowry Y, SQ-2 and Damascus. **Prices:** $500 to $20,000. **Remarks:** Full-time maker; designer and inventor. First knife sold in 1991. **Mark:** Name and state.

O'QUINN, W. LEE
2654 Watson St., Elgin, SC 29045, Phone: 803-438-8322, wleeoquinn@bellsouth.net; Web: www.creativeknifeworks.com
Specialties: Hunters, utility, working, tactical and neck knives. **Technical:** Grinds ATS-34, CPM-154, 5160, D2, 1095 and damascus steels. **Prices:** Start at $100. **Remarks:** Member of South Carolina Association of Knifemakers. **Mark:** O'Quinn.

ORFORD, BEN
Nethergreen Farm, Ridgeway Cross, Malvern, Worcestershire, ENGLAND WR13 5JS, Phone: 44 01886 880410, web: www.benorford.com
Specialties: Working knives for woodcraft and the outdoorsman, made to his own designs. **Patterns:** Mostly flat Scandinavian grinds, full and partial tang. Also makes specialist woodcraft tools and hook knives. Custom leather sheaths by Lois, his wife. **Technical:** Grinds and forges 01, EN9, EN43, EN45 plus recycled steels. Heat treats. **Prices:** $25 - $650. **Remarks:** Full-time maker; first knife made in 1997. **Mark:** Celtic knot with name underneath.

ORTON, RICH
1218 Cary Ave.r., Wilmington, CA 90744, Phone: 310-549-2990, rorton2@ca.rr.com
Specialties: Straight knives only. **Patterns:** Fighters, hunters, skinners. **Technical:** Grinds ATS-34. Heat treats by Paul Bos.**Prices:** $100 to $1000. **Remarks:** Full-time maker; first knife sold in 1992. Doing business as Orton Knife Works. **Mark:** Rich Orton/ Maker/Wilmington, CA./Orton Knifeworks.

OSBORNE, DONALD H
5840 N McCall, Clovis, CA 93611, Phone: 559-299-9483, Fax: 559-298-1751, oforge@sbcglobal.net
Specialties: Traditional working using straight knives and folder of his design. **Patterns:** Working straight knives, Bowies, hunters, camp knives and folders. **Technical:** Forges carbon steels and makes Damascus. Grinds ATS-34, 154CM, and 440C. **Prices:** $150 and up. **Remarks:** Part-time maker. **Mark:** Last name logo and J.S.

OTT, FRED
1257 Rancho Durango Rd, Durango, CO 81303, Phone: 970-375-9669, fredsknives@wildblue.net
Patterns: Bowies, hunters tantos and daggers. **Technical:** Forges 1086M, W2 and Damascus. **Prices:** $250 to $2,000. **Remarks:** Full-time maker. **Mark:** Last name.

OTT, TED
154 Elgin Woods Ln., Elgin, TX 78621, Phone: 512-413-2243, tedottknives@aol.com
Specialties: Fixed blades, chef knives, butcher knives, bowies, fillet and hunting knives

Technical: Use mainly CPM powder steel, also ATS-34 and D-2. **Prices:** $250 - $1000, depending on embellishments, including scrimshaw and engraving. **Remarks:** Part-time maker; sold first knife in 1993. Won world cutting competition title in 2010 and 2012, along with the Bladesports championship. **Mark:** Ott Knives Elgin Texas.

OUYE, KEITH

PO Box 25307, Honolulu, HI 96825, Phone: 808-395-7000, keith@keithouyeknives.com; Web: www.keithouyeknives.com
Specialties: Folders with 1/8 blades and titanium handles. **Patterns:** Tactical design with liner lock and flipper. **Technical:** Blades are stainless steel ATS 34, CPM154 and S30V. Titanium liners (.071) and scales 3/16 pivots and stop pin, titanium pocket clip. Heat treat by Paul Bos.**Prices:** $495 to $995, with engraved knives starting at $1,200. **Remarks:** Engraving done by C.J. Cal, Bruce Shaw, Lisa Tomlin and Tom Ferry. Retired, so basically a full time knifemaker. Sold fixed blade in 2004 and first folder in 2005. **Mark:** Ouye/ Hawaii with steel type on back side **Other:** Selected by Blade Magazine (March 2006 issue) as one of five makers to watch in 2006.

OVERALL, JASON

111 Golfside Cir., Sanford, FL 32773, Phone: 407-883-5800, Larevo@gmail.com; Web: www.larevoknives.com, Instagram: larevoknives
Specialties: High-grade tactical and dress tactical folders and fixed blades. **Technical:** Stock removal method of blade making with various stainless steels and stainless damascus, and uses titanium, zirconium, Timascus, Mokuti, Mokume and other high-performance alloys. Manmade and natural handle materials used, and offers custom-designed pocket clips. **Prices:** $650 and up, depending on materials and details. **Mark:** Combined L and K.

OVEREYNDER, T R

1800 S. Davis Dr, Arlington, TX 76013, Phone: 817-277-4812, trovereynder@gmail.com or tom@overeynderknives.com; Web: www.overeynderknives.com
Specialties: Highly finished collector-grade knives. Multi-blades. **Patterns:** Fighters, Bowies, daggers, locking folders, 70 percent collector-grade multi blade slip joints, 25 percent interframe, 5 percent fixed blade **Technical:** Grinds CPM-D2, CPM-S60V, CPM-S30V, CPM-154, CPM-M4, BG-42, CTS-XHP, PSF27, RWL-34 and vendor supplied damascus. Has been making titanium-frame folders since 1977. **Prices:** $800 to $2,500, some to $9,000. **Remarks:** Full-time maker; first knife sold in 1977. Doing business as TRO Knives. **Mark:** T.R. OVEREYNDER KNIVES, city and state.

OWEN, DAVID J.A.

30 New Forest Rd., Forest Town, Johannesburg, SOUTH AFRICA, Phone: +27-11-486-1086; cell: +27-82-990-7178, djaowen25@gmail.com
Specialties: Steak knife sets, carving sets, bird-and-trout knives, top-end hunting knives, LinerLock folders. **Patterns:** Variety of knives and techniques. **Technical:** Stock-removal method, freehand hollow and flat grinds, exotic handle materials such as African hardwoods, giraffe bone, hippo tooth and warthog tusk. **Prices:** $150 and up. **Remarks:** Full-time maker since 1993. **Mark:** Two knives back-to-back with words "Owen" and "original" acid etched above and below the knives.

OWENS, DONALD

2274 Lucille Ln, Melbourne, FL 32935, Phone: 321-254-9765

OWENS, JOHN

P.O. Box 455, Buena Vista, CO 81211, Phone: 719-207-0067
Specialties: Hunters. **Prices:** $225 to $425 some to $700. **Remarks:** Spare-time maker. **Mark:** Last name.

OWNBY, JOHN C

708 Morningside Tr., Murphy, TX 75094-4365, Phone: 972-442-7352, john@johnownby.com; Web: www.johnownby.com
Specialties: Hunters, utility/camp knives. **Patterns:** Hunters, locking folders and utility/camp knives. **Technical:** 440C, D2 and ATS-34. All blades are flat ground. Prefers natural materials for handles—exotic woods, horn and antler. **Prices:** $150 to $350; some to $500. **Remarks:** Part-time maker; first knife sold in 1993. Doing business as John C. Ownby Handmade Knives. **Mark:** Name, city, state.

OYSTER, LOWELL R

543 Grant Rd, Corinth, ME 04427, Phone: 207-884-8663
Specialties: Traditional and original designed multi-blade slip-joint folders. **Patterns:** Hunters, minis, camp and fishing knives. **Technical:** Grinds O1; heat-treats. **Prices:** $55 to $450; some to $750. **Remarks:** Full-time maker; first knife sold in 1981. **Mark:** A scallop shell.

P

PACKARD, RONNIE

301 White St., Bonham, TX 75418, Phone: 903-227-3131, packardknives@gmail.com; Web: www.packardknives.com
Specialties: Bowies, folders (lockback, slip joint, frame lock, Hobo knives) and hunters of all sizes. **Technical:** Grinds 440C, ATS-34, D2 and stainless damascus. Makes own sheaths, does heat treating and sub-zero quenching in shop. **Prices:** $160 to $2,000. **Remarks:** Part-time maker; first knife sold in 1975. **Mark:** Last name over year.

PADILLA, GARY

PO Box 5706, Bellingham, WA 98227, Phone: 360-756-7573, gkpadilla@yahoo.com
Specialties: Unique knives of all designs and uses. **Patterns:** Hunters, kitchen knives, utility/camp knives and obsidian ceremonial knives. **Technical:** Grinds 440C, ATS-34 and damascus, with limited flintknapped obsidian. **Prices:** Discounted from $50 to $200 generally. **Remarks:** Retired part-time maker; first knife sold in 1977. **Mark:** Stylized name.

PAGE, LARRY

1200 Mackey Scott Rd, Aiken, SC 29801-7620, Phone: 803-648-0001
Specialties: Working knives of his design. **Patterns:** Hunters, boots and fighters. **Technical:** Grinds ATS-34. **Prices:** Start at $85. **Remarks:** Part-time maker; first knife sold in 1983. **Mark:** Name, city and state in oval.

PAGE, REGINALD

6587 Groveland Hill Rd, Groveland, NY 14462, Phone: 716-243-1643
Specialties: High-art straight knives and one-of-a-kind folders of his design. **Patterns:** Hunters, locking folders and slip-joint folders. **Technical:** Forges O1, 5160 and his own Damascus. Prefers natural handle materials but will work with Micarta. **Remarks:** Spare-time maker; first knife sold in 1985. **Mark:** First initial, last name.

PAINTER, TONY

87 Fireweed Dr, Whitehorse, YT, CANADA Y1A 5T8, Phone: 867-633-3323, yukonjimmies@gmail.com; Web: www.tonypainterdesigns.com
Specialties: One-of-a-kind knives, some fancy, fixed and folders. **Patterns:** No fixed patterns. **Technical:** Grinds ATS-34, D2, O1, S30V, Damascus. Prefers to use exotic woods and other natural materials. Micarta and G10 on working knives. **Prices:** Starting at $200. **Remarks:** Full-time knifemaker and carver. First knife sold in 1996. **Mark:** Two stamps used: initials TP in a circle and painter.

PALIKKO, J-T

B30 B1, Suomenlinna, 00190 Helsinki, FINLAND, Phone: +358-400-699687, jt@kp-art.fi; Web: www.art-helsinki.com
Specialties: One-of-a-kind knives and swords. **Patterns:** Own puukko models, hunters, integral & semi-integral knives, swords & other historical weapons and friction folders. **Technical:** Forges 52100 & other carbon steels, Damasteel stainless damascus & RWL-34, makes own damascus steel, makes carvings on walrus ivory and antler. **Prices:** Starting at $250. **Remarks:** Full-time maker; first knife sold in 1989. **Mark:** JT

PALM, RIK

10901 Scripps Ranch Blvd, San Diego, CA 92131, Phone: 858-530-0407, rikpalm@knifesmith.com; Web: www.knifesmith.com
Specialties: Sole authorship of one-of-a-kind unique art pieces, working/using knives and sheaths. **Patterns:** Carved nature themed knives, camp, hunters, friction folders, tomahawks, and small special pocket knives. **Technical:** Makes own Damascus, grinds 5160H, 1084, 1095, W2, O1. Does his own heat treating including clay hardening. **Prices:** $80 and up. **Remarks:** American Bladesmith Society Journeyman Smith. First blade sold in 2000. **Mark:** Stamped, hand signed, etched last name signature.

PALMER, TAYLOR

TAYLOR-MADE SCENIC KNIVES INC., 1607 E. 450 S, Blanding, UT 84511, Phone: 435-678-2523, taylormadewoodeu@citlink.net
Specialties: Bronze carvings inside of blade area. **Prices:** $250 and up. **Mark:** Taylor Palmer Utah.

PANAK, PAUL S

6103 Leon Rd., Andover, OH 44003, Phone: 330-442-2724, burn@burnknives.com; Web: www.burnknives.com
Specialties: Italian-styled knives. DA OTF's, Italian style stilettos. **Patterns:** Vintage-styled Italians, fighting folders and high art gothic-styles all with various mechanisms. **Technical:** Grinds ATS-34, 154 CM, 440C and Damascus. **Prices:** $800 to $3000. **Remarks:** Full-time maker, first knife sold in 1998. **Mark:** "Burn."

PANCHENKO, SERGE

5927 El Sol Way, Citrus Heights, CA 95621, Phone: 916-588-8821, serge@sergeknives.com Web: www.sergeknives.com
Specialties: Unique art knives using natural materials, copper and carbon steel for a rustic look. **Patterns:** Art knives, tactical folders, Japanese- and relic-style knives. **Technical:** Forges carbon steel, grinds carbon and stainless steels. **Prices:** $100 to $800. **Remarks:** Part-time maker, first knife sold in 2008. **Mark:** SERGE

PARDUE, JOE

PO Box 569, Hillister, TX 77624, Phone: 409-429-7074, Fax: 409-429-5657, joepardue@hughes.net; Web: www.melpardueknives.com/Joepardueknives/index.htm

PARDUE, MELVIN M

4461 Jerkins Rd., Repton, AL 36475, Phone: 251-248-2686, mpardue@frontiernet.net; Web: www.pardueknives.com
Specialties: Folders, collectable, combat, utility and tactical. **Patterns:** Lockback, liner lock, push button; all blade and handle patterns. **Technical:** Grinds 154CM, 440C, 12C27. Forges mokume and Damascus. Uses titanium. **Prices:** $400 to $1600. **Remarks:** Full-time maker, Guild member, ABS member, AFC member. First knife made in 1957; first knife sold professionally in 1974. **Mark:** Mel Pardue.

PARKER, CLIFF

6350 Tulip Dr, Zephyrhills, FL 33544, Phone: 813-973-1682, cooldamascus@aol.com Web: cliffparkerknives.com
Specialties: Damascus gent knives. **Patterns:** Locking liners, some straight knives. **Technical:** Mostly use 1095, 1084, 15N20, 203E and powdered steel. **Prices:** $700 to $2100. **Remarks:** Making own Damascus and specializing in mosaics; first knife sold in 1996. Full-time beginning in 2000. **Mark:** CP.

PARKER, J E

11 Domenica Cir, Clarion, PA 16214, Phone: 814-226-4837, jimparkerknives@hotmail.com Web:www.jimparkerknives.com
Specialties: Fancy/embellished, traditional and working straight knives of his design and to customer specs. Engraving and scrimshaw by the best in the business. **Patterns:**

custom knifemakers

Bowies, hunters and LinerLock® folders. **Technical:** Grinds 440C, 440V, ATS-34 and nickel Damascus. Prefers mastodon, oosik, amber and malachite handle material. **Prices:** $75 to $5200. **Remarks:** Full-time maker; first knife sold in 1991. Doing business as Custom Knife. **Mark:** J E Parker and Clarion PA stamped or etched in blade.

PARKER, ROBERT NELSON
1527 E Fourth St, Royal Oak, MI 48067, Phone: 248-545-8211, rnparkerknives@gmail.com or rnparkerknives@wowway.com; Web: www.classicknifedesign.com
Specialties: Traditional working and using straight knives of his design. **Patterns:** Chutes, subhilts, hunters, and fighters. **Technical:** Grinds CPM-154, CPM-D2, BG-42 and ATS-34, no forging, hollow and flat grinds, full and hidden tangs. Hand-stitched leather sheaths. **Prices:** $400 to $2,000, some to $3,000. **Remarks:** Full-time maker; first knife sold in 1986. I do forge sometimes. **Mark:** Full name.

PARKINSON, MATTHEW
DRAGON'S BREATH FORGE, 10 Swiss Ln., Wolcott, CT 06716, Phone: 203-879-1786, swordmatt@yahoo.com and info@fallinghammerproductions.com; Web: www.dragonsbreathforge.com
Specialties: Knives, swords and axes from the 7th-19th centuries, as well as kitchen knives. **Technical:** Forges blades in a number of steels, including 1084, W1, 80CrV2, L6 and his own damascus in 1095/15N20 and 8670/1095. Specializes in the low-layer, multi-bar Viking style of pattern welding. **Prices:** Knives start at $200 and swords at $1,000. **Remarks:** First knife made in 1990, "Forged In Fire" champion, winning the first aired episode (katana making) on History Channel. **Mark:** Connected MP in a shield, and in the past used simply a connected MP. Viking-era blades are marked with the runes for M&P.

PARKS, BLANE C
15908 Crest Dr, Woodbridge, VA 22191, Phone: 703-221-4680
Specialties: Knives of his design. **Patterns:** Boots, Bowies, daggers, fighters, hunters, kitchen knives, locking and slip-joint folders, utility/camp knives, letter openers and friction folders. **Technical:** Grinds ATS-34, 440C, D2 and other carbon steels. Offers filework, silver wire inlay and wooden sheaths. **Prices:** Start at $250 to $650; some to $1000. **Remarks:** Part-time maker; first knife sold in 1993. Doing business as B.C. Parks Knives. **Mark:** First and middle initials, last name.

PARKS, JOHN
3539 Galilee Church Rd, Jefferson, GA 30549, Phone: 706-367-4916
Specialties: Traditional working and using straight knives of his design. **Patterns:** Hunters, integral bolsters, and personal knives. **Technical:** Forges 1095 and 5168. **Prices:** $275 to $600; some to $800. **Remarks:** Part-time maker; first knife sold in 1989. **Mark:** Initials.

PARLER, THOMAS O
11 Franklin St, Charleston, SC 29401, Phone: 803-723-9433

PARRISH, ROBERT
271 Allman Hill Rd, Weaverville, NC 28787, Phone: 828-645-2864
Specialties: Heavy-duty working knives of his design or to customer specs. **Patterns:** Survival and duty knives; hunters and fighters. **Technical:** Grinds 440C, D2, O1 and commercial Damascus. **Prices:** $200 to $300; some to $6000. **Remarks:** Part-time maker; first knife sold in 1970. **Mark:** Initials connected, sometimes with city and state.

PARRISH III, GORDON A
940 Lakloey Dr, North Pole, AK 99705, Phone: 907-488-0357, ga-parrish@gci.net
Specialties: Classic and high-art straight knives of his design and to customer specs; working and using knives. **Patterns:** Bowies and hunters. **Technical:** Grinds tool steel and ATS-34. Uses mostly Alaskan handle materials. **Prices:** Starting at $300. **Remarks:** Spare-time maker; first knife sold in 1980. **Mark:** Last name, FBKS. ALASKA

PARSONS, LARRY
539 S. Pleasant View Dr., Mustang, OK 73064, Phone: 405-376-9408, l.j.parsons@sbcglobal.net; parsonssaddleshop.com
Specialties: Variety of sheaths from plain leather, geometric stamped, also inlays of various types. **Prices:** Starting at $35 and up

PARSONS, PETE
5905 High Country Dr., Helena, MT 59602, Phone: 406-202-0181, Parsons14@MT.net; Web: www.ParsonsMontanaKnives.com
Specialties: Forged utility blades in straight steel or Damascus (will grind stainless on customer request). Folding knives of my own design. **Patterns:** Hunters, fighters, Bowies, hikers, camp knives, everyday carry folders, tactical folders, gentleman's folders. Some customer designed pieces. **Technical:** Forges carbon steel, grinds carbon steel and some stainless. Forges own Damascus. **Mark:** Left side of blade PARSONS stamp or Parsons Helena, MT etch.

PARTRIDGE, JERRY D.
P.O. Box 977, DeFuniak Springs, FL 32435, Phone: 850-520-4873, jerry@partridgeknives.com; Web: www.partridgeknives.com
Specialties: Fancy and working straight knives and straight razors of his designs. **Patterns:** Hunters, skinners, fighters, chef's knives, straight razors, neck knives, and miniatures. **Technical:** Grinds 440C, ATS-34, carbon Damascus, and stainless Damascus. **Prices:** $250 and up, depending on materials used. **Remarks:** Part-time maker, first knife sold in 2007. **Mark:** Partridge Knives logo on the blade; Partridge or Partridge Knives engraved in script.

PASSMORE, JIMMY D
316 SE Elm, Hoxie, AR 72433, Phone: 870-886-1922

PATRICK, BOB
12642 24A Ave, S. Surrey, BC, CANADA V4A 8H9, Phone: 604-538-6214, Fax: 604-

888-2683, bob@knivesonnet.com; Web: www.knivesonnet.com
Specialties: Maker's designs only, No orders. **Patterns:** Bowies, hunters, daggers, throwing knives. **Technical:** D2, 5160, Damascus. **Prices:** Good value. **Remarks:** Full-time maker; first knife sold in 1987. Doing business as Crescent Knife Works. **Mark:** Logo with name and province or Crescent Knife Works.

PATRICK, CHUCK
4650 Pine Log Rd., Brasstown, NC 28902, Phone: 828-837-7627, chuckandpeggypatrick@gmail.com Web: www.chuckandpeggypatrick.com
Specialties: Period pieces. **Patterns:** Hunters, daggers, tomahawks, pre-Civil War folders. **Technical:** Forges hardware, his own cable and Damascus, available in fancy pattern and mosaic. **Prices:** $150 to $1000; some higher. **Remarks:** Full-time maker. **Mark:** Hand-engraved name or flying owl.

PATRICK, PEGGY
4650 Pine Log Rd., Brasstown, NC 28902, Phone: 828-837-7627, chuckandpeggypatrick@gmail.com Web: www.chuckandpeggypatrick.com
Specialties: Authentic period and Indian sheaths, braintan, rawhide, beads and quill work. **Technical:** Does own braintan, rawhide; uses only natural dyes for quills, old color beads.

PATRICK, WILLARD C
PO Box 5716, Helena, MT 59604, Phone: 406-458-6552, wilamar@mt.net
Specialties: Working straight knives and one-of-a-kind art knives of his design or to customer specs. **Patterns:** Hunters, Bowies, fish, patch and kitchen knives. **Technical:** Grinds ATS-34, 1095, O1, A2 and Damascus. **Prices:** $100 to $2000. **Remarks:** Full-time maker; first knife sold in 1989. Doing business as Wil-A-Mar Cutlery. **Mark:** Shield with last name and a dagger.

PATTAY, RUDY
8739 N. Zurich Way, Citrus Springs, FL 34434, Phone: 516-318-4538, dolphin51@att.net; Web: www.pattayknives.com
Specialties: Fancy and working straight knives of his design. **Patterns:** Bowies, hunters, utility/camp knives, drop point, skinners. **Technical:** Hollow-grinds ATS-34, 440C, O1. Offers commercial Damascus, stainless steel soldered guards; fabricates guard and butt cap on lathe and milling machine. Heat-treats. Prefers synthetic handle materials. Offers hand-sewn sheaths. **Prices:** $100 to $350; some to $500. **Remarks:** Full-time maker; first knife sold in 1990. **Mark:** First initial, last name in sorcerer logo.

PATTERSON, PAT
Box 246, Barksdale, TX 78828, Phone: 830-234-3586, pat@pattersonknives.com
Specialties: Traditional fixed blades and LinerLock folders. **Patterns:** Hunters and folders. **Technical:** Grinds 440C, ATS-34, D2, O1 and Damascus. **Prices:** $250 to $1000. **Remarks:** Full-time maker. First knife sold in 1991. **Mark:** Name and city.

PATTON, DICK AND ROB
6803 View Ln, Nampa, ID 83687, Phone: 208-468-4123, grpatton@pattonknives.com; Web: www.pattonknives.com
Specialties: Custom Damascus, hand forged, fighting knives, Bowie and tactical. **Patterns:** Mini Bowie, Merlin Fighter, Mandrita Fighting Bowie. **Prices:** $100 to $2000.

PATTON, PHILLIP
PO BOX 113, Yoder, IN 46798, phillip@pattonblades.com Web: www.pattonblades.com
Specialties: Tactical fixed blades, including fighting, camp, and general utility blades. Also makes Bowies and daggers. Known for leaf and recurve blade shapes. **Technical:** Forges carbon, stainless, and high alloy tool steels. Makes own damascus using 1084/15n20 or O1/L6. Makes own carbon/stainless laminated blades. For handle materials, prefers high end woods and sythetics. Uses 416 ss and bronze for fittings. **Prices:** $175 - $1000 for knives; $750 and up for swords. **Remarks:** Full-time maker since 2005. Two-year backlog. ABS member. **Mark:** "Phillip Patton" with Phillip above Patton.

PAULO, FERNANDES R
Raposo Tavares No 213, Lencois Paulista, SP, BRAZIL 18680, Phone: 014-263-4281
Specialties: An apprentice of Jose Alberto Paschoarelli, his designs are heavily based on the later designs. **Technical:** Grinds tool steels and stainless steels. Part-time knifemaker. **Prices:** Start from $100. **Mark:** P.R.F.

PAWLOWSKI, JOHN R
19380 High Bluff Ln., Barhamsville, VA 23011, Phone: 757-870-4284 or 804-843-2223, Fax: 757-223-5935, bigjohnknives@yahoo.com; Web: www.bigjohnknives.com
Specialties: Traditional working and using straight knives and folders. **Patterns:** Hunters, Bowies, fighters and camp knives. **Technical:** Stock removal, grinds 440C, ATS-34, 154CM and buys Damascus. **Prices:** $400 and up. **Remarks:** Part-time maker, first knife sold in 1983, Knifemaker Guild Member. **Mark:** Big John, Virginia.

PAYNE, TRAVIS
T-BONE'S CUSTOM CREATIONS, 1588 CR 2655, Telephone, TX 75488, Phone: 903-640-6484, tbone7599@yahoo.com; Web: tbonescustomcreations.com
Specialties: Full-time maker of fixed blades, specializing in a unique style of castration knives, but also hunting and everyday carry (EDC's). **Technical:** Prefers 440C, PSF27, CPM 154 and Damasteel blade steels. **Prices:** $200 to $1,000. **Remarks:** Full-time maker since 1993.

PEAGLER, RUSS
PO Box 1314, Moncks Corner, SC 29461, Phone: 803-761-1008 or 843-312-7371, rpeagler1@homesc.com or rfpeagler1@gmail.com
Specialties: Traditional working straight knives of his design and to customer specs. **Patterns:** Hunters, fighters, boots. **Technical:** Hollow-grinds 440C, ATS-34 and O1; uses Damascus steel. Prefers bone handles. **Prices:** $85 to $300; some to $500. **Remarks:** Spare-time maker; first knife sold in 1983. **Mark:** Initials.

PEARCE, LOGAN
1013 Dogtown Rd, De Queen, AR 71832, Phone: 580-212-0995, night_everclear@hotmail.com; Web: www.pearceknives.com
Specialties: Edged weapons, art knives, stright working knives. **Patterns:** Bowie, hunters, tomahawks, fantasy, utility, daggers, and slip-joint. **Technical:** Fprges 1080, L6, 5160, 440C, steel cable, and his own Damascus. **Prices:** $35 to $500. **Remarks:** Full-time maker; first knife sold in 1992. Doing business as Pearce Knives **Mark:** Name

PEASE, W D
657 Cassidy Pike, Ewing, KY 41039, Phone: 606-845-0387, Web: www.wdpeaseknives.com
Specialties: Display-quality working folders. **Patterns:** Fighters, tantos and boots; locking folders and interframes. **Technical:** Grinds ATS-34 and commercial Damascus; has own side-release lock system. **Prices:** $500 to $1000; some to $3000. **Remarks:** Full-time maker; first knife sold in 1970. **Mark:** First and middle initials, last name and state. W. D. Pease Kentucky.

PEDERSEN, OLE
23404 W. Lake Kayak Dr., Monroe, WA 98272, Phone: 425-931-5750, ole@pedersenknives.com; www.pedersenknives.com
Specialties: Fixed blades of own design. **Patterns:** Hunters, working and utility knives. **Technical:** Stock removal, hollow grinds CPM 154 and stainless steel, 416 stainless fittings, makes own custom sheaths. Handles are mostly stabilized burl wood, some G-10. Heat treats and tempers own knives. **Prices:** $275 to $500. **Remarks:** Full-time maker; sold first knife in 2012. **Mark:** Ole Pedersen - Maker.

PEELE, BRYAN
219 Ferry St, PO Box 1363, Thompson Falls, MT 59873, Phone: 406-827-4633, banana_peele@yahoo.com
Specialties: Fancy working and using knives of his design. **Patterns:** Hunters, Bowies and fighters. **Technical:** Grinds 440C, ATS-34, D2, O1 and commercial Damascus. **Prices:** $110 to $300; some to $900. **Remarks:** Part-time maker; first knife sold in 1985. **Mark:** The Elk Rack, full name, city, state.

PELLEGRIN, MIKE
MP3 Knives, 107 White St., Troy, IL 62294-1126, Phone: 618-667-6777, Web: MP3knives.com
Specialties: Lockback folders with stone inlays, and one-of-a-kind art knives with stainless steel or damascus handles. **Technical:** Stock-removal method of blade making using 440C, Damasteel or high-carbon damascus blades. **Prices:** $800 and up. **Remarks:** Making knives since 2000. **Mark:** MP (combined) 3.

PENDRAY, ALFRED H
13950 NE 20th St, Williston, FL 32696, Phone: 352-528-6124
Specialties: Working straight knives and folders; period pieces. **Patterns:** Fighters and hunters, axes, camp knives and tomahawks. **Technical:** Forges Wootz steel; makes his own Damascus; makes traditional knives from old files and rasps. **Prices:** $125 to $1000; some to $3500. **Remarks:** Part-time maker; first knife sold in 1954. **Mark:** Last initial in horseshoe logo.

PENNINGTON, C A
163 Kainga Rd, Kainga Christchurch, NEW ZEALAND 8009, Phone: 03-3237292, capennington@xtra.co.nz
Specialties: Classic working and collectors knives. Folders a specialty. **Patterns:** Classical styling for hunters and collectors. **Technical:** Forges his own all tool steel Damascus. Grinds D2 when requested. **Prices:** $240 to $2000. **Remarks:** Full-time maker; first knife sold in 1988. Color brochure $3. **Mark:** Name, country.

PEPIOT, STEPHAN
73 Cornwall Blvd, Winnipeg, MB, CANADA R3J-1E9, Phone: 204-888-1499
Specialties: Working straight knives in standard patterns. **Patterns:** Hunters and camp knives. **Technical:** Grinds 440C and industrial hack-saw blades. **Prices:** $75 to $125. **Remarks:** Spare-time maker; first knife sold in 1982. Not currently taking orders. **Mark:** PEP.

PERRY, CHRIS
1654 W. Birch, Fresno, CA 93711, Phone: 559-246-7446, chris.perry4@comcast.net
Specialties: Traditional working/using straight knives of his design. **Patterns:** Boots, hunters and utility/camp knives. **Technical:** Grinds ATS-34, Damascus, 416ss fittings, silver and gold fittings, hand-rubbed finishes. **Prices:** Starting at $250. **Remarks:** Part-time maker, first knife sold in 1995. **Mark:** Name above city and state.

PERRY, JIM
Hope Star PO Box 648, Hope, AR 71801, jenn@comfabinc.com

PERRY, JOHN
9 South Harrell Rd, Mayflower, AR 72106, Phone: 501-470-3043, jpknives@cyberback.com
Specialties: Investment grade and working folders; Antique Bowies and slip joints. **Patterns:** Front and rear lock folders, liner locks, hunters and Bowies. **Technical:** Grinds CPM440V, D2 and making own Damascus. Offers filework. **Prices:** $375 to $1200; some to $3500. **Remarks:** Part-time maker; first knife sold in 1991. Doing business as Perry Custom Knives. **Mark:** Initials or last name in high relief set in a diamond shape.

PERRY, JOHNNY
PO Box 35, Inman, SC 29349, Phone: 864-431-6390, perr3838@bellsouth.net **Mark:** High Ridge Forge.

PERSSON, CONNY
PL 588, Loos, SWEDEN 82050, Phone: +46 657 10305, Fax: +46 657 413 435, connyknives@swipnet.se; Web: www.connyknives.com
Specialties: Mosaic Damascus. **Patterns:** Mosaic Damascus. **Technical:** Straight knives and folders. **Prices:** $1000 and up. **Mark:** C. Persson.

PETEAN, FRANCISCO AND MAURICIO
R. Dr. Carlos de Carvalho Rosa 52, Birigui, SP, BRAZIL 16200-000, Phone: 0186-424786
Specialties: Classic knives to customer specs. **Patterns:** Bowies, boots, fighters, hunters and utility knives. **Technical:** Grinds D6, 440C and high-carbon steels. Prefers natural handle material. **Prices:** $70 to $500. **Remarks:** Full-time maker; first knife sold in 1985. **Mark:** Last name, hand made.

PETERS, DANIEL
5101 Flager St., El Paso, TX 79938, Phone: 360-451-9386, dan@danpeterscustomknives.com; www.danpeterscustomknives.com
Specialties: Hunters, skinners, tactical and combat knives. **Patterns:** Drop points, daggers, folders, hunters, skinners, Kukri style and fillet knives, often to customer's specs. **Technical:** CPM S35VN, CPM 3V, CPM 154 and a few other high-end specialty steels. **Prices:** $75 for bottle openers, and $150 and up on all others. **Remarks:** Part-time maker, full-time military. Member of Georgia Custom Knifemakers Guild and The Knifemakers' Guild. **Mark:** Peters USA etched or engraved with crossed knives.

PETERSEN, DAN L
10610 SW 81st St, Auburn, KS 66402, Phone: 785-220-8043, dan@petersenknives.com; Web: www.petersenknives.com
Specialties: Period pieces and forged integral hilts on hunters and fighters. Vitreous enameling on guards and buttcaps. **Patterns:** Texas-style Bowies, boots and hunters in high-carbon and Damascus steel. **Technical:** Precision heat treatments. Bainite blades with mantensite cores. **Prices:** $800 to $10,000. **Remarks:** First knife sold in 1978. ABS Master Smith. **Mark:** Stylized initials.

PETERSON, CHRIS
Box 143, 2175 W Rockyford, Salina, UT 84654, Phone: 435-529-7194
Specialties: Working straight knives of his design. **Patterns:** Large fighters, boots, hunters and some display pieces. **Technical:** Forges O1 and meteor. Makes and sells his own Damascus. Engraves, scrimshaws and inlays. **Prices:** $150 to $600; some to $1500. **Remarks:** Full-time maker; first knife sold in 1986. **Mark:** A drop in a circle with a line through it.

PETERSON, LLOYD (PETE) C
64 Halbrook Rd, Clinton, AR 72031, Phone: 501-893-0000, wmblade@cyberback.com
Specialties: Miniatures and mosaic folders. **Prices:** $250 and up. **Remarks:** Lead time is 6-8 months. **Mark:** Pete.

PFANENSTIEL, DAN
1824 Lafayette Ave, Modesto, CA 95355, Phone: 209-575-5937, dpfan@sbcglobal.net
Specialties: Japanese tanto, swords. One-of-a-kind knives. **Technical:** Forges simple carbon steels, some Damascus. **Prices:** $200 to $1000. **Mark:** Circle with wave inside.

PHILIPPE, D A
3024 Stepping Stone Path, The Villages, FL 32163, Phone: 352-633-9676, dave.philippe@yahoo.com
Specialties: Traditional working straight knives. **Patterns:** Hunters, trout and bird, camp knives etc. **Technical:** Grinds ATS-34, 440C, A-2, Damascus, flat and hollow ground. Exotic woods and antler handles. Brass, nickel silver and stainless components. **Prices:** $125 to $800. **Remarks:** Full-time maker, first knife sold in 1984. **Mark:** First initial, last name.

PHILLIPS, ALISTAIR
Amaroo, ACT, AUSTRALIA 2914, alistair.phillips@knives.mutantdiscovery.com; Web: http://knives.mutantdiscovery.com
Specialties: Slipjoint folders, forged or stock removal fixed blades. **Patterns:** Single blade slipjoints, smaller neck knives, and hunters. **Technical:** Flat grnds O1, ATS-34, and forged 1055. **Prices:** $80 to $400. **Remarks:** Part-time maker, first knife made in 2005. **Mark:** Stamped signature.

PHILLIPS, DENNIS
16411 West Bennet Rd, Independence, LA 70443, Phone: 985-878-8275
Specialties: Specializes in fixed blade military combat tacticals.

PHILLIPS, DONAVON
905 Line Prairie Rd., Morton, MS 39117, Phone: 662-907-0322, bigdknives@gmail.com
Specialties: Flat ground, tapered tang working/using knives. **Patterns:** Hunters, Capers, Fillet, EDC, Field/Camp/Survival, Competition Cutters. Will work with customers on custom designs or changes to own designs. **Technical:** Stock removal maker using CPM-M4, CPM-154, and other air-hardening steels. Will use 5160 or 52100 on larger knives. G-10 or rubber standard, will use natural material if requested including armadillo. Kydex sheath is standard, outsourced leather available.†Heat treat is done by maker. **Prices:** $100 - $1000. **Remarks:** Part-time/hobbyist maker. First knife made in 2004; first sold 2007. **Mark:** Mark is etched, first and last name forming apex of triangle, city and state at the base, D in center.

PICA, DANIEL
SCREECH OWL KNIVES, 109 Olde Farm Rd., Pittsboro, NC 27312, Phone: 919-542-2335, screechowlknives@gmail.com; Web: www.screechowlknives.com
Specialties: Outdoor/sportsman's blades and tactical/EDC knives, also folders, excelling in fit and finish, and making each knife an heirloom tool to be passed down from generation to generation. **Patterns:** Wharncliffe blades, small EDC/neck knives, Bushcrafter, bird & trout knives, skinners and two sizes of fillet knives for large- and medium-sized fish. **Technical:** Stock removal maker using mainly CPM 154, O1 and CPM

3V steels, all work done by hand, in-house heat-treating and sheath work. **Prices:** $200 to $1,000-plus. **Remarks:** Full-time maker as of January 2015; first knife made in 2013. **Mark:** Side profile of an owl head looking down the blade of the knife.

PICKENS, SELBERT

2295 Roxalana Rd, Dunbar, WV 25064, Phone: 304-744-4048

Specialties: Using knives. **Patterns:** Standard sporting knives. **Technical:** Stainless steels; stock removal method. **Prices:** Moderate. **Remarks:** Part-time maker. **Mark:** Name.

PICKETT, TERRELL

66 Pickett Ln, Lumberton, MS 39455, Phone: 601-794-6125, pickettfence66@bellsouth.net

Specialties: Fix blades, camp knives, Bowies, hunters, & skinners. Forge and stock removal and some firework. **Technical:** 5160, 1095, 52100, 440C and ATS-34. **Prices:** Range from $150 to $550. **Mark:** Logo on stock removal T.W. Pickett and on forged knives Terrell Pickett's Forge.

PIENAAR, CONRAD

19A Milner Rd, Bloemfontein, Free State, SOUTH AFRICA 9300, Phone: 027 514364180, Fax: 027 514364180

Specialties: Fancy working and using straight knives and folders of his design, to customer specs and in standard patterns. **Patterns:** Hunters, locking folders, cleavers, kitchen and utility/camp knives. **Technical:** Grinds 12C27, D2 and ATS-34. Uses some Damascus. Embellishments; scrimshaws; inlays gold. Knives come with wooden box and custom-made leather sheath. **Prices:** $300 to $1000. **Remarks:** Part-time maker; first knife sold in 1981. Doing business as C.P. Knifemaker. Makes slip joint folders and liner locking folders. **Mark:** Initials and serial number.

PIERCE, HAROLD L

106 Lyndon Lane, Louisville, KY 40222, Phone: 502-429-5136

Specialties: Working straight knives, some fancy. **Patterns:** Big fighters and Bowies. **Technical:** Grinds D2, 440C, 154CM; likes sub-hilts. **Prices:** $150 to $450; some to $1200. **Remarks:** Full-time maker; first knife sold in 1982. **Mark:** Last name with knife through the last initial.

PIERCE, RANDALL

903 Wyndam, Arlington, TX 76017, Phone: 817-468-0138

PIERGALLINI, DANIEL E

4011 N. Forbes Rd, Plant City, FL 33565, Phone: 813-754-3908 or 813-967-1471, coolnifedad@wildblue.net; Web: www.piergalliniknives.com

Specialties: Traditional and fancy straight knives and folders of his design or to customer's specs. **Patterns:** Hunters, fighters, skinners, working and camp knives. **Technical:** Grinds 440C, O1, D2, ATS-34, some Damascus; forges his own mokume. Uses natural handle material. **Prices:** $450 to $800; some to $1800. **Remarks:** Full-time maker; sold first knife in 1994. **Mark:** Last name, city, state or last name in script.

PIESNER, DEAN

1786 Sawmill Rd, Conestogo, ON, CANADA N0B 1N0, Phone: 519-664-3648, dean47@rogers.com

Specialties: Classic and period pieces of his design and to customer specs. **Patterns:** Bowies, skinners, fighters and swords. **Technical:** Forges 5160, 52100, steel Damascus and nickel-steel Damascus. Makes own mokume gane with copper, brass and nickel silver. Silver wire inlays in wood. **Prices:** Start at $150. **Remarks:** Full-time maker; first knife sold in 1990. **Mark:** First initial, last name, JS.

PITMAN, DAVID

PO Drawer 2566, Williston, ND 58802, Phone: 701-572-3325

PITT, DAVID F

Anderson, CA 96007, Phone: 530-357-2393, handcannons@tds.net; Web: www.bearpawcustoms.blademakers.com

Specialties: Fixed blade, hunters and hatchets. Flat ground mirror finish. **Patterns:** Hatchets with gut hook, small gut hooks, guards, bolsters or guard less. **Technical:** Grinds A2, 440C, 154CM, ATS-34, D2. **Prices:** $150 to $1,000. **Remarks:** All work done in-house including heat treat, and all knives come with hand-stitched, wet-fromed sheaths. **Mark:** Bear paw with David F. Pitt Maker.

PLOPPERT, TOM

1407 2nd Ave. SW, Cullman, AL 35055, Phone: 256-962-4251, tomploppert3@bellsouth.net

Specialties: Highly finished single- to multiple-blade slip-joint folders in standard and traditional patterns, some lockbacks. **Technical:** Hollow grinds CPM-154, 440V, damascus and other steels upon customer request. Uses elephant ivory, mammoth ivory, bone and pearl. **Mark:** Last name stamped on main blade.

PLUNKETT, RICHARD

29 Kirk Rd, West Cornwall, CT 06796, Phone: 860-672-3419; Toll free: 888-KNIVES-8

Specialties: Traditional, fancy folders and straight knives of his design. **Patterns:** Slip-joint folders and small straight knives. **Technical:** Grinds O1 and stainless steel. Offers many different file patterns. **Prices:** $150 to $450. **Remarks:** Full-time maker; first knife sold in 1994. **Mark:** Signature and date under handle scales.

PODMAJERSKY, DIETRICH

9219 15th Ave NE, Seattle, WA 98115, Phone: 206-552-0763, podforge@gmail.com; Web: podforge.com

Specialties: Straight and folding knives that use fine engraving and materials to create technically intricate, artistic visions. **Technical:** Stainless and carbon steel blades, with titanium and precious metal fittings, including Japanese ornamental alloys. **Prices:** $500 and up.

POIRIER, RICK

1149 Sheridan Rd., McKees Mills, New Brunswick E4V 2W7, CANADA, Phone: 506-525-2818, ripknives@gmail.com; Web: www.ripcustomknives.com

Specialties: Working straight knives of his design or to customer specs, hunters, fighters, bowies, utility, camp, tantos and short swords. **Technical:** Forges own damascus and cable damascus using 1084, 15N20, O1 and mild steel. Forges/grinds mostly O1 and W2. Varied handle materials inlcude G-10, Micarta, wood, bone, horn and Japanese cord wrap. **Prices:** $200 and up. **Remarks:** Full-time maker, apprenticed under ABS master smith Wally Hayes; first knife sold in 1998. **Marks:** R P (pre. 2007), RIP (2007 on), also etches gravestone RIP.

POLK, CLIFTON

4625 Webber Creek Rd, Van Buren, AR 72956, Phone: 479-474-3828, cliffpolkknives1@aol.com; Web: www.polkknives.com

Specialties: Fancy working folders. **Patterns:** One blades spring backs in five sizes, LinerLock®, automatics, double blades spring back folder with standard drop & clip blade or bird knife with drop and vent hook or cowboy's knives with drop and hoof pick and straight knives. **Technical:** Uses D2 & ATS-34. Makes all own Damascus using 1084, 1095, O1, 15N20, 5160. Using all kinds of exotic woods. Stag, pearls, ivory, mastodon ivory and other bone and horns. **Prices:** $200 to $3000. **Remarks:** Retired fire fighter, made knives since 1974. **Mark:** Polk.

POLK, RUSTY

5900 Wildwood Dr, Van Buren, AR 72956, Phone: 870-688-3009, polkknives@yahoo.com; Web: www.facebook.com/polkknives

Specialties: Skinners, hunters, Bowies, fighters and forging working knives fancy Damascus, daggers, boot knives, survival knives, and folders. **Patterns:** Drop point, and forge to shape. **Technical:** ATS-34, 440C, Damascus, D2, 51/60, 1084, 15N20, does all his forging. **Prices:** $200 to $2000. **Mark:** R. Polk

POLLOCK, WALLACE J

806 Russet Valley Dr., Cedar Park, TX 78613, Phone: 512-918-0528, jarlsdad@gmail.com; Web: www.pollackknives.com

Specialties: Using knives, skinner, hunter, fighting, camp knives. **Patterns:** Use his own patterns or yours. Traditional hunters, daggers, fighters, camp knives. **Technical:** Grinds ATS-34, D-2, BG-42, makes own Damascus, D-2, O-1, ATS-34, prefer D-2, handles exotic wood, horn, bone, ivory. **Remarks:** Full-time maker, sold first knife 1973. **Prices:** $250 to $2500. **Mark:** Last name, maker, city/state.

POLZIEN, DON

1912 Inler Suite-L, Lubbock, TX 79407, Phone: 806-791-0766, blindinglightknives.net

Specialties: Traditional Japanese-style blades; restores antique Japanese swords, scabbards and fittings. **Patterns:** Hunters, fighters, one-of-a-kind art knives. **Technical:** 1045-1050 carbon steels, 440C, D2, ATS-34, standard and cable Damascus. **Prices:** $150 to $2500. **Remarks:** Full-time maker. First knife sold in 1990. **Mark:** Oriental characters inside square border.

PONZIO, DOUG

10219 W State Rd 81, Beloit, WI 53511, Phone: 608-313-3223, prfgdoug@hughes.net; Web: www.ponziodamascus.com

Specialties: Mosaic Damascus, stainless Damascus. **Mark:** P.F.

POOLE, MARVIN O

PO Box 552, Commerce, GA 30529, Phone: 803-225-5970

Specialties: Traditional working/using straight knives and folders of his design and in standard patterns. **Patterns:** Bowies, fighters, hunters, locking folders, bird and trout knives. **Technical:** Grinds 440C, D2, ATS-34. **Prices:** $50 to $150; some to $750. **Remarks:** Part-time maker; first knife sold in 1980. **Mark:** First initial, last name, year, serial number.

POTIER, TIMOTHY F

PO Box 711, Oberlin, LA 70655, Phone: 337-639-2229, tpotier@hotmail.com

Specialties: Classic working and using straight knives to customer specs; some collectible. **Patterns:** Hunters, Bowies, utility/camp knives and belt axes. **Technical:** Forges carbon steel and his own Damascus; offers filework. **Prices:** $300 to $1800; some to $4000. **Remarks:** Part-time maker; first knife sold in 1981. **Mark:** Last name, MS.

POTTER, BILLY

6323 Hyland Dr., Dublin, OH 43017, Phone: 614-589-8324, potterknives@yahoo.com; Web: www.potterknives.com

Specialties: Working straight knives; his design or to customers patterns. **Patterns:** Bowie, fighters, utilities, skinners, hunters, folding lock blade, miniatures and tomahawks. **Technical:** Grinds and forges, carbon steel, L6, O-1, 1095, 5160, 1084 and 52000. Grinds 440C stainless. Forges own Damascus. Handles: prefers exotic hardwood, curly and birdseye maples. Bone, ivory, antler, pearl and horn. Some scrimshaw. **Prices:** Start at $100 up to $800. **Remarks:** Part-time maker; first knife sold 1996. **Mark:** First and last name (maker).

POWELL, ROBERT CLARK

PO Box 321, 93 Gose Rd., Smarr, GA 31086, Phone: 478-994-5418

Specialties: Composite bar Damascus blades. **Patterns:** Art knives, hunters, combat, tomahawks. **Patterns:** Hand forges all blades. **Prices:** $300 and up. **Remarks:** ABS Journeyman Smith. **Mark:** Powell.

POWERS, WALTER R.

PO BOX 82, Lolita, TX 77971, Phone: 361-874-4230, carlyn@laward.net Web: waltscustomknives.blademakers.com

Specialties: Skinners and hunters. **Technical:** Uses mainly CPM D2, CPM 154, CPM S35VN and 52100, but will occasionally use 3V. Stock removal. **Prices:** $160 - $225. **Remarks:** Part-time maker; first knife made in 2002. **Mark:** WP

PRATER, MIKE
PRATER AND COMPANY, 81 Sanford Ln., Flintstone, GA 30725, Phone: 706-820-7300, cmprater@aol.com; Web: www.pratercustoms.com
Specialties: Customizing factory knives. **Patterns:** Buck knives, case knives, hen and rooster knives. **Technical:** Manufacture of mica pearl. **Prices:** Varied. **Remarks:** First knife sold in 1980. **Mark:** Mica pearl.

PRESSBURGER, RAMON
59 Driftway Rd, Howell, NJ 07731, Phone: 732-363-0816
Specialties: BG-42. Only knifemaker in U.S.A. that has complete line of affordable hunting knives made from BG-42. **Patterns:** All types hunting styles. **Technical:** Uses all steels; main steels are D-2 and BG-42. **Prices:** $75 to $500. **Remarks:** Full-time maker; has been making hunting knives for 30 years. Makes knives to your patterning. **Mark:** NA.

PRESTI, MATT
5280 Middleburg Rd, Union Bridge, MD 21791, Phone: 410-775-1520; Cell: 240-357-3592
Specialties: Hunters and chef's knives, fighters, bowies, and period pieces.**Technical:** Forges 5160, 52100, 1095, 1080, W2, and O1 steels as well as his own Damascus. Does own heat treating and makes sheaths. Prefers natural handle materials, particularly antler and curly maple. **Prices:** $150 and up. **Remarks:** Part-time knifemaker who made his first knife in 2001. **Mark:** MCP.

PRICE, DARRELL MORRIS
92 Union, Plymouth, Devon, ENGLAND PL1 3EZ, Phone: 0752 223546
Specialties: Traditional Japanese knives, Bowies and high-art knives. **Technical:** Nickel Damascus and mokume. **Prices:** $1000 to $4000. **Remarks:** Part-time maker; first knife sold in 1990. **Mark:** Initials and Japanese name—Kuni Shigae.

PRICE, TIMMY
PO Box 906, Blairsville, GA 30514, Phone: 706-745-5111

PRIDGEN JR., LARRY
PO Box 127, Davis, OK 73030, Phone: 229-457-6522, pridgencustomknives@gmail.com Web: www.pridgencustomknives.com
Specialties: Custom folders. **Patterns:** Bowie, fighter, skinner, trout, liner lock, and custom orders. **Technical:** I do stock removal and use carbon and stainless Damascus and stainless steel. **Prices:** $300 and up. **Remarks:** Each knife comes with a hand-crafted custom sheath and life-time guarantee. **Mark:** Distinctive logo that looks like a brand with LP and a circle around it.

PRIMOS, TERRY
932 Francis Dr, Shreveport, LA 71118, Phone: 318-686-6625, tprimos@sport.rr.com or terry@primosknives.com; Web: www.primosknives.com
Specialties: Traditional forged straight knives. **Patterns:** Hunters, Bowies, camp knives, and fighters. **Technical:** Forges primarily 1084 and 5160; also forges Damascus. **Prices:** $250 to $600. **Remarks:** Full-time maker; first knife sold in 1993. **Mark:** Last name.

PRINSLOO, THEUNS
PO Box 2263, Bethlehem, Free State, SOUTH AFRICA 9700, Phone: 27824663885, theunsmes@yahoo.com; Web: www.theunsprinsloo.co.za
Specialties: Handmade folders and fixed blades. **Technical:** Own Damascus and mokume. I try to avoid CNC work, laser cutting and machining as much as possible. **Prices:** $650 and up. **Mark:** Handwritten name with bushman rock art and mountain scene.

PRITCHARD, RON
613 Crawford Ave, Dixon, IL 61021, Phone: 815-284-6005
Specialties: Plain and fancy working knives. **Patterns:** Variety of straight knives, locking folders, interframes and miniatures. **Technical:** Grinds 440C, 154CM and commercial Damascus. **Prices:** $100 to $200; some to $1500. **Remarks:** Part-time maker; first knife sold in 1979. **Mark:** Name and city.

PROVENZANO, JOSEPH D
39043 Dutch Lane, Ponchatoula, LA 70454, Phone: 225-615-4846, gespro61@gmail.com
Specialties: Working straight knives and folders in standard patterns. **Patterns:** Hunters, Bowies, folders, camp and fishing knives. **Technical:** Grinds ATS-34, 440C, 154CM, CPM-S60V, CPM-S90V, CPM-3V and damascus. Hollow-grinds hunters. **Prices:** $125 to $300; some to $1,000. **Remarks:** Part-time maker; first knife sold in 1980. **Mark:** Joe-Pro.

PROVOST, J.C.
1634 Lakeview Dr., Laurel, MS 39440, Phone: 601-498-1143, jcprovost2@gmail.com; Web: www.jcprovost.com
Specialties: Classic working straight knives and folders. **Patterns:** Hunters, skinners, bowies, daggers, fighters, fillet knives, chef's and steak knives, folders and customs. **Technical:** Grinds 440C, CPM-154 and commercial damascus. **Prices:** $175 and up. **Remarks:** Part-time maker; first knife made in 1979. Taught by R.W. Wilson. **Mark:** Name, city and state.

PRUYN, PETER
Brothersville Custom Knives, 110 Reel La., Grants Pass, OR 97527, Phone: 631-793-9052, Fax: 541-479-1889, brothersvilleknife@gmail.com Web: brothersvilleknife.com
Specialties: Chef knives and fighters in damascus and san mai, as well as stainless steels. **Patterns:** Fixed-blade knives of all styles, some folding models. **Technical:** Damascus, high-carbon and stainless steels; does own heat treating. **Prices:** $200 to $2,000, with a discount to active and retired military personnel. **Remarks:** Full-time maker, first knife sold in 2009. **Mark:** Anvil with "Brothersville" crested above.

PUDDU, SALVATORE
Via Lago Bunnari #12, 09045 Quartu Sant 'Elena, (Cagliari) Sardinia, ITALY, Phone: 0039-070-892208, salvatore.puddu@tin.it
Specialties: Custom knives. **Remarks:** Full-time maker.

PULIS, VLADIMIR
CSA 230-95, 96701 Kremnica, SLOVAKIA, Phone: 00421 903 340076, vpulis@gmail.com; Web: www.vpulis.host.sk
Specialties: Fancy and high-art straight knives of his design. **Patterns:** Daggers and hunters. **Technical:** Forges Damascus steel. All work done by hand. **Prices:** $250 to $3000; some to $10,000. **Remarks:** Full-time maker; first knife sold in 1990. **Mark:** Initials in sixtagon.

PURSLEY, AARON
8885 Coal Mine Rd, Big Sandy, MT 59520, Phone: 406-378-3200
Specialties: Fancy working knives. **Patterns:** Locking folders, straight hunters and daggers, personal wedding knives and letter openers. **Technical:** Grinds O1 and 440C; engraves. **Prices:** $900 to $2500. **Remarks:** Full-time maker; first knife sold in 1975. **Mark:** Initials connected with year.

PURVIS, BOB AND ELLEN
2416 N Loretta Dr, Tucson, AZ 85716, Phone: 520-795-8290, repknives2@cox.net
Specialties: Hunter, skinners, Bowies, using knives, gentlemans folders and collectible knives. **Technical:** Grinds ATS-34, 440C, Damascus, Dama steel, heat-treats and cryogenically quenches. We do gold-plating, salt bluing, scrimshawing, filework and fashion handmade leather sheaths. Materials used for handles include exotic woods, mammoth ivory, mother-of-pearl, G-10 and Micarta. **Prices:** $165 to $800. **Remarks:** Knifemaker since retirement in 1984. Selling them since 1993. **Mark:** Script or print R.E. Purvis ~ Tucson, AZ or last name only.

Q

QUAKENBUSH, THOMAS C
2426 Butler Rd, Ft Wayne, IN 46808, Phone: 219-483-0749

QUARTON, BARR
PO Box 4335, McCall, ID 83638, Phone: 208-634-3641
Specialties: Plain and fancy working knives; period pieces. **Patterns:** Hunters, tantos and swords. **Technical:** Forges and grinds 154CM, ATS-34 and his own Damascus. **Prices:** $180 to $450; some to $4500. **Remarks:** Part-time maker; first knife sold in 1978. Doing business as Barr Custom Knives. **Mark:** First name with bear logo.

QUESENBERRY, MIKE
110 Evergreen Cricle, Blairsden, CA 96103, Phone: 775-233-1527, quesenberryknives@gmail.com; Web: www.quesenberryknives.com
Specialties: Hunters, daggers, bowies and integrals. **Technical:** Forges 52100 and W2. Makes own damascus. Will use stainless on customer requests. Does own heat-treating and own leather work. **Prices:** Starting at $400. **Remarks:** Part-time maker. ABS member since 2006. ABS master bladesmith. **Mark:** Last name.

R

RABUCK, JASON
W3080 Hay Lake Road, Springbrook, WI 54875, Phone: 715-766-8220, sales@rabuckhandmadeknives.com; web: www.rabuckhandmadeknives.com
Patterns: Hunters, skinners, camp knives, fighters, survival/tactical, neck knives, kitchen knives. Include whitetail antler, maple, walnut, as well as stabilized woods and micarta. **Technical:** Flat grinds 1095, 5160, and 0-1 carbon steels. Blades are finished with a hand-rubbed satin blade finish. Hand stitched leather sheaths specifically fit to each knife. Boot clips, swivel sheaths, and leg ties include some of the available sheath options. **Prices:** $140 - $560. **Remarks:** Also knife restoration (handle replacement, etc.) Custom and replacement sheath work available for any knife. **Mark:** "RABUCK" over a horseshoe

RACHLIN, LESLIE S
412 Rustic Ave., Elmira, NY 14905, Phone: 607-733-6889, lrachlin@stry.rr.com
Specialties: Classic and working kitchen knives, carving sets and outdoors knives. **Technical:** Grinds 440C or cryogenically heat-treated A2. **Prices:** $65 to $1,400. **Remarks:** Spare-time maker; first knife sold in 1989. Doing business as Tinkermade Knives. **Mark:** LSR

RADER, MICHAEL
23706 7th Ave. SE, Ste. D, Bothell, WA 98021, michael@raderblade.com; Web: www.raderblade.com
Specialties: Swords, kitchen knives, integrals. **Patterns:** Non traditional designs. Inspired by various cultures. **Technical:** Damascus is made with 1084 and 15N-20, forged blades in 52100, W2 and 1084.**Prices:** $350 - $5,000 **Remarks:** ABS Journeyman Smith **Mark:** ABS Mastersmith Mark "Rader" on one side, "M.S." on other

RADOS, JERRY F
134 Willie Nell Rd., Columbia, KY 42728, Phone: 606-303-3334, jerry@radosknives.com Web: www.radosknives.com
Specialties: Deluxe period pieces. **Patterns:** Hunters, fighters, locking folders, daggers and camp knives. **Technical:** Forges and grinds his own Damascus which he sells commercially; makes pattern-welded Turkish Damascus. **Prices:** Start at $900. **Remarks:** Full-time maker; first knife sold in 1981. **Mark:** Last name.

RAFN, DAN C.
Norholmvej 46, 7400 Herning, DENMARK, contact@dcrknives.com Web: www.dcrknives.com

custom knifemakers

Specialties: One of a kind collector art knives of own design. **Patterns:** Mostly fantasy style fighters and daggers. But also swords, hunters, and folders. **Technical:** Grinds RWL-34, sleipner steel, damasteel, and hand forges Damascus. **Prices:** Start at $500. **Remarks:** Part-time maker since 2003. **Mark:** Rafn. or DCR. or logo.

RAGSDALE, JAMES D
160 Clear Creek Valley Tr., Ellijay, GA 30536, Phone: 706-636-3180, jimmarrags@etcmail.com
Specialties: Fancy and embellished working knives of his design or to customer specs. **Patterns:** Hunters, folders and fighters. **Technical:** Grinds 440C, ATS-34 and A2. Uses some Damascus **Prices:** $150 and up. **Remarks:** Full-time maker; first knife sold in 1984. **Mark:** Fish symbol with name above, town below.

RAINVILLE, RICHARD
126 Cockle Hill Rd, Salem, CT 06420, Phone: 860-859-2776, w1jo@comcast.net
Specialties: Traditional working straight knives. **Patterns:** Outdoor knives, including fishing knives. **Technical:** L6, 400C, ATS-34. **Prices:** $100 to $800. **Remarks:** Full-time maker; first knife sold in 1982. **Mark:** Name, city, state in oval logo.

RALEY, R. WAYNE
825 Poplar Acres Rd, Collierville, TN 38017, Phone: 901-853-2026

RALPH, DARREL
DDR CUSTOM KNIVES, 12034 S. Profit Row, Forney, TX 75126, Phone: 469-728-7242, ddr@darrelralph.com; Web: www.darrelralph.com
Specialties: Tactical and tactical dress folders and fixed blades. **Patterns:** Daggers, fighters and swords. **Technical:** High tech. Forges his own damascus, nickel and high-carbon. Uses mokume and damascus, mosaics and special patterns. Engraves and heat treats. Prefers pearl, ivory and abalone handle material; uses stones and jewels. **Prices:** $600 to $30,000. **Remarks:** Full-time maker; first knife sold in 1987. Doing business as Briar Knives. **Mark:** DDR.

RAMONDETTI, SERGIO
VIA MARCONI N 24, CHIUSA DI PESIO (CN), ITALY 12013, Phone: 0171 734490, Fax: 0171 734490, info@ramon-knives.com Web: www.ramon-knives.com
Specialties: Folders and straight knives of his design. **Patterns:** Utility, hunters and skinners. **Technical:** Grinds RWL-34 and Damascus. **Prices:** $500 to $2000. **Remarks:** Part-time maker; first knife sold in 1999. **Mark:** Logo (S.Ramon) with last name.

RAMOS, STEVEN
2466 Countryside Ln., West Jordan, UT 84084, Phone: 801-913-1696, srknives88@gmail.com; Web: www.stevenramosknives.com
Specialties: Mirror finishes, complex filework, tapered tangs, genuine polished gemstone handles, all original and unique blade designs. **Patterns:** Fixed, full-tang hunters/utility, fighters, modified bowies, daggers, cooking and chef's knives, personalized wedding cake knives and art pieces. **Technical:** Stock removal, predominantly using CPM 154 stainless steel, but also 440C, D2, 154CM and others. Mostly polished gemstone handles, but also Micarta, G-10 and various woods. Sheaths and custom display stands with commemorative engravings also available. **Prices:** $400 to $3,000. **Remarks:** Full-time maker. **Mark:** Signature "Steven Ramos" laser etched on blade.

RAMSEY, RICHARD A
8525 Trout Farm Rd, Neosho, MO 64850, Phone: 417-592-1494, rams@hughes.net or ramseyknives@gmail.com; Web: www.ramseyknives.com
Specialties: Drop point hunters. **Patterns:** Various Damascus. **Prices:** $125 to $1500. **Mark:** RR double R also last name-RAMSEY.

RANDALL, PATRICK
Patrick Knives, 160 Mesa Ave., Newbury Park, CA 91320, Phone: 805-390-5501, pat@patrickknives.com; Web: www.patrickknives.com
Specialties: Chef's and kitchen knives, bowies, hunters and utility folding knives. **Technical:** Preferred materials include 440C, 154CM, CPM-3V, 1084, 1095 and ATS-34. Handle materials include stabilized wood, Micarta, stag and jigged bone. **Prices:** $125 to $225. **Remarks:** Part-time maker since 2005.

RANDALL, STEVE
3438 Oak Ridge Cir., Lincolnton, NC 28092, Phone: 704-472-4957, steve@ksrblades.com; Web: www.ksrblades.com
Specialties: Mostly working straight knives and one-of-a-kind pieces, some fancy fixed blades. **Patterns:** Bowies, hunters, choppers, camp and utility knives. **Technical:** Forged high-carbon-steel blades: 5160, 52100, W2 and damascus patterns. **Prices:** $275 and up. **Remarks:** Part-time maker, first knife sold in 2009. Earned journeyman smith rating in 2012. Doing business as Knives By Steve Randall or KSR Blades. **Mark:** KS Randall on left side, JS on right side.

RANDALL JR., JAMES W
11606 Keith Hall Rd, Keithville, LA 71047, Phone: 318-925-6480, Fax: 318-925-1709, jw@jwrandall.com; Web: www.jwrandall.com
Specialties: Collectible and functional knives. **Patterns:** Bowies, hunters, daggers, swords, folders and combat knives. **Technical:** Forges 5160, 1084, O1 and his Damascus. **Prices:** $400 to $8000. **Remarks:** Part-time. First knife sold in 1998. **Mark:** JW Randall, MS.

RANDALL MADE KNIVES
4857 South Orange Blossom Trail, Orlando, FL 32839, Phone: 407-855-8075, Fax: 407-855-9054, Web: http://www.randallknives.com
Specialties: Working straight knives. **Patterns:** Hunters, fighters and Bowies. **Technical:** Forges and grinds O1 and 440B. **Prices:** $170 to $550; some to $450. **Remarks:** Full-time maker; first knife sold in 1937. **Mark:** Randall made, city and state in scimitar logo.

RANDOW, RALPH
7 E. Chateau Estates Dr., Greenbrier, AR 72058, Phone: 318-729-3368, randow3368@gmail.com

RANKL, CHRISTIAN
Possenhofenerstr 33, Munchen, GERMANY 81476, Phone: 0049 01 71 3 66 26 79, Fax: 0049 8975967265, Web: http://www.german-knife.com/german-knifemakers-guild.html
Specialties: Tail-lock knives. **Patterns:** Fighters, hunters and locking folders. **Technical:** Grinds ATS-34, D2, CPM1440V, RWL 34 also stainless Damascus. **Prices:** $450 to $950; some to $2000. **Remarks:** Part-time maker; first knife sold in 1989. **Mark:** Electrochemical etching on blade.

RAPP, STEVEN J
8033 US Hwy 25-70, Marshall, NC 28753, Phone: 828-649-1092
Specialties: Gold quartz; mosaic handles. **Patterns:** Daggers, Bowies, fighters and San Francisco knives. **Technical:** Hollow- and flat-grinds 440C and Damascus. **Prices:** Start at $500. **Remarks:** Full-time maker; first knife sold in 1981. **Mark:** Name and state.

RAPPAZZO, RICHARD
142 Dunsbach Ferry Rd, Cohoes, NY 12047, Phone: 518-783-6843
Specialties: Damascus locking folders and straight knives. **Patterns:** Folders, dirks, fighters and tantos in original and traditional designs. **Technical:** Hand-forges all blades; specializes in Damascus; uses only natural handle materials. **Prices:** $400 to $1500. **Remarks:** Part-time maker; first knife sold in 1985. **Mark:** Name, date, serial number.

RARDON, A D
1589 SE Price Dr, Polo, MO 64671, Phone: 660-354-2330
Specialties: Folders, miniatures. **Patterns:** Hunters, buck skinners, Bowies, miniatures and daggers. **Technical:** Grinds O1, D2, 440C and ATS-34. **Prices:** $150 to $2000; some higher. **Remarks:** Full-time maker; first knife sold in 1954. **Mark:** Fox logo.

RARDON, ARCHIE F
1589 SE Price Dr, Polo, MO 64671, Phone: 660-354-2330
Specialties: Working knives. **Patterns:** Hunters, Bowies and miniatures. **Technical:** Grinds O1, D2, 440C, ATS-34, cable and Damascus. **Prices:** $50 to $500. **Remarks:** Part-time maker. **Mark:** Boar hog.

RASSENTI, PETER
218 Tasse, St-Eustache, Quebec J7P 4C2, CANADA, Phone: 450-598-6250, guireandgimble@hotmail.com
Specialties: Tactical mono-frame folding knives.

RAY, ALAN W
1287 FM 1280 E, Lovelady, TX 75851, awray@rayzblades.com; Web: www.rayzblades.com
Specialties: Working straight knives of his design. **Patterns:** Hunters. **Technical:** Forges O1, L6 and 5160 for straight knives. **Prices:** $200 to $1000. **Remarks:** Full-time maker; first knife sold in 1979. **Mark:** Stylized initials.

RAYMOND, MICHAEL
4000 Weber Rd., Malabar, FL 32950, Phone: 321-300-5515, michael@michaelraymondknives.com; Web: www.michaelraymondknives.com
Specialties: Integral folding knives with bushings and washer pivot construction. All parts made in-house. **Technical:** Uses Bohler M390, Crucible 20CV and Uddeholm Elmax steels. **Prices:** $1,200+. **Remarks:** Full-time maker; first folder made in late 2011, graduate of machinist school and apprentice tool & die maker.

REBELLO, INDIAN GEORGE
358 Elm St, New Bedford, MA 02740-3837, Phone: 508-999-7090, indgeo@juno.com; Web: www.indiangeorgesknives.com
Specialties: One-of-a-kind fighters and Bowies. **Patterns:** To customer's specs, hunters and utilities. **Technical:** Forges his own Damascus, 5160, 52100, 1084, 1095, cable and O1. Grinds S30V, ATS-34, 154CM, 440C, D2 and A2. **Prices:** Starting at $250. **Remarks:** Full-time maker, first knife sold in 1991. Doing business as Indian George's Knives. Founding father and President of the Southern New England Knife-Makers Guild. Member of the N.C.C.A. **Mark:** Indian George's Knives.

RED, VERNON
2020 Benton Cove, Conway, AR 72034, Phone: 501-450-7284, knivesvr@conwaycorp.net
Specialties: Lock-blade folders, as well as fixed-blade knives of maker's own design or customer's. **Patterns:** Hunters, fighters, Bowies, folders. **Technical:** Hollow grind, flat grind, stock removal and forged blades. Uses 440C, D-2, A-2, ATS-34, 1084, 1095, and Damascus. **Prices:** $225 and up. **Remarks:** Made first knife in 1982, first folder in 1992. Member of (AKA) Arkansas Knives Association. **Mark:** Last name.

REDD, BILL
2647 West 133rd Circle, Broomfield, Colorado 80020, Phone: 303-469-9803, unlimited_design@msn.com
Prices: Contact maker. **Remarks:** Full-time custom maker, member of PKA and RMBC (Rocky Mountain Blade Collectors). **Mark:** Redd Knives, Bill Redd.

REDDIEX, BILL
27 Galway Ave, Palmerston North, NEW ZEALAND, Phone: 06-357-0383, Fax: 06-358-2910
Specialties: Collector-grade working straight knives. **Patterns:** Traditional-style Bowies and drop-point hunters. **Technical:** Grinds 440C, D2 and O1; offers variety of grinds and finishes. **Prices:** $130 to $750. **Remarks:** Full-time maker; first knife sold in 1980. **Mark:** Last name around kiwi bird logo.

REEVES, J.R.
5181 South State Line, Texarkana, AR 71854, Phone: 870-773-5777, jos123@ netscape.com
Specialties: Working straight knives of my design or customer design if a good flow. **Patterns:** Hunters, fighters, bowies, camp, bird, and trout knives. **Technical:** Forges and grinds 5160, 1084, 15n20, L6, 52100 and some damascus. Also some stock removal 440C, 01, D2, and 154 CM steels. I offer flat or hollow grinds. Natural handle material to include Sambar stag, desert Ironwood, sheep horn, other stabilized exotic woods and ivory. Custom filework offered. **Prices:** $200 - $1500. **Remarks:** Full-time maker, first knife sold in 1985. **Mark:** JR Reeves.

REGEL, JEAN-LOUIS
les ichards, Saint Leger de Fougeret, FRANCE 58120, Phone: 0033-66-621-6185, jregel2@hotmail.com
Specialties: Bowies, camp knives, swords and folders. **Technical:** Forges own Wootz steel by hand, and damascus and high-carbon blade steels. **Remarks:** American Bladesmith Society journeyman smith. **Mark:** Jean-louis on right side of blade.

REGGIO JR., SIDNEY J
PO Box 851, Sun, LA 70463, Phone: 985-886-1397
Specialties: Miniature classic and fancy straight knives of his design or in standard patterns. **Patterns:** Fighters, hunters and utility/camp knives. **Technical:** Grinds 440C, ATS-34 and commercial Damascus. Engraves; scrimshaws; offers filework. Hollow grinds most blades. Prefers natural handle material. Offers handmade sheaths. **Prices:** $85 to $250; some to $500. **Remarks:** Part-time maker; first knife sold in 1988. Doing business as Sterling Workshop. **Mark:** Initials.

REID, JIM
6425 Cranbrook St. NE, Albuquerque, NM 87111, jhrabq7@Q.com
Specialties: Fixed-blade knives.**Patterns:** Hunting, neck, and cowboy bowies. **Technical:** A2, D2, and damascus, stock removal. **Prices:** $125 to $300. **Mark:** Jim Reid over New Mexico zia sign.

RENNER, TERRY
TR Blades, Inc., 707 13th Ave. Cir. W, Palmetto, FL 34221, Phone: 941-729-3226; 941-545-6320, terrylmusic@gmail.com Web: www.trblades.com
Specialties: High art folders and straight-blades, specialty locking mechanisms. Designer of the Neckolas knife by CRKT. Deep-relief carving.**Technical:** Prefer CPM154, S30V, 1095 carbon, damascus by Rob Thomas, Delbert Ealey, Bertie Reitveld, Todd Fischer, Joel Davis. Does own heat treating. **Remarks:** Full-time maker as of 2005. Formerly in bicylce manufacturing business, with patents for tooling and fixtures. President of the Florida Knifemaker's Association since 2009. **Mark:** TR* stylized

REPKE, MIKE
4191 N. Euclid Ave., Bay City, MI 48706, Phone: 517-684-3111
Specialties: Traditional working and using straight knives of his design or to customer specs; classic knives; display knives. **Patterns:** Hunters, Bowies, skinners, fighters boots, axes and swords. **Technical:** Grind 440C. Offer variety of handle materials. **Prices:** $99 to $1500. **Remarks:** Full-time makers. Doing business as Black Forest Blades. **Mark:** Knife logo.

REVERDY, NICOLE AND PIERRE
5 Rue de L'egalite', Romans, FRANCE 26100, Phone: 334 75 05 10 15, Web: http://www.reverdy.com
Specialties: Art knives; legend pieces. Pierre and Nicole, his wife, are creating knives of art with combination of enamel on pure silver (Nicole) and poetic Damascus (Pierre) such as the "La dague a la licorne." **Patterns:** Daggers, folding knives Damascus and enamel, Bowies, hunters and other large patterns. **Technical:** Forges his Damascus and "poetic Damascus"; where animals such as unicorns, stags, dragons or star crystals appear, works with his own EDM machine to create any kind of pattern inside the steel with his own touch. **Prices:** $2000 and up. **Remarks:** Full-time maker since 1989; first knife sold in 1986. Nicole (wife) collaborates with enamels. **Mark:** Reverdy.

REVISHVILI, ZAZA
2102 Linden Ave, Madison, WI 53704, Phone: 608-243-7927
Specialties: Fancy/embellished and high-art straight knives and folders of his design. **Patterns:** Daggers, swords and locking folders. **Technical:** Uses Damascus; silver filigree, silver inlay in wood; enameling. **Prices:** $1000 to $9000; some to $15,000. **Remarks:** Full-time maker; first knife sold in 1987. **Mark:** Initials, city.

REXFORD, TODD
4531 W. Hwy. 24, Florissant, CO 80816, Phone: 719-492-2282, rexfordknives@ gmail.com; Web: www.rexfordknives.com
Specialties: Dress tactical and tactical folders and fixed blades. **Technical:** I work in stainless steels, stainless damascus, titanium, Stellite and other high performance alloys. All machining and part engineering is done in house.

REXROAT, KIRK
12 Crow Ln., Banner, WY 82832, Phone: 307-689-5430, rexroatknives@gmail.com; Web: www.rexroatknives.com
Specialties: Using and collectible straight knives and folders of his design or to customer specs. **Patterns:** Bowies, hunters, folders. **Technical:** Forges damascus patterns, mosaic and 52100. Does own engraving. **Prices:** $400 and up. **Remarks:** Part-time maker, master smith in the ABS; first knife sold in 1984. Doing business as Rexroat Knives. Designs and builds prototypes for Al Mar Knives. **Mark:** Last name.

REYNOLDS, DAVE
1404 Indian Creek, Harrisville, WV 26362, Phone: 304-643-2889, wvreynolds@ zoomintevnet.net
Specialties: Working straight knives of his design. **Patterns:** Bowies, kitchen and utility knives. **Technical:** Grinds and forges L6, 1095 and 440C. Heat-treats. **Prices:** $50 to $85; some to $175. **Remarks:** Full-time maker; first knife sold in 1980. Doing business as Terra-Gladius Knives. **Mark:** Mark on special orders only; serial number on all knives.

REYNOLDS, JOHN C
#2 Andover HC77, Gillette, WY 82716, Phone: 307-682-6076
Specialties: Working knives, some fancy. **Patterns:** Hunters, Bowies, tomahawks and buck skinners; some folders. **Technical:** Grinds D2, ATS-34, 440C and forges own Damascus and knives. Scrimshaws. **Prices:** $200 to $3000. **Remarks:** Spare-time maker; first knife sold in 1969. **Mark:** On ground blades JC Reynolds Gillette WY, on forged blades, initials make the mark-JCR.

RHEA, LIN
413 Grant 291020, Prattsville, AR 72129, Phone: 870-942-6419, lwrhea@rheaknives. com; Web: www.rheaknives.com
Specialties: Traditional and early American styled Bowies in high carbon steel or Damascus. **Patterns:** Bowies, hunters and fighters. **Technical:** Filework wire inlay. Sole authorship of construction, Damascus and embellishment. **Prices:** $280 to $1500. **Remarks:** Serious part-time maker and rated as a Master Smith in the ABS.

RHO, NESTOR LORENZO
Primera Junta 589, Junin, Buenos Aires, ARGENTINA CP 6000, Phone: +54-236-15-4670686, info@cuchillosrho.com.ar; Web: www.cuchillosrho.com.ar
Specialties: Classic and fancy straight knives of his design. **Patterns:** Bowies, fighters and hunters. **Technical:** Grinds 420C, 440C, 1084, 5160, 52100, L6 and W1. Offers semi-precious stones on handles, acid etching on blades and blade engraving. **Prices:** $120 to $600, collector's pieces up to $3,000. **Remarks:** Full-time maker; first knife sold in 1975. **Mark:** Name.

RIBONI, CLAUDIO
Via L Da Vinci, Truccazzano (MI), ITALY, Phone: 02 95309010, Web: www.riboni-knives.com

RICARDO ROMANO, BERNARDES
Ruai Coronel Rennò 1261, Itajuba MG, BRAZIL 37500, Phone: 0055-2135-622-5896
Specialties: Hunters, fighters, Bowies. **Technical:** Grinds blades of stainless and tools steels. **Patterns:** Hunters. **Prices:** $100 to $700. **Mark:** Romano.

RICHARD, RAYMOND
31047 SE Jackson Rd., Gresham, OR 97080, Phone: 503-663-1219, rayskee13@ hotmail.com; Web: www.hawknknives.com
Specialties: Hand-forged knives, tomahawks, axes, and spearheads, all one-of-a-kind. **Prices:** $200 and up, some to $3000. **Remarks:** Full-time maker since 1994. **Mark:** Name on spine of blades.

RICHARDS, CHUCK
7243 Maple Tree Lane SE, Salem, OR 97317, Phone: 503-569-5549, woodchuckforge@gmail.com; Web: www.acrichardscustomknives.com
Specialties: Fixed blade Damascus. One-of-a-kind. **Patterns:** Hunters, fighters. **Prices:** $300 to $1,500+ **Remarks:** Likes to work with customers on a truly custom knife. **Mark:** A.C. Richards J.S. or ACR J.S.

RICHARDS, RALPH (BUD)
6413 Beech St, Bauxite, AR 72011, Phone: 501-602-5367, DoubleR042@aol.com; Web: www.ralphrichardscustomknives.com
Specialties: Forges 55160, 1084, and 15N20 for Damascus. S30V, 440C, and others. Wood, mammoth, giraffe and mother of pearl handles.

RICHARDSON, PERCY
1508 Atkinson Dr., Lufkin, TX 75901, Phone: 936-288-1690 or 936-634-1690, richardsonknives@yahoo.com; Web: americasfightingshipsknives.com or richardsonhandmadeknives.com
Specialties: Knives forged from steel off old ships. **Patterns:** Slip joints, lockbacks, hunters, bowies, mostly knives forged from steel from old Navy ships. **Prices:** $300 to $2,000. **Remarks:** Five-year project of ships knives, 2014 until 2019. **Mark:** Richardson over five-point star and Lone Star USA.

RICHARDSON III, PERCY (RICH)
1508 Atkinson Dr., Lufkin, TX 75901, Phone: 318-455-5309 or 936-634-1690, prichardson100@yahoo.com; Web: www.facebook.com/PRichKnives
Specialties: Straight knives of others' damascus, laser etching, some stabilized woods. **Patterns:** Hunters, skinners, small bowies and fighters. **Technical:** Stock removal, hollow grinds using CPM 154, ATS 34, 440C and damascus blade steels. **Prices:** $150 to $600. **Remarks:** Full-time maker, first knife made in 1995. **Mark:** Rich with year after on backbone of blade.

RICHARDSON JR., PERCY
1508 Atkinson Dr., Lufkin, TX 75901, Phone: 936-288-1690, Percy@ Richardsonhandmadeknives.com; Web: www.Richardsonhandmadeknives.com
Specialties: Working straight knives and folders. **Patterns:** Hunters, skinners, bowies, fighters and folders. **Technical:** Mostly grinds CPM-154. **Prices:** $175 - $750 some bowies to $1200. **Remarks:** Full-time maker, first knife sold in 1990. Doing business as Richardsons Handmade Knives. **Mark:** Texas star with last name across it.

RICHERSON, RON
P.O. Box 51, Greenburg, KY 42743, Phone: 270-405-0491, Fax: 270-932-5601, RRicherson1@windstream.net
Specialties: Collectible and functional fixed blades, locking liners, and autos of his design. **Technical:** Grinds ATS-34, S30V, S60V, CPM-154, D2, 440, high carbon steel,

and his and others' Damascus. Prefers natural materials for handles and does both stock removal and forged work, some with embellishments. **Prices:** $250 to $850, some higher. **Remarks:** Full-time maker. Member American Bladesmith Society. Made first knife in September 2006, sold first knife in December 2006. **Mark:** Name in oval with city and state. Also name in center of oval Green River Custom Knives.

RICKE, DAVE
1209 Adams St, West Bend, WI 53090, Phone: 262-334-5739
  Specialties: Working knives; period pieces. **Patterns:** Hunters, boots, Bowies; locking folders and slip joints. **Technical:** Grinds ATS-34, A2, 440C and 154CM. **Prices:** $145 and up. **Remarks:** Full-time maker; first knife sold in 1976. **Mark:** Last name.

RICKS, KURT J.
Darkhammer Forge, 29 N. Center, Trenton, UT 84338, Phone: 435-563-3471, kopsh@ hotmail.com; http://darkhammerworks.tripod.com
  Specialties: Fixed blade working knives of all designs and to customer specs. **Patterns:** Fighters, daggers, hunters, swords, axes, and spears. **Technical:** Uses a coal fired forge. Forges high carbon, tool and spring steels. Does own heat treat on forge. Prefers natural handle materials. Leather sheaths available. **Prices:** Start at $50 plus shipping. **Remarks:** A knife should be functional first and pretty second. Part-time maker; first knife sold in 1994. **Mark:** Initials.

RIDER, DAVID M
PO Box 5946, Eugene, OR 97405-0911, Phone: 541-343-8747

RIDGE, TIM
SWAMP FOX KNIVES, 1282 W. Creston Rd., Crossville, TN 38571, Phone: 931-484-0216, swampfoxknives@frontiernet.net; www.swampfoxknives.com
  Specialties: Handforged historical American knives circa 1700 to 1865, colonial through Civil War eras. **Technical:** Forges 1095, 5160, 1084 and 1075 high-carbon steels. **Prices:** $135 to $2,000, depending on style and size of knife. **Remarks:** Full-time maker for 17 years. **Mark:** Patented running fox with TR in the body.

RIDLEY, ROB
RR1, Sundre, AB, CANADA T0M 1X0, Phone: 405-556-1113, rob@rangeroriginal.com; www.rangeroriginal.com, www.knifemaker.ca
  Specialties: The knives I make are mainly fixed blades, though I'm exploring the complex world of folders. **Technical:** I favour high-end stainless alloys and exotic handle materials because a knife should provide both cutting ability and bragging rights. **Remarks:** I made my first knife in 1998 and still use that blade today. I've gone from full time, to part time, to hobby maker, but I still treasure time in the shop or spent with other enthusiasts. Operates Canadian Knifemakers Supply

RIEPE, RICHARD A
17604 E 296 St, Harrisonville, MO 64701

RIETVELD, BERTIE
PO Box 53, Magaliesburg, GT, SOUTH AFRICA 1791, Phone: 2783 232 8766, bertie@ rietveldknives.com; Web: www.rietveldknives.com
  Specialties: Art daggers, Bolster lock folders, Persian designs, embraces elegant designs. **Patterns:** Mostly one-of-a-kind. **Technical:** Sole authorship, work only in own Damascus, gold inlay, blued stainless fittings. **Prices:** $500 - $8,000 **Remarks:** First knife made in 1979. Annual shows attended: ECCKS, Blade Show, Milan Show, South African Guild Show. **Marks:** Logo is elephant in half circle with name, enclosed in Stanhope lens

RIGNEY JR., WILLIE
191 Colson Dr, Bronston, KY 42518, Phone: 606-679-4227
  Specialties: High-tech period pieces and fancy working knives. **Patterns:** Fighters, boots, daggers and push knives. **Technical:** Grinds 440C and 154CM; buys Damascus. Most knives are embellished. **Prices:** $150 to $1500; some to $10,000. **Remarks:** Full-time maker; first knife sold in 1978. **Mark:** First initial, last name.

RINKES, SIEGFRIED
Am Sportpl 2, Markterlbach, GERMANY 91459

RITCHIE, ADAM
Koi Knifeworks, 10925 Sheridan Ave. S, Bloomington, MN 55431, Phone: 651-503-2818, adamkara2@earthlink.net
  Specialties: Japanese-influenced fixed blades. **Patterns:** Small utility knives to larger hunter/tactical pieces, Kwaikens, tantos and Kiridashis. **Technical:** Flat and convex grinds O1 tool steel and 1095, differentially heat treated to 58-60 Rockwell hardness. **Prices:** $150-$1,000. **Remarks:** Part-time maker, full-time firefighter/EMT/FEO. **Mark:** Koi Knifeworks in circle around Kanji or Koi.

RIZZI, RUSSELL J
37 March Rd, Ashfield, MA 01330, Phone: 413-625-2842
  Specialties: Fancy working and using straight knives and folders of his design or to customer specs. **Patterns:** Hunters, locking folders and fighters. **Technical:** Grinds 440C, D2 and commercial Damascus. **Prices:** $150 to $750; some to $2500. **Remarks:** Part-time maker; first knife sold in 1990. **Mark:** Last name, Ashfield, MA.

ROBBINS, BILL
2160 E. Fry Blvd., Ste. C5, Sierra Vista, AZ 85635-2794, billrknifemaker@aol.com
  Specialties: Plain and fancy working straight knives. Makes to his designs and most anything you can draw. **Patterns:** Hunting knives, utility knives, and Bowies. **Technical:** Grinds ATS-34, 440C, tool steel, high carbon, buys Damascus. **Prices:** $70 to $450. **Remarks:** Part-time maker, first knife sold in 2001. **Mark:** Last name or desert scene with name.

ROBBINS, HOWARD P
1310 E. 310th Rd., Flemington, MO 65650, Phone: 417-282-5055, ARobb1407@aol.com

  Specialties: High-tech working knives with clean designs, some fancy. **Patterns:** Folders, hunters and camp knives. **Technical:** Grinds 440C. Heat-treats; likes mirror finishes. Offers leatherwork. **Prices:** $100 to $500; some to $1000. **Remarks:** Full-time maker; first knife sold in 1982. **Mark:** Name, city and state.

ROBBINS, LANDON
2370 State Hwy. U, Crane, MO 65633, Phone: 417-207-4290, lwrobbins71@gmail.com
  Specialties: Fixed blades using high-carbon damascus. **Patterns:** Hunters, bowies and fighters. **Technical:** Hand-forged, flat-ground 1084, 1074, 5160, 52100 and maker's own damascus. **Prices:** $300 and up. **Remarks:** Part-time maker, ABS journeyman smith. **Mark:** Robbins with an arrow under name.

ROBERTS, CHUCK
PO Box 7174, Golden, CO 80403, Phone: 303-642-2388, chuck@crobertsart.com; Web: www.crobertsart.com
  Specialties: Price daggers, large Bowies, hand-rubbed satin finish. **Patterns:** Bowies and California knives. **Technical:** Grinds 440C, 5160 and ATS-34. Handles made of stag, ivory or mother-of-pearl. **Prices:** $1250. **Remarks:** Full-time maker. Company name is C. Roberts - Art that emulates the past. **Mark:** Last initial or last name.

ROBERTS, JACK
10811 Sagebluff Dr, Houston, TX 77089, Phone: 281-481-1784, jroberts59@ houston.rr.com
  Specialties: Hunting knives and folders, offers scrimshaw by wife Barbara. **Patterns:** Drop point hunters and LinerLock® folders. **Technical:** Grinds 440-C, offers file work, texturing, natural handle materials and Micarta. **Prices:** $200 to $800 some higher. **Remarks:** Part-time maker, sold first knife in 1965. **Mark:** Name, city, state.

ROBERTS, T. C. (TERRY)
142131 Lake Forest Heights Rd., Siloam Springs, AR 72761, Phone: 479-373-6502, carolcroberts@cox.net
  Specialties: Working straight knives and folders of the maker's original design. **Patterns:** Bowies, daggers, fighters, locking folders, slip joints to include multiblades and whittlers. **Technical:** Grinds all types of carbon and stainless steels and commercially available Damascus. Works in stone and casts in bronze and silver. Some inlays and engraving. **Prices:** $250 - $3500. **Remarks:** Full-time maker; sold first knife in 1983. **Mark:** Stamp is oval with initials inside.

ROBERTSON, LEO D
3728 Pleasant Lake Dr, Indianapolis, IN 46227, Phone: 317-882-9899, ldr52@juno.com
  Specialties: Hunting and folders. **Patterns:** Hunting, fillet, Bowie, utility, folders and tantos. **Technical:** Uses ATS-34, 154CM, 440C, 1095, D2 and Damascus steels. **Prices:** Fixed knives $75 to $350, folders $350 to $600. **Remarks:** Handles made with stag, wildwoods, laminates, mother-of-pearl. Made first knife in 1990. Member of American Bladesmith Society. **Mark:** Logo with full name in oval around logo.

ROBINSON, CALVIN
5501 Twin Creek Circle, Pace, FL 32571, Phone: 850 572 1504, calvin@ calvinrobinsonknives.com; Web: www.CalvinRobinsonKnives.com
  Specialties: Working knives of my own design. **Patterns:** Hunters, fishing, folding and kitchen and purse knives. **Technical:** Now using 14C28N stainless blade steel, as well as 12C27, 13C26 and D2. **Prices:** $180 to $2500. **Remarks:** Full-time maker. Knifemakers' Guild Board of Directors. **Mark:** Robinson.

ROBINSON, CHUCK
SEA ROBIN FORGE, 1423 Third Ave., Picayune, MS 39466, Phone: 601-798-0060, robi5515@bellsouth.net
  Specialties: Deluxe period pieces and working / using knives of his design and to customer specs. **Patterns:** Bowies, fighters, hunters, utility knives and original designs. **Technical:** Forges own damascus, 52100, O1, W2, L6, A2 and 1070 thru 1095. **Prices:** Start at $250. **Remarks:** First knife 1958. **Mark:** Fish logo, anchor and initials C.R.

ROBINSON III, REX R
10531 Poe St, Leesburg, FL 34788, Phone: 352-787-4587
  Specialties: One-of-a-kind high-art automatics of his design. **Patterns:** Automatics, liner locks and lock back folders. **Technical:** Uses tool steel and stainless Damascus and mokume; flat grinds. Hand carves folders. **Prices:** $1800 to $7500. **Remarks:** First knife sold in 1988. **Mark:** First name inside oval.

ROCHFORD, MICHAEL R
PO Box 577, Dresser, WI 54009, Phone: 715-755-3520, mrrochford@centurytel.net
  Specialties: Working straight knives and folders. Classic Bowies and Moran traditional. **Patterns:** Bowies, fighters, hunters: slip-joint, locking and liner locking folders. **Technical:** Grinds ATS-34, 440C, 154CM and D-2; forges W2, 5160, and his own Damascus. Offers metal and metal and leather sheaths. Filework and wire inlay. **Prices:** $150 to $1000; some to $2000. **Remarks:** Part-time maker; first knife sold in 1984. **Mark:** Name.

RODDENBERRY, CHARLES
SUWANNEE RIVER KNIFE, 160 Elm St. NE, Live Oak, FL 32064, Phone: 386-362-5641, suwanneeknife@yahoo.com; Web: Facebook.com: Suwannee River Knife & Jewelry
  Patterns: Small three-finger fixed blades, friction folders and miniatures. **Technical:** Uses forging and stock removal methods of blademaking, with preferred steels currently being 1095, L6, 52100 and D2. **Prices:** $50 to $500. **Remarks:** Full-time knifemaker since 2012; first knife made in 2000 under the tutoring of Paul Martrildonno, with further training by Billy Brown. **Mark:** Simple skull face hot stamped.

RODDY, ROY "TIM"
7640 Hub-Bedford Rd., Hubbard, OH 44425, Phone: 330-770-5921, pfr2rtr@hotmail.com
  Specialties: Any type of knife a customer wants, large knives, small knives and anything

in between. **Patterns:** Hunters, fighters, martial arts knives, hide-outs, neck knives, throwing darts and locking-liner folders. Leather or Kydex sheaths with exotic-skin inlays. **Technical:** 440C, D2, ATS-34 or damascus blade steels. **Remarks:** Started making knives 25 years ago. **Mark:** Railroad sign (circle with an X inside and an R on either side of the X).

RODEBAUGH, JAMES L
P.O. Box 404, Carpenter, WY 82054, Phone: 307-649-2394, jlrodebaugh@gmail.com

RODEWALD, GARY
447 Grouse Ct, Hamilton, MT 59840, Phone: 406-363-2192
Specialties: Bowies of his design as inspired from historical pieces. **Patterns:** Hunters, Bowies and camp/combat. Forges 5160 1084 and his own Damascus of 1084, 15N20, field grade hunters AT-34-440C, 440V, and BG42. **Prices:** $200 to $1500. **Remarks:** Sole author on knives, sheaths done by saddle maker. **Mark:** Rodewald.

RODKEY, DAN
18336 Ozark Dr, Hudson, FL 34667, Phone: 727-863-8264
Specialties: Traditional straight knives of his design and in standard patterns. **Patterns:** Boots, fighters and hunters. **Technical:** Grinds 440C, D2 and ATS-34. **Prices:** Start at $200. **Remarks:** Full-time maker; first knife sold in 1985. Doing business as Rodkey Knives. **Mark:** Etched logo on blade.

ROEDER, DAVID
426 E. 9th Pl., Kennewick, WA 99336, d.roeder1980@yahoo.com
Specialties: Fixed blade field and exposition grade knives. **Patterns:** Favorite styles are Bowie and hunter. **Technical:** Forges primarily 5160 and 52100. Makes own Damascus. **Prices:** Start at $150. **Remarks:** Made first knife in September, 1996. **Mark:** Maker's mark is a D and R with the R resting at a 45-degree angle to the lower right of the D.

ROGERS, RAY
PO Box 126, Wauconda, WA 98859, Phone: 509-486-8069, knives @rayrogers.com; Web: www.rayrogers.com
Specialties: LinerLock® folders. Asian and European professional chef's knives. **Patterns:** Rayzor folders, chef's knives and cleavers of his own and traditional designs, drop point hunters and fillet knives. **Technical:** Stock removal S30V, 440, 1095, O1 Damascus and other steels. Does all own heat treating, clay tempering, some forging G-10, Micarta, carbon fiber on folders, stabilized burl woods on fixed blades. **Prices:** $300 to $700. **Remarks:** Knives are made one-at-a-time to the customer's order. Happy to consider customizing knife designs to suit your preferences and sometimes create entirely new knives when necessary. As a full-time knifemaker is willing to spend as much time as it takes (usually through email) discussing the options and refining details of a knife's design to insure that you get the knife you really want.

ROGERS, RICHARD
PO Box 769, Magdalena, NM 87825, Phone: 575-838-7237, r.s.rogersknives@gmail.com; Web: www.richardrogersknives.com
Specialties: Folders. **Patterns:** Modern slip joints, LinerLocks and frame-locks. **Prices:** $300 and up. **Mark:** Last name.

ROGHMANS, MARK
607 Virginia Ave, LaGrange, GA 30240, Phone: 706-885-1273
Specialties: Classic and traditional knives of his design. **Patterns:** Bowies, daggers and fighters. **Technical:** Grinds ATS-34, D2 and 440C. **Prices:** $250 to $500. **Remarks:** Part-time maker; first knife sold in 1984. Doing business as LaGrange Knife. **Mark:** Last name and/or LaGrange Knife.

ROHDE, DANIEL S.
25692 County Rd. 9, Winona, MN 55987, Phone: 507-312-6664, rohdeedge@gmail.com; Web: www.rohdeedge.com
Specialties: High performance fixed blades, chef's knives and slip-joint folders. **Patterns:** Loveless- and Fowler-style hunters, SharkTail and other hunting, EDC and chef's knives. **Technical:** Highly thermal cycled and forged 52100 and 1095, and AEB-L for a stainless steel. **Prices:** $100 to $400, some to $1,200, with the typical EDC knife going for about $185. **Remarks:** HEPK apprentice smith, part-time maker, and consistent, repeatable performance is the goal. **Mark:** Electro-etched last name (typically).

ROHN, FRED
7675 W Happy Hill Rd, Coeur d'Alene, ID 83814, Phone: 208-667-0774
Specialties: Hunters, boot knives, custom patterns. **Patterns:** Drop points, double edge, etc. **Technical:** Grinds 440 or 154CM. **Prices:** $85 and up. **Remarks:** Part-time maker. **Mark:** Logo on blade; serial numbered.

ROLLERT, STEVE
PO Box 65, Keenesburg, CO 80643-0065, Phone: 303-732-4858, steve@doveknives.com; Web: www.doveknives.com
Specialties: Highly finished working knives. **Patterns:** Variety of straight knives; locking folders and slip-joints. **Technical:** Forges and grinds W2, 1095, ATS-34 and his pattern-welded, cable Damascus and nickel Damascus. **Prices:** $300 to $1000; some to $3000. **Remarks:** Full-time maker; first knife sold in 1980. Doing business as Dove Knives. **Mark:** Last name in script.

ROMEIS, GORDON
1521 Coconut Dr., Fort Myers, FL 33901, Phone: 239-940-5060, gordonromeis@gmail.com Web: Romeisknives.com
Specialties: Smaller using knives. **Patterns:** I have a number of standard designs that include both full tapered tangs and narrow tang knives. Custom designs are welcome. Many different types. No folders. **Technical:** Standard steel is 440C. Also uses Alabama Damascus steel. **Prices:** Start at $165. **Remarks:** I am a part-time maker however I do try to keep waiting times to a minimum. **Mark:** Either my name, city, and state or simply ROMEIS depending on the knife.

RONZIO, N. JACK
PO Box 248, Fruita, CO 81521, Phone: 970-858-0921

ROOSEVELT, RUSSELL
398 County Rd. 450 E, Albion, IL 62806-4753, Phone: 618-445-3226 or 618-302-7272, rroosevelt02@gmail.com
Specialties: Using straight knives of his design and to customers' specs. **Patterns:** Hunters, utility and camp knives. **Technical:** Forges 1084 and high-carbon damascus. **Prices:** $250 to $1,200. **Remarks:** Part-time maker, first knife sold in 1999. **Mark:** Full name left side, ABS JS stamp right side.

ROOT, GARY
644 East 14th St, Erie, PA 16503, Phone: 814-459-0196
Specialties: Damascus Bowies with hand carved eagles, hawks and snakes for handles. Few folders made. **Patterns:** Daggers, fighters, hunter/field knives. **Technical:** Using handforged Damascus from Ray Bybar Jr (M.S.) and Robert Eggerling. Grinds D2, 440C, 1095 and 5160. Some 5160 is hand forged. **Prices:** $80 to $300 some to $1000. **Remarks:** Full time maker, first knife sold in 1976. **Mark:** Name over Erie, PA.

ROSE, BOB
PO BOX 126, Wagontown, PA 19376, Phone: 484-883-3925, bobmedit8@comcast.net Web: www.bobroseknives.com
Patterns: Bowies, fighters, drop point hunters, daggers, bird and trout, camp, and other fixed blade styles. **Technical:** Mostly using 1095 and damascus steel, desert ironwood and other top-of-the-line exotic woods as well as mammoth tooth. **Prices:** $49 - $300. **Remarks:** Been making and selling knives since 2004. "Knife Making is a meditation technique for me."

ROSE, DEREK W
14 Willow Wood Rd, Gallipolis, OH 45631, Phone: 740-446-4627

ROSE II, DOUN T.
Ltc US Special Operations Command (ret.), 1795/96 W Sharon Rd SW, Fife Lake, MI 49633, Phone: 231-645-1369, rosecutlery@gmail.com; Web: www.rosecutlery.com
Specialties: Straight working, collector and presentation knives to a high level of fit and finish. Design in collaboration with customer. **Patterns:** Field knives, Scagel, bowies, tactical, period pieces, axes and tomahawks, fishing and hunting spears and fine kitchen cutlery. **Technical:** Forged and billet ground, high carbon and stainless steel appropriate to end use. Steel from leading industry sources. Some period pieces from recovered stock. Makes own damascus (to include multi-bar and mosaic) and mokume gane. **Remarks:** Full-time maker, ABS since 2000, William Scagel Memorial Scholarship 2002, Bill Moran School of Blade Smithing 2003, apprentice under Master Blacksmith Dan Nickels at Black Rock Forge current. Working at Crooked Pine Forge. **Mark:** Last name ROSE in block letters with five petal "wild rose" in place of O. Doing business as Rose Cutlery.

ROSENBAUGH, RON
2806 Stonegate Dr, Crystal Lake, IL 60012, Phone: 815-477-9233 or 815-345-1633, ron@rosenbaughknives.com; Web: www.rosenbaughknives.com
Specialties: Fancy and plain working knives using own designs, collaborations, and traditional patterns. **Patterns:** Bird, trout, boots, hunters, fighters, some Bowies. **Technical:** Grinds high alloy stainless, tool steels, and Damascus; forges 1084,5160, 52100, carbon and spring steels. **Prices:** $150 to $1000. **Remarks:** Full-time maker, first knife sold in 2004. **Mark:** Last name, logo, city.

ROSS, STEPHEN
534 Remington Dr, Evanston, WY 82930, Phone: 307-799-7653
Specialties: One-of-a-kind collector-grade classic and contemporary straight knives and folders of his design and to customer specs; some fantasy pieces. **Patterns:** Combat and survival knives, hunters, boots and folders. **Technical:** Grinds stainless and tool steels. Engraves, scrimshaws. Makes leather sheaths. **Prices:** $160 to $3000. **Remarks:** Part-time maker; first knife sold in 1971. **Mark:** Last name in modified Roman; sometimes in script.

ROSS, TIM
3239 Oliver Rd, Thunder Bay, ON, CANADA P7G 1S9, Phone: 807-935-2667, Fax: 807-935-3179, rosscustomknives@gmail.com
Specialties: Fixed blades, natural handle material. **Patterns:** Hunting, fishing, Bowies, fighters. **Technical:** 440C, D2, 52100, Cable, 5160, 1084, L6, W2. **Prices:** $150 to $750 some higher. **Remarks:** Forges and stock removal. **Mark:** Ross Custom Knives.

ROSSDEUTSCHER, ROBERT N
133 S Vail Ave, Arlington Heights, IL 60005, Phone: 847-577-0404, Web: www.rnrknives.com
Specialties: Frontier-style and historically inspired knives. **Patterns:** Trade knives, Bowies, camp knives and hunting knives, tomahawks and lances. **Technical:** Most knives are hand forged, a few are stock removal. **Prices:** $135 to $1500. **Remarks:** Journeyman Smith of the American Bladesmith Society. **Mark:** Back-to-back "R's", one upside down and backwards, one right side up and forward in an oval. Sometimes with name, town and state; depending on knife style.

ROTELLA, RICHARD A
643 75th St., Niagara Falls, NY 14304, richarpo@roadrunner.com
Specialties: Highly finished working knives of his own design, as well as some Loveless-style designs. **Patterns:** Hunters, fishing, small game, utility, fighters and boot knives. **Technical:** Grinds ATS-34, 154CM, CPM 154 and 440C. **Prices:** $150 to $600. **Remarks:** Part-time maker; first knife sold in 1977. Sells completed knives only and does not take orders; makes about 70 knives a year. **Mark:** Name and city.

ROUGEAU, DERICK
1465 Cloud Peak Dr., Sparks, NV 89436, Phone: 775-232-6167, derick@rougeauknives.com; Web: www.rougeauknives.com
Specialties: A wide range of original designs from practical to tactical and traditional. **Patterns:** Bowies, hunters, fighters, bushcraft blades, tantos, machetes, chef's knives, tomahawks, hatchets, swords, neck and tool knives. Also makes assorted accessories and other cool items. **Technical:** Using stock-removal process. Flat and hollow grinds using a wide range of steels from damascus to 1080, 1095, 5160, 6150, O1, D2, ATS 34, CPM 154 and other CPM stainless steels. Does own heat treating, leather work and Kydex, and uses synthetic materials, stabilized woods and antler. **Prices:** $250 to $650 or more. **Remarks:** Part-time maker, full-time artist/designer. **Mark:** "DR" logo in front of "ROUGEAU."

ROULIN, CHARLES
113 B Rt. de Soral, Geneva, SWITZERLAND 1233, Phone: 022-757-4479, Fax: 079-218-9754, charles.roulin@bluewin.ch; Web: www.coutelier-roulin.com
Specialties: Fancy high-art straight knives and folders of his design. **Patterns:** Bowies, locking folders, slip-joint folders and miniatures. **Technical:** Grinds 440C, ATS-34 and D2. Engraves; carves nature scenes and detailed animals in steel, ivory, on handles and blades. **Prices:** $500 to $3000; some to Euro: 14,600. **Remarks:** Full-time maker; first knife sold in 1988. **Mark:** Symbol of fish with name or name engraved.

ROUSH, SCOTT
Big Rock Forge, 30955 Hove Ln., Washburn, WI 54891, Phone: 715-682-2844, scott@bigrockforge.com; Web: bigrockforge.com
Specialties: Forged blades representing a diversity of styles from trasditional hunters, fighters, camp knives, and EDC's to artistic pieces of cultural and historical inspiration with an emphasis in unique materials. **Technical:** Forges Aldo 1084, W2, low MN 1075, stainless/high carbon san mai, wrought iron/high carbon san mai, damascus. **Prices:** $85 to $1000 **Remarks:** Full-time maker; first knife sold in 2010.**Mark:** Stamped initials (SAR) set in a diamond.

ROWE, FRED
BETHEL RIDGE FORGE, 3199 Roberts Rd, Amesville, OH 45711, Phone: 866-325-2164, fred.rowe@bethelridgeforge.com; Web: www.bethelridgeforge.com
Specialties: Damascus and carbon steel sheath knives. **Patterns:** Bowies, hunters, fillet small kokris. **Technical:** His own Damascus, 52100, O1, L6, 1095 carbon steels, mosaics. **Prices:** $200 to $2000. **Remarks:** All blades are clay hardened. **Mark:** Bethel Ridge Forge.

ROYER, KYLE
9021 State Hwy. M, Clever, MO 65631, Phone: 417-247-5572, royerknifeworks@live.com; Web: www.kyleroyerknives.com
Specialties: Folders and fixed-blade knives. **Technical:** Mosaic damascus and engraving. **Prices:** $350 to $7,500. **Remarks:** ABS master smith. **Mark:** K~ROYER~MS.

ROZAS, CLARK D
1436 W "G" St, Wilmington, CA 90744, Phone: 310-518-0488
Specialties: Hand forged blades. **Patterns:** Pig stickers, toad stabbers, whackers, choppers. **Technical:** Damascus, 52100, 1095, 1084, 5160. **Prices:** $200 to $600. **Remarks:** A.B.S. member; part-time maker since 1995. **Mark:** Name over dagger.

RUA, GARY
400 Snell St., Apt. 2, Fall River, MA 02721, Phone: 508-677-2664
Specialties: Working straight knives of his design. 1800 to 1900 century standard patterns. **Patterns:** Bowies, hunters, fighters, and patch knives. **Technical:** Forges and grinds. Damascus, 5160, 1095, old files. Uses only natural handle material. **Prices:** $350 - $2000. **Remarks:** Part-time maker. (Harvest Moon Forge) **Mark:** Last name.

RUANA KNIFE WORKS
Box 520, Bonner, MT 59823, Phone: 406-258-5368, Fax: 406-258-2895, info@ruanaknives.com; Web: www.ruanaknives.com
Specialties: Working knives and period pieces. **Patterns:** Variety of straight knives. **Technical:** Forges 5160 chrome alloy for Bowies and 1095. **Prices:** $300 and up. **Remarks:** Full-time maker; first knife sold in 1938. For free catalog email regular mailing address to info@ruanaknives.com **Mark:** Name.

RUCKER, THOMAS
30222 Mesa Valley Dr., Spring, TX 77386, Phone: 832-216-8122, admin@knivesbythomas.com Web: www.knivesbythomas.com
Specialties: Personal design and custom design. Hunting, tactical, folding knives, and cutlery. **Technical:** Design and grind ATS34, D2, O1, Damascus, and VG10. **Prices:** $150 - $5,000. **Remarks:** Full-time maker and custom scrimshaw and engraving done by wife, Debi Rucker. First knife done in 1969; first design sold in 1975 **Mark:** Etched logo and signature.

RUPERT, BOB
301 Harshaville Rd, Clinton, PA 15026, Phone: 724-573-4569, rbrupert@aol.com
Specialties: Wrought period pieces with natural elements. **Patterns:** Elegant straight blades, friction folders. **Technical:** Forges colonial 7; 1095; 5160; diffuse mokume-gane and Damascus. **Prices:** $150 to $1500; some higher. **Remarks:** Part-time maker; first knife sold in 1980. Evening hours studio since 1980. Likes simplicity that disassembles. **Mark:** R etched in Old English.

RUPLE, WILLIAM H
201 Brian Dr., Pleasanton, TX 78064, Phone: 830-569-0007, bknives@devtex.net
Specialties: Multi-blade folders, slip joints, some lock backs. **Patterns:** Like to reproduce old patterns. Offers filework and engraving. **Technical:** Grinds CPM-154 and other carbon and stainless steel and commercial Damascus. **Prices:** $950 to $2500. **Remarks:** Full-time maker; first knife sold in 1988. **Mark:** Ruple.

RUSNAK, JOSEF
Breclavska 6, 323 00 Plzen, CZECH REPUBLIC, Phone: 00420721329442, rusnak.josef@centrum.cz; Web: http://knife.guaneru.cz
Specialties: Highly artistically designed knives. **Patterns:** Straight knives and folders. Collaboration with Buddy Weston. **Technical:** Engraving in high-quality steel and organic materials (mammoth tusk, giraffe bone, mother-of-pearl, bone), miniature sculpting, casting (Au, Ag, bronze). **Prices:** $1,000 and up. **Remarks:** Part-time maker; first knife sold in 1994. **Mark:** Signature.

RUSS, RON
5351 NE 160th Ave, Williston, FL 32696, Phone: 352-528-2603, RussRs@aol.com
Specialties: Damascus and mokume. **Patterns:** Ladder, rain drop and butterfly **Technical:** Most knives, including Damascus, are forged from 52100-E. **Prices:** $65 to $2500. **Mark:** Russ.

RUSSELL, MICK
4 Rossini Rd, Pari Park, Port Elizabeth, EC, SOUTH AFRICA 6070
Specialties: Art knives. **Patterns:** Working and collectible bird, trout and hunting knives defense knives and folders. **Technical:** Grinds D2, 440C, ATS-34 and Damascus. Offers mirror or satin finishes. **Prices:** Start at $100. **Remarks:** Full-time maker; first knife sold in 1986. **Mark:** Stylized rhino incorporating initials.

RUSSELL, TOM
6500 New Liberty Rd, Jacksonville, AL 36265, Phone: 205-492-7866
Specialties: Straight working knives of his design or to customer specs. **Patterns:** Hunters, folders, fighters, skinners, Bowies and utility knives. **Technical:** Grinds D2 440C and ATS-34; offers filework. **Prices:** $75 to $225. **Remarks:** Part-time maker; first knife sold in 1987. Full-time tool and die maker. **Mark:** Last name with tulip stamp.

RUTH, MICHAEL G
3101 New Boston Rd, Texarkana, TX 75501, Phone: 903-832-7166/cell:903-277-3663, Fax: 903-832-4710, mike@ruthknives.com; Web: www.ruthknives.com
Specialties: Hunters, bowies & fighters. Damascus & carbon steel. **Prices:** $375 & up **Mark:** Last name.

RUTH, JR., MICHAEL
5716 Wilshire Dr., Texarkana, TX 75503, Phone: 903-293-2663, michael@ruthlesscustomknives.com; Web: www.ruthlesscustomknives.com
Specialties: Custom hand-forged blades, utilizing high carbon and Damascus steels. **Patterns:** Bowies, hunters and fighters ranging from field to presentation-grade pieces. **Technical:** Steels include 5160, 1084, 15n20, W-2, 1095, and O-1. Handle materials include a variety of premium hardwoods, stag, assorted ivories and micarta.**Mark:** 8-pointed star with capital "R" in center.

RUUSUVUORI, ANSSI
Verkkotie 38, Piikkio, FINLAND 21500, Phone: 358-50-520 8057, anssi.ruusuvuori@akukon.fi; Web: www.arknives.suntuubi.com
Specialties: Traditional and modern puukko knives and hunters. Sole author except for Damascus steel.**Technical:** Forges mostly 1080 steel and grinds RWL-34. **Prices:** $200 to $500; some to $1200. **Remarks:** Part-time maker.**Mark:** A inside a circle (stamped)

RYBAR JR., RAYMOND B
2328 S. Sunset Dr., Camp Verde, AZ 86322, Phone: 928-567-6372
Specialties: Straight knives or folders with customers name, logo, etc. in mosaic pattern. **Patterns:** Common patterns plus mosaics of all types. **Technical:** Forges own Damascus. Primary forging of self smelted steel - smelting classes. **Prices:** $200 to $1200; Bible blades to $10,000. **Remarks:** Master Smith (A.B.S.) Primary focus toward Biblicaly themed blades **Mark:** Rybar or stone church forge or Rev. 1:3 or R.B.R. between diamonds.

RYDBOM, JEFF
PO Box 548, Annandale, MN 55302, Phone: 320-274-9639, jry1890@hotmail.com
Specialties: Ring knives. **Patterns:** Hunters, fighters, Bowie and camp knives. **Technical:** Straight grinds O1, A2, 1566 and 5150 steels. **Prices:** $150 to $1000. **Remarks:** No pinning of guards or pommels. All silver brazed. **Mark:** Capital "C" with J R inside.

RYUICHI, KUKI
504-7 Tokorozawa-Shinmachi, Tokorozawa-city, Saitama, JAPAN, Phone: 042-943-3451

RZEWNICKI, GERALD
8833 S Massbach Rd, Elizabeth, IL 61028-9714, Phone: 815-598-3239

S

SAINDON, R BILL
233 Rand Pond Rd, Goshen, NH 03752, Phone: 603-863-1874, dayskier71@aol.com
Specialties: Collector-quality folders of his design or to customer specs. **Patterns:** Latch release, LinerLock® and lockback folders. **Technical:** Offers limited amount of own Damascus; also uses Damas makers steel. Prefers natural handle material, gold and gems. **Prices:** $500 to $4000. **Remarks:** Full-time maker; first knife sold in 1981. Doing business as Daynia Forge. **Mark:** Sun logo or engraved surname.

SAKMAR, MIKE
4337 E. Grand River Ave. #113, Howell, MI 48843, Phone: 517-546-6388, Fax: 517-546-6399, sakmarent@yahoo.com; Web: www.sakmarenterprises.com
Specialties: Mokume in various patterns and alloy combinations. **Patterns:** Bowies, fighters, hunters and integrals. **Technical:** Grinds ATS-34, Damascus and high-carbon tool steels. Uses mostly natural handle materials—elephant ivory, walrus ivory, stag,

wildwood, oosic, etc. Makes mokume for resale. **Prices:** $250 to $2500; some to $4000. **Remarks:** Part-time maker; first knife sold in 1990. Supplier of mokume. **Mark:** Last name.

SALLEY, JOHN D

3965 Frederick-Ginghamsburg Rd., Tipp City, OH 45371, Phone: 937-698-4588, Fax: 937-698-4131

Specialties: Fancy working knives and art pieces. **Patterns:** Hunters, fighters, daggers and some swords. **Technical:** Grinds ATS-34, 12C27 and W2; buys Damascus. **Prices:** $85 to $1000; some to $6000. **Remarks:** Part-time maker; first knife sold in 1979. **Mark:** First initial, last name.

SALTER, GREGG

Salter Fine Cutlery, POB 384571, Waikoloa, HI 96738-4571, Phone: 808-883-0128, salterfinecutlery@gmail.com; Web: www.salterfinecutlery.com

Specialties: Custom, made-to-order cutlery and custom display boxes, including kitchen knife sets, steak knife sets, carving sets, chef's knives and collectible knives and swords. Work in collaboration with several individual bladesmiths who create blades to our specifications. **Technical:** Variety of steels available, including VG-10, Aogami Super, R2, OU-31, YSS White Paper Shirogami, YSS Aogami Blue Paper and Tamahagane (swords). Damascus patterns, hammered and laser-etched patterns, and, in the case of swords, hand-etched scenes available. **Prices:** Range widely, from approximately $250 to over $1 million in the case of one spectacular collectible. Average price for chef's knives in the $500-$750 range. **Remarks:** Full-time business making a range of products based around knives. **Mark:** Hawaiian koa tree with crossed chef's knives and the outline of a crown between them.

SAMPSON, LYNN

381 Deakins Rd, Jonesborough, TN 37659, Phone: 423-348-8373

Specialties: Highly finished working knives, mostly folders. **Patterns:** Locking folders, slip-joints, interframes and two-blades. **Technical:** Grinds D2, 440C and ATS-34; offers extensive filework. **Prices:** Start at $300. **Remarks:** Full-time maker; first knife sold in 1982. **Mark:** Name and city in logo.

SANDBERG, RONALD B

24784 Shadowwood Ln, Brownstown, MI 48134-9560, Phone: 734-671-6866, msc2009@comcast.net

Specialties: Good looking and functional hunting knives, filework, mixing of handle materials. **Patterns:** Hunters, skinners and Bowies. **Prices:** $120 and up. **Remarks:** Full lifetime workmanship guarantee. **Mark:** R.B. SANDBERG

SANDERS, BILL

335 Bauer Ave, PO Box 957, Mancos, CO 81328, Phone: 970-533-7223, Fax: 970-533-7390, billsand@frontier.net; Web: www.billsandershandmadeknives.com

Specialties: Survival knives, working straight knives, some fancy and some fantasy, of his design. **Patterns:** Hunters, boots, utility knives, using belt knives. **Technical:** Grinds 440C, ATS-34 and commercial Damascus. Provides wide variety of handle materials. **Prices:** $170 to $800. **Remarks:** Full-time maker. Formerly of Timberline Knives. **Mark:** Name, city and state.

SANDOW, BRENT EDWARD

50 O'Halloran Road, Howick, Auckland, NEW ZEALAND 2014, Phone: 64 9 537 4166, knifebug@vodafone.co.nz; Web: www.brentsandowknives.com

Specialties: Tactical fixed blades, hunting, camp, Bowie. **Technical:** All blades made by stock removal method. **Prices:** From US $200 upward. **Mark:** Name etched or engraved.

SANDS, SCOTT

2 Lindis Ln, New Brighton, Christchurch 9, NEW ZEALAND

Specialties: Classic working and fantasy swords. **Patterns:** Fantasy, medieval, celtic, viking, katana, some daggers. **Technical:** Forges own Damascus; 1080 and L6; 5160 and L6; O1 and L6. All hand-polished, does own heat-treating, forges non-Damascus on request. **Prices:** $1500 to $15,000+. **Remarks:** Full-time maker; first blade sold in 1996. **Mark:** Stylized Moon.

SANFORD, DICK

151 London Ln., Chehalis, WA 98532, Phone: 360-748-2128, richardsanfo364@centurytel.net

Remarks: Ten years experience hand forging knives

SANGSTER, JOE

POB 312, Vienna, GA 31092, Phone: 229-322-3407, ssangster@sowega.net; Web: www.sangsterknives.com

Specialties: Gent's **LinerLock folders with filework. Patterns:** Traditional LinerLock folders, hunters, skinners and kitchen knives. **Technical:** Grinds ATS-34, CPM 134, 440C and commercial damascus. Handle materials of mammoth ivory, mammoth tooth, pearl, oosic, coral and exotic burl woods. **Prices:** $250 to $500, some up to $1,200. **Remarks:** Full-time maker; first knife sold in 2003. **Mark:** name or name, city and state.

SANTA, LADISLAV "LASKY"

Stara Voda 264/10, 97637 Hrochot, SLOVAKIA, Phone: +421-907-825-2-77, lasky@lasky.sk; Web: www.lasky.sk

Specialties: Damascus hunters, daggers and swords. **Patterns:** Various damascus patterns. **Prices:** $300 to $6,000 U.S. **Mark:** L or Lasky.

SANTIAGO, ABUD

Av Gaona 3676 PB, Buenos Aires, ARGENTINA 1416, Phone: 5411 4612 8396, info@phi-sabud.com; Web: www.phi-sabud.com/blades.html

SANTINI, TOM

101 Clayside Dr, Pikeville, NC 27863, Phone: 586-354-0245, tomsantiniknives@hotmail.com; Web: www.tomsantiniknives.com

Specialties: working/using straight knives, tactical, and some slipjoints **Technical:** Grinds ATS-34, S-90-V, D2, and damascus. I handstitch my leather sheaths. **Prices:** $150 - $500. **Remarks:** Full-time maker, first knife sold in 2004. **Mark:** Full name.

SARGANIS, PAUL

2215 Upper Applegate Rd, Jacksonville, OR 97530, Phone: 541-899-2831, paulsarganis@hotmail.com; Web: www.sarganis.50megs.com

Specialties: Hunters, folders, Bowies. **Technical:** Forges 5160, 1084. Grinds ATS-34 and 440C. **Prices:** $120 to $500. **Remarks:** Spare-time maker, first knife sold in 1987. **Mark:** Last name.

SASS, GARY N

803 W. Main St., Sharpsville, PA 16150, Phone: 724-866-6165, gnsass@yahoo.com

Specialties: Working straight knives of his design or to customer specifications. **Patterns:** Hunters, fighters, utility knives, push daggers. **Technical:** Grinds 440C, ATS-34 and Damascus. Uses exotic wood, buffalo horn, warthog tusk and semi-precious stones. **Prices:** $50 to $250, some higher. **Remarks:** Part-time maker. First knife sold in 2003. **Mark:** Initials G.S. formed into a diamond shape or last name.

SAVIANO, JAMES

124 Wallis St., Douglas, MA 01516, Phone: 508-476-7644, jimsaviano@gmail.com

Specialties: Straight knives. **Patterns:** Hunters, bowies, fighters, daggers, short swords. **Technical:** Hand-forged high-carbon and my own damascus steel. **Prices:** Starting at $300. **Remarks:** ABS mastersmith, maker since 2000, sole authorship. **Mark:** Last name or stylized JPS initials.

SAWBY, SCOTT

480 Snowberry Ln, Sandpoint, ID 83864, Phone: 208-263-4253, scotmar3@gmail.com; Web: www.sawbycustomknives.com

Specialties: Folders, working and fancy. **Patterns:** Locking folders, patent locking systems and interframes. **Technical:** Grinds D2, 440C, CPM154, ATS-34, S30V, and Damascus. **Prices:** $700 to $3000. **Remarks:** Full-time maker; first knife sold in 1974. **Mark:** Last name, city and state.

SCARROW, WIL

c/o Scarrow's Custom Stuff, PO Box 1036, Gold Hill, OR 97525-1036, Phone: 541-855-1236, willsknife@gmail.com

Specialties: Carving knives and tools, and some mini wood lathe tools. **Patterns:** Carving, fishing, hunting, skinning, utility, swords and Bowies. **Technical:** Forges and grinds: A2, W1, O1, 5160 and 1095. Offers some filework. **Prices:** $45 and up. **Remarks:** Spare-time maker; first knife made/sold in 1983. One month turnaround on orders. Doing business as Scarrow's Custom Stuff (Gold Hill, OR, USA). Carving knives available at Raven Dog Enterprises. Contact at Ravedog@aol.com. **Mark:** SC with arrow and year made.

SCHALLER, ANTHONY BRETT

5609 Flint Ct. NW, Albuquerque, NM 87120, Phone: 505-899-0155, brett@schallerknives.com; Web: www.schallerknives.com

Specialties: Straight knives and locking-liner folders of his design and in standard patterns. **Patterns:** Boots, fighters, utility knives and folders. **Technical:** Grinds CPM154, S30V, and stainless Damascus. Offers filework, hand-rubbed finishes and full and narrow tangs. Prefers exotic woods or Micarta for handle materials, G-10 and carbon fiber for handle materials. **Prices:** $100 to $350; some to $500. **Remarks:** Part-time maker; first knife sold in 1990. **Mark:** A.B. Schaller - Albuquerque NM - handmade.

SCHEID, MAGGIE

124 Van Stallen St, Rochester, NY 14621-3557

Specialties: Simple working straight knives. **Patterns:** Kitchen and utility knives; some miniatures. **Technical:** Forges 5160 high-carbon steel. **Prices:** $100 to $200. **Remarks:** Part-time maker; first knife sold in 1986. **Mark:** Full name.

SCHEMPP, ED

PO Box 1181, Ephrata, WA 98823, Phone: 509-754-2963, Fax: 509-754-3212, edschempp@yahoo.com

Specialties: Mosaic Damascus and unique folder designs. **Patterns:** Primarily folders. **Technical:** Grinds CPM440V; forges many patterns of mosaic using powdered steel. **Prices:** $100 to $400; some to $2000. **Remarks:** Part-time maker; first knife sold in 1991. Doing business as Ed Schempp Knives. **Mark:** Ed Schempp Knives over five heads of wheat, city and state.

SCHEMPP, MARTIN

PO Box 1181, 5430 Baird Springs Rd NW, Ephrata, WA 98823, Phone: 509-754-2963, Fax: 509-754-3212

Specialties: Fantasy and traditional straight knives of his design, to customer specs and in standard patterns; Paleolithic-styles. **Patterns:** Fighters and Paleolithic designs. **Technical:** Uses opal, Mexican rainbow and obsidian. Offers scrimshaw. **Prices:** $15 to $100; some to $250. **Remarks:** Spare-time maker; first knife sold in 1995. **Mark:** Initials and date.

SCHEURER, ALFREDO E FAES

Av Rincon de los Arcos 104, Col Bosque Res del Sur, Distrito Federal, MEXICO 16010, Phone: 5676 47 63

Specialties: Fancy and fantasy knives of his design. **Patterns:** Daggers. **Technical:** Grinds stainless steel; casts and grinds silver. Sets stones in silver. **Prices:** $2000 to $3000. **Remarks:** Spare-time maker; first knife sold in 1989. **Mark:** Symbol.

SCHIPPNICK, JIM

PO Box 326, Sanborn, NY 14132, Phone: 716-731-3715, ragnar@ragweedforge.com; Web: www.ragweedforge.com

custom knifemakers

Specialties: Nordic, early American, rustic. **Mark:** Runic R. **Remarks:** Also imports Nordic knives from Norway, Sweden and Finland.

SCHLUETER, DAVID
2136 Cedar Gate Rd., Madison Heights, VA 24572, Phone: 434-384-8642, drschlueter@hotmail.com

Specialties: Japanese-style swords. **Patterns:** Larger blades. O-tanto to Tachi, with focus on less common shapes. **Technical:** Forges and grinds carbon steels, heat-treats and polishes own blades, makes all fittings, does own mounting and finishing. **Prices:** Start at $3000. **Remarks:** Sells fully mounted pieces only, doing business as Odd Frog Forge. **Mark:** Full name and date.

SCHMITZ, RAYMOND E
PO Box 1787, Valley Center, CA 92082, Phone: 760-749-4318

SCHNEIDER, CRAIG M
5380 N Amity Rd, Claremont, IL 62421, Phone: 217-377-5715, raephtownslam@att.blackberry.net

Specialties: Straight knives and folders of his own design. **Patterns:** Bowies, hunters, tactical, bird & trout. **Technical:** Forged high-carbon steel and Damascus. Flat grind and differential heat treatment use a wide selection of handle, guard and bolster material, also offers leather sheaths. **Prices:** $150 to $3,500. **Remarks:** Part-time maker; first knife sold in 1985. **Mark:** Stylized initials with Schneider Claremont IL.

SCHNEIDER, HERMAN J.
14084 Apple Valley Rd, Apple Valley, CA 92307, Phone: 760-946-9096

Specialties: Presentation pieces, Fighters, Hunters. **Prices:** Starting at $900. **Mark:** H.J. Schneider-Maker or maker's last name.

SCHOEMAN, CORRIE
Box 28596, Danhof, Free State, SOUTH AFRICA 9310, Phone: 027 51 4363528 Cell: 027 82-3750789, corries@intekom.co.za

Specialties: High-tech folders of his design or to customer's specs. **Patterns:** Linerlock folders and automatics. **Technical:** ATS-34, Damascus or stainless Damascus with titanium frames; prefers exotic materials for handles. **Prices:** $650 to $2000. **Remarks:** Full-time maker; first knife sold in 1984. All folders come with filed liners and back and jeweled inserts. **Mark:** Logo in knife shape engraved on inside of back bar.

SCHOENFELD, MATTHEW A
RR #1, Galiano Island, BC, CANADA V0N 1P0, Phone: 250-539-2806

Specialties: Working knives of his design. **Patterns:** Kitchen cutlery, camp knives, hunters. **Technical:** Grinds 440C. **Prices:** $85 to $500. **Remarks:** Part-time maker; first knife sold in 1978. **Mark:** Signature, Galiano Is. B.C., and date.

SCHOENINGH, MIKE
49850 Miller Rd, North Powder, OR 97867, Phone: 541-856-3239

SCHOLL, TIM
1389 Langdon Rd, Angier, NC 27501, Phone: 910-897-2051, tschollknives@live.com; Web: www.timschollcustomknives.com

Specialties: Fancy and working/using straight knives and folders of his design and to customer specs. **Patterns:** Bowies, hunters, tomahawks, daggers & fantasy knives. **Technical:** Forges high carbon and tool steel makes Damascus, grinds ATS-34 and D2 on request. **Prices:** $150 to $6000. **Remarks:** Part-time maker; first knife sold in 1990. Doing business as Tim Scholl Custom Knives. Member North Carolina Custom Knifemakers Guild. American Bladesmith Society journeyman smith. **Mark:** S pierced by arrow.

SCHORSCH, KENDALL
693 Deer Trail Dr., Jourdanton, TX 78026, Phone: 830-770-0205, schorschknives@gmail.com; Web: www.schorschknives.com

Specialties Slip-joint folders and straight blades. Patterns: Single- and double-blade trappers and straight hunting knives, all with or without filework. **Technical:** Grinds CPM 154, ATS-34, D2 and damascus. **Prices:** $350 to $750 and up. **Remarks:** Full-time maker; first knife sold in 2010. **Mark:** Stamped SCHORSCH on the tang or Schorsch Knives etched in a circle with an Arrow "S" in the center.

SCHOW, LYLE
2103 Ann Ave., Harrisonville, MO 64701, Phone: 816-738-9849, rocktips17@yahoo.com; Web: www.LDknives.com

Specialties: Bowies, hunters, skinners, camp knives and some folders. **Technical:** Forges hunters and big knives, and practices stock-removal method of blade making on small blades. Uses high-carbon steels such as 1075, 1080, 1084, 1095 and W2, makes his own damascus and stainless/high-carbon San Mai steel. **Prices:** $110 to $2,000. **Remarks:** Part-time maker; started making knives in 2009. **Mark:** Maker's initials LDS configured together in the center, with LYLE D. in an arch on the top and SCHOW in an upward arch on the bottom.

SCHRADER, ROBERT
55532 Gross De, Bend, OR 97707, Phone: 541-598-7301

Specialties: Hunting, utility, Bowie. **Patterns:** Fixed blade. **Prices:** $150 to $600.

SCHRAP, ROBERT G
CUSTOM LEATHER KNIFE SHEATH CO., 7024 W Wells St, Wauwatosa, WI 53213-3717, Phone: 414-771-6472 or 414-379-6819, Fax: 414-479-9765, knifesheaths@aol.com; Web: www.customsheaths.com

Specialties: Leather knife sheaths. **Prices:** $38 to $150. **Mark:** Schrap in oval.

SCHREINER, TERRY
4310 W. Beech St., Duncan, OK 73533, Phone: 580-255-4880, Rhino969@hotmail.com

Specialties Hunters, bird-and-trout knives, handforged, one-of-a-kind bowies. Patterns: Hunters and bird-and-trout knives. **Technical:** Stainless damascus, Damasteel, hand-forged carbon damascus and RWL stainless steels, with handle materials mostly natural, including stag, mastodon ivory, horn and wood. **Prices:** $350 to $1,500. **Remarks:** Part-time maker. **Mark:** TerryJack Knives; TSchreiner with interlocking T&S.

SCHROEN, KARL
4042 Bones Rd, Sebastopol, CA 95472, Phone: 707-823-4057, Web: www.schroenknives.com

Specialties: Using knives made to fit. **Patterns:** Sgian dubhs, carving sets, wood-carving knives, fishing knives, kitchen knives and new cleaver design. **Technical:** Forges D2, CPM S30V and 204P. **Prices:** $150 to $6000. **Remarks:** Full-time maker; first knife sold in 1968. Author of The Hand Forged Knife. **Mark:** Last name.

SCHUCHMANN, RICK
1251 Wilson Dunham Hill Rd., New Richmond, OH 45157, Phone: 513-553-4316

Specialties: Replicas of antique and out-of-production Scagels and Randalls, primarily miniatures. **Patterns:** All sheath knives, mostly miniatures, hunting and fighting knives, some daggers and hatchets. **Technical:** Stock removal, 440C and O1 steel. Most knives are flat ground, some convex. **Prices:** $175 to $600 and custom to $4000. **Remarks:** Part-time maker, sold first knife in 1997. Knives on display in the Randall Museum. Sheaths are made exclusively at Sullivan's Holster Shop, Tampa, FL **Mark:** SCAR.

SCHUTTE, NEILL
01 Moffet St., Fichardt Park, Bloemfontein, SOUTH AFRICA 9301, Phone: +27(0) 82 787 3429, neill@schutteknives.co.za; www.schutteknives.co.za

Specialties: Bob Loveless-style knives, George Herron fighters, custom designs and designs/requests from clients. **Technical:** Mainly stock removal of Bohler N690, RWL-34 and ATS-34, if available, blade steels. Uses the materials clients request. **Prices:** $450 to $1,250. **Remarks:** Full-time maker; first knife made at 10 years old, seriously started knifemaking in 2008. **Mark:** Kneeling archer/bowman (maker's surname, Schutte, directly translates to archer or bowman.)

SCHWARTZ, AARON
4745 B Asdee Ln., Woodbridge, VA 22192, Phone: 908-256-3869, big_hammer_forge@yahoo.com; Web: www.bighammerforge.com

Specialties Fantasy custom designs and one-off custom pieces to order. Technical: Stock-removal method of blade making. **Remarks:** Made first knife around eight years ago.

SCHWARZER, LORA SUE
POB 6, Crescent City, FL 32112, Phone: 904-307-0872, auntielora57@yahoo.com

Specialties: Scagel style knives. **Patterns:** Hunters and miniatures **Technical:** Forges 1084 and Damascus. **Prices:** Start at $400. **Remarks:** Part-time maker; first knife sold in 1997. Journeyman Bladesmith, American Bladesmith Society. Now working with Steve Schwarzer on some projects.**Mark:** Full name - JS on reverse side.

SCHWARZER, STEPHEN
POB 6, Crescent City, FL 32112, Phone: 904-307-0872, schwarzeranvil@gmail.com; Web: www.steveschwarzer.com

Specialties: Mosaic Damascus and picture mosaic in folding knives. All Japanese blades are finished working with Wally Hostetter considered the top Japanese lacquer specialist in the U.S.A. Also produces a line of carbon steel skinning knives at $300. **Patterns:** Folders, axes and buckskinner knives. **Technical:** Specializes in picture mosaic Damascus and powder metal mosaic work. Sole authorship; all work including carving done in-house. Most knives have file work and carving. Hand carved steel and precious metal guards. **Prices:** $1500 to $5000, some higher; carbon steel and primitive knives much less. **Remarks:** Full-time maker; first knife sold in 1976, considered by many to be one of the top mosaic Damascus specialists in the world. Mosaic Master level work. I am now working with Lora Schwarzer on some projects. **Mark:** Schwarzer + anvil.

SCIMIO, BILL
4554 Creek Side Ln., Spruce Creek, PA 16683, Phone: 814-632-3751, sprucecreekforge@gmail.com Web: www.sprucecreekforge.com

Specialties: Hand-forged primitive-style knives with curly maple, antler, bone and osage handles.

SCORDIA, PAOLO
Via Terralba 144, Torrimpietra, Roma, ITALY 00050, Phone: 06-61697231, paolo.scordia@uni.net; Web: www.scordia-knives.com

Specialties: Working, fantasy knives, Italian traditional folders and fixed blades of own design. **Patterns:** Any. **Technical:** Forge mosaic Damascus, forge blades, welds own mokume and grinds ATS-34, etc. use hardwoods and Micarta for handles, brass and nickel-silver for fittings. Makes sheaths. **Prices:** $200 to $2000, some to $4000. **Remarks:** Part-time maker; first knife sold in 1988. **Mark:** Sun and moon logo and ititials.

SCROGGS, JAMES A
108 Murray Hill Dr, Warrensburg, MO 64093, Phone: 660-747-2568, jscroggsknives@embarqmail.com

Specialties: Straight knives, prefers light weight. **Patterns:** Hunters, hideouts, and fighters. **Technical:** Grinds CPM-154 stainless plus experiments in steel. Prefers handles of walnut in English, bastonge, American black. Also uses myrtle, maple, Osage orange. **Prices:** $200 to $1000. **Remarks:** 1st knife sold in 1985. Full-time maker. Won "Best Hunter Award" at Branson Hammer-In & Knife Show for 2012 and 2014. **Mark:** SCROGGS in block or script.

SCULLEY, PETER E
340 Sunset Dr, Rising Fawn, GA 30738, Phone: 706-398-0169

SEATON, DAVID D
1028 South Bishop Ave, #237, Rolla, MO 65401, Phone: 573-465-3193, aokcustomknives@gmail.com
Specialties: Gentleman's and Lady's folders. **Patterns:** Liner lock folders of own design and to customer specs, lock backs, slip joints, some stright knives, tactical folders, skinners, fighters, and utility knives. **Technical:** Grinds ATS 34, O1, 1095, 154CM, CPM154, commercial Damascus. Blades are mostly flat ground, some hollow ground. Does own heat treating, tempering, and Nitre Bluing. Prefers natural handle materials such as ivory, mother of pearl, bone, and exotic woods, some use of G10 and micarta on hard use knives. Use gem stones, gold, silver on upscale knives, offers some carving, filework, and engrving. **Prices:** $150 to $600 avg; some to $1500 and up depending on materials and embellishments. **Remarks:** First knife sold in 2002, part-time maker, doing business at AOK Custom Knives. **Mark:** full or last name engraved on blade.

SEIB, STEVE
7914 Old State Road, Evansville, IN 47710, Phone: 812-867-2231, sseib@insightbb.com
Specialties: Working straight knives. **Pattern:** Skinners, hunters, bowies and camp knives. **Technical:** Forges high-carbon and makes own damascus. **Remarks:** Part-time maker. ABS member. **Mark:** Last name.

SELF, ERNIE
950 O'Neill Ranch Rd, Dripping Springs, TX 78620-9760, Phone: 512-940-7134, ernieself@yahoo.com
Specialties: Traditional and working straight knives and folders of his design and in standard patterns. **Patterns:** Hunters, locking folders and slip-joints. **Technical:** Grinds 440C, D2, 440V, ATS-34 and Damascus. Offers fancy filework. **Prices:** $250 to $1000; some to $2500. **Remarks:** Full-time maker; first knife sold in 1982. Also customizes Buck 110's and 112's folding hunters. **Mark:** In oval shape - Ernie Self Maker Dripping Springs TX.

SELLEVOLD, HARALD
PO Box 4134, Sandviken S Kleivesmau:2, Bergen, NORWAY N5835, Phone: 47 55-310682, haraldsellevold@gmail.com; Web:knivmakeren.com
Specialties: Norwegian-styles; collaborates with other Norse craftsmen. **Patterns:** Distinctive ferrules and other mild modifications of traditional patterns; Bowies and friction folders. **Technical:** Buys Damascus blades; blacksmiths his own blades. Semi-gemstones used in handles; gemstone inlay. **Prices:** $350 to $2000. **Remarks:** Full-time maker; first knife sold in 1980. **Mark:** Name and country in logo.

SELZAM, FRANK
Martin Reinhard Str 23, Bad Koenigshofen, GERMANY 97631, Phone: 09761-5980, frankselzam.de
Specialties: Hunters, working knives to customers specs, hand tooled and stitched leather sheaths large stock of wood and German stag horn. **Patterns:** Mostly own design. **Technical:** Forged blades, own Damascus, also stock removal stainless. **Prices:** $250 to $1500. **Remarks:** First knife sold in 1978. **Mark:** Last name stamped.

SENTZ, MARK C
4084 Baptist Rd, Taneytown, MD 21787, Phone: 410-756-2018
Specialties: Fancy straight working knives of his design. **Patterns:** Hunters, fighters, folders and utility/camp knives. **Technical:** Forges 1085, 1095, 5160, 5155 and his Damascus. Most knives come with wood-lined leather sheath or wooden presentation sheath. **Prices:** Start at $275. **Remarks:** Full-time maker; first knife sold in 1989. Doing business as M. Charles Sentz Gunsmithing, Inc. **Mark:** Last name.

SERAFEN, STEVEN E
24 Genesee St, New Berlin, NY 13411, Phone: 607-847-6903
Specialties: Traditional working/using straight knives of his design and to customer specs. **Patterns:** Bowies, fighters, hunters. **Technical:** Grinds ATS-34, 440C, high-carbon steel. **Prices:** $175 to $600; some to $1200. **Remarks:** Part-time maker; first knife sold in 1990. **Mark:** First and middle initial, last name in script.

SEVECEK, PAVEL
Lhota u Konice 7, BRODEK U KONICE, 79845 CZECH REPUBLIC, Phone: 00420 603 545333, seva.noze@seznam.cz; Web: www.sevaknives.cz
Specialties Production of handforged mosaic damascus knives, all including the plastic engravings and sheaths of his own exclusive work. **Prices:** $800 and up. **Remarks:** First knife sold in 2001. **Mark:** Logo SP in blade.

SEVEY CUSTOM KNIFE
94595 Chandler Rd, Gold Beach, OR 97444, Phone: 541-247-2649, sevey@charter.net; Web: www.seveyknives.com
Specialties: Fixed blade hunters. **Patterns:** Drop point, trailing paint, clip paint, full tang, hidden tang. **Technical:** D-2, and ATS-34 blades, stock removal. Heat treatment by Paul Bos. **Prices:** $225 and up depending on overall length and grip material. **Mark:** Sevey Custom Knife.

SEWARD, BEN
471 Dogwood Ln., Austin, AR 72007, Phone: 501-416-1543, sewardsteel@gmail.com; Web: www.bensewardknives.com
Specialties: Forged blades, mostly bowies and fighters. **Technical:** Forges high-carbon steels such as 1075 and W2. **Remarks:** First knife made in 2005; ABS journeyman smith and member Arkansas Knifemakers Association.

SFREDDO, RODRIGO MENEZES
Rua 7 De Setembro 66 Centro, Nova Petropolis, RS, BRAZIL 95150-000, Phone: 011-55-54-303-303-90, r.sfreddoknives@gmail.com; www.sbcutelaria.org.br
Specialties: Integrals, bowies, hunters, dirks & swords. **Patterns:** Forges his own Damascus and 52100 steel. **Technical:** Specialized in integral knives and Damascus. **Prices:**

From $350 and up. Most around $750 to $1000. **Remarks:** Considered by many to be the Brazil's best bladesmith. ABS SBC Member. **Mark:** S. Sfreddo on the left side of the blade.

SHADLEY, EUGENE W
209 NW 17th Street, Grand Rapids, MN 55744, Phone: 218-999-7197 or 218-244-8628, Fax: call first, ShadleyKnives@hotmail.com
Specialties: Gold frames are available on some models. **Patterns:** Whittlers, stockman, sowbelly, congress, trapper, etc. **Technical:** Grinds ATS-34, 416 frames. **Prices:** Starts at $600, some models up to $15,000. **Remarks:** Full-time maker; first knife sold in 1985. Doing business as Shadley Knives. **Mark:** Last name.

SHADMOT, BOAZ
MOSHAV PARAN D N, Arava, ISRAEL 86835, srb@arava.co.il

SHARP, DAVID
17485 Adobe St., Hesperia, CA 92345, Phone: 520-370-1899, sharpwerks@gmail.com or david@sharpwerks.com; Web: www.sharpwerks.com
Specialties: Fixed blades. **Patterns:** Original and real Loveless pattern utilities, hunters and fighters. **Technical:** Stock removal, tool steel and stainless steel, hollow grind, machine finish, full polish, various handle materials. **Prices:** $300 to $1,500. **Remarks:** Part-time maker, first knife sold in 2011. **Mark:** "Sharpwerks" on original designs; "D. Sharp" on Loveless designs.

SHARRIGAN, MUDD
111 Bradford Rd, Wiscasset, ME 04578-4457, Phone: 207-882-9820, Fax: 207-882-9835
Specialties: Custom designs; repair straight knives, custom leather sheaths. **Patterns:** Daggers, fighters, hunters, crooked knives and seamen working knives; traditional Scandinavian-styles. **Technical:** Forges 1095, 5160, and W2. **Prices:** $50 to $325; some to $1200. **Remarks:** Full-time maker; first knife sold in 1982. **Mark:** Swallow tail carving. Mudd engraved.

SHEEHY, THOMAS J
4131 NE 24th Ave, Portland, OR 97211-6411, Phone: 503-493-2843
Specialties: Hunting knives and ulus. **Patterns:** Own or customer designs. **Technical:** 1095/01 and ATS-34 steel. **Prices:** $35 to $200. **Remarks:** Do own heat treating; forged or ground blades. **Mark:** Name.

SHEELY, "BUTCH" FOREST
15784 Custar Rd., Grand Rapids, OH 43522, Phone: 419-308-3471, sheelyblades@gmail.com
Specialties: Traditional bowies and pipe tomahawks. **Patterns:** Bowies, hunters, integrals, dirks, axes and hawks. **Technical:** Forges 5160, 52100, 1084, 1095, and Damascus.**Prices:** $150 to $1500;**Remarks:** Full-time bladesmith part-time blacksmith; first knife sold in 1982. ABS Journeysmith, sole author of all knives and hawks including hand sewn leather sheaths, doing business as Beaver Creek Forge. **Mark:** First and last name above Bladesmith.

SHEETS, STEVEN WILLIAM
6 Stonehouse Rd, Mendham, NJ 07945, Phone: 201-543-5882

SHIFFER, STEVE
PO Box 471, Leakesville, MS 39451, Phone: 601-394-4425, aiifish2@yahoo.com; Web: wwwchoctawplantationforge.com
Specialties: Bowies, fighters, hard use knives. **Patterns:** Fighters, hunters, combat/utility knives. Walker pattern LinerLock® folders. Allen pattern scale and bolster release autos. **Technical:** Most work forged, stainless stock removal. Makes own Damascus. O1 and 5160 most used also 1084, 154cm, s30v. **Prices:** $125 to $1000. **Remarks:** First knife sold in 2000, all heat treatment done by maker. Doing business as Choctaw Plantation Forge. **Mark:** Hot mark sunrise over creek.

SHIGENO, MAMORU
2-12-3 Hirosehigashi, Sayama-shi, Saitama, 350-1320, JAPAN, shigeno-knife@tbc.t-com.ne.jp; Web: http://www2.tbb.t-com.ne.jp/shigeno-knife/
Specialties: Fixed blades. **Patterns:** Hunters, boot knives, fighters, including most Loveless patterns, bowies and others. **Technical:** Stock removal of ATS-34. **Prices:** $700 to $3,000 and up. **Remarks:** Full-time maker; first knife sold in 2003. **Mark:** SHIGENO (last name).

SHINOSKY, ANDY
3117 Meanderwood Dr, Canfield, OH 44406, Phone: 330-702-0299, andrew@shinosky.com; Web: www.shinosky.com
Specialties: Collectable folders and interframes. **Patterns:** Drop point, spear point, trailing point, daggers. **Technical:** Grinds ATS-34 and Damascus. Prefers natural handle materials. Most knives are engraved by Andy himself. **Prices:** Start at $800. **Remarks:** Part-time maker/engraver. First knife sold in 1992. **Mark:** Name.

SHINOZAKI, AKIO
24-10 Jyouseigaoka 2-chome, Munakata-city, Fukuoka-ken, JAPAN 811-3404, Phone: 81-940-32-6768, shinozakiknife4152@ab.auone-net.jp
Specialties: One-of-a-kind straight knives and locking folders. **Patterns:** Hunters, skinners, bowies and utility knives of maker's own design and to customer's specifications. **Technical:** Stock removal method of blade making using ATS-34, CPM S30V, CV134 and SPG2 steels, mirror polishes. Handle materials are stag, exotic woods, Micarta and mammoth ivory. **Prices:** $350 to $800, with bowies and fighters starting at $1,200 and up. **Remarks:** Full-time maker; first knife sold in 1987. **Mark:** Akio S or Akio Shinozaki.

SHIPLEY, STEVEN A
800 Campbell Rd Ste 137, Richardson, TX 75081, Phone: 972-644-7981, Fax: 972-644-7985, steve@shipleysphotography.com

custom knifemakers

Specialties: Hunters, skinners and traditional straight knives. **Technical:** Hand grinds ATS-34, 440C and Damascus steels. Each knife is custom sheathed by his son, Dan. **Prices:** $175 to $2000. **Remarks:** Part-time maker; like smooth lines and unusual handle materials. **Mark:** S A Shipley.

SHOEMAKER, CARROLL
380 Yellowtown Rd, Northup, OH 45658, Phone: 740-446-6695
Specialties: Working/using straight knives of his design. **Patterns:** Hunters, utility/camp and early American backwoodsmen knives. **Technical:** Grinds ATS-34; forges old files, 01 and 1095. Uses some Damascus; offers scrimshaw and engraving. **Prices:** $100 to $175; some to $350. **Remarks:** Spare-time maker; first knife sold in 1977. **Mark:** Name and city or connected initials.

SHOEMAKER, SCOTT
316 S Main St, Miamisburg, OH 45342, Phone: 513-859-1935
Specialties: Twisted, wire-wrapped handles on swords, fighters and fantasy blades; new line of seven models with quick-draw, multi-carry Kydex sheaths. **Patterns:** Bowies, boots and one-of-a-kinds in his design or to customer specs. **Technical:** Grinds A6 and ATS-34; buys Damascus. Hand satin finish is standard. **Prices:** $100 to $1500; swords to $8000. **Remarks:** Part-time maker; first knife sold in 1984. **Mark:** Angel wings with last initial, or last name.

SHOGER, MARK O
POB 778, Kalama, WA 98625, Phone: 503-816-8615, mosdds@msn.com
Specialties: Working and using straight knives and folders of his design; fancy and embellished knives. **Patterns:** Hunters, Bowies, daggers and folders. **Technical:** Forges 01, W2, 1084, 5160, 52100 and 1084/15n20 pattern weld. **Remarks:** Spare-time maker. **Mark:** Last name "Shoger" or stamped last initial over anvil.

SHROPSHIRE, SHAWN
PO Box 453, Piedmont, OK 73078, Phone: 405-833-5239, shawn@sdsknifeworks.com; Web: www.sdsknifeworks.com
Specialties: Working straight knives and frontier style period pieces. **Patterns:** Bowies, hunters, skinners, fighters, patch/neck knives. **Technical:** Grinds D2, 154CM and some Damascus, forges 1084, 5160. **Prices:** Starting at $125. **Remarks:** Part-time maker; first knife sold in 1997. Doing business at SDS Knifeworks. **Mark:** Etched "SDS Knifeworks - Oklahoma" in an oval or "SDS" tang stamp.

SHULL, JAMES
5146 N US 231 W, Rensselaer, IN 47978, Phone: 219-866-0436, nbjs@netnitco.net Web: www.shullhandforgedknives.com
Specialties: Working knives of hunting, fillet, Bowie patterns. **Technical:** Forges or uses 1095, 5160, 52100 & 01. **Prices:** $100 to $300. **Remarks:** DBA Shull Handforged Knives. **Mark:** Last name in arc.

SIBERT, SHANE
PO BOX 241, Gladstone, OR 97027, Phone: 503-650-2082, shane.sibert@comcast.net Web: www.sibertknives.com
Specialties: Innovative knives designed for hostile environments, lightweight hiking and backpacking knives for outdoorsman and adventurers, progressive fixed blade combat and fighting knives. One-of-a-kind knives of various configurations. Titanium frame lock folders. **Patterns:** Modern configurations of utility/camp knives, bowies, modified spear points, daggers, tantos, recurves, clip points and spine serrations. **Technical:** Stock removal. Specializes in CPM S30V, CPM S35VN, CPM D2, CPM 3V, stainless damascus. Micarta, G-10, stabilized wood and titanium. **Prices:** $200 - $1000, some pieces $1500 and up. **Remarks:** Full-time maker, first knife sold in 1994. **Mark:** Stamped "SIBERT" and occasionally uses electro-etch with oval around last name.

SIBRIAN, AARON
4308 Dean Dr, Ventura, CA 93003, Phone: 805-642-6950
Specialties: Tough working knives of his design and in standard patterns. **Patterns:** Makes a "Viper utility"—a kukri derivative and a variety of straight using knives. **Technical:** Grinds 440C and ATS-34. Offers traditional Japanese blades; soft backs, hard edges, temper lines. **Prices:** $60 to $100; some to $250. **Remarks:** Spare-time maker; first knife sold in 1989. **Mark:** Initials in diagonal line.

SIMMONS, H R
1100 Bay City Rd, Aurora, NC 27806, Phone: 252-916-2241
Specialties: Working/using straight knives of his design. **Patterns:** Fighters, hunters and utility/camp knives. **Technical:** Forges and grinds Damascus and L6; grinds ATS-34. **Prices:** $150 and up. **Remarks:** Part-time maker; first knife sold in 1987. Doing business as HRS Custom Knives, Royal Forge and Trading Company. **Mark:** HRS.

SIMONELLA, GIANLUIGI
Via Battiferri 33, Maniago, ITALY 33085, Phone: 01139-427-730350
Specialties: Traditional and classic folding and working/using knives of his design and to customer specs. **Patterns:** Bowies, fighters, hunters, utility/camp knives. **Technical:** Forges ATS-34, D2, 440C. **Prices:** $250 to $400; some to $1000. **Remarks:** Full-time maker; first knife sold in 1988. **Mark:** Wilson.

SINCLAIR, J E
520 Francis Rd, Pittsburgh, PA 15239, Phone: 412-793-5778
Specialties: Fancy hunters and fighters, liner locking folders. **Patterns:** Fighters, hunters and folders. **Technical:** Flat-grinds and hollow grind, prefers hand rubbed satin finish. Uses natural handle materials. **Prices:** $185 to $800. **Remarks:** Part-time maker; first knife sold in 1995. **Mark:** First and middle initials, last name and maker.

SINYARD, CLESTON S
27522 Burkhardt Dr, Elberta, AL 36530, Phone: 334-987-1361, nimoforge1@gulftel.com; Web: www.knifemakersguild
Specialties: Working straight knives and folders of his design. **Patterns:** Hunters, buckskinners, Bowies, daggers, fighters and all-Damascus folders. **Technical:** Makes Damascus from 440C, stainless steel, D2 and regular high-carbon steel; forges "forefinger pad" into hunters and skinners. **Prices:** In Damascus $450 to $1500; some $2500. **Remarks:** Full-time maker; first knife sold in 1980. Doing business as Nimo Forge. **Mark:** Last name, U.S.A. in anvil.

SIROIS, DARRIN
Tactical Combat Tools, 6182 Lake Trail Dr., Fayetteville, NC 28304, Phone: 910-730-0536, knives@tctknives.com; www.tctknives.com
Specialties: Tactical fighters, hunters and camp knives. **Technical:** Stock removal method of blade making, using D2 and 154CM steels. Entire process, including heat treat, done in-house. **Prices:** $80 to $750. **Remarks:** Part-time maker; first knife sold in 2008. **Mark:** Letters TCT surrounded by a triangle, or "Delta Tactical Combat Tools."

SISKA, JIM
48 South Maple St, Westfield, MA 01085, Phone: 413-642-3059, siskaknives@comcast.net
Specialties: Traditional working straight knives, no folders. **Patterns:** Hunters, fighters, Bowies and one-of-a-kinds; folders. **Technical:** Grinds D2, A2, 154CM and ATS-34, buys damascus and forges some blades. Likes exotic woods. **Prices:** $300 and up. **Remarks:** Part-time. **Mark:** Siska in Old English, or for forged blades, a hammer over maker's name.

SJOSTRAND, KEVIN
1541 S Cain St, Visalia, CA 93292, Phone: 559-625-5254
Specialties: Traditional and working/using straight knives and folders of his design or to customer specs. **Patterns:** Fixed blade hunters, Bowies, utility/camp knives. **Technical:** Grinds ATS-34, 440C and 1095. Prefers high polished blades and full tang. Natural and stabilized hardwoods, Micarta and stag handle material. **Prices:** $250 to $400. **Remarks:** Part-time maker; first knife sold in 1992. **Mark:** SJOSTRAND

SKIFF, STEVEN
SKIFF MADE BLADES, PO Box 537, Broadalbin, NY 12025, Phone: 518-883-4875, skiffmadeblades @hotmail.com; Web: www.skiffmadeblades.com
Specialties: Custom using/collector grade straight blades and LinerLock® folders of maker's design or customer specifications. **Patterns:** Hunters, utility/camp knives, tactical/fancy art folders. **Prices:** Straight blades $225 and up. Folders $450 and up. **Technical:** Stock removal hollow ground ATS-34, 154 CM, S30V, and tool steel. Damascus-Devon Thomas, Robert Eggerling, Mike Norris and Delbert Ealy. Nickel silver and stainless in-house heat treating. Handle materials: man made and natural woods (stabilized). Horn shells sheaths for straight blades, sews own leather and uses sheaths by "Tree-Stump Leather." **Remarks:** First knife sold 1997. Started making folders in 2000. **Mark:** SKIFF on blade of straight blades and in inside of backspacer on folders.

SLEE, FRED
9 John St, Morganville, NJ 07751, Phone: 732-591-9047
Specialties: Working straight knives, some fancy, to customer specs. **Patterns:** Hunters, fighters, fancy daggers and folders. **Technical:** Grinds D2, 440C and ATS-34. **Prices:** $285 to $1100. **Remarks:** Part-time maker; first knife sold in 1980. **Mark:** Letter "S" in Old English.

SLOAN, DAVID
PO BOX 83, Diller, NE 68342, Phone: 402-793-5755, sigp22045@hotmail.com
Specialties: Hunters, choppers and fighters. **Technical:** Forged blades of W2, 1084 and Damascus. **Prices:** Start at $225. **Remarks:** Part-time maker, made first knife in 2002, received JS stamp 2010. **Mark:** Sloan JS.

SLOAN, SHANE
4226 FM 61, Newcastle, TX 76372, Phone: 940-846-3290
Specialties: Collector-grade straight knives and folders. **Patterns:** Uses stainless Damascus, ATS-34 and 12C27. Bowies, lockers, slip-joints, fancy folders, fighters and period pieces. **Technical:** Grinds D2 and ATS-34. Uses hand-rubbed satin finish. Prefers rare natural handle materials. **Prices:** $250 to $6500. **Remarks:** Full-time maker; first knife sold in 1985. **Mark:** Name and city.

SLOBODIAN, SCOTT
PO Box 1498, San Andreas, CA 95249, Phone: 209-286-1980, Fax: 209-286-1982, info@slobodianswords.com; Web: www.slobodianswords.com
Specialties: Japanese-style knives and swords, period pieces, fantasy pieces and miniatures. **Patterns:** Small kweikens, tantos, wakazashis, katanas, traditional samurai swords. **Technical:** Flat-grinds 1050, commercial Damascus. **Prices:** Prices start at $1500. **Remarks:** Full-time maker; first knife sold in 1987. **Mark:** Blade signed in Japanese characters and various scripts.

SMALE, CHARLES J
509 Grove Ave, Waukegan, IL 60085, Phone: 847-244-8013

SMALL, ED
Rt 1 Box 178-A, Keyser, WV 26726, Phone: 304-298-4254, coldanvil@gmail.com
Specialties: Working knives of his design; period pieces. **Patterns:** Hunters, daggers, buckskinners and camp knives; likes one-of-a-kinds, very primitive bowies. **Technical:** Forges and grinds W2, L6 and his own Damascus. **Prices:** $150 to $1500. **Remarks:** Full-time maker; first knife sold in 1978. **Mark:** Script initials connected.

SMART, STEVE
907 Park Row Cir, McKinney, TX 75070-3847, Phone: 214-882-0441, Fax: 972-548-7151
Specialties: Working/using straight knives and folders of his design, to customer specs

and in standard patterns. **Patterns:** Bowies, hunters, kitchen knives, locking folders, utility/camp, fishing and bird knives. **Technical:** Grinds ATS-34, D2, 440C and O1. Prefers mirror polish or satin finish; hollow-grinds all blades. All knives come with sheath. Offers some filework. **Prices:** $95 to $225; some to $500. **Remarks:** Spare-time maker; first knife sold in 1983. **Mark:** Name, Custom, city and state in oval.

SMIT, GLENN

627 Cindy Ct, Aberdeen, MD 21001, Phone: 410-272-2959, wolfsknives@comcast. net; Web: www.facebook.com/Wolf'sKnives

    Specialties: Working and using straight and folding knives of his design or to customer specs. Customizes and repairs all types of cutlery. Exclusive maker of Dave Murphy Style knives. **Patterns:** Hunters, Bowies, daggers, fighters, utility/camp, folders, kitchen knives and miniatures, Murphy combat, C.H.A.I.K., Little 88 and Tiny 90-styles. **Technical:** Grinds 440C, ATS-34, O1, A2 also grinds 6AL4V titanium allox for blades. Reforges commercial Damascus and makes cast aluminum handles. **Prices:** Miniatures start at $50; full-size knives start at $100. **Remarks:** Spare-time maker; first knife sold in 1986. Doing business as Wolf's Knives. **Mark:** G.P. SMIT, with year on reverse side, Wolf's Knives-Murphy's way with date.

SMITH, CHRIS

POB 351, Burgin, KY 40310, Phone: 859-948-1505, fireman6152000@yahoo.com; Web: Facebook.com: CS&Sons

    Technical: Stock removal method of blade making using mainly simple carbon steels like 1080, 1084, 5160 and some damascus, has done a few forged knives. **Prices:** $100 to $500. **Remarks:** Part-time maker since June of 2014. **Mark:** Maker's initials in his own cursive script, the same way he has signed his work since he was in art class in elementary school.

SMITH, J D

22 Ledge St., Melrose, MA 02176, Phone: 857-492-5324, mamboslave@yahoo.com

    Specialties: Fighters, Bowies, Persian, locking folders and swords. **Patterns:** Bowies, fighters and locking folders. **Technical:** Forges and grinds D2, his Damascus, O1, 52100 etc. and wootz-pattern hammer steel. **Prices:** $500 to $2000; some to $5000. **Remarks:** Full-time maker; first knife sold in 1987. Doing business as Hammersmith. **Mark:** Last initial alone in cartouche.

SMITH, J.B.

21 Copeland Rd., Perkinston, MS 39573, Phone: 228-380-1851

    Specialties: Traditional working knives for the hunter and fisherman. **Patterns:** Hunters, Bowies, and fishing knives; copies of 1800 period knives. **Technical:** Grinds ATS-34, 440C. **Prices:** $100 to $800. **Remarks:** Full-time maker, first knife sold in 1972. **Mark:** J.B. Smith MAKER PERKINSTON, MS.

SMITH, JERRY W.

Jerry W. Smith Knives, 1950 CR 5120, Willow Springs, MO 65793, Phone: 417-252-7463, jwdeb93@gmail.com; Web: www.jerrywsmith.com

    Specialties: Loveless-style knives, folders/slip joints. **Patterns:** Sway backs and drop-point hunters. **Technical:** Steels used D2, A2, O1, 154CM and CPM 154. Stock removal, heat treat in house, all leather work in house. **Prices:** Start at $200. **Remarks:** Full-time knifemaker. First knife made in 2004. **Mark:** Jerry W Smith USA.

SMITH, JOHN M

3450 E Beguelin Rd, Centralia, IL 62801, Phone: 618-249-6444, jknife@frontiernet.net

    Specialties: Folders. **Patterns:** Folders. **Prices:** $250 to $2500. **Remarks:** First knife sold in 1980. Not taking orders at this time on fixed blade knives. Part-time maker. **Mark:** Etched signature or logo.

SMITH, JOHN W

1322 Cow Branch Rd, West Liberty, KY 41472, Phone: 606-743-3599, jwsknive@mrtc.com; Web: www.jwsmithknives.com

    Specialties: Fancy and working locking folders of his design or to customer specs. **Patterns:** Interframes, traditional and daggers. **Technical:** Grinds 530V and his own Damascus. Offers gold inlay, engraving with gold inlay, hand-fitted mosaic pearl inlay and filework. Prefers hand-rubbed finish. Pearl and ivory available. **Prices:** Utility pieces $375 to $650. Art knives $1200 to $10,000. **Remarks:** Full-time maker. **Mark:** Initials engraved inside diamond.

SMITH, JOSH

Box 753, Frenchtown, MT 59834, Phone: 406-626-5775, joshsmithknives@gmail. com; Web: www.joshsmithknives.com

    Specialties: Mosaic, Damascus, LinerLock folders, automatics, Bowies, fighters, etc. **Patterns:** All kinds. **Technical:** Advanced Mosaic and Damascus. **Prices:** $450 and up. **Remarks:** A.B.S. Master Smith. **Mark:** Josh Smith with last two digits of the current year.

SMITH, LACY

PO BOX 188, Jacksonville, AL 36265, Phone: 256-310-4619, sales@smith-knives. com; Web: www.smith-knives.com

    Specialties: All styles of fixed-blade knives. **Technical:** Stock removal method of blade making. **Prices:** $100 and up. **Mark:** Circle with three dots and three S's on inside.

SMITH, LENARD C

PO Box D68, Valley Cottage, NY 10989, Phone: 914-268-7359

SMITH, MICHAEL J

1418 Saddle Gold Ct, Brandon, FL 33511, Phone: 813-431-3790, smithknife@hotmail.com; Web: www.smithknife.com

    Specialties: Fancy high art folders of his design. **Patterns:** Locking locks and automatics. **Technical:** Uses ATS-34, non-stainless and stainless Damascus; hand carves folders, prefers ivory and pearl. Hand-rubbed satin finish. Liners are 6AL4V titanium. **Prices:** $500 to $3000. **Remarks:** Full-time maker; first knife sold in 1989. **Mark:** Name, city, state.

SMITH, NEWMAN L.

865 Glades Rd Shop #3, Gatlinburg, TN 37738, Phone: 423-436-3322, thesmithshop@aol.com; Web: www.thesmithsshop.com

    Specialties: Collector-grade and working knives. **Patterns:** Hunters, slip-joint and lock-back folders, some miniatures. **Technical:** Grinds O1 and ATS-34; makes fancy sheaths. **Prices:** $165 to $750; some to $1000. **Remarks:** Full-time maker; first knife sold in 1984. Partners part-time to handle Damascus blades by Jeff Hurst; marks these with SH connected. **Mark:** First and middle initials, last name.

SMITH, RALPH L

525 Groce Meadow Rd, Taylors, SC 29687, Phone: 864-444-0819, ralph_smith1@charter.net; Web: www.smithhandcraftedknives.com

    Specialties: Working knives: straight and folding knives. Hunters, skinners, fighters, bird, boot, Bowie and kitchen knives. **Technical:** Concave Grind D2, ATS 34, 440C, steel hand finish or polished. **Prices:** $125 to $350 for standard models. **Remarks:** First knife sold in 1976. KMG member since 1981. SCAK founding member and past president. **Mark:** SMITH handcrafted knives in SC state outline.

SMITH, RAYMOND L

217 Red Chalk Rd, Erin, NY 14838, Phone: 607-795-5257, Bladesmith@wildblue.net; Web: www.theanvilsedge.com

    Specialties: Working/using straight knives and folders to customer specs and in standard patterns; period pieces. **Patterns:** Bowies, hunters, slip joints. **Technical:** Forges 5160, 52100, 1018, 15N20, 1084, ATS 34. Damascus and wire cable Damascus. Filework. **Prices:** $125 to $1500; estimates for custom orders. **Remarks:** Full-time maker; first knife sold in 1991. ABS Master Smith. Doing business as The Anvils Edge. **Mark:** Ellipse with RL Smith, Erin NY MS in center.

SMITH, RICK

BEAR BONE KNIVES, 1843 W Evans Creek Rd., Rogue River, OR 97537, Phone: 541-582-4144, BearBoneSmith@msn.com; Web: www.bearbone.com

    Specialties: Classic, historical style Bowie knives, hunting knives and various contemporary knife styles. **Technical:** Blades are either forged or made by stock removal method depending on steel used. Also forge weld wire Damascus. Does own heat treating and tempering using digital even heat kiln. Stainless blades are sent out for cryogenic "freeze treat." Preferred steels are O1, tool, 5160, 1095, 1084, ATS-34, 154CM, 440C and various high carbon Damascus. **Prices:** $350 to $1500. Custom leather sheaths available for knives. **Remarks:** Full-time maker since 1997. Serial numbers no longer put on knives. Official business name is "Bear Bone Knives." **Mark:** Early maker's mark was "Bear Bone" over capital letters "RS" with downward arrow between letters and "Hand Made" underneath letters. Mark on small knives is 3/8 circle containing "RS" with downward arrow between letters. Current mark since 2003 is "R Bear Bone Smith" arching over image of coffin Bowie knife with two shooting stars and "Rogue River, Oregon" underneath.

SMITH, SHAWN

2644 Gibson Ave, Clouis, CA 93611, Phone: 559-323-6234, kslc@sbcglobal.net

    Specialties: Working and fancy straight knives. **Patterns:** Hunting, trout, fighters, skinners. **Technical:** Hollow grinds ATS-34, 154CM, A-2. **Prices:** $150.00 and up. **Remarks:** Part time maker. **Mark:** Shawn Smith handmade.

SMITH, STUART

Smith Hand Forged Knives, 32 Elbon Rd., Blairgowrie, Gauteng, SOUTH AFRICA 2123, Phone: +27 84 248 1324, samuraistu@forgedknives.co.za; www.forgedknives. co.za

    Specialties: Hand-forged bowie knives and puukos in high-carbon steel and maker's own damascus. **Patterns:** Bowies, puukos, daggers, hunters, fighters, skinners and swords. **Technical:** Forges 5160, 1070, 52100 and SilverSteel, and maker's own damascus from 5160 and Bohler K600 nickel tool steel. Fitted guards and threaded pommels. Own heat treating. Wood and bronze carving. Own sheaths and custom sheaths. **Prices:** $150 to $1,500. **Remarks:** Full-time maker since 2004; first knife sold in 2000. **Mark:** Stamped outline of an anvil with SMITH underneath on right side of knife. For 2014, anvil and surname with 10Yrs.

SMOCK, TIMOTHY E

1105 N Sherwood Dr, Marion, IN 46952, Phone: 765-664-0123

SNODY, MIKE

910 W. Young Ave., Aransas Pass, TX 78336, Phone: 361-443-0161, snodyknives@yahoo.com; Web: www.snodygallery.com

    Specialties: High performance straight knives in traditional and Japanese-styles. **Patterns:** Skinners, hunters, tactical, Kwaiken and tantos. **Technical:** Grinds BG42, ATS-34, 440C and A2. Offers full or tapered tangs, upgraded handle materials such as fossil ivory, coral and exotic woods. Traditional diamond wrap over stingray on Japanese-style knives. Sheaths available in leather or Kydex. **Prices:** $100 to $1000. **Remarks:** Part-time maker; first knife sold in 1999. **Mark:** Name over knife maker.

SNOW, BILL

4824 18th Ave, Columbus, GA 31904, Phone: 706-576-4390, tipikw@knology.net

    Specialties: Traditional working/using straight knives and folders of his design and to customer specs. Offers engraving and scrimshaw. **Patterns:** Bowies, fighters, hunters and folders. **Technical:** Grinds ATS-34, 440V, 440C, 420V, CPM350, BG42, A2, D2, 5160, 52100 and O1; forges if needed. Cryogenically quenches all steels; inlaid handles; some integrals; leather or Kydex sheaths. **Prices:** $125 to $700; some to $3500. **Remarks:** Now also have 530V, 10V and 3V steels in use. Full-time maker; first knife sold in 1958. Doing business as Tipi Knife works. **Mark:** Old English scroll "S" inside a tipi.

SOAPER, MAX H.
2375 Zion Rd, Henderson, KY 42420, Phone: 270-827-8143
Specialties: Primitive Longhunter knives, scalpers, camp knives, cowboy Bowies, neck knives, working knives, period pieces from the 18th century. **Technical:** Forges 5160, 1084, 1095; all blades differentially heat treated. **Prices:** $80 to $800. **Remarks:** Part-time maker since 1989. **Mark:** Initials in script.

SOILEAU, DAMON
POB 7292, Kingsport, TN 37664, Phone: 423-297-4665, oiseaumetalarts@gmail.com; Web: www.oiseaumetalarts.etsy.com
Specialties: Natural and exotic materials, slip-joint folders, fixed blades, hidden tang and full tang, hand engraving. **Patterns:** Slip-joint folders, hunters, skinners and art knives. **Technical:** Stock removal of damascus, forges W2, O1 and 1084. **Prices:** $150 to $2,000. **Remarks:** Full-time maker and hand engraver. **Mark:** Hand engraved last name on spine of blade, or inside back spring of folders.

SONNTAG, DOUGLAS W
902 N 39th St, Nixa, MO 65714, Phone: 417-693-1640, dougsonntag@gmail.com
Specialties: Working knives; art knives. **Patterns:** Hunters, boots, straight working knives; Bowies, some folders, camp/axe sets. **Technical:** Grinds D2, ATS-34, forges own Damascus; does own heat treating. **Prices:** $225 and up. **Remarks:** Full-time maker; first knife sold in 1986. **Mark:** Etched name in arch.

SONNTAG, JACOB D
14148 Trisha Dr., St. Robert, MO 65584, Phone: 573-336-4082, Jake0372@live.com
Specialties: Working knives, some art knives. **Patterns:** Hunters, bowies, and tomahawks. **Technical:** Grinds D2, ATS34 and Damascus. Forges some Damascus and tomahawks; does own heat treating. **Prices:** $200 and up. **Remarks:** Part-time maker; first knife sold in 2010. **Mark:** Etched name or stamped

SONNTAG, KRISTOPHER D
902 N 39th St, Nixa, MO 65714, Phone: 417-838-8327, kriss@buildit.us
Specialties: Working fixed blades, hunters, skinners, using knives. **Patterns:** Hunters, bowies, skinners. **Technical:** Grinds D2, ATS 34, Damascus. Makes some Damascus; does own heat treating. **Prices:** $200 and up.**Remarks:** Part-time maker; first knife sold in 2010. **Mark:** Etched name or stamped

SONTHEIMER, G DOUGLAS
14821 Dufief Mill Rd., Gaithersburg, MD 20878, Phone: 301-948-5227
Specialties: Fixed blade knives. **Patterns:** Whitetail deer, backpackers, camp, claws, fillet, fighters. **Technical:** Hollow Grinds. **Prices:** $500 and up. **Remarks:** Spare-time maker; first knife sold in 1976. **Mark:** LORD.

SORNBERGER, JIM
25126 Overland Dr, Volcano, CA 95689, Phone: 209-295-7819, sierrajs@volcano.net
Specialties: Master engraver making classic San Francisco-style knives. Collectible straight knives. **Patterns:** Fighters, daggers, bowies, miniatures, hunters, custom canes and LinerLock folders. **Technical:** Grinds 440C, 154CM and ATS-34; engraves, carves and embellishes. **Prices:** $500 to $35,000 in gold with gold quartz inlays. **Remarks:** Full-time maker; first knife sold in 1970. Master engraver. **Mark:** First initial, last name, city and state.

SOWELL, BILL
100 Loraine Forest Ct, Macon, GA 31210, Phone: 478- 994-9863, billsowell@reynoldscable.net
Specialties: Antique reproduction Bowies, forging Bowies, hunters, fighters, and most others. Also folders. **Technical:** Makes own Damascus, using 1084/15N20, also making own designs in powder metals, forges 5160-1095-1084, and other carbon steels, grinds ATS-34. **Prices:** Starting at $150 and up. **Remarks:** Part-time maker. Sold first knife in 1998. Does own leather work. ABS Master Smith. **Mark:** Iron Horse Forge - Sowell - MS.

SPAKE, JEREMY
6128 N. Concord Ave., Portland, OR 97217-4735, jeremy@spakeknife.com; Web: www.spakeknife.com, www.instagram.com/jspake
Specialties: Handmade hidden-tang fixed blade knives. **Patterns:** Utility, hunting and Nordic-influenced knives, kitchen cutlery and others as the occasion arises. **Technical:** Concentration on forged three-layer laminated blades with high-carbon steel cores. Also forges high-carbon mono-steel blades. Stock removal on occasion. For handles, prefers a variety fo stabilized woods and premium natural materials. **Prices:** $350 to $500 and up. **Remarks:** Part-time maker; first knife sold in 2012. American Bladesmith Society member. **Mark:** Last name etched or stamped in Gotham typeface.

SPARKS, BERNARD
PO Box 73, Dingle, ID 83233, Phone: 208-847-1883, dogknifeii@juno.com; Web: www.sparksknives.com
Specialties: Maker engraved, working and art knives. Straight knives and folders of his own design. **Patterns:** Locking inner-frame folders, hunters, fighters, one-of-a-kind art knives. **Technical:** Grinds 530V steel, 440-C, 154CM, ATS-34, D-2 and forges by special order; triple temper, cryogenic soak. Mirror or hand finish. New Liquid metal steel. **Prices:** $300 to $2000. **Remarks:** Full-time maker, first knife sold in 1967. **Mark:** Last name over state with a knife logo on each end of name. Prior 1980, stamp of last name.

SPICKLER, GREGORY NOBLE
5614 Mose Cir, Sharpsburg, MD 21782, Phone: 301-432-2746

SPINALE, RICHARD
4021 Canterbury Ct, Lorain, OH 44053, Phone: 440-282-1565
Specialties: High-art working knives of his design. **Patterns:** Hunters, fighters, daggers and locking folders. **Technical:** Grinds 440C, ATS-34 and 07; engraves. Offers gold bolsters and other deluxe treatments. **Prices:** $300 to $1000; some to $3000. **Remarks:** Spare-time maker; first knife sold in 1976. **Mark:** Name, address, year and model number.

SPIVEY, JEFFERSON
9244 W Wilshire, Yukon, OK 73099, Phone: 405-371-9304, jspivey5@cox.net
Specialties: The Saber tooth: a combination hatchet, saw and knife. **Patterns:** Built for the wilderness, all are one-of-a-kind. **Technical:** Grinds chromemoly steel. The saw tooth spine curves with a double row of biangular teeth. **Prices:** Start at $275. **Remarks:** First knife sold in 1977. As of September 2006 Spivey knives has resumed production of the Sabertooth knife (one word trademark).**Mark:** Name and serial number.

SPRAGG, WAYNE E
252 Oregon Ave, Lovell, WY 82431, Phone: 307-548-7212
Specialties: Working straight knives, some fancy. **Patterns:** Folders. **Technical:** Forges carbon steel and makes Damascus. **Prices:** $200 and up. **Remarks:** All stainless heat-treated by Paul Bos. Carbon steel in shop heat treat. **Mark:** Last name front side w/s initials on reverse side.

SPROKHOLT, ROB
Burgerweg 5, Gatherwood, NETHERLANDS 1754 KB Burgerbrug, Phone: 0031 6 51230225, Fax: 0031 84 2238446, info@gatherwood.nl; Web: www.gatherwood.nl
Specialties: One-of-a-kind knives. Top materials collector grade, made to use. **Patterns:** Outdoor knives (hunting, sailing, hiking), Bowies, man's surviving companions MSC, big tantos, folding knives. **Technical:** Handles mostly stabilized or oiled wood, ivory, Micarta, carbon fibre, G10. Stiff knives are full tang. Characteristic one row of massive silver pins or tubes. Folding knives have a LinerLock® with titanium or Damascus powdersteel liner thumb can have any stone you like. Stock removal grinder: flat or convex. Steel 440-C, RWL-34, ATS-34, PM damascener steel. **Prices:** Start at 320 euro. **Remarks:** Writer of the first Dutch knifemaking book, supply shop for knife enthusiastic. First knife sold in 2000. **Mark:** Gatherwood in an eclipse etched blade or stamped in an intarsia of silver in the spine.

SQUIRE, JACK
350 W. 7th St., McMinnville, OR 97182-5509, Phone: 503-472-7290

ST. AMOUR, MURRAY
2066 Lapasse Rd., Beachburg, Ontario, CANADA K0J 1C0, Phone: 613-587-4194, knives@nrtco.net; Web: www.st-amourknives.com
Specialties: Hunters, fish knives, outdoor knives, bowies and some collectors' pieces. **Technical:** Steels include CPM S30V, CPM S90V, CPM 154, 154CM and ATS 34. **Remarks:** Full-time maker; first sold in 1992. **Mark:** St. Amour over Canada or small print st. amour.

ST. CLAIR, THOMAS K
12608 Fingerboard Rd, Monrovia, MD 21770, Phone: 301-482-0264

STAFFORD, RICHARD
104 Marcia Ct, Warner Robins, GA 31088, Phone: 912-923-6372, Fax: Cell: 478-508-5821, rnrstafford@cox.net
Specialties: High-tech straight knives and some folders. **Patterns:** Hunters in several patterns, fighters, boots, camp knives, combat knives and period pieces. **Technical:** Grinds ATS-34 and 440C. Machine satin finish offered. **Prices:** Starting at $150. **Remarks:** Part-time maker; first knife sold in 1983. **Mark:** R. W. STAFFORD GEORGIA.

STAINTHORP, GUY
4 Fisher St, Brindley Ford, Stroke-on-Trent, ENGLAND ST8 7QJ, Phone: 07946 469 888, guystainthorp@hotmail.com Web: http://stainthorpknives.co.uk/index.html
Specialties: Tactical and outdoors knives to his own design. **Patterns:** Hunting, survival and occasionally folding knives. **Technical:** Grinds RWL-34, O1, S30V, Damasteel. Micarta, G10 and stabilised wood/bone for handles. **Prices:** $200 - $1000. **Remarks:** Full-time knifemaker. **Mark:** Squared stylised GS over "Stainthorp".

STALCUP, EDDIE
PO Box 2200, Gallup, NM 87305, Phone: 505-863-3107, sharon.stalcup@gmail.com
Specialties: Working and fancy hunters, bird and trout. Special custom orders. **Patterns:** Drop point hunters, locking liner and multi blade folders. **Technical:** ATS-34, 154 CM, 440C, CPM 154 and S30V. **Prices:** $150 to $1500. **Remarks:** Scrimshaw, exotic handle material, wet formed sheaths. Membership Arizona Knife Collectors Association. Southern California blades collectors & professional knife makers assoc. **Mark:** E.F. Stalcup, Gallup, NM.

STANCER, CHUCK
62 Hidden Ranch Rd NW, Calgary, AB, CANADA T3A 5S5, Phone: 403-295-7370, stancerc@telusplanet.net
Specialties: Traditional and working straight knives. **Patterns:** Bowies, hunters and utility knives. **Technical:** Forges and grinds most steels. **Prices:** $175 and up. **Remarks:** Part-time maker. **Mark:** Last name.

STANFORD, PERRY
405N Walnut #9, Broken Arrow, OK 74012, Phone: 918-251-7983 or 866-305-5690, stanfordoutdoors@valornet.com; Web: www.stanfordoutdoors.homestead.com
Specialties: Drop point, hunting and skinning knives, handmade sheaths. **Patterns:** Stright, hunting, and skinners. **Technical:** Grinds 440C, ATS-34 and Damascus. **Prices:** $65 to $275. **Remarks:** Part-time maker, first knife sold in 2007. Knifemaker supplier, manufacturer of paper sharpening systems. Doing business as Stanford Outdoors. **Mark:** Company name and nickname.

STANLEY, JOHN
604 Elm St, Crossett, AR 71635, Phone: 970-304-3005
Specialties: Hand forged fixed blades with engraving and carving. **Patterns:** Scottish

dirks, skeans and fantasy blades. **Technical:** Forge high-carbon steel, own Damascus. Prices $70 to $500. **Remarks:** All work is sole authorship. Offers engraving and carving services on other knives and handles. **Mark:** Varies.

STAPLETON, WILLIAM E
BUFFALO 'B' FORGE, 5425 Country Ln, Merritt Island, FL 32953
Specialties: Classic and traditional knives of his design and customer spec. **Patterns:** Hunters and using knives. **Technical:** Forges, O1 and L6 Damascus, cable Damascus and 5160; stock removal on request. **Prices:** $150 to $1000. **Remarks:** Part-time maker, first knife sold 1990. Doing business as Buffalo "B" Forge. **Mark:** Anvil with S initial in center of anvil.

STATES, JOSHUA C
43905 N 16th St, New River, AZ 85087, Phone: 623-826-3809, Web: www.dosgatosforge.com
Specialties: Design and fabrication of forged working and art knives from O1 and my own damascus. Stock removal from 440C and CM154 upon request. Folders from 440C, CM154 and Damascus. Flat and Hollow grinds. Knives made to customer specs and/or design.**Patterns:** Bowies, hunters, daggers, chef knives, and exotic shapes. **Technical:** Damascus is 1095, 1084, O1 and 15N20. Carved or file-worked fittings from various metals including my own mokume gane and Damascus.**Prices:** $250 and up. **Remarks:** Part-time maker with waiting list. First knife sold in 2006. **Mark:** Initials JCS in small oval, or States in italisized script. Unmarked knives come with certificate of authorship.

STECK, VAN R
260 W Dogwood Ave, Orange City, FL 32763, Phone: 407-416-1723, van@thudknives.com
Specialties: Specializing in double-edged grinds. Free-hand grinds: folders, spears, bowies, swords and miniatures. **Patterns:** Tomahawks with a crane for the spike, tactical merged with nature.**Technical:** Hamon lines, folder lock of own design, the arm-lock! **Prices:** $50 - $1500. **Remarks:** Builds knives designed by Laci Szabo or builds to customer design. Studied with Reese Weiland on folders and automatics. **Mark:** GEISHA holding a sword with initials and THUD KNIVES in a circle.

STEGALL, KEITH
701 Outlet View Dr, Wasilla, AK 99654, Phone: 907-376-0703, kas5200@yahoo.com
Specialties: Traditional working straight knives. **Patterns:** Most patterns. **Technical:** Grinds 440C and 154CM. **Prices:** $100 to $300. **Remarks:** Spare-time maker; first knife sold in 1987. **Mark:** Name and state with anchor.

STEGNER, WILBUR G
9242 173rd Ave SW, Rochester, WA 98579, Phone: 360-273-0937, wilbur@wgsk.net; Web: www.wgsk.net
Specialties: Working/using straight knives and folders of his design. **Patterns:** Hunters and locking folders. **Technical:** Makes his own Damascus steel. **Prices:** $100 to $1000; some to $5000. **Remarks:** Full-time maker; first knife sold in 1979. Google search key words:-"STEGNER KNIVES." Best folder awards NWKC 2009, 2010 and 2011. **Mark:** First and middle initials, last name in bar over shield logo.

STEIER, DAVID
7722 Zenith Way, Louisville, KY 40219, Phone: 502-969-8409, umag300@aol.com; Web: www.steierknives.com
Specialties: Folding LinerLocks, Bowies, slip joints, lockbacks, and straight hunters. **Technical:** Stock removal blades of 440C, ATS-34, and Damascus from outside sources like Robert Eggerling and Mike Norris. **Prices:** $150 for straight hunters to $1400 for fully decked-out folders. **Remarks:** First knife sold in 1979. **Mark:** Last name STEIER.

STEIGER, MONTE L
Box 186, Genesee, ID 83832, Phone: 208-285-1769, montesharon@genesee-id.com
Specialties: Traditional working/using straight knives of all designs. **Patterns:** Hunters, utility/camp knives, fillet and chefs. Carving sets and steak knives. **Technical:** Grinds 1095, O1, 440C, ATS-34. Handles of stacked leather, natural wood, Micarta or pakkawood. Each knife comes with right- or left-handed sheath. **Prices:** $110 to $600. **Remarks:** Spare-time maker; first knife sold in 1988. Retired librarian **Mark:** First initial, last name, city and state.

STEIGERWALT, KEN
507 Savagehill Rd, Orangeville, PA 17859, Phone: 570-683-5156, Web: www.steigerwaltknives.com
Specialties: Elaborate carving and inlays, primarily in Art Deco design. **Patterns:** Folders, button locks and rear locks. **Technical:** Uses CPM 154, CPM S35V, RWL-34 and damascus steels. **Prices:** $500 to $10,000. **Remarks:** Full-time maker; first knife sold in 1981. **Mark:** Kasteigerwalt

STEINAU, JURGEN
Julius-Hart Strasse 44, Berlin, GERMANY 01162, Phone: 372-6452512, Fax: 372-645-2512
Specialties: Fantasy and high-art straight knives of his design. **Patterns:** Boots, daggers and switch-blade folders. **Technical:** Grinds 440B, 2379 and X90 Cr.Mo.V. 78. **Prices:** $1500 to $2500; some to $3500. **Remarks:** Full-time maker; first knife sold in 1984. **Mark:** Symbol, plus year, month day and serial number.

STEINBERG, AL
5244 Duenas, Laguna Woods, CA 92653, Phone: 949-951-2889, lagknife@fea.net
Specialties: Fancy working straight knives to customer specs. **Patterns:** Hunters, Bowies, fishing, camp knives, push knives and high end kitchen knives. **Technical:** Grinds O1, 440C and 154CM. **Prices:** $60 to $2500. **Remarks:** Full-time maker; first knife sold in 1972. **Mark:** Signature, city and state.

STEINBRECHER, MARK W
1122 92nd Place, Pleasant Prairie, WI 53158-4939
Specialties: Daggers, pocket knives, fighters and gents of his own design or to customer specs. **Technical:** Hollow grinds ATS-34, O1 other makers Damascus. Uses natural handle materials: stag, ivories, mother-of-pearl. File work and some inlays. **Prices:** $500 to $1200, some to $2500. **Remarks:** Part-time maker, first folder sold in 1989. **Mark:** Name etched or handwritten on ATS-34; stamped on Damascus.

STEINGASS, T.K.
334 Silver Lake Rd., Bucksport, ME 04416, Phone: 304-268-1161, tksteingass@frontier.com; Web: http://steingassknives.com
Specialties: Loveless style hunters and fighters and sole authorship knives: Man Knife, Silent Hunter, and Silent Fighter. Harpoon Grind Camp Knife and Harpoon Grind Man Hunter. **Technical:** Stock removal, use CPM 154, S3V and occasionally 1095 or O1 for camp choppers.**Prices:** $200 to $500. **Remarks:** Part-time maker; first knife made in 2010. **Mark:** STEINGASS.

STEKETEE, CRAIG A
871 NE US Hwy 60, Billings, MO 65610, Phone: 417-744-2770, stekknives04@yahoo.com
Specialties: Classic and working straight knives and swords of his design. **Patterns:** Bowies, hunters, and Japanese-style swords. **Technical:** Forges his own Damascus; bronze, silver and Damascus fittings, offers filework. Prefers exotic and natural handle materials. **Prices:** $200 to $4000. **Remarks:** Full-time maker. **Mark:** STEK.

STEPHAN, DANIEL
2201 S Miller Rd, Valrico, FL 33594, Phone: 727-580-8617, knifemaker@verizon.net
Specialties: Art knives, one-of-a-kind.

STERLING, MURRAY
693 Round Peak Church Rd, Mount Airy, NC 27030, Phone: 336-352-5110, Fax: Fax: 336-352-5105, sterck@surry.net; Web: www.sterlingcustomknives.com
Specialties: Single and dual blade folders. Interframes and integral dovetail frames. **Technical:** Grinds ATS-34 or Damascus by Mike Norris and/or Devin Thomas. **Prices:** $400 to $1,200. **Remarks:** Full-time maker; first knife sold in 1991. **Mark:** Last name stamped.

STERLING, THOMAS J
ART KNIVES BY, POB 1621, Coupeville, WA 98239, Phone: 360-678-9269, Fax: 360-678-9269, netsuke@comcast.net; Web: www.sterlingsculptures.com
Specialties: Since 2003, Tom Sterling has created one-of-a-kind, ultra-quality art knives, jewelry and assorted doodads using high-quality precious and semi-precious materials, steel, titanium, shibuichi and shakudo. His work is often influenced by the traditions of Japanese netsuke and a unique fusion of cultures and styles. Tom's highly sought-after engraving skills reflect stylistically integrated choices of materials and contrasting inlays for a unique presentation style. **Prices:** $300 to $14,000. **Remarks:** Limited output ensures highest quality artwork and exceptional levels of craftsmanship. **Mark:** TJSterling.

STEYN, PETER
PO Box 76, Welkom, Freestate, SOUTH AFRICA 9460, Phone: 27573522015, Fax: 27573523566, Web:www.petersteynknives.com email:info@petersteynknives.com
Specialties: Fixed blade knives of own design, all with hand-stitched leather sheaths. Folding knives of own design supplied with soft pouches. **Patterns:** Fixed blades: hunters and skinners. Folding knives: friction folders, slip joints and lockbacks. **Technical:** Grinds 12C27 and Damasteel. Blades are bead-blasted in plain or patterned finish. Ceramic wash also available in satin or antiqued finish. Grind syle is convex, concave on the obverse, and convex on the reverse. Works with a wide variety of handle materials, prefers exotic woods and synthetics. **Prices:** $150 to $650. **Remarks:** Full-time maker, first knife sold 2005, member of South African Guild. **Mark:** Letter 'S' in shape of pyramid with full name above and 'Handcrafted' below.

STICE, DOUGLAS W
PO Box 12815, Wichita, KS 67277, Phone: 316-295-6855, doug@sticecraft.com; Web: www.sticecraft.com
Specialties: Working fixed blade knives of own design. **Patterns:** Tacticals, hunters, skinners,utility, and camp knives. **Technical:** Grinds CPM154CM, 154CM, CPM3V, Damascus; uses 18" contact grinds where wheel for hollow grinds, also flat. **Prices:** $100 to $750. **Remarks:** Full-time maker; first professional knife made in 2009. All knives have serial numbers and include certificate of authenticity. **Mark:** Stylized "Stice" stamp.

STIDHAM, DANIEL
3106 Mill Cr. Rd., Gallipolis, Ohio 45631, Phone: 740-446-1673, danstidham@yahoo.com
Specialties: Fixed blades, folders, Bowies and hunters. **Technical:** 440C, Alabama Damascus, 1095 with filework. **Prices:** Start at $150. **Remarks:** Has made fixed blades since 1961, folders since 1986. Also sells various knife brands.**Mark:** Stidham Knives Gallipolis, Ohio 45631.

STIMPS, JASON M
374 S Shaffer St, Orange, CA 92866, Phone: 714-744-5866

STIPES, DWIGHT
2651 SW Buena Vista Dr, Palm City, FL 34990, Phone: 772-597-0550, dwightstipes@adelphia.net
Specialties: Traditional and working straight knives in standard patterns. **Patterns:** Boots, Bowies, daggers, hunters and fighters. **Technical:** Grinds 440C, D2 and D3 tool steel. Handles of natural materials, animal, bone or horn. **Prices:** $75 to $150. **Remarks:** Full-time maker; first knife sold in 1972. **Mark:** Stipes.

STOKES, ED
22614 Cardinal Dr, Hockley, TX 77447, Phone: 713-351-1319
Specialties: Working straight knives and folders of all designs. **Patterns:** Boots, Bowies, daggers, fighters, hunters and miniatures. **Technical:** Grinds ATS-34, 440C and D2. Offers decorative butt caps, tapered spacers on handles and finger grooves, nickel-silver inlays, handmade sheaths. **Prices:** $185 to $290; some to $350. **Remarks:** Full-time maker; first knife sold in 1973. **Mark:** First and last name, Custom Knives with Apache logo.

STONE, JERRY
PO Box 1027, Lytle, TX 78052, Phone: 830-709-3042
Specialties: Traditional working and using folders of his design and to customer specs; fancy knives. **Patterns:** Fighters, hunters, locking folders and slip joints. Also make automatics. **Technical:** Grinds 440C and ATS-34. Offers filework. **Prices:** $175 to $1000. **Remarks:** Full-time maker; first knife sold in 1973. **Mark:** Name over Texas star/town and state underneath.

STORCH, ED
RR 4, Mannville, AB, CANADA T0B 2W0, Phone: 780-763-2214, storchknives@gmail.com; Web: www.storchknives.com
Specialties: Working knives, fancy fighting knives, kitchen cutlery and art knives. Knifemaking classes. **Patterns:** Working patterns, Bowies and folders. **Technical:** Forges his own Damascus. Grinds ATS-34. Builds friction folders. Salt heat treating. **Prices:** $100 to $3,000 (U.S.). **Remarks:** Full-time maker; first knife sold in 1984. Classes taught in stock-removal, and damascus and sword making. **Mark:** Last name.

STORMER, BOB
34354 Hwy E, Dixon, MO 65459, Phone: 636-734-2693, bs34354@gmail.com
Specialties: Straight knives, using collector grade. **Patterns:** Bowies, skinners, hunters, camp knives. **Technical:** Forges 5160, 1095. **Prices:** $200 to $500. **Remarks:** Part-time maker, ABS Journeyman Smith 2001. **Mark:** Setting sun/fall trees/initials.

STOUT, CHARLES
RT3 178 Stout Rd, Gillham, AR 71841, Phone: 870-386-5521

STOUT, JOHNNY
1205 Forest Trail, New Braunfels, TX 78132, Phone: 830-606-4067, johnny@stoutknives.com; Web: www.stoutknives.com, Facebook-Johnny Stout, Instagram-Stout Handmade Knives
Specialties: Folders, some fixed blades. Working knives, some fancy. **Patterns:** Hunters, automatics, LinerLocks and slip joints. **Technical:** Grinds stainless and carbon steels; forges some Damascus. **Prices:** $450 to $895; some to $6,500. **Remarks:** Full-time maker; first knife sold in 1983. Hosts semi-annual Guadalupe Forge Hammer-in and Knifemakers Rendezvous. **Mark:** Name and city in logo.

STRAIGHT, KENNETH J
11311 103 Lane N, Largo, FL 33773, Phone: 813-397-9817

STRANDE, POUL
Soster Svenstrup Byvej 16, Viby Sj., Dastrup, DENMARK 4130, Phone: 46 19 43 05, Fax: 46 19 53 19, Web: www.poulstrande.com
Specialties: Classic fantasy working knives; Damasceret blade, Nikkel Damasceret blade, Lamineret: Lamineret blade with Nikkel. **Patterns:** Bowies, daggers, fighters, hunters and swords. **Technical:** Uses carbon steel and 15C20 steel. **Prices:** NA. **Remarks:** Full-time maker; first knife sold in 1985. **Mark:** First and last initials.

STRAUB, SALEM F.
324 Cobey Creek Rd., Tonasket, WA 98855, Phone: 509-486-2627, vorpalforge@hotmail.com Web: www.prometheanknives.com
Specialties: Elegant working knives, fixed blade hunters, utility, skinning knives; liner locks. Makes own horsehide sheaths. **Patterns:** A wide range of syles, everything from the gentleman's pocket to the working kitchen, integrals, Bowies, folders, check out my website to see some of my work for ideas. **Technical:** Forges several carbon steels, 52100, W1, etc. Grinds stainless and makes/uses own damascus, cable, san mai, stadard patterns. Likes clay quenching, hamons, hand rubbed finishes. Flat, hollow, or convex grinds. Prefers synthetic handle materials. Hidden and full tapered tangs. **Prices:** $150 - $600, some higher. **Remarks:** Full-time maker. Doing what it takes to make your knife ordering and buying experience positive and enjoyable; striving to exceed expectations. All knives backed by lifetime guarantee. **Mark:** "Straub" stamp or "Promethean Knives" etched. Some older pieces stamped "Vorpal" though no longer using this mark. **Other:** Feel free to call or e-mail anytime. I love to talk knives.

STRICKLAND, DALE
1440 E Thompson View, Monroe, UT 84754, Phone: 435-896-8362
Specialties: Traditional and working straight knives and folders of his design and to customer specs. **Patterns:** Hunters, folders, miniatures and utility knives. **Technical:** Grinds Damascus and 440C. **Prices:** $120 to $350; some to $500. **Remarks:** Part-time maker; first knife sold in 1991. **Mark:** Oval stamp of name, Maker.

STRIDER, MICK
STRIDER KNIVES, 565 Country Club Dr., Escondido, CA 92029, Phone: 760-471-8275, Fax: 503-218-7069, striderguys@striderknives.com; Web: www.striderknives.com

STRONG, SCOTT
1599 Beaver Valley Rd, Beavercreek, OH 45434, Phone: 937-426-9290
Specialties: Working knives, some deluxe. **Patterns:** Hunters, fighters, survival and military-style knives, art knives. **Technical:** Forges and grinds O1, A2, D2, 440C and ATS-34. Uses no solder; most knives disassemble. **Prices:** $75 to $450; some to $1500. **Remarks:** Spare-time maker; first knife sold in 1983. **Mark:** Strong Knives.

STROYAN, ERIC
Box 218, Dalton, PA 18414, Phone: 717-563-2603
Specialties: Classic and working/using straight knives and folders of his design. **Patterns:** Hunters, locking folders, slip-joints. **Technical:** Forges Damascus; grinds ATS-34, D2. **Prices:** $200 to $600; some to $2000. **Remarks:** Part-time maker; first knife sold in 1968. **Mark:** Signature or initials stamp.

STUART, MASON
24 Beech Street, Mansfield, MA 02048, Phone: 508-339-8236, smasonknives@verizon.net Web: smasonknives.com, Facebook.com/S. Mason Custom Knives
Specialties: Straight knives of his design, standard patterns. **Patterns:** Bowies, hunters, fighters and neck knives. **Technical:** Forges and grinds. Damascus, 5160, 1095, 1084, old files. Uses only natural handle material. **Prices:** $350 - 2,000. **Remarks:** Part-time maker. **Mark:** First initial and last name.

STUART, STEVE
Box 168, Gores Landing, ON, CANADA K0K 2E0, Phone: 905-440-6910, stevestuart@xplornet.com
Specialties: Straight knives. **Patterns:** Tantos, fighters, skinners, file and rasp knives. **Technical:** Uses 440C, CPM154, CPMS30V, Micarta and natural handle materials. **Prices:** $60 to $400. **Remarks:** Part-time maker. **Mark:** SS.

STUCKY, DANIEL
37924 Shenandoah Loop, Springfield, OR 97478, Phone: 541-747-6496, stuckyj1@msn.com, www.stuckyknives.com
Specialties: Tactical, fancy and everyday carry folders, fixed-blade hunting knives, trout, bird and fillet knives. **Technical:** Stock removal maker. Steels include but are not limited to damascus, CPM 154, CPM S30V, CPM S35VN, 154CM and ATS-34. **Prices:** Start at $300 and can go to thousands, depending on materials used. **Remarks:** Full-time maker; first knife sold in 1999. **Mark:** Name over city and state.

STYREFORS, MATTIAS
Unbyn 23, Boden, SWEDEN 96193, infor@styrefors.com
Specialties: Damascus and mosaic Damascus. Fixed blade Nordic hunters, folders and swords. **Technical:** Forges, shapes and grinds Damascus and mosaic Damascus from mostly UHB 15N20 and 20C with contrasts in nickel and 15N20. Hardness HR 58. **Prices:** $800 to $3000. **Remarks:** Full-time maker since 1999. International reputation for high end Damascus blades. Uses stabilized Arctic birch and willow burl, horn, fossils, exotic materials, and scrimshaw by Viveca Sahlin for knife handles. Hand tools and hand stitches leather sheaths in cow raw hide. Works in well equipped former military forgery in northern Sweden. **Mark:** MS.

SUEDMEIER, HARLAN
762 N 60th Rd, Nebraska City, NE 68410, Phone: 402-873-4372
Patterns: Straight knives. **Technical:** Forging hi carbon Damascus. **Prices:** Starting at $175. **Mark:** First initials & last name.

SUGIHARA, KEIDOH
4-16-1 Kamori-Cho, Kishiwada City, Osaka, JAPAN F596-0042, Fax: 0724-44-2677
Specialties: High-tech working straight knives and folders of his design. **Patterns:** Bowies, hunters, fighters, fishing, boots, some pocket knives and liner-lock folders. **Technical:** Grinds ATS-34, COS-25, buys Damascus and high-carbon steels. Prices $60 to $4000. **Remarks:** Full-time maker, first knife sold in 1980. **Mark:** Initial logo with fish design.

SUGIYAMA, EDDY K
2361 Nagayu, Naoirimachi Naoirigun, Oita, JAPAN, Phone: 0974-75-2050
Specialties: One-of-a-kind, exotic-style knives. **Patterns:** Working, utility and miniatures. **Technical:** CT rind, ATS-34 and D2. **Prices:** $400 to $1200. **Remarks:** Full-time maker. **Mark:** Name or cedar mark.

SUMMERS, ARTHUR L
1310 Hess Rd, Concord, NC 28025, Phone: 704-787-9275 Cell: 704-305-0735, arthursummers88@hotmail.com
Specialties: Drop points, clip points, straight blades. **Patterns:** Hunters, Bowies and personal knives. **Technical:** Grinds ATS-34, CPM-D2, CPM-154 and damascus. **Prices:** $250 to $1000. **Remarks:** Full-time maker; first knife sold in 1988. **Mark:** Serial number is the date.

SUMMERS, DAN
2675 NY Rt. 11, Whitney Pt., NY 13862, Phone: 607-692-2391, dansumm11@gmail.com
Specialties: Period knives and tomahawks. **Technical:** All hand forging. **Prices:** Most $100 to $400.

SUMMERS, DENNIS K
827 E. Cecil St, Springfield, OH 45503, Phone: 513-324-0624
Specialties: Working/using knives. **Patterns:** Fighters and personal knives. **Technical:** Grinds 440C, A2 and D2. Makes drop and clip point. **Prices:** $75 to $200. **Remarks:** Part-time maker; first knife sold in 1995. **Mark:** First and middle initials, last name, serial number.

SUNDERLAND, RICHARD
Av Infraganti 23, Col Lazaro Cardenas, Puerto Escondido, OA, MEXICO 71980, Phone: 011 52 94 582 1451, sunamerica@prodigy.net.mx7
Specialties: Personal and hunting knives with carved handles in oosic and ivory. **Patterns:** Hunters, Bowies, daggers, camp and personal knives. **Technical:** Grinds 440C, ATS-34 and O1. Handle materials of rosewoods, fossil mammoth ivory and oosic. **Prices:** $150 to $1000. **Remarks:** Part-time maker; first knife sold in 1983. Doing business as Sun Knife Co. **Mark:** SUN.

SURLS, W. ALLEN

W.A. SURLS KNIVES, 3889 Duncan Ives Dr., Buford, GA 30519, Phone: 678-897-1624, wasknives@gmail.com

Patterns: Bushcraft knives, traditional fixed blades, Loveless patterns, skinners and gent's knives. **Technical:** Stock removal method of blade making with occasional forging, using CPM 154, A2 and O1 steels. **Prices:** $150 to $1,200. **Remarks:** Full-time maker; first blade ground in May of 2013. Owner and operator of W.A. Surls Knives, and vice president of Fiddleback Forge Inc. **Mark:** Current mark is "W.A. Surls," with early production pieces marked "WAS."

SUTTON, S RUSSELL

4900 Cypress Shores Dr, New Bern, NC 28562, Phone: 252-637-3963, srsutton@suddenlink.net; Web: www.suttoncustomknives.com

Specialties: Straight knives and folders to customer specs and in standard patterns. **Patterns:** Boots, hunters, interframes, slip joints and locking liners. **Technical:** Grinds ATS-34, 440C and stainless Damascus. **Prices:** $220 to $2000. **Remarks:** Full-time maker; first knife sold in 1992. Provides relief engraving on bolsters and guards. **Mark:** Etched last name.

SWARZ-BURT, PETER T.

FALLING HAMMER PRODUCTIONS, LLC, 10 Swiss Ln., Wolcott, CT 06716, Phone: 203-879-1786, dragonsbreathforge@gmail.com; Web: www.fallinghammerproductions.com or www.dragonsbreathforge.com

Specialties: Makes own Wootz and other crucible steels, specializing in unusual blade shapes with a focus on Indian and Middle Eastern weapons; historical reproductions from all regions. **Patterns:** Designs focus on utility and comfort. **Technical:** Uses 5160, L6, 10xx, and his own Wootz and damascus steels. Forges closely to shape. **Prices:** $150 to $2,000 (knives) and $500 to $5,000 (swords). **Remarks:** Full-time blacksmith and bladesmith; first knife made in 1992. **Mark:** PTSB combined to look like a snake twined around a sword on one side of ricasso, and the Dragon's Breath Forge symbol that looks like a talon on the other side.

SWEARINGEN, KURT

22 Calvary Rd., Cedar Crest, NM 87008, Phone: 575-613-0500, kurt@swearingenknife.com; Web: www.swearingenknife.com

Specialties: Traditional hunting and camp knives, as well as slip-joint and lockback folders of classic design with an emphasis on utility. Hand-carved and tooled sheaths accompany each knife. **Patterns:** Loveless-style hunters, Scagel folders, as well as original designs. **Technical:** Grinds CPM 154 for all standard hunting models and D2 for all folders. Smiths W2 for forged hunters, and 5160 or 1084 for camp knives. **Prices:** Standard models in CPM 154 start at $320, including a custom sheath. **Remarks:** Serious part-time maker and ABS journeyman smith, I personally test each knife in my shop and in the field during hunting season (hunters) and in my work as a forester (camp knives).

SWEAZA, DENNIS

4052 Hwy 321 E, Austin, AR 72007, Phone: 501-941-1886, knives4den@aol.com

SWENSON, LUKE

SWENSON KNIVES, 1667 Brushy Creek Dr., Lakehills, TX 78063, Phone: 210-722-3227, luke@swensonknives.com; Web: www.swensonknives.com

Specialties: Small hunting knives, concentrating on traditional multi-blade slip joints. **Technical:** Stock-removal method of blade making. Flat grinds A2 tool steel for fixed blades, and hollow grinds CPM 154 for slip-joint folders. Credits Bill Ruple for mentoring him in the making slip knives. **Prices:** $275 to $675. **Remarks:** Part-time maker/full-time firefighter; first knife made in 2003. Starting to do some traditional lockback patterns also. **Mark:** Name and city where maker lives.

SWYHART, ART

509 Main St, PO Box 267, Klickitat, WA 98628, Phone: 509-369-3451, swyhart@gorge.net; Web: www.knifeoutlet.com/swyhart.htm

Specialties: Traditional working and using knives of his design. **Patterns:** Bowies, hunters and utility/camp knives. **Technical:** Forges 52100, 5160 and Damascus 1084 mixed with either 15N20 or O186. Blades differentially heat-treated with visible temper line. **Prices:** $75 to $250; some to $350. **Remarks:** Part-time maker; first knife sold in 1983. **Mark:** First name, last initial in script.

SYLVESTER, DAVID

465 Sweede Rd., Compton, QC, CANADA J0B 1L0, Phone: 819-837-0304, david@swedevilleforge.com Web: swedevilleforge.com

Patterns: I hand forge all my knives and I like to make hunters and integrals and some Bowies and fighters. I work with W2, 1084, 1095, and my damascus. **Prices:** $200 - $1500. **Remarks:** Part-time maker. ABS Journeyman Smith. **Mark:** D.Sylvester

SYMONDS, ALBERTO E

Rambla M Gandhi 485, Apt 901, Montevideo, URUGUAY 11300, Phone: 011 598 27103201, Fax: 011 598 2 7103201, albertosymonds@hotmail.com

Specialties: All kinds including puukos, nice sheaths, leather and wood. **Prices:** $300 to $2200. **Mark:** AESH and current year.

SYSLO, CHUCK

3418 South 116 Ave, Omaha, NE 68144, Phone: 402-333-0647, ciscoknives@cox.net

Specialties: Hunters, working knives, daggers and misc. **Patterns:** Hunters, daggers and survival knives; locking folders. **Technical:** Flat-grinds D2, 440C and 154CM; hand polishes only. **Prices:** $250 to $1,000; some to $3,000. **Remarks:** Part-time maker; first knife sold in 1978. Uses many natural materials. Making some knives, mainly retired from knifemaking. **Mark:** CISCO in logo.

SZCZERBIAK, MACIEJ

Crusader Forge Knives, PO Box 2181, St. George, UT 84771, Phone: 435-574-2193, crusaderforge@yahoo.com; Web: www.crusaderforge.com

Patterns: Drop-point, spear-point and tanto fixed blades and tactical folders. **Technical:** Stock removal using CPM-S30V and D2 steels. Knives designed with the technical operator in mind, and maintain an amazing balance in the user's hand. **Prices:** $300 to $2,500. **Remarks:** First knife made in 1999.

SZILASKI, JOSEPH

School of Knifemaking, 52 Woods Dr., Pine Plains, NY 12567, Phone: 518-398-0309, joe@szilaski.com; Web: www.szilaski.com

Specialties: Straight knives, folders and tomahawks of his design, to customer specs and in standard patterns. Many pieces are one-of-a-kind. Offers knifemaking classes for all levels in 4,000-square-foot shop. Courses are in forging, grinding, damascus, tomahawk engraving and carving. **Patterns:** Bowies, daggers, fighters, hunters, art knives and early American styles. **Technical:** Forges A2, D2, O1 and damascus. **Prices:** $450 to $4,000; some to $10,000. **Remarks:** Full-time maker; first knife sold in 1990. ABS master smith. **Mark:** Snake logo.

T

TABER, DAVID E.

51 E. 4th St., Ste. 300, Winona, MN 55987, Phone: 507-450-1918, dtaber@qwestoffice.net

Specialties: Traditional slip joints, primarily using and working knives. **Technical:** Blades are hollow ground on a 20" wheel, ATS-34 and some damascus steel. **Remarks:** Full-time orthodontist, part-time maker; first knife made in January 2011. **Mark:** dr.t.

TABOR, TIM

18925 Crooked Lane, Lutz, FL 33548, Phone: 813-948-6141, taborknives.com

Specialties: Fancy folders, Damascus Bowies and hunters. **Patterns:** My own design folders & customer requests. **Technical:** ATS-34, hand forged Damascus, 1084, 15N20 mosaic Damascus, 1095, 5160 high carbon blades, flat grind, file work & jewel embellishments. **Prices:** $175 to $1500. **Remarks:** Part-time maker, sold first knife in 2003. **Mark:** Last name

TAKACH, ANDREW

1390 Fallen Timber Rd., Elizabeth, PA 15037, Phone: 724-691-2271, a-takach@takachforge.com; Web: www.takachforge.com

Specialties: One-of-a-kind fixed blade working knives (own design or customer's). Mostly all fileworked. **Patterns:** Hunters, skinners, caping, fighters, and designs of own style. **Technical:** Forges mostly 5160, 1090, 01, an down pattern welded Damascus, nickle Damascus, and cable and various chain Damascus. Also do some San Mai. **Prices:** $100 to $350, some over $550. **Remarks:** Doing business as Takach Forge. First knife sold in 2004. **Mark:** Takach (stamped).

TALLY, GRANT

26961 James Ave, Flat Rock, MI 48134, Phone: 313-414-1618

Specialties: Straight knives and folders of his design. **Patterns:** Bowies, daggers, fighters. **Technical:** Grinds ATS-34, 440C and D2. Offers filework. **Prices:** $250 to $1000. **Remarks:** Part-time maker; first knife sold in 1985. Doing business as Tally Knives. **Mark:** Tally (last name).

TAMATSU, KUNIHIKO

5344 Sukumo, Sukumo City, Kochi-ken, JAPAN 788-0000, Phone: 0880-63-3455, ktamatsu@mb.gallery.ne.jp; Web: www.knife.tamatu.net

Specialties: Loveless-style fighters, sub-hilt fighters and hunting knives. **Technical:** Mirror-finished ATS-34, BG-42 and CPM-S30V blades. **Prices:** $400 to $2,500. **Remarks:** Part-time maker, making knives for eight years. **Mark:** Electrical etching of "K. Tamatsu."

TAMBOLI, MICHAEL

12447 N 49 Ave, Glendale, AZ 85304, Phone: 602-978-4308, mnbtamboli@gmail.com

Specialties: Miniatures, some full size. **Patterns:** Miniature hunting knives to fantasy art knives. **Technical:** Grinds ATS-34 & Damascus. **Prices:** $75 to $500; some to $2000. **Remarks:** Full time maker; first knife sold in 1978. **Mark:** Initials, last name, last name city and state, MT Custom Knives or Mike Tamboli in Japanese script.

TASMAN, KERLEY

9 Avignon Retreat, Pt Kennedy, WA, AUSTRALIA 6172, Phone: 61 8 9593 0554, Fax: 61 8 9593 0554, taskerley@optusnet.com.au

Specialties: Knife/harness/sheath systems for elite military personnel and body guards. **Patterns:** Utility/tactical knives, hunters small game and presentation grade knives. **Technical:** ATS-34 and 440C, Damascus, flat and hollow grids. **Prices:** $200 to $1800 U.S. **Remarks:** Will take presentation grade commissions. Multi award winning maker and custom jeweler. **Mark:** Maker's initials.

TAYLOR, BILLY

10 Temple Rd., Petal, MS 39465, Phone: 601-544-0041

Specialties: Straight knives of his design. **Patterns:** Bowies, skinners, hunters and utility knives. **Technical:** Flat-grinds 440C, ATS-34 and 154CM. **Prices:** $60 to $300. **Remarks:** Part-time maker; first knife sold in 1991. **Mark:** Full name, city and state.

TAYLOR, C. GRAY

560 Poteat Ln., Fall Branch, TN 37656, Phone: 423-348-8304 or 423-765-6434, graysknives@aol.com; Web: www.cgraytaylor.com

Specialties: Traditonal multi-blade lobster folders, also art display Bowies and daggers. **Patterns:** Orange Blossom, sleeveboard and gunstocks. **Technical:** Grinds. **Prices:** Upscale. **Remarks:** Full-time maker; first knife sold in 1975. **Mark:** Name, city and state.

custom knifemakers

TAYLOR, SHANE

42 Broken Bow Ln, Miles City, MT 59301, Phone: 406-234-7175, shane@taylorknives.com; Web: www.taylorknives.com
Specialties: One-of-a-kind fancy Damascus straight knives and folders. **Patterns:** Bowies, folders and fighters. **Technical:** Forges own mosaic and pattern welded Damascus. **Prices:** $450 and up. **Remarks:** ABS Master Smith, full-time maker; first knife sold in 1982. **Mark:** First name.

TEDFORD, STEVEN J.

14238 Telephone Rd., Colborne, ON, CANADA K0K 1S0, Phone: 613-689-7569, firebornswords@yahoo.com; Web: www.steventedfordknives.com
Specialties: Handmade custom fixed blades, specialty outdoors knives. **Patterns:** Swept Survival Bowie, large, medium and small-size field-dressing/hunting knives, drop-point skinners, and world-class fillet knives. **Technical:** Exclusively using ATS-34 stainless steel, Japanese-inspired, free-hand ground, zero-point edge blade design. **Prices:** All knives are sold wholesale directly from the shop starting at $150 to $500+. **Remarks:** Tedford Knives; Function is beauty. Every knife is unconditionally guaranteed for life.

TENDICK, BEN

798 Nadine Ave, Eugene, OR 97404, Phone: 541-912-1280, bentendick@gmail.com; Web: www.brtbladeworks.com
Specialties: Hunter/utility, tactical, bushcraft, and kitchen. **Technical:** Preferred steel - L6, 5160, and 15N20. Stock Removal. **Prices:** $130 to $700. **Remarks:** Part-time; has been making knives since early 90's but started seriously making knives in 2010. In business at BRT Bladeworks, no website yet but can be found on Facebook. **Mark:** Initials (BRT) with B backwards and T between the B and R, and also use last name.

TERRILL, STEPHEN

16357 Goat Ranch Rd, Springville, CA 93265, Phone: 559-920-2722, steve@slterrillknives.com; Web: www.slterrillknives.com
Specialties: Deluxe working straight knives and folders. **Patterns:** Fighters, tantos, boots, locking folders and axes; traditional oriental patterns. **Technical:** Forged and stock removal of 1095, 5160, Damascus, stock removal ATS-34. **Prices:** $400 and up. **Remarks:** Full-time maker, semi-retired; first knife sold in 1972. **Mark:** Name, name-city-state.

TERZUOLA, ROBERT

10121 Eagle Rock NE, Albuquerque, NM 87122, Phone: 505-856-7077, terzuola@earthlink.net
Specialties: Working folders of his design; period pieces. **Patterns:** High-tech utility, defense and gentleman's folders. **Technical:** Grinds CPM154 and damascus. Offers titanium, carbon fiber and G10 composite for side-lock folders and tactical folders. **Prices:** $1,200 to $3,000. **Remarks:** Full-time maker; first knife sold in 1980. **Mark:** Mayan dragon head, name.

TESARIK, RICHARD

Pisecnik 87, 614 00 Brno, Czech Republic, Phone: 00420-602-834-726, rtesarik@gmail.com; Web: www.tesarikknives.com
Specialties: Handmade art knives. **Patterns:** Daggers, hunters and LinerLock or back-lock folders. **Technical:** Grinds RWL-34, N690 and stainless or high-carbon damascus. Carves on blade, handle and other parts. I prefer fossil material and exotic wood, don't use synthetic material. **Prices:** $600 to $2,000. **Remarks:** Part-time maker, full-time hobby; first knife sold in 2009. **Mark:** TR.

THAYER, DANNY O

8908S 100W, Romney, IN 47981, Phone: 765-538-3105, dot61h@juno.com
Specialties: Hunters, fighters, Bowies. **Prices:** $250 and up.

THEVENOT, JEAN-PAUL

16 Rue De La Prefecture, Dijon, FRANCE 21000
Specialties: Traditional European knives and daggers. **Patterns:** Hunters, utility-camp knives, daggers, historical or modern style. **Technical:** Forges own Damascus, 5160, 1084. **Remarks:** Part-time maker. ABS Master Smith. **Mark:** Interlocked initials in square.

THIE, BRIAN

13250 150th St, Burlington, IA 52601, Phone: 319-850-2188, thieknives@gmail.com; Web: www.mepotelco.net/web/tknives
Specialties: Working using knives from basic to fancy. **Patterns:** Hunters, fighters, camp and folders. **Technical:** Forges blades and own Damascus. **Prices:** $250 and up. **Remarks:** ABS Journeyman Smith, part-time maker. Sole author of blades including forging, heat treat, engraving and sheath making. **Mark:** Last name hand engraved into the blade, JS stamped into blade.

THILL, JIM

10242 Bear Run, Missoula, MT 59803, Phone: 406-251-5475, bearrunmt@hotmail.com
Specialties: Traditional and working/using knives of his design. **Patterns:** Fighters, hunters and utility/camp knives. **Technical:** Grinds D2 and ATS-34; forges 10-95-85, 52100, 5160, 10 series, reg. Damascus-mosaic. Offers hand cut sheaths with rawhide lace. **Prices:** $145 to $350; some to $1250. **Remarks:** Full-time maker; first knife sold in 1962. **Mark:** Running bear in triangle.

THOMAS, BOB

Sunset Forge, 3502 Bay Rd., Ferndale, WA 98248, Phone: 360-201-0160, Fax: 360-366-5723, sunsetforge@rockisland.com

THOMAS, DAVID E

8502 Hwy 91, Lillian, AL 36549, Phone: 251-961-7574, redbluff@gulftel.com
Specialties: Bowies and hunters. **Technical:** Hand forged blades in 5160, 1095 and own Damascus. **Prices:** $400 and up. **Mark:** Stylized DT, maker's last name, serial number.

THOMAS, DEVIN

PO Box 568, Panaca, NV 89042, Phone: 775-728-4363, hoss@devinthomas.com; Web: www.devinthomas.com
Specialties: Traditional straight knives and folders in standard patterns. **Patterns:** Bowies, fighters, hunters. **Technical:** Forges stainless Damascus, nickel and 1095. Uses, makes and sells mokume with brass, copper and nickel-silver. **Prices:** $300 to $1200. **Remarks:** Full-time maker; first knife sold in 1979. **Mark:** First and last name, city and state with anvil, or first name only.

THOMAS, KIM

PO Box 531, Seville, OH 44273, Phone: 330-769-9906
Specialties: Fancy and traditional straight knives of his design and to customer specs; period pieces. **Patterns:** Boots, daggers, fighters, swords. **Technical:** Forges own Damascus from 5160, 1010 and nickel. **Prices:** $135 to $1500; some to $3000. **Remarks:** Part-time maker; first knife sold in 1986. Doing business as Thomas Iron Works. **Mark:** KT.

THOMAS, ROCKY

1716 Waterside Blvd, Moncks Corner, SC 29461, Phone: 843-761-7761
Specialties: Traditional working knives in standard patterns. **Patterns:** Hunters and utility/camp knives. **Technical:** ATS-34 and commercial Damascus. **Prices:** $130 to $350. **Remarks:** Spare-time maker; first knife sold in 1986. **Mark:** First name in script and/or block.

THOMPSON, KENNETH

4887 Glenwhite Dr, Duluth, GA 30136, Phone: 770-446-6730
Specialties: Traditional working and using knives of his design. **Patterns:** Hunters, Bowies and utility/camp knives. **Technical:** Forges 5168, O1, 1095 and 52100. **Prices:** $75 to $1500; some to $2500. **Remarks:** Part-time maker; first knife sold in 1990. **Mark:** P/W; or name, P/W, city and state.

THOMPSON, LEON

3400 S.W. Dilley Rd., Forest Grove, OR 97116, Phone: 503-357-2573, lsthomp@msn.com
Specialties: Working knives. **Patterns:** Locking folders, slip-joints and liner locks. **Technical:** Grinds ATS-34, D2 and 440C. **Prices:** $450 to $1000. **Remarks:** Full-time maker; first knife sold in 1976. **Mark:** First and middle initials, last name, city and state.

THOMPSON, LLOYD

PO Box 1664, Pagosa Springs, CO 81147, Phone: 970-264-5837
Specialties: Working and collectible straight knives and folders of his design. **Patterns:** Straight blades, lock back folders and slip joint folders. **Technical:** Hollow-grinds ATS-34, D2 and O1. Uses sambar stag and exotic woods. **Prices:** $150 to upscale. **Remarks:** Full-time maker; first knife sold in 1985. Doing business as Trapper Creek Knife Co. **Remarks:** Offers three-day knife-making classes. **Mark:** Name.

THOMPSON, TOMMY

4015 NE Hassalo, Portland, OR 97232-2607, Phone: 503-235-5762
Specialties: Fancy and working knives; mostly liner-lock folders. **Patterns:** Fighters, hunters and liner locks. **Technical:** Grinds D2, ATS-34, CPM440V and T15. Handles are either hardwood inlaid with wood banding and stone or shell, or made of agate, jasper, petrified woods, etc. **Prices:** $75 to $500; some to $1000. **Remarks:** Part-time maker; first knife sold in 1987. Doing business as Stone Birds. Knife making temporarily stopped due to family obligations. **Mark:** First and last name, city and state.

THOMSEN, LOYD W

25241 Renegade Pass, Custer, SD 57730, Phone: 605-673-2787, loydt@yahoo.com; Web: horseheadcreekknives.com
Specialties: High-art and traditional working/using straight knives and presentation pieces of his design and to customer specs; period pieces. Hand carved animals in crown of stag on handles and carved display stands. **Patterns:** Bowies, hunters, daggers and utility/camp knives. **Technical:** Forges and grinds 1095HC, 1084, L6, 15N20, 440C stainless steel, nickel 200; special restoration process on period pieces. Makes sheaths. Uses natural materials for handles. **Prices:** $350 to $1000. **Remarks:** Full-time maker; first knife sold in 1995. Doing business as Horsehead Creek Knives. **Mark:** Initials and last name over a horse's head.

THORBURN, ANDRE E.

P.O. Box 1748, Bela Bela, Warmbaths, LP, SOUTH AFRICA 0480, Phone: 27-82-650-1441, Fax: 27-86-750-2765, andrethorburn@gmail.com; Web: www.thorburnknives.co.za
Specialties: Working and fancy folders of own design to customer specs. **Technical:** Uses RWL-34, Damasteel, CPM steels, Bohler N690, and carbon and stainless damascus. **Prices:** Starting at $350. **Remarks:** Full-time maker since 1996; first knife sold in 1990. Member of South African, Italian, and German guilds. **Mark:** Initials and name in a double circle.

THOUROT, MICHAEL W

T-814 Co Rd 11, Napoleon, OH 43545, Phone: 419-533-6832, Fax: 419-533-3516, mike2row@henry-net.com; Web: wwwsafariknives.com
Specialties: Working straight knives to customer specs. Designed two-handled skinning ax and limited edition engraved knife and art print set. **Patterns:** Fishing and fillet knives, Bowies, tantos and hunters. **Technical:** Grinds O1, D2, 440C and Damascus. **Prices:** $200 to $5000. **Remarks:** Part-time maker; first knife sold in 1968. **Mark:** Initials.

THUESEN, ED

21211 Knolle Rd, Damon, TX 77430, Phone: 979-553-1211, Fax: 979-553-1211
Specialties: Working straight knives. **Patterns:** Hunters, fighters and survival knives. **Technical:** Grinds D2, 440C, ATS-34 and Vascowear. **Prices:** $150 to $275; some to

$600. **Remarks:** Part-time maker; first knife sold in 1979. Runs knifemaker supply business. **Mark:** Last name in script.

TIENSVOLD, ALAN L
PO Box 355, 3277 U.S. Hwy. 20, Rushville, NE 69360, Phone: 308-360-0613, tiensvoldknives@gpcom.net
Specialties: Working knives, tomahawks and period pieces, high end Damascus knives. **Patterns:** Random, ladder, twist and many more. **Technical:** Hand forged blades, forges own Damascus. **Prices:** Working knives start at $300. **Remarks:** Received Journeyman rating with the ABS in 2002. Does own engraving and fine work. **Mark:** Tiensvold hand made U.S.A. on left side, JS on right.

TIENSVOLD, JASON
PO Box 795, Rushville, NE 69360, Phone: 308-360-2217, jasontiensvoldknives@yahoo.com
Specialties: Working and using straight knives of his design; period pieces. Gentlemen folders, art folders. Single action automatics. **Patterns:** Hunters, skinners, Bowies, fighters, daggers, liner locks. **Technical:** Forges own Damascus using 15N20 and 1084, 1095, nickel, custom file work. **Prices:** $200 to $4000. **Remarks:** Full-time maker, first knife sold in 1994; doing business under Tiensvold Custom Knives. **Mark:** J. Tiensvold on left side, MS on right.

TIGHE, BRIAN
12-111 Fourth Ave, Suite 376 Ridley Square, St. Catharines, ON, CANADA L2S 3P5, Phone: 905-892-2734, Web: www.tigheknives.com
Specialties: Folding knives, bearing pivots. High tech tactical folders. **Patterns:** Boots, daggers and locking. **Technical:** BG-42, RWL-34, Damasteel, 154CM, S30V, CPM 440V and CPM 420V. Prefers natural handle material inlay; hand finishes. **Prices:** $450 to $4000. **Remarks:** Full-time maker; first knife sold in 1989. **Mark:** Etched signature.

TILL, CALVIN E AND RUTH
1010 Maple St., Lot 4, Chadron, NE 69337-6967, Phone: 308-430-2231
Specialties: Straight knives, hunters, Bowies; no folders **Patterns:** Training point, drop point hunters, Bowies. **Technical:** ATS-34 sub zero quench RC59, 61. **Prices:** $700 to $1200. **Remarks:** Sells only the absolute best knives they can make. Manufactures every part in their knives. **Mark:** RC Till. The R is for Ruth, the C for Calvin.

TILTON, JOHN
24041 Hwy 383, Iowa, LA 70647, Phone: 337-582-6785, john@jetknives.com
Specialties: Bowies, camp knives, skinners and folders. **Technical:** All forged blades. Makes own Damascus. **Prices:** $150 and up. **Remarks:** ABS Journeyman Smith. **Mark:** Initials J.E.T.

TINDERA, GEORGE
BURNING RIVER FORGE, 751 Hadcock Rd, Brunswick, OH 44212-2648, Phone: 330-220-6212
Specialties: Straight knives; his designs. **Patterns:** Personal knives; classic Bowies and fighters. **Technical:** Hand-forged high-carbon; his own cable and pattern welded Damascus. **Prices:** $125 to $600. **Remarks:** Spare-time maker; sold first knife in 1995. Natural handle materials.

TINGLE, DENNIS P
19390 E Clinton Rd, Jackson, CA 95642, Phone: 209-223-4586, dtknives@earthlink.net
Specialties: Swords, fixed blades: small to medium, tomahawks. **Technical:** All blades forged. **Remarks:** ABS, JS. **Mark:** D. Tingle over JS.

TIPPETTS, COLTEN
4515 W. Long Meadow Dr., Hidden Springs, ID 83714, Phone: 208-473-1474, coltentippetts@gmail.com; Web: www.ctknives.webs.com
Specialties: Fancy and working fixed blades and folders of his own design or to customer specifications. **Patterns:** Hunters and skinners, fighters, tactical blades and lockback folders. **Technical:** Grinds BG-42 and CPM S30V, and forges O1. **Prices:** $200 to $1,000. **Remarks:** Full-time maker; first knife sold in 1996. **Mark:** Fused initials.

TOBOLAK, LIBOR
NO COMPROMISE DESIGN, 635 N. Twin Oaks Valley Rd., Ste. 20, San Marcos, CA 92069, Phone: 201-668-9885, nocompromisedesign@gmail.com; Web: www. nocompromisedesign.com; Facebook: No Compromise Design

TODD, RICHARD C
375th LN 46001, Chambersburg, IL 62323, Phone: 217-327-4380, ktodd45@yahoo.com
Specialties: Multi blade folders and silver sheaths. **Patterns:** Jewel setting and hand engraving. **Mark:** RT with letter R crossing the T or R Todd.

TOICH, NEVIO
Via Pisacane 9, Rettorgole di Caldogna, Vincenza, ITALY 36030, Phone: 0444-985065, Fax: 0444-301254
Specialties: Working/using straight knives of his design or to customer specs. **Patterns:** Bowies, hunters, skinners and utility/camp knives. **Technical:** Grinds 440C, D2 and ATS-34. Hollow-grinds all blades and uses mirror polish. Offers hand-sewn sheaths. Uses wood and horn. **Prices:** $120 to $300; some to $450. **Remarks:** Spare-time maker; first knife sold in 1989. Doing business as Custom Toich. **Mark:** Initials and model number punched.

TOKAR, DANIEL
Box 1776, Shepherdstown, WV 25443
Specialties: Working knives; period pieces. **Patterns:** Hunters, camp knives, buckskinners, axes, swords and battle gear. **Technical:** Forges L6, 1095 and his Damascus; makes mokume, Japanese alloys and bronze daggers; restores old edged weapons. **Prices:** $25 to $800; some to $3000. **Remarks:** Part-time maker; first knife sold in 1979. Doing business as The Willow Forge. **Mark:** Arrow over rune and date.

TOMBERLIN, BRION R
ANVIL TOP CUSTOM KNIVES, 825 W Timberdell, Norman, OK 73072, Phone: 405-202-6832, anviltopp@aol.com
Specialties: Handforged blades, working pieces, standard classic patterns, some swords and customer designs. **Patterns:** Bowies, hunters, fighters, Persian and eastern-styles. Likes Japanese blades. **Technical:** Forges 1050, 1075, 1084, 1095, 5160, some forged stainless, also does some stock removal in stainless. Also makes own damascus. **Prices:** $350 to $4,000. Higher and up for swords and custom pieces. **Remarks:** Part-time maker, ABS master smith. Prefers natural handle materials, hand-rubbed finishes. Likes temper lines. **Mark:** BRION with MS.

TOMEY, KATHLEEN
146 Buford Pl, Macon, GA 31204, Phone: 478-746-8454, ktomey@tomeycustomknives.com; Web: www.tomeycustomknives.com
Specialties: Hunters, skinners, daily users in fixed blades, plain and embellished. Tactical neck and belt carry. Japanese influenced. Bowies. **Technical:** Grinds O1, ATS-34, flat or hollow grind, filework, satin and mirror polish finishes. High quality leather sheaths with tooling. Kydex with tactical. **Prices:** $150 to $500. **Remarks:** Almost full-time maker. **Mark:** Last name in diamond.

TONER, ROGER
531 Lightfoot Pl, Pickering, ON, CANADA L1V 5Z8, Phone: 905-420-5555
Specialties: Exotic sword canes. **Patterns:** Bowies, daggers and fighters. **Technical:** Grinds 440C, D2 and Damascus. Scrimshaws and engraves. Silver cast pommels and guards in animal shapes; twisted silver wire inlays. Uses semi-precious stones. **Prices:** $200 to $2000; some to $3000. **Remarks:** Part-time maker; first knife sold in 1982. **Mark:** Last name.

TORRES, HENRY
2329 Moody Ave., Clovis, CA 93619, Phone: 559-297-9154, Web: www.htknives.com
Specialties: Forged high-performance hunters and working knives, Bowies, and fighters. **Technical:** 52100 and 5160 and makes own Damascus. **Prices:** $350 to $3000. **Remarks:** Started forging in 2004. Has mastersmith with American Bladesmith Association.

TOSHIFUMI, KURAMOTO
3435 Higashioda, Asakura-gun, Fukuoka, JAPAN, Phone: 0946-42-4470

TOWELL, DWIGHT L
2375 Towell Rd, Midvale, ID 83645, Phone: 208-355-2419
Specialties: Solid, elegant working knives; art knives, high quality hand engraving and gold inlay. **Patterns:** Hunters, Bowies, daggers and folders. **Technical:** Grinds 154CM, ATS-34, 440C and other maker's Damascus. **Prices:** Upscale. **Remarks:** Full-time maker. First knife sold in 1970. Member of AKI. **Mark:** Towell, sometimes hand engraved.

TOWNSEND, ALLEN MARK
6 Pine Trail, Texarkana, AR 71854, Phone: 870-772-8945

TOWNSLEY, RUSSELL
PO BOX 91, Floral, AR 72534-0091, Phone: 870-307-8069, circleTRMtownsley@yahoo.com
Specialties: Using knives of his own design. **Patterns:** Hunters, skinners, folders. **Technical:** Hollow grinds D2 and O1. Handle material - antler, tusk, bone, exotic woods. **Prices:** Prices start at $125. **Remarks:** Arkansas knifemakers association. Sold first knife in 2009. Doing business as Circle-T knives. **Mark:** Encircled T.

TRACE RINALDI CUSTOM BLADES
1470 Underpass Rd, Plummer, ID 83851, Trace@thrblades.com; Web: www.thrblades.com
Technical: Grinds S30V, 3V, A2 and talonite fixed blades. **Prices:** $300-$1000. **Remarks:** Tactical and utility for the most part. **Mark:** Diamond with THR inside.

TRIBBLE, SKYLAR
Cold Handle Custom Knives, 1413 Alabama St., Leakesville, MS 39451, Phone: 601-394-3490, skylartribble@yahoo.com
Specialties: Fixed blades only. **Patterns:** From small neck knives to large bowie knives. **Technical:** Mainly uses repurposed steels from old files and high-carbon steels, and recently started using 154CM and CPM 154 stainless steels that he enjoys working with. Does both stock removal and forging, saying it's up to the customer. **Prices:** $50+ (up to around $600). **Remarks:** Part-time maker and full-time student; first knife made in 2009 at 13 years old. **Mark:** C with H and K on the tail of the C (for Cold Handle Custom Knives).

TRINDLE, BARRY
1660 Ironwood Trail, Earlham, IA 50072-8611, Phone: 515-462-1237
Specialties: Engraved folders. **Patterns:** Mostly small folders, classical-styles and pocket knives. **Technical:** 440 only. Engraves. Handles of wood or mineral material. **Prices:** Start at $1000. **Mark:** Name on tang.

TRISLER, KENNETH W
6256 Federal 80, Rayville, LA 71269, Phone: 318-728-5541

TRITZ, JEAN-JOSE
Pinneberger Chaussee 48, Hamburg, GERMANY 22523, Phone: +49(40) 49 78 21, jeanjosetritz@aol.com; www.tritz-messer.com
Specialties: Scandinavian knives, Japanese kitchen knives, friction folders, swords. **Patterns:** Puukkos, Tollekniven, Hocho, friction folders, swords. **Technical:** Forges tool steels, carbon steels, 52100 Damascus, mokume, San Maj. **Prices:** $200 to $2000; some higher. **Remarks:** Full-time maker; first knife sold in 1989. Does own leatherwork, prefers natural materials. Sole authorship. Speaks French, German, English, Norwegian. **Mark:** Initials in monogram.

TROUT, GEORGE H.
727 Champlin Rd, Wilmington, OH 45177, Phone: 937-382-2331, gandjtrout@msn.com
Specialties: Working knives, some fancy. **Patterns:** Hunters, drop points, Bowies and fighters. **Technical:** Stock removal: ATS-34, 440C Forged: 5160, W2, 1095, O1 Full integrals: 440C, A2, O1. **Prices:** $150 and up. **Remarks:** Makes own sheaths and mosaic pins. Fileworks most knives. First knife 1985. **Mark:** Etched name and state on stock removal. Forged: stamped name and forged.

TRUJILLO, ALBERT M B
2035 Wasmer Cir, Bosque Farms, NM 87068, Phone: 505-869-0428, trujilloscutups@comcast.net
Specialties: Working/using straight knives of his design or to customer specs. **Patterns:** Hunters, skinners, fighters, working/using knives. File work offered. **Technical:** Grinds ATS-34, D2, 440C, S30V. Tapers tangs, all blades cryogenically treated. **Prices:** $75 to $500. **Remarks:** Part-time maker; first knife sold in 1997. **Mark:** First and last name under logo.

TRUNCALI, PETE
966 Harmony Circle, Nevada, TX 75173, Phone: 214-763-7127, truncaliknives@yahoo.com Web: www.truncaliknives.com
Specialties: Lockback folders and automatics. Does business as Truncali Custom Knives.

TSCHAGER, REINHARD
S. Maddalena di Sotto 1a, Bolzano, ITALY 39100, Phone: 0471-975005, Fax: 0471-975005, reinhardtschager@virgilio.it
Specialties: Classic, high-art, collector-grade straight knives of his design. **Patterns:** Jewel knife, daggers, and hunters. **Technical:** Grinds ATS-34, D2 and Damascus. Oval pins. Gold inlay. Offers engraving. **Prices:** $900 to $2000; some to $3000. **Remarks:** Spare-time maker; first knife sold in 1979. **Mark:** Gold inlay stamped with initials.

TUCH, WILLIAM
Troy Studios, 1220 S.W. Morrison St., Lobby A, Portland, OR 97205, Phone: 503-504-1261, tuchknives@gmail.com; Web: www.tuchknives.com
Specialties: Folding knives and daggers, mostly ornate. **Patterns:** One-of-a-kind locking knives, lockbacks, side locks, switchblades, miniatures and more. **Technical:** Flat and hollow grinds, ornate sculpture. All knives are hand filed and hand polished. Materials vary. **Prices:** $1,800 to $10,000 and up. **Remarks:** Full-time maker since 2004. **Mark:** TUCH.

TUOMINEN, PEKKA
Pohjois-Keiteleentie 20, Tossavanlahti, FINLAND 72930, Phone: 358405167853, puukkopekka@luukku.com; Web: www.puukkopekka.com
Specialties: Puukko knives. **Patterns:** Puukkos, hunters, leukus, and folders. **Technical:** Forges silversteel, 1085, 52100, and makes own Damascus 15N20 and 1095. Grinds RWL-34 and ATS-34. **Prices:** Starting at $300. **Remarks:** Full-time maker. **Mark:** PEKKA; earlier whole name.

TURECEK, JIM
12 Elliott Rd, Ansonia, CT 06401, Phone: 203-734-8406, jturecek@sbcglobal.net
Specialties: Exotic folders, art knives and some miniatures. **Patterns:** Trout and bird knives with split bamboo handles and one-of-a-kind folders. **Technical:** Grinds and forges stainless and carbon damascus. All knives are handmade using no computer-controlled machinery. **Prices:** $2,000 to $10,000. **Remarks:** Full-time maker; first knife sold in 1983. **Mark:** Last initial in script, or last name.

TURNBULL, RALPH A
14464 Linden Dr, Spring Hill, FL 34609, Phone: 352-688-7089, tbull2000@bellsouth.net; Web: www.turnbullknives.com
Specialties: Fancy folders. **Patterns:** Primarily gents pocket knives. **Technical:** Wire EDM work on bolsters. **Prices:** $300 and up. **Remarks:** Full-time maker; first knife sold in 1973. **Mark:** Signature or initials.

TURNER, KEVIN
17 Hunt Ave, Montrose, NY 10548, Phone: 914-739-0535
Specialties: Working straight knives of his design and to customer specs; period pieces. **Patterns:** Daggers, fighters and utility knives. **Technical:** Forges 5160 and 52100. **Prices:** $90 to $500. **Remarks:** Part-time maker; first knife sold in 1991. **Mark:** Acid-etched signed last name and year.

TURNER, MIKE
3065 Cedar Flat Rd., Williams, OR 97544, Phone: 541-846-0204, mike@turnerknives.com Web: www.turnerknives.com
Specialties: Forged and stock removed full tang, hidden and thru tang knives. **Patterns:** Hunters, fighters, Bowies, boot knives, skinners and kitchen knives. **Technical:** I make my own damascus. **Prices:** $200 - $1,000. **Remarks:** Part-time maker, sold my first knife in 2008, doing business as Mike Turner Custom Knives. **Mark:** Name, City, & State.

TYRE, MICHAEL A
1219 Easy St, Wickenburg, AZ 85390, Phone: 928-684-9601/602-377-8432, mtyre86@gmail.com; Web: www.miketyrecustomknives.com
Specialties: Quality folding knives, upscale gents folders, one-of-a-kind collectable models. **Patterns:** Working fixed blades for hunting, kitchen and fancy bowies. Forging my own damascus patterns. **Technical:** Grinds, prefers hand-rubbed satin finishes and uses natural handle materials. **Prices:** $250 to $1,300. **Remarks:** ABS journeyman smith.

TYSER, ROSS
1015 Hardee Court, Spartanburg, SC 29303, Phone: 864-585-7616
Specialties: Traditional working and using straight knives and folders of his design and in standard patterns. **Patterns:** Bowies, hunters and slip-joint folders. **Technical:** Grinds 440C and commercial Damascus. Mosaic pins; stone inlay. Does filework and scrimshaw. Offers engraving and cut-work and some inlay on sheaths. **Prices:** $45 to $125; some to

$400. **Remarks:** Part-time maker; first knife sold in 1995. Doing business as RT Custom Knives. **Mark:** Stylized initials.

U

UCHIDA, CHIMATA
977-2 Oaza Naga Shisui Ki, Kumamoto, JAPAN 861-1204

UPTON, TOM
Little Rabbit Forge, 1414 Feast Pl., Rogers, AR 72758, Phone: 479-636-6755, Web: www.upton-knives.com
Specialties: Working fixed blades. **Patterns:** Hunters, utility, fighters, bowies and small hatchets. **Technical:** Forges 5160, 1084 and W2 blade steels, or stock removal using D2, 440C and 154CM. Performs own heat treat. **Prices:** $150 and up. **Remarks:** Part-time maker; first knife sold in 1977. Member of the Knife Group Association. **Mark:** Name (Small Rabbit logo), city and state, etched or stamped.

URBACH, SCOTT
19135 E. Oxford Dr., Aurora, CO 80013, Phone: 303-882-1875, urbach@comcast.net or laughingcoyoteknives@gmail.com; Web: www.facebook.com/laughingcoyoteknivescolorado
Specialties: Unique hard-use working knives. **Patterns:** Western, cowboy and traditional historic bowies, fighters, mountain man styles, camp knives and hunters. **Technical:** Customer's choice of steel, from high-end carbon to custom damascus, including natural handle material and leather or Kydex sheaths. Specializes in repurposing discarded steel from old saws, kitchen knives, auto parts, etc., as well as repairing damaged knives that would otherwise be discarded. **Prices:** $50 to $300+. **Remarks:** Part-time maker looking to transition to full time; first knife sold in 2014. **Mark:** Petroglyph Coyote with last name.

V

VAGNINO, MICHAEL
1415 W. Ashland Ave., Visalia, CA 93277, Phone: 559-636-0501; cell: 559-827-7802, mike@mvknives.com; Web: www.mvknives.com
Specialties: Folders and straight knives, working and fancy. **Patterns:** Folders--locking liners, slip joints, lock backs, double and single action autos. Straight knives--hunters, Bowies, camp and kitchen. **Technical:** Forges 52100, W2, 15N20 and 1084. Grinds stainless. Makes own damascus and does engraving. **Prices:** $300 to $4,000 and above. **Remarks:** Full-time maker, ABS Mastersmith. **Mark:** Logo, last name.

VAIL, DAVE
554 Sloop Point Rd, Hampstead, NC 28443, Phone: 910-270-4456
Specialties: Working/using straight knives of his own design or to the customer's specs. **Patterns:** Hunters/skinners, camp/utility, fillet, Bowies. **Technical:** Grinds ATS-34, 440C, 154 CM and 1095 carbon steel. **Prices:** $90 to $450. **Remarks:** Part-time maker. Member of NC Custom Knifemakers Guild. **Mark:** Etched oval with "Dave Vail Hampstead NC" inside.

VALLOTTON, BUTCH AND AREY
621 Fawn Ridge Dr, Oakland, OR 97462, Phone: 541-459-2216, Fax: 541-459-7473
Specialties: Quick opening knives w/complicated mechanisms. **Technical:** Tactical, fancy, working, and some art knives. **Technical:** Grinds all steels, uses others' Damascus. Uses Spectrum Metal. **Prices:** From $350 to $4500. **Remarks:** Full-time maker since 1984; first knife sold in 1981. Co/designer, Applegate Fairbarn folding w/Bill Harsey. **Mark:** Name w/viper head in the "V."

VALLOTTON, RAINY D
1295 Wolf Valley Dr, Umpqua, OR 97486, Phone: 541-459-0465
Specialties: Folders, one-handed openers and art pieces. **Patterns:** All patterns. **Technical:** Stock removal all steels; uses titanium liners and bolsters; uses all finishes. **Prices:** $350 to $3500. **Remarks:** Full-time maker. **Mark:** Name.

VALLOTTON, SHAWN
621 Fawn Ridge Dr, Oakland, OR 97462, Phone: 503-459-2216
Specialties: Left-hand knives. **Patterns:** All styles. **Technical:** Grinds 440C, ATS-34 and Damascus. Uses titanium. Prefers bead-blasted or anodized finishes. **Prices:** $250 to $1400. **Remarks:** Full-time maker. **Mark:** Name and specialty.

VALLOTTON, THOMAS
621 Fawn Ridge Dr, Oakland, OR 97462, Phone: 541-459-2216
Specialties: Custom autos. **Patterns:** Tactical, fancy. **Technical:** File work, uses Damascus, uses Spectrum Metal. **Prices:** From $350 to $700. **Remarks:** Full-time maker. Maker of ProtŽgé 3 canoe. **Mark:** T and a V mingled.

VAN CLEVE, STEVE
Box 372, Sutton, AK 99674, Phone: 907-745-3038, Fax: 907-745-8770, sucents@mtaonline.net; Web: www.alaskaknives.net

VAN DE MANAKKER, THIJS
Koolweg 34, Holland, NETHERLANDS, Phone: 0493539369, www.ehijsvandemanakker.com
Specialties: Classic high-art knives. **Patterns:** Swords, utility/camp knives and period pieces. **Technical:** Forges soft iron, carbon steel and Bloomery Iron. Makes own Damascus, Bloomery Iron and patterns. **Prices:** $20 to $2000; some higher. **Remarks:** Full-time maker; first knife sold in 1969. **Mark:** Stylized "V."

VAN DEN BERG, NEELS
166 Van Heerdan St., Capital Park, Pretoria, Gauteng, SOUTH AFRICA, Phone: +27(0)12-326-5649 or +27(0)83-451-3105, neels@blackdragonforge.com; Web: http://www.blackdragonforge.com or http://www.facebook.com/neels.vandenberg
Specialties: Handforged damascus and high-carbon steel axes, hunters, swords and art

knives. **Patterns:** All my own designs and customer collaborations, from axes, hunters, choppers, bowies, swords and folders to one-off tactical prototypes. **Technical:** Flat and hollow grinding. Handforges high-carbon steels and maker's own damascus. Also works in high-carbon stainless steels. **Prices:** $50 to $1,000. **Remarks:** Part-time maker; first knife sold in Oct. 2009. **Mark:** Stylized capital letter "N" resembling a three-tier mountain, normally hot stamped in forged blades.

VAN DEN ELSEN, GERT
Purcelldreef 83, Tilburg, NETHERLANDS 5012 AJ, Phone: 013-4563200, gvdelsen@home.nl
Specialties: Fancy, working/using, miniatures and integral straight knives of the maker's design or to customer specs. **Patterns:** Bowies, fighters, hunters and Japanese-style blades. **Technical:** Grinds ATS-34 and 440C; forges Damascus. Offers filework, differentially tempered blades and some mokume-gane fittings. **Prices:** $350 to $1000; some to $4000. **Remarks:** Part-time maker; first knife sold in 1982. Doing business as G-E Knives. **Mark:** Initials GE in lozenge shape.

VAN DER WESTHUIZEN, PETER
PO Box 1698, Mossel Bay, SC, SOUTH AFRICA 6500, Phone: 27 446952388, pietvdw@telkomsa.net
Specialties: Working knives, folders, daggers and art knives. **Patterns:** Hunters, skinners, bird, trout and sidelock folders. **Technical:** Sandvik, 12627. Damascus indigenous wood and ivory. **Prices:** From $450 to $5500. **Remarks:** First knife sold in 1987. Full-time since 1996. **Mark:** Initial & surname. Handmade RSA.

VAN DIJK, RICHARD
76 Stepney Ave Rd 2, Harwood Dunedin, NEW ZEALAND, Phone: 0064-3-4780401, Web: www.hoihoknives.com
Specialties: Damascus, Fantasy knives, sgiandubhs, dirks, swords, and hunting knives. **Patterns:** Mostly one-offs, anything from bird and trout to swords, no folders. **Technical:** Forges mainly own Damascus, some 5160, O1, 1095, L6. Prefers natural handle materials, over 40 years experience as goldsmith, handle fittings are often made from sterling silver and sometimes gold, manufactured to cap the handle, use gemstones if required. Makes own sheaths. **Prices:** $300 and up. **Remarks:** Full-time maker, first knife sold in 1980. Doing business as HOIHO KNIVES. **Mark:** Stylized initials RvD in triangle.

VAN EIZENGA, JERRY W
4281 Cleveland, Nunica, MI 49448, Phone: 616-638-2275
Specialties: Hand forged blades, Scagel patterns and other styles. **Patterns:** Camp, hunting, bird, trout, folders, axes, miniatures. **Technical:** 5160, 52100, 1084. **Prices:** Start at $250. **Remarks:** Part-time maker, sole author of knife and sheath. First knife made 1970s. ABS member who believes in the beauty of simplicity. **Mark:** J.S. stamp.

VAN ELDIK, FRANS
Ho Flaan 3, Loenen, NETHERLANDS 3632 BT, Phone: 0031 294 233 095, Fax: 0031 294 233 095
Specialties: Fancy collector-grade straight knives and folders of his design. **Patterns:** Hunters, fighters, boots and folders. **Technical:** Forges and grinds D2, 154CM, ATS-34 and stainless Damascus. **Prices:** Start at $450. **Remarks:** Spare-time maker; first knife sold in 1979. Knifemaker 30 years, 25 year member of Knifemakers Guild. **Mark:** Lion with name and Amsterdam.

VAN HEERDEN, ANDRE
P.O. Box 905-417, Garsfontein, Pretoria, GT, SOUTH AFRICA 0042, Phone: 27 82 566 5030, andrevh@iafrica.com; Web: www.andrevanheerden.com
Specialties: Fancy and working folders of his design to customer specs. **Technical:** Grinds RWL34, 19C27, D2, carbon and stainless Damascus. **Prices:** Starting at $350. **Remarks:** Part-time maker, first knife sold in 2003. **Mark:** Initials and name in a double circle.

VAN REENEN, IAN
003 Harvard St, Amarillo, TX 79109, Phone: 806-236-8333, ianvanreenen@suddenlink.net Web: www.ianvanreenencustomknives.com
Specialties: Pocketknives and hunting knives. **Patterns:** Tactical pocketknives. **Technical:** 14C28N, 12C27 and ATS-34 blade steels. **Prices:** $600 to $1,500. **Remarks:** Specializing in tactical pocketknives. **Mark:** IVR with TEXAS underneath.

VAN RYSWYK, AAD
AVR KNIVES, Werf Van Pronk 8, Vlaardingen, NETHERLANDS 3134 HE, Phone: +31 10 4742952, info@avrknives.com; Web: www.avrknives.com
Specialties: High-art interframe folders of his design. **Patterns:** Hunters and locking folders. **Technical:** Uses semi-precious stones, mammoth ivory, iron wood, etc. **Prices:** $550 to $3800. **Remarks:** Full-time maker; first knife sold in 1993.

VANCE, DAVID
646 Bays Bend Rd., West Liberty, KY 41472, Phone: 606-743-1465 and 606-362-339, dtvance@mrtc.com; Web: www.facebook.com/ddcutlery
Specialties: Custom hunting or collectible knives, folders and fixed blades, also unique bullet casing handle pins and filework. **Patterns:** Maker's design or made to customers' specifications. **Technical:** Uses stock removal method on 1095 steel. **Remarks:** Part-time maker; first knife made in 2006. **Mark:** Cursive D&D.

VANDERFORD, CARL G
290 Knob Creek Rd, Columbia, TN 38401, Phone: 931-381-1488
Specialties: Traditional working straight knives and folders of his design. **Patterns:** Hunters, Bowies and locking folders. **Technical:** Forges and grinds 440C, O1 and wire Damascus. **Prices:** $60 to $125. **Remarks:** Part-time maker; first knife sold in 1987. **Mark:** Last name.

VANDERKOLFF, STEPHEN
5 Jonathan Crescent, Mildmay, ON, CANADA N0g 2JO, Phone: 519-367-3401, steve@vanderkolffknives.com; Web: www.vanderkolffknives.com
Specialties: Fixed blades from gent's pocketknives and drop hunters to full sized Bowies and art knives. **Technical:** Primary blade steel 440C, Damasteel or custom made Damascus. All heat treat done by maker and all blades hardness tested. Handle material: stag, stabilized woods or MOP. **Prices:** $150 to $1200. **Remarks:** Started making knives in 1998 and sold first knife in 2000. Winner of the best of show art knife 2005 Wolverine Knife Show.

VANDEVENTER, TERRY L
1915 Timberlake Pl., Byram, MS 39272, Phone: 601-371-7414, vandeventerterry@gmail.com; Web: www.vandeventerknives.com
Specialties: Bowies, hunters, camp knives, friction folders. **Technical:** 1084, 1095, 15N20 and L6 steels. Damascus and mokume. Natural handle materials. **Prices:** $600 to $3000. **Remarks:** Sole author; makes everything here. First ABS MS from the state of Mississippi. **Mark:** T.L. Vandeventer (silhouette of snake underneath). MS on ricasso.

VANHOY, ED AND TANYA
24255 N Fork River Rd, Abingdon, VA 24210, Phone: 276-944-4885, vanhoyknives@centurylink.net
Specialties: Traditional and working/using straight knives and folders and innovative locking mechanisms. **Patterns:** Fighters, straight knives, folders, hunters, art knives and Bowies. **Technical:** Grinds ATS-34 and carbon/stainless steel Damascus; forges carbon and stainless Damascus. Offers filework and engraving with hammer and chisel. **Prices:** $250 to $3000. **Remarks:** Full-time maker; first knife sold in 1977. Wife also engraves. Doing business as Van Hoy Custom Knives. **Mark:** Acid etched last name.

VARDAMAN, ROBERT
2406 Mimosa Lane, Hattiesburg, MS 39402, Phone: 601-268-3889, rvx222@gmail.com
Specialties: Working straight knives, mainly integrals, of his design or to customer specs. **Patterns:** Mainly integrals, bowies and hunters. **Technical:** Forges 52100, W2 and 1084. Filework. **Prices:** $250 to $1,000. **Remarks:** Part-time maker. First knife sold in 2004. **Mark:** Last name, last name with Mississippi state logo.

VASQUEZ, JOHNNY DAVID
1552 7th St, Wyandotte, MI 48192, Phone: 734-837-7733, trollhammerv@aol.com

VEIT, MICHAEL
3289 E Fifth Rd, LaSalle, IL 61301, Phone: 815-223-3538, whitebear@starband.net
Specialties: Damascus folders. **Technical:** Engraver, sole author. **Prices:** $2500 to $6500. **Remarks:** Part-time maker; first knife sold in 1985. **Mark:** Name in script.

VELARDE, RICARDO
7240 N Greenfield Dr, Park City, UT 84098, Phone: 435-901-1773, velardeknives@mac.com Web: www.velardeknives.com
Specialties: Investment grade integrals and interframs. **Patterns:** Boots, fighters and hunters; hollow grind. **Technical:** BG on Integrals. **Prices:** $1450 to $5200. **Remarks:** First knife sold in 1992. **Mark:** First initial and last name.

VELICK, SAMMY
3457 Maplewood Ave, Los Angeles, CA 90066, Phone: 310-663-6170, metaltamer@gmail.com
Specialties: Working knives and art pieces. **Patterns:** Hunter, utility and fantasy. **Technical:** Stock removal and forges. **Prices:** $100 and up. **Mark:** Last name.

VENSILD, HENRIK
Gl Estrup, Randersvei 4, Auning, DENMARK 8963, Phone: +45 86 48 44 48
Specialties: Classic and traditional working and using knives of his design; Scandinavian influence. **Patterns:** Hunters and using knives. **Technical:** Forges Damascus. Hand makes handles, sheaths and blades. **Prices:** $350 to $1000. **Remarks:** Part-time maker; first knife sold in 1967. **Mark:** Initials.

VERONIQUE, LAURENT
Avenue du Capricorne, 53, 1200 Bruxelles, BELGIUM, Phone: 0032-477-48-66-73, whatsonthebench@gmail.com
Specialties: Fixed blades and friction folders. **Patterns:** Bowies, camp knives, ladies' knives and maker's own designs. **Technical:** Maker's own San Mai steel with a Blue Paper Steel edge and pure-nickel-and-O1 outer layers, called "Nickwich" (nickel in sandwich), and damascus, numerical milling embellishments and inlays, and hand-fashioned sheaths. **Prices:** Start at $350. **Remarks:** Part-time maker since 2005, ABS journeyman smith since 2013.

VESTAL, CHARLES
26662 Shortsville Rd., Abingdon, VA 24210, Phone: 276-492-3262, charles@vestalknives.com; Web: www.vestalknives.com
Specialties: Hunters and double ground fighters in traditional designs and own designs. **Technical:** Grinds CPM-154, ATS-134, 154-CM and other steels. **Prices:** $300 to $1000, some higher. **Remarks:** First knife sold in 1995.

VIALLON, HENRI
Les Belins, Thiers, FRANCE 63300, Phone: 04-73-80-24-03, Fax: 04 73-51-02-02
Specialties: Folders and complex Damascus **Patterns:** His draws. **Technical:** Forge. **Prices:** $1000 to $5000. **Mark:** H. Viallon.

VICKERS, DAVID
11620 Kingford Dr., Montgomery, TX 77316, Phone: 936-537-4900, jdvickers@gmail.com
Specialties: Working/using blade knives especially for hunters. His design or to customer

specs. **Patterns:** Hunters, skinners, camp/utility. **Technical:** Grinds ATS-34, 440C, and D-2. Uses stag, various woods, and micarta for handle material. Hand-stitched sheaths. **Remarks:** Full-time maker. **Prices:** $125 - $350. **Mark:** VICKERS

VIELE, H J
88 Lexington Ave, Westwood, NJ 07675, Phone: 201-666-2906, h.viele@verizon.net
Specialties: Folding knives of distinctive shapes. **Patterns:** High-tech folders and one-of-a-kind. **Technical:** Grinds ATS-34 and S30V. **Prices:** Start at $575. **Remarks:** Full-time maker; first knife sold in 1973. **Mark:** Japanese design for the god of war.

VILAR, RICARDO
Al. dos Jasmins 243, Mairipora, SP, BRAZIL 07600-000, Phone: +55 (15) 8133-0196, ricardovilar@gmail.com; Web: rvilarknives.com.br
Specialties: Straight working knives to customer specs. **Patterns:** Bowies, fighters and utility/camp knives. **Technical:** Grinds D6, ATS-34 and 440C stainless. **Prices:** $80 to $200. **Remarks:** Part-time maker; first knife sold in 1993. **Mark:** Percor over sword and circle.

VILAR, RICARDO AUGUSTO FERREIRA
Rua Alemada Dos Jasmins NO 243, Parque Petropolis, Mairipora, SP, BRAZIL 07600-000, Phone: 011-55-11-44-85-43-46, ricardovilar@ig.com.br
Specialties: Traditional Brazilian-style working knives of the Sao Paulo state. **Patterns:** Fighters, hunters, utility, and camp knives, welcome customer design. Specialize in the "true" Brazilian camp knife "Soracabana." **Technical:** Forges only with sledge hammer to 100 percent shape in 5160 and 52100 and his own Damascus steels. Makes own sheaths in the "true" traditional "Paulista"-style of the state of Sao Paulo. **Remarks:** Full-time maker. **Prices:** $250 to $600. Uses only natural handle materials. **Mark:** Special designed signature styled name R. Vilar.

VILLA, LUIZ
R. Com. Miguel Calfat 398, Itaim Bibi, SP, BRAZIL 04537-081, Phone: 011-8290649
Specialties: One-of-a-kind straight knives and jewel knives of all designs. **Patterns:** Bowies, hunters, utility/camp knives and jewel knives. **Technical:** Grinds D6, Damascus and 440C; forges 5160. Prefers natural handle material. **Prices:** $70 to $200. **Remarks:** Part-time maker; first knife sold in 1990. **Mark:** Last name and serial number.

VILPPOLA, MARKKU
Jaanintie 45, Turku, FINLAND 20540, Phone: +358 (0)50 566 1563, markku@mvforge.fi Web: www.mvforge.fi
Specialties: All kinds of swords and knives. **Technical:** Forges silver steel, CO, 8%, nickel, 1095, A203E, etc. Mokume (sterling silver/brass/copper). Bronze casting (sand casting, lost-wax casting). **Prices:** Starting at $200.

VINING, BILL
9 Penny Lane, Methuen, MA 01844, Phone: 978-688-4729, billv@medawebs.com; Web: www.medawebs.com/knives
Specialties Liner locking folders. **Slip joints & lockbacks. Patterns:** Likes to make patterns of his own design. **Technical:** S30V, 440C, ATS-34. Damascus from various makers. **Prices:** $450 and up. **Remarks:** Part-time maker. **Mark:** VINING or B. Vining.

VISTE, JAMES
EDGEWISE FORGE, 9745 Dequindre, Hamtramck, MI 48212, Phone: 313-587-8899, edgewiseforge@hotmail.com
Mark: EWF touch mark.

VISTNES, TOR
Svelgen, NORWAY N-6930, Phone: 047-57795572
Specialties: Traditional and working knives of his design. **Patterns:** Hunters and utility knives. **Technical:** Grinds Uddeholm Elmax. Handles made of rear burls of different Nordic stabilized woods. **Prices:** $300 to $1100. **Remarks:** Part-time maker; first knife sold in 1988. **Mark:** Etched name and deer head.

VITALE, MACE
925 Rt 80, Guilford, CT 06437, Phone: 203-457-5591, Web: www.laurelrockforge.com
Specialties: Hand forged blades. **Patterns:** Hunters, utility, chef, Bowies and fighters. **Technical:** W2, 1095, 1084, L6. Hand forged and finished. **Prices:** $100 to $1000. **Remarks:** American Bladesmith Society, Journeyman Smith. Full-time maker; first knife sold 2001. **Mark:** MACE.

VOGT, DONALD J
9007 Hogans Bend, Tampa, FL 33647, Phone: 813-973-3245, vogtknives@verizon.net
Specialties: Art knives, folders, automatics. **Technical:** Uses Damascus steels for blade and bolsters, filework, hand carving on blade bolsters and handles. Other materials used: jewels, gold, mother-of-pearl, gold-lip pearl, black-lip pearl, ivory. **Prices:** $4,000 to $10,000. **Remarks:** Part-time maker; first knife sold in 1997. **Mark:** Last name.

VOGT, PATRIK
Kungsvagen 83, Halmstad, SWEDEN 30270, Phone: 46-35-30977
Specialties: Working straight knives. **Patterns:** Bowies, hunters and fighters. **Technical:** Forges carbon steel and own Damascus. **Prices:** From $100. **Remarks:** Not currently making knives. **Mark:** Initials or last name.

VOORHIES, LES
14511 Lk Mazaska Tr, Faribault, MN 55021, Phone: 507-332-0736, lesvor@msn.com; Web: www.lesvoorhiesknives.com
Specialties: Steels. **Patterns:** Liner locks & autos. **Technical:** ATS-34 Damascus. **Prices:** $250 to $1200. **Mark:** L. Voorhies.

VOSS, BEN
2212 Knox Rd. 1600 Rd. E, Victoria, IL 61485-9644, Phone: 309-879-2940

Specialties: Fancy working knives of his design. **Patterns:** Bowies, fighters, hunters, boots and folders. **Technical:** Grinds 440C, ATS-34 and D2. **Prices:** $35 to $1200. **Remarks:** Part-time maker; first knife sold in 1986. **Mark:** Name, city and state.

VOTAW, DAVID P
305 S State St, Pioneer, OH 43554, Phone: 419-737-2774
Specialties: Working knives; period pieces. **Patterns:** Hunters, Bowies, camp knives, buckskinners and tomahawks. **Technical:** Grinds O1 and D2. **Prices:** $100 to $200; some to $500. **Remarks:** Part-time maker; took over for the late W.K. Kneubuhler. Doing business as W-K Knives. **Mark:** WK with V inside anvil.

W

WACHOLZ, DOC
95 Anne Rd, Marble, NC 28905, Phone: 828-557-1543, killdrums@aol.com; web: rackforge.com
Specialties: Forged tactical knives and tomahawks. **Technical:** Use 52100 and 1084 high carbon steel; make own Damascus; design and dew own sheaths. Grind up and down fashion on a 3" wheel. **Prices:** $300 to $800. **Remarks:** Part-time maker; started forging in 1999, with ABS master Charles Ochs.. **Mark:** Early knives stamped RACK, newer knives since 2005 stamped WACHOLZ.

WADA, YASUTAKA
2-6-22 Fujinokidai, Nara City, Nara, JAPAN 631-0044, Phone: 0742 46-0689
Specialties: Fancy and embellished one-of-a-kind straight knives of his design. **Patterns:** Bowies, daggers and hunters. **Technical:** Grinds ATS-34. All knives hand-filed and flat grinds. **Prices:** $400 to $2500; some higher. **Remarks:** Part-time maker; first knife sold in 1990. **Mark:** Owl eyes with initial and last name underneath or last name.

WAGAMAN, JOHN K
107 E Railroad St, Selma, NC 27576, Phone: 919-965-9659, Fax: 919-965-9901
Specialties: Fancy working knives. **Patterns:** Bowies, miniatures, hunters, fighters and boots. **Technical:** Grinds D2, 440C, 154CM and commercial Damascus; inlays mother-of-pearl. **Prices:** $110 to $2000. **Remarks:** Part-time maker; first knife sold in 1975. **Mark:** Last name.

WAIDE, RUSTY
Triple C Knives, PO Box 499, Buffalo, MO 65622, Phone: 417-345-7231, Fax: 417-345-1911, wrrccc@yahoo.com
Specialties: Custom-designed hunting knives and cowboy working knives in high-carbon and damascus steels. **Prices:** $150 to $450. **Remarks:** Part-time maker; first knife sold in 2010. **Mark:** Name.

WAITES, RICHARD L
PO Box 188, Broomfield, CO 80038, Phone: 303-324-2905, Fax: 303-465-9971, dickknives@aol.com
Specialties: Working fixed blade knives of all kinds including "paddle blade" skinners. Hand crafted sheaths, some upscale and unusual. **Technical:** Grinds 440C, damascus and D2. **Prices:** $100 to $500. **Remarks:** Part-time maker. First knife sold in 1998. Doing business as R.L. Waites Knives. **Mark:** Oval etch with first and middle initial and last name on top and city and state on bottom. Memberships; Professional Knifemakers Association and Rocky Mountain Blade Collectors Club.

WALKER, BILL
431 Walker Rd, Stevensville, MD 21666, Phone: 410-643-5041

WALKER, DON
2850 Halls Chapel Rd, Burnsville, NC 28714, Phone: 828-675-9716, dlwalkernc@gmail.com

WALKER, JIM
22 Walker Ln, Morrilton, AR 72110, Phone: 501-354-3175, jwalker46@att.net
Specialties: Period pieces and working/using knives of his design and to customer specs. **Patterns:** Bowies, fighters, hunters, camp knives. **Technical:** Forges 5160, O1, L6, 52100, 1084, 1095. **Prices:** Start at $450. **Remarks:** Full-time maker; first knife sold 1993. **Mark:** Three arrows with last name/MS.

WALKER, MICHAEL L
925-A Paseo del, Pueblo Sur Taos, NM 87571, Phone: 505-751-3409, Fax: 505-751-3417, metalwerkr@msn.com
Specialties: Innovative knife designs and locking systems; titanium and SS furniture and art. **Patterns:** Folders from utility grade to museum quality art; others upon request. **Technical:** State-of-the-art materials: titanium, stainless Damascus, gold, etc. **Prices:** $3500 and above. **Remarks:** Designer/MetalCrafts; full-time professional knifemaker since 1980; four U.S. patents; invented LinerLock® and was awarded registered U.S. trademark no. 1,585,333. **Mark:** Early mark MW, Walker's Lockers by M.L. Walker; current M.L. Walker or Michael Walker.

WALL, GREG
4753 Michie Pebble Hill Rd., Michie, TN 38357, Phone: 662-415-2909, glwall36@hotmail.com, www.wallhandmadeknives.com
Specialties: Working straight knives. **Patterns:** Classic hollow-handle survival knives, Ek-style fighters, drop-point hunters and big 7's models. **Technical:** Stock removal method of blade making, convex and flat grinds, using O1 tool steels and 440C stainless steel. **Prices:** $295 to $395. **Remarks:** First knife made and sold in 1983.

WALLINGFORD JR., CHARLES W
9024 Old Union Rd, Union, KY 41091, Phone: 859-384-4141, Web: www.cwknives.com
Specialties: 18th and 19th century styles, patch knives, rifleman knives. **Technical:** 10 and 5160 forged blades. **Prices:** $125 to $300. **Mark:** CW.

WARD, CHUCK

□ BOX 2272, 1010 E North St, Benton, AR 72018-2272, Phone: 501-778-4329, ␣uckbop@aol.com

Specialties: Traditional working and using straight knives and folders of his design. **Technical:** Grinds 440C, D2, A2, ATS-34 and O1; uses natural and composite handle materials. **Prices:** $90 to $400, some higher. **Remarks:** Part-time maker; first knife sold in 1990. **Mark:** First initial, last name.

WARD, KEN

␣25 Lee Roze Ln, Grants Pass, OR 97527, Phone: 541-956-8864

Specialties: Working knives, some to customer specs. **Patterns:** Straight, axes, Bowies, buckskinners and miniatures. **Technical:** Grinds ATS-34, Damascus. **Prices:** $100 to $700. **Remarks:** Part-time maker; first knife sold in 1977. **Mark:** Name.

WARD, RON

□ BOX 21, Rose Hill, VA 24281, Phone: 276-445-4757

Specialties: Classic working and using straight knives, fantasy knives. **Patterns:** Bowies, hunter, fighters, and utility/camp knives. **Technical:** Grinds 440C, 154CM, ATS-34, uses composite and natural handle materials. **Prices:** $50 to $750. **Remarks:** Part-time maker, first knife sold in 1992. Doing business as Ron Ward Blades. **Mark:** RON WARD BLADES.

WARD, TOM

␣4 Village Rd., Wilmot, NH 03287, Phone: 508-277-3190, tempestcraft@gmail.com; ␣eb: www.tempestcraft.com

Specialties: Axes and pattern welding, multi-billet twist constructions. Open to all commissions. **Technical:** Forges to shape, generally using 15N20, 1095 and 1084 blade steels. **Prices:** $400 for mono-steel hunting/camping knives to $3,000 and up on elaborate pieces. **Remarks:** Full-time maker; first knife made in 2008. **Mark:** An ornate T.

WARD, W C

␣7 Glenn St, Clinton, TN 37716, Phone: 615-457-3568

Specialties: Working straight knives; period pieces. **Patterns:** Hunters, Bowies, swords and kitchen cutlery. **Technical:** Grinds O1. **Prices:** $85 to $150; some to $500. **Remarks:** Part-time maker; first knife sold in 1969. He styled the Tennessee Knife Maker. **Mark:** TKM.

WARDELL, MICK

␣ Clovelly Rd, Bideford, N Devon, ENGLAND EX39 3BU, wardellknives@hotmail. ␣.uk Web: www.wardellscustomknives.com

Specialties: Spring back folders and a few fixed blades. **Patterns:** Locking and slip-joint folders, Bowies. **Technical:** Grinds stainless Damascus and RWL34. Heat-treats. **Prices:** $300 to $2500. **Remarks:** Full-time maker; first knife sold in 1986. Takes limited Comissions. **Mark:** Wardell.

WARDEN, ROY A

␣75 Tanglewood Rd, Union, MO 63084, Phone: 314-583-8813, rwarden@yhti.net

Specialties: Complex mosaic designs of "EDM wired figures" and "stack up" patterns and "lazer cut" and "torch cut" and "sawed" patterns combined. **Patterns:** Mostly "all mosaic" folders, automatics, fixed blades. **Technical:** Mosaic Damascus with all tool steel edges. **Prices:** $100 to $1000. **Remarks:** Part-time maker; first knife sold in 1987. **Mark:** WARDEN stamped or initials connected.

WARE, J.D.

␣alle 40 #342 x 47 y 49, Colonia Benito Juarez Norte, Merida, Yucatan, MEXICO ␣7119, jdware@jdwareknives.com; Web: www.jdwareknives.com

Specialties: Coin knives, slip-joint folders, chef's knives and hunting/camping/fishing knives. **Technical:** Practices stock-removal and forging methods of blade making using O1, 440C and D2 blade steels. **Prices:** Start at $200. **Remarks:** Full-time maker; first knife made in 1976. **Mark:** Usually etched "JD Ware, Artesano, Merida Yucatan, Hecho a Mano, Mexico."

WARE, TOMMY

␣58 Idlewilde, Onalaska, TX 77360, Phone: 936-646-4649

Specialties: Traditional working and using straight knives, folders and automatics of his design and to customer specs. **Patterns:** Hunters, automatics and locking folders. **Technical:** Grinds ATS-34, 440C and D2. Offers engraving and scrimshaw. **Prices:** $425 to $650; some to $1500. **Remarks:** Full-time maker; first knife sold in 1990. Doing business as Wano Knives. **Mark:** Last name inside oval, business name above, city and state below, year on side.

WARREN, AL

␣423 Sante Fe Circle, Roseville, CA 95678, Phone: 916-257-5904, Fax: 215-318-␣945, al@warrenknives.com; Web: www.warrenknives.com

Specialties: Working straight knives and folders, some fancy. **Patterns:** Hunters, Bowies, fillets, lockback, folders & multi blade. **Technical:** Grinds ATS-34 and S30V.440V. **Prices:** $225 to $2,500.**Remarks:** Full-time maker; first knife sold in 1978. **Mark:** First and middle initials, last name.

WARREN, ALAN AND CARROLL

␣605 S.E. 69th Ave., Portland, OR 97206, Phone: 503-788-6863 or 503-926-3559, ␣anwarrenknives@yahoo.com

Specialties: Mostly one-of-a-kind straight knives, bird & trout knives, skinners, fighters, bowies, daggers, short swords and LinerLock folders (tactical and gent's). My designs or custom. **Technical:** Hollow and flat grinds 154CM, ATS-34, CPM-S30V, O1, 5160 and others. Uses just about all handle materials available. Makes custom-to-fit, hand-tooled and hand stitched leather sheaths, some with skin inlays or hard inlays to match knife handle materials such as G-10, Micarta, ironwood, ivory, stag, etc. **Prices:** $200 to $1,800, some to $3,595. **Remarks:** Full-time maker for nine years; first knife sold in 1998. **Mark:** Name, state, USA.

WARREN, DANIEL

571 Lovejoy Rd, Canton, NC 28716, Phone: 828-648-7351

Specialties: Using knives. **Patterns:** Drop point hunters. **Prices:** $200 to $500. **Mark:** Warren-Bethel NC.

WASHBURN, ARTHUR D

ADW CUSTOM KNIVES, 211 Hinman St / PO Box 625, Pioche, NV 89043, Phone: 775-962-5463, knifeman@lcturbonet.com; Web: www.adwcustomknives.com

Specialties: Locking liner folders. **Patterns:** Slip joint folders (single and multiplied), lock-back folders, some fixed blades. Do own heat-treating; Rockwell test each blade. **Technical:** Carbon and stainless Damascus, some 1084, 1095, AEBL, 12C27, S30V. **Prices:** $200 to $1000 and up. **Remarks:** Sold first knife in 1997. Part-time maker. **Mark:** ADW enclosed in an oval or ADW.

WASHBURN JR., ROBERT LEE

636 75th St., Tuscaloosa, AL 35405, Phone: 435-619-4432, Fax: 435-574-8554, rlwashburn@excite.com; Web: www.washburnknives.net

Specialties: Hand-forged period, Bowies, tactical, boot and hunters. **Patterns:** Bowies, tantos, loot hunters, tactical and folders. **Prices:** $100 to $2500. **Remarks:** All hand forged. 52100 being his favorite steel. **Mark:** Washburn Knives W.

WATANABE, MELVIN

1297 Kika St., Kailua, HI 96734, Phone: 808-429-9403, meltod808@yahoo.com

Specialties: Fancy folding knives. Some hunters. **Patterns:** Liner-locks and hunters. **Technical:** Grinds ATS-34, stainless Damascus. **Prices:** $350 and up. **Remarks:** Part-time maker, first knife sold in 1985. **Mark:** Name and state.

WATANABE, WAYNE

PO Box 3563, Montebello, CA 90640, wwknives@yahoo.com

Specialties: Straight knives in Japanese-styles. One-of-a-kind designs; welcomes customer designs. **Patterns:** Tantos to katanas, Bowies. **Technical:** Flat grinds A2, O1 and ATS-34. Offers hand-rubbed finishes and wrapped handles. **Prices:** Start at $200. **Remarks:** Part-time maker. **Mark:** Name in characters with flower.

WATERS, GLENN

11 Shinakawa Machi, Hirosaki City, JAPAN 036, Phone: 0172-886741, watersglenn@hotmail.com; Web: www.glennwaters.com

Specialties: One-of-a-kind collector-grade highly embellished art knives. Mostly folders with a few fixed blades and up-market tactical flippers. **Patterns:** Locking-liner folders and collectible flippers and fixed art knives. **Technical:** Grinds blades from Damasteel, VG-10, CowryX, ZDP-189, San Mai from ZDP-189 and VG-10, and Super Gold 2 powdered stainless by Takefu. Does own engraving, gold inlaying and stone setting, filework and carving. Gold and Japanese precious metal fabrication. Prefers exotic material, high karat gold, silver, Shyaku Dou, Shibu Ichi Gin, precious gemstones. **Prices:** Upscale. **Remarks:** Designs and makes one-of-a-kind highly embellished art knives, often with fully engraved handles and blades that tell a story. A jeweler by trade for 20 years before starting to make knives in 1993. First knife sold in 1994. **Mark:** On knives before 2010, Glenn Waters maker Japan or Glenn in Japanese. Knives since 2010 uses a new engraved logo that says Glenn in Japanese.

WATSON, BERT

9315 Meade St., Westminster, CO 80031, Phone: 303-587-3064, watsonbd21960@q.com

Specialties: Working/using straight knives of his design and to customer specs. **Patterns:** Hunters, utility/camp knives. **Technical:** Grinds O1, ATS-34, 440C, D2, A2 and others. **Prices:** $150 to $800. **Remarks:** Full-time maker. **Mark:** GTK and/or Bert.

WATSON, BILLY

440 Forge Rd, Deatsville, AL 36022, Phone: 334-365-1482, hilldweller44@att.net

Specialties: Working and using straight knives and folders of his design; period pieces. **Patterns:** Hunters, Bowies and utility/camp knives. **Technical:** Forges and grinds his own Damascus, 1095, 5160 and 52100. **Prices:** $40 to $1500. **Remarks:** Full-time maker; first knife sold in 1970. **Mark:** Last name.

WATSON, DANIEL

350 Jennifer Ln, Driftwood, TX 78619, Phone: 512-847-9679, info@angelsword.com; Web: http://www.angelsword.com

Specialties: One-of-a-kind knives and swords. **Patterns:** Hunters, daggers, swords. **Technical:** Hand-purify and carbonize his own high-carbon steel, pattern-welded Damascus, cable and carbon-induced crystalline Damascus. Teehno-Wootz™ Damascus steel, heat treats including cryogenic processing. European and Japanese tempering. **Prices:** $125 to $25,000. **Remarks:** Full-time maker; first knife sold in 1979. **Mark:** "Angel Sword" on forged pieces; "Bright Knight" for stock removal. Avatar on Techno-Wootz™ Damascus. Bumon on traditional Japanese blades.

WATSON, PETER

66 Kielblock St, La Hoff, NW, SOUTH AFRICA 2570, Phone: 018-84942

Specialties: Traditional working and using straight knives and folders of his design. **Patterns:** Hunters, locking folders and utility/camp knives. **Technical:** Sandvik and 440C. **Prices:** $120 to $250; some to $1500. **Remarks:** Part-time maker; first knife sold in 1989. **Mark:** Buffalo head with name.

WATSON, TOM

1103 Brenau Terrace, Panama City, FL 32405, Phone: 850-785-9209, tom@tomwatsonknives.com; Web: www.tomwatsonknives.com

Specialties: Utility/tactical LinerLocks and flipper folders. **Patterns:** Various patterns. **Technical:** Grinds D2 and CPM-154. **Prices:** $375 and up. **Remarks:** In business since 1978. **Mark:** Name and city.

WATTELET, MICHAEL A
PO Box 649, 125 Front, Minocqua, WI 54548, Phone: 715-356-3069, redtroll@ frontier.com
Specialties: Working and using straight knives of his design and to customer specs; fantasy knives. **Patterns:** Daggers, fighters and swords. **Technical:** Grinds 440C and L6; forges and grinds O1. Silversmith. **Prices:** $75 to $1000; some to $5000. **Remarks:** Full-time maker; first knife sold in 1966. Doing business as M and N Arts Ltd. **Mark:** First initial, last name.

WATTS, JOHNATHAN
9440 S. Hwy. 36, Gatesville, TX 76528, Phone: 254-223-9669
Specialties: Traditional folders. **Patterns:** One and two blade folders in various blade shapes. **Technical:** Grinds ATS-34 and Damascus on request. **Prices:** $120 to $400. **Remarks:** Part-time maker; first knife sold in 1997. **Mark:** J Watts.

WATTS, RODNEY
Watts Custom Knives, 1100 Hwy. 71 S, Hot Springs, SD 57747, Phone: 605-890-0645, wattscustomknives@yahoo.com; www.wattscustomknives.com
Specialties: Fixed blades and some folders, most of maker's own designs, some Loveless and Johnson patterns. **Technical:** Stock removal method of blade making, using CPM 154 and ATS-34 steels. **Prices:** $450 to $1,100. **Remarks:** Part-time maker; first knife made in 2007. Won "Best New Maker" award at the 2011 BLADE Show. **Mark:** Watts over Custom Knives.

WEBSTER, BILL
58144 West Clear Lake Rd, Three Rivers, MI 49093, Phone: 269-244-2873, wswebster_5@msn.com Web: www.websterknifeworks.com
Specialties: Working and using straight knives, especially for hunters. His patterns are custom designed. **Patterns:** Hunters, skinners, camp knives, Bowies and daggers. **Technical:** Hand-filed blades made of D2 steel only, unless other steel is requested. Preferred handle material is stabilized and exotic wood and stag. Sheaths are hand-sewn by Bill Dehn in Three Rivers, MI. **Prices:** $75 to $500. **Remarks:** Part-time maker, first knife sold in 1978. **Mark:** Originally WEB stamped on blade, at present, Webster Knifeworks Three Rivers, MI laser etched on blade.

WEEKS, RYAN
PO Box 1101, Bountiful, UT 84001, Phone: 801-755-6789, ryan@ryanwknives.com; Web: www.ryanwknives.com
Specialties: Military and Law Enforcement applications as well as hunting and utility designs. **Patterns:** Fighters, bowies, hunters, and custom designs, I use man made as well as natural wood and exotic handle materials. **Technical:** Make via forge and stock removal methods, preferred steel includes high carbon, CPM154 CM and ATS34, Damascus and San Mai. **Prices:** $160 to $750. **Remarks:** Part-time maker; Business name is "Ryan W. Knives." First knife sold in 2009. **Mark:** Encircled "Ryan" beneath the crossed "W" UTAH, USA.

WEEVER, JOHN
150 Valley View St., Glen Rose, TX 76043, Phone: 254-898-9595, john.weever@ gmail.com; Web: WeeverKnives.com
Specialties: Traditional hunters (fixed blade, slip joint, and lockback) and tactical. **Patterns:** See website. **Technical:** Types of steel: S30V, Damascus or customer choice. Handles in mammoth ivory, oosic, horn, sambar, stag, etc. Sheaths in exotic leathers. **Prices:** $400 to $1200. **Remarks:** Stock removal maker full-time; began making knives in 1985. Member of knifemakers guild. **Mark:** Tang stamp: head of charging elephant with ears extended and WEEVER curved over the top.

WEHNER, RUDY
297 William Warren Rd, Collins, MS 39428, Phone: 601-765-4997
Specialties: Reproduction antique Bowies and contemporary Bowies in full and miniature. **Patterns:** Skinners, camp knives, fighters, axes and Bowies. **Technical:** Grinds 440C, ATS-34, 154CM and Damascus. **Prices:** $100 to $500; some to $850. **Remarks:** Full-time maker; first knife sold in 1975. **Mark:** Last name on Bowies and antiques; full name, city and state on skinners.

WEILAND JR., J REESE
PO Box 2337, Riverview, FL 33568, Phone: 813-671-0661, RWPHIL413@verizon.net; Web: www.reeseweilandknives.com
Specialties: Hawk bills; tactical to fancy folders. **Patterns:** Hunters, tantos, Bowies, fantasy knives, spears and some swords. **Technical:** Grinds ATS-34, 154CM, 440C, D2, O1, A2, Damascus. Titanium hardware on locking liners and button locks. **Prices:** $150 to $4000. **Remarks:** Full-time maker, first knife sold in 1978. Knifemakers Guild member since 1988.

WEINAND, GEROME M
14440 Harpers Bridge Rd, Missoula, MT 59808, Phone: 406-543-0845
Specialties: Working straight knives. **Patterns:** Bowies, fishing and camp knives, large special hunters. **Technical:** Grinds O1, 440C, ATS-34, 1084, L6, also stainless Damascus, Aebl and 304; makes all-tool steel Damascus; Dendritic D2 from powdered steel. Heat-treats. **Prices:** $30 to $100; some to $500. **Remarks:** Full-time maker; first knife sold in 1982. **Mark:** Last name.

WEINSTOCK, ROBERT
PO Box 170028, San Francisco, CA 94117-0028, Phone: 415-731-5968, robertweinstock@att.net
Specialties: Folders, slip joins, lockbacks, autos. **Patterns:** Daggers, folders. **Technical:** Grinds A2, O1 and 440C. Chased and hand-carved blades and handles. Also using various Damascus steels from other makers. **Prices:** $3000 to 7000. **Remarks:** Full-time maker; first knife sold in 1994. **Mark:** Last name carved in steel.

WEISS, CHARLES L
PO BOX 1037, Waddell, AZ 85355, Phone: 623-935-0924, weissknife@live.com
Specialties: High-art straight knives and folders; deluxe period pieces. **Patterns:** Daggers, fighters, boots, push knives and miniatures. **Technical:** Grinds 440C, 154CM and ATS-34. **Prices:** $300 to $1200; some to $2000. **Remarks:** Full-time maker; first knife sold in 1975. **Mark:** Name and city.

WELLING, RONALD L
15446 Lake Ave, Grand Haven, MI 49417, Phone: 616-846-2274
Specialties: Scagel knives of his design or customer specs. **Patterns:** Hunters, camp knives, miniatures, bird, trout, folders, double edged, hatchets, skinners and some art pieces. **Technical:** Forges Damascus 1084 and 1095. Antler, ivory and horn. **Prices:** $25 to $3000. **Remarks:** Full-time maker. ABS Journeyman maker. **Mark:** First initials and name and last name. City and state. Various scagel kris (1or 2).

WELLING, WILLIAM
Up-armored Knives, 5437 Pinecliff Dr., West Valley, NY 14171, Phone: 716-942-6031, uparmored@frontier.net; Web: www.up-armored.com
Specialties: Innovative tactical fixed blades each uniquely coated in a variety of Up-armored designed patterns and color schemes. Convexed edged bushcraft knives for the weekend camper, backpacker, or survivalist. Knives developed specifically for tactical operators. Leather- and synthetic-suede-lined Kydex sheaths. **Patterns:** Modern sample of time tested designs as well as contemporary developed cutting tools. **Technical:** Stock removal specializing in tested 1095CV and 5160 steels. **Prices:** $200 to $500. **Remarks:** Part-time maker; first knife sold in 2010. **Mark:** Skull rounded up by Up-Armored USA.

WERTH, GEORGE W
5223 Woodstock Rd, Poplar Grove, IL 61065, Phone: 815-544-4408
Specialties: Period pieces, some fancy. **Patterns:** Straight fighters, daggers and Bowies. **Technical:** Forges and grinds O1, 1095 and his Damascus, including mosaic patterns. **Prices:** $200 to $650; some higher. **Remarks:** Full-time maker. Doing business as Fox Valley Forge. **Mark:** Name in logo or initials connected.

WESCOTT, CODY
5330 White Wing Rd, Las Cruces, NM 88012, Phone: 575-382-5008
Specialties: Fancy and presentation grade working knives. **Patterns:** Hunters, locking folders and Bowies. **Technical:** Hollow-grinds D2 and ATS-34; all knives file worked. Offers some engraving. Makes sheaths. **Prices:** $110 to $500; some to $1200. **Remarks:** Full-time maker; first knife sold in 1982. **Mark:** First initial, last name.

WEST, CHARLES A
1315 S Pine St, Centralia, IL 62801, Phone: 618-532-2777
Specialties: Classic, fancy, high tech, period pieces, traditional and working/using straight knives and folders. **Patterns:** Bowies, fighters and locking folders. **Technical:** Grinds ATS-34, O1 and Damascus. Prefers hot blued finishes. **Prices:** $100 to $1000; some to $2000. **Remarks:** Full-time maker; first knife sold in 1963. Doing business as West Custom Knives. **Mark:** Name or name, city and state.

WESTBERG, LARRY
305 S Western Hills Dr, Algona, IA 50511, Phone: 515-368-1974, westberg@ netmumail.com
Specialties: Traditional and working straight knives of his design and in standard patterns. **Patterns:** Bowies, hunters, fillets and folders. **Technical:** Grinds 440C, D2 and 1095. Heat-treats. Uses natural handle materials. **Prices:** $85 to $600; some to $1000. **Remarks:** Part-time maker; first knife sold in 1987. **Mark:** Last name-town and state.

WETTEN, BOBBY
550 W. Caracas Ave., Hershey, PA 17033, Phone: 717-439-7686, bobwetten@gmail. com; Web: https://bobbywett.wordpress.com
Patterns: Forged hunters, camp knives, bowies, fighters and tomahawks. Likes to make pieces that blend into nature. **Technical:** Forges 10xx, 5160 and W2 steels, occasionally doing stock removal pieces. Father-in-law Paul Wittle makes sheaths. **Prices:** $30 to $1,500. **Remarks:** First knife completed in 2006; ABS journeyman smith. **Mark:** BobbyWett (one word, no spaces).

WHEELER, GARY
351 Old Hwy 48, Clarksville, TN 37040, Phone: 931-552-3092, LR22SHTR@charter.net
Specialties: Working to high end fixed blades. **Patterns:** Bowies, Hunters, combat knives, daggers and a few folders. **Technical:** Forges 5160, 1095, 52100 and his own Damascus. **Prices:** $125 to $2000. **Remarks:** Full-time maker since 2001, first knife sold in 1985 collaborates/works at B&W Blade Works. ABS Journeyman Smith 2008. **Mark:** Stamped last name.

WHEELER, NICK
140 Studebaker Rd., Castle Rock, WA 98611, Phone: 360-967-2357, merckman99@ yahoo.com
Specialties: Bowies, integrals, fighters, hunters and daggers. **Technical:** Forges W2, W1, 1095, 52100 and 1084. Makes own damascus, from random pattern to complex mosaics. Also grinds stainless and other more modern alloys. Does own heat-treating and leather work. Also commissions leather work from Paul Long. **Prices:** Start at $250. **Remarks:** Full-time maker; ABS member since 2001. Journeyman bladesmith. **Mark:** Last name.

WHEELER, ROBERT
289 S Jefferson, Bradley, IL 60915, Phone: 815-932-5854, b2btaz@brmemc.net

WHIPPLE, WESLEY A
1002 Shoshoni St, Thermopolis, WY 82443, Phone: 307-921-2445, wildernessknife@yahoo.com
Specialties: Working straight knives, some fancy. **Patterns:** Hunters, Bowies, camp

knives, fighters. **Technical:** Forges high-carbon steels, Damascus, offers relief carving and silver wire inlay and checkering. **Prices:** $300 to $1400; some higher. **Remarks:** Full-time maker; first knife sold in 1989. A.K.A. Wilderness Knife and Forge. **Mark:** Last name/JS.

WHITE, BRYCE
1415 W Col Glenn Rd, Little Rock, AR 72210, Phone: 501-821-2956
Specialties: Hunters, fighters, makes Damascus, file work, handmade only. **Technical:** L6, 1075, 1095, O1 steels used most. **Patterns:** Will do any pattern or use his own. **Prices:** $200 to $300. Sold first knife in 1995. **Mark:** White.

WHITE, CALEB A.
502 W. River Rd. #88, Hooksett, NH 03106, Phone: 603-340-4716, caleb@ calebwhiteknives.com; www.calebwhiteknives.com
Specialties: Hunters, tacticals, dress knives, daggers and utilitarian pieces. **Patterns:** Multiple. **Technical:** Mostly stock removal, preferring high-carbon steels. **Prices:** $275 to $4,100. **Remarks:** Full-time maker. **Mark:** Derivation of maker's last name, replacing the "T" with a symbol loosely based on the Templars' cross and shield.

WHITE, DALE
525 CR 212, Sweetwater, TX 79556, Phone: 325-798-4178, dalew@taylortel.net
Specialties: Working and using knives. **Patterns:** Hunters, skinners, utilities and Bowies. **Technical:** Grinds 440C, offers file work, fancy pins and scrimshaw by Sherry Sellers. **Prices:** From $45 to $300. **Remarks:** Sold first knife in 1975. **Mark:** Full name, city and state.

WHITE, LOU
7385 Red Bud Rd NE, Ranger, GA 30734, Phone: 706-334-2273

WHITE, RICHARD T
359 Carver St, Grosse Pointe Farms, MI 48236, Phone: 313-881-4690

WHITE, RUSSELL D.
4 CR 8240, Rienzi, MS 38865, Phone: 662-416-3461, rwhite292@gmail.com; Facebook: Handmade Knives by Russell White
Patterns: Hunters, bowies and camp knives using natural handle materials and micarta. **Technical:** Forges 1084, 15N20, 52100, 5160, O1 and damascus. **Prices:** Start at $200. **Remarks:** Part-time maker; first knife sold in 2010. ABS journeyman smith, sole authorship knifemaker offering handmade leather sheaths if wanted. **Mark:** R. White, J.S. on ricasso.

WHITENECT, JODY
Halifax County, Elderbank, NS, CANADA B0N 1K0, Phone: 902-384-2511
Specialties: Fancy and embellished working/using straight knives of his design and to customer specs. **Patterns:** Bowies, fighters and hunters. **Technical:** Forges 1095 and O1; forges and grinds ATS-34. Various filework on blades and bolsters. **Prices:** $200 to $400; some to $800. **Remarks:** Part-time maker; first knife sold in 1996. **Mark:** Longhorn stamp or engraved.

WHITESELL, J. DALE
P.O. Box 455, Stover, MO 65078, Phone: 573-569-0753, dalesknives@yahoo.com; Web: whitesell-knives.webs.com
Specialties: Fixed blade working knives,a nd some collector pieces. **Patterns:** Hunting and skinner knives, camp knives, and kitchen knives. **Technical:** Blades ground from O1, 1095, and 440C in hollow, flat and saber grinds. Wood, bone, deer antler, and G10 are basic handle materials. **Prices:** $100 to $450. **Remarks:** Part-time maker, first knife sold in 2003. Doing business as Dale's Knives. All knives have serial number to indicate steel (since June 2010).**Mark:** Whitesell on the left side of the blade.

WHITLEY, L WAYNE
675 Carrow Rd, Chocowinity, NC 27817-9495, Phone: 252-946-5648

WHITLEY, WELDON G
308 N Robin Ave, Odessa, TX 79764, Phone: 432-530-0448, Fax: 432-530-0048, wgwhitley@juno.com
Specialties: Working knives of his design or to customer specs. **Patterns:** Hunters, folders and various double-edged knives. **Technical:** Grinds 440C, 154CM and ATS-34. **Prices:** $150 to $1250. **Mark:** Name, address, road-runner logo.

WHITTAKER, ROBERT E
PO Box 204, Mill Creek, PA 17060
Specialties: Using straight knives. Has a line of knives for buckskinners. **Patterns:** Hunters, skinners and Bowies. **Technical:** Grinds O1, A2 and D2. Offers filework. **Prices:** $35 to $100. **Remarks:** Part-time maker; first knife sold in 1980. **Mark:** Last initial or full initials.

WHITTAKER, WAYNE
1900 Woodland Ct, Metamore, MI 48455, Phone: 810-797-5315, lindorwayne@yahoo.com
Specialties: Liner locks and autos.**Patterns:** Folders. **Technical:** Damascus, mammoth, ivory, and tooth. **Prices:** $500 to $1500. **Remarks:** Full-time maker. **Mark:** Inside of backbar.

WICK, JONATHAN P.
541 E. Calle Narcisco, Hereford, AZ 85615, Phone: 520-227-5228, vikingwick@aol.com
Specialties: Fixed blades, pocketknives, neck knives, hunters, bowies, fighters, Roman-style daggers with full tangs, stick tangs and some integrals, and leather-lined, textured copper sheaths. **Technical:** Forged blades and own damascus and mosaic damascus, along with shibuichi, mokume, lost wax casting. **Prices:** $250 - $1800 and up. **Remarks:**

Full-time maker, ABS member, sold first knife in 2008. **Mark:** J P Wick, also on small blades a JP over a W.

WICKER, DONNIE R
2544 E 40th Ct, Panama City, FL 32405, Phone: 904-785-9158
Specialties: Traditional working and using straight knives of his design or to customer specs. **Patterns:** Hunters, fighters and slip-joint folders. **Technical:** Grinds 440C, ATS-34, D2 and 154CM. Heat-treats and does hardness testing. **Prices:** $90 to $200; some to $400. **Remarks:** Part-time maker; first knife sold in 1975. **Mark:** First and middle initials, last name.

WIGGINS, BILL
105 Kaolin Lane, Canton, NC 28716, Phone: 828-226-2551, wncbill@bellsouth.net Web: www.wigginsknives.com
Specialties: Forged working knives. **Patterns:** Hunters, Bowies, camp knives and utility knives of own design or will work with customer on design. **Technical:** Forges 1084 and 52100 as well as making own Damascus. **Prices:** $250 - $1500. **Remarks:** Part-time maker. First knife sold in 1989. ABS board member. **Mark:** Wiggins

WILBURN, AARON
2521 Hilltop Dr., #364, Redding, CA 96002, Phone: 530-227-2827, wilburnforge@yahoo.com; Web: www.wilburnforge.com
Patterns: Daggers, bowies, fighters, hunters and slip-joint folders. **Technical:** Forges own damascus and works with high-carbon steel. **Prices:** $500 to $5,000. **Remarks:** Full-time maker and ABS master smith. **Mark:** Wilburn Forge.

WILKINS, MITCHELL
15523 Rabon Chapel Rd, Montgomery, TX 77316, Phone: 936-588-2696, mwilkins@consolidated.net

WILLEY, WG
14210 Sugar Hill Rd, Greenwood, DE 19950, Phone: 302-349-4070, Web: www. willeyknives.com
Specialties: Fancy working straight knives. **Patterns:** Small game knives, Bowies and throwing knives. **Technical:** Grinds 440C and 154CM. **Prices:** $350 to $600; some to $1500. **Remarks:** Part-time maker; first knife sold in 1975. Owns retail store. **Mark:** Last name inside map logo.

WILLIAMS, JASON L
PO Box 67, Wyoming, RI 02898, Phone: 401-539-8353, Fax: 401-539-0252
Specialties: Fancy and high tech folders of his design, co-inventor of the Axis Lock. **Patterns:** Fighters, locking folders, automatics and fancy pocket knives. **Technical:** Forges Damascus and other steels by request. Uses exotic handle materials and precious metals. Offers inlaid spines and gemstone thumb knobs. **Prices:** $1000 and up. **Remarks:** Full-time maker; first knife sold in 1989. **Mark:** First and last initials on pivot.

WILLIAMS, MICHAEL
333 Cherrybark Tr., Broken Bow, OK 74728, Phone: 580-420-3051, hforge@pine-net.com; Web: www.williamscustomknives.com
Specialties: Functional, personalized, edged weaponry. Working and collectible art. **Patterns:** Bowies, hunters, camp knives, daggers, others. **Technical:** Forges high carbon steel and own forged Damascus. **Prices:** $500 - $12000. **Remarks:** Full-time ABS Master Smith. **Mark:** Williams MS.

WILLIAMS, ROBERT
15962 State Rt. 267, East Liverpool, OH 43920, Phone: 203-979-0803, wurdmeister@gmail.com; Web: www.customstraightrazors.com
Specialties: Custom straight razors with a philosophy that form must follow function, so shaving performance drives designs and aesthetics. **Technical:** Stock removal and forging, working with 1095, O1 and damascus. Natural handle materials and synthetics, accommodating any and all design requests and can incorporate gold inlays, scrimshaw, hand engraving and jewel setting. All work done in maker's shop, sole-source maker shipping worldwide. **Remarks:** Full-time maker; first straight razor in 2005. **Mark:** Robert Williams - Handmade, USA with a hammer separating the two lines.

WILLIAMS JR., RICHARD
1440 Nancy Circle, Morristown, TN 37814, Phone: 615-581-0059
Specialties: Working and using straight knives of his design or to customer specs. **Patterns:** Hunters, dirks and utility/camp knives. **Technical:** Forges 5160 and uses file steel. Hand-finish is standard; offers filework. **Prices:** $80 to $180; some to $250. **Remarks:** Spare-time maker; first knife sold in 1985. **Mark:** Last initial or full initials.

WILLIAMSON, TONY
Rt 3 Box 503, Siler City, NC 27344, Phone: 919-663-3551
Specialties: Flint knapping: knives made of obsidian flakes and flint with wood, antler or bone for handles. **Patterns:** Skinners, daggers and flake knives. **Technical:** Blades have width/thickness ratio of at least 4 to 1. Hafts with methods available to prehistoric man. **Prices:** $58 to $160. **Remarks:** Student of Errett Callahan. **Mark:** Initials and number code to identify year and number of knives made.

WILLIS, BILL
RT 7 Box 7549, Ava, MO 65608, Phone: 417-683-4326
Specialties: Forged blades, Damascus and carbon steel. **Patterns:** Cable, random or ladder lamented. **Technical:** Professionally heat treated blades. **Prices:** $75 to $600. **Remarks:** Lifetime guarantee on all blades against breakage. All work done by maker; including leather work. **Mark:** WF.

WILLUMSEN, MIKKEL
Nyrnberggade 23, S Copenhagen, DENMARK 2300, Phone: 4531176333, mw@willumsen-cph.com Web: www.wix.com/willumsen/urbantactical
Specialties: Folding knives, fixed blades, and balisongs. Also kitchen knives. **Patterns:**

custom knifemakers

Primarily influenced by design that is function and quality based. Tactical style knives inspired by classical designs mixed with modern tactics. **Technical:** Uses CPM 154, RW 134, S30V, and carbon fiber titanium G10 for handles. **Prices:** Starting at $600.

WILSON, CURTIS M
PO Box 383, Burleson, TX 76097, Phone: 817-295-3732, cwknifeman2026@att.net; Web: www.cwilsonknives.com

Specialties: Traditional working/using knives, fixed blade, folders, slip joint, LinerLock® and lock back knives. Art knives, presentation grade Bowies, folder repair, heat treating services. Sub-zero quench. **Patterns:** Hunters, camp knives, military combat, single and multi-blade folders. Dr's knives large or small or custom design knives. **Technical:** Grinds ATS-34, 440C 52100, D2, S30V, CPM 154, mokume gane, engraves, scrimshaw, sheaths leather of kykex heat treating and file work. **Prices:** $150-750. **Remarks:** Part-time maker since 1984. Sold first knife in 1993. **Mark:** Curtis Wilson in ribbon or Curtis Wilson with hand made in a half moon.

WILSON, JAMES G
PO Box 4024, Estes Park, CO 80517, Phone: 303-586-3944

Specialties: Bronze Age knives; Medieval and Scottish-styles; tomahawks. **Patterns:** Bronze knives, daggers, swords, spears and battle axes; 12-inch steel Misericorde daggers, sgian dubhs, "his and her" skinners, bird and fish knives, capers, boots and daggers. **Technical:** Casts bronze; grinds D2, 440C and ATS-34. **Prices:** $49 to $400; some to $1300. **Remarks:** Part-time maker; first knife sold in 1975. **Mark:** WilsonHawk.

WILSON, MIKE
1416 McDonald Rd, Hayesville, NC 28904, Phone: 828-389-8145

Specialties: Fancy working and using straight knives of his design or to customer specs, folders. **Patterns:** Hunters, Bowies, utility knives, gut hooks, skinners, fighters and miniatures. **Technical:** Hollow grinds 440C, 1095, D2, XHP and CPM-154. Mirror finishes are standard. Offers filework. **Prices:** $130 to $600. **Remarks:** Full-time maker; first knife sold in 1985. **Mark:** Last name.

WILSON, P.R. "REGAN"
805 Janvier Rd., Scott, LA 70583, Phone: 504-427-1293, pat71ss@cox.net; www.acadianawhitetailtaxidermy.com

Specialties: Traditional working knives. **Patterns:** Old-school working knives, trailing points, drop points, hunters, boots, etc. **Technical:** 440C, ATS-34 and 154CM steels, all hollow ground with mirror or satin finishes. **Prices:** Start at $175 with sheath. **Remarks:** Mentored by Jim Barbee; first knife sold in 1988; lessons and guidance offered in maker's shop. **Mark:** Name and location with "W" in center of football-shaped logo.

WILSON, RON
2639 Greenwood Ave, Morro Bay, CA 93442, Phone: 805-772-3381

Specialties: Classic and fantasy straight knives of his design. **Patterns:** Daggers, fighters, swords and axes, mostly all miniatures. **Technical:** Forges and grinds Damascus and various tool steels; grinds meteorite. Uses gold, precious stones and exotic wood. **Prices:** Vary. **Remarks:** Part-time maker; first knives sold in 1995. **Mark:** Stamped first and last initials.

WILSON, RW
PO Box 2012, Weirton, WV 26062, Phone: 304-723-2771, rwknives@comcast.net or rwknives@hotmail.com; Web: www.rwwilsonknives.com, Facebook: RW Wilson Knives

Specialties: Custom-made knives and tomahawks. **Patterns:** Bowies, drop-point hunters, skinners, tomahawks and more. **Technical:** Grinds. **Prices:** $7 to $5,000. **Remarks:** First knife sold in 1966. Made tomahawks for the movie "Jeremiah Johnson." **Mark:** "RW Wilson" above a tomahawk and "Weirton WV" under tomahawk.

WILSON, STAN
8931 Pritcher Rd, Lithia, FL 33547, Phone: 727-461-1992, swilson@stanwilsonknives.com; Web: www.stanwilsonknives.com

Specialties: Fancy folders and automatics of his own design. **Patterns:** Locking liner folders, single and dual action autos, daggers. **Technical:** Stock removal, uses Damascus, stainless and high carbon steels, prefers ivory and pearl, Damascus with blued finishes and filework. **Prices:** $400 and up. **Remarks:** Member of Knifemakers Guild and Florida Knifemakers Association. Full-time maker will do custom orders. **Mark:** Name in script.

WILSON, VIC
9130 Willow Branch Dr, Olive Branch, MS 38654, Phone: 901-591-6550, vdubjr55@earthlink.net; Web: www.knivesbyvic.com

Specialties: Classic working and using knives and folders. **Patterns:** Hunters, boning, utility, camp, my patterns or customers. **Technical:** Grinds O1 and D2. Also does own heat treating. Offer file work and decorative liners on folders. Fabricate custom leather sheaths for all knives. **Prices:** $150 to $400. **Remarks:** Part-time maker, first knife sold in 1989. **Mark:** Etched V over W with oval circle around it, name, Memphis, TN.

WINGO, GARY
240 Ogeechee, Ramona, OK 74061, Phone: 918-536-1067, wingg_2000@yahoo.com; Web: www.geocities.com/wingg_2000/gary.html

Specialties: Folder specialist. Steel 440C, D2, others on request. Handle bone-stag, others on request. **Patterns:** Trapper three-blade stockman, four-blade congress, single-and two-blade barlows. **Prices:** 150 to $400. **Mark:** First knife sold 1994. Steer head with Wingo Knives or Straight line Wingo Knives.

WINGO, PERRY
22 55th St, Gulfport, MS 39507, Phone: 228-863-3193

Specialties: Traditional working straight knives. **Patterns:** Hunters, skinners, Bowies and fishing knives. **Technical:** Grinds 440C. **Prices:** $75 to $1000. **Remarks:** Full-time maker; first knife sold in 1988. **Mark:** Last name.

WINKLER, DANIEL
PO Box 2166, Blowing Rock, NC 28605, Phone: 828-295-9156, danielwinkler@bellsouth.net; Web: www.winklerknives.com

Specialties: Forged cutlery styled in the tradition of an era past as well as producing a custom-made stock removal line. **Patterns:** Fixed blades, friction folders, lock back folders, and axes/tomahawks. **Technical:** Forges, grinds, and heat treats carbon steels, specialty steels, and his own Damascus steel. **Prices:** $350 to $4000+. **Remarks:** Full-time maker since 1988. Exclusively offers leatherwork by Karen Shook. ABS Master Smith; Knifemakers Guild voting member. **Mark:** Hand forged: Dwinkler; Stock removal: Winkler Knives

WINN, MARVIN
Maxcutter Custom Knives, 587 Winn Rd., Sunset, LA 70584, Phone: 214-471-7012, maxcutter03@yahoo.com Web: www.maxcutterknives.com

Patterns: Hunting knives, some tactical and some miniatures. **Technical:** 1095, 5160, 154 CM, 12C27, CPM S30V, CPM 154, CTS-XHP and CTS-40CP blade steels, damascus or to customer's specs. Stock removal. **Prices:** $200 to $2,000. **Remarks:** Part-time maker. First knife made in 2002. **Mark:** Name and state.

WINN, TRAVIS A.
558 E 3065 S, Salt Lake City, UT 84106, Phone: 801-467-5957

Specialties: Fancy working knives and knives to customer specs. **Patterns:** Hunters, fighters, boots, Bowies and fancy daggers, some miniatures, tantos and fantasy knives. **Technical:** Grinds D2 and 440C. Embellishes. **Prices:** $125 to $500; some higher. **Remarks:** Part-time maker; first knife sold in 1976. **Mark:** TRAV stylized.

WINSTON, DAVID
1671 Red Holly St, Starkville, MS 39759, Phone: 601-323-1028

Specialties: Fancy and traditional knives of his design and to customer specs. **Patterns:** Bowies, daggers, hunters, boot knives and folders. **Technical:** Grinds 440C, ATS-34 and D2. Offers filework; heat-treats. **Prices:** $40 to $750; some higher. **Remarks:** Part-time maker; first knife sold in 1984. Offers lifetime sharpening for original owner. **Mark:** Last name.

WIRTZ, ACHIM
Mittelstrasse 58, Wuerselen, GERMANY 52146, Phone: 0049-2405-462-486, wootz@web.de

Specialties: Medieval, Scandinavian and Middle East-style knives. **Technical:** Forged blades only, Damascus steel, Wootz, Mokume. **Prices:** Start at $200. **Remarks:** Part-time maker. First knife sold in 1997. **Mark:** Stylized initials.

WISE, DONALD
304 Bexhill Rd, St Leonardo-On-Sea, East Sussex, ENGLAND TN3 8AL

Specialties: Fancy and embellished working straight knives to customer specs. **Patterns:** Hunters, Bowies and daggers. **Technical:** Grinds Sandvik 12C27, D2 D3 and O1 Scrimshaws. **Prices:** $110 to $300; some to $500. **Remarks:** Full-time maker; first knife sold in 1983. **Mark:** KNIFECRAFT.

WITHERS, TIM
WITHERS KNIVES, 4625 N. Granada Ln., Linden, CA 95236, tim@withersknives.com; Web: www.withersknives.com

Specialties: Loveless and original designs. **Patterns:** Bowies, fighters, hunters, daggers and custom pieces. **Technical:** Stock removal method of blade making using ATS-34, 440C, 1095 and CPM 154 steels, and with hollow and flat grinds. Heat-treating includes sub-zero quenching done in-house. Every blade Rockwell Hardness tested. Uses Micarta, exotic wood, stag and mother-of-pearl handles, and each knife comes with a quality 8-9-ounce leather sheath, also made in-house. **Prices:** $350 to $1,100. **Remarks:** Part time maker; first knife completed in 2011. **Mark:** TIM WITHERS over LINDEN, CA.

WOLF, BILL
4618 N 79th Ave, Phoenix, AZ 85033, Phone: 623-910-3147, bwcustomknives143@gmail.com Web: billwolfcustomknives.com

Specialties: Investment grade knives. **Patterns:** Own designs or customer's. **Technical:** Grinds stainless and all steels. **Prices:** $400 to ? **Remarks:** First knife made in 1988. **Mark:** WOLF

WOLF JR., WILLIAM LYNN
4006 Frank Rd, Lagrange, TX 78945, Phone: 409-247-4626

WOOD, ALAN
Greenfield Villa, Greenhead, Brampton, ENGLAND CA8 7HH, info@alanwoodknives.com; Web: www.alanwoodknives.com

Specialties: High-tech working straight knives of his design. **Patterns:** Hunters, utility camp and bushcraft knives. **Technical:** Grinds 12C27, RWL-34, stainless Damascus an O1. Blades are cryogenic treated. **Prices:** $200 to $800; some to $1,200. **Remarks:** Full time maker; first knife sold in 1979. Not currently taking orders. **Mark:** Full name wit stag tree logo.

WOOD, OWEN DALE
6492 Garrison St, Arvada, CO 80004-3157, Phone: 303-456-2748, wood.owen@gmail.com; Web: www.owenwoodknives.net

Specialties: Folding knives and daggers. **Patterns:** Own Damascus, specialties in 45 composite blades. **Technical:** Materials: Damascus stainless steel, exotic metals, gol rare handle materials. **Prices:** $1000 to $9000. **Remarks:** Folding knives in art deco an art noveau themes. Full-time maker from 1981. **Mark:** OWEN WOOD.

WOOD, WEBSTER
22041 Shelton Trail, Atlanta, MI 49709, Phone: 989-785-2996, mainganikan@src-milp.com

Specialties: Works mainly in stainless; art knives, Bowies, hunters and folders. **Remark**

Full-time maker; first knife sold in 1980. Retired guild member. All engraving done by maker. **Mark:** Initials inside shield and name.

WORLEY, JOEL A., J.S.

PO BOX 64, Maplewood, OH 45340, Phone: 937-638-9518, jaworleyknives@gmail.com **Specialties:** Bowies, hunters, fighters, utility/camp knives also period style friction folders. **Patterns:** Classic styles, recurves, his design or customer specified. **Technical:** Most knives are fileworked and include a custom made leather sheath. Forges 5160, W2, Cru forge V, files own Damascus of 1080 and 15N20. **Prices:** $250 and up. **Remarks:** Part-time maker. ABS journeyman smith. First knife sold in 2005. **Mark:** First name, middle initial and last name over a shark incorporating initials.

WRIGHT, KEVIN

671 Leland Valley Rd W, Quilcene, WA 98376-9517, Phone: 360-765-3589, kevinw@ptpc.com **Specialties:** Fancy working or collector knives to customer specs. **Patterns:** Hunters, boots, buckskinners, miniatures. **Technical:** Forges and grinds L6, 1095, 440C and his own Damascus. **Prices:** $75 to $500; some to $2000. **Remarks:** Part-time maker; first knife sold in 1978. **Mark:** Last initial in anvil.

WRIGHT, L.T.

130b Warren Ln., Wintersville, OH 43953, Phone: 740-317-1404, lt@ltwrightknives.com; Web: www.ltwrightknives.com **Specialties:** Hunting, bushcraft and tactical knives. **Patterns:** Drop-point hunters, spear-point bushcraft and tactical. **Technical:** Grinds A2, D2 and O1. **Remarks:** Full-time maker.

WRIGHT, RICHARD S

PO Box 201, 111 Hilltop Dr, Carolina, RI 02812, Phone: 401-364-3579, rswswitchblades@hotmail.com; Web: www.richardswright.com **Specialties:** Bolster release switchblades, tactical automatics. **Patterns:** Folding fighters, gents pocket knives, one-of-a-kind high-grade automatics. **Technical:** Reforges and grinds various makers Damascus. Uses a variety of tool steels. Uses natural handle material such as ivory and pearl, extensive file-work on most knives. **Prices:** $850 and up. **Remarks:** Full-time knifemaker with background as a gunsmith. Made first folder in 1991. **Mark:** RSW on blade, all folders are serial numbered.

WRIGHT, ROBERT A

21 Wiley Bottom Rd, Savannah, GA 31411, Phone: 912-777-7864; Cell: 912-656-9085, maker@robwrightknives.com; Web: www.RobWrightKnives.com **Specialties:** Hunting, skinning, fillet, fighting and tactical knives. **Patterns:** Custom designs by client and/or maker. **Technical:** All types of steel, including CPM-S30V, D2, 440C, O1 tool steel and damascus upon request, as well as exotic wood and other high-quality handle materials. **Prices:** $200 and up depending on cost of steel and other materials. **Remarks:** Full-time maker, member of The Knifemakers' Guild and Georgia Custom Knifemaker's Guild. **Mark:** Etched maple leaf with maker's name: R.A. Wright.

WRIGHT, TIMOTHY

PO Box 3746, Sedona, AZ 86340, Phone: 928-282-4180 **Specialties:** High-tech folders and working knives. **Patterns:** Interframe locking folders, non-inlaid folders, straight hunters and kitchen knives. **Technical:** Grinds BG-42, AEB-L, K190 and Cowry X; works with new steels. All folders can disassemble and are furnished with tools. **Prices:** $150 to $1800; some to $3000. **Remarks:** Full-time maker; first knife sold in 1975. **Mark:** Last name and type of steel used.

WUERTZ, TRAVIS

2487 E Hwy 287, Casa Grande, AZ 85222, Phone: 520-723-4432

WULF, DERRICK

25 Sleepy Hollow Rd, Essex, VT 05452, Phone: 802-777-8766, dickwulf@yahoo.com Web: www.dicksworkshop.com **Specialties:** Makes predominantly forged fixed blade knives using carbon steels and his own Damascus. **Mark:** "WULF".

WYATT, WILLIAM R

Box 237, Rainelle, WV 25962, Phone: 304-438-5494 **Specialties:** Classic and working knives of all designs. **Patterns:** Hunters and utility knives. **Technical:** Forges and grinds saw blades, files and rasps. Prefers stag handles. **Prices:** $45 to $95; some to $350. **Remarks:** Part-time maker; first knife sold in 1990. **Mark:** Last name in star with knife logo.

WYLIE, TOM

Peak Knives, 2 Maun Close, Sutton-In-Ashfield, Notts, England NG17 5JG, tom@peakknives.com **Specialties:** Knives for adventure sports and hunting, mainly fixed blades. **Technical:** Damasteel or European stainless steel used predominantly, handle material to suit purpose, embellished as required. Work can either be all handmade or CNC machined. **Prices:** $450+. **Remarks:** Pro-Am maker. **Mark:** Ogram "tinne" in circle of life, sometimes with addition of maker's name.

Y

YASHINSKI, JOHN L

207 N Platt, PO Box 1284, Red Lodge, MT 59068, Phone: 406-446-3916 **Specialties:** Indian knife sheaths, beaded, tacked, painted rawhide sheaths, antiqued to look old, old beads and other parts, copies of originals. Write with color copies to be made. **Prices:** $100 to $600. Call to discuss price variations.

YESKOO, RICHARD C

76 Beekman Rd, Summit, NJ 07901

YONEYAMA, CHICCHI K.

5-19-8 Nishikicho, Tachikawa-City, Tokyo, JAPAN 190-0022, Phone: 081-1-9047449370, chicchi.ky1007@gmail.com; Web: https://sites.google.com/site/chicchiyoneyama/ **Specialties:** Folders, hollow ground, lockback and slip-joint folders with interframe handles. **Patterns:** Pocketknives, desk and daily-carry small folders. **Technical:** Stock-removal method on ATS-34, 440C, V10 and SG2/damascus blade steels. **Prices:** $300 to $1,000 and up. **Remarks:** Full-time maker; first knife sold in 1999. **Mark:** Saber tiger mark with logos/Chicchi K. Yoneyama.

YORK, DAVID C

PO Box 3166, Chino Valley, AZ 86323, Phone: 928-636-1709, dmatj@msn.com **Specialties:** Working straight knives and folders. **Patterns:** Prefers small hunters and skinners; locking folders. **Technical:** Grinds D2. **Prices:** $75 to $300; some to $600. **Remarks:** Part-time maker; first knife sold in 1975. **Mark:** Last name.

YOSHIHARA, YOSHINDO

8-17-11 Takasago Katsushi, Tokyo, JAPAN

YOSHIKAZU, KAMADA

540-3 Kaisaki Niuta-cho, Tokushima, JAPAN, Phone: 0886-44-2319

YOSHIO, MAEDA

3-12-11 Chuo-cho tamashima, Kurashiki-city, Okayama, JAPAN, Phone: 086-525-2375

YOUNG, BUD

Box 336, Port Hardy, BC, CANADA V0N 2P0, Phone: 250-949-6478 **Specialties:** Fixed blade, working knives, some fancy. **Patterns:** Drop-points to skinners. **Technical:** Hollow or flat grind, 5160, 440C, mostly ATS-34, satin finish. Using supplied damascus at times. **Prices:** $150 to $2000 CDN. **Remarks:** Spare-time maker; making knives since 1962; first knife sold in 1985. Not taking orders at this time, sell as produced. **Mark:** Name.

YOUNG, CLIFF

Fuente De La Cibeles No 5, Atascadero, San Miguel De Allende, GJ, MEXICO 37700, Phone: 011-52-415-2-57-11 **Specialties:** Working knives. **Patterns:** Hunters, fighters and fishing knives. **Technical:** Grinds all; offers D2, 440C and 154CM. **Prices:** Start at $250. **Remarks:** Part-time maker; first knife sold in 1980. **Mark:** Name.

YOUNG, GEORGE

713 Pinoak Dr, Kokomo, IN 46901, Phone: 765-457-8893 **Specialties:** Fancy/embellished and traditional straight knives and folders of his design and to customer specs. **Patterns:** Hunters, fillet/camp knives and locking folders. **Technical:** Grinds 440C, CPM440V, and stellite 6K. Fancy ivory, black pearl and stag for handles. Filework: all stellite construction (6K and 25 alloys). Offers engraving. **Prices:** $350 to $750; some $1500 to $3000. **Remarks:** Full-time maker; first knife sold in 1954. Doing business as Young's Knives. **Mark:** Last name integral inside Bowie.

YOUNG, JOHN

483 E. 400 S, Ephraim, UT 84627, Phone: 435-340-1417 or 435-283-4555 **Patterns:** Fighters, hunters and bowies. **Technical:** Stainless steel blades, including ATS-34, 440C and CTS-40CP. **Prices:** $800 to $5,000. **Remarks:** Full-time maker since 2006; first knife sold in 1997. **Mark:** Name, city and state.

YOUNG, RAYMOND L

CUTLER/BLADESMITH, 2922 Hwy 188E, Mt. Ida, AR 71957, Phone: 870-867-3947 **Specialties:** Cutler-Bladesmith, sharpening service. **Patterns:** Hunter, skinners, fighters, no guard, no ricasso, chef tools. **Technical:** Edge tempered 1095, 516C, mosaic handles, water buffalo and exotic woods. **Prices:** $100 and up. **Remarks:** Federal contractor since 1995. Surgical steel sharpening. **Mark:** R.

YURCO, MICKEY

PO Box 712, Canfield, OH 44406, Phone: 330-533-4928, shorinki@aol.com **Specialties:** Working straight knives. **Patterns:** Hunters, utility knives, Bowies and fighters, push knives, claws and other hideouts. **Technical:** Grinds 440C, ATS-34 and 154CM; likes mirror and satin finishes. **Prices:** $20 to $500. **Remarks:** Part-time maker; first knife sold in 1983. **Mark:** Name, steel, serial number.

Z

ZAFEIRIADIS, KONSTANTINOS

Dionyson Street, Marathon Attiki, GREECE 19005, Phone: 011-30697724-5771 or 011-30697400-6245 **Specialties:** Fixed blades, one-of-a-kind swords with bronze fittings made using the lost wax method. **Patterns:** Ancient Greek, central Asian, Viking, bowies, hunting knives, fighters, daggers. **Technical:** Forges 5160, O1 and maker's own damascus. **Prices:** $1,100 and up. **Remarks:** Full-time maker; first knife sold in 2010. **Mark:** (backward K)ZK.

ZAHM, KURT

488 Rio Casa, Indialantic, FL 32903, Phone: 407-777-4860 **Specialties:** Working straight knives of his design or to customer specs. **Patterns:** Daggers, fancy fighters, Bowies, hunters and utility knives. **Technical:** Grinds D2, 440C; likes filework. **Prices:** $75 to $1000. **Remarks:** Part-time maker; first knife sold in 1985. **Mark:** Last name.

ZAKABI, CARL S

PO Box 893161, Mililani Town, HI 96789-0161, Phone: 808-626-2181 **Specialties:** User-grade straight knives of his design, cord wrapped and bare steel handles exclusively. **Patterns:** Fighters, hunters and utility/camp knives. **Technical:**

custom knifemakers

Grinds 440C and ATS-34. **Prices:** $90 to $400. **Remarks:** Spare-time maker; first knife sold in 1988. Doing business as Zakabi's Knifeworks LLC. **Mark:** Last name and state inside a Hawaiian sharktooth dagger.

ZAKHAROV, GLADISTON
Rua Pernambuca, 175-Rio Comprido (Long River), Jacaret-SP, BRAZIL 12302-070, Phone: 55 12 3958 4021, Fax: 55 12 3958 4103, arkhip@terra.com.br; Web: www.arkhip.com.br
Specialties: Using straight knives of his design. **Patterns:** Hunters, kitchen, utility/camp and barbecue knives. **Technical:** Grinds his own "secret steel." **Prices:** $30 to $200. **Remarks:** Full-time maker. **Mark:** Arkhip Special Knives.

ZBORIL, TERRY
5320 CR 130, Caldwell, TX 77836, Phone: 979-535-4157, tzboril@tconline.net
Specialties: ABS Journeyman Smith.

ZEMBKO III, JOHN
140 Wilks Pond Rd, Berlin, CT 06037, Phone: 860-828-3503, johnzembko@hotmail.com
Specialties: Working knives of his design or to customer specs. **Patterns:** Likes to use stabilized high-figured woods. **Technical:** Grinds ATS-34, A2, D2; forges O1, 1095; grinds Damasteel. **Prices:** $50 to $400; some higher. **Remarks:** First knife sold in 1987. **Mark:** Name.

ZEMITIS, JOE
14 Currawong Rd, Cardiff Heights, NSW, AUSTRALIA 2285, Phone: +610249549907 or +614034599396, jjvzem@bigpond.com
Specialties: Traditional working straight knives. **Patterns:** Hunters, Bowies, tantos, fighters and camp knives. **Technical:** Grinds O1, D2, W2 and 440C. Embellishes; offers engraving. **Prices:** $150 to $3000. **Remarks:** Full-time maker; first knife sold in 1983. **Mark:** First initial, last name and country, or last name.

ZERMENO, WILLIAM D.
9131 Glenshadow Dr, Houston, TX 77088, Phone: 281-726-2459, will@wdzknives.com Web: www.wdzknives.com
Specialties: Tactical/utility folders and fixed blades. **Patterns:** Frame lock and liner lock folders the majority of which incorporate flippers and utility fixed blades. **Technical:** Grinds CPM 154, S30V, 3V and stainless Damascus. **Prices:** $250 - $600. **Remarks:** Part-time maker, first knife sold in 2008. Doing business as www.wdzknives.com. **Mark:** WDZ over logo.

ZIEBA, MICHAEL
95 Commercial St., #4, Brooklyn, NY 11222, Phone: 347-335-9944, ziebametal@gmail.com; Web: www.ziebaknives.com or www.brooklynknives.com
Specialties: High-end kitchen knives under maker's last name, ZIEBA, also tactical knives under HUSSAR name. **Technical:** Uses stainless steels: CPM S30V, CPM S35VN, CPM S60V, CPM D2 and AEB-L, and high-carbon steels: 52100 and Aogami #2. Forges carbon steel in his shop. **Remarks:** Full-time maker. Marks: Feather logo (kitchen knives only with 24k gold as a standard), ZIEBA (kitchen knives and folders) and "H" Hussar (tactical).

ZIMA, MICHAEL F
732 State St, Ft. Morgan, CO 80701, Phone: 970-867-6078, Web: http://www.zimaknives.com

Specialties: Working and collector quality straight knives and folders. **Patterns:** Hunters, lock backs, LinerLock®, slip joint and automatic folders. **Technical:** Grinds Damascus, 440C, ATS-34 and 154CM. **Prices:** $200 and up. **Remarks:** Full-time maker; first knife sold in 1982. **Mark:** Last name.

ZIMMERMAN, NATHAN
416 S. Comanche Ln., Waukesha, WI 53188, Phone: 262-510-3563, zimknives@gmail.com; Web: www.zimknives.com
Specialties: Custom high-end chef's knives. Large, elaborate fantasy weapons. **Patterns:** Unique matching sets of kitchen knives, as well as various hunters, fighters and utility knives. **Technical:** Thin-ground AEB-L chef's knives, forged 1084 knives with hamons (temper lines). Uses burls, Micartas, bone and horn. Favorite handle materials include ebony, African blackwood, bog oak and ironwood. **Prices:** Start at $200. **Remarks:** Full-time maker and knife sharpener; first knife sold in 2012. **Mark:** Hand-chiseled Z with dash. Signature on forged blades.

ZINKER, BRAD
BZ KNIVES, 1591 NW 17 St, Homestead, FL 33030, Phone: 305-216-0404, bzinker@gmail.com
Specialties: Fillets, folders and hunters. **Technical:** Uses ATS-34 and stainless Damascus. **Prices:** $200 to $600. **Remarks:** Voting member of Knifemakers Guild and Florida Knifemakers Association. **Mark:** Offset connected initials BZ.

ZIRBES, RICHARD
Neustrasse 15, Niederkail, GERMANY 54526, Phone: 0049 6575 1371, r.zirbes@freenet.de Web: www.zirbes-knives.com www.zirbes-messer.de
Specialties: Fancy embellished knives with engraving and self-made scrimshaw (scrimshaw made by maker). High-tech working knives and high-tech hunters, boots, fighters and folders. All knives made by hand. **Patterns:** Boots, fighters, hunters. **Technical:** Uses only the best steels for blade material like CPM-T 440V, CPM-T 420V, ATS-34, D2, C440, stainless Damascus or steel according to customer's desire. **Prices:** Working knives and hunters: $200 to $600. Fancy embellished knives with engraving and/or scrimshaw: $800 to $3000. **Remarks:** Part-time maker; first knife sold in 1991. Member of the German Knifemaker Guild. **Mark:** Zirbes or R. Zirbes.

ZOWADA, TIM
4509 E Bear River Rd, Boyne Falls, MI 49713, Phone: 231-838-4120, timzowada@gmail.com; Web: www.tzknives.com
Specialties: Working knives and straight razors. **Technical:** Forges O1, L6, his own Damascus and smelted steel "Michi-Gane". **Prices:** $200 to $2500; some to $5000. **Remarks:** Full-time maker; first knife sold in 1980. **Mark:** Gothic, lower case "TZ"

ZSCHERNY, MICHAEL
1840 Rock Island Dr, Ely, IA 52227, Phone: 319-321-5833, zschernyknives@aol.com
Specialties: Quality folders--slip joints and flipper folders. **Patterns:** Liner-lock and lock-back folders in titanium, working straight knives. **Technical:** Grinds ATS-34 and commercial damascus, prefers natural materials such as pearls and ivory. Uses Timascus, mokume, san mai and carbon fibers. **Prices:** Start at $600. **Remarks:** Full-time maker, first knife sold in 1978. **Mark:** Last name with image of a scorpion.

AK

Barlow, Jana Poirier	Anchorage
Brennan, Judson	Delta Junction
Breuer, Lonnie	Wasilla
Broome, Thomas A	Kenai
Chamberlin, John A	Anchorage
Cornwell, Jeffrey	Anchorage
Desrosiers, Adam	Petersburg
Desrosiers, Haley	Petersburg
Dufour, Arthur J	Anchorage
England, Virgil	Anchorage
Flint, Robert	Anchorage
Gouker, Gary B	Sitka
Harding, Jacob	Fairbanks
Harvey, Mel	Nenana
Hibben, Westley G	Anchorage
Hook, Bob	North Pole
Kelsey, Nate	Palmer
Knapp, Mark	Fairbanks
Lance, Bill	Palmer
Lance, Lucas	Wasilla
Malaby, Raymond J	Juneau
Mcfarlin, Eric E	Kodiak
Miller, Nate	Fairbanks
Miller, Terry	Healy
Mirabile, David	Juneau
Moore, Marve	Willow
Parrish Iii, Gordon A	North Pole
Stegall, Keith	Wasilla
Van Cleve, Steve	Sutton

AL

Alverson, Tim (R.V.)	Arab
Batson, James	Huntsville
Baxter, Dale	Trinity
Bell, Tony	Woodland
Brothers, Dennis L.	Oneonta
Coffman, Danny	Jacksonville
Conn Jr., C T	Attalla
Daniels, Alex	Town Creek
Dark, Robert	Oxford
Deibert, Michael	Trussville
Durham, Kenneth	Cherokee
Elrod, Roger R	Enterprise
Gilbreath, Randall	Dora
Golden, Randy	Montgomery
Grizzard, Jim	Oxford
Hammond, Jim	Birmingham
Heeter, Todd S.	Mobile
Howard, Durvyn M.	Hokes Bluff
Howell, Keith A.	Oxford
Howell, Len	Opelika
Howell, Ted	Wetumpka
Huckabee, Dale	Maylene
Hulsey, Hoyt	Attalla
Mccullough, Jerry	Georgiana
Mcnees, Jonathan	Northport
Militano, Tom	Jacksonville
Morris, C H	Frisco City
Pardue, Melvin M	Repton
Ploppert, Tom	Cullman
Russell, Tom	Jacksonville
Vinyard, Cleston S	Elberta
Smith, Lacy	Jacksonville
Thomas, David E	Lillian
Washburn Jr., Robert Lee	Tuscaloosa
Watson, Billy	Deatsville

AR

Anders, David	Center Ridge
Ardwin, Corey	Bryant
Barker, Reggie	Taylor
Barnes Jr., Cecil C.	Center Ridge
Brown, Jim	Little Rock
Browning, Steven W	Benton
Bullard, Benoni	Bradford
Bullard, Tom	Flippin
Chambers, Ronny	Beebe
Cook, James R	Nashville
Copeland, Thom	Nashville
Cox, Larry	Murfreesboro
Crawford, Pat And Wes	West Memphis
Crotts, Dan	Elm Springs
Crowell, James L	Mtn. View
Dozier, Bob	Springdale
Duvall, Fred	Benton
Echols, Rodger	Nashville
Edge, Tommy	Cash
Ferguson, Lee	Hindsville
Fisk, Jerry	Nashville
Fitch, John S	Clinton
Flournoy, Joe	El Dorado
Foster, Ronnie E	Morrilton
Foster, Timothy L	El Dorado
Frizzell, Ted	West Fork
Gadberry, Emmet	Hattieville
Greenaway, Don	Fayetteville
Herring, Morris	Dyer
Hutchinson, Alan	Conway
Kirkes, Bill	Little Rock
Koster, Daniel	Bentonville
Krein, Tom	Gentry
Lawrence, Alton	De Queen
Lemoine, David C	Mountain Home
Livesay, Newt	Siloam Springs
Lunn, Gail	Mountain Home
Lunn, Larry A	Mountain Home
Lynch, Tad	Beebe
Maringer, Tom	Springdale
Martin, Hal W	Morrilton
Massey, Roger	Texarkana
Newberry, Allen	Lowell
Newton, Ron	London
Nolte, Barbie	Lowell
Nolte, Steve	Lowell
Olive, Michael E	Leslie
Passmore, Jimmy D	Hoxie
Pearce, Logan	De Queen
Perry, Jim	Hope
Perry, John	Mayflower
Peterson, Lloyd (Pete) C	Clinton
Polk, Clifton	Van Buren
Polk, Rusty	Van Buren
Randow, Ralph	Greenbrier
Red, Vernon	Conway
Reeves, J.R.	Texarkana
Rhea, Lin	Prattsville
Richards, Ralph (Bud)	Bauxite
Roberts, T. C. (Terry)	Siloam Springs
Seward, Ben	Austin
Stanley, John	Crossett
Stout, Charles	Gillham
Sweaza, Dennis	Austin
Townsend, Allen Mark	Texarkana
Townsley, Russell	Floral
Upton, Tom	Rogers
Walker, Jim	Morrilton
Ward, Chuck	Benton
White, Bryce	Little Rock
Young, Raymond L	Mt. Ida

AZ

Allan, Todd	Glendale
Ammons, David C	Tucson
Bennett, Glen C	Tucson
Birdwell, Ira Lee	Congress
Boye, David	Dolan Springs
Cheatham, Bill	Laveen
Dawson, Barry	Prescott Valley
Dawson, Lynn	Prescott Valley
Deubel, Chester J.	Tucson
Dodd, Robert F	Camp Verde
Fuegen, Larry	Prescott
Genovese, Rick	Tonto Basin
Goo, Tai	Tucson
Hancock, Tim	Scottsdale
Harris, John	Quartzsite
Hoel, Steve	Pine
Holder, D'Alton	Wickenburg
Jackson, Laramie	Claysprings
Jensen, Eli	Prescott
Karp, Bob	Phoenix
Kiley, Mike And Jandy	Chino Valley
Kopp, Todd M	Apache Jct.
Lee, Randy	St. Johns
Mcfall, Ken	Lakeside
Mcfarlin, J W	Lake Havasu City
Miller, Michael	Kingman
Montell, Ty	Thatcher
Mooney, Mike	Queen Creek
Newhall, Tom	Tucson
Purvis, Bob And Ellen	Tucson
Robbins, Bill	Sierra Vista
Rybar Jr., Raymond B	Camp Verde
States, Joshua C	New River
Tamboli, Michael	Glendale
Tyre, Michael A	Wickenburg
Weiss, Charles L	Waddell
Wick, Jonathan P.	Hereford
Wolf, Bill	Phoenix
Wright, Timothy	Sedona
Wuertz, Travis	Casa Grande
York, David C	Chino Valley

CA

Abegg, Arnie	Huntington Beach
Adkins, Richard L	Mission Viejo
Andrade, Don Carlos	Los Osos
Athey, Steve	Riverside
Barnes, Gregory	Altadena
Barnes, Roger	Bay Point
Barnes, Roger	Bay Point
Barron, Brian	San Mateo
Begg, Todd M.	Petaluma
Benson, Don	Escalon
Berger, Max A.	Carmichael
Bolduc, Gary	Corona
Bost, Roger E	Palos Verdes
Boyd, Francis	Berkeley
Breshears, Clint	Manhattan Beach
Brooks, Buzz	Los Angles
Brous, Jason	Buellton
Browne, Rick	Upland
Bruce, Richard L.	Yankee Hill
Butler, Bart	Ramona
Cabrera, Sergio B	Wilmington
Cantrell, Kitty D	Ramona
Caston, Darriel	Folsom
Caswell, Joe	Newbury
Clinco, Marcus	Venice
Coffey, Bill	Clovis
Coleman, John A	Citrus Heights
Colwell, Kevin	Cheshire
Connolly, James	Oroville
Cucchiara, Matt	Fresno
Davis, Charlie	Lakeside
De Maria Jr., Angelo	Carmel Valley
Dion, Greg	Oxnard
Dobratz, Eric	Laguna Hills
Doolittle, Mike	Novato
Driscoll, Mark	La Mesa
Dwyer, Duane	Escondido
Ellis, William Dean	Sanger
Emerson, Ernest R	Harbor City
English, Jim	Jamul
Ernest, Phil (Pj)	Whittier
Essegian, Richard	Fresno
Felix, Alexander	Torrance
Ferguson, Jim	Lakewood
Finney, Garett	Loomis
Forrest, Brian	Descanso
Fraley, D B	Dixon
Fred, Reed Wyle	Sacramento
Freeman, Matt	Fresno
Freer, Ralph	Seal Beach
Fulton, Mickey	Willows
Girtner, Joe	Brea
Grayman, Mike	Lake Arrowhead
Guarnera, Anthony R	Quartzhill
Hall, Jeff	Paso Robles
Hardy, Scott	Placerville
Harris, Jay	Redwood City
Helton, Roy	San Diego
Herndon, Wm R "Bill"	Acton
Hink Iii, Les	Stockton
Hoy, Ken	North Fork

Humenick, Roy	Rescue
Jacks, Jim	Covina
Jackson, David	Lemoore
Jensen, John Lewis	Pasadena
Johnson, Randy	Turlock
Kazsuk, David	Menifee
Kelly, Dave	Los Angeles
Keyes, Dan	Chino
Kilpatrick, Christian A	Citrus Hieghts
Koster, Steven C	Huntington Beach
Larson, Richard	Turlock
Leland, Steve	Fairfax
Lin, Marcus	Mission Viejo
Lockett, Sterling	Burbank
Luchini, Bob	Palo Alto
Maccaughtry, Scott F.	Camarillo
Mackie, John	Whittier
Massey, Ron	Joshua Tree
Mata, Leonard	San Diego
Maxwell, Don	Clovis
Mcabee, William	Colfax
Mcclure, Michael	Menlo Park
Mcgrath, Patrick T	Westchester
Melin, Gordon C	La Mirada
Meloy, Sean	Lemon Grove
Montano, Gus A	San Diego
Morgan, Jeff	Santee
Moses, Steven	Santa Ana
Mutz, Jeff	Rancho Cucamonga
Naten, Greg	Bakersfield
Orton, Rich	Wilmington
Osborne, Donald H	Clovis
Palm, Rik	San Diego
Panchenko, Serge	Citrus Heights
Perry, Chris	Fresno
Pfanenstiel, Dan	Modesto
Pitt, David F	Anderson
Quesenberry, Mike	Blairsden
Randall, Patrick	Newbury Park
Rozas, Clark D	Wilmington
Schmitz, Raymond E	Valley Center
Schneider, Herman J.	Apple Valley
Schroen, Karl	Sebastopol
Sharp, David	Hesperia
Sibrian, Aaron	Ventura
Sjostrand, Kevin	Visalia
Slobodian, Scott	San Andreas
Smith, Shawn	Clouis
Sornberger, Jim	Volcano
Steinberg, Al	Laguna Woods
Stimps, Jason M	Orange
Strider, Mick	Escondido
Terrill, Stephen	Springville
Tingle, Dennis P	Jackson
Tobolak, Libor	San Marcos
Torres, Henry	Clovis
Vagnino, Michael	Visalia
Velick, Sammy	Los Angeles
Warren, Al	Roseville
Watanabe, Wayne	Montebello
Weinstock, Robert	San Francisco
Wilburn, Aaron	Redding
Wilson, Ron	Morro Bay
Withers, Tim	Linden

CO

Anderson, Mel	Hotchkiss
Booco, Gordon	Hayden
Brock, Kenneth L	Allenspark
Burrows, Chuck	Durango
Corich, Vance	Morrison
Davis, Don	Loveland
Dennehy, John D	Greeley
Dill, Robert	Loveland
Fairly, Daniel	Bayfield
Fredeen, Graham	Colorado Springs
Fronefield, Daniel	Peyton
Graham, Levi	Greeley
High, Tom	Alamosa
Hockensmith, Dan	Berthoud
Hughes, Ed	Grand Junction
Hughes, Tony	Littleton

Irie, Michael L	Colorado Springs
Kitsmiller, Jerry	Montrose
Leck, Dal	Hayden
Mcwilliams, Sean	Carbondale
Miller, Hanford J	Lakespur
Miller, M A	Northglenn
Nolen, Steve	Longmont
Ott, Fred	Durango
Owens, John	Buena Vista
Rexford, Todd	Florissant
Roberts, Chuck	Golden
Rollert, Steve	Keenesburg
Ronzio, N. Jack	Fruita
Sanders, Bill	Mancos
Thompson, Lloyd	Pagosa Springs
Urbach, Scott	Aurora
Waites, Richard L	Broomfield
Watson, Bert	Westminster
Wilson, James G	Estes Park
Wood, Owen Dale	Arvada
Zima, Michael F	Ft. Morgan
Redd, Bill	Broomfield

CT

Buebendorf, Robert E	Monroe
Chapo, William G	Wilton
Cross, Kevin	Portland
Framski, Walter P	Prospect
Jean, Gerry	Manchester
Loukides, David E	Cheshire
Meyer, Christopher J	Tolland
Parkinson, Matthew	Wolcott
Plunkett, Richard	West Cornwall
Rainville, Richard	Salem
Swarz-Burt, Peter T.	Wolcott
Turecek, Jim	Ansonia
Vitale, Mace	Guilford
Zembko Iii, John	Berlin

DE

Willey, Wg	Greenwood

FL

Adams, Les	Cape Coral
Alexander,, Oleg, And Cossack Blades	Wellington
Anders, Jerome	Miramar
Angell, Jon	Hawthorne
Atkinson, Dick	Wausau
Barnes, Gary L.	Defuniak Springs
Barry Iii, James J.	West Palm Beach
Beers, Ray	Lake Wales
Benjamin Jr., George	Kissimmee
Bosworth, Dean	Key Largo
Bradley, John	Pomona Park
Bray Jr., W Lowell	New Port Richey
Brown, Harold E	Arcadia
Butler, John	Havana
Clark, Jason	O'Brien
D'Andrea, John	Citrus Springs
Davis, John H.	Fruitland Park
Davis Jr., Jim	Zephyrhills
Dietzel, Bill	Middleburg
Dintruff, Chuck	Plant City
Dotson, Tracy	Baker
Ellerbe, W B	Geneva
Ellis, Willy B	Tarpon Springs
Enos Iii, Thomas M	Orlando
Fowler, Charles R	Ft McCoy
Franklin, Mike	Clermont
Gallagher, Scott	Santa Rosa Beach
Gamble, Roger	Newberry
Gardner, Robert	West Palm Beach
Ghio, Paolo	Pensacola
Goers, Bruce	Lakeland
Granger, Paul J	Largo
Greene, Steve	Intercession City
Griffin Jr., Howard A	Davie
Grospitch, Ernie	Orlando
Heaney, John D	Haines City
Heitler, Henry	Tampa
Hodge Iii, John	Palatka
Hostetler, Larry	Fort Pierce

Hostetter, Wally	San Mateo
Humphreys, Joel	Lake Placid
Hunter, Richard D	Alachua
Hytovick, Joe "Hy"	Dunnellon
Jernigan, Steve	Milton
Johanning Custom Knives, Tom	Sarasota
Johnson, John R	Plant City
King, Bill	Tampa
Krapp, Denny	Apopka
Levengood, Bill	Tampa
Long, Glenn A	Dunnellon
Lovestrand, Schuyler	Vero Beach
Lozier, Don	Ocklawaha
Lyle Iii, Ernest L	Chiefland
Mandt, Joe	St. Petersburg
Mason, Bill	Hobe Sound
Mcdonald, Robert J	Loxahatchee
Miller, Ronald T	Largo
Miller, Steve	Clearwater
Newton, Larry	Jacksonville
Ochs, Charles F	Largo
Overall, Jason	Sanford
Owens, Donald	Melbourne
Parker, Cliff	Zephyrhills
Partridge, Jerry D.	DeFuniak Springs
Pattay, Rudy	Citrus Springs
Pendray, Alfred H	Williston
Philippe, D A	The Villages
Piergallini, Daniel E	Plant City
Randall Made Knives,	Orlando
Raymond, Michael	Malabar
Renner, Terry	Palmetto
Robinson, Calvin	Pace
Robinson Iii, Rex R	Leesburg
Roddenberry, Charles	Live Oak
Rodkey, Dan	Hudson
Romeis, Gordon	Fort Myers
Russ, Ron	Williston
Schwarzer, Lora Sue	Crescent City
Schwarzer, Stephen	Crescent City
Smith, Michael J	Brandon
Stapleton, William E	Merritt Island
Steck, Van R	Orange City
Stephan, Daniel	Valrico
Stipes, Dwight	Palm City
Straight, Kenneth J	Largo
Tabor, Tim	Lutz
Turnbull, Ralph A	Spring Hill
Vogt, Donald J	Tampa
Watson, Tom	Panama City
Weiland Jr., J Reese	Riverview
Wicker, Donnie R	Panama City
Wilson, Stan	Lithia
Zahm, Kurt	Indialantic
Zinker, Brad	Homestead

GA

Arrowood, Dale	Sharpsburg
Ashworth, Boyd	Powder Springs
Barker, John	Cumming
Barker, Robert G.	Bishop
Beaver, Dirk	Ellijay
Bentley, C L	Albany
Bish, Hal	Jonesboro
Brach, Paul	Cumming
Bradley, Dennis	Blairsville
Buckner, Jimmie H	Putney
Busbie, Jeff	Bloomingdale
Cambron, Henry	Dallas
Chamblin, Joel	Concord
Crockford, Jack	Chamblee
Daniel, Travis E	Thomaston
Davidson, Scott	Alto
Davis, Steve	Powder Springs
Fowler, Stephan	Acworth
Frost, Dewayne	Barnesville
Gaines, Buddy	Commerce
Glover, Warren D	Cleveland
Greene, David	Covington
Hammond, Hank	Leesburg
Hammond, Ray	Buford
Hardy, Douglas E	Franklin

Hensley, Wayne	Conyers	Tippetts, Colten	Hidden Springs	Craig, Roger L	Topeka
Hewitt, Ronald "Cotton"	Adel	Towell, Dwight L	Midvale	Culver, Steve	Meriden
Hinson And Son, R	Columbus	Trace Rinaldi Custom Blades,	Plummer	Darpinian, Dave	Olathe
Hoffman, Kevin L	Savannah			Dawkins, Dudley L	Topeka
Hossom, Jerry	Duluth	**IL**		Dick, Dan	Hutchinson
Kimsey, Kevin	Cartersville	Armour, Dave	Auburn	Evans, Phil	Columbus
King, Fred	Cartersville	Bloomer, Alan T	Maquon	Finley, Jon M.	Leawood
Knott, Steve	Guyton	Camerer, Craig	Chesterfield	Hegwald, J L	Humboldt
Landers, John	Newnan	Cook, Louise	Ozark	Herman, Tim	Olathe
Lockett, Lowell C.	Canton	Cook, Mike	Ozark	Keranen, Paul	Tacumseh
Lonewolf, J Aguirre	Demorest	Detmer, Phillip	Breese	King Jr., Harvey G	Alta Vista
Mathews, Charlie And Harry	Statesboro	Dicristofano, Anthony P	Melrose Park	Kraft, Steve	Abilene
Mcgill, John	Blairsville	Eaker, Allen L	Paris	Lamb, Curtis J	Ottawa
Mitchell, James A	Columbus	Hall, Scott M.	Geneseo	Magee, Jim	Salina
Moncus, Michael Steven	Smithville	Hawes, Chuck	Weldon	Petersen, Dan L	Auburn
Parks, John	Jefferson	Heath, William	Bondville	Stice, Douglas W	Wichita
Poole, Marvin O	Commerce	Hill, Rick	Maryville		
Powell, Robert Clark	Smarr	Kovar, Eugene	Evergreen Park	**KY**	
Prater, Mike	Flintstone	Kulis, David S.	Chicago	Addison, Kyle A	Hazel
Price, Timmy	Blairsville	Leone, Nick	Pontoon Beach	Baskett, Barbara	Eastview
Ragsdale, James D	Ellijay	Markley, Ken	Sparta	Baskett, Lee Gene	Eastview
Roghmans, Mark	LaGrange	Meers, Andrew	Carbondale	Bybee, Barry J	Cadiz
Sangster, Joe	Vienna	Meier, Daryl	Carbondale	Carter, Mike	Louisville
Sculley, Peter E	Rising Fawn	Myers, Paul	Wood River	Downing, Larry	Bremen
Snow, Bill	Columbus	Myers, Steve	Carlinville	Dunn, Steve	Smiths Grove
Sowell, Bill	Macon	Nowland, Rick	Waltonville	Edwards, Mitch	Glasgow
Stafford, Richard	Warner Robins	Pellegrin, Mike	Troy	Finch, Ricky D	West Liberty
Surls, W. Allen	Buford	Pritchard, Ron	Dixon	Fister, Jim	Simpsonville
Thompson, Kenneth	Duluth	Roosevelt, Russell	Albion	France, Dan	Cawood
Tomey, Kathleen	Macon	Rosenbaugh, Ron	Crystal Lake	Frederick, Aaron	West Liberty
White, Lou	Ranger	Rossdeutscher, Robert N	Arlington Heights	Greco, John	Greensburg
Wright, Robert A	Savannah	Rzewnicki, Gerald	Elizabeth	Hibben, Daryl	LaGrange
		Schneider, Craig M	Claremont	Hibben, Gil	LaGrange
HI		Smale, Charles J	Waukegan	Hoke, Thomas M	LaGrange
Evans, Vincent K And Grace	Keaau	Smith, John M	Centralia	Holbrook, H L	Sandy Hook
Gibo, George	Hilo	Todd, Richard C	Chambersburg	Jeffries, Mike	Louisville
Lui, Ronald M	Honolulu	Veit, Michael	LaSalle	Keeslar, Joseph F	Almo
Mann, Tim	Honokaa	Voss, Ben	Victoria	Pease, W D	Ewing
Matsuoka, Scot	Mililani	Werth, George W	Poplar Grove	Pierce, Harold L	Louisville
Mayo Jr., Tom	Waialua	West, Charles A	Centralia	Rados, Jerry F	Columbia
Mitsuyuki, Ross	Honolulu	Wheeler, Robert	Bradley	Richerson, Ron	Greenburg
Onion, Kenneth J	Kaneohe			Rigney Jr., Willie	Bronston
Ouye, Keith	Honolulu	**IN**		Smith, Chris	Burgin
Salter, Gregg	Waikoloa	Ball, Ken	Mooresville	Smith, John W	West Liberty
Watanabe, Melvin	Kailua	Barkes, Terry	Edinburgh	Soaper, Max H.	Henderson
Zakabi, Carl S	Mililani Town	Barrett, Rick L. (Toshi Hisa)	Goshen	Steier, David	Louisville
		Bose, Reese	Shelburn	Vance, David	West Liberty
IA		Bose, Tony	Shelburn	Wallingford Jr., Charles W	Union
Brooker, Dennis	Chariton	Chaffee, Jeff L	Morris		
Brower, Max	Boone	Claiborne, Jeff	Franklin	**LA**	
Clark, Howard F	Runnells	Cramer, Brent	Wheatland	Blaum, Roy	Covington
Cockerham, Lloyd	Denham Springs	Crowl, Peter	Waterloo	Caldwell, Bill	West Monroe
Helscher, John W	Washington	Curtiss, David	Granger	Calvert Jr., Robert W (Bob)	Rayville
Lainson, Tony	Council Bluffs	Damlovac, Sava	Indianapolis	Capdepon, Randy	Carencro
Lewis, Bill	Riverside	Darby, Jed	Greensburg	Capdepon, Robert	Carencro
Mckiernan, Stan	Lamoni	Fitzgerald, Dennis M	Fort Wayne	Chauvin, John	Scott
Miller, James P	Fairbank	Fraps, John R	Indianapolis	Dake, C M	New Orleans
Thie, Brian	Burlington	Good, D.R.	Tipton	Dake, Mary H	New Orleans
Trindle, Barry	Earlham	Harding, Chad	Solsberry	Durio, Fred	Opelousas
Westberg, Larry	Algona	Imel, Billy Mace	New Castle	Faucheaux, Howard J	Loreauville
Zscherny, Michael	Ely	Johnson, C E Gene	Chesterton	Fontenot, Gerald J	Mamou
		Kain, Charles	Indianapolis	Gorenflo, James T (Jt)	Baton Rouge
ID		Keeslar, Steven C	Hamilton	Graves, Dan	Shreveport
Alderman, Robert	Sagle	Keeton, William L	Laconia	Johnson, Gordon A.	Choudrant
Bair, Mark	Firth	Kinker, Mike	Greensburg	Ki, Shiva	Baton Rouge
Bloodworth Custom Knives,	Meridian	Largin, Ken	Connersville	Laurent, Kermit	LaPlace
Burke, Bill	Boise	Mayville, Oscar L	Marengo	Lemaire, Ryan M.	Abbeville
Eddy, Hugh E	Caldwell	Miller, Levi	Howe	Leonard, Randy Joe	Sarepta
Farr, Dan	Post Falls	Minnick, Jim & Joyce	Middletown	Mitchell, Max Dean And Ben	Leesville
Hackney, Dana A.	Naples	Patton, Phillip	Yoder	Phillips, Dennis	Independence
Hawk, Grant And Gavin	Idaho City	Quakenbush, Thomas C	Ft Wayne	Potier, Timothy F	Oberlin
Hogan, Thomas R	Boise	Robertson, Leo D	Indianapolis	Primos, Terry	Shreveport
Horton, Scot	Buhl	Seib, Steve	Evansville	Provenzano, Joseph D	Ponchatoula
Howe, Tori	Athol	Shull, James	Rensselaer	Randall Jr., James W	Keithville
Mann, Michael L	Spirit Lake	Smock, Timothy E	Marion	Reggio Jr., Sidney J	Sun
Metz, Greg T	Cascade	Thayer, Danny O	Romney	Tilton, John	Iowa
Patton, Dick And Rob	Nampa	Young, George	Kokomo	Trisler, Kenneth W	Rayville
Quarton, Barr	McCall			Wilson, P.R. "Regan"	Scott
Rohn, Fred	Coeur d'Alene	**KS**		Winn, Marvin	Sunset
Sawby, Scott	Sandpoint	Bradburn, Gary	Wichita		
Sparks, Bernard	Dingle	Burrows, Stephen R	Humboldt	**MA**	
Steiger, Monte L	Genesee	Chard, Gordon R	Iola	Banaitis, Romas	Medway

Cooper, Paul	Woburn
Dailey, G E	Seekonk
Dugdale, Daniel J.	Walpole
Gedraitis, Charles J	Holden
Grossman, Stewart	Clinton
Hinman, Theodore	Greenfield
Jarvis, Paul M	Cambridge
Johnson, Timothy A.	Worcester
Khalsa, Jot Singh	Millis
Klein, Kevin	Boston
Kubasek, John A	Easthampton
Lapen, Charles	W. Brookfield
Little, Larry	Spencer
Martin, Randall J	Bridgewater
Mcluin, Tom	Dracut
Moore, Michael Robert	Lowell
Rebello, Indian George	New Bedford
Rizzi, Russell J	Ashfield
Rua, Gary	Fall River
Saviano, James	Douglas
Siska, Jim	Westfield
Smith, J D	Melrose
Stuart, Mason	Mansfield
Vining, Bill	Methuen

MD

Aylor, Erin Lutzer	Myersville
Bagley, R. Keith	White Plains
Barnes, Aubrey G.	Hagerstown
Cohen, N J (Norm)	Baltimore
Dement, Larry	Prince Fredrick
Fuller, Jack A	New Market
Gossman, Scott	Whiteford
Hart, Bill	Pasadena
Heard, Tom	Waldorf
Hendrickson, E Jay	Frederick
Hendrickson, Shawn	Knoxville
Kreh, Lefty	"Cockeysville"
Mccarley, John	Taneytown
Mcgowan, Frank E	Sykesville
Merchant, Ted	White Hall
Nicholson, R. Kent	Monkton
Nuckels, Stephen J	Hagerstown
Presti, Matt	Union Bridge
Sentz, Mark C	Taneytown
Smit, Glenn	Aberdeen
Sontheimer, G Douglas	Gaithersburg
Spickler, Gregory Noble	Sharpsburg
St. Clair, Thomas K	Monrovia
Walker, Bill	Stevensville

ME

Bohrmann, Bruce	Yarmouth
Breda, Ben	Hope
Ceprano, Peter J.	Auburn
Coombs Jr., Lamont	Bucksport
Gray, Daniel	Brownville
Hillman, Charles	Friendship
Leavitt Jr., Earl F	E. Boothbay
Oyster, Lowell R	Corinth
Sharrigan, Mudd	Wiscasset
Steingass, T.K.	Bucksport

MI

Ackerson, Robin E	Buchanan
Alcorn, Douglas A.	Chesaning
Andrews, Eric	Grand Ledge
Arms, Eric	Tustin
Behnke, William	Kingsley
Booth, Philip W	Ithaca
Carr, Tim	Muskegon
Carroll, Chad	Grant
Cashen, Kevin R	Hubbardston
Cook, Mike A	Portland
Cousino, George	Onsted
Cowles, Don	Royal Oak
Doyle, John	Gladwin
Ealy, Delbert	Indian River
Erickson, Walter E.	Atlanta
Gordon, Larry B	Farmington Hills
Gottage, Dante	Clinton Twp.
Gottage, Judy	Clinton Twp.

Haas, Randy	Marlette
Harm, Paul W	Attica
Harrison, Brian	Cedarville
Hartman, Arlan (Lanny)	Baldwin
Hoffman, Jay	Munising
Hughes, Daryle	Nunica
Lankton, Scott	Ann Arbor
Lark, David	Kingsley
Logan, Iron John	Leslie
Marsh, Jeremy	Ada
Mills, Louis G	Ann Arbor
Morris, Michael S.	Yale
Nevling, Mark	Owosso
Noren, Douglas E	Springlake
Parker, Robert Nelson	Royal Oak
Repke, Mike	Bay City
Rose Ii, Doun T.	Fife Lake
Sakmar, Mike	Howell
Sandberg, Ronald B	Brownstown
Tally, Grant	Flat Rock
Van Eizenga, Jerry W	Nunica
Vasquez, Johnny David	Wyandotte
Viste, James	Hamtramck
Webster, Bill	Three Rivers
Welling, Ronald L	Grand Haven
White, Richard T	Grosse Pointe Farms
Whittaker, Wayne	Metamore
Wood, Webster	Atlanta
Zowada, Tim	Boyne Falls

MN

Andersen, Karl B.	Warba
Burns, Robert	Carver
Davis, Joel	Albert Lea
Hagen, Doc	Pelican Rapids
Hansen, Robert W	Cambridge
Hebeisen, Jeff	Hopkins
Johnson, Jerry L	Worthington
Johnson, Keith R.	Bemidji
Johnson, R B	Clearwater
Knipschield, Terry	Rochester
Leblanc, Gary E	Little Falls
Maines, Jay	Wyoming
Mesenbourg, Nick	Inver Grove Heights
Metsala, Anthony	Princeton
Mickley, Tracy	North Mankato
Ritchie, Adam	Bloomington
Rohde, Daniel S.	Winona
Rydbom, Jeff	Annandale
Shadley, Eugene W	Grand Rapids
Taber, David E.	Winona
Voorhies, Les	Faribault

MO

Abernathy, Lance	North Kansas City
Allred, Elvan	St. Charles
Andrews, Russ	Sugar Creek
Betancourt, Antonio L.	St. Louis
Braschler, Craig W.	Zalma
Buxton, Bill	Kaiser
Chinnock, Daniel T.	Union
Cover, Jeff	Potosi
Cover, Raymond A	Mineral Point
Dippold, Al	Perryville
Duncan, Ron	Cairo
Eaton, Frank L Jr	Farmington
Ehrenberger, Daniel Robert	Mexico
Engle, William	Boonville
Hanson, Kyle S.	Success
Hanson Iii, Don L.	Success
Harrison, Jim (Seamus)	St. Louis
Kinnikin, Todd	Pacific
Knickmeyer, Hank	Cedar Hill
Knickmeyer, Kurt	Cedar Hill
Krause, Jim	Farmington
Lee, Ethan	Sturgeon
Martin, Tony	Arcadia
Mccrackin, Kevin	House Spings
Mccrackin And Son, V J	House Spings
Miller, William (Bill)	Warsaw
Mosier, David	Independence
Mulkey, Gary	Branson

Muller, Jody	Goodson
Newcomb, Corbin	Moberly
Ramsey, Richard A	Neosho
Rardon, A D	Polo
Rardon, Archie F	Polo
Riepe, Richard A	Harrisonville
Robbins, Howard P	Flemington
Robbins, Landon	Crane
Royer, Kyle	Clever
Schow, Lyle	Harrisonville
Scroggs, James A	Warrensburg
Seaton, David D	Rolla
Smith, Jerry W.	Willow Springs
Sonntag, Douglas W	Nixa
Sonntag, Jacob D	St. Robert
Sonntag, Kristopher D	Nixa
Steketee, Craig A	Billings
Stormer, Bob	Dixon
Waide, Rusty	Buffalo
Warden, Roy A	Union
Whitesell, J. Dale	Stover
Willis, Bill	Ava

MS

Black, Scott	Picayune
Boleware, David	Carson
Cohea, John M	Nettleton
Davis, Jesse W	Coldwater
Davison, Todd A.	Kosciusko
Evans, Bruce A	Booneville
Flynt, Robert G	Gulfport
Jones, Jack P.	Ripley
Lamey, Robert M	Biloxi
Lebatard, Paul M	Vancleave
May, Charles	Aberdeen
Mayo Jr., Homer	Biloxi
Nichols, Chad	Blue Springs
Phillips, Donavon	Morton
Pickett, Terrell	Lumberton
Provost, J.C.	Laurel
Robinson, Chuck	Picayune
Shiffer, Steve	Leakesville
Smith, J.B.	Perkinston
Taylor, Billy	Petal
Tribble, Skylar	Leakesville
Vandeventer, Terry L	Byram
Vardaman, Robert	Hattiesburg
Wehner, Rudy	Collins
White, Russell D.	Rienzi
Wilson, Vic	Olive Branch
Wingo, Perry	Gulfport
Winston, David	Starkville

MT

Barnes, Jack	Whitefish
Barnes, Wendell	Clinton
Barth, J.D.	Alberton
Beam, John R.	Kalispell
Beaty, Robert B.	Missoula
Behring, James	Missoula
Bell, Don	Lincoln
Bizzell, Robert	Butte
Brooks, Steve R	Walkerville
Caffrey, Edward J	Great Falls
Campbell, Doug	McLeod
Carlisle, Jeff	Simms
Christensen, Jon P	Stevensville
Colter, Wade	Colstrip
Conklin, George L	Ft. Benton
Conti, Jeffrey D	Judith Gap
Crowder, Robert	Thompson Falls
Curtiss, Steve L	Eureka
Dunkerley, Rick	Lincoln
Eaton, Rick	Broadview
Ellefson, Joel	Manhattan
Fassio, Melvin G	Lolo
Forthofer, Pete	Whitefish
Fritz, Erik L	Forsyth
Gallagher, Barry	Lincoln
Harkins, J A	Conner
Hintz, Gerald M	Helena
Hulett, Steve	West Yellowstone

Kauffman, Dave	Clancy
Kelly, Steven	Bigfork
Mcguane Iv, Thomas F	Bozeman
Mckee, Neil	Stevensville
Moyer, Russ	Havre
Nedved, Dan	Kalispell
Olson, Joe	Great Falls
Parsons, Pete	Helena
Patrick, Willard C	Helena
Peele, Bryan	Thompson Falls
Pursley, Aaron	Big Sandy
Rodewald, Gary	Hamilton
Ruana Knife Works,	Bonner
Smith, Josh	Frenchtown
Taylor, Shane	Miles City
Thill, Jim	Missoula
Weinand, Gerome M	Missoula
Yashinski, John L	Red Lodge

NC

Baker, Herb	Eden
Barefoot, Joe W.	Wilmington
Best, Ron	Stokes
Bisher, William (Bill)	Denton
Brackett, Jamin	Fallston
Britton, Tim	Winston-Salem
Busfield, John	Roanoke Rapids
Craddock, Mike	Thomasville
Crist, Zoe	Flat Rock
Drew, Gerald	Mill Spring
Gaddy, Gary Lee	Washington
Gahagan, Kyle	Moravian Falls
Gingrich, Justin	Wade
Goode, Brian	Shelby
Greene, Chris	Shelby
Gross, W W	Archdale
Hall, Ken	Waynesville
Hege, John B.	Danbury
Hoffman, Liam	Newland
Johnson, Tommy	Troy
Livingston, Robert C	Murphy
Maynard, William N.	Fayetteville
Mcghee, E. Scott	Clarkton
Mclurkin, Andrew	Raleigh
Mcnabb, Tommy	Bethania
Mcrae, J Michael	Mint Hill
Neely, Jonathan	Greensboro
Nichols, Calvin	Raleigh
Parrish, Robert	Weaverville
Patrick, Chuck	Brasstown
Patrick, Peggy	Brasstown
Pica, Daniel	Pittsboro
Randall, Steve	Lincolnton
Rapp, Steven J	Marshall
Santini, Tom	Pikeville
Scholl, Tim	Angier
Simmons, H R	Aurora
Sirois, Darrin	Fayetteville
Sterling, Murray	Mount Airy
Summers, Arthur L	Concord
Sutton, S Russell	New Bern
Vail, Dave	Hampstead
Wacholz, Doc	Marble
Wagaman, John K	Selma
Walker, Don	Burnsville
Warren, Daniel	Canton
Whitley, L Wayne	Chocowinity
Wiggins, Bill	Canton
Williamson, Tony	Siler City
Wilson, Mike	Hayesville
Winkler, Daniel	Blowing Rock

ND

Kommer, Russ	Fargo
Pitman, David	Williston

NE

Archer, Ray And Terri	Omaha
Hielscher, Guy	Alliance
Jokerst, Charles	Omaha
Lyons, William R. (Bill)	Palisade
Marlowe, Charles	Omaha

Moore, Jon P	Aurora
Sloan, David	Diller
Suedmeier, Harlan	Nebraska City
Syslo, Chuck	Omaha
Tiensvold, Alan L	Rushville
Tiensvold, Jason	Rushville
Till, Calvin E And Ruth	Chadron

NH

Hudson, C Robbin	Rochester
Jonas, Zachary	Wilmot
Saindon, R Bill	Goshen
Ward, Tom	Wilmot
White, Caleb A.	Hooksett

NJ

Fisher, Lance	Pompton Lakes
Grussenmeyer, Paul G	Cherry Hill
Knowles, Shawn	Great Meadows
Lesswing, Kevin	Bayonne
Licata, Steven	Boonton
Mccallen Jr., Howard H	So Seaside Park
Nadeau, Brian	Stanhope
Pressburger, Ramon	Howell
Sheets, Steven William	Mendham
Slee, Fred	Morganville
Viele, H J	Westwood
Yeskoo, Richard C	Summit

NM

Black, Tom	Albuquerque
Burnley, Lucas	Albuquerque
Chavez, Ramon	Belen
Cherry, Frank J	Albuquerque
Cordova, Joey	Bernalillo
Cordova, Joseph G	Bosque Farms
Cumming, Bob	Cedar Crest
Digangi, Joseph M	Los Ojos
Duran, Jerry T	Albuquerque
Dyess, Eddie	Roswell
Fisher, Jay	Clovis
Garner, George	Albuquerque
Goode, Bear	Navajo Dam
Gunter, Brad	Tijeras
Hartman, Tim	Albuquerque
Hethcoat, Don	Clovis
Kimberley, Richard L.	Santa Fe
Leu, Pohan	Rio Rancho
Lewis, Tom R	Carlsbad
Lynn, Arthur	Galisteo
Macdonald, David	Los Lunas
Meshejian, Mardi	Santa Fe
Reid, Jim	Albuquerque
Rogers, Richard	Magdalena
Schaller, Anthony Brett	Albuquerque
Stalcup, Eddie	Gallup
Swearingen, Kurt	Cedar Crest
Terzuola, Robert	Albuquerque
Trujillo, Albert M B	Bosque Farms
Walker, Michael L	Pueblo Sur Taos
Wescott, Cody	Las Cruces

NV

Barnett, Van	Reno
Bingenheimer, Bruce	Spring Creek
Cameron, Ron G	Logandale
Dellana,	Reno
George, Tom	Henderson
Hrisoulas, Jim	Henderson
Kreibich, Donald L.	Reno
Nishiuchi, Melvin S	Las Vegas
Rougeau, Derick	Sparks
Thomas, Devin	Panaca
Washburn, Arthur D	Pioche

NY

Baker, Wild Bill	Boiceville
Castellucio, Rich	Amsterdam
Cimms, Greg	Pleasant Valley
Daly, Michael	Brooklyn
Davis, Barry L	Castleton
Gregory, Matthew M.	Glenwood
Hobart, Gene	Windsor

Johnson, Mike	Orient
Johnston, Dr. Robt	Rochester
Lamothe, Jordan	Granville
Lamothe, Jordan	Granville
Levin, Jack	Brooklyn
Loos, Henry C	New Hyde Park
Ludwig, Richard O	Maspeth
Lupole, Jamie G	Kirkwood
Manaro, Sal	Holbrook
Maragni, Dan	Georgetown
Mccornock, Craig	Willow
Meerdink, Kurt	Barryville
Merola, Jim	Brooklyn
Miller, Chelsea Grace	Brooklyn
Nazz, Theo "Rock"	New York
Page, Reginald	Groveland
Rachlin, Leslie S	Elmira
Rappazzo, Richard	Cohoes
Rotella, Richard A	Niagara Falls
Scheid, Maggie	Rochester
Schippnick, Jim	Sanborn
Serafen, Steven E	New Berlin
Skiff, Steven	Broadalbin
Smith, Lenard C	Valley Cottage
Smith, Raymond L	Erin
Summers, Dan	Whitney Pt.
Szilaski, Joseph	Pine Plains
Turner, Kevin	Montrose
Welling, William	West Valley
Zieba, Michael	Brooklyn

OH

Busse, Jerry	Wauseon
Coffee, Jim	Norton
Collins, Lynn M	Elyria
Coppins, Daniel	Cambridge
Cottrill, James I	Columbus
Crews, Randy	Patriot
Downing, Tom	Cuyahoga Falls
Downs, James F	Powell
Etzler, John	Grafton
Francis, John D	Ft. Loramie
Gittinger, Raymond	Tiffin
Glover, Ron	Cincinnati
Greiner, Richard	Green Springs
Hinderer, Rick	Shreve
Humphrey, Lon	Newark
Imboden Ii, Howard L.	Dayton
Johnson, Wm. C. "Bill"	Enon
Jones, Roger Mudbone	Waverly
Kiefer, Tony	Pataskala
Landis, David E. Sr.	Galion
Longworth, Dave	Felicity
Maienknecht, Stanley	Sardis
Marshall, Rex	Wilmington
Mcdonald, Rich	Hillboro
Mcgroder, Patrick J	Madison
Mercer, Mike	Lebanon
Morgan, Tom	Beloit
Munjas, Bob	Waterford
O'Machearley, Michael	Wilmington
Panak, Paul S	Andover
Potter, Billy	Dublin
Roddy, Roy "Tim"	Hubbard
Rose, Derek W	Gallipolis
Rowe, Fred	Amesville
Salley, John D	Tipp City
Schuchmann, Rick	New Richmond
Sheely, "Butch" Forest	Grand Rapids
Shinosky, Andy	Canfield
Shoemaker, Carroll	Northup
Shoemaker, Scott	Miamisburg
Spinale, Richard	Lorain
Strong, Scott	Beavercreek
Summers, Dennis K	Springfield
Thomas, Kim	Seville
Thourot, Michael W	Napoleon
Tindera, George	Brunswick
Trout, George H.	Wilmington
Votaw, David P	Pioneer
Williams, Robert	East Liverpool
Worley, Joel A., J.S.	Maplewood

Wright, L.T.	Wintersville
Yurco, Mickey	Canfield
Stidham, Daniel	Gallipolis

OK

Baker, Ray	Sapulpa
Cleveland, Mike	Mustang
Coye, Bill	Tulsa
Crenshaw, Al	Eufaula
Crowder, Gary L	Sallisaw
Damasteel Stainless Damascus,	Norman
Darby, David T	Cookson
Dill, Dave	Bethany
Duff, Bill	Poteau
Dunlap, Jim	Sallisaw
Gepner, Don	Norman
Haze, Jeff	Skiatook
Heimdale, J E	Tulsa
Kennedy Jr., Bill	Yukon
Kirk, Ray	Tahlequah
Lairson Sr., Jerry	Ringold
Martin, John Alexander	Okmulgee
Mcclure, Jerry	Norman
Menefee, Ricky Bob	Blanchard
Midgley, Ben	Wister
Miller, Michael E	Chandler
Parsons, Larry	Mustang
Pridgen Jr., Larry	Davis
Schreiner, Terry	Duncan
Shropshire, Shawn	Piedmont
Spivey, Jefferson	Yukon
Stanford, Perry	Broken Arrow
Tomberlin, Brion R	Norman
Williams, Michael	Broken Bow
Wingo, Gary	Ramona

OR

Allen, Jim	Bend
Bell, Gabriel	Coquille
Bell, Michael	Coquille
Berg, Lee	Roseburg
Bochman, Bruce	Grants Pass
Brandt, Martin W	Springfield
Buchanan, Thad	Powell Butte
Buchanan, Zac	Eugene
Buchner, Bill	Idleyld Park
Busch, Steve	Oakland
Carter, Murray M	Hillsboro
Coon, Raymond C	Damascus
Dixon Jr., Ira E	Cave Junction
Emmerling, John	Gearheart
Frank, Heinrich H	Newport
Goddard, Wayne	Eugene
Harsey, William H	Creswell
Horn, Jess	Eugene
House, Cameron	Salem
Kelley, Gary	Aloha
Lake, Ron	Eugene
Lewis, Mike	Coquille
Little, Gary M	Broadbent
Magruder, Jason	Medford
Martin, Gene	Williams
Ochs, Eric	Sherwood
Olson, Darrold E	McMinnville
Pruyn, Peter	Grants Pass
Richard, Raymond	Gresham
Richards, Chuck	Salem
Rider, David M	Eugene
Sarganis, Paul	Jacksonville
Scarrow, Wil	Gold Hill
Schoenigh, Mike	North Powder
Schrader, Robert	Bend
Sevey Custom Knife,	Gold Beach
Sheehy, Thomas J	Portland
Sibert, Shane	Gladstone
Smith, Rick	Rogue River
Spake, Jeremy	Portland
Squire, Jack	McMinnville
Stucky, Daniel	Springfield
Tendick, Ben	Eugene
Thompson, Leon	Forest Grove
Thompson, Tommy	Portland

Tuch, William	Portland
Turner, Mike	Williams
Vallotton, Butch And Arey	Oakland
Vallotton, Rainy D	Umpqua
Vallotton, Shawn	Oakland
Vallotton, Thomas	Oakland
Ward, Ken	Grants Pass
Warren, Alan And Carroll	Portland
Kurt, David	Molalla

PA

Anderson, Gary D	Spring Grove
Anderson, Tom	Manchester
Appleby, Robert	Shickshinny
Bennett, Brett C	Reinholds
Besedick, Frank E	Monongahela
Blystone, Ronald L.	Creekside
Candrella, Joe	Warminster
Clark, D E (Lucky)	Johnstown
Corkum, Steve	Littlestown
Darby, Rick	Levittown
Evans, Ronald B	Middleton
Frey Jr., W Frederick	Milton
Fry, Dean	Wellsboro
Godlesky, Bruce F.	Apollo
Goldberg, David	Ft Washington
Gottschalk, Gregory J	Carnegie
Harner Iii, "Butch" Lloyd R.	Littlestown
Heinz, John	Upper Black Eddy
Johnson, John R	New Buffalo
Kolenko, Vladimir	Huntingdon Valley
Krammes, Jeremy	Schuylkill Haven
Malloy, Joe	Freeland
Marlowe, Donald	Dover
Mensch, Larry C	Milton
Miller, Rick	Rockwood
Moore, Ted	Elizabethtown
Morett, Donald	Lancaster
Nealy, Bud	Stroudsburg
Neilson, J	Towanda
Nguyen, Mike	Pittsburgh
Ogden, Bill	Avis
Parker, J E	Clarion
Root, Gary	Erie
Rose, Bob	Wagontown
Rupert, Bob	Clinton
Sass, Gary N	Sharpsville
Scimio, Bill	Spruce Creek
Sinclair, J E	Pittsburgh
Steigerwalt, Ken	Orangeville
Stroyan, Eric	Dalton
Takach, Andrew	Elizabeth
Wetten, Bobby	Hershey
Whittaker, Robert E	Mill Creek

RI

Dickison, Scott S	Portsmouth
Jacques, Alex	Warwick
Mchenry, William James	Wyoming
Olszewski, Stephen	Coventry
Williams, Jason L	Wyoming
Wright, Richard S	Carolina

SC

Beatty, Gordon H.	Seneca
Branton, Robert	Awendaw
Cox, Sam	Gaffney
Denning, Geno	Gaston
Estabrook, Robbie	Conway
Frazier, Jim	Wagener
Gainey, Hal	Greenwood
George, Harry	Aiken
Gregory, Michael	Belton
Hendrix, Jerry	Clinton
Hendrix, Wayne	Allendale
Hucks, Jerry	Moncks Corner
Kay, J Wallace	Liberty
Knight, Jason	Harleyville
Kreger, Thomas	Lugoff
Langley, Gene H	Florence
Lutz, Greg	Greenwood
Manley, David W	Central

Miles Jr., C R "Iron Doctor"	Lugoff
Odom Jr., Victor L.	North
O'Quinn, W. Lee	Elgin
Page, Larry	Aiken
Parler, Thomas O	Charleston
Peagler, Russ	Moncks Corner
Perry, Johnny	Inman
Smith, Ralph L	Taylors
Thomas, Rocky	Moncks Corner
Tyser, Ross	Spartanburg

SD

Boley, Jamie	Parker
Boysen, Raymond A	Rapid Ciy
Ferrier, Gregory K	Rapid City
Thomsen, Loyd W	Custer
Watts, Rodney	Hot Springs

TN

Accawi, Fuad	Oak Ridge
Adams, Jim	Cordova
Bailey, Joseph D.	Nashville
Bartlett, Mark	Lawrenceburg
Blanchard, G R (Gary)	Dandridge
Breed, Kim	Clarksville
Brend, Walter	Etowah
Burris, Patrick R	Athens
Byrd, Wesley L	Evensville
Canter, Ronald E	Jackson
Casteel, Dianna	Monteagle
Casteel, Douglas	Monteagle
Claiborne, Ron	Knox
Conley, Bob	Jonesboro
Coogan, Robert	Smithville
Corby, Harold	Johnson City
Elishewitz, Allen	Lenoir City
Ewing, John H	Clinton
Fitz, Andrew A. Sr. And Jr.	Milan
Hale, Lloyd	Pulaski
Harley, Larry W	Bristol
Hughes, Dan	Spencer
Hurst, Jeff	Rutledge
Hutcheson, John	Chattanooga
Johnson, David A	Pleasant Shade
Johnson, Ryan M	Signal Mountain
Kemp, Lawrence	Ooltewah
Kilroy, Kyle	Knoxville
Kistner, Dee	Crossville
Levine, Bob	Tullahoma
Mccarty, Harry	Blaine
Mcdonald, W.J. "Jerry"	Germantown
Moulton, Dusty	Loudon
Oates, Lee	Bethpage
Raley, R. Wayne	Collierville
Ridge, Tim	Crossville
Sampson, Lynn	Jonesborough
Smith, Newman L.	Gatlinburg
Soileau, Damon	Kingsport
Taylor, C. Gray	Fall Branch
Vanderford, Carl G	Columbia
Wall, Greg	Michie
Ward, W C	Clinton
Wheeler, Gary	Clarksville
Williams Jr., Richard	Morristown

TX

Alexander, Eugene	Ganado
Aplin, Spencer	Brazoria
Appleton, Ron	Bluff Dale
Ashby, Douglas	Dallas
Baker, Tony	Allen
Barnes, Marlen R.	Atlanta
Barr, Judson C.	Irving
Batts, Keith	Hooks
Blackwell, Zane	Eden
Blum, Kenneth	Brenham
Bradley, Gayle	Weatherford
Bratcher, Brett	Plantersville
Brewer, Craig	Killeen
Broadwell, David	Wichita Falls
Brooks, Michael	Lubbock
Brown, Douglas	Fort Worth

Budell, Michael	Brenham
Bullard, Randall	Canyon
Burden, James	Burkburnett
Buzek, Stanley	Waller
Callahan, F Terry	Boerne
Carey, Peter	Lago Vista
Carpenter, Ronald W	Jasper
Carter, Fred	Wichita Falls
Champion, Robert	Amarillo
Chase, John E	Aledo
Chew, Larry	Weatherford
Childers, David	Montgomery
Churchman, T W (Tim)	Bandera
Cole, James M	Bartonville
Connor, John W	Odessa
Connor, Michael	Winters
Cooke, Mark	Spring
Cornett, Brian	McKinney
Costa, Scott	Spicewood
Crain, Jack W	Granbury
Crouch, Bubba	Pleasanton
Crowner, Jeff	Plano
Darcey, Chester L	College Station
De Mesa, John	Lewisville
Dean, Harvey J	Rockdale
Debaud, Jake	Plano
Delong, Dick	Centerville
Dietz, Howard	New Braunfels
Dominy, Chuck	Colleyville
Dyer, David	Granbury
Eldridge, Allan	Ft. Worth
Epting, Richard	College Station
Eriksen, James Thorlief	Garland
Evans, Carlton	Fort Davis
Fant Jr., George	Atlanta
Ferguson, Jim	San Angelo
Fisher, Josh	Murchison
Foster, Al	Magnolia
Foster, Norvell C	Marion
Fritz, Jesse	Slaton
Fry, Jason	Hawley
Fuller, Bruce A	Blanco
Gann, Tommy	Canton
Garner, Larry W	Tyler
Gatlin, Steve	Schwartz
George, Les	Corpus Christi
Graham, Gordon	New Boston
Green, Bill	Sachse
Griffin, John	Hockley
Grimes, Mark	Bedford
Guinn, Terry	Eastland
Halfrich, Jerry	San Marcos
Hamlet Jr., Johnny	Clute
Hand, Bill	Spearman
Hawkins, Buddy	Texarkana
Hawkins Jr., Charles R.	San Angelo
Hawley, Troy G.	Ivanhoe
Haynes, Jerry	Gunter
Hays, Mark	Austin
Hemperley, Glen	Willis
Hicks, Gary	Tuscola
Hill, Steve E	Spring Branch
Horrigan, John	Burnet
Howell, Jason G	Lake Jackson
Hudson, Robert	Humble
Hughes, Lawrence	Plainview
Hunt, Raymon E.	Irving
Huse, James D. Ii	Buda
Jackson, Charlton R	San Antonio
Maksik Jr., Michael	Fredericksburg
Mangtanong, Suchat	Dripping Springs
Keller, Bill	San Antonio
Lance, Dan	Weatherford
Laplante, Brett	McKinney
Lay, L J	Burkburnett
Lemcke, Jim L	Houston
Lennon, Dale	Alba
Lister Jr., Weldon E	Boerne
Love, Ed	San Antonio
Lovett, Michael	Mound
Luchak, Bob	Channelview
Lucie, James R	Austin

Luckett, Bill	Weatherford
Majors, Charlie	Montgomery
Martin, Michael W	Beckville
Mcconnell Jr., Loyd A	Marble Falls
Merz Iii, Robert L	Katy
Minchew, Ryan	Midland
Mitchell, Wm Dean	Warren
Moen, Jerry	Dallas
Moore, James B	Ft. Stockton
Neely, Greg	Bellaire
O'Brien, Mike J.	San Antonio
Ogletree Jr., Ben R	Livingston
Ott, Ted	Elgin
Overeynder, T R	Arlington
Ownby, John C	Murphy
Packard, Ronnie	Bonham
Pardue, Joe	Hillister
Patterson, Pat	Barksdale
Payne, Travis	Telephone
Peters, Daniel	El Paso
Pierce, Randall	Arlington
Pollock, Wallace J	Cedar Park
Polzien, Don	Lubbock
Powers, Walter R.	Lolita
Ralph, Darrel	Forney
Ray, Alan W	Lovelady
Richardson, Percy	Lufkin
Richardson Iii, Percy (Rich)	Lufkin
Richardson Jr., Percy	Lufkin
Roberts, Jack	Houston
Rucker, Thomas	Spring
Ruple, William H	Pleasanton
Ruth, Michael G	Texarkana
Ruth, Jr., Michael	Texarkana
Schorsch, Kendall	Jourdanton
Self, Ernie	Dripping Springs
Shipley, Steven A	Richardson
Sloan, Shane	Newcastle
Smart, Steve	McKinney
Snody, Mike	Aransas Pass
Stokes, Ed	Hockley
Stone, Jerry	Lytle
Stout, Johnny	New Braunfels
Swenson, Luke	Lakehills
Thuesen, Ed	Damon
Truncali, Pete	Nevada
Van Reenen, Ian	Amarillo
Vickers, David	Montgomery
Ware, Tommy	Onalaska
Watson, Daniel	Driftwood
Watts, Johnathan	Gatesville
Weever, John	Glen Rose
White, Dale	Sweetwater
Whitley, Weldon G	Odessa
Wilkins, Mitchell	Montgomery
Wilson, Curtis M	Burleson
Wolf Jr., William Lynn	Lagrange
Zboril, Terry	Caldwell
Zermeno, William D.	Houston

UT

Allred, Bruce F	Layton
Black, Earl	Salt Lake City
Carter, Shayne	Payson
Ence, Jim	Richfield
Ennis, Ray	Ogden
Erickson, L.M.	Ogden
Hunter, Hyrum	Aurora
Johnson, Steven R	Manti
Jorgensen, Carson	Mt Pleasant
Lang, David	Kearns
Maxfield, Lynn	Layton
Nell, Chad	St. George
Nielson, Jeff V	Monroe
Nunn, Gregory	Castle Valley
Palmer, Taylor	Blanding
Peterson, Chris	Salina
Ramos, Steven	West Jordan
Ricks, Kurt J.	Trenton
Strickland, Dale	Monroe
Szczerbiak, Maciej	St. George
Velarde, Ricardo	Park City
Weeks, Ryan	Bountiful
Winn, Travis A.	Salt Lake City
Young, John	Ephraim
Jenkins, Mitch	Manti
Johnson, Jerry	Spring City

VA

Apelt, Stacy E	Norfolk
Arbuckle, James M	Yorktown
Ball, Butch	Floyd
Ballew, Dale	Bowling Green
Barnhill, Wess	Spotsylvania
Batson, Richard G.	Rixeyville
Beverly Ii, Larry H	Spotsylvania
Catoe, David R	Norfolk
Davidson, Edmund	Goshen
Foster, Burt	Bristol
Goodpasture, Tom	Ashland
Harley, Richard	Bristol
Harris, Cass	Bluemont
Hedrick, Don	Newport News
Hendricks, Samuel J	Maurertown
Holloway, Paul	Norfolk
Jones, Barry M And Phillip G	Danville
Jones, Enoch	Warrenton
Kearney, Jarod	Swoope
Klein, Kieran	Check
Martin, Herb	Richmond
Mccoun, Mark	DeWitt
Metheny, H A "Whitey"	Spotsylvania
Mills, Michael	Colonial Beach
Murski, Ray	Reston
Norfleet, Ross W	Providence Forge
Parks, Blane C	Woodbridge
Pawlowski, John R	Barhamsville
Schlueter, David	Madison Heights
Schwartz, Aaron	Woodbridge
Vanhoy, Ed And Tanya	Abingdon
Vestal, Charles	Abingdon
Ward, Ron	Rose Hill

VT

Bensinger, J. W.	Marshfield
Haggerty, George S	Jacksonville
Kelso, Jim	Worcester
Wulf, Derrick	Essex

WA

Amoureux, A W	Northport
Ber, Dave	San Juan Island
Berglin, Bruce	Mount Vernon
Bromley, Peter	Spokane
Brothers, Robert L	Colville
Brunckhorst, Lyle	Bothell
Buckner, Tom	Olympia
Bump, Bruce D.	Walla Walla
Butler, John R	Shoreline
Campbell, Dick	Colville
Chamberlain, Jon A	E. Wenatchee
Conway, John	Kirkland
Crowthers, Mark F	Rolling Bay
D'Angelo, Laurence	Vancouver
Davis, John	Selah
De Wet, Kobus	Yakima
Diaz, Jose	Ellensburg
Diskin, Matt	Freeland
Erickson, Daniel	Snohomish
Ferry, Tom	Auburn
Gray, Bob	Spokane
Gray, Robb	Seattle
Greenfield, G O	Everett
Hansen, Lonnie	Spanaway
House, Gary	Ephrata
Keyes, Geoff P.	Duvall
Leeper, Dan	Olympia
Lisch, David K	Yelm
Norton, Don	Port Townsend
O'Malley, Daniel	Seattle
Padilla, Gary	Bellingham
Pedersen, Ole	Monroe
Podmajersky, Dietrich	Seattle
Rader, Michael	Bothell

directory

Roeder, David — Kennewick
Rogers, Ray — Wauconda
Sanford, Dick — Chehalis
Schempp, Ed — Ephrata
Schempp, Martin — Ephrata
Shoger, Mark O — Kalama
Stegner, Wilbur G — Rochester
Sterling, Thomas J — Coupeville
Straub, Salem F. — Tonasket
Swyhart, Art — Klickitat
Thomas, Bob — Ferndale
Wheeler, Nick — Castle Rock
Wright, Kevin — Quilcene

WI

Boyes, Tom — West Bend
Brandsey, Edward P — Janesville
Bruner, Fred Jr. — Fall Creek
Carr, Joseph E. — Menomonee Falls
Coats, Ken — Stevens Point
Delarosa, Jim — Waterford
Deyong, Clarence — Sturtevant
Franklin, Larry — Stoughton
Haines, Jeff — Mayville
Hoffman, Jess — Shawano
Johnson, Richard — Germantown
Kanter, Michael — New Berlin
Kohls, Jerry — Princeton
Kolitz, Robert — Beaver Dam
Lary, Ed — Mosinee
Lerch, Matthew — Sussex
Maestri, Peter A — Spring Green
Martin, Cory — Racine
Martin, Peter — Waterford
Mikolajczyk, Glen — Caledonia
Millard, Fred G — Richland Center
Montgomery, Stephen R. — Madison
Nelson, Ken — Racine
Niemuth, Troy — Sheboygan
Ponzio, Doug — Beloit
Rabuck, Jason — Springbrook
Revishvili, Zaza — Madison
Ricke, Dave — West Bend
Rochford, Michael R — Dresser
Roush, Scott — Washburn
Schrap, Robert G — Wauwatosa
Steinbrecher, Mark W — Pleasant Prairie
Wattelet, Michael A — Minocqua
Zimmerman, Nathan — Waukesha

WV

Derr, Herbert — St. Albans
Drost, Jason D — French Creek
Drost, Michael B — French Creek
Elliott, Jerry — Charleston
Groves, Gary — Canvas
Jeffries, Robert W — Red House
Liegey, Kenneth R — Millwood
Maynard, Larry Joe — Crab Orchard
Morris, Eric — Beckley
Pickens, Selbert — Dunbar
Reynolds, Dave — Harrisville
Small, Ed — Keyser
Tokar, Daniel — Shepherdstown
Wilson, Rw — Weirton
Wyatt, William R — Rainelle

WY

Amos, Chris — Riverton
Ankrom, W.E. — Cody
Banks, David L. — Riverton
Barry, Scott — Laramie
Bartlow, John — Sheridan
Casey, Kevin — Lander
Deveraux, Butch — Riverton
Draper, Audra — Riverton
Draper, Mike — Riverton
Fowler, Ed A. — Riverton
Friedly, Dennis E — Cody
Kilby, Keith — Cody
Oliver, Todd D — Cheyenne
Rexroat, Kirk — Banner

Reynolds, John C — Gillette
Rodebaugh, James L — Carpenter
Ross, Stephen — Evanston
Spragg, Wayne E — Lovell
Whipple, Wesley A — Thermopolis

ARGENTINA

Ayarragaray, Cristian L. — Parana, Entre Rios
Bertolami, Juan Carlos — Neuquen
Gibert, Pedro — San Martin de los Andes, Neuquen
Kehiayan, Alfredo — Maschwitz, Buenos Aires
Montenegro, Facundo — Merlo (5881) San Luis
Rho, Nestor Lorenzo — Junin, Buenos Aires
Santiago, Abud — Buenos Aires

AUSTRALIA

Barnett, Bruce — Mundaring, WA
Bennett, Peter — Engadine, NSW
Brodziak, David — Albany, WA
Crawley, Bruce R — Croydon, VIC
Cross, Robert — Tamworth, NSW
Del Raso, Peter — Mt. Waverly, VIC
Fludder, Keith — Tahmoor, New South Wales
Gerner, Thomas — Walpole, WA
Giljevic, Branko — New South Wales
Green, William (Bill) — View Bank, VIC
Harvey, Max — Western Australia 6149
Hedges, Dee — Bedfordale, WA
Husiak, Myron — Altona, VIC
K B S, Knives — North Castlemaine, VIC
Maisey, Alan — Vincentia, NSW
Mcintyre, Shawn — Hawthornm, E VIC
Phillips, Alistair — Amaroo, ACT
Tasman, Kerley — Pt Kennedy, WA
Zemitis, Joe — Cardiff Heights, NSW

BELGIUM

Dox, Jan — Schoten
Laurent, Veronique — Brussels
Lurquin, Samuel — Binches
Monteiro, Victor — Maleves Ste Marie
Veronique, Laurent — Bruxelles

BRAZIL

Bodolay, Antal — Belo Horizonte, MG
Boeck, Sandro Eduardo — Cachoeira do Sul - RS
Bossaerts, Carl — Ribeirao Preto, SP
Campos, Ivan — Tatui, SP
Cecchini, Gustavo T. — Sao Jose Rio Preto SP
Dionatam, Franco — Ibitinga-SP
Dionatam, Franco — Jardim Filadelfia, Ibitinga-SP
Dorneles, Luciano Oliverira — Nova Petropolis, RS
Gaeta, Angelo — Centro Jau, SP-CEP: 14.201310
Garcia, Mario Eiras — Caxingui, SP
Glasser, Roger Cesar — 679 - Sao Paulo - SP
Goncalves, Luiz Gustavo — 124A - Sao Paulo - SP
Ikoma, Flavio — Presidente Prudente, SP
Lala, Paulo Ricardo P And Lala, Roberto P. — Presidente Prudente, SP
Neto Jr.,, Nelson And De Carvalho, Henrique M. — Braganca Paulista, SP
Paulo, Fernandes R — Lencois Paulista, SP
Petean, Francisco And Mauricio — Birigui, SP
Ricardo Romano, Bernardes — Itajuba MG
Sfreddo, Rodrigo Menezes — Nova Petropolis, RS
Vilar, Ricardo — Mairipora, SP
Vilar, Ricardo Augusto Ferreira — Mairipora, SP
Villa, Luiz — Itaim Bibi, SP
Zakharov, Gladiston — Jacaret-SP

CANADA

Arnold, Joe — London, ON
Beauchamp, Gaetan — Stoneham, QC
Beets, Marty — Williams Lake, BC
Bell, Donald — Bedford, NS
Berg, Lothar — Kitchener ON
Beshara, Brent (Besh) — NL
Boos, Ralph — Edmonton, AB
Bourbeau, Jean Yves — Ile Perrot, QC
Bradford, Garrick — Kitchener, ON
Bucharsky, Emil — Spruce Grove, Alberta
Daley, Mark — Waubaushene, Ontario
Dallyn, Kelly — Calgary, AB

De Braga, Jose C. — Trois Rivieres, QC
Debraga, Jovan — Quebec
Deringer, Christoph — Cookshire, QC
Desaulniers, Alain — Cookshire, QC
Diotte, Jeff — LaSalle, ON
Doiron, Donald — Messines, QC
Doucette, R — Brantford, ON
Doussot, Laurent — St. Bruno, QC
Downie, James T — Ontario
Friesen, Dave J — British Columbia
Frigault, Rick — Golden Lake, ON
Ganshorn, Cal — Regina, SK
Garvock, Mark W — Balderson, ON
Gilbert, Chantal — Quebec City, QC
Haslinger, Thomas — British Columbia V1B 3G7
Hayes, Wally — Essex, ON
Hindmarch, Garth — Carlyle, SK
Hofer, Louis — Rose Prairie, BC
Jobin, Jacques — Levis, QC
Kaczor, Tom — Upper London, ON
Lambert, Kirby — Regina, SK
Langley, Mick — Qualicum Beach, BC
Lay, R J (Bob) — Logan Lake, BC
Leber, Heinz — Hudson's Hope, BC
Lemelin, Stephanie — Brossard
Lightfoot, Greg — Kitscoty, AB
Linklater, Steve — Aurora, ON
Loerchner, Wolfgang — Bayfield, ON
Maneker, Kenneth — Galiano Island, BC
Marchand, Rick — Lunenburg, Nova Scotia
Marzitelli, Peter — Langley, BC
Massey, Al — Mount Uniacke, NS
Mckenzie, David Brian — Campbell River, BC
Miville-Deschenes, Alain — Quebec
Moeller, Harald — Parksville, BC
Moizis, Stan — Delta, British Columbia (BC)
Nease, William — LaSalle, ON
Niro, Frank — Kamloops, B.C.
O'Hare, Sean — Grand Manan, NB
Olson, Rod — Nanton, AB
Painter, Tony — Whitehorse, YT
Patrick, Bob — S. Surrey, BC
Pepiot, Stephan — Winnipeg, MB
Piesner, Dean — Conestogo, ON
Poirier, Rick — New Brunswick E4V 2W7
Rassenti, Peter — Quebec J7P 4C2
Ridley, Rob — Sundre, AB
Ross, Tim — Thunder Bay, ON
Schoenfeld, Matthew A — Galiano Island, BC
St. Amour, Murray — Beachburg, Ontario
Stancer, Chuck — Calgary, AB
Storch, Ed — Mannville, AB
Stuart, Steve — Gores Landing, ON
Sylvester, David — Compton, QC
Tedford, Steven J. — Colborne, ON
Tighe, Brian — St. Catharines, ON
Toner, Roger — Pickering, ON
Vanderkolff, Stephen — Mildmay, ON
Whitenect, Jody — Elderbank, NS
Young, Bud — Port Hardy, BC

CZECH REPUBLIC

Kislinger, Milos — Dobronin 314 58812
Rusnak, Josef — 323 00 Plzer
Sevecek, Pavel — Brodek U Konice
Tesarik, Richard — 614 00 Brn

DENMARK

Andersen, Henrik Lefolii — Fredensbor
Anso, Jens — Sporup
Rafn, Dan C. — 7400 Hernin
Strande, Poul — Dastru
Vensild, Henrik — Aunin
Willumsen, Mikkel — S Copenhage

ENGLAND

Bailey, I.R. — Colkir
Barker, Stuart — Wigston, Leiceste
Boden, Harry — Derbyshir
Ducker, Brian — Colkir
Farid, Mehr R — Ken
Harrington, Roger — East Susse

Nowacki, Stephen R.	Southampton, Hampshire
Orford, Ben	Worcestershire
Price, Darrell Morris	Devon
Stainthorp, Guy	Stroke-on-Trent
Wardell, Mick	N Devon
Wise, Donald	East Sussex
Wood, Alan	Brampton
Wylie, Tom	Sutton-In-Ashfield, Notts

FINLAND

Hankala, Jukka	39580 Riitiala
Nylund, Erik	65320 Vaasa
Palikko, J-T	00190 Helsinki
Ruusuvuori, Anssi	Piikkio
Tuominen, Pekka	Tossavanlahti
Vilppola, Markku	Turku

FRANCE

Bennica, Charles	Moules et Baucels
Chomilier, Alain And Joris	Clermont-Ferrand
Doursin, Gerard	Pernes les Fontaines
Grangette, Alain	23210 Azat-Chatenet
Graveline, Pascal And Isabelle	Moelan-sur-Mer
Headrick, Gary	Juan Les Pins
Laroche, Jean-Marc	78160 Marly le Roi
Madrulli, Mme Joelle	Salon De Provence
Regel, Jean-Louis	Saint Leger de Fougeret
Reverdy, Nicole And Pierre	Romans
Thevenot, Jean-Paul	Dijon
Viallon, Henri	Thiers

GERMANY

Boehlke, Guenter	56412 Grobholbach
Borger, Wolf	Graben-Neudorf
Dell, Wolfgang	Owen-Teck
Drumm, Armin	Dornstadt
Faust, Joachim	Goldkronach
Fruhmann, Ludwig	Burghausen
Greiss, Jockl	Schenkenzell
Hehn, Richard Karl	Dorrebach
Herbst, Peter	Lauf a.d. Pegn.
Joehnk, Bernd	Kiel
Kressler, D F	D-28832 Achim
Rankl, Christian	Munchen
Rinkes, Siegfried	Markterlbach
Selzam, Frank	Bad Koenigshofen
Steinau, Jurgen	Berlin
Tritz, Jean-Jose	Hamburg
Wirtz, Achim	Wuerselen
Zirbes, Richard	Niederkail

GREECE

Ioannis-Minas, Filippou	Athens
Zafeiriadis, Konstantinos	Marathon Attiki

IRELAND

Moore, Davy	Quin, Co Clare

ISRAEL

Shadmot, Boaz	Arava

ITALY

Ameri, Mauro	Genova
Ballestra, Santino	Ventimiglia
Bertuzzi, Ettore	Bergamo
Bonassi, Franco	Pordenone
Esposito, Emmanuel	Buttigliera Alta TO
Fogarizzu, Boiteddu	Pattada
Frizzi, Leonardo	Firenze
Garau, Marcello	Oristano
Giagu, Salvatore And Deroma Maria Rosaria Pattada (SS)	
Mainolfi, Dr. Riccardo	Positano (SA)
Moro, Corrado	Torino
Mura, Denis	Cascina (Pi)
Puddu, Salvatore	(Cagliari) Sardinia
Ramondetti, Sergio	CHIUSA DI PESIO (CN)
Riboni, Claudio	Truccazzano (MI)
Scordia, Paolo	Roma
Simonella, Gianluigi	Maniago
Toich, Nevio	Vincenza
Tschager, Reinhard	Bolzano

JAPAN

Aida, Yoshihito	Tokyo
Ebisu, Hidesaku	Hiroshima
Fujikawa, Shun	Osaka
Fukuta, Tak	Gifu
Hara, Koji	Gifu
Hirayama, Harumi	Saitama
Hiroto, Fujihara	Hiroshima
Isao, Ohbuchi	Fukuoka
Ishihara, Hank	Chiba
Kagawa, Koichi	Kanagawa
Kanki, Iwao	Hyogo
Kansei, Matsuno	Gifu
Kato, Shinichi	Aichi
Katsumaro, Shishido	Hiroshima
Keisuke, Gotoh	Oita
Koyama, Captain Bunshichi	Aichi
Makoto, Kunitomo	Hiroshima
Matsuno, Kansei	Gifu-City
Matsusaki, Takeshi	Nagasaki
Michinaka, Toshiaki	Tottori
Narasada, Mamoru	NAGANO
Ryuichi, Kuki	Saitama
Shigeno, Mamoru	Saitama, 350-1320
Shinozaki, Akio	Fukuoka-ken
Sugihara, Keidoh	Osaka
Sugiyama, Eddy K	Oita
Tamatsu, Kunihiko	Kochi-ken
Toshifumi, Kuramoto	Fukuoka
Uchida, Chimata	Kumamoto
Wada, Yasutaka	Nara
Waters, Glenn	Hirosaki City
Yoneyama, Chicchi K.	Tokyo
Yoshihara, Yoshindo	Tokyo
Yoshikazu, Kamada	Tokushima
Yoshio, Maeda	Okayama

MEXICO

Scheurer, Alfredo E Faes	Distrito Federal
Sunderland, Richard	Puerto Escondido, OA
Ware, J.D.	Merida, Yucatan
Young, Cliff	San Miguel De Allende, GJ

Namibia

Naude, Louis	Okahandja

NETHERLANDS

Brouwer, Jerry	Alkmaar
Sprokholt, Rob	Gatherwood
Van De Manakker, Thijs	Holland
Van Den Elsen, Gert	Tilburg
Van Eldik, Frans	Loenen
Van Ryswyk, Aad	Vlaardingen

NEW ZEALAND

Bassett, David J.	Auckland
Gunther, Eddie	Auckland
Jansen Van Vuuren, Ludwig	Dunedin
Knapton, Chris C.	Henderson, Aukland
Pennington, C A	Kainga Christchurch
Reddiex, Bill	Palmerston North
Sandow, Brent Edward	Auckland
Sands, Scott	Christchurch 9
Van Dijk, Richard	Harwood Dunedin

NICARAGUA

Morales, Ramon	Managua

NORWAY

Bache-Wiig, Tom	Eivindvik
Sellevold, Harald	Bergen
Vistnes, Tor	Svelgen

RUSSIA

Kharlamov, Yuri	Tula

SLOVAKIA

Albert, Stefan	Filakovo 98604
Bojtos, Arpad	98403 Lucenec
Kovacik, Robert	Tomasovce 98401
Mojzis, Julius	98511 Halic
Pulis, Vladimir	96701 Kremnica
Santa, Ladislav "Lasky"	97637 Hrochot

SOUTH AFRICA

Arm-Ko Knives,	Marble Ray , KZN
Baartman, George	Bela-Bela, LP
Bauchop, Robert	Munster, KN
Beukes, Tinus	Vereeniging, GT
Bezuidenhout, Buzz	Malvern, KZN
Boardman, Guy	New Germany, KZN
Brown, Rob E	Port Elizabeth, EC
Burger, Fred	Munster, KZN
Burger, Tiaan	Pretoria, GT
Culhane, Sean K.	Horizon, Roodepoort, 1740
Dickerson, Gavin	Petit, GT
Fellows, Mike	Riversdale 6670
Grey, Piet	Naboomspruit, LP
Harvey, Kevin	Belfast, LP
Herbst, Gawie	Akasia, GT
Herbst, Thinus	Akasia, GT
Horn, Des	Onrusrivier, WC
Klaasee, Tinus	George, WC
Kojetin, W	Germiston, GT
Lancaster, C G	Free State
Liebenberg, Andre	Randburg, GT
Mackrill, Stephen	Johannesburg, GT
Mahomedy, A R	Marble Ray, KZN
Mahomedy, Humayd A.R.	Marble Ray, KZN
Mitchell, Alan	Randburg, Gauteng
Oelofse, Tinus	Glenstantia, Pretoria
Owen, David J.A.	Johannesburg
Pienaar, Conrad	Free State
Prinsloo, Theuns	Free State
Rietveld, Bertie	Magaliesburg, GT
Russell, Mick	Port Elizabeth, EC
Schoeman, Corrie	Free State
Schutte, Neill	Bloemfontein
Smith, Stuart	Gauteng
Steyn, Peter	Freestate
Thorburn, Andre E.	Warmbaths, LP
Van Den Berg, Neels	Pretoria, Gauteng
Van Der Westhuizen, Peter	Mossel Bay, SC
Van Heerden, Andre	Pretoria, GT
Watson, Peter	La Hoff, NW

SOUTH AUSTRALIA

Edmonds, Warrick	Adelaide Hills

SPAIN

Goshovskyy, Vasyl	Castellon de la Plana

SWEDEN

Bergh, Roger	Bygdea
Eklund, Maihkel	Farila
Embretsen, Kaj	Edsbyn
Hedlund, Anders	Brastad
Henningsson, Michael	430 83 Vrango (Gothenburg)
Hogstrom, Anders T	37011 Backaryd
Johansson, Anders	Grangesberg
Lundstrom, Jan-Ake	Dals-Langed
Lundstrom, Torbjorn (Tobbe)	Are
Nilsson, Jonny Walker	93391 Arvidsjaur
Nordell, Ingemar	FŠrila
Persson, Conny	Loos
Styrefors, Mattias	Boden
Vogt, Patrik	Halmstad

SWITZERLAND

Roulin, Charles	Geneva

UNITED KINGDOM

Hague, Geoff	Quarley, Hampshire
Horne, Grace	Sheffield
Maxen, Mick	Hatfield, Herts

URUGUAY

Gonzalez, Leonardo Williams	Maldonado
Symonds, Alberto E	Montevideo

ZIMBABWE

Burger, Pon	Bulawayo

Knifemakers listed here are in good standing with these organizations.

the knifemakers' guild
2016 membership

a Les Adams, Mike "Whiskers" Allen

b Robert K. Bagley, Tony Baker, Robert Ball, James J. Barry, III, John Bartlow, Barbara Baskett, Gene Baskett, Michael S. Blue, Arpad Bojtos, Tony Bose, Dennis Bradley, W. Lowell Bray, Jr., Fred Bruner, Jr., John Busfield

c Harold J. "Kit" Carson, Michael Carter, Dianna Casteel, Douglas Casteel, Daniel Chinnock, Richard Clow, Kenneth R. Coats, George Cousino, Pat Crawford, Kevin Cross, Daniel Cummings

d George Dailey, Alex K. Daniels, Edmund Davidson, Scott Davidson, John H. Davis, Steve Davis, David Dodds, Tom Downing, James Downs, Will Dutton

e Jim Elliott, William B. Ellis, James T. Eriksen, Carlton R. Evans

f Cliff Fendley, Lee Ferguson, Robert G. Flynt, John R. Fraps

g Steve Gatlin, Warren Glover, Gregory J. Gottschalk

h Philip (Doc) L. Hagen, Jim Hammond, Rade Hawkins, Earl Jay Hendrickson, Wayne G. Hensley, Gil Hibben, Wesley G. Hibben, Kevin Hoffman, Larry Hostetler, Rob Hudson, Roy Humenic

i Billy Mace Imel, Michael Irie

j Brad Johnson, Jerry L. Johnson, Ronald B. Johnson, Steven R. Johnson, William "Bill" C. Johnson, Lonnie L. Jones

k William L. Keeton, Bill Kennedy, Jr., Bill King, Harvey King, Jeff Knox

l Tim "Chops" Lambkin, Ed Lary, Paul M. LeBetard, Gary E. LeBlanc, David C. Lemoine, William S. Letcher, Jack Levin, Bob Levine, Ken Linton, Don Lozier, Bill Luckett, Gail Lunn, Ernest Lyle

m Stephen Mackrill, Riccardo Mainolfi, Joe Malloy, Herbert A. Martin, Charlie B. Mathews, Harry S. Mathews, Ken McFall, Ted Merchant, Robert L. Merz, III, Toshiaki Michinaka, James P. Miller, Stephen C. Miller, Jerry Moen, Kyle Moen, Jeff Morgan, Stephen D. Myers

n Bud Nealy, Larry Newton, Ross W Norfleet

o Clifford W. O'Dell, Charles F. Ochs, III, Ben R. Ogletree, Sean O'Hare, Jr., Warren Osborne, T. R. Overeynder, John E. Owens

p Larry Page, Cliff Parker, Jerry Partridge, John R. Pawlowski, W. D. Pease, Michael Pellegrin, Alfred Pendray, James J. Pengov, Jr., John W. PerMar, John Perry, Daniel Piergallini, Leon Pittman, Otakar Pok, Larry Pridgen, Jr., Joseph R. Prince

r James D. Ragsdale, Simone Raimondi, Steven Rapp, Carl E. Rechsteiner, Lin Rhea, Joseph Calvin Robinson, Michael Rochford, Gordon Romeis, A.G. Russell

s Michael A. Sakmar, Joseph A. Sangster, Kenneth Savage, Scott W. Sawby, Juergen Schanz, Mike Schirmer, Mark C. Sentz, Eugene W. Shadley, John I Shore, Jim Siska, Steven C. Skiff, Ralph Smith, James Rodney Sornberger, David Steier, Murray Sterling, Douglas W. Stice, Russ Sutton

t Leon Thompson, Bobby L. Toole, Reinhard Tschager, Ralph Turnbull

v Charles Vestal, Donald Vogt

w George A. Walker, Charles B. Ward, John S. Weever, Wayne Whittaker, Stan Wilson, Daniel Winkler, Marvin Winn

y George L. Young, Mike Yurco

z Brad Zinker

abs master smith listing

a David Anders, Gary D. Anderson, E. R. Russ Andrews II

b Gary Barnes, Aubrey G. Barnes Sr., James L. Batson, Jimmie H. Buckner, Bruce D. Bump, Bill Burke, Bill Buxton

c Ed Caffrey, Murray M. Carter, Kevin R. Cashen, Hsiang Lin (Jimmy) Chin, Jon Christensen, Howard F. Clark, Wade Colter, Michael Connor, James R. Cook, Joseph G. Cordova, Jim Crowell, Steve Culver

d Sava Damlovac, Harvey J. Dean, Christoph Deringer, Adam DesRosiers, Bill Dietzel, Audra L. Draper, Rick Dunkerley, Steve Dunn, Kenneth Durham

e Dave Ellis

f Robert Thomas Ferry III, Jerry Fisk, John S. Fitch, Joe Flournoy, Don Fogg—retired, Burt Foster, Ronnie E. Foster, Larry D. Fuegen, Bruce A. Fuller, Jack A. Fuller

g Tommy Gann, Bert Gaston, Thomas Gerner, Greg Gottschalk

h Tim Hancock, Don L. Hanson III, Heather Harvey, Kevin Harvey, Wally Hayes, E. Jay Hendrickson, Don Hethcoat, John Horrigan, Gary House, Rob Hudson

j Jim L. Jackson—retired

k Joseph F. Keeslar, Keith Kilby, Ray Kirk, Hank Knickmeyer, Jason Knight, Bob Kramer

l Jerry Lairson Sr.

m J. Chris Marks, John Alexander Martin, Roger D. Massey, Victor J. McCrackin, Shawn McIntyre, Hanford J. Miller, Wm Dean Mitchell

n Greg Neely, J. Neilson, Ron Newton, Douglas E. Noren

o Charles F. Ochs III

p Alfred Pendray, Dan Petersen Ph.D., Alex Dwight Phillips, Timothy Potier

q Mike Quesenberry

r Michael Rader, J. W. Randall, Kirk Rexroat, Linden W. Rhea, James L. Rodebaugh, Kyle Royer, Raymond B. Rybar Jr.

s James P. Saviano, Stephen C. Schwarzer, Mark C. Sentz, Rodrigo Menezes Sfreddo, J.D. Smith, Josh Smith, Raymond L. Smith, Bill Sowell, Charles Stout, Joseph Szilaski

t Shane Taylor, Jean-paul Thevenot, Jason Tiensvold, Brion Tomberlin, P. J. Tomes, Henry Torres

v Michael V. Vagnino Jr., Terry L. Vandeventer

w James L. Walker, Daniel Warren, Aaron Michael Wilburn, Michael L. Williams, Daniel Winkler

professional knifemaker's association

Mike Allen, Pat Ankrom, Shane Paul Atwood, Eddie J. Baca, D. Scott Barry, John Bartlow, Donald Bell, Tom Black, Justin Bridges, Kenneth L. Brock, Lucas Burnley, Craig Camerer, Tim S. Cameron, Ken Cardwell, David Clark, Vance Corich, Del Corsi, Culpepper & Co., John Easter, Ray W. Ennis, Lee Ferguson, Chuck Fraley, Graham Fredeen, Bob Glassman, Levi Graham, Bob Ham, Alford "Alf" Hanna, James Helm, Wayne Hensley, Gary Hicks, Guy E. Hielscher, Jay Higgins, Mike L. Irie, Mitch Jenkins, Harvey King, Todd Kopp, Jim Krause, Tom Krein, Scott Kuntz, Tim "Chops" Lambkin, James R. Largent, Ken Linton, Arthur Lynn, Jim Magee, Jerry & Sandy McClure, Mardi Meshejian, Clayton Miller, Michael Miller, Tyree L. Montell, Mike Mooney, Steve Myers, Robert Nash, Fred A. Ott, William Pleins, James L. Poplin, Bill Post, Calvin Powell, Steve Powers, Peter Pruyn, Bill Redd, Jim Reid, Steve Rollert, David Ruana, Dennis "Bud" Ruana, Don Ruana, Walter Scherar, Terry Schreiner, M.L. "Pepper" Seaman, Eugene Solomonik, Eddie F. Stalcup, Craig Steketee, Douglas Stice, Mark Strauss, Kurt Swearingen, James D. Thrash, Ed Thuesen, Albert Trujillo, Pete Truncali, Charles Turnage, Mike Tyre, Dick Waites, James Walton, Al Warren, Rodney Watts, Hans Weinmueller, Harold J. Wheeler, Jacob Wilson, R.W. Wilson, Michael C. Young, Monte Zavatta, Russ Zima, Daniel F. Zvonek

state/regional associations

arizona knife collectors association

Lee Beene, Larry Braasch, Bill Cheatam, Bob Dodd, Gary Fields, Tim Hancock, Bob Haskins, D'Alton Holder, Gerard Hurst, Todd M. Kopp, Mike Mooney, Jim Ort, Brian Quinn, Ray Rybar, Paul Vandine, Jim Yarbrough

australian knifemakers guild inc.

Peter Bald, Bruce Barnett, Alex Bean, Walter Bidgood, Matt Black, Scott Broad, David Brodziak, Matt Brook, Zac Cheong, Stephen Cooper, Peter Del Raso, Michael Fechner, Keith Fludder, John Foxwell, Alfred Frater, Adam Fromholtz, Thomas Gerner, Branko Giljevic, James Gladstone, Peter Gordon, Karim Haddad, Mal Hannan, Jamie Harrington, Rod Harris, Glenn Michael Henke, Robert Herbert, Joe Kiss, Michael Masion, Maurie, McCarthy, Shawn McIntyre, Will Morrison, Garry Odgers, Adam Parker, Terri Parker, Jeff Peck, Alistair Phillips, Fred Rowley, Wayne Saunders, Doug Timbs, Stewart Townsend, Rob Wakelin, Jason Weightman, Ross Yeats, Joe Zemitis

california knifemakers association

Paul Anderson, Stewart Anderson, Elmer Art, Kendell Banks, Harold Bishop, Gary Bolduc, Anton Bosch, Roger Bost, Sean P. Bourke, John Burens, Mike Butcher, Joe Caswell, Jon Chabot, Marcus Clinco, George Cummings, Mike Daly, Capt. J-C Demirdjian, Mike Desensi, Albert M. Dorado Sr., Frank Dunkin, Vern Edler III, Eddie Escobar, Chuck Faulkner, Alex Felix, Jim Ferguson, Marcus Flores, Lowell Ford, Brian Forrest, Randy Freer, Bill Fried, Joe Girtner, John Glueck, Corey Gray, Richard Grimm, Ron Gue, Eva Gulbrandsen, Rich Hale, Tim Harbert, John Harris, Roy Helton, Daniel Hernandez, Wm. R. 'Bill' Herndon, Neal A. Hodges, Jerid Johnson, Lawrence Johnson, David Kazsuk, Paul Kelso, Bernie Kerkvliet, Steve Koster, Tom Lewis, Robert Liguori, John Mackie, Bob McCready, Gordon Melin, Jim Merritt, David Moody, Russ Moody, Gerald Morgan, Jeff Morgan, Tim Musselman, Jeff Mutz, Helen Nauert, Aram Nigoghossian, Bruce Oakley, Rich Orton, John Powers, Robert Reid, E.J. Robison, Valente Rosas, Clark Rozas, H.J. Schneider, Laurence Segel, Mikhail Shindel, Sam Silva, Matt Steeneken, Alexander Strickland, Bill Stroman, Reinhardt Swanson, Tony Swatton, Billy Tinkley, Scott Tolman, William Tracy, Bill Traylor, Tru-grit, Mike Tyre, Wayne Watanabe, Martin Wells, Blaine Whitney, Tim Withers, Trent Wong

canadian knifemakers guild

Gaetan Beauchamp, Charles Bennica, Paul Bold, Paolo Brignone, Mark Daley, Jose deBraga, Christoph Deringer, Alain Desaulniers, Rob Douglas, Jason Duclos, James Emmons, Emmanuel Esposito, Paul-Aime Fortier, Rick Frigault, Aaron Gough, Sharla and Shawn Hansen, Wally Hayes, Gil Hibben, Des Horn, Suchat Jangtanong, Nathan Knowles, Kirby Lambert, Stephanie Lemelin, Matthew Lerch, Steve Linklater, Elizabeth Loerchner, Wolfgang Loerchner, David MacDonald, Mike Mossington, William Nease, Rod Olson, Warren Osborne, Simone Raimondi, Steven Rapp, David Riccardo, Murray St. Amour, Paul Savage, Eugene Shadley, John W. Smith, Ken Steigerwalt, Jurgen Steinau, Brian Tighe, Libor Tobolak, Stephen Vanderkolff, Craig Wheatley, Murray White

finnish knifemakers guild

Tonu Arrak, Jukka Hankala, Pasi Jaakonaho, Arto Liukko, Jari Liukko, Erik Nylund, Jakob Nylund, Simon Nylund, JT Palikko, J-P Peltonen, Anssi Ruusuvuori, Teuvo Sorvari, Pekka Tuominen, Rauno Vainionpaa, Kay Vikstrom, Markku Vilppola

florida knifemaker's association

James J. Barry III, Terry Betts, Dennis Blaine, Dennis Blankenhem, Dean Bosworth, W. Lowell Bray Jr., Michael Buell, Patrick Burris, Lowell Cobb, John H. Davis, Jim Elliott, Tom M. Enos, Ernie Grospitch, Larry Hostetler, Joe "Hy" Hytovick, Tom Ivey, Mark James, Richard Johnson, Paul S. Kent, George Lambert, William (Bill) Letcher, Ernie Lyle, Steve Miller, James Mustain, Larry Newton, Dan Piergallini, Marvin Powell, Jr., Carlo Raineri, Roland Robidoux, Ann Sheffield/Sheffield Knifemaker's Supply, Jimmie Smith, Martin Snailgrove, Dale Thomas, John Thorsby, Ralph Turnbull, Louis M. Vallet, Voodoo Daggers, Don Vogt, ned Whitner, Stan Wilson, Denny Young, Maggie Young, Brad Zinker

georgia custom knifemakers' guild

Don R. Adams, Doug Adams, Larry Akins, Adam Andreasen, Joel Atkinson, Paul Brach, Dennis Bradley, Bobby Bragg, Steve Brazeale, Aaron Brewer, Marsha Brewer, Jerry Brinegar, James Brooker, Brian Brown, Mike Brown, Robert Busbee, Jeff Busbie, G.H. Caldwell, Henry Cambron, Rob Carper, Paul Chastain, Frank Chikey, Jim Collins, Jerry Costin, Nola Costin, Scott Davidson, Carol W. Dutton, Dan Eastland, Kerrie Edwards, Emory Fennell, Jarrett Fleming, Dylan Fletcher, Stephan Fowler, Jack Frost, Grady Gentles, Warren Glover, Jim Hamer, George Hancox, Rade Hawkins, Rebecca Hensley, Wayne Hensley, Ronald Hewitt, Kevin Hoffman, Jimmy Kirkland, Christopher Linton, Damon Lusky, Charlie Mathews, Harry Mathews, Vince McDowell, Larry McEachern, Russell McNabb, David McNeal, James Mitchell, Ralph Mitchell, Sandy Morrisey, Daniel Moye, Dan Peters, James Poplin, Joan Poythress, Carey Quinn, Jim Ragsdale, Nathan Raptis, Eddie Ray, Carl Rechsteiner, Adam Reese, David Roberts, Andy Roy, Joe Sangster, Jamey Saunders, Craig Schneeberger, Randy Scott, Ken Simmons, Jim Small, Dave Smith, Johnny Smith, Bill Snow, Luke Snyder, Brian Sorensen, Richard Stafford, Derek Stepp, Allen Suris, Cliff Thrower, Don Tommey, Owen Welch, Alex Whetsel, David White, Gerald White, Michael Wiesner, Chris Wilkes, Mike Wilson, Robert A. Wright, Judy Yoon

kansas custom knifemakers association

Roger Ball, James W. "Jim" Bevan, William Bevan, Gary Bradburn, Claude Campbell, Clint Childers, Roger Craig, Jacob Culver, Steve Culver, Mike Curran, Dave Darpinian, Richard Davis, Dan Dick, Ed Day, Laural "Shorty" Ediger, Jacob Ellis, Phil Evans, Andy Garrett, Jim Glines, Ernie Grospitch, Jim Haller Jr., Jim Haller Sr., Steve Hansen, Billy Helton, Jon Finley, Ross Jagears, Chris Jones, Donald Judd, Carolyn Kaberline, Paul Keranen, Harvey King, Ray Kirk, Doug Klaus, Troy Klaus, Bob Kneisler, Kelly Kneisler, Knives N' Such (Tom and Susie Durham), Tom Lyles, Bill Lyons, Matt Manley, Gilbert Masters, Bruce Miller, Channing "Red" Morford, Joe O'Neill, Dan L. Peterson, Lister Potter, John Sandy, Robert Schornick, M.L. "Pepper" Seaman, Joe Skupa, David Sloane, Eric Showalter, Michael Sparta, Greg Steinert, Douglas Stice, Frank Weiss, Jeff Wells, Kevin Werth, Jim Wharton, Wesley Workman, Roy C. Young III, Tony Zanussi

knife group association of oklahoma

Mike "Whiskers" Allen, Howard Allman, David Anders, Rocky Anderson, Dale Atkerson, Richard Barchenger, Roy Brinsfield, Troy Brown, Tom Buchanan, F. L. Clowdus, Charles Conner, Bill Coye, Gary Crowder, Steve Culver, Marc Cullip, David Darby, Voyne Davis, Dan Dick, Lynn Drury, Bill Duff, Steve Elmenhorst, Beau Erwin, David Etchieson, Harry Fentress, Lee Ferguson, Linda Ferguson, Gary Gloden, Steve Hansen, Paul Happy, Calvin Harkins, Billy Helton, Ed Hites, Tim Johnston, Les Jones, Jim Keen, Bill Kennedy, Stew Killiam, Andy Kirk, Ray Kirk, Nicholas Knack, Jerry Lairson, Sr., Al Lawrence, Ken Linton, Newt Livesay, Ron Lucus, Matt Manley, John Martin, Jerry McClure, Sandy McClure, Jim McGuinn, Gary McNeill, Rick Menefee, Ben Midgley, Michael E. Miller, Roy Miller, Ray Milligan, Gary Mulkey, Allen Newberry, Jerald Nickels, Jerry Parkhurst, Chris Parson, Larry Parsons, Jerry Paul, Paul Piccola, Cliff Polk, Ron Reeves, Lin Rhea, Gary Robertson, Mike Ruth, Dan Schneringer, Terry Schreiner, Allen Shafer, Shawn Shropshire, Randell Sinnett, Clifford Smith, Doug Sonntag, Michel Sparkman, Perry Stanford, Jeremy Steely, Douglas Stice, Mike Stott, Michael Tarango, Don Thompson, Brian Tomberlin, Tom Upton, Chuck Ward, Jesse Webb, Jesse Webb, Rob Weber, Joe Wheeler, Bill Wiggins, Joe Wilkie, Daniel Zvonek

knifemakers' guild of southern africa

Jeff Angelo, John Arnold, George Baartman, Francois Basson, Rob Bauchop, George Beechey, Arno Bernard, Buzz Bezuidenhout, Harucus Blomerus, Chris Booysen, Thinus Bothma, Ian Bottomley, Peet Bronkhorst, Rob Brown, Fred Burger, Sharon Burger, Trevor Burger, William Burger, Brian Coetzee, Rucus Coetzee, Jack Connan, Larry Connelly, Andre de Beer, André de Villiers, Melodie de Witt, Gavin Dickerson, Roy Dunseith, Johan Ellis, Bart Fanoy, Mike Fellows, Werner Fourie, Andrew Frankland, Brian Geyer, Ettoré Gianferrari, Dale Goldschmidt, Stan Gordon, Nick Grabe, John Grey, Piet Grey, Heather Harvey, Kevin Harvey, Dries Hattingh, Gawie Herbst, Thinus Herbst, Greg Hesslewood, Rupert Holtshausen, Des Horn, Oubaas Jordaan, Nkosilathi Jubane, Billy Kojetin, Mark Kretschmer, Andre Lesch, Steven Lewis, Garry Lombard, Steve Lombard, Ken Madden, Abdur-Rasheed Mahomedy, Peter Mason, Shelley Mason, Francois Massyn, Edward Mitchell, George Muller, Günther Muller, Deon Nel, Tom Nelson, Andries Olivier, Christo Oosthuizen, Johan Oosthuysen, Cedric Pannell, Willie Paulsen, Nico Pelzer, Conrad Pienaar, David Pienaar, Jan Potgieter, Lourens Prinsloo, Theuns Prinsloo, Hilton Purvis, Derek Rausch, Chris Reeve, Martin Reeves, Bertie Rietveld, Melinda Rietveld, Dean Riley, John Robertson, Neels Roos, Corrie Schoeman, Neill Schutte, Eddie Scott, Harvey Silk, Mike Skellern, Toi Skellern, Carel Smith, Stuart Smith, Ken Smythe, Graham Sparks, Kosie Steenkamp, Willem Steenkamp, Peter Steyn, Peter Szkolnik, André Thorburn, Hennie Van Brakel, Fanie Van Der Linde, Johan van der Merwe, Van van der Merwe, Lieben Van Der Sandt, Marius Van der Vyver, Louis Van der Walt, Johann Van Deventer, Cor Van Ellinckhuijzen, Andre van Heerden, Ben Venter, Willie Venter, Gert Vermaak, René Vermeulen, Erich Vosloo, Jan Wahl, Desmond, Waldeck, Albie Wantenaar, Henning Wilkinson, John Wilmot, Wollie Wolfaardt, Owen Wood

montana knifemaker's association

Peter C. Albert, Gordon Alcorn, Chet Allinson, Marvin Allinson, Tim & Sharyl Alverson, Bill Amoureux, Wendell Barnes, Jim & Kay Barth, Bob & Marian Beaty, Donald Bell, Brett Bennett, Raymond Bernier, Bruce Bingenheimer, Robert Bizzell, BladeGallery, Chuck Bragg, Frederick Branch, Peter Bromley, Emil Bucharsky, Thomas and Linda Buckner, Bruce & Kay Bump, Chuck and Brenda Bybee, Jim & Kate Carroll, Rocco Chicarilli & Linda McNeese, Clayton Christofferson, Seth Coughlin, Bob Crowder, John Davis, John Doyal, Rich & Jacque Duxbury, Kevin Easley, Arnold Erhardt, Daniel Erickson, Mel & Darlene Fassio, E.V. Ford, Stephen & Kathy Garger, Chris & Jolene Giarde, Robb & Brandis Gray, Dana & Sandy Hackney, Doc & Lil Hagen, Gary & Betsy Hannon, Tedd Harris, Roger & Diane Hatt, Cal Heinrich, Sam & Joy Hensen, Gerald & Pamela Hintz, Tori Howe, Kevin Hutchins, Karl Jermunson, Keith Johnson, Don Kaschmitter, Steven Kelly, Jay Kemble, Dan & Penny Kendrick, Monte Koppes, Sheridan Lee, David Lisch, James Luman, Robert Martin, Neil McKee, Larry McLaughlin, Mac & Nancy McLaughlin, Phillip Moen, Daniel O'Malley, Tim Olds, Joe Olson, Collin Paterson, James Petri, Tim & Becca Pierce, Riley Pitchford, James Poling, Richard Prusz, Greg Rabatin, Jim Raymond, Darren Reeves, Tom Rickard and Cathy Capps,

Ryan Robison, Ruana Knifeworks, Dean Schroeder, Rachel Slade, Gordon St. Clair, Terry Steigers, George Stemple, Dan & Judy Stucky, Art & Linda Swyhart, Jim Thill, James & Sharon Thompson, Dennis & Dora VanDyke, Bill & Lori Waldrup, Jonathan & Doris Walther, Michael Wattelet, Gerome & Darlene Weinand, Walter Wengrzynek, Daniel & Donna Westlind, Richard Wheeler, Sheldon & Edna Wickersham, Dave Wilkes, Randy Williams, R.W. Wilson, Mike & Seana Young

new england bladesmiths guild

Rick Barrett, Kevin Cashen, Mike Davis, Don Fogg, Burt Foster, Ric Furrer, Brian Lyttle, Bill McGrath, W.D. Pease, Jake Powning, Jim Siska, Tim Zowada

north carolina custom knifemakers' guild

Joe Aker, Dr. James Batson, Wayne Bernauer, Tom Beverly, William "Bill" Bisher, Jamin Brackett, William P. Brixon, Jr., Mark Carey, Barry Clodfelter, Travis Daniel, David Diggs, Jeffrey W. Foster, Jimmy Freeman, Russell Gardner, Anthony Griffin, Ken Hall, Mark Hall, Ed Halligan, Koji Hara, John B. Hege, Lian Hoffman, Terrill Hoffman, Jesse Houser, B.R. Hughes, Dan Johnson, Tommy Johnson, Barry and Phillip Jones, Frank Joyce, Jake Kirks, Michael Lamb, Dr. Jim Lucie, Robert Luck, Stuart Maynard, Scott McGhee, Arthur McNeil, Carl Mickey Jr., William Morris, Randy Nance, Ron Newton, Victor L. Odom Jr., J.D. Palmer Jr., Howard Peacock, Daniel Pica, James Poplin, Murphy Ragsdale, Steve Randall, Bruce Ryan, Joel Sandifer, Tim Scholl, Andy Sharpe, William Shoaf, Harland Simmons, Jeff Simmons, Darrin Sirois, Gene Smith, Charles E. Staples Jr., Murray Sterling, Arthur Summers, Russell Sutton, Jed Taylor, Bruce Turner, Ed & Tanya Van Hoy, Christopher M. Williams, Michael Wilson, Daniel Winkler.

ohio knifemakers association

Raymond Babcock, Van Barnett, Steve Bottorff, Harold A. Collins, Larry Detty, Tom Downing, Jim Downs, Patty Ferrier, Jeff Flannery, James Fray, Bob Foster, Raymond Guess, Scott Hamrie, Rick Hinderer, Curtis Hurley, Ed Kalfayan, Michael Koval, Judy Koval, Gene Loro, Larry Lunn, Stanley Maienknecht, Dave Marlott, Mike Mercer, David Morton, Patrick McGroder, Charles Pratt, Darrel Ralph, Roy Roddy, Michael Sheppard, Carroll Shoemaker, Clifton Smith, Jerry Smith, John Smith, Art Summers, Jan Summers, Donald Tess, Dale Warther, John Wallingford, Earl Witsaman, Joanne Yurco, Mike Yurco

saskatchewan knifemakers guild

Dennis Allenback, Vern Alton, David Beck, Marty Beets, Dan Bowers, Clarence Broeksma, Irv Brunas, Emil Bucharsky, Jim Clow, Murray Cook, Don Crane, Jonathan Crane, Bob Crowder, Jim Dahlin, Cole Dale, Kim Davis, Kevin Donald, Jordan Doucette, Brian Drayton, Ray Fehler, Cal Ganshorn, Kaila Garchinski, Brandon Gray, Gary Greer, Wayne Hamilton, Kent Hanmer, Diane and Roger Hatt, Robert Hazell, Garth Hindmarch, Rolf Holzkaemper, Chris Johnson, Rod Johnson, Cliff Kaufmann, Donald Kreuger, Nathan Kunkel, Paul Laronge, Bryan Lipp, Jared Longard, Pat Macnamara, Chris Mathie, Len Meeres, Brian Mercer, Cory Miller, Robert Minnes, Ralph Mitton, Ron Nelson, Morris Nesdole, Ben Parry, Blaine Parry, Greg Penner, John Perron, Gary D. Peterson, Barry Popick, Jim Quickfall, Rob Robson, Pat de la Sablonniere, Robert Sainsbury, Kim Senft, Bob Serban, Carter Smyth, Don Spasoff, Ed Storch, Jim Takenaka, Isaac Tamlin, Tim Vanderwekken, Jay West, Merle Williams

south carolina association of knifemakers

Douglas Bailey, Ken Black, Dick Brainard, Bobby Branton, Richard Bridwell, Dan Cannady, Rodger Casey, Robert L. Davis, Geno Denning, Charlie Douan, Eddy T. Elsmore, Robert D. Estabrook, Lewis A. Fowler, Jim Frazier, Wayne Hendrix, T.J. Hucks, Johnny Johnson, Lonnie Jones, John Keaton, Col. Thomas Kreger, Gene Langley, David Manley, C.R. Miles, Gene Miller, Barry L. Myers, Paul G. Nystrom, Lee O'Quinn, Victor Odom Jr., Larry Page, Johnny L. Perry, James Rabb, Ricky Rankin, Jerry Riddle, Rick Rockwood, John Sarratt, Ralph L. Smith, David Stroud, Rocky Thomas, Justin Walker, Mickey Walker, H. Syd Willis Jr.

photo index

A

ALCORN, GORDON 141
ANDERSEN, KARL 161
ANDRADE, DON CARLOS 88, 97
ANDREWS, E. RUSS, II 171
APPLEBY, ROBERT L., JR. 102, 123, 136
APPLETON, RON 137, 138
ARMOUR, DAVE 123
ASHBY, DOUG 139

B

BALL, BUTCH 63
BANKS, DAVID L. 170
BARRETT, RICK 63, 92, 160
BARRY, D. SCOTT 88, 149
BASKETT, GENE 163
BATTLE HORSE KNIVES 66
BEGG, TODD 63
BEHNKE, BILL 86, 95, 122
BEHRING, JAMES 102
BELL, GABRIEL 135
BENNICA, CHARLES 154
BERRY, CHRIS 105
BEST, RON 60, 84
BEST, RONALD 155
BETANCOURT, ANTONIO 153
BOECK, SANDRO 159, 171
BRADLEY, DENNIS 104, 114, 120, 128
BRADLEY, GAYLE 83
BRADY, SANDRA 152
BRASCHI, LUCA 139
BREDA, BEN 107
BREWER, CRAIG 115
BRODZIAK, DAVID 87, 125, 133
BROWN, PAUL K. 156
BUCHANAN, ZAC 89, 119, 127
BUCKNER, TOM 59
BUMP, BRUCE 159, 169
BURKE, BILL 58, 161

C

CALDWELL, HARRY, IV 138
CAMERER, CRAIG 91
CAROTHERS, NATHAN 111
CARR, KEN 103
CARROLL, TOMMY 77
CARTER, SHAYNE 71
CASEY, KEVIN 103, 154
CASHEN, KEVIN 75, 109, 128, 134
CHEWIWI, ALVIN 138
CHOMILIER, ALAIN 87, 148, 158
CHOMILIER, JORIS 87, 148, 158
CHRISTENSEN, JON 165
CLAIBORNE, JEFF 83, 114
CLARK, JASON 61, 67
CLOW, RICK 95
COFFEE, JIM 125
COFFEY, BILL 74
COHEA, JOHN 133
COHEN, N.J. "NORM" 90
COLTER, WADE 146
COOK, JAMES 164
COVER, RAY, JR. 140
COX, LARRY 78, 167

COYE, BILL 62
CRADDOCK, MIKE 68
CRAWFORD, WES 61
CROSS, KEVIN 59, 167
CROWDER, BOB 111

D

DAVIDSON, EDMUND 74
DAVIDSON, JERE 143
DAVIS, BARRY 79, 147
DAVIS, JOHN 99
DEAN, HARVEY 59, 99, 120
DEIBERT, MICHAEL 73, 76
DESROSIERS, ADAM 165
DEVERAUX, BUTCH 119
DICKINSON, NATHAN 143
DIONATAM, FRANCO 157
DOYLE, JOHN 69
DUFF, BILL 81, 94, 110
DUNKERLEY, RICK 148, 157
DUNN, STEVE 140
DUVALL, FRED 68, 88

E

EATON, RICK 144
ELLIS, BILLY 139
ENGLAND, VIRGIL 75
ERICKSON, CURT 76, 147
ERICKSON, KEN 116
ESPOSITO, EMMANUEL 79, 155
EVANS, PHIL 99

F

FASSIO, MEL 114
FINLEY, JON 122, 153, 171
FISCHER, CLYDE 121
FISHER, JOSH 120
FISK, JERRY 125, 167
FLORIAN, SEAN 62
FOGARIZZU, TORE 163
FOWLER, STEPHAN 129
FRANK, BRAM 88
FREDERICK, AARON 89
FREEMAN, JEFF 89
FRISILLO, AL 142
FRITZ, ERIK 105
FRY, JASON 77, 123
FRY, TRAVIS 111
FUEGEN, LARRY 84, 136, 147

G

GALLAGHER, SCOTT 69
GAMBA, LORENZO 143
GEORGE, LES 66, 94, 112
GLASSER, ROGER CESAR 167
GRAHAM, LEVI 135
GREGORY, MATT 104
GREGORY, MATTHEW 117
GRIFFIN, JOHN 84, 149
GROVES, GARY 71, 125

H

HAGEN, DOC 117
HAINES, JEFF 104
HAINES, JERRY 158, 166

HALL, KEN 69, 168
HALL, SCOTT 94, 121
HANSON, DON, III 71, 168
HANSON, KYLE 90
HARTSFIELD, PHILL 96
HASLINGER, THOMAS 58, 109, 118
HAWES, CHUCK 114
HAWKINS, CHARLES R., JR. 105
HAZE, JEFF 89, 129
HEADRICK, GARY 81
HEARD, TOM 78, 152
HEETER, TODD 67
HENNINGSSON, MICHAEL 145
HETHCOAT, DON 134
HIBBEN, GIL 73
HILL, STEVE 159, 171
HINDMARCH, GARTH 101, 105, 121
HOFFMAN, KEVIN 81
HOFFMAN, LIAM 97, 104
HOGSTROM, ANDERS 85, 106, 110, 170
HOLBROOK, H.L. 107, 124
HORRIGAN, JOHN 76, 119, 162, 170
HOSSOM, JERRY 91, 107
HOSTETTER, WALLY 98
HUCKABEE, DALE 101, 105
HUGHES, TONY 168
HUNT, RAYMON 115
HUTCHINSON, ALAN 73, 100

J

JACKSON, LARAMIE 86, 131, 153, 171
JANGTANONG, SUCHAT 147
JARVIS, PAUL 96
JENSEN, DON 152
JENSEN, ELI 104
JENSEN, PETER 152
JOHNSON, STEVE 70, 118, 127, 155, 163
JONAS, ZACK 106

K

KELLY, STEVE 82
KENNEDY, BILL, JR. 132
KEYES, GEOFF 113, 124
KING, HARVEY 121
KIRKES, BILL 101, 103, 119, 170
KISLINGER, MILOS 161
KLAUSE, TURTLE 145
KNAPP, MARK 93, 103, 128
KNIGHT, JASON 97, 170
KNOX, JEFF 69, 93, 107
KOIKE, NORIO 145
KOSTER, STEVEN 101, 166
KRAUSE, JIM 132
KULIS, DAVID 83
KULIS, DAVID S. 64
KURT, DAVID 109

L

LAKE, RON 154
LALA, RICK 83
LAMBERT, KIRBY 64
LAMOTHE, JORDAN 70, 106
LANCE, DAN 123, 169
LEBATARD, PAUL 70, 124, 134
LEMELIN, STEPHANIE 142

LERCH, MATTHEW 84, 162
LEWIS, TOM 106, 153
LIN, MARCUS 73, 118, 126
LISCH, DAVID 158, 166
LITZ, MATT .142
LOERCHNER, ELIZABETH. 136
LONG, TAN 112, 140
LOVELESS, BOB 95
LOVESTRAND, SCHUYLER. 70
LUCKETT, BILL 92
LUNN, GAIL .158
LURQUIN, SAM 72, 108
LUSK, PAUL 85
LYNCH, TAD .74
LYNN, ARTHUR 72

M

MARTIN, CORY 79
MARTINDALE, GARY 95
MARTIN, PETER 77, 159, 161
MARTIN, R.J. .65
MATSUOKA, SCOT 60, 82
MATSUSAKI, TAKESHI 94, 116
MCCLURE, JERRY. 85
MCCLURE, MICHAEL 58, 118, 127
MCGHEE, E. SCOTT. 72
MCGINNIS, TOM 100
MCNEES, JONATHAN 61
MEROLA, JIM 109
MESHEJIAN, MARDI. 98
MILLER, BILL 112, 146
MILLER, KURTZ 152
MILLER, LEVI 115
MILLER, STEVE. 94, 102, 133
MILLER, WILLIAM 72
MITCHELL, ALAN 112
MITSUYUKI, ROSS 172
MOEN, JERRY. 62, 81
MOIZIS, STAN 66
MONTGOMERY, CHRIS. 123
MULKEY, GARY. 77
MULLER, JODY 142
MURA, DENIS 135

N

NADEAU, BRIAN 61, 80
NEILSON, J. 129, 168
NELL, CHAD .80
NEVLING, MARK 134
NEWTON, LARRY 82
NEWTON, RON 132, 156, 165
NIRO, FRANK. 82
NOREN, DOUG. 77
NOWACKI, STEPHEN. 92, 95, 101
NYLUND, ERIK 151

O

OCHS, ERIC. 64, 93, 148, 172
O'HARE, SEAN 84, 108
OHLEMANN, BOB 91
OLSON, JOE 155
OLSZEWSKI, STEPHEN. 136
ONION, KEN. .92
OTT, FRED. .165
OVEREYNDER, T.R.. 137

P

PALIKKO, J.T.. . . . . .114, 122, 168
PARKER, CLIFF 79, 157
PAYNE, TRAVIS. 132
PEARCE, LOGAN 75, 86, 121, 149
PELLEGRIN, MIKE. 81
PENA, ENRIQUE 149
PERRY, JOHN 116
PETERS, DAN 111, 131
PETERSEN, DAN 169
PICA, DANIEL 89
PLUMER, KATHERINE. 138
PODMAJERSKY, DIETRICH 92
POIRIER, RICK 109
PRICE, JARED 67
PROVOST, JIM 108, 117, 166
PRUYN, PETER 160
PULISOVA, ANDREA 150
PULIS, VLADIMIR 147, 164

Q

QUESENBERRY, MIKE. 120

R

RAMON, BRAM. 145
RAMOS, STEVEN 131
RANDALL, J.W.. 159
RANDALL, STEVE. 73, 160
RAYMOND, MICHAEL 85
REGEL, JEAN-LOUIS. 100
REGEL, JEAN-LUIS. 158
REVERDY, PIERRE 137
RHEA, LIN 71, 100, 108, 126
RIETVELD, BERTIE 75
ROBBINS, LANDON. 71
ROBINSON, CALVIN 79, 115
RODEBAUGH, JAMES 133
ROGERS, RICHARD. 63, 78, 91
ROOT, GARY 97, 146
ROSENBAUGH, RON 107, 122, 153
RUPLE, BILL 115
RUSNAK, JOSEF 136, 146, 149
RUUSUVUORI, ANSSI. 96
RYBAR, RAY .76

S

SCHEMPP, ED 166
SCHOEMAN, CORRIE 87
SCHUTTE, NEILL. 91
SCROGGS, JAMES 102
SELLERS, SHERRY 151
SEMONES, DAVID 151
SEVECEK, PAVEL 156
SHARP, DAVID. 62, 93
SHAW, BRUCE 140
SHIGENO, MAMORU 126
SIBERT, SHANE 90, 111
SKAGGS, RON. 144
SMITH, JOHN W.. 162
SMITH, ROBERT P.. 169
SMITH, STUART 68
SMITTY'S DESIGNS 151
SOBRAL, ARIEL 69
SOBRAL, CLAUDIO 69
SORNBERGER, JIM. 87
SOUTHARD, BRAD 65
SPAKE, JEREMY 58, 98, 103, 110

STATES, JOSHUA 112
STEIGERWALT, KEN 155, 163, 169
STEINGASS, TIMOTHY 120
STEINGASS, T.K.. 113
STERLING, MURRAY 80
STERLING, TOM 144
STONE, LINDA KARST 150, 151
STONER, SAMUEL, JR. 87, 124
STOUT, JOHNNY 167
SURLS, ALLEN 126
SWEARINGEN, KURT 131
SWENSON, LUKE 116

T

TABER, DAVID. 116
TABOR, TIM. .58
TAYLOR, C. GRAY 82
TEDFORD, STEVEN J.. 108
TENDICK, BEN 70, 90
TERZUOLA, BOB 67
TESARIK, RICHARD 86, 137
TESARIK, VERONIKA 140
THORBURN, MARIETJIE 144
TIGHE, BRIAN 60
TOMBERLIN, BRION 98
TOMLIN, LISA 141, 142
TOWELL, DWIGHT 76, 139
TSCHAGER, REINHARD 141, 157, 163, 165
TUCH, WILLIAM 137
TUOMINEN, PEKKA. 117
TYRE, MIKE. 172

V

VAN EIZENGA, JERRY. 172
VAN RYSWYK, AAD 162
VESTAL, CHARLES 124
VITALE, MACE. 100

W

WAIDE, RUSTY 135
WALDROP, MARK 141
WALKER, MICHAEL 67, 154
WARENSKI-ERICKSON, JULIE . . .141, 143, 144
WATERS, GLENN. 80, 145, 157
WATSON, DANIEL 97, 147
WATTS, RODNEY 86
WELLING, RON. 113, 172
WHEELER, NICK 74
WILBURN, AARON 113, 172
WILIAMS, GARY "GARBO". 150
WILLIAMS, LEE. 64, 65
WILSON, R.W.. 117
WILSON, STAN 65
WINKLER, DANIEL 129
WINN, MARVIN 125
WITHERS, TIM 127
WOOD, OWEN 154
WRIGHT, RICHARD. 93
WULF, DERRICK 74

Y

YOUNG, JOHN. 127

Z

ZIEBA, MICHAEL 59, 63, 90, 98, 161
ZIEBA, MIKE 113
ZOWADA, TIM. 106
ZSCHERNY, MIKE 65

The firms listed here are special in the sense that they make or market special kinds of knives made in facilities they own or control either in the U.S. or overseas. Or they are special because they make knives of unique design or function. The second phone number listed is the fax number.

sporting cutlers

A.G. RUSSELL KNIVES INC
2900 S. 26th St
Rogers, AR 72758-8571
800-255-9034
fax 479-631-8493
ag@agrussell.com; www.agrussell.com
The oldest knife mail-order company, highest quality. Free catalog available. In these catalogs you will find the newest and the best. If you like knives, this catalog is a must

AL MAR KNIVES
PO Box 2295
Tualatin, OR 97062-2295
503-670-9080; fax 503-639-4789
info@almarknives.com;
www.almarknives.com
Featuring our Ultralight™ series of knives. Sere 2000™ Shrike, Sere™, Operator™, Nomad™ and Ultralight series™

ATLANTA CUTLERY CORP.
2147 Gees Mill Rd., Box 839
Conyers, GA 30013
770-922-7500; fax 770-918-2026
custserv@atlantacutlery.com;
www.atlantacutlery.com
Outdoor sporting and hunting knives, mail order

BARK RIVER KNIVES
6911 County Road 426 M.5 Road
Escanaba, MI 49829
906-789-1801
jacquie@barkriverknives.com
www.barkriverknifetool.com
Family-owned business producing bushcraft, hunting, Canadian, deluxe game, professional guide, search & rescue and EDC knives

BEAR & SON CUTLERY, INC.
111 Bear Blvd. SW
Jacksonville, AL 36265
256-435-2227; fax 256-435-9348
www.bearandsoncutlery.com
Bear Jaws®, three sizes of multi-tools, cutlery, hunting and pocketknives in traditional and innovative patterns and designs

BECK'S CUTLERY & SPECIALTIES
51 Highland Trace Ln.
Benson, NC 27504
919-902-9416
beckscutlery@embarqmail.com;
www.beckscutlery.com

BENCHMADE KNIFE CO. INC.
300 Beavercreek Rd
Oregon City, OR 97045
800-800-7427
info@benchmade.com;
www.benchmade.com
Sports, utility, law enforcement, military, gift and semi custom

BERETTA U.S.A. CORP.
17601 Beretta Dr.
Accokeek, MD 20607
301-283-2191
www.berettausa.com
Full range of hunting & specialty knives

BLACKHAWK PRODUCTS GROUP
6160 Commander Pkwy.
Norfolk, VA 23502
757-436-3101; fax 757-436-3088
cs@blackhawk.com
www.blackhawk.com
Leading manufacturer of tactical sheaths and knives

BLADE-TECH INDUSTRIES
5530 184th St. E, Ste. A
Puyallup, WA 98375
253-655-8059; fax 253-655-8066
tim@blade-tech.com
www.blade-tech.com

BLUE GRASS CUTLERY, INC.
20 E Seventh St, PO Box 156
Manchester, OH 45144
937-549-2602; 937-549-2709 or 2603
sales@bluegrasscutlery.com;
www.bluegrasscutlery.com
Manufacturer of Winchester Knives, John Primble Knives and many contract lines

BOKER USA INC
1550 Balsam St.
Lakewood, CO 80214-5917
800-992-6537; 303-462-0668
sales@bokerusa.com; www.bokerusa.com
Wide range of fixed-blade and folding knives for hunting, military, tactical and general use

BROUS BLADES
POB 550
Buellton, CA 93427
805-717-7192
contact@brousblades.com
www.brousblades.com
Custom and semi-custom knives

BROWNING
One Browning Place
Morgan, UT 84050
800-333-3504; Customer Service:
801-876-2711 or 800-333-3288
www.browning.com
Outdoor hunting & shooting products

BUCK KNIVES INC.
660 S Lochsa St
Post Falls, ID 83854-5200
800-326-2825; Fax: 800-733-2825
www.buckknives.com
Sports cutlery

BULLDOG BRAND KNIVES
P.O. Box 23852
Chattanooga, TN 37422
423-894-5102; fax 423-892-9165
Fixed blade and folding knives for hunting and general use

BUSSE COMBAT KNIFE CO.
11651 Co Rd 12
Wauseon, OH 43567
419-923-6471; 419-923-2337
www.bussecombat.com
Simple & very strong straight knife designs for tactical & expedition use

CAMILLUS C/O ACME UNITED CORP.
60 Round Hill Rd.
Fairfield, CT 06824
800-835-2263
orders@shopatron.com
www.camillusknives.com

CANAL STREET CUTLERY
30 Canal St.
Ellenville, NY 12428
845-647-5900
info@canalstreetcutlery.com
www.canalstreetcutlery.com
Manufacturers of pocket and hunting knives finished to heirloom quality

CAS IBERIA
650 Industrial Blvd
Sale Creek, TN 37373
800-635-9366
www.casiberia.com
Extensive variety of fixed-blade and folding knives for hunting, diving, camping, military and general use. Japanese swords and European knives

CASE, W.R. & SONS CUTLERY CO.
50 Owens Way
Bradford, PA 16701
800-523-6350; Fax: 814-368-1736
consumer-relations@wrcase.com
www.wrcase.com
Folding pocket knives

CHRIS REEVE KNIVES
2949 S. Victory View Way
Boise, ID 83709-2946
208-375-0367; Fax: 208-375-0368
crkinfo@chrisreeve.com;
www.chrisreeve.com
Makers of the Sebenza, Umnumzaan and Mnandi folding knives, the legendary Green Beret knife and other military knives

COAST CUTLERY CO
8033 N.E. Holman
Portland, OR 97218
800-426-5858; Fax: 503-234-4422
www.coastportland.com
Variety of fixed-blade and folding knives and multi-tools for hunting, camping and general use

COLD STEEL INC
6060 Nicolle St.
Ventura, CA 93003
800-255-4716 or 805-642-9727
sales@coldsteel.com
www.coldsteel.com
Wide variety of folding lockbacks and fixed-blade hunting, fishing and neck knives, as well as bowies, kukris, tantos, throwing knives, kitchen knives and swords

COLONIAL KNIFE, A DIVISION OF COLONIAL CUTLERY INT.
61 Dewey Ave.
Warwick, RI 02886
401-421-6500; Fax: 401-737-0054
stevep@colonialknifecorp.com
www.colonialknifecorp.com
Collectors edition specialty knives. Special promotions.

Old cutler, barion, trappers, military knives. Industrial knives-electrician.

CONDOR™ TOOL & KNIFE
7557 W. Sand Lake Rd., #106
Orlando, FL 32819
407-354-3488; Fax: 407-354-3489
rtj2@att.net; www.condortk.com

CRAWFORD KNIVES, LLC
205 N Center
West Memphis, AR 72301
870-732-2452
www.crawfordknives.com
Folding knives for tactical and general use

CRKT
18348 SW 126th Place
Tualatin, OR 97062
800-891-3100; fax 503-682-9680
info@crkt.com; www.crkt.com
Complete line of sport, work and tactical knives

CUTCO CORPORATION
1116 E. State St.
Olean, NY 14760
716-372-3111
www.cutco.com
Household cutlery / sport knives

DPX GEAR INC.
2321 Kettner Blvd.
San Diego, CA 92101
619-780-2600; fax: 619-780-2605
www.dpxgear.com
Hostile environment survival knives and tools

EMERSON KNIVES, INC.
1234 254th St.
Harbor City, CA 90710
310-539-5633; fax: 310-539-5609
www.emersonknives.com
Hard use tactical knives; folding & fixed blades

ESEE KNIVES
POB 99
Gallant, AL 35972
256-613-0372
www.eseeknives.com
Survival and tactical knives

EXTREMA RATIO
Mauro Chiostri/Maurizio Castrati
Via Tourcoing 40/p
Prato (PO) 59100
ITALY
0039 0576 584639; fax: 0039 0576 584312
info@extremaratio.com
Tactical/military knives and sheaths, blades and sheaths to customers specs

FALLKNIVEN
Granatvägen 8
S-961 43 Boden
SWEDEN
46-(0)-921 544 22; Fax: 46-(0)-921 544 33
info@fallkniven.se; www.fallkniven.com
High quality stainless knives

FAMARS USA
2091 Nooseneck Hill Rd., Ste. 200
Coventry, RI 02816
855-FAMARS1 (326-2771)
www.famarsusa.com
FAMARS has been building guns for over 50 years. Known for innovative design, quality and craftsmanship. New lines of gentleman's knives, tactical fixed blades and folders, hunters and utility pieces.

FOX KNIVES USA
9918 162nd St. Ct. E, Ste. 14
Puyallup, WA 98375
303-263-2468
www.foxknivesusa.com
Designer, manufacturer and distributor of high-quality cutlery

FROST CUTLERY CO
PO Box 22636
Chattanooga, TN 37422
800-251-7768
www.frostcutlery.com
Wide range of fixed-blade and folding knives with a multitude of handle materials

GATCO SHARPENERS/TIMBERLINE
PO Box 600
Getzville, NY 14068
716-646-5700; fax: 716-646-5775
gatco@gatcosharpeners.com;
www.gatcosharpeners.com
Manufacturer of the GATCO brand of knife sharpeners and Timberline brand of knives

GERBER LEGENDARY BLADES
14200 SW 72nd Ave
Portland, OR 97223
503-403-1143; fax: 307-857-4702
www.gerbergear.com
Knives, multi-tools, axes, saws, outdoor products

GINSU/DOUGLAS QUIKUT
118 E. Douglas Rd.
Walnut Ridge, AR 72476
800-982-5233; fax: 870-886-9162
www.douglasquikut.com
Household cutlery

GROHMANN KNIVES
PO Box 40
116 Water St
Pictou, Nova Scotia B0K 1H0
CANADA
888-7KNIVES; Fax: 902-485-5872
www.grohmannknives.com
Fixed-blade belt knives for hunting and fishing, folding pocketknives for hunting and general use. Household cutlery.

H&B FORGE CO.
235 Geisinger Rd
Shiloh, OH 44878
419-895-1856
www.hbforge.com
Special order throwing knives and tomahawks, camp stoves, muzzleloading accroutements

HALLMARK CUTLERY
POB 220
Kodak, TN 37764
866-583-3912; fax: 901-405-0948
www.hallmarkcutlery.com
Traditional folders, tactical folders and fixed blades, multi-tools, shotgun shell knives, Bad Blood, Robert Klaas and Chief brand knives, and Super Premium care products

HISTORIC EDGED WEAPONRY
1021 Saddlebrook Dr
Hendersonville, NC 28739
828-692-0323; fax: 828-692-0600
histwpn@bellsouth.net
Antique knives from around the world; importer of puukko and other knives from Norway, Sweden, Finland and Lapland; also edged weaponry book "Travels for Daggers" by Eiler R. Cook

JOY ENTERPRISES-FURY CUTLERY
Port Commerce Center III
1862 M.L. King Jr. Blvd
Riviera Beach, FL 33404
800-500-3879; fax: 561-863-3277
mail@joyenterprises.com;
www.joyenterprises.com;
www.furycutlery.com
Fury™ Mustang™ extensive variety of fixed-blade and folding knives for hunting, fishing, diving, camping, military and general use; novelty key-ring knives. Muela Sporting Knives. Fury Tactical, Muela of Spain, Mustang Outdoor Adventure

KA-BAR KNIVES INC
200 Homer St
Olean, NY 14760
800-282-0130; fax: 716-790-7188
info@ka-bar.com; www.ka-bar.com *Manufacture of law enforcement, military, hunting and outdoor knives*

KAI USA LTD.
18600 S.W. Teton Ave.
Tualatin, OR 97062
800-325-2891; fax 503-682-7168
info@kai-usa.com
www.kershawknives.com
Manufacturer of high-quality, lifetime-guaranteed knives. Kai USA brands include Kershaw Knives for everyday carrying, hunting, fishing and other outdoor use; Zero Tolerance Knives for professional use; and Shun Cutlery, providing premium-quality kitchen knives

KATZ KNIVES, INC.
10924 Mukilteo Speedway #287
Mukilteo, WA 98275
480-786-9334; fax 460-786-9338
katzkn@aol.com; www.katzknives.com

KELLAM KNIVES WORLDWIDE
P.O. Box 3438
Lantana, FL 33465
800-390-6918
info@kellamknives.com;
www.kellamknives.com
Largest selection of Finnish knives, handmade and production

KLOTZLI (MESSER KLOTZLI)
Hohengasse 3 CH 3400
Burgdorf
SWITZERLAND
41-(34)-422-23 78
info@klotzli.com; www.klotzli.com
High-tech folding knives for tactical and general use

KNIGHTS EDGE LTD.
5696 N. Northwest Highway
Chicago, IL 60646-6136
773-775-3888; fax 773-775-3339
sales@knightsedge.com;
www.knightsedge.com
Medieval weaponry, swords, suits of armor, katanas, daggers

KNIVES OF ALASKA, INC.
Charles or Jody Allen
3100 Airport Dr
Denison, TX 75020
903-786-7366; fax 903-786-7371
info@knivesofalaska.com;
www.knivesofalaska.com
High quality hunting & outdoorsmen's knives

KNIVES PLUS
2467 Interstate 40 West
Amarillo, TX 79109
800-359-6202
www.knivesplus.com
Retail cutlery and cutlery accessories since 1987; free catalog available

LANSKY KNIFE, TOOL & SHARPENERS
POB 800
Buffalo, NY 14231
716-877-7511; fax 716-877-6955
cfire@lansky.com
www.lansky.com
Knives, multi-tools, survival axes, sharpeners

LEATHERMAN TOOL GROUP, INC.
12106 N.E. Ainsworth Cir.
Portland, OR 97220-0595
800-847-8665; fax 503-253-7830
info@leatherman.com;
www.leatherman.com
Multi-tools

LONE STAR WHOLESALE
2401 Interstate 40 W
Amarillo, TX 79109
806-836-9540; fax 806-359-1603
sales@lswtexas.com
www.lswtexas.com
Great prices, dealers only, most major brands

MANTIS KNIVES
520 Cameron St.
Placentia, CA 92870
714-996-9673
gwest@mantis.bz
www.mantisknives.com
Manufacturer of utility, karambit, fixed and folding blades, and Neccessikeys

MARBLE ARMS C/O BLUE RIDGE KNIVES
166 Adwolfe Rd.
Marion, VA 24354-6664
276-783-6143
onestop@blueridgeknives.com
www.blueridgeknives.com

MASTER CUTLERY INC
700 Penhorn Ave
Secaucus, NJ 07094
888-227-7229; fax 888-271-7228
www.mastercutlery.com
Largest variety in the knife industry

MEYERCO USA
4481 Exchange Service Dr.
Dallas, TX 75236
214-467-8949; fax 214-467-9241
www.meyercousa.com
Folding tactical,rescue and speed-assisted pocketknives; fixed-blade hunting and fishing designs; multi-function camping tools and machetes

MICROTECH KNIVES
300 Chestnut Street Ext.
Bradford, PA 16701
814-363-9260; Fax: 814-363-9030
info@microtechknives.com
www.microtechknives.com
Manufacturers of the highest quality production knives

MISSION KNIVES
13771 Newhope St.
Garden Grove, CA 92843
714-638-4692; fax 714-638-4621
info@missionknives.com
www.missionknives.com

Manufacturer of titanium and steel knives and tools with over 20 years in business. Tactical, combat, military, law enforcement, EOD units, survivalist, diving, recreational straight blades, folding blades and mine probes, and more.

MOKI KNIFE COMPANY LTD.
15 Higashisenbo
Seki City GIFU
Pref JAPAN
575-22-4185; fax 575-24-5306
information@moki.co.jp
www.moki.co.jp
Pocketknives, folders, fixed-blade knives and gent's knives

MUSEUM REPLICAS LTD.
P.O. Box 840, 2147 Gees Mill Rd
Conyers, GA 30012
800-883-8838; fax: 770-388-0246
www.museumreplicas.com
Historically accurate and battle-ready swords and daggers

NEMESIS KNIVES, LLC
179 Niblick Rd., #180
Paso Robles, CA 93446
562-594-4740
info@nemesis-knives.com
www.nemesis-knives.com
Semi-custom and production kinves

ONTARIO KNIFE CO.
26 Empire St.
Franklinville, NY 14737
800-222-5233; fax 716-676-5535
knifesales@ontarioknife.com
www.ontarioknife.com
Fixed blades, tactical folders, military and hunting knives, machetes

OUTDOOR EDGE CUTLERY CORP.
9500 W. 49th Ave., #A-100
Wheat Ridge, CO 80033
800-447-3343; 303-530-7667
moreinfo@outdooredge.com;
www.outdooredge.com

PACIFIC SOLUTION MARKETING, INC.
1220 E. Belmont St.
Ontario, CA 91761
Tel: 877-810-4643
Fax: 909-930-5843
sales@pacificsolution.com
www.pacificsolution.com
Wide range of folding pocket knives, hunting knives, tactical knives, novelty knives, medieval armor and weapons as well as hand forged samurai swords and tantos.

PARAGON SPORTS
867 Broadway at 18th St.
New York, NY 10003
800-961-3030 or 212-255-8889
customerservice@paragonsports.com
www.paragonsports.com
Folders, fixed blades, hunters, multi-tools, tool knives, handmade fixed blades and folders from top makers

PRO-TECH KNIVES LLC
17115 Alburtis Ave.
Artesia, CA 90701-2616
562-860-0678
service@protechknives.com
www.protechknives.com
Manufacturer specializing in automatic knives for police, military and discriminating collectors

QUEEN CUTLERY COMPANY
507 Chestnut St.
Titusville, PA 16354

814-827-3673; fax: 814-827-9693
jmoore@queencutlery.com
www.queencutlery.com
Pocketknives, collectibles, Schatt & Morgan, Robeson, club knives

RANDALL MADE KNIVES
4857 South Orange Blossom Trail
Orlando, FL 32839
407-855-8075; fax 407-855-9054
grandall@randallknives.com;
www.randallknives.com
Handmade fixed-blade knives for hunting, fishing, diving, military and general use

REMINGTON ARMS CO., INC.
870 Remington Drive
Madison, NC 27025-0700
800-243-9700
www.remington.com

RUKO LLC.
PO Box 38
Buffalo, NY 14207-0038
800-611-4433; fax 905-826-1353
info@rukoproducts.com
www.rukoproducts.com

SANTA FE STONEWORKS
3790 Cerrillos Rd.
Santa Fe, NM 87507
800-257-7625
knives@rt66.com
www.santafestoneworks.com
Gemstone handles

SARCO KNIVES LLC
449 Lane Dr
Florence AL 35630
256-766-8099; fax 256-766-7246
www.TriEdgeKnife.com
Etching and engraving services, club knives, etc. New knives, antique-collectible knives

SARGE KNIVES
2720 E. Phillips Rd.
Greer, SC 29650
800-454-7448; fax 864-331-0752
cgaines@sargeknives.com
www.sargeknives.com
High-quality, affordable pocketknives, hunting, fishing, camping and tactical. Custom engraving for promotional knives or personalized gifts

SOG SPECIALTY KNIVES & TOOLS, INC.
6521 212th St SW
Lynnwood, WA 98036
425-771-6230; fax 425-771-7689
sogsales@sogknives.com
www.sogknives.com
SOG assisted technology, Arc-Lock, folding knives, specialized fixed blades, multi-tools

SPARTAN BLADES, LLC
625 S.E. Service Rd.
Southern Pines, NC 28387
910-757-0035
contact@spartanbladesusa.com
www.spartanbladesusa.com
Tactical, combat, fighter, survival and field knives

SPYDERCO, INC.
820 Spyderco Way
Golden, CO 80403
800-525-7770; fax 303-278-2229
sales@spyderco.com
www.spyderco.com
Knives, sharpeners and accessories

directory

STONE RIVER GEAR
75 Manor Rd.
Red Hook, NY 12571
203-470-2526; fax 866-258-7202
info@stonerivergear.com
www.stonerivergear.com
Fighters, tactical, survival and military knives, household cutlery, hunting knives, pocketknives, folders and utility tools

SWISS ARMY BRANDS INC.
15 Corporate Dr.
Orangeburg, NY 10962
800-431-2994
customer.service@swissarmy.com
www.swissarmy.com
Folding multi-blade designs and multi-tools for hunting, fishing, camping, hiking, golfing and general use. One of the original brands (Victorinox) of Swiss Army Knives

TAYLOR BRANDS LLC
1043 Fordtown Road
Kingsport, TN 37663
800-251-0254; fax 423-247-5371

info@taylorbrandsllc.com
www.taylorbrandsllc.com
Smith & Wesson Knives, Old Timer, Uncle Henry and Schrade.

TIMBERLINE KNIVES
7223 Boston State Rd.
Boston, NY 14075
800-liv-sharp; fax 716-646-5775
www.timberlineknives.com
High technology production knives for professionals, sporting, tradesmen and kitchen use

TRU-BALANCE KNIFE CO. EAST
PO Box 807
Awendaw, SC 29429
843-928-3624
Manufacturing and sale of throwing knives

UNITED CUTLERY
475 U.S. Hwy. 319 S
Moultrie, GA 31768
800-548-0835; fax 229-551-0182
customerservice@unitedcutlery.com
www.unitedcutlery.com

Wholesale only; pocket, sportsman knives, licensed movie knives, swords, exclusive brands

WILLIAM HENRY STUDIO
3200 NE Rivergate St
McMinnville, OR 97128
503-434-9700; Fax: 503-434-9704
www.williamhenry.com
Semi-production, handmade knives

WUU JAU CO. INC
2600 S Kelly Ave
Edmond, OK 73013
405-359-5031; fax 405-340-5965
mail@wuujau.com; www.wuujau.com
Wide variety of imported fixed-blade and folding knives for hunting, fishing, camping and general use. Wholesale to knife dealers only

XIKAR INC
3305 Terrace, PO Box 025757
Kansas City MO 64111-3637
888-266-1193; fax 917-464-6398
info@xikar.com; www.xikar.com
Gentlemen's cutlery and accessories

importers

A.G. RUSSELL KNIVES INC
2900 S. 26th St.
Rogers, AR 72758-8571
800-255-9034
fax 479-631-8493
ag@agrussell.com; www.agrussell.com
The oldest knife mail-order company, highest quality. Free catalog available. In these catalogs you will find the newest and the best. If you like knives, this catalog is a must. Celebrating over 40 years in the industry

ADAMS INTERNATIONAL KNIFEWORKS
8710 Rosewood Hills
Edwardsville, IL 62025
Importers & foreign cutlers

ATLANTA CUTLERY CORP.
P.O.Box 839
Conyers, Ga 30012
770-922-7500; Fax: 770-918-2026
custserve@atlantacutlery.com;
www.atlantacutlery.com
Exotic knives from around the world

BAILEY'S
PO Box 550
Laytonville, CA 95454
800-322-4539; 707-984-8115
baileys@baileys-online.com;
www.baileys-online.com

BELTRAME, FRANCESCO
Fratelli Beltrame F&C snc Via dei Fabbri 15/B-
33085 MANIAGO (PN)
ITALY
39 0427 701859
www.italianstiletto.com

BOKER USA, INC.
1550 Balsam St
Lakewood, CO 80214-5917
800-992-6537; 303-462-0668
sales@bokerusa.com; www.bokerusa.com
Ceramic blades

CAMPOS, IVAN DE ALMEIDA
R. Stelio M. Loureiro, 205
Centro, Tatui
BRAZIL
00-55-15-33056867
www.ivancampos.net

C.A.S. IBERIA
650 Industrial Blvd
Sale Creek, TN 37373
800-635-9366; fax 423-332-7248
mhillian@casiberia.com; www.casiberia.com

CATOCTIN CUTLERY
PO Box 188
Smithsburg, MD 21783

CLASSIC INDUSTRIES
1325 Howard Ave, Suite 408
Burlingame, CA 94010

COAST CUTLERY CO.
8033 N.E. Holman
Portland, OR 97218
800-426-5858
staff@coastcutlery.com;
www.coastcutlery.com

COLUMBIA PRODUCTS CO.
PO Box 1333
Sialkot 51310
PAKISTAN

COLUMBIA PRODUCTS INT'L
PO Box 8243
New York, NY 10116-8243
201-854-3054; Fax: 201-854-7058
nycolumbia@aol.com; http://www.
columbiaproducts.homestead.com/cat.html
Pocket, hunting knives and swords of all kinds

COMPASS INDUSTRIES, INC.
104 E. 25th St
New York, NY 10010
800-221-9904; Fax: 212-353-0826
jeff@compassindustries.com;
www.compassindustries.com
Imported pocket knives

CONAZ COLTELLERIE
American Office
4179 Cristal Lake Dr.
Deerfield Beach, FL 33064
561-809-9701 or 754-423-3356
Fax: 954-781-3693
susanna@consigliscarperia.com;
www.consigliscarperia.it
Handicraft workmanship of knives of the ancient Italian tradition. Historical and collection knives

CONSOLIDATED CUTLERY CO., INC.
696 NW Sharpe St
Port St. Lucie, FL 34983
772-878-6139

CRAZY CROW TRADING POST
PO Box 847
Pottsboro, TX 75076
800-786-6210; Fax: 903-786-9059
info@crazycrow.com; www.crazycrow.com
Solingen blades, knife making parts & supplies

DER FLEISSIGEN BEAVER
(The Busy Beaver)
Harvey Silk
PO Box 1166
64343 Griesheim
GERMANY
49 61552231; 49 6155 2433
Der.Biber@t-online.de
Retail custom knives. Knife shows in Germany & UK

EXTREMA RATIO
Mauro Chiostri; Mavrizio Castrati
Via Tourcoing 40/p
59100 Prato (PO)
ITALY
0039 0576 58 4639; fax 0039 0576 584312
info@extremaratio.com;
www.extremaratio.com
Tactical & military knives manufacturing

ALLKNIVEN
Granatvagen 8
961 43 Boden
SWEDEN
46 (0) 921 544 22; fax +46 (0) 921 544 33
info@fallkniven.se
www.fallkniven.com
High quality knives

REDIANI COLTELLI FINLANDESI
Via Lago Maggiore 41
21038 Leggiuno
ITALY

MESSER MESSERFABRIK GMBH, JOHANNES
Raiffeisenstr 15
71349 Winnenden
GERMANY
9-7195-1808-29
info@giesser.de; www.giesser.de
Professional butchers and chef's knives

HIMALAYAN IMPORTS
3495 Lakeside Dr
Reno, NV 89509
775-825-2279
unclebill@himalayan-imports.com; www.himalayan-imports.com

IVAN DE ALMEIDA CAMPOS-KNIFE DEALER
R. Xi De Agosto
107, Centro, Tatui, Sp 18270
BRAZIL
55-15-251-8092; 55-15-251-4896
campos@bitweb.com.br
Custom knives from all Brazilian knifemakers

JOY ENTERPRISES
1862 Martin Luther King Jr. Blvd.
Riviera Beach, FL 33404
561-863-3205; fax 561-863-3277
mail@joyenterprises.com;
www.joyenterprises.com
Fury™, Mustang™, Hawg Knives, Muela

KELLAM KNIVES WORLDWIDE
POB 3438
Lantana, FL 33465
561-588-3185 or 800-390-6918
info@kellamknives.com;
www.kellamknives.com
Knives from Finland; own line of knives

KNIFE IMPORTERS, INC.
1307 Conroy Ln
Manchaca, TX 78652
512-282-6860, Fax: 512-282-7504
Wholesale only

KNIGHTS EDGE LTD.
5696 N Northwest Hwy
Chicago, IL 60646
773-775-3888; fax 773-775-3339
www.knightsedge.com
Exclusive designers of our Rittersteel, Stagesteel and Valiant Arms and knightedge lines of weapon

LEISURE PRODUCTS CORP.
PO Box 1171
Sialkot-51310
PAKISTAN

L. C. RISTINEN
Suomi Shop
7533 Co Hwy 38
Frazee MN 56544

218-538-6633; 218-538-6633
icrist@wcta.net
Scandinavian cutlery custom antique, books and reindeer antler

LINDER, CARL NACHF.
Erholungstr. 10
D-42699 Solingen
GERMANY
212 33 0 856; Fax: 212 33 71 04
info@linder.de; www.linder.de

MARTTIINI KNIVES
PO Box 44 (Marttiinintie 3)
96101 Rovaniemi
FINLAND

MATTHEWS CUTLERY
POB 2768
Moultrie, GA 31776
800-251-0123; fax 877-428-3599
www.matthewscutlery.com
Wholesale of major brands

MESSER KLÖTZLI
PO Box 104
Hohengasse 3, 3400 Burgdorf
SWITZERLAND
0041 (0)34 422 23 78; fax 0041 (0)34 422 76 93; info@klotzli.com; www.klotzli.com

MUSEUM REPLICAS LIMITED
2147 Gees Mill Rd
Conyers, GA 30012
800-883-8838; fax 770-388-0246
mrw@museumreplicas.com
www.museumreplicas.com
Subsidiary of Atlanta Cutlery. Battle-ready swords and other historic edged weapons, as well as clothing, jewelry and accessories.

NICHOLS CO.
Pomfret Rd
South Pomfret, VT 05067
Import & distribute knives from EKA (Sweden), Helle (Norway), Brusletto (Norway), Roselli (Finland). Also market Zippo products, Snow, Nealley axes and hatchets and snow & Neally axes

NORMARK CORP.
Craig Weber
10395 Yellow Circle Dr
Minnetonka, MN 55343

PIELCU
Parque Empresarial Campollano
Avenida 2a Numero 25 (esquina con C/E)
02007 Albacete
SPAIN
+34 967 523 568; fax +34 967 523 569
pielcu@pielcu.com; www.grupopielcu.com
Tactical, outdoor, fantasy and sporting knives

PRODUCTORS AITOR, S.A.
Izelaieta 17
48260 Ermua
SPAIN
943-170850; 943-170001
info@aitor.com
Sporting knives

PROFESSIONAL CUTLERY SERVICES
9712 Washburn Rd
Downey, CA 90241
562-803-8778; 562-803-4261
Wholesale only. Full service distributor of domestic & imported brand name cutlery. Exclusive U.S. importer for both Marto Swords and Battle Ready Valiant Armory edged weapons

SVORD KNIVES
Smith Rd., RD 2
Waiuku, South Auckland
NEW ZEALAND
64 9 2358846; fax 64 9 2356483
www.svord.com

SWISS ARMY BRANDS INC.
15 Corporate Dr.
Orangeburg, NY 10962
800-431-2994 or 914-425-4700
customer.service@swissarmy.com
www.swissarmy.com
Importer and distributor of Victorinox's Swiss Army brand

TAYLOR BRANDS, LLC
1043 Fordtown Road
Kingsport, TN 37663
800-251-0254; fax 423-247-5371
info@taylorbrandsllc.com;
www.taylorbrandsllc.com
Fixed-blade and folding knives for tactical, rescue, hunting and general use. Also provides etching, engraving, scrimshaw services.

UNITED CUTLERY
475 U.S. Hwy. 319 S
Moultrie, GA 31768
800-548-0835 or 229-890-6669; fax 229-551-0182
customerservice@unitedcutlery.com www.unitedcutlery.com
Harley-Davidson ®, Colt ®, Stanley ®, U21 ®, Rigid Knives ®, Outdoor Life ®, Ford ®, hunting, camping, fishing, collectible & fantasy knives

VICTORINOX SWISS ARMY, INC.
7 Victoria Dr.
Monroe, CT 06468
203-929-6391
renee.hourigan@swissarmy.com
www.swissarmy.com
Genuine Swiss Army Knives and Swiss Watches

WORLD CLASS EXHIBITION KNIVES
Cary Desmon
941-504-2279
www.withoutequal.com
Carries an extensive line of Pius Lang knives

ZWILLING J.A. HENCKELS LLC
171 Saw Mill River Rd
Hawthorne, NY 10532
914-747-0300; fax 914-747-1850
info@jahenckels.com;
www.jahenckels.com
Zwilling, Henckels International, Miyabi, Staub, Demeyere kitchen cutlery, scissors, shears, gadgets, cookware, flatware

knifemaking supplies

FRICAN IMPORT CO.
Alan Zanotti
22 Goodwin Rd
Plymouth, MA 02360
508-746-8552; 508-746-0404
africanimport@aol.com
Ivory

ALABAMA DAMASCUS STEEL
PO Box 54
WELLINGTON, AL 36279
256-310-4619 or 256-282-7988
sales@alabamadamascussteel.com
www.alabamadamascussteel.com
*We are a manufacturer of damascus steel billets &
blades. We also offer knife supplies. We can custom
make any blade design that the customer wants. We can
also make custom damascus billets per customer specs.*

ALPHA KNIFE SUPPLY
425-868-5880; Fax: 425-898-7715
chuck@alphaknifesupply.com;
www.alphaknifesupply.com
Inventory of knife supplies

AMERICAN SIEPMANN CORP.
65 Pixley Industrial Parkway
Rochester, NY 14624
585-247-1640; Fax: 585-247-1883
www.siepmann.com
*CNC blade grinding equipment, grinding wheels,
production blade grinding services. Sharpening stones
and sharpening equipment*

ANKROM EXOTICS
Pat Ankrom
306 1/2 N. 12th
Centerville, IA 52544
641-436-0235
ankromexotics@hotmail.com
www.ankromexotics.com
*Stabilized handle material; Exotic burls and hardwoods
from around the world; Stabilizing services available*

ATLANTA CUTLERY CORP.
P.O.Box 839
Conyers, Ga 30012
770-922-7500; Fax: 770-918-2026
custserve@atlantacutlery.com;
www.atlantacutlery.com

BLADEMAKER, THE
Gary Kelley
17485 SW Phesant Ln
Beaverton, OR 97006
503-649-7867
garykelley@theblademaker.com;
www.theblademaker.com
*Period knife and hawk blades for hobbyists & re-enactors
and in dendritic D2 steel. "Ferroulithic" steel-stone spear
point, blades and arrowheads*

BOONE TRADING CO., INC.
PO Box 669
562 Coyote Rd
Brinnon, WA 98320
800-423-1945; Fax: 360-796-4511
bella@boonetrading.com
www.boonetrading.com
Ivory of all types, bone, horns

BORGER, WOLF
Benzstrasse 8
76676 Graben-Neudorf
GERMANY

wolf@messerschmied.de;
www.messerschmied.de

BOYE KNIVES
PO Box 1238
Dolan Springs, AZ 86441-1238
800-853-1617 or 928-272-0903
boye@citlink.net
www.boyeknives.com
Dendritic steel and Dendritic cobalt

BRONK'S KNIFEWORKS
Lyle Brunckhorst
Country Village
23706 7th Ave SE, Suite B
Bothell, WA 98021
425-402-3484
bronks@bronksknifeworks.com;
www.bronksknifeworks.com
Damascus steel

CRAZY CROW TRADING POST
PO Box 847
Pottsboro, TX 75076
800-786-6210; Fax: 903-786-9059
info@crazycrow.com; www.crazycrow.com
Solingen blades, knife making parts & supplies

CULPEPPER & CO.
Joe Culpepper
P.O. Box 690
8285 Georgia Rd.
Otto, NC 28763
828-524-6842; Fax: 828-369-7809
info@culpepperco.com
www.knifehandles.com
www.stingrayproducts.com
www.oldschoolknifeworks.com
*Mother of pearl, bone, abalone, stingray, dyed stag,
blacklip, ram's horn, mammoth ivory, coral, scrimshaw*

CUTLERY SPECIALTIES
6819 S.E. Sleepy Hollow Lane
Stuart, FL 34997-4757
772-219-0436 or 800-229-5530
Dennis13@aol.com
www.restorationproduct.com
*Exclusive distributor for Renaissance Wax/Polish and
other restoration products*

DAMASCUS USA
149 Deans Farm Rd
Tyner, NC 27980-9718
252-333-0349
rob@damascususa.com;
www.damascususa.com
*All types of damascus cutlery steel, including 100 percent
finished damascus blade blanks*

DAN'S WHETSTONE CO., INC.
418 Hilltop Rd
Pearcy, AR 71964
501-767-1616; fax 501-767-9598
questions@danswhetstone.com;
www.danswhetstone.com
Natural abrasive Arkansas stone products

**DIAMOND MACHINING TECHNOLOGY,
  INC. (DMT)**
85 Hayes Memorial Dr
Marlborough, MA 01752
800-666-4DMT
dmtcustomercare@dmtsharp.com;
www.dmtsharp.com
*Knife and tool sharpener—diamond, ceramic and easy
edge guided sharpening kits*

DIGEM DIAMOND SUPPLIERS
7303 East Earll Drive
Scottsdale, Arizona 85251
602-620-3999
eglasser@cox.net
*#1 international diamond tool provider. Every diamond
tool you will ever need 1/16th of an inch to 11'x9'. BURR
CORE DRILLS, SAW BLADES, MILLING SHAPES, AND
WHEELS*

DIXIE GUN WORKS, INC.
1412 West Reelfoot Ave.
Union City, TN 38281
731-885-0700; Fax: 731-885-0440
www.dixiegunworks.com
Knife and knifemaking supplies

EZE-LAP DIAMOND PRODUCTS
3572 Arrowhead Dr
Carson City, NV 89706
775-888-9500; Fax: 775-888-9555
sales@eze-lap.com; www.eze-lap.com
Diamond coated sharpening tools

FINE TURNAGE PRODUCTIONS
Charles Turnage
1210 Midnight Drive
San Antonio, TX 78260
210-352-5660
info@fineturnage.com
www.fineturnage.com
*Specializing in stabilized mammoth tooth and bone,
mammoth ivory, fossil brain coral, meteorite, etc.*

FLITZ INTERNATIONAL, LTD.
821 Mohr Ave
Waterford, WI 53185
800-558-8611; Fax: 262-534-2991
info@flitz.com; www.flitz.com
Metal polish, buffing pads, wax

FORTUNE PRODUCTS, INC.
2010A Windy Terrace
Cedar Park, TX 78613
800-742-7797; Fax: 800-600-5373
www.accusharp.com
AccuSharp knife sharpeners

GALLERY HARDWOODS
Larry Davis, Eugene, OR
www.galleryhardwoods.com
Stabilized exotic burls and woods

GILMER WOOD CO.
2211 NW St Helens Rd
Portland, OR 97210
503-274-1271; Fax: 503-274-9839
www.gilmerwood.com

GIRAFFEBONE KNIFE SUPPLY
3052 Isim Rd.
Norman, OK 73026
888-804-0683
sandy@giraffebone.com;
www.giraffebone.com
Exotic handle materials

GLENDO CORPORATION/GRS TOOLS
D.J. Glaser
900 Overlander Rd.
Emporia, KS 66801
620-343-1084; Fax: 620-343-9640
glendo@glendo.com; www.grstools.com
Engraving, equipment, tool sharpener, books/videos

HALPERN TITANIUM INC.
Les and Marianne Halpern

PO Box 214
4 Springfield St
Three Rivers, MA 01080
888-283-8627; Fax: 413-289-2372
info@halperntitanium.com;
www.halperntitanium.com
Titanium, carbon fiber, G-10, fasteners; CNC milling

HAWKINS KNIFE MAKING SUPPLIES
110 Buckeye Rd
Fayetteville, GA 30214
770-964-1023
Sales@hawkinsknifemakingsupplies.com
www.HawkinsKnifeMakingSupplies.com
All styles

HILTARY INDUSTRIES
6060 East Thomas Road
Scottsdale, AZ 85251
Office: 480-945-0700
Fax: 480-945-3333
usgrc@usgrc.biz, eglasser@cox.net
OEM manufacturer, knife and sword importer, appraiser, metal supplier, diamond products, stag, meteorite, reconstituted gems, exotic wood, leather and bone

HOUSE OF TOOLS LTD.
#54-5329 72 Ave. S.E.
Calgary, Alberta
CANADA T2C 4X
403-640-4594; Fax: 403-451-7006
www.houseoftools.net

INDIAN JEWELERS SUPPLY CO.
Mail Order: 601 E Coal Ave
Gallup, NM 87301-6005
2105 San Mateo Blvd NE
Albuquerque, NM 87110-5148
800-545-6540; fax: 888-722-4172
orders@ijsinc.com; www.ijsinc.com
Handle materials, tools, metals

INTERAMCO INC.
5210 Exchange Dr
Flint, MI 48507
810-732-8181; 810-732-6116
solutions@interamco.com
Knife grinding and polishing

JANTZ SUPPLY / KOVAL KNIVES
PO Box 584
309 West Main
Davis, OK 73030
800-351-8900; 580-369-3082
jantz@jantzusa.com
www.knifemaking.com
Pre shaped blades, kit knives, complete knifemaking supply line

JMD INTERNATIONAL
2985 Gordy Pkwy., Unit 405
Marietta, GA 30066
678-969-9147; Fax: 770-640-9852
knifesupplies@gmail.com;
www.knifesupplies.com;
Serving the cutlery industry with the finest selection of India stag, buffalo horn, mother-of-pearl and smooth white bone

JOHNSON, R.B.
I.B.S. Int'l. Folder Supplies, Box 11
Clearwater, MN 55320
320-558-6128; 320-558-6128
www.foldingknifesupplies.com
Threaded pivot pins, screws, taps, etc.

JOHNSON WOOD PRODUCTS
34897 Crystal Rd
Strawberry Point, IA 52076
563-933-6504

K&G FINISHING SUPPLIES
1972 Forest Ave
Lakeside, AZ 85929
928-537-8877; fax: 928-537-8066
csinfo@knifeandgun.com;
www.knifeandgun.com
Full service supplies

KOWAK IVORY
Roland and Kathy Quimby
(May-Sept): PO Box 350
Ester, AK 99725
907-479-9335
(Oct-April)
Green Valley, AZ 85662
520-207-6620
sales@kowakivory.com;
www.kowakivory.com
Fossil ivories

LITTLE GIANT POWER HAMMER
Roger Rice
6414 King Rd.
Nebraska City, NE 68410
402-873-6603
www.littlegianthammer.com
Rebuilds hammers and supplies parts

LIVESAY, NEWT
3306 S Dogwood St
Siloam Springs, AR 72761
479-549-3356; 479-549-3357
Combat utility knives, titanium knives, sportsmen knives, custom made orders taken on knives and after market Kydex© sheaths for commercial or custom cutlery

M MILLER ORIGINALS
Michael Miller
3030 E. Calle Cedral
Kingman AZ 86401
928-757-1359
mike@mmilleroriginals.com;
www.mmilleroriginals.com
Supplies stabilized juniper burl blocks and scales, mosaic damascus, damascus

MARKING METHODS, INC.
Sales
301 S. Raymond Ave
Alhambra, CA 91803-1531
626-282-8823; Fax: 626-576-7564
sales@markingmethods.com;
www.markingmethods.com
Knife etching equipment & service

MASECRAFT SUPPLY CO.
254 Amity St
Meriden, CT 06450
800-682-5489; Fax: 203-238-2373
info@masecraftsupply.com;
www.masecraftsupply.com
Natural & specialty synthetic handle materials & more

MEIER STEEL
Daryl Meier
75 Forge Rd
Carbondale, IL 62903
618-549-3234; Fax: 618-549-6239
www.meiersteel.com

NICO, BERNARD
PO Box 5151
Nelspruit 1200
SOUTH AFRICA
011-2713-7440099; 011-2713-7440099
bernardn@iafrica.com

NORRIS, MIKE
Rt 2 Box 242A

Tollesboro, KY 41189
606-798-1217
Damascus steel

NORTHCOAST KNIVES
17407 Puritas Ave
Cleveland, Ohio 44135
www.NorthCoastKnives.com
Tutorials and step-by-step projects. Entry level knifemaking supplies.

OSO FAMOSO
PO Box 654
Ben Lomond, CA 95005
831-336-2343
oso@osofamoso.com;
www.osofamoso.com
Mammoth ivory bark

OZARK CUTLERY SUPPLY
5230 S. MAIN ST.
Joplin, MO 64804
417-782-4998
ozarkcutlery@gmail.com
28 years in the cutlery business, Missouri's oldest cutlery firm

PARAGON INDUSTRIES, L.P.
2011 South Town East Blvd
Mesquite, TX 75149-1122
800-876-4328 or 972-288-7557
info@paragonweb.com;
www.paragonweb.com
Heat treating furnaces for knifemakers

POPLIN, JAMES / POP'S KNIVES & SUPPLIES
1654 S. Smyrna Church Rd.
Washington, GA 30673
706-678-5408
www.popsknifesupplies.com

PUGH, JIM
PO Box 711
917 Carpenter
Azle, TX 76020
817-444-2679; Fax: 817-444-5455
Rosewood and ebony Micarta blocks, rivets for Kydex sheaths, 0-80 screws for folders

RADOS, JERRY
134 Willie Nell Rd.
Columbia, KY 42728
606-303-3334
jerryr@ttlv.net
www.radosknives.com
Damascus steel

REACTIVE METALS STUDIO, INC.
PO Box 890
Clarksdale, AZ 86324
800-876-3434; 928-634-3434; Fax: 928-634-6734
info@reactivemetals.com; www.reactivemetals.com

R. FIELDS ANCIENT IVORY
Donald Fields
790 Tamerlane St
Deltona, FL 32725
386-532-9070
donaldbfields@earthlink.net
Selling ancient ivories; Mammoth, fossil & walrus

RICK FRIGAULT CUSTOM KNIVES
1189 Royal Pines Rd.
Golden Lake, Ontario
CANADA K0J 1X0
613-401-2869
jill@mouseworks.net
www.rfrigaultknives.ca
Selling padded zippered knife pouches with an option to

personalize the outside with the marker, purveyor, stores-address, phone number, email web-site or any other information needed. Available in black cordura, mossy oak camo in sizes 4"x2" to 20"x4.5"

RIVERSIDE MACHINE
201 W Stillwell Ave.
DeQueen, AR 71832
870-642-7643; Fax: 870-642-4023
uncleal@riversidemachine.net
www.riversidemachine.net

ROCKY MOUNTAIN KNIVES
George L. Conklin
PO Box 902, 615 Franklin
Ft. Benton, MT 59442
406-622-3268; Fax: 406-622-3410
bbgrus@ttc-cmc.net
Working knives

SAKMAR, MIKE
903 S. Latson Rd. #257
Howell, MI 48843
517-546-6388; Fax: 517-546-6399
sakmarent@yahoo.com
www.sakmarenterprises.com
Mokume bar stock. Retail & wholesale

SANDPAPER, INC. OF ILLINOIS
P.O. Box 2579
Glen Ellyn, IL 60138
630-629-3320; Fax: 630-629-3324
sandinc@aol.com; www.sandpaperinc.com
Abrasive belts, rolls, sheets & discs

SCHMIEDEWERKSTATTE
Markus Balbach e.K.
Heinrich-Worner-Str. 1-3
35789 Weilmunster-Laubuseschbach,
Germany
06475-8911 Fax: 912986
Damascus steel

SENTRY SOLUTIONS LTD.
PO Box 214
Wilton, NH 03086
800-546-8049; Fax: 603-654-3003
info@sentrysolutions.com;
www.sentrysolutions.com
Knife care products

**SHEFFIELD KNIFEMAKERS
SUPPLY, INC.**
PO Box 741107
Orange City, FL 32774
386-775-6453; fax: 386-774-5754
email@sheffieldsupply.com;
www.sheffieldsupply.com

SHINING WAVE METALS
PO Box 563

Snohomish, WA 98291
425-334-5569
info@shiningwave.com;
www.shiningwave.com
A full line of mokume-gane in precious and non-precious metals for knifemakers, jewelers and other artists

SMITH'S
747 Mid-America Blvd.
Hot Springs, AR 71913-8414
501-321-2244; Fax: 501-321-9232
sales@smithsproducts.com
www.smithsproducts.com

STAMASCUS KNIFEWORKS INC.
Ed VanHoy
24255 N Fork River Rd
Abingdon, VA 24210
276-944-4885; Fax: 276-944-3187
stamascus@centurylink.net
www.stamascusknifeworks.com
Blade steels

POUL STRANDE
Søster Svenstrup Byvej 16
4130 Viby Sjælland
Denmark
45 46 19 43 05; Fax: 45 46 19 53 19
www.poulstrande.com

STOVER, JEFF
PO Box 43
Torrance, CA 90507
310-486-0976
edgedealer@aol.com;
www.edgedealer.com
Fine custom knives, top makers

TEXAS KNIFEMAKERS SUPPLY
10649 Haddington Suite 180
Houston TX 77043
713-461-8632; Fax: 713-461-8221
sales@texasknife.com;
www.texasknife.com
Complete line of knifemaking supplies, equipment, and custom heat treating

TRU-GRIT, INC.
760 E Francis St., Unit N
Ontario, CA 91761
909-923-4116; Fax: 909-923-9932
www.trugrit.com
The latest in Norton and 3/M ceramic grinding belts. Also Super Flex, Trizact, Norax and Micron belts to 3000 grit. All of the popular belt grinders. Buffers and variable speed motors. ATS-34, 440C, BG-42, CPM S-30V, 416 and Damascus steel

TWO FINGER KNIFE, LLC
4574 N. Haroldsen Dr.
Idaho Falls, ID 83401
208-523-7436; Fax: 208-523-7436

twofingerknife@gmail.com www.
twofingerknife.com
USA-forged and hand-ground finished damascus blades, and blades in 5160, 1095, 52100, D2, 440C, ATS 34, ELMAX and other steels. Finishes sword blades, sword-cane blades, damascus bar stock and tomahawk heads. Offers folder kits, custom sheaths, in-house heat treating.

WASHITA MOUNTAIN WHETSTONE CO.
PO Box 20378
Hot Springs, AR 71903-0378
501-525-3914; Fax: 501-525-0816
wmw@hsnp

WEILAND, J. REESE
PO Box 2337
Riverview, FL 33568
813-671-0661
rwphil413@verizon.net
www.reeseweilandknives.com
Folders, straight knives, etc.

WILSON, R.W.
PO Box 2012
113 Kent Way
Weirton, WV 26062
304-723-2771
rwknives@hotmail.com

WOOD CARVERS SUPPLY, INC.
PO Box 7500
Englewood, FL 34295
800-284-6229
teamwcs@yahoo.com
www.woodcarverssupply.com
Over 2,000 unique wood carving tools

WOOD LAB
Michael Balaskovitz
2471 6th St.
Muskegon Hts., MI 49444
616-322-5846
woodlabgroup@gmail.com
www.woodlab.biz
Acrylic stabilizing services and materials

**WOOD STABILIZING SPECIALISTS INT'L,
LLC**
2940 Fayette Ave
Ionia, IA 50645
800-301-9774; 641-435-4746
mike@stabilizedwood.com;
www.stabilizedwood.com
Processor of acrylic impregnated materials

ZOWADA CUSTOM KNIVES
Tim Zowada
4509 E. Bear River Rd
Boyne Falls, MI 49713
231-881-5056
tim@tzknives.com; www.tzknives.com
Damascus, pocket knives, swords, Lower case gothic tz logo

mail order, sales, dealers and purveyors

A.G. RUSSELL KNIVES INC
2900 S. 26th St
Rogers, AR 72758-8571
800-255-9034 or 479-631-0130
fax 479-631-8493
ag@agrussell.com; www.agrussell.com
The oldest knife mail-order company, highest quality. Free catalog available. In these catalogs you will find the newest and the best. If you like knives, this catalog is a must

ARIZONA CUSTOM KNIVES
Julie Maguire
3670 U.S. 1 S, Suite 260-F
St. Augustine, FL 32086

904-826-4178
sharptalk@arizonacustomknives.com; www.
arizonacustomknives.com
Color catalog $5 U.S. / $7 Foreign

ARTKNIVES.COM
Fred Eisen Leather & Art Knives
129 S. Main St.
New Hope, PA 18938
215-862-5988
fredeisen@verizon.net
www.artknives.com
Handmade knives from over 75 makers/high-quality manufacturers, leather sheath maker

ATLANTA CUTLERY CORP.
P.O.Box 839
Conyers, Ga 30012
770-922-7500; Fax: 770-918-2026
custserv@atlantacutlery.com; www.
atlantacutlery.com

BECK'S CUTLERY SPECIALTIES
51 Highland Trace Ln.
Benson, NC 27504
919-902-9416
beckscutlery@embarqmail.com;
www.beckscutlery.com
Knives

BLADE HQ
400 S. 1000 E, Ste. E
Lehi, UT 84043
888-252-3347 or 801-768-0232
questions@bladehq.com
www.bladehq.com
*Online destination for knives and gear, specializing in law
enforcement and military, including folders, fixed blades,
custom knives, asisted-opening folders, automatics,
butterfly knives, hunters, machetes, multi-tools, axes,
knife cases, paracord, sharpeners, sheaths, lubricants
and supplies*

BLADEART.COM
14216 S.W. 136 St.
Miami, FL 33186
305-255-9176
sales@bladeart.com
www.bladeart.com
Custom knives, swords and gear

BLADEGALLERY.COM
107 Central Way
Kirkland, WA 98033
425-889-5980 or 877-56BLADE
info@bladegallery.com;
www.bladegallery.com
*Bladegallery.com specializes in handmade, one-of-a-kind
knives from around the world. We have an emphasis on
forged knives and high-end gentlemen's folders*

BLADEOPS, LLC
1352 W. 7800 S
West Jordan, UT 84088
888-EZ BLAD (392-5233)
trevor@bladeops.com
www.bladeops.com
*Online dealer of all major brands of automatic knives,
butterfly knives, spring-assisted folders, throwing
knives, manual folders, survival and self-defense knives,
sharpeners and paracord*

BLUE RIDGE KNIVES
166 Adwolfe Rd
Marion, VA 24354
276-783-6143; fax 276-783-9298
onestop@blueridgeknives.com;
www.blueridgeknives.com
Wholesale distributor of knives

BOB'S TRADING POST
308 N Main St
Hutchinson, KS 67501
620-669-9441
bobstradingpost@cox.net;
www.bobstradingpostinc.com
*Tad custom knives with Reichert custom sheaths one at a
time, one of a kind*

BOONE TRADING CO., INC.
PO Box 669
562 Coyote Rd
Brinnon, WA 98320
800-423-1945; Fax: 360-796-4511
bella@boonetrading.com
www.boonetrading.com
Ivory of all types, bone, horns

CARMEL CUTLERY
Dolores & 6th
PO Box 1346
Carmel, CA 93921
831-624-6699; 831-624-6780
sanford@carmelcutlery.com;
www.carmelcutlery.com
*Quality custom and a variety of production pocket knives,
swords; kitchen cutlery; personal grooming items*

CLASSIC CUTLERY
66 N. Adams St., Ste. 1
Manchester, NH 03104
classiccutlery@earthlink.net
www.classiccutleryusa.com
*Private-label zip-up knife cases and all brands of
production cutlery and outdoor gear*

CUTLERY SHOPPE
3956 E Vantage Pointe Ln
Meridian, ID 83642-7268
800-231-1272; Fax: 208-884-4433
orders@cutleryshoppe.com;
www.cutleryshoppe.com
Discount pricing on top quality brands

CUTTING EDGE, THE
2900 South 26th St
Rogers, AR 72758-8571
800-255-9034; Fax: 479-631-8493
ce_info@cuttingedge.com;
www.cuttingedge.com
*After-market knives since 1968. They offer about 1,000
individual knives for sale each month. Subscription by
first class mail, in U.S $20 per year, Canada or Mexico
by air mail, $25 per year. All overseas by air mail, $40 per
year. The oldest and the most experienced in the business
of buying and selling knives. They buy collections of any
size, take knives on consignment. Every month there are
4-8 pages in color featuring the work of top makers*

DENTON, JOHN W.
703 Hiawassee Estates Dr.
Hiawassee, GA 30546
706-781-8479
jwdenton@windstream.net
www.bobloveleessknives.com
Loveless knives

EDGEDEALER.COM
PO BOX 43
TORRANCE, CA 90507
310-532-2166
edgedealer1@yahoo.com
www.edgedealer.com
Antiques

EPICUREAN EDGE
107 Central Way
Kirkland, WA 98033
425-889-5980
info@epicedge.com
www.epicedge.com
*Specializing in handmade and one-of-a-kind kitchen
knives from around the world*

EXQUISITEKNIVES.COM
770 Sycamore Ave., Ste. 122, Box 451
Vista, CA 92083
760-945-7177
mastersmith@cox.net
www.exquisiteknives.com and
www.robertloveless.com
Purveyor of high-end custom knives

**FAZALARE INTERNATIONAL
ENTERPRISES**
PO Box 7062
Thousand Oaks, CA 91359
805-496-2002
ourfaz@aol.com
*Handmade multiblades; older Case; Fight'n Rooster;
Bulldog brand & Cripple Creek*

FROST CUTLERY CO.
PO Box 22636
Chattanooga, TN 37422
800-251-7768
www.frostcutlery.com

GODWIN, INC. G. GEDNEY
PO Box 100
Valley Forge, PA 19481
610-783-0670; Fax: 610-783-6083
sales@gggodwin.com
www.gggodwin.com
18th century reproductions

GPKNIVES, LLC
2230 Liebler Rd.
Troy, IL 62294
866-667-5965
gpk@gpknives.com
www.gpknives.com
*Serving law enforcement, hunters, sportsmen and
collectors*

**GRAZYNA SHAW/QUINTESSENTIAL
CUTLERY**
POB 11
Clearwater, MN 55320
320-217-9002
gshaw@quintcut.com
www.quintcut.com
*Specializing in investment-grade custom knives and early
makers*

GUILD KNIVES
Donald Guild
320 Paani Place 1A
Paia, HI 96779
808-877-3109
don@guildknives.com;
www.guildknives.com
Purveyor of custom art knives

HOUSE OF BLADES
6451 N.W. Loop 820
Ft. Worth, TX 76135
817-237-7721
sales@houseofblades.com
www.houseofbladestexas.com
*Handmades, pocketknives, hunting knives, antique and
collector knives, swords, household cutlery and knife-
related items.*

**JENCO SALES, INC. / KNIFE IMPORTERS,
INC. / WHITE LIGHTNING**
PO Box 1000
11307 Conroy Ln
Manchaca, TX 78652
800-531-5301; fax 800-266-2373
jencosales@sbcglobal.net
*Wholesale distributor of domestic and imported cutlery
and sharpeners*

KELLAM KNIVES WORLDWIDE
POB 3438
Lantana, FL 33465
800-390-6918; 561-588-3185
info@kellamknives.com;
www.kellamknives.com
*Largest selection of Finnish knives; own line of folders
and fixed blades*

KNIFEART.COM
13301 Pompano Dr
Little Rock AR 72211
501-221-1010
connelley@knifeart.com
www.knifeart.com
*Large internet seller of custom knives & upscale
production knives*

directory

KNIFECENTER
5201 Lad Land Dr.
Fredericksburg, VA 22407
800-338-6799 or 301-486-0901
info@knifecenter.com
www.knifecenter.com

KNIFEPURVEYOR.COM LLC
919-295-1283
mdonato@knifepurveyor.com
www.knifepurveyor.com
Owned and operated by Michael A. Donato (full-time knife purveyor since 2002). We buy, sell, trade, and consign fine custom knives. We also specialize in buying and selling valuable collections of fine custom knives. Our goal is to make every transaction a memorable one.

KNIVES PLUS
2467 I 40 West
Amarillo, TX 79109
806-359-6202
salessupport@knivesplus.com
www.knivesplus.com
Retail cutlery and cutlery accessories since 1987

KRIS CUTLERY
2314 Monte Verde Dr
Pinole, CA 94564
510-758-9912 Fax: 510-758-9912
kriscutlery@aol.com; www.kriscutlery.com
Japanese, medieval, Chinese & Philippine

LONE STAR WHOLESALE
2401 Interstate 40 W
Amarillo, TX 79109
806-836-9540; fax 806-359-1603
sales@lswtexas.com
www.lswtexas.com
Nationwide distributor of knives, knife accessories and knife-related tools

MATTHEWS CUTLERY
PO Box 2768
Moultrie, GA 31776
800-251-0123; fax 877-428-3599
www.matthewscutlery.com

MOORE CUTLERY
PO Box 633
Lockport, IL 60441
708-301-4201
www.moorecutlery.com
Owned & operated by Gary Moore since 1991 (a full-time dealer). Purveyor of high quality custom & production knives

MUSEUM REPLICAS LIMITED
2147 Gees Mill Rd
Conyers, GA 30012
800-883-8838
www.museumreplicas.com
Historically accurate and battle ready swords & daggers

NEW GRAHAM KNIVES
560 Virginia Ave.
Bluefield, VA 24605
276-326-1384
mdye@newgraham.com
www.newgraham.com
Wide selection of knives from over 75 manufacturers, knife sharpening and maintenance accessories

NORDIC KNIVES
436 1st St., Ste. 203A
Solvang, CA 93463
805-688-3612; fax 805-688-1635
info@nordicknives.com
www.nordicknives.com
Custom and Randall knives

PARKERS' KNIFE COLLECTOR SERVICE
6715 Heritage Business Court
Chattanooga, TN 37421
423-892-0448; fax 423-892-9165
www.bulldogknives.org
Online and mail order dealer specializing in collectible knives, including Bulldog Knives, Weidmannsheil and Parker Eagle Brand. Parkers' Greatest Knife Show On Earth

PLAZA CUTLERY, INC.
3333 S. Bristol St., Suite 2060
South Coast Plaza
Costa Mesa, CA 92626
866-827-5292; 714-549-3932
dan@plazacutlery.com;
www.plazacutlery.com
Largest selection of knives on the west coast. Custom makers from beginners to the best. All customs, William Henry, Strider, Reeves, Randalls & others available online, by phone

ROBERTSON'S CUSTOM CUTLERY
4960 Sussex Dr
Evans, GA 30809
706-650-0252; 706-860-1623
customknives@comcast.net
www.robertsoncustomcutlery.com
World class custom knives, custom knife entrepreneur

RUMMELL, HANK
10 Paradise Lane
Warwick, NY 10990
845-769-7273
hank@newyorkcustomknives.com;
www.newyorkcustomknives.com

SCHENK KNIVES
4574 N. Haroldsen Dr.
Idaho Falls, ID 83401
208-523-2026
schenkknives@gmail.com
www.schenkknives.com
High-performance factory custom knives. All models offered in the USA forged from damascus steel, forged 52100 bearting steel and ELMAX stainless steel.

SMOKY MOUNTAIN KNIFE WORKS, INC.
2320 Winfield Dunn Pkwy
PO Box 4430
Sevierville, TN 37864
800-564-8374; 865-453-5871
info@smkw.com; www.smkw.com
The world's largest knife showplace, catalog and website

TRUE NORTH KNIVES
82 Blair Park Rd. #955
Williston, VT 05495
866-748-9985
info@TNKUSA.com
www.TNKUSA.com
Custom and production knife purveyor

VOYLES, BRUCE
PO Box 22007
Chattanooga, TN 37422
423-238-6753
bruce@jbrucevoyles.com;
www.jbrucevoyles.com
Knives, knife auctions

knife services

appraisers
Levine, Bernard, P.O. Box 2404, Eugene, OR, 97402, 541-484-0294, brlevine@ix.netcom.com
Russell, A.G., Knives Inc, 2900 S. 26th St., Rogers, AR 72758-8571, phone 800-255-9034 or 479-631-0130, fax 479-631-8493, ag@agrussell.com, www.agrussell.com
Voyles, J. Bruce, PO Box 22007, Chattanooga, TN 37422, 423-238-6753, bruce@jbrucevoyles.com, www.jbrucevoyles.com

custom grinders
McGowan Manufacturing Company, 4720 N. La Cholla Blvd., #190, Tucson, AZ, 85705, 800-342-4810, 520-219-0884, info@mcgowanmfg.com, www.mcgowanmfg.com, Knife sharpeners, hunting axes
Peele, Bryan, The Elk Rack, 215 Ferry St. P.O. Box 1363, Thompson Falls, MT, 59873
Schlott, Harald, Zingster Str. 26, 13051 Berlin, GERMANY, 049 030 9293346, harald.schlott@T-online.de, Custom grinder, custom handle artisan, display case/box maker, etcher, scrimshander
Wilson, R.W., P.O. Box 2012, Weirton, WV, 26062, 304-723-2771 rwknives@comcast.net, www.rwwilsonknives.com

custom handles
Cooper, Jim, 1221 Cook St, Ramona, CA, 92065-3214, 760-789-1097, (760) 788-7992, jamcooper@aol.com
Burrows, Chuck, dba Wild Rose Trading Co, 102 Timber Ln., Durango, CO, 81303, 970-317-5592, chuck@wrtleather.com, www.wrtleather.com
Fields, Donald, 790 Tamerlane St, Deltona, FL, 32725, 386-532-9070, donaldfields@earthlink.net, Selling ancient ivories; mammoth & fossil walrus
Grussenmeyer, Paul G., 310 Kresson Rd, Cherry Hill, NJ, 08034, 856-428-1088, 856-428-8997, pgrussentne@comcast.net, www.pgcarvings.com
Holland, Dennis K., 4908-17th Pl., Lubbock, TX, 79416
Imboden II, Howard L., Hi II Originals, 620 Deauville Dr., Dayton, OH, 45429, 513-439-1536
Kelso, Jim, 577 Collar Hill Rd, Worcester, VT, 05682, 802-229-4254, (802) 229-0595
Marlatt, David, 67622 Oldham Rd., Cambridge, OH, 43725, 740-432-7549
Mead, Dennis, 2250 E. Mercury St., Inverness, FL, 34453-0514
Myers, Ron, 6202 Marglenn Ave., Baltimore, MD, 21206, 410-866-6914
Schlott, Harald, Zingster Str. 26, 13051 Berlin, GERMANY, 049 030 9293346, harald.schlott@T-online.de, Custom grinder, custom handle artisan, display case/box maker, etcher, scrimshander

...ell, Barry A., 4801 96th St. N., St. Petersburg, FL, 33708-3740
...lotton, A., 621 Fawn Ridge Dr., Oakland, OR, 97462, 541-459-2216
...tson, Silvia, 350 Jennifer Lane, Driftwood, TX, 78619
...derness Forge, 315 North 100 East, Kanab, UT, 84741, 435-644-3674,
 bhatting@xpressweb.com
...liams, Gary, (GARBO), PO Box 210, Glendale, KY, 42740-2010 270-369-6752,
 scrimbygarbo@gmail.com, www.scrimbygarbo.com

isplay cases and boxes

...'s Custom Cases, P O Box 603, Montague, CA, 96064, 541-727-7223,
 billscustomcases@earthlink.net, www.billscustomcases.com
...lpepper & Company, 8285 Georgia Rd., Otto, NC, 28763 828-524-6842,
 info@culpepperco.com, www.knifehandles.com
...Lean, Lawrence, 12344 Meritage Ct, Rancho Cucamonga, CA, 91739,
 714-848-5779, lmclean@charter.net
...ler, Michael K., M&M Kustom Krafts, 28510 Santiam Highway, Sweet Home,
 OR, 97386
...ler, Robert, P.O. Box 2722, Ormond Beach, FL, 32176
...tichek, Joseph L., W9377 Co. TK. D, Beaver Dam, WI, 53916
...bbins, Wayne, 11520 Inverway, Belvidere, IL, 61008
...D Enterprises, 20 East Seventh St, Manchester, OH, 45144, 855-876-9693,
 937-549-2602, sales@s-denterprises.com, www.s-denterprises.com, Display
 case/ box maker. Manufacturer of aluminum display, chipboard type displays,
 wood displays. Silk screening or acid etching for logos on product
...hlott, Harald, Zingster Str. 26, 13051 Berlin, GERMANY, 049 030 9293346,
 harald.schlott@T-online.de, Custom grinder, custom handle artisan, display
 case/box maker, etcher, scrimshander

ngravers

...am, Tim, 1705 Witzel Ave., Oshkosh, WI, 54902, 920-235-4589,
 www.adlamengraving.com
...corn, Gordon, 10573 Kelly Canyon Rd., Bozeman, MT 59715, 406-586-1350,
 alcorncustom@yahoo.com, www.alcornengraving.com
...ano, Sam, 45 Catalpa Trace, Covington, LA, 70433, alfano@gmail.com,
 www.masterengraver.com
...ron, David, Baron Engraving, 62 Spring Hill Rd., Trumbull, CT, 06611,
 203-452-0515, sales@baronengraving.com, www.baronengraving.com,
 Polishing, plating, inlays, artwork
...tes, Billy, 2302 Winthrop Dr. SW, Decatur, AL, 35603, bbrn@aol.com,
 www.angelfire.com/al/billybates
...ir, Jim, PO Box 64, 59 Mesa Verde, Glenrock, WY, 82637, 307-436-8115,
 jblairengrav@msn.com, www.jimblairengraving.com
...oysen, Chris, South Africa, +27-73-284-1493, chris@cbknives.com,
 www.cbknives.com
...ristensen, Bruce, 3072 W. Millerama Ave., West Valley City, UT 84119,
 801-966-0805, cengraver@gmail.com
...urchill, Winston G., RFD Box 29B, Proctorsville, VT 05153, www.wchurchill.com
...llins, Michael, 405-392-2273, info@michaelcollinsart.com,
 www.michaelcollinsart.com
...ver, Raymond A., 1206 N. Third St., Festus, MO 63010 314-808-2508
 cover@sbcglobal.net, http://learningtoengrave.com
...Lorge, Ed, 6734 W Main St, Houma, LA, 70360, 985-223-0206,
 delorge@triparish.net, http://www.eddelorge.com
...ckson, John W., PO Box 49914, Sarasota, FL, 34230, 941-952-1907
...lbare, Elizabeth, PO Box 502, Dubois, WY, 82513-0502 edolbare@hotmail.com,
 http://www.scrimshaw-engraving.com/
...wning, Jim, PO Box 4224, Springfield, MO, 65803, 417-865-5953,
 handlebar@thegunengraver.com, www.thegunengraver.com, engraver and
 scrimshaw artist
...arte, Carlos, 108 Church St., Rossville, CA, 95678, 916-782-2617
 carlossilver@surewest.net, www.carlossilver.com
...bber, Michael W., 11 S. Green River Rd., Evansville, IN, 47715, 812-454-0271,
 m.dubber@firearmsengraving.com, www.firearmsengraving.com
...ton, Rick, 313 Dailey Rd., Broadview, MT 59015, 406-667-2405,
 rick@eatonknives.com, www.eatonknives.com
...lund, Maihkel, Föne Stam V9, S-820 41 Färila, SWEDEN, info@art-knives.com,
 www.art-knives.com
...ridge, Allan, 7731 Four Winds Dr., Ft. Worth, TX 76133, 817-370-7778
...s, Willy B, Willy B's Customs, 1025 Hamilton Ave., Tarpon Springs, FL, 34689,
 727-942-6420, wbflashs@verizon.net, www.willyb.com
...nnery Gun Engraving, Jeff, 11034 Riddles Run Rd., Union, KY, 41091,
 859-384-3127, engraving@fuse.net, www.flannerygunengraving.com
...urnet, Geoffroy, 820 Paxinosa Ave., Easton, PA, 18042, 610-559-0710,

ggournet@yahoo.com, www.gournetusa.com
Halloran, Tim, 316 Fenceline Dr., Blue Grass, IA 52726 563-260-8464,
 vivtim@msn.com, http://halloranengraving.com
Hands, Barry Lee, 30608 Fernview Ln., Bigfork, MT 59911, 406-249-4334,
 barry_hands@yahoo.com, www.barryleehands.com
Holder, Pat, 18910 McNeil Ranch Rd., Wickenburg, AZ 85390, 928-684-2025
 dholderknives@commspeed.net, www.dholder.com
Ingle, Ralph W., 151 Callan Dr., Rossville, GA, 30741, 706-858-0641,
 riengraver@aol.com
Johns, Bill, 1716 8th St, Cody, WY, 82414, 307-587-5090,
 http://billjohnsengraver.com
Kelso, Jim, 577 Collar Hill Rd, Worcester, VT, 05682, 802-229-4254,
 jimkelsojournal@gmail.com, www.jimkelso.com
Koevenig, Eugene and Eve, Koevenig's Engraving Service, Rabbit Gulch, Box 55,
 Hill City, SD, 57745-0055
Kostelnik, Joe and Patty, RD #4, Box 323, Greensburg, PA, 15601
Kudlas, John M., 55280 Silverwolf Dr, Barnes, WI, 54873, 715-795-2031,
 jkudlas@cheqnet.net, Engraver, scrimshander
Lark, David, 6641 Schneider Rd., Kingsley, MI 49649, Phone: 231-342-1076
 dblark58@yahoo.com
Larson, Doug, Dragon's Fire Studio, Percival, IA, Phone: 402-202-3703 (cell)
 dragonsfirestudio@hotmail.com
Limings Jr., Harry, 5793 Nichels Ln., Johnstown, OH, 43031-9576
Lindsay, Steve, 3714 West Cedar Hill, Kearney, NE, 68845, Phone: 308-236-7885
 steve@lindsayengraving.com, www.lindsayengraving.com
Lurth, Mitchell, 1317 7th Ave., Marion, IA 52302, Phone: 319-377-1899
 www.lurthengraving.com
Lyttle, Brian, Box 5697, High River AB CANADA, T1V 1M7, Phone: 403-558-3638,
 brian@lyttleknives.com, www.lyttleknives.com
Lytton, Simon M., 19 Pinewood Gardens, Hemel Hempstead, Hertfordshire HP1
 1TN, ENGLAND, 01-442-255542, simonlyttonengraver@virginmedia.com
Markow, Paul, 130 Spinnaker Ridge Dr. SW, B206, Huntsville, AL 35824,
 256-513-9790, paul.markow@gmail.com, sites.google.com/site/
 artistictouch2010/engraving
Mason, Joe, 146 Value Rd, Brandon, MS, 39042, 601-519-8850,
 masonjoe@bellsouth.net, www.joemasonengraving.com
McCombs, Leo, 1862 White Cemetery Rd., Patriot, OH, 45658
McDonald, Dennis, 8359 Brady St., Peosta, IA, 52068
McLean, Lawrence, 12344 Meritage Ct, Rancho Cucamonga, CA, 91739,
 714-848-5779, lmclean@charter.net
Meyer, Chris, 39 Bergen Ave., Wantage, NJ, 07461, 973-875-6299
Minnick, Joyce, 144 N. 7th St., Middletown, IN, 47356, 765-354-4108
Morgan, Tandie, P.O. Box 693, 30700 Hwy. 97, Nucla, CO, 81424
Morton, David A., 1110 W. 21st St., Lorain, OH, 44052
Moulton, Dusty, 135 Hillview Ln, Loudon, TN, 37774, 865-408-9779,
 dusty@moultonknives.com, www.moultonknives.com
Muller, Jody & Pat, 3359 S. 225th Rd., Goodson, MO, 65663, 417-852-4306/417-
 752-3260, mullerforge2@hotmail.com, www.mullerforge.com
Nelida, Toniutti, via G. Pasconi 29/c, Maniago 33085 (PN), ITALY
Nilsson, Jonny Walker, Akkavare 16, 93391 Arvidsjaur, SWEDEN, +(46) 702-
 144207, 0960.13048@telia.com, www.jwnknives.com
Parke, Jeff, 1365 Fort Pierce Dr. #3, St. George, UT 84790, Phone: 435-421-1692
 jeffrey_parke@hotmail.com, https://www.facebook.com/jeff.parke1
Patterson, W.H., P.O. Drawer DK, College Station, TX, 77841
Peri, Valerio, Via Meucci 12, Gardone V.T. 25063, ITALY
Pilkington Jr., Scott, P.O. Box 97, Monteagle, TN, 37356, 931-924-3400,
 scott@pilkguns.com, www.pilkguns.com
Pulisova, Andrea, CSA 230-95, 96701 Kremnica, Slovakia, Phone: 00421
 903-340076 vpulis@gmail.com
Rabeno, Martin, Spook Hollow Trading Co, 530 Eagle Pass, Durango, CO, 81301
Raftis, Andrew, 2743 N. Sheffield, Chicago, IL, 60614
Riccardo, David, Riccardo Fine Hand Engraving, Buckley, MI, Phone:
 231-269-3028, riccardoengraving@acegroup.cc, www.riccardoengraving.com
Roberts, J.J., 7808 Lake Dr., Manassas, VA, 20111, 703-330-0448,
 jjrengraver@aol.com
Robidoux, Roland J., DMR Fine Engraving, 25 N. Federal Hwy. Studio 5, Dania, FL,
 33004
Rosser, Bob, Hand Engraving, 2809 Crescent Ave Ste 20, Birmingham, AL, 35209,
 205-870-4422, brengraver1@gmail.com, www.hand-engravers.com
Rudolph, Gil, 20922 Oak Pass Ave, Tehachapi, CA, 93561, 661-822-4949
Rundell, Joe, 6198 W. Frances Rd., Clio, MI, 48420
Schönert, Elke, 18 Lansdowne Pl., Central, Port Elizabeth, SOUTH AFRICA
Shaw, Bruce, P.O. Box 545, Pacific Grove, CA, 93950, 831-646-1937,
 831-644-0941, shawdogs@aol.com
Simmons, Rick W., 3323 Creek Manor Dr., Kingwood, TX, 77339, 504-261-8450,

exhibitiongrade@gmail.com www.bespokeengraving.com

Slobodian, Barbara, 4101 River Ridge Dr., PO Box 1498, San Andreas, CA 95249, 209-286-1980, fax 209-286-1982, barbara@dancethetide.com. Specializes in Japanese-style engraving.

Small, Jim, 2860 Athens Hwy., Madison, GA 30650, 706-818-1245, smallengrave@aol.com

Smith, Ron, 5869 Straley, Ft. Worth, TX, 76114

Smitty's Engraving, 21320 Pioneer Circle, Harrah, OK, 73045, 405-454-6968, mail@smittys-engraving.us, www.smittys-engraving.us

Soileau, Damon, P.O. Box 7292, Kingsport, TN 37664 423-297-4665, oiseaumetalarts@gmail.com, www.oiseaumetalarts.etsy.com

Spode, Peter, Tresaith Newland, Malvern, Worcestershire WR13 5AY, ENGLAND

Swartley, Robert D., 2800 Pine St., Napa, CA, 94558

Takeuchi, Shigetoshi, 21-14-1-Chome kamimuneoka Shiki shi, 353 Saitama, JAPAN

Theis, Terry, 21452 FM 2093, Harper, TX, 78631, 830-864-4438

Valade, Robert B., 931 3rd Ave., Seaside, OR, 97138, 503-738-7672, (503) 738-7672

Waldrop, Mark, 14562 SE 1st Ave. Rd., Summerfield, FL, 34491

Warenski-Erickson, Julie, 590 East 500 N., Richfield, UT, 84701, 435-627-2504, julie@warenskiknives.com, www.warenskiknives.com

Warren, Kenneth W., P.O. Box 2842, Wenatchee, WA, 98807-2842, 509-663-6123, (509) 663-6123

Whitmore, Jerry, 1740 Churchill Dr., Oakland, OR, 97462

Winn, Travis A., 558 E. 3065 S., Salt Lake City, UT, 84106, 801-467-5957

Zima, Russ, 7291 Ruth Way, Denver, CO, 80221, 303-657-9378, rzima@rzengraving.com, www.rzengraving.com

etchers

Baron Engraving, David Baron, 62 Spring Hill Rd., Trumbull, CT, 06611, 203-452-0515 sales@baronengraving.com, www.baronengraving.com

Fountain Products, 492 Prospect Ave., West Springfield, MA, 01089, 413-781-4651

Hayes, Dolores, P.O. Box 41405, Los Angeles, CA, 90041

Holland, Dennis, 4908 17th Pl., Lubbock, TX, 79416

Kelso, Jim, 577 Collar Hill Rd, Worcester, VT, 05682, 802-229-4254, jimkelsojournal@gmail.com, www.jimkelso.com

Larstein, Francine, Francine Etched Knives, 368 White Rd., Watsonville, CA, 95076, 800-557-1525/831-426-6046, francine@francinetchedknives.com, www.francinetchedknives.com

Lefaucheux, Jean-Victor, Saint-Denis-Le-Ferment, 27140 Gisors, FRANCE

Myers, Ron, 6202 Marglenn Ave., Baltimore, MD, 21206, (acid) etcher

Nilsson, Jonny Walker, Akkavare 16, 93391 Arvidsjaur, SWEDEN, +(46) 702-144207, 0960.13048@telia.com, www.jwnknives.com

Schlott, Harald, Zingster Str. 26, 13051 Berlin, GERMANY, 049 030 9293346, harald.schlott@T-online.de, Custom grinder, custom handle artisan, display case/box maker, etcher, scrimshander

Vallotton, A., Northwest Knife Supply, 621 Fawn Ridge Dr., Oakland, OR, 97462

Watson, Silvia, 350 Jennifer Lane, Driftwood, TX, 78619

heat treaters

Bodycote Inc., 443 E. High St., London, OH 43140 740-852-5000, chris.gattie@bodycote.com, www.bodycote.com

Kazou, Okaysu, 12-2 1 Chome Higashi, Ueno, Taito-Ku, Tokyo, JAPAN, 81-33834-2323, 81-33831-3012

O&W Heat Treat Inc., One Bidwell Rd., South Windsor, CT, 06074, 860-528-9239, (860) 291-9939, owht1@aol.com

Pacific Heat Treating, attn: B.R. Holt, 1238 Birchwood Drive, Sunnyvale, CA, 94089, 408-736-8500, www.pacificheattreating.com

Paul Bos Heat Treating c/o Paul Farner, Buck Knives: 660 S. Lochsa St., Post Falls, ID 83854, 208-262-0500, Ext. 211 / fax 800-733-2825, pfarner@buckknives.com, or contact Paul Bos direct: 928-232-1656, paulbos@buckknives.com

Progressive Heat Treating Co., 2802 Charles City Rd, Richmond, VA, 23231, 804-717-5353, 800-868-5457, sales@pecgears.com

Texas Heat Treating Inc., 155 Texas Ave., Round Rock, TX, 78680, 512-255-5884, buster@texasheattreating.com, www.texasheattreating.com

Texas Knifemakers Supply, 10649 Haddington, Suite 180, Houston, TX, 77043, 713-461-8632, sales@texasknife.com, www.texasknife.com

Tinker Shop, The, 1120 Helen, Deer Park, TX, 77536, 713-479-7286

Valley Metal Treating Inc., 355 S. East End Ave., Pomona, CA, 91766, 909-623-6316, ray@valleymt.net

Wilson, R.W., P.O. Box 2012, Weirton, WV, 26062, 304-723-2771 rwknives@comcast.net, rwwilsonknives.com

leather workers

Abramson, David, 116 Baker Ave, Wharton, NJ, 07885, 973-713-9776, lifter4him1@aol.com, www.liftersleather.com

Burrows, Chuck, dba Wild Rose Trading Co, 102 Timber Ln., Durango, CO 8130?, 970-317-5592, wrtc@wrtcleather.com, www.wrtcleather.com

Clements' Custom Leathercraft, Chas, 1741 Dallas St., Aurora, CO 80010, Phone: 303-364-0403, chasclements@comcast.net

Cole, Dave, 620 Poinsetta Dr., Satellite Beach, FL 32937, 321-773-1687, www.dcknivesandleather.blademakers.com. Custom sheath services.

CowCatcher Leatherworks, 2045 Progress Ct., Raleigh, NC 27608, Phone: 919-833-8262 cowcatcher1@ymail.com, www.cowcatcher.us

Cubic, George, GC Custom Leather Co., 10561 E. Deerfield Pl., Tucson, AZ, 857?, 520-760-0695, gcubic@aol.com

Dawkins, Dudley, 221 N. Broadmoor Ave, Topeka, KS, 66606-1254, 785-817-9343, dawkind@reagan.com, ABS member/knifemaker forges straight knives

Evans, Scott V, Edge Works Mfg, 1171 Halltown Rd, Jacksonville, NC, 28546, 910-455-9834, fax 910-346-5660, support@tacticalholsters.com, www.tacticalholsters.com

Genske, Jay, 283 Doty St, Fond du Lac, WI, 54935, 920-921-8019/Cell Phone 920-579-0144, jaygenske@hotmail.com, http: //genskeknives.weebly.com, Custom Grinder, Custom Handle Artisan

Green River Leather, 1098 Legion Park Road, PO BOX 190, Greensburg, KY, 427?, Phone: 270-932-2212 fax: 270-299-2471 email: info@greenriverleather.com

John's Custom Leather, John R. Stumpf, 523 S. Liberty St, Blairsville, PA, 1571?, 724-459-6802, 724-459-5996, www.jclleather.com

Kravitt, Chris, Treestump Leather, 443 Cave Hill Rd., Waltham, ME, 04605-870?, 207-584-3000, sheathmkr@aol.com, www.treestumpleather.com, Reference Tree Stump Leather

Layton, Jim, 2710 Gilbert Avenue, Portsmouth, OH, 45662, 740-353-6179

Lee,Sonja and Randy, P.O. Box 1873, 270 N 9th West, St. Johns, AZ, 85936, 92?-337-2594, 928-337-5002, randylee.knives@yahoo.com, info@randyleeknives.com, Custom knifemaker; www.randyleeknives.com

Long, Paul, Paul Long Custom Leather, 108 Briarwood Ln. W, Kerrville, TX, 78028, 830-367-5536, PFL@cebridge.net

Lott, Sherry, 1098 Legion Park Road, PO BOX 190, Greensburg, KY, 42743, Phone: 270-932-2212 fax: 270-299-2471 email: info@greenriverleather.com sherrylott@alltel.net

Mason, Arne, 258 Wimer St., Ashland, OR, 97520, 541-482-2260, (541) 482-7785, am@arnemason.com, www.arnemason.com

Metheny, H.A. "Whitey", 7750 Waterford Dr., Spotsylvania, VA 22551, 540-582-3228 Cell 540-842-1440, fax 540-582-3095, hametheny@aol.com, http://whitey.methenyknives.com

Morrissey, Martin, 4578 Stephens Rd., Blairsville, GA, 30512

Niedenthal, John Andre, Beadwork & Buckskin, Studio 3955 NW 103 Dr., Coral Springs, FL, 33065-1551, 954-345-0447, a_niedenthal@hotmail.com

Neilson, Tess, 187 Cistern Ln., Towanda, PA 18848, 570-721-0470, mountainhollow@epix.net, www.mountainhollow.net, Doing business as Neilson's Mountain Hollow

Parsons, Larry, 539 S. Pleasant View Dr., Mustang, OK 73064 405-376-9408 l.j.parsons@sbcglobal.net, www.parsonssaddleshop.com

Red's Custom Leather, Ed Todd, 9 Woodlawn Rd., Putnam Valley, NY 10579, 845-528-3783, redscustomleather@redscustomleather.com, www.redscustomleather.com

Rowe, Kenny, Rowe's Leather, 3219 Hwy 29 South, Hope, AR, 71801, 870-777-8216, fax 870-777-0935, rowesleather@yahoo.com, www.rowesleather.com

Schrap, Robert G., Custom Leather Knife Sheaths, 7024 W. Wells St., Wauwatosa, WI, 53213, 414-771-6472, fax 414-479-9765, rschrap@aol.com, www.customsheaths.com

Strahin, Robert, 401 Center St., Elkins, WV, 26241, 304-636-0128, rstrahin@copper.net, *Custom Knife Sheaths

Walker, John, 17 Laber Circle, Little Rock, AR, 72210, 501-455-0239, john.walker@afbic.com

miscellaneous

Robertson, Kathy, Impress by Design, PO Box 1367, Evans, GA, 30809-1367, 706-650-0982, (706) 860-1623, impressbydesign@comcast.net, Advertising graphic designer

Strahin, Robert, 401 Center St., Elkins, WV, 26241, 304-636-0128, rstrahin@copper.net, *Custom Knife Sheaths

photographers

Alfano, Sam, 36180 Henery Gaines Rd., Pearl River, LA, 70452

Allen, John, Studio One, 3823 Pleasant Valley Blvd., Rockford, IL, 61114

Bilal, Mustafa, Turk's Head Productions, 908 NW 50th St., Seattle, WA, 98107-3634, 206-782-4164, (206) 783-5677, info@turkshead.com, www.turkshead.com, Graphic design, marketing & advertising

Bogaerts, Jan, Regenweg 14, 5757 Pl., Liessel, HOLLAND

Box Photography, Doug, 1804 W Main St, Brenham, TX, 77833-3420

Brown, Tom, 6048 Grants Ferry Rd., Brandon, MS, 39042-8136

Butman, Steve, P.O. Box 5106, Abilene, TX, 79608

Calidonna, Greg, 205 Helmwood Dr., Elizabethtown, KY, 42701

Campbell, Jim, 7935 Ranch Rd., Port Richey, FL, 34668

Cooper, Jim, Sharpbycoop.com Photography, 9 Mathew Court, Norwalk, CT 06851, jcooper@sharpbycoop.com, www.sharpbycoop.com

Courtice, Bill, P.O. Box 1776, Duarte, CA, 91010-4776

Crosby, Doug, RFD 1, Box 1111, Stockton Springs, ME, 04981

Danko, Michael, 3030 Jane Street, Pittsburgh, PA, 15203

Davis, Marshall B., P.O. Box 3048, Austin, TX, 78764

Earley, Don, 1241 Ft. Bragg Rd., Fayetteville, NC, 28305

Ehrlich, Linn M., 1850 N Clark St #1008, Chicago, IL, 60614, 312-209-2107

Etzler, John, 11200 N. Island Rd., Grafton, OH, 44044

Fahrner, Dave, 1623 Arnold St., Pittsburgh, PA, 15205

Faul, Jan W., 903 Girard St. NE, Rr. Washington, DC, 20017

Fedorak, Allan, 28 W. Nicola St., Amloops BC CANADA, V2C 1J6

Fox, Daniel, Lumina Studios, 6773 Industrial Parkway, Cleveland, OH, 44070, 440-734-2118, (440) 734-3542, lumina@en.com, lumina-studios.com

Francesco Pachi, Loc. Pometta 1, 17046 Sassello (SV) ITALY Tel-fax: 0039 019 724581, info@pachi-photo.com, www.pachi-photo.com

Freiberg, Charley, PO Box 42, Elkins, NH, 03233, 603-526-2767, charleyfreiberg@tds.net, charleyfreibergphotography.com

Gardner, Chuck, 116 Quincy Ave., Oak Ridge, TN, 37830

Gawryla, Don, 1105 Greenlawn Dr., Pittsburgh, PA, 15220

Goffe Photographic Associates, 3108 Monte Vista Blvd., NE, Albuquerque, NM, 87106

Hanusin, John, Reames-Hanusin Studio, PO Box 931, Northbrook, IL, 60065 0931, 847-564-2706

Hodge, Tom, 7175 S US Hwy 1 Lot 36, Titusville, FL, 32780-8172, 321-267-7989, egdoht@hotmail.com

Molter, Wayne V., 125 Lakin Ave., Boonsboro, MD, 21713, 301-416-2855, mackwayne@hotmail.com

Hopkins, David W, Hopkins Photography inc, 201 S Jefferson, Iola, KS, 66749, 620-365-7443, nhoppy@netks.net

LaFleur, Gordon, 111 Hirst, Box 1209, Parksville BC CANADA, V0R 270

Lear, Dale, 6544 Cora Mill Rd, Gallipolis, OH, 45631, 740-245-5482, dalelear@yahoo.com, Ebay Sales

LeBlanc, Paul, No. 3 Meadowbrook Cir., Melissa, TX, 75454

Lester, Dean, 2801 Junipero Ave Suite 212, Long Beach, CA, 90806-2140

Leviton, David A., A Studio on the Move, P.O. Box 2871, Silverdale, WA, 98383, 360-697-3452

Long, Gary W., 3556 Miller's Crossroad Rd., Hillsboro, TN, 37342, 931-596-2275

Martin, Cory, 4249 Taylor Harbor #7, Racine, WI 53403, 262-352-5392, info@corymartinimaging.com, www.corymartinimaging.com

McCollum, Tom, P.O. Box 933, Lilburn, GA, 30226

Mitch Lum Website and Photography, 22115 NW Imbrie Dr. #298, Hillsboro, OR 97124, mitch@mitchlum.com, www.mitchlum.com, 206-356-6813

Moake, Jim, 18 Council Ave., Aurora, IL, 60504

Moya Inc., 4212 S. Dixie Hwy., West Palm Beach, FL, 33405

Norman's Studio, 322 S. 2nd St., Vivian, LA, 71082

Owens, William T., Box 99, Williamsburg, WV, 24991

Pachi, Francesco, Loc. Pometta 1, 17046 Sassello (SV) ITALY Tel-fax: 0039 019 724581, info@pachi-photo.com, www.pachi-photo.com

Palmer Studio, 2008 Airport Blvd., Mobile, AL, 36606

Payne, Robert G., P.O. Box 141471, Austin, TX, 78714

Pigott, John, 9095 Woodprint LN, Mason, OH, 45040

Point Seven, 6450 Weatherfield Ct., Unit 2A, Maumee, OH, 43537, 312-420-4647 pointseven@pointsevenstudios.com, www.ericegglyphotography.com

Rob Andrew Photography, Rob Szajkowski, 7960 Silverton Ave., Ste. 125, San Diego, CA 92126, 760-920-6380, robandrewphoto@gmail.com, www.robandrewphoto.com

Professional Medica Concepts, Patricia Mitchell, P.O. Box 0002, Warren, TX, 77664, 409-547-2213, pm0909@wt.net

Rasmussen, Eric L., 1121 Eliason, Brigham City, UT, 84302

Rhoades, Cynthia J., Box 195, Clearmont, WY, 82835

Rice, Tim, PO Box 663, Whitefish, MT, 59937

Richardson, Kerry, 2520 Mimosa St., Santa Rosa, CA, 95405, 707-575-1875, kerry@sonic.net, www.sonic.net/~kerry

Ross, Bill, 28364 S. Western Ave. Suite 464, Rancho Palos Verdes, CA, 90275

Rubicam, Stephen, 14 Atlantic Ave., Boothbay Harbor, ME, 04538-1202

Rush, John D., 2313 Maysel, Bloomington, IL, 61701

Schreiber, Roger, 429 Boren Ave. N., Seattle, WA, 98109

Semmer, Charles, 7885 Cyd Dr., Denver, CO, 80221

Silver Images Photography, 2412 N Keystone, Flagstaff, AZ, 86004

Slobodian, Scott, 4101 River Ridge Dr., P.O. Box 1498, San Andreas, CA, 95249, 209-286-1980, (209) 286-1982, www.slobodianswords.com

Smith, Earl W., 5121 Southminster Rd., Columbus, OH, 43221

Smith, Randall, 1720 Oneco Ave., Winter Park, FL, 32789

Storm Photo, 334 Wall St., Kingston, NY, 12401

Surles, Mark, P.O. Box 147, Falcon, NC, 28342

Third Eye Photos, 140 E. Sixth Ave., Helena, MT, 59601

Thurber, David, P.O. Box 1006, Visalia, CA, 93279

Tighe, Brian, 12-111 Fourth Ave., Ste. 376 Ridley Square, St. Catharines ON CANADA, L2S 3P5, 905-892-2734, www.tigheknives.com

Towell, Steven L., 3720 N.W. 32nd Ave., Camas, WA, 98607, 360-834-9049, sltowell@netscape.net

Verno Studio, Jay, 3030 Jane Street, Pittsburgh, PA, 15203

Ward, Chuck, 1010 E North St, PO Box 2272, Benton, AR, 72018, 501-778-4329, chuckbop@aol.com

Wise, Harriet, 242 Dill Ave., Frederick, MD, 21701

Worley, Holly, Worley Photography, 6360 W David Dr, Littleton, CO, 80128-5708, 303-257-8091, 720-981-2800, hsworley@aol.com, Products, Digital & Film

scrimshanders

Adlam, Tim, 1705 Witzel Ave., Oshkosh, WI, 54902, 920-235-4589, ctimadlam@new.rr.com, www.adlamengraving.com

Alpen, Ralph, 7 Bentley Rd., West Grove, PA, 19390, 610-869-7141

Anderson, Terry Jack, 10076 Birnamwoods Way, Riverton, UT, 84065-9073

Ashworth, Boyd, 1510 Bullard Pl., Powder Springs, GA 30127, 404-583-5652, boydashworthknives@comcast.net, www.boydashworthknives.com

Bailey, Mary W., 3213 Jonesboro Dr., Nashville, TN, 37214, Phone: 615-889-3172 mbscrim@aol.com

Baker, Duane, 2145 Alum Creek Dr., Cambridge Park Apt. #10, Columbus, OH, 43207

Barrows, Miles, 524 Parsons Ave., Chillicothe, OH, 45601

Brady, Sandra, Scrimshaw by Sandra Brady, 9608 Monclova Rd., Monclova, OH 43542, 419-866-0435, 419-261-1582 sandy@sandrabradyart.com, www.sandrabradyart.com

Beauchamp, Gaetan, 125 de la Riviere, Stoneham, QC, G3C 0P6, CANADA, 418-848-1914, fax 418-848-6859, knives@gbeauchamp.ca, www.gbeauchamp.ca

Bellet, Connie, PO Box 151, Palermo, ME, 04354 0151, 207-993-2327, phwhitehawk@gwl.net

Benade, Lynn, 2610 Buckhurst Dr, Beachwood, OH, 44122, 216-464-0777, llbnc17@aol.com

Bonshire, Benita, 1121 Burlington Dr., Muncie, IN, 47302

Boone Trading Co. Inc., P.O. Box 669, Brinnon, WA, 98320, 800-423-1945, bella@boonetrading.com, www.boonetrading.com

Bryan, Bob, 1120 Oak Hill Rd., Carthage, MO, 64836

Burger, Sharon, Glenwood, Durban KZN, South Africa, cell: +27 83 7891675, scribble@iafrica.com, www.sharonburger-scrimshaw.co.za/

Byrne, Mary Gregg, 1018 15th St., Bellingham, WA, 98225-6604

Cable, Jerry, 332 Main St., Mt. Pleasant, PA, 15666

Caudill, Lyle, 7626 Lyons Rd., Georgetown, OH, 45121

Cole, Gary, PO Box 668, Naalehu, HI, 96772, 808-929-9775, 808-929-7371

Collins, Michael, Rt. 3075, Batesville Rd., Woodstock, GA, 30188

Conover, Juanita Rae, P.O. Box 70442, Eugene, OR, 97401, 541-747-1726 or 543-4851, juanitaraeconover@yahoo.com

Courtnage, Elaine, Box 473, Big Sandy, MT, 59520

Cover Jr., Raymond A., 1206 N. 3rd St., Festus, MO, 63010, Phone: 314-808-2508 cover@sbcglobal.net, learningtoengravecom

Cox, J. Andy, 116 Robin Hood Lane, Gaffney, SC, 29340

Dietrich, Roni, Wild Horse Studio, 1257 Cottage Dr, Harrisburg, PA, 17112, 717-469-0587, ronimd@aol

Dolbare, Elizabeth, PO Box 502, Dubois, WY, 82513-0502

Eklund, Maihkel, Föne Stam V9, S-82041 Färila, SWEDEN, +46 6512 4192, info@art-knives.com, www.art-knives.com

Eldridge, Allan, 1424 Kansas Lane, Gallatin, TN, 37066

Ellis, Willy B., Willy B's Customs by William B Ellis, Tarpon Springs, FL, 34689, 727-942-6420, wbflashs@verizon.net, www.willyb.com

Fisk, Dale, Box 252, Council, ID, 83612, dafisk@ctcweb.net

Foster Enterprises, Norvell Foster, P.O. Box 200343, San Antonio, TX, 78220

Fountain Products, 492 Prospect Ave., West Springfield, MA, 01089

Gill, Scott, 925 N. Armstrong St., Kokomo, IN, 46901

Hands, Barry Lee, 30608 Fernview Ln., Bigfork, MT, 59911, 406-249-4334, barry_hands@yahoo.com, www.barryleehands.com

Hargraves Sr., Charles, RR 3 Bancroft, Ontario CANADA, K0L 1C0

Harless, Star, c/o Arrow Forge, P.O. Box 845, Stoneville, NC, 27048-0845

Harrington, Fred A., Summer: 2107 W Frances Rd, Mt Morris MI 48458 8215, Winter: 3725 Citrus, St. James City, FL, 33956, Winter 239-283-0721, Summer 810-686-3008

Hergert, Bob, 12 Geer Circle, Port Orford, OR, 97465, 541-332-3010, hergert@harborside.com, www.scrimshander.com

Hielscher, Vickie, 6550 Otoe Rd, P.O. Box 992, Alliance, NE, 69301, 308-762-4318, g-hielsc@bbcwb.net

High, Tom, 5474 S. 112.8 Rd., Alamosa, CO, 81101, 719-589-2108, rmscrimshaw@gmail.com, www.rockymountainscrimshaw.com, Wildlife Artist

Himmelheber, David R., 11289 40th St. N., Royal Palm Beach, FL, 33411

Holland, Dennis K., 4908-17th Place, Lubbock, TX, 79416

Hutchings, Rick "Hutch", 3007 Coffe Tree Ct, Crestwood, KY, 40014, 502-241-2871, baron1@bellsouth.net

Imboden II, Howard L., 620 Deauville Dr., Dayton, OH, 45429, 937-439-1536, Guards by the "Last Wax Technic"

Johnson, Corinne, W3565 Lockington, Mindora, WI, 54644

Johnston, Kathy, W. 1134 Providence, Spokane, WA, 99205

Karst Stone, Linda, 903 Tanglewood Ln, Kerrville, TX, 78028-2945, 830-896-4678, 830-257-6117, linda@karstone.com, www.karstone.com

Kelso, Jim, 577 Collar Hill Rd, Worcester, VT 05682, 802-229-4254 kelsomaker@gmail.com, www.jimkelso.com

Koevenig, Eugene and Eve, Koevenig's Engraving Service, Rabbit Gulch, Box 55, Hill City, SD, 57745-0055

Kostelnik, Joe and Patty, RD #4, Box 323, Greensburg, PA 15601

Lemen, Pam, 3434 N. Iroquois Ave., Tucson, AZ, 85705

Martin, Diane, 28220 N. Lake Dr., Waterford, WI, 53185

McDonald, René Cosimini-, 14730 61 Court N., Loxahatchee, FL, 33470

McFadden, Berni, 2547 E Dalton Ave, Dalton Gardens, ID, 83815-9631

McGowan, Frank, 12629 Howard Lodge Dr., Winter Add-2023 Robin Ct Sebring FL 33870, Sykesville, MD, 21784, 863-385-1296

McGrath, Gayle, PMB 232 15201 N Cleveland Ave, N Ft Myers, FL, 33903

McLaran, Lou, 603 Powers St., Waco, TX, 76705

McWilliams, Carole, P.O. Box 693, Bayfield, CO, 81122

Mitchell, James, 1026 7th Ave., Columbus, GA, 31901

Moore, James B., 1707 N. Gillis, Stockton, TX, 79735

Ochonicky, Michelle "Mike", Stone Hollow Studio, 31 High Trail, Eureka, MO, 63025, 636-938-9570, www.stonehollowstudio.com

Ochs, Belle, 124 Emerald Lane, Largo, FL, 33771, 727-536-3827, contact@oxforge.com, www.oxforge.com

Pachi, Mirella, Localita Pometta 1, 17046 Sassello (SV), ITALY, +39 019 72 00 86, www.pachi-photo.com

Parish, Vaughn, 103 Cross St., Monaca, PA, 15061

Peterson, Lou, 514 S. Jackson St., Gardner, IL, 60424

Pienaar, Conrad, 19A Milner Rd., Bloemfontein 9300, SOUTH AFRICA, Phone: 027 514364180 fax: 027 514364180

Poag, James H., RR #1 Box 212A, Grayville, IL, 62844

Polk, Trena, 4625 Webber Creek Rd., Van Buren, AR, 72956

Pulisova, Andrea, CSA 230-95, 96701 Kremnica, Slovakia, Phone: 00421 903-340076 vpulis@gmail.com, www.vpulis.host.sk

Purvis, Hilton, P.O. Box 371, Noordhoek, 7979, SOUTH AFRICA, 27 21 789 1114, hiltonp@telkomsa.net, http://capeknifemakersguild.com/?page_id=416

Ramsey, Richard, 8525 Trout Farm Rd, Neosho, MO, 64850

Ristinen, Lori, 14256 County Hwy 45, Menahga, MN, 56464, 218-538-6608, lori@loriristinen.com, www.loriristinen.com

Roberts, J.J., 7808 Lake Dr., Manassas, VA, 22111, 703-330-0448, jjrengraver@aol.com, www.angelfire.com/va2/engraver

Rudolph, Gil, 20922 Oak Pass Ave, Tehachapi, CA, 93561, 661-822-4949

Rundell, Joe, 6198 W. Frances Rd., Clio, MI, 48420

Satre, Robert, 518 3rd Ave. NW, Weyburn SK CANADA, S4H 1R1

Schlott, Harald, Zingster Str. 26, 13051 Berlin, +49 030 929 33 46, GERMANY, harald.schlott@web.de, www.gravur-kunst-atelier.de

Schulenburg, E.W., 25 North Hill St., Carrollton, GA, 30117

Schwallie, Patricia, 4614 Old Spartanburg Rd. Apt. 47, Taylors, SC, 29687

Selent, Chuck, P.O. Box 1207, Bonners Ferry, ID, 83805

Semich, Alice, 10037 Roanoke Dr., Murfreesboro, TN, 37129

Shostle, Ben, 1121 Burlington, Muncie, IN, 47302

Smith, Peggy, 676 Glades Rd., #3, Gatlinburg, TN, 37738

Smith, Ron, 5869 Straley, Ft. Worth, TX, 76114

Steigerwalt, Jim, RD#3, Sunbury, PA, 17801

Stuart, Stephen, 15815 Acorn Circle, Tavares, FL, 32778, 352-343-8423, (352) 343-8916, inkscratch@aol.com

Talley, Mary Austin, 2499 Countrywood Parkway, Memphis, TN, 38016, matalley@midsouth.rr.com

Thompson, Larry D., 23040 Ave. 197, Strathmore, CA, 93267

Toniutti, Nelida, Via G. Pascoli, 33085 Maniago-PN, ITALY

Trout, Lauria Lovestrand, 1136 19th St. SW, Vero Beach, FL 32962, 772-778-0282, lovestranded@aol.com

Tucker, Steve, 3518 W. Linwood, Turlock, CA, 95380

Tyser, Ross, 1015 Hardee Court, Spartanburg, SC, 29303

Velasquez, Gil, Art of Scrimshaw, 7120 Madera Dr., Goleta, CA, 93117

Williams, Gary, PO Box 210, Glendale, KY, 42740, 270-369-6752, scrimbygarbo@gmail.com, scrimbygarbo.com

Winn, Travis A., 558 E. 3065 S., Salt Lake City, UT 84106, 801-467-5957

Young, Mary, 4826 Storeyland Dr., Alton, IL, 62002

organizations

AMERICAN BLADESMITH SOCIETY
c/o Office Manager, Cindy Sheely; P. O. Box 160, Grand Rapids, Ohio 43522; cindy@americanbladesmith.com; (419) 832-0400; Web: www.americanbladesmith.com

AMERICAN KNIFE & TOOL INSTITUTE
Jan Billeb, Comm. Coordinator, AKTI, 22 Vista View Ln., Cody, WY 82414; 307-587-8296, akti@akti.org; www. akti.org

AMERICAN KNIFE THROWERS ALLIANCE
c/o Bobby Branton; POB 807; Awendaw, SC 29429; akta@akta-usa.com, www.AKTA-USA.com

ARIZONA KNIFE COLLECTOR'S ASSOCIATION
c/o Mike Mooney, President, 19432 E. Cloud Rd., Quen Creek, AZ 85142; Phone: 480-244-7768, mike@moonblades.com, Web: www.arizonaknifecollectors.org

ART KNIFE COLLECTOR'S ASSOCIATION
c/o Mitch Weiss, Pres.; 2211 Lee Road, Suite 104; Winter Park, FL 32789

BAY AREA KNIFE COLLECTOR'S ASSOCIATION
c/o Larry Hirsch, 5339 Prospect Rd. #129, San Jose, CA 95129, bladeplay@earthlink.net, Web: www.bakcainc.org

ARKANSAS KNIFEMAKERS ASSOCIATION
David Etchieson, 60 Wendy Cove, Conway, AR 72032; Phone: 501-554-2582, arknifeassn@yahoo.com, Web: www.arkansasknifemakers.com

AUSTRALASIAN KNIFE COLLECTORS
PO BOX 149 CHIDLOW 6556 WESTERN AUSTRALIA TEL: (08) 9572 7255; FAX: (08) 9572 7266. International Inquiries: TEL: + 61 8 9572 7255; FAX: + 61 8 9572 7266; akc@knivesaustralia.com.au, www.knivesaustralia.com.au

CALIFORNIA KNIFEMAKERS ASSOCIATION
c/o Clint Breshears, Membership Chairman; 1261 Keats St; Manhattan Beach CA 90266; 310-372-0739; breshears1@verizon.net
Dedicated to teaching and improving knifemaking

CANADIAN KNIFEMAKERS GUILD
c/o Wolfgang Loerchner; PO Box 255, Bayfield, Ont., CANADA N0M 1G0; 519-565-2196; info@canadianknifemakersguild.com, www.canadianknifemakersguild.com

CUSTOM KNIFE COLLECTORS ASSOCIATION

c/o Kevin Jones, PO Box 5893, Glen Allen, VA 23058-5893;
E-mail: customknifecollectorsassociation@yahoo.com; Web:
www.customknifecollectorsassociation.com
*The purpose of the CKCA is to recognize and promote the artistic
significance of handmade knives, to advnace their collection and
conservation, and to support the creative expression of those who make
them. Open to collectors, makers purveyors, and other collectors. Has
members from eight countries. Produced a calednar which features
custom knives either owned or made by CKCA members.*

CUTTING EDGE, THE

2900 S. 26th St., Rogers, AR 72758; 479-631-0130; 800-255-
9034; ce_info@cuttingedge.com, www.cuttingedge.com
*After-market knives since 1968. We offer about 1,000 individual knives each month.
The oldest and the most experienced in the business of buying and selling knives. We
buy collections of any size, take knives on consignment or we will trade. Web: www.
cuttingedge.com*

FLORIDA KNIFEMAKERS ASSOCIATION

c/o President John H. Davis, (209) 740-7125; johndavis@custom-
knifemaker.com, floridaknifemakers@gmail.com, Web: www.
floridaknifemakers.org

JAPANESE SWORD SOCIETY OF THE U.S.

PO Box 712; Breckenridge, TX 76424, barry@hennick.ca, www.
jssus.org

KNIFE COLLECTORS CLUB INC, THE

2900 S. 26th St, Rogers, AR 72758; 479-631-0130; 800-255-
9034; ag@agrussell.com; Web: www.agrussell.com/kcc-one-
year-membership-usa-/p/KCC/
*The oldest and largest association of knife collectors. Issues limited edition knives,
both handmade and highest quality production, in very limited numbers. The very
earliest was the CM-1, Kentucky Rifle*

KNIFEMAKERS' GUILD, THE

c/o Gene Baskett, Knifemakers Guild, 427 Sutzer Creek Rd., La
Grange, KY 42732; 270-862-5019; Web: www.knifemakersguild.
com

KNIFEMAKERS GUILD OF SOUTHERN AFRICA, THE

c/o Andre Thorburn; PO Box 1748; Bela Bela, Warmbaths, LP,
SOUTH AFRICA 0480; +27 82 650 1441 andrethorburn@gmail.
com; Web: www.kgsa.co.za

MONTANA KNIFEMAKERS' ASSOCIATION, THE

1439 S. 5th W, Missoula, MT 59801; 406-728-2861;
macnancymclaughlin@yahoo.com, Web: www.
montanaknifemakers.com
Annual book of custom knife makers' works and directory of knife making supplies; $19.99

NATIONAL KNIFE COLLECTORS ASSOCIATION

PO Box 21070; Chattanooga, TN 37424, 423-667-8199;
nkcalisa@hotmail.com; Web: www.nkcalisa.wix.com/nkca-
website-2

NEO-TRIBAL METALSMITHS

5920 W. Windy Lou Ln., Tucson, AZ 85742; Phone: 520-744-9777,
taigoo@msn.com, Web: www.neo-tribalmetalsmiths.com

NEW ENGLAND CUSTOM KNIFE ASSOCIATION

Vickie Gray, Treasurer, 686 Main Rd, Brownville, ME 04414;
Phone: 207-965-2191, Web: www.necka.net

NORTH CAROLINA CUSTOM KNIFEMAKERS GUILD

c/o Tim Scholl, President, 1389 Langdon Rd., Angier, NC 27501,
910-897-2051, tschollknives@live.com, Web: www.ncknifeguild.org

NORTH STAR BLADE COLLECTORS

PO Box 20523, Bloomington, MN 55420; info@nsbc.us, Web:
www.nsbc.us

OHIO KNIFEMAKERS ASSOCIATION

c/o Jerry Smith, Anvils and Ink Studios, P.O. Box 151,
Barnesville, Ohio 43713; jerry_smith@anvilsandinkstudios.com,
Web: www.oocities.org/ohioknives/

OREGON KNIFE COLLECTORS ASSOCIATION

Web: www.oregonknifeclub.org

ROCKY MOUNTAIN BLADE COLLECTORS ASSOCIATION

Mike Moss. Pres., P.O. Box 324, Westminster, CO 80036;
rmbladecollectors@gmail.com, Web: www.rmbladecollectors.org

SOUTH CAROLINA ASSOCIATION OF KNIFEMAKERS

c/o Col. Tom Kreger, President, (803) 438-4221; tdkreger@
bellsouth.net, Web: www.southcarolinaassociationofknifemakers.
org

SOUTHERN CALIFORNIA BLADES KNIFE COLLECTORS CLUB

SC Blades, PO Box 231112, Encinitas, CA 92023-1112; Phone:
619-417-4329, scblades@att.net, Web: www.scblades.org

THE WILLIAM F. MORAN JR. MUSEUM & FOUNDATION

4204 Ballenger Creek Pike, Frederick, MD 21703, info@
billmoranmuseum.com, www.williammoranmuseum.com

Publications

AUTOMATIC KNIFE RESOURCE

c/o Lantama Cutlery, POB 721, Montauk, NY 11954; 631-668-
5995; info@latama.net, Web: www.thenewsletter.com,
*Unique compilation and archive for the switchblade/automatic knife fan.
Sheldon Levy's Newsletter was first published in 1992, and was a labor of
love from its inception and has remained informative and insightful.*

BLADE AND BLADE'S COMPLETE KNIFE GUIDE

700 E. State St., Iola, WI 54990-0001; 715-445-4612; Web:
www.blademag.com, www.KnifeForums.com, www.ShopBlade.
com, facebook.com/blademag
*The world's No. 1 knife magazine. The most indepth knife magazine on the market,
covering all aspects of the industry, from knifemaking to production knives and
handmade pieces. With 13 issues per year, BLADE® boasts twice the distribution of its
closest competitor.*

CUTLERY NEWS JOURNAL (BLOG)

http://cutlerynewsjournal.wordpress.com
*Covers significant happenings from the world of knife collecting, in addition to
editorials, trends, events, auctions, shows, cutlery history, and reviews*

KNIFE MAGAZINE

PO Box 3395, Knoxville, TN 37927; Phone: 865-397-1955,
knifepub@knifeworld.com, www.knifeworld.com
Since 1977, a monthly knife publication covering all types of knives

KNIVES ILLUSTRATED

22840 Savi Ranch Pkwy. #200, Yorba Linda, CA 92887; Phone:
714-200-1963; bmiller@engagedmediainc.com; Web: www.
knivesillustrated.com
*All encompassing publication focusing on factory knives, new handmades, shows and
industry news*

THE LEATHER CRAFTERS & SADDLERS JOURNAL

222 Blackburn St., Rhinelander, WI 54501; Phone: 715-
362-5393; info@leathercraftersjournal.com, Web: www.
leathercraftersjournal.com
Bi-monthly how-to leathercraft magazine